MONEY, BANKING,

and th
CAN
FINA
SYST

EIGHTH

MONEY, BANKING,

and the
CANADIAN FINANCIAL SYSTEM

EIGHTH EDITION

H.H. Binhammer
Professor Emeritus
The Royal Military College of Canada

Peter S. Sephton
University of New Brunswick
and Queen's School of Business
Queen's University

NELSON

™

THOMSON LEARNING

AUSTRALIA   CANADA   MEXICO   SINGAPORE   SPAIN   UNITED KINGDOM   UNITED STATES

NELSON

THOMSON LEARNING

Money, Banking, and the Canadian
Financial System, Eighth Edition
by H.H. Binhammer and Peter S. Sephton

Editorial Director and Publisher:
Evelyn Veitch

Acquisitions Editor:
Paul Manley/Gary Bennett

Marketing Manager:
Anthony Rezek

Senior Project Editor:
Karina TenVeldhuis

Production Editor:
Tracy Bordian/Marcia Miron

Production Coordinator:
Hedy Sellers

Art Director:
Angela Cluer

Cover Design:
Linda Neale

Cover Image:
FPG International LLC

Copy Editor:
Dawn Hunter

Proofreader:
Jim Zimmerman

Senior Composition Analyst:
Zenaida Diores

Printer:
Transcontinental Printing Inc.

**Canadian Cataloguing in
Publication Data**

Binhammer, H. H., 1927–
 Money, banking and the
Canadian financial system

8th ed.
Includes bibliographical references
and index.
ISBN 0-17-616856-7

1. Finance - Canada. 2. Banks and
banking - Canada. 3. Monetary
policy - Canada. 4. Finance. I.
Sephton, Peter S. II. Title.

HG185.C2B5 2000
332'.0971   C00-932807-6

CREDITS

Bank of Canada
Information is adapted and repro-
duced with the permission of the
Minister of Public Works and
Government Services, 2000.

*Canada Deposit Insurance
Corporation*
Information is reproduced with the
permission of the Canada Deposit
Insurance Corporation.

Canadian Payments Association
The CPA is not responsible for the
accuracy or reliability of the repro-
duction of the information.

Government of Canada
Information is reproduced with the
permission of the Minister of
Public Works and Government
Services, 2000.

*Office of the Superintendent of
Financial Institutions*
Data reflected at the OSFI website
has been provided by the companies themselves and the OSFI can
make no claim as to the accuracy
of the information provided.

Statistics Canada
Statistics Canada information is
used with the permission of the
Minister of Industry, as Minister
responsible for Statistics Canada.
Information on the availability of
the wide range of data from
Statistics Canada can be obtained
from Statistics Canada's Regional
Offices, its World Wide Web site at
http://www.statscan.ca, and its toll-
free access number
1-800-263-1136.

To Susan, Jennifer, and William with love.

P.S.S.

To my grandchildren, Sarah and Robert Gates, with love.

H.H.B.

$\mathscr{C}$ONTENTS

PREFACE

The new millennium will see changes in the Canadian financial sector that few could have imagined 30 years ago. Indeed, as we complete this, the eighth edition of the book, the federal government has just announced sweeping reforms for the financial services sector in Canada. As might be expected, the reforms have been embraced by some and denounced by others. Such is the nature of economic policymaking, particularly when it comes to issues relating to money—who has it, who can control its creation, and how it can be used to generate income and wealth.

This edition builds on the last, retaining its pedagogical features, which include learning objectives at the beginning of each chapter, margin definitions of important terms, and the use of boxes to discuss topical issues and to provide background information. Every discipline has its own language, and we have found that the margin definitions help students manage the "lingo" of the financial world. At the end of every chapter we repeat these key terms, with their definitions appearing again in the glossary at the end of the book.

The more significant changes in this edition include

- adding an introductory chapter outlining our approach, with an aggregate demand–aggregate supply model to motivate discussion
- analyzing exchange rates earlier in the book
- moving much of the material on Canadian monetary history to appendices
- including more review questions
- combining previous chapters on central bank policy instruments into a single chapter
- devoting a single chapter to the demand for money
- discussing the Euro and its impact
- discussing the pros and cons of moving to a common North American currency
- updating the current monetary policy and regulatory environments
- adding margin graphics indicating associated Web content at the book's Website, <http://money.nelson.com>

www.

Supplements

This book has its own Web site where instructors and students can search for information on money, banking, and financial markets in Canada and around the world. Students will appreciate the online, autograded, multiple-choice tutorials—akin to an online study guide. The tutorials help students determine which chapters and topics they need to focus their preparation on, and provide sample tests for students.

This book also has a computerized test bank for instructors to use in student evaluation. A hard copy is available, if requested. PowerPoint lectures and an Instructor's Manual containing answers to all of the review questions round out the list of available supplements. We've tried to make both teaching and learning the material as enjoyable as possible!

Acknowledgments

We owe a debt of gratitude to many people who have contributed in the preparation of this edition. We are grateful to our colleagues for their generosity, and to Joseph Atta-Mensah of the Bank of Canada, for hearing us out and setting us straight. We have also benefited from comments on the seventh edition by Dale Box, University College of the Fraser Valley; Kum Hon Chu, Memorial University; Duane Rockerbie, University of Lethbridge; James Savary, York University, Glendon College; and Lance Shandler, Kwantlen University College. Anthony Bassett and Mustapha Kichane kindly provided comments that substantially improved the final version of the text, as did Linda Williams, former student par excellence and the author of the PowerPoint slides and the Instructor's Manual. Finally, we express our thanks to the editors and production staff at Nelson Thomson Learning, especially Paul Manley (acquisitions editor) and Karina TenVeldhuis (senior project editor).

H.H. Binhammer   P.S. Sephton
Kingston, Ontario   Fredericton, New Brunswick

$\mathscr{A}$N $\mathscr{I}$NTRODUCTION TO $\mathscr{M}$ONEY, $\mathscr{B}$ANKING, AND THE $\mathscr{C}$ANADIAN $\mathscr{F}$INANCIAL $\mathscr{S}$YSTEM

After reading this chapter you should be able to
1. *Describe the importance of the financial system to the economy*
2. *Provide a role for monetary policy in the management of aggregate demand*
3. *Outline our approach to further study*

Why Study Money, Banking, and the Canadian Financial System?

Every day, the media bombard us with new information on financial markets and how those markets will affect our future. Our aim in this book is to provide you with a framework that will help you to understand the importance of the financial system, how it operates, why it plays a central role in the economy, why governments get involved in regulating financial markets and their participants, the roles that monetary policy can and cannot play, how international factors contribute to and constrain the system, and the history and evolution of Canada's monetary system. When you finish studying the book, you should have a firm grasp of the fundamental issues and should more fully appreciate the roles that money and the financial system play in your life.

WHAT IF? To start to grasp the importance of money and the financial system, consider what your daily routine would consist of if you had to be self-sufficient; there would be no supermarkets where you could buy food, no clothing stores, no dentists or hairstylists, no lawyers (some might think this a *good thing*, to paraphrase Martha Stewart), and no economists (we'll remain silent on this one). Your daily routine would be much different from what it is today. Let's suppose you need a tooth pulled, and that you cannot manage to

1

do the job on your own (there are some things that even economists won't do). What would you do? Obviously, you would need to find someone whose skills included pulling teeth, and that person would need to be willing to provide the service to you—perhaps in exchange for something you own or some service you could provide.

As we will learn in Chapter 2, the type of economy we have just described is based on a **double coincidence of wants**—each party must need what the other has to offer before trade can take place.

Money allows us to move beyond self-sufficiency. You could pay the person specializing in pulling teeth with **money**—we will see an exact definition of money in Chapter 2—and you would no longer be limited to trading goods and services for goods and services. Trades could take place based on transferring ownership of some form of generalized purchasing power (money), and this transfer of ownership would allow individuals to specialize in what they do best.

Trading money for goods and services allows people to expand their opportunities to produce and consume.

It appears that money, however we define it, is useful; it provides a valuable service. So do financial markets—markets in which money and closely related assets are traded. To understand why, consider the following example. Suppose you want to buy some land from someone who is willing to trade the land for money. Let's further suppose that you have enough of what we're calling money to buy a large parcel of land, but that you are concerned about being robbed on your way to trade the money for the land. Having the ability to trade the money for the land in a well-organized market means you simply transfer the ownership of the land for the ownership of the money. The transaction is immune from robbery. The financial markets provide a valuable service and increase the scope of possible transactions in the economy.

We think you are getting the picture, but just to make sure, let's consider one more example. Suppose you don't have enough money to buy all the land you want right now. Why? Let's say you are an apple farmer, and the apples won't be ready to harvest for another five months. You want to buy the land now. If you could borrow money against the income you will make selling the apples in the future, you might be able to buy the land today. A financial market that allows people to borrow and lend provides for a greater number of transactions—it widens the scope of possible trades—and society is better off. Thus, financial markets provide valuable services to the economy.

REGULATION   In a system just beginning to use money as a payment instrument, it won't be long before some people realize they can benefit from creating counterfeit money (all those robbers who find themselves out of business as people move to trading on organized financial markets!). The risk of physical injury is small (compared to other illegal activities), and the potential for gain is immense. Other people will realize that it has become easier to sell products that many in society view as being detrimental to its welfare (illegal drugs, prostitution). "Shady operators" may decide to operate their own financial markets in which competing goods and services—perhaps of dubious quality—are bought and sold, borrowed, and lent. All these factors suggest that the government, as an agent for the people, might decide to intervene in the

double coincidence of wants a situation in which two or more individuals have what others want, and trade accordingly

money anything that provides monetary functions

www.

BOX 1–1 BACKGROUNDER

Economic Development and Money

There are some interesting parallels between the monetary system, globalization, and growth in the twentieth century and over the period from 1100 to 1300, called the "commercial revolution" by some economic historians. These similarities serve as a reminder that underlying economic forces have operated and contributed to shaping history long before economics was recognized as a (social) science.

The commercial revolution was a period of rapid output growth, urbanization, population growth, and technological innovation that transformed key parts of Western Europe from an autarkic and feudal economy to a vibrant commercial one. The progress made during that period led to European economic and political hegemony of subsequent centuries. The seeds of many legal and economic institutions that prevail today were also sown back then.

One striking resemblance between the commercial revolution and the period of rapid economic growth during the gold standard era and since the Second World War is the performance of the monetary and financial systems. During the commercial revolution, the emerging nation-states took control over issuance of coins and provided the infrastructure for the accelerating pace of interregional and international trade. The state regained monetary control by competing with private coin producers and proliferated during the eleventh century. The state prevailed because it was able to circulate a stable, reputable, and therefore universally accepted medium of exchange that catered to the merchant community's demand. By 1250, gold coins were being issued and a truly international currency (the Florentine Florin) emerged. A process of regional monetary integration and an era of price stability were inaugurated.

The stability of the monetary system and rates of exchange allowed the development of banks and, in particular, bills of exchange that facilitated international transactions and contributed to the rise in trade volumes, which facilitated the process of division of labour and specialization. There was also a substantial amount of foreign lending to governments. The result of these developments enabled the European periphery, most notably England, to reap the fruits of economic growth. While hard data are lacking, one can speak of a process of convergence within Europe and convergence between Europe and the more advanced regions of the world at that time—China and the Orient.

By the late thirteenth century, growth rates started to decline and many regions descended into economic crisis.[1] Much like the reaction of states in the interwar period and during the Great Depression, many states abandoned and others were forced to abandon stable monetary policies. Parallel to the increase in warfare, many states took recourse to inflationary finance, and monetary wars raged for almost two centuries. Foreign lending also collapsed, as did international trade credit, and the most prominent Italian banks were forced into bankruptcy. As in the 1930s, monetary disintegration and exchange rate volatility exacerbated the decline in output and delayed recovery.

---

1. Historians do not agree on the reasons for this decline. Some suspect that climatic change had a significant impact, while others argue that the fall of the Crusader state and the decline in trade across to the Orient are to blame. And some think that the rapid increase in population, not matched by sustained productivity growth, sent Europe into a Malthusian trap.

SOURCE: International Monetary Fund, *World Economic Outlook*, May 2000, p. 164.

marketplace to guarantee that money retains its value and that financial markets operate to support common standards and morals. In a democracy, that's what governments do: They act as an agent for the people—at least in theory. So, government intervention has a role to play in financial markets and in the issuance of money, as well as in the regulation of money and the financial markets. Much debate centres on what should be regulated and how. For now, we think you'll agree that there is a role for intervention—perhaps a limited role, but a role nevertheless.

DEVELOPING COUNTRIES   Sometimes, the easiest way to appreciate the value provided by money and financial markets is to turn on the television, or surf the Net, and learn about the struggles developing countries endure to increase the welfare of their citizens. Those nations with well-functioning financial systems appear to grow much faster than do their developing counterparts. Economic development depends critically on the infrastructure provided by the financial system, since the system supports the efficient allocation of society's resources (as long as corrupt government officials are removed). Without the ability to trade and transact—critical roles played by money and the financial system—no amount of development assistance is going to help a country move beyond its most rudimentary, agrarian base.

INFRASTRUCTURE   One of our other objectives in this book is to describe Canada's financial infrastructure—the various types, functions, and roles of financial institutions and markets. A well-developed and efficient financial infrastructure is an important base for a well-functioning economy. As we will learn, monetary policy depends critically on that infrastructure.

We think you'll agree that money and financial markets provide value to society. Now let's delve deeper to understand some important economic variables and to see the ways in which money and financial markets are central to the economy.

Aggregate Demand Management

Do you remember playing the game Mouse Trap™? A player dropped a marble down a chute, and it would travel along a path, knocking down levers, and making contact with the trap, which, if you dropped the marble just right, would fall on the mouse, thereby winning the game. Economic policy is a lot like this game. The authorities have objectives they want to achieve: high economic growth, low unemployment, and low inflation, to name just a few. The government has at its disposal an arsenal of policy instruments, and it uses those instruments to hit as many of its objectives as possible.

Figure 1–1 shows the history of Canadian output growth over the past 40 years. As you can see, real output generally rises year over year, but sometimes the economy goes through periods of recession in which real output actually falls. Consider Figure 1–2, a plot of the Canadian unemployment rate. You can see that the unemployment rate cycles up and down over the business cycle,

BOX 1–2 BACKGROUNDER

When Is a Dollar a Dollar?

CAN'T PAY TAX IN PESOS, COURT RULES

CALGARIAN SAW A BAR MISSING IN AGENCY'S DOLLAR SYMBOL

BY PAUL WALDIE

James Weber thought he had found the ultimate tax loophole.

Last year, the Calgary resident paid a $110 650 tax bill with 110 650 Colombian pesos, worth about $75.

Mr. Weber argued that the dollar sign used by the Canada Customs and Revenue Agency is incorrect because it has only one bar through it instead of two.

A dollar sign with one bar, he claimed, denoted Colombian pesos (as well as several currencies in other South American countries), but not Canadian dollars.

Tax officials didn't buy the argument, and last August they seized Mr. Weber's BMW motorcycle along with his motorcycle helmet, jacket, and pants.

But Mr. Weber continued to argue that he'd paid what he owed, and the case ended up in the Federal Court of Canada.

At a hearing last month, Mr. Weber filed 50 documents to back up his claim that the only official sign for a Canadian dollar is the one with two bars through it. His supporting documents included banking dictionaries, Oxford and Webster's dictionaries, Bank of Canada material dating back to 1910, and even the *British North America Act,* which, he said, "utilizes the icons for the class of dollars—S with two vertical bars—six times."

All the documents prove, he alleged, that "this financial symbol has been accepted as the financial symbol for the Canadian dollar."

While the Federal Court judges applauded Mr. Weber for raising an intriguing argument, they still ruled against him.

The court noted that one of Mr. Weber's own documents proved that Canada also uses a dollar sign with one bar. A complete version of one of the Webster's dictionaries Mr. Weber cited "illustrates the Canadian dollar sign also to be a one-bar dollar sign," the court ruled. The judges noted that Mr. Weber had edited the text to exclude the symbol.

"The whole exercise may be summed up by saying that neither the Canadian tax system nor, indeed, the Canadian economy, ought to be held hostage to a typesetter's selection, at any given time, of what is considered a pleasing and useful typeface for a dollar sign," the court ruled.

"Were Mr. Weber's gambit to have been successful one might, in April, expect a high demand in Canada for Colombian pesos, pushing the Colombian peso far beyond the present worth of less than a thousandth of a cent. As it is, taxpayers, including [Mr. Weber], will have to pay taxes this year in Canadian dollars."

The *Encyclopedia of Word and Phrase Origins* says the dollar symbol probably derives from "the twisted Pillars of Hercules stamped with a scroll around them on [Spanish] pieces of eight." Another possibility is that the symbol is a corruption of Ps, the Spanish contraction of peso.

SOURCE: Paul Waldie, "Can't Pay Tax in Pesos, Court Rules," *National Post*, March 22, 2000, p. A10. Reprinted by permission.

FIGURE 1–1 **CANADIAN ECONOMIC GROWTH**

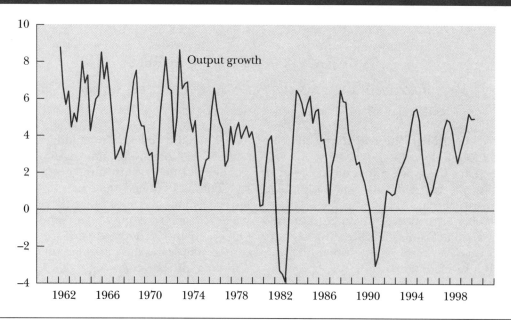

SOURCE: Statistics Canada, CANSIM Database, Series D14872, June 2000.

FIGURE 1–2 **UNEMPLOYMENT IN CANADA**

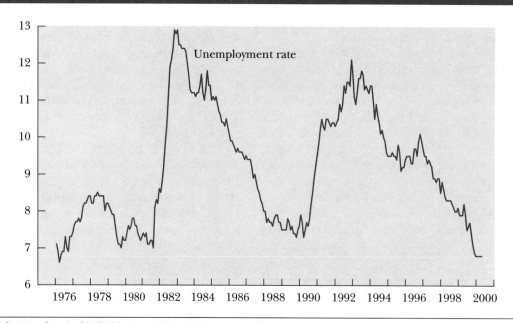

SOURCE: Statistics Canada, CANSIM Database, Series D980745, June 2000.

and that there are prolonged periods during which the unemployment rate appears to remain relatively high. One of the objectives of macroeconomic policy is to dampen recessions and lessen their severity, but as we will see, there's much more to policy than simply moderating fluctuations in output and unemployment. For example, in Canada and many other industrialized nations today, monetary policy is aimed at maintaining a low and stable rate of inflation.

Figure 1–3 plots the Canadian inflation rate and the Canadian interest rate since 1979. You can see that both the inflation rate and the interest rate have been highly volatile over about half of the past 25 years. It also appears that interest rates and inflation move in unison over time. One of our aims in this book is to help you understand the nature of the relationship between interest rates and the rate of inflation. If you examine the past 10 years of data in Figure 1–3, you will see that Canada has enjoyed a period of relatively low and stable inflation, and interest rates have followed a similar path. Was this simply good luck, or was monetary policy designed to achieve these objectives? At what cost to society? We will spend quite a bit of time learning why the Bank of Canada has embarked on a policy of attaining **price stability**—by which we mean a low and stable rate of inflation. We will answer questions such as

price stability *a policy aimed at maintaining a low and stable rate of inflation*

- Why is low and stable inflation reflected in interest rates, and how are the two related?
- What are the benefits of having low interest rates and a stable and low inflation rate?

FIGURE 1–3 CANADIAN INFLATION AND INTEREST RATES

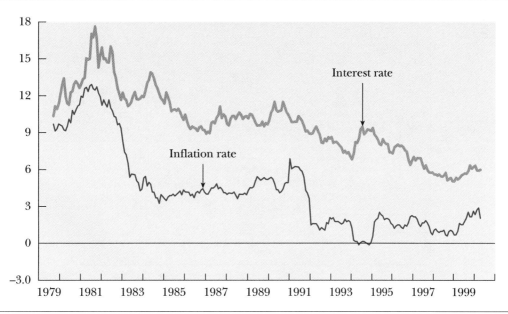

SOURCE: Statistics Canada, CANSIM Database, Series P119500 and B14013, June 2000.

Being able to answer these questions is an important, tangible benefit of studying *Money, Banking, and the Canadian Financial System.*

ECONOMIC POLICY   One way in which governments intervene in markets is through **aggregate demand management policies**—policies that raise or lower the level of aggregate demand in the economy. Consider Figure 1–4, a plot of aggregate demand and aggregate supply curves for an economy. The vertical axis measures the overall price level in the economy, while the horizontal axis measures the quantity of real output produced in one year. The intersection of aggregate demand and aggregate supply tells us the level of equilibrium income and the equilibrium price level. If the authorities want to achieve a higher level of real income, they can shift the aggregate demand curve to the right, with the economy moving from point *A* to point *B*. Note that both output and the price level rise because of this expansionary policy. You can also see that as the level of aggregate demand rises, the price level eventually rises more than real income rises, with a further shift in aggregate demand taking the economy to point *C*.

aggregate demand management policies
economic policies aimed at manipulating the level of aggregate demand in the economy

FIGURE 1–4   EQUILIBRIUM IN THE AGGREGATE DEMAND-AGGREGATE SUPPLY MODEL

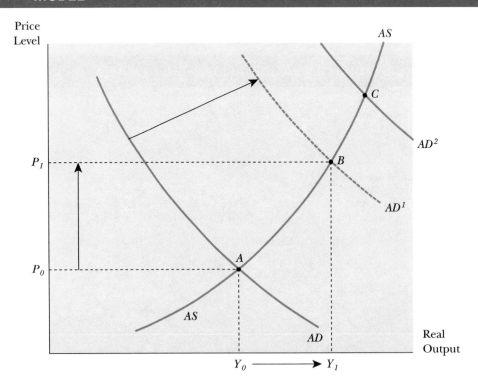

Aggregate demand and aggregate supply jointly determine equilibrium output and the price level. As aggregate demand rises, proportionately more of these changes are reflected in the price level.

FIGURE 1–5 **FAILURE OF POLICY TO RAISE OUTPUT**

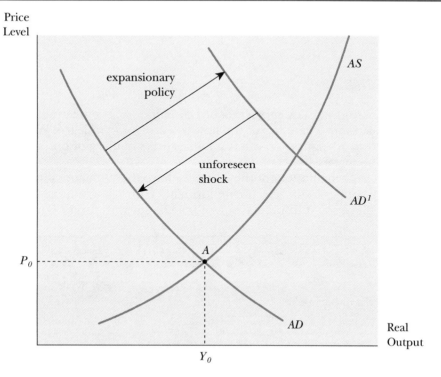

An expansion policy can raise aggregate demand. An unforeseen reduction in demand can offset the expansionary impact of that policy initiative.

Monetary policy is one tool of demand management policy. Through the judicious choice of policy instruments, the authorities manipulate aggregate demand to achieve their objectives for the target variables. At least, in theory, this is how things are supposed to work. As we will see, policies can fail to accomplish their objectives in several ways. Figure 1–5 demonstrates how economic policy might not work as expected.

Suppose the government wanted output to rise, and it implemented an expansionary policy that, ceteris paribus,[1] would shift the aggregate demand curve to the right. Just as the aggregate demand curve is about to shift to the right, think about what happens if the foreign demand for Canadian goods falls unexpectedly. This drop shifts the aggregate demand curve back from where it would have been, and the government would fail to meet its target for national income.

In other chapters, we'll examine how monetary policy can be used to affect aggregate demand, consider the various channels through which monetary

1. Recall that the Latin phrase *ceteris paribus* means "holding all other things constant." When we consider one change to our economic models, we invoke this assumption so that we can trace how the change affects the system.

policy might work, and examine the history of monetary policy in Canada for the lessons we can learn from the past. It is an exciting time to be studying *Money, Banking, and the Canadian Financial System*!

What's to Come

In studying any subject, be it economics or engineering, you need to have a firm understanding of the how you are going to learn. We think our "big picture" in Figure 1–6 offers an attractive summary of our approach to learning the material.

At the bottom of the figure we have the ultimate objectives of policy: high output growth, low unemployment, and a low and stable rate of inflation (there could be others, but we'll be happy with three). These are the targets—

FIGURE 1–6   THE BIG PICTURE: A PLAN FOR STUDY

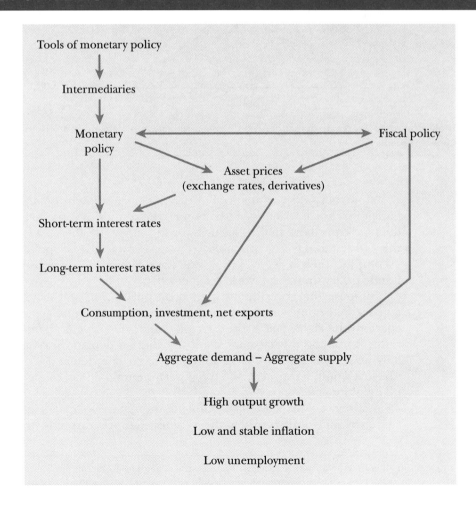

in our Mouse Trap game, they represent the mouse that we want to trap. Working back from this link, we see the aggregate demand–aggregate supply model of output and price determination. You can see that both fiscal policy and monetary policy directly affect this model. Moving back another stage takes us to important determinants of aggregate demand: consumption, investment, and net exports (exports minus imports). Given targets for the level of aggregate demand, the authorities create intermediate targets for these three components of aggregate demand. How is this accomplished?

Move up another level. Long-term interest rates, we will see, determine how households choose to smooth consumption over time and affect the willingness of firms to undertake investment projects. Thus, we need to examine how long-term interest rates are set. We will demonstrate that long-term interest rates are partly a function of current and expected future short-term interest rates, and that we need to consider the role that exchange rates play in international investment strategies. In today's global economy, almost every financial market is tied to other markets through the potential for cross-market trades, which take place with the click of a button on your mouse. If we are buying Canadian dollars using Japanese yen, we might be able to benefit from price discrepancies across markets in Toronto, New York, and Tokyo. Our theories linking long-term interest rates to short-term interest rates need to consider these international factors, particularly given that Canada has a relatively small, open economy.

To see how interest rates are determined, we'll look at the decisions facing investors. Portfolio optimization models will help us to understand how and why investors choose to hold many different assets in their "asset basket." These models require that we examine the role that the authorities play in regulating financial markets. Since there are several different types of financial actors, or intermediaries, we'll need to examine how they behave and how (and why) regulatory bodies treat them differently. Then we'll look at how the tools of monetary policy affect financial intermediaries. Today, in the new millennium, central bank policy is implemented by changing the behaviour of the financial intermediaries. The central bank sits back (most of the time), and allows the marketplace to work, in much the same way parents do by requiring children to do their chores before they receive their allowance, thereby assuring good behaviour (as long as the allowance is high enough).

We'll finish off with some monetary history and a review of Bank of Canada policy so that you'll have a firm grasp of the current state of monetary policy in Canada.

Figure 1–6 provides us with a roadmap for our travels. Let's get started by asking some questions about what we mean when we say "money," and delve into a deceptively simple question: What is money?

KEY TERMS

aggregate demand management
  policies

double coincidence of wants
money

price stability

REVIEW QUESTIONS

1. Figure 1–3 plots the Canadian inflation rate and an interest rate for the past 20 years. It appears that the two rates move together over time. Why?
2. How can the aggregate demand–aggregate supply model be used to explain recessions and economic booms? What are some of the factors that economists consider when they determine by how much a policy variable needs to be changed to achieve a certain target for output?

3. The "big picture" in Figure 1–6 provides an outline for the book. Explain, using an example, how the central bank might trace the effects of a change in the money supply on the ultimate objectives of monetary policy.
4. Figure 1–6 indicates that there are three objectives of monetary policy. Can you name two others? Explain why the central bank might be concerned with your choices.

SELECTED READINGS

Bank of Canada. *Monetary Policy Report* (May 2000).

Colander, D., and P. Sephton. *Macroeconomics,* First Canadian Edition. Toronto: McGraw Hill Ryerson, 1996.

CHAPTER TWO

MONEY, MONETARY STANDARDS, AND PAYMENTS SYSTEMS

After reading this chapter you should be able to
1. Outline the nature and functions of money
2. Discuss the evolution of and kinds of money
3. Describe the composition of the Canadian money supply
4. Provide a historical record of what North Americans have used as money over the past 200 years
5. Explain the payments system and its evolution
6. List several ways in which technological changes affect money and the payments system

The Nature and Functions of Money

Probably no subject is more widely discussed than money. Many of us are familiar with the popular saying that "money makes the world go around," but what do we mean when we use the term "money"? What is money? Where does it come from? Why does it matter? What does money do for us? Why do we always want more money than we have? We will try to address these questions in this chapter.

When we think about money, we need to consider the different roles that money plays in the economy. Anything can serve as **money** as long as it performs three important functions: as a standard unit of account, as a medium of exchange, and as a store of value.

money anything that fulfils monetary functions

A STANDARD UNIT OF ACCOUNT   An economy without money is a **barter economy**: one good has to be exchanged for another, which in turn may be exchanged for yet another, and so on. The terms of exchange depend on the values placed on goods by those entering into the various exchanges. The primitive way of establishing values was to compare the size or quantity of the items to be exchanged. For example, the value of one cow could be expressed

barter economy an economy without money— all trade is based on the exchange of goods and services as two goats or five cubic metres of wheat. The ratios of exchange between goods express their **relative prices**.

In an economy without money, the number of ratios of exchange is given by the simple formula

$$\frac{N(N-1)}{2}$$

relative prices
the price of one good relative to another

absolute price
the price of one good in terms of the price of money

where N is the number of goods. Applying this formula in a strictly barter economy, with 100 items to exchange, you would wind up with 4950 different relative prices. You would need a computer to remember all these prices! Fortunately, there is an alternative: the standard unit of account. In a monetary economy, money performs this function.

Money serves as a "numeraire," or yardstick, for measuring value in exchange. In an economy with money, each good or service has just one price expressed in terms of money. We call this its **absolute price**. The money price of one good in terms of the money price of another good expresses its relative price. Consider the above example, with 100 items to be exchanged. If one of these items functions as money, we now have only 99 absolute prices instead of 4950 relative prices. The formula for determining the number of ratios of exchange between goods is now $(N-1)$.

The unit of account is used for more than just measuring value in exchange. It also functions as a measure for specifying the value of deferred, or future, payment. Contracts calling for future payment are normally expressed in terms of the standard unit of account. If dollars are the standard unit of account and your sister borrows five dollars from you, she owes you five dollars. You usually do not tell her that she owes you five nights of doing your chores (although that might be a good bargain).

When we measure weight, the unit of account is the gram; when we measure distance, it is the metre. In either case the unit of account is an abstract phenomenon. Similarly, our monetary unit, the dollar, can be considered a purely abstract unit of account. For example, when an accountant enters a dollar into a ledger, the dollar has no physical presence. Historically, however, measures of the values of things have been expressed in both abstract and physical units. In early Canada, for example, beaver skins were the standard measure of value. Today, our dollar, in addition to being used as an abstract unit of account, may also have a physical presence. Such is the case when we hand over coins and Bank of Canada notes (currency) for items we purchase.

The introduction of money to express and compare the value of goods and services was probably as significant for the economic development of society as was the invention of the wheel for technology. Money prices provide an efficient information system that allows us to formulate and to order our preferences and, ultimately, to make our choices.

www.

double coincidence of wants
a situation in which two or more individuals have what others want and trade accordingly

A MEDIUM OF EXCHANGE   Without money to provide a generally acceptable medium of exchange, our only alternative is to barter. Suppose a farmer wants to trade a cow for a horse. First, she must search for someone who wants to sell a horse, but even if the farmer finds such a person, a trade cannot be concluded unless the other person also wants to buy a cow. Hence, direct exchange can take place only when a **double coincidence of wants** exists.

Without this coincidence, the farmer must engage in intermediate trades before finally exchanging the cow for a horse. For instance, she may start by trading the cow for some goats. The next step could be finding someone who will exchange some wheat for these goats. The wheat can then be traded for some pigs, which in turn can finally be traded for the horse. All these intermediate trades can be avoided with the introduction of money, since money serves as a generally acceptable medium of exchange and thereby eliminates the need for a double coincidence of wants. With money, the farmer only has to make two trades: the cow for money, and the money for the horse. Best of all, the time and effort previously required to gather information in the search for advantageous intermediate trades can be used in more productive ways.

Money provides generalized purchasing power because it is a "bearer of options," making it possible to separate the decision to buy from the decision to sell. The freedom that the use of money allows has been the very foundation of our market system and of the efficient use of our resources. When the possibilities of trade are limited to barter, each household tends to strive for self-sufficiency. The production advantages of occupational specialization and division of labour cannot be exploited effectively. Furthermore, without the use of money, workers have to be paid for their services in kind. Such a method of payment can result in waste, or what economists call an inefficient allocation of resources. Waste occurs when, in payment for their services, workers receive goods they can neither consume nor readily trade for other goods they both need and desire.

liquidity *the nearness to money or ease with which an asset can be sold or converted into money on short notice at a predictable price with little cost*

liquid *an asset is liquid when it can be converted into money quickly with little cost*

A STORE OF VALUE   Money is but one of many things that may serve as a store of value. Land, buildings, stocks, bonds, and precious metals, to mention only a few examples, are also stores of value. The things that we hold as part of our wealth are called *assets*. Money is different from other assets, however, in that it is a liquid store of value. **Liquidity** refers to the relative ease and small transaction costs associated with using an asset to make payments. When an asset is also the generally acceptable medium of exchange, it is said to be perfectly **liquid.**

Although money need not be perfectly liquid to be a store of value, we expect it to have superior liquidity relative to other assets. As such, money has low transaction costs in terms of its command over other resources, and the value of money is relatively more stable than the value of other things that could be used to store wealth. Because of these attributes money provides a temporary abode for purchasing power: It is held in the interim between receiving payment and making payment.

Monetary Standards

When we speak of a country's monetary standard, we refer to the entire set of laws and practices that have established that country's ultimate, or standard, money. Nonstandard money is credit money, which represents promises to pay a designated amount of standard money. Credit money can be issued by the government in the form of paper promises to pay standard money, or in the form of subsidiary coin redeemable in standard money. Banks have traditionally been the most important source of credit money. At one time banks issued bank notes, which were promises by the bank to supply standard money on demand. When governments and their agencies took over the issue of notes for circulation, the banks' chief form of credit money became their demand deposits (chequing accounts).

A country's monetary standard depends on what that country designates as standard money. Although many modifications exist, there are only two basic standards: (1) commodity standards, and (2) credit, or inconvertible "managed" paper standards.

Commodity Standards

**commodity
standard**
*a monetary
system in which
the value of the
monetary unit is
kept equal to the
value of a spe-
cific quantity of a
particular com-
modity or group
of commodities*

A **commodity standard** is a monetary system in which the value of the monetary unit is kept equal to the value of a specific quantity of a particular commodity or group of commodities. Of all the commodities that have been used as a base for monetary systems, precious metals, especially gold and silver, have the longest history. Metallic standards based on only one metal are known as monometallic standards; those founded on two metals are known as bimetallic standards. Monometallic standards using silver (silver standard) were popular in China, India, and Central and South America. Gold has played a more important role in Western nations, particularly the United Kingdom, France, the United States, and Canada. In the late nineteenth century and early twentieth century, the monometallic gold standard was considered a sign of monetary maturity.

MONOMETALLIC STANDARDS   Monometallic standards achieved their greatest degree of sophistication when gold served as standard money. In its purest form a monometallic standard is also a metallic coin standard. The two major modifications of the metallic coin standard are the *bullion standard* and the *exchange standard*, both of which developed while gold was the standard metal. A country is said to have a **metallic coin standard** when its monetary authorities follow certain requisites:

**metallic coin
standard**
*a monetary
system in which
the value of the
monetary unit is
kept equal to the
value of a spe-
cific metal*

1. The country's monetary unit of account is defined by statute to contain a specific quantity of the metallic commodity. For example, when the United Kingdom operated on the gold coin standard before the First World War, the sovereign was declared equivalent to 123.2744 grains of fine gold. Before 1933, when the United States was on a gold coin standard, the dollar was defined as containing 25.8 grains of gold nine-tenths fine, or 23.22 grains of fine gold.

2. Under a "full" (also referred to as a "pure" or "free") monometallic coin standard, free coinage (of metal to coin) and free convertibility (of coin to metal) must prevail in an unlimited amount. Free coinage means that the public has the right to take unlimited quantities of the standard metal to the national treasury or its agency and have it minted into coin at no cost and at a rate fixed by the definition of the unit of account. Free convertibility means that the public is free to take metallic coins from its hoards

and out of circulation and convert them to industrial use or into bullion. Free coinage, free convertibility, and the additional requirement allowing export and import of the standard metal in coin and bullion ensure equality between the face value of coins and the value of the metal of which they are composed. For example, when the United States was minting $10 gold pieces of 232.2 grains of fine gold, the $10 gold coin had the same value as 232.2 grains of unminted fine gold in the gold commodity market. Only under a full (or pure) coin standard where coinage is free, or gratuitous, will there be complete equality between the face value of the coin and its metal content. Under the gold coin standard, some countries charged a fee called **brassage** to cover the costs of coinage, while others absorbed the cost of operating the mint but charged for the alloys used in hardening coins. Some countries also charged a fee for exchanging coin for unminted metal. The fees charged produced only slight discrepancies between the value of the coins and the market value of an equivalent amount of unminted metal. Values did vary, however, when mints were operated to produce seigniorage, or profit.

brassage a fee charged to cover the costs of coinage

3. Another requisite of a metallic coin standard is that all other types of money are redeemable at par into metal coin. In the countries that adopted a silver or gold standard, the circulation of full-bodied coins was supplemented with other kinds of money or nonstandard money in the form of token-coin and credit or paper money. Nonstandard money was introduced because full-bodied metal coins could not be minted into small enough denominations to provide small change. Nonstandard money also allowed countries to expand their money supply beyond the limits imposed by the strict amount of the metal available. As long as people were confident that the nonstandard money would be redeemed in standard money and that the value of credit money of various denominations would at all times have value equal to metal coins of the same denominations, they were willing to hold substantial amounts of nonstandard money and not exercise their redemption rights. Under normal conditions, the monetary authorities could meet the redemption requirement without holding an amount of the money metal equal to the value of the nonstandard money issued. As long as the authorities could gauge public confidence, they could issue nonstandard money in excess of the standard money available to them, thus expanding the total money supply beyond the limits imposed by the strict amount of the metal available.

Public acceptance of nonstandard money made modifications of the monometallic coin standard possible. The first of these modifications was the bullion standard. When convenience made paper money and token-coin the day-to-day medium of exchange, coins remained in the vaults of the treasury and the banks and in the hands of hoarders. Since there was no real advantage to the treasury or banks in holding standard money as coin rather than as bullion, minting of coin became an unnecessary expense. The monometallic coin standard was modified, therefore, to the bullion standard. When unlimited amounts of coin were no longer available to the public, metal hoarding declined, making it possible to conserve the supply of standard money. With more metal left in their hands, the monetary authorities were able to maintain a larger money circulation. The production of the monetary metal, especially gold, did not increase at a rate demanded by the expansion of economic activity. Thus, the amount of the metal that the monetary authorities could obtain through the reduction of hoarding became an important factor in the expansion of the total money supply.

monometallic bullion standard a form of metallic coin standard

The requisites of a **monometallic bullion standard** are:

1. All kinds of credit money, which provide the only medium of exchange, are redeemable at par in bullion—uncoined metal in the form of bars. However, since gold bars have traditionally been made in minimum sizes containing many hundred ounces of the precious metal, redemption is limited to those who can afford to exchange a relatively large amount of credit money. The gold bullion standard has sometimes been called "the rich man's gold standard." It was adopted by the United Kingdom in 1925 and by France in 1928.

2. As under a coin standard, the country's money unit of account is defined by statute to contain a specific quantity of the metallic commodity.

3. The government no longer coins the standard metal. It does, however, undertake to buy and sell unlimited quantities of the standard metal at an established price. This provision, along with the free import and export of the metal, ensures equality between the value of the monetary unit and the domestic and foreign market value of the corresponding quantity of the metal.

metallic exchange standard a form of metallic coin standard

The **metallic exchange standard**, like the bullion standard, is another modification of the metallic standard made by countries in an attempt to remain on a commodity standard at a time when the stock of the standard metal did not increase at the rate required for the desired expansion of economic activity. This situation occurred after the First World War, when the standard metal was gold. The requisites of a metallic exchange standard are:

1. As under both a coin and a bullion standard, the country's money unit of account is defined by statute to contain a specific quantity of the metallic commodity.

2. Either the country maintains no metallic reserves at home and depends entirely on the metallic reserves of other countries for its standard money, or, as is usually the case, the country maintains partial metallic reserves at home and supplements them by reserves held in the form of short-term investments in a foreign country. The government or its agency does not undertake to buy and sell metallic coin or bullion. Instead, the government undertakes to buy and sell, at an established price, unlimited quantities of drafts (or bills of exchange) against the reserves it maintains in foreign financial institutions. These drafts are in turn convertible into metallic coin or bullion in the foreign country.

Under an exchange standard, a country links its nonstandard money indirectly to metal by making it convertible into foreign currency or foreign claims that are directly convertible into metal. For example, when India adopted a gold exchange standard, most of its standard money was held in British pounds invested in London. Indian nonstandard money was still as good as gold because the Indian monetary authorities could meet the convertibility requirement by selling India's London investments (reserves) for British pounds, which were convertible into gold. For individuals, convertibility was slow and cumbersome, but for India as a whole there were inherent advantages. Even with few or no metallic reserves of its own, it could remain on a commodity standard. Instead of holding gold, which is sterile, pays no interest, and involves a storage cost, the country maintained its reserves of standard money in the form of liquid foreign investments that earned interest and could be converted into metal if necessary.

3. All kinds of credit money, the only medium of exchange, are redeemable at par in metallic drafts convertible into metal abroad. This provision, along with a free market of the metallic commodity, including free export and import, ensures that the value of the nonstandard money is fixed to the value of the metal serving as standard money.

bimetallic standard a metallic coin standard based on two metals

A **bimetallic standard** differs from a monometallic standard in that two metals (usually gold and silver) instead of one are used as standard money. Historically, the transition from a monometallic to a bimetallic standard was made as a method of increasing the stock of standard money. In the United States, bimetallism was also advocated by the "silverites," who wanted an assured market for U.S. silver mines. The characteristics of a bimetallic standard are:

1. The country's standard monetary unit is defined by statute to contain a specific quantity of each of two metals. For example, when the United States first formally adopted a monetary standard in 1792, it chose a bimetallic standard; the dollar was defined as containing either 24.75 grains of fine gold or 371.25 grains of fine silver. This established a fixed ratio, or mint ratio, of 15:1 for the two metals in their use as money.

2. Both metals may be coined, in which case they circulate as money, and all other kinds of circulating money are fully and freely convertible to coin of either metal. If bullion rather than coin is the standard, convertibility is in terms of bullion.

3. If the two metals are coined, coinage must be free. Convertibility of coin to either metal must be permitted, and so must the free import and export of both metals. The convertibility requirement and the free market for both metals must also apply if bullion rather than coin is used for the monetary base. For two metals to coexist in a monetary system, their mint and market ratios must be the same. We have already noted that the mint ratio is defined by statute. The market ratio is the relative bullion price of the two metals determined in the open market. If the mint and market ratios differ, one of the metals will be drained out of the monetary system. The metal that the mint ratio undervalues (in terms of the market ratio) will always tend to disappear; only the metal that the mint ratio overvalues will then be left in the monetary system. An example will illustrate this phenomenon, which is known as Gresham's Law.[1]

---

1. Gresham's Law is named after Sir Thomas Gresham (1519–79), Queen Elizabeth I's Chancellor of the Exchequer, who formulated the theory that "cheap money" drives "dear money" out of circulation.

Let us assume that the mint ratio is established at 15:1; that is, gold as money is worth 15 times as much as silver. Suppose further that the market ratio (or relative free-market price) of the metals as commodities is 16:1; gold as bullion is worth 16 times as much as silver. It will now be profitable for speculators and traders to take silver to the mint in exchange for gold, and take the gold thus acquired and exchange it in the free market at the market value of 16:1. The result will be that with gold flowing into the commodity market and silver into the monetary system, the monetary authorities will be left with little or no gold. The country, though still legally on a bimetallic standard, is de facto on a monometallic standard. Later chapters will provide other examples of **Gresham's Law** at work.

Gresham's Law
bad money drives good money out of circulation

In the example above we explained the difficulties of maintaining a bimetallic standard when the mint ratio and the market ratio diverge. These divergencies are more acute when the foreign and domestic market prices of the two metals differ. In addition, different countries may establish different mint ratios—resulting in the flow of one metal to one country, and of the other metal to another country.

BOX 2–1   BACKGROUNDER

Buddy, Can You Spare an Ingot? The History of Coinage

Early coin, particularly silver and gold, allowed cheating. The weight of a coin was reduced by removing a thin layer of metal from around the edge of the coin, a practice called *clipping*. Clipping was prevented in the seventeenth century by milling the coin. A milled coin has a serrated edge that makes clipping easily noticeable. Milling also put a stop to the more difficult, and therefore less usual, practice of *hollowing* coin. Once clipping and hollowing were prevented, *sweating* began. Sweating was the practice of putting coins in a leather bag and shaking them vigorously over heat to collect small amounts of metallic dust in the bag. The only apparent effect this process had on the coins was that of normal wear.

Once coinage came to play an important role in the economy of the ancient world, political sovereigns assumed the prerogative of minting. The avowed intention was to protect the public interest by providing a uniform, readily recognizable, honest system of coins. In reality, because the state frequently used its monopoly on minting to make a profit by debasing the coinage, those good intentions were often thwarted. Where the state did not take over the minting of coins completely, private merchants were allowed to mint their own coin; alternatively, the state would mint money and allow a few merchants the exclusive right to distribute it. In either case, the merchants paid the state a fee, or seigniorage, for the privilege. In some places where there was free coinage, seigniorage was not imposed.

The first coin minted was full-bodied, which meant that the value written on its face was equal to the value of the metal that composed the coin. With the passage of time, society began to think not about the coin's intrinsic content, but almost entirely in terms of the government stamp on the coin. This made it possible for the government to issue coins of the same gross value and bearing the same stamp on their faces, but containing a smaller proportion of the precious metal. This practice is known as debasement.

Because of their high values, precious metals could not readily be minted into coin

BOX 2–1   BACKGROUNDER (*continued*)

for use in small transactions. To overcome this problem, subsidiary coins were minted from different metals. An early example of subsidiary coinage may be found in the ancient empires of Persia and Rome, where gold coins were the medium of exchange for large transactions, while silver and bronze coins were used for the smaller everyday transactions.

Interestingly, a reverse example is found in early Roman monetary history, where the principal coin was copper. Since the copper coin was unsuitable for large transactions, the silver denarius was introduced in 269 B.C. as a subsidiary coin to facilitate transactions of large value.

Advantages and Disadvantages of Metallic Standards

Advocates of commodity standards, particularly metallic standards, have emphasized the importance of the discipline these standards impose on a country's monetary authorities. Insofar as these standards operate in an automatic way, the authorities cannot manage the total money supply. The money supply changes automatically, in some fixed proportion to changes in the stock of the standard monetary metal available to the monetary authorities. The proportion by which the money supply thus changes depends on the public's confidence in the monetary system and the amount of metal reserves held against each unit of nonstandard money. Under normal circumstances, when the public is confident that the nonstandard money it holds can ultimately be converted into the standard metal, the authorities will need to hold only a relatively small proportion of metallic reserves. In other words, a quantity of nonstandard money can be issued without an equal amount of the metal being held as reserves. For a metallic standard to operate automatically, however, metallic reserves must always be held in some designated fixed proportion to the nonstandard money. Thus, for example, if the metal reserve ratio is fixed at 50 percent, an increase of one unit in the metal reserves must be matched by an increase of two monetary units in the total money supply. In this way, a change in the total money supply takes place as the automatic result of a change in the metal reserve.

Expansion and contraction of the metal reserves, and therefore of the total money supply, can be due to several factors: the metal is imported (or exported), domestic production increases (or begins), or the amounts hoarded or used for nonmonetary purposes change. Proponents of a metallic standard argue that the total money supply must bear a fixed relation to some fundamental factors explaining the economy, and that these factors are reflected in the causes for changes in the supply of monetary metal noted above. History has shown, however, that the changes in the money supply that have been produced by the so-called "automatic working" of metal standards have not always been the changes needed by the economy. The fluctuations in the stock of monetary reserves due to the factors noted need not be the same as the desired changes in economic activity. Nor are these fluctuations necessarily related to the nation's capacity to produce and consume. Surely this capacity, not the amount of the standard metal available to the monetary authorities, should govern the size of the money stock.

Another virtue claimed for the metallic standard is that it maintains long-run stability in the price level. This argument, made by those who favour gold, is based on two propositions: the stability of the world's monetary stock, and the inverse relationship between the output of gold and its price level. The gold stocks available for monetary purposes have been relatively stable because they have been accumulated over the centuries, and because the production of any one year has represented only a small fraction of the available stocks. Even in 1940, the year of the greatest output of gold, total production amounted to less than 5 percent of the existing monetary stocks. The average yearly increment to the total gold stock is about 2 percent. It is contended, therefore, that a price system based on a relatively constant metallic foundation, such as gold, ought to be more stable than one based on a foundation subject to greater variation. The weakness of this argument lies in the fact that while the global stock of gold has shown relatively small annual fluctuation, the supply in an individual country may vary considerably. A country can experience dramatic changes in its stock of the money metal because of its export to and its import from other countries, or because of the discovery of gold within its borders. The implications of these flows for an individual country will be considered later in the book, when we will deal with the international gold standard.

We have observed that one of the requisites for all the kinds of metallic standards is that the standard money of the country be defined by statute to contain a specific quantity of the metallic commodity. This requirement, together with the one of convertibility at a fixed price, means that the price at which the metal may be sold is also fixed. According to one commonly held theory, as prices in general move up, the output of the monetary metal will decline because its costs of production increase along with the rise in price level. The decline in output of the money metal will produce a reduction in the total money supply, which in turn will depress the demand for goods and services and a rise in prices generally. Similarly, if prices in general fall, gold production will become more profitable and will increase; the money supply will then increase, preventing any further fall in the price level. This mechanism assumes a direct relationship between the money supply and the price level and that the production of the monetary metal is turned off and on in response to changes in the cost of its production. We shall discuss the relationship between the money supply and the price level later, when we consider the **quantity theory of money**. For now it is enough to say that in the short run, a proportional relationship may not exist between the money supply and the general price level.

Although the output of gold and the price level tend to move in opposite directions, this movement may be relatively slow. To expand metal production, more equipment is needed to mine and process the metal in less accessible areas and from poorer quality ores. These factors may delay any immediate increase in gold available for monetary purposes. Alternatively, the general rise in prices may not significantly discourage gold production. The producer, having incurred greater fixed costs by installing new machinery, will probably

quantity theory of money *the theory that the quantity of money or its growth is an important determinant of money income in the short run and of the price level in the long run*

continue its increased output as long as its variable costs are being met, even though the general price rise has reduced profits.

Finally, it is argued that a metallic standard and, here again, one based on gold, promotes confidence in a monetary system because gold is almost universally desired for its intrinsic value; that is to say, gold has a value in itself aside from its monetary use. If gold should lose its acceptability as money, it can be made into jewellery, tableware, and the like. This is not the case with irredeemable paper money, which is worthless once its monetary value is lost.

We mentioned earlier that variants of the gold coin standard were introduced because of the shortage of gold for monetary purposes. Scarcity of the monetary metal has been one of the more important shortcomings of monometallic standards. Indeed, the scarcity of the metal and the consequent loss of confidence in its availability have led to "scrambles" for gold and the downfall of the gold standard.

SYMMETALLIC STANDARD AND COMMODITY RESERVE STANDARD

symmetallism when the monetary unit of account is defined as a combination of two metals in some specific proportion to each other

Toward the end of the nineteenth century, a plan known as **symmetallism** was proposed as a solution to the problem inherent in a bimetallic standard. Because of the difficulty in maintaining a mint ratio that would always correspond to the market ratio, it was proposed that the monetary unit of account be defined as a combination of the two metals in some specific proportion to each other. The monetary unit might be a specified weight of silver plus a specified weight of gold. You can visualize a bar containing a defined amount of grains of the two metals—or even better, think of a shiny new toonie, with its silver-coloured outer ring and its darker inner ring. The market price of silver to that of gold could vary, but the price of the particular combination of metals defined as the monetary unit would remain the same.

commodity reserve standard when the monetary unit of account is defined in terms of a fixed combination of storable commodities other than metals

A natural extension of a symmetallic standard is a **commodity reserve standard**. This type of standard has been proposed as a means of stabilizing the purchasing power of money. Under such a standard, the monetary unit of account would be defined in terms of a fixed combination of storable commodities other than metals. These commodities would be combined into a bundle consisting of a specified quantity of each commodity chosen. Such a bundle would be given a fixed value. If the market price of the aggregate quantity of goods composing the bundle were to fall below this fixed value, the monetary authorities would purchase these commodities in the open market and place them in storage. If the market price of the bundle of commodities were to rise above the fixed value, the authorities would sell some of their reserve of these commodities in the open market. Thus, the price of the bundle of commodities would be stabilized. If basic commodities were chosen to compose the bundle, the general price level would also be stabilized.

fiat money money that has no value in non-money use; it usually derives value from government decree of legal tender

Inconvertible Paper Standards

paper standards paper money whose value is derived by government fiat

Paper money has been referred to as a creature of the state. It has been called **fiat money** because it circulates by government decree. Government decree must, however, be accompanied by public acceptance before paper will circulate successfully. **Paper standards** first developed out of the breakdown of con-

BOX 2–2   BACKGROUNDER

Will That Be Cash, Cattle, or Coin? What We've Used as Money.

We know that the first type of money was commodity money. Its main role was to provide a standard unit of account. In early pastoral societies everything was valued in terms of cattle, a symbol of wealth and prestige. The use of cattle as money, however, had weaknesses. There was, for instance, no standard cow, bull, or ox, and since cattle are not readily divisible, small transactions could not be made. For large payments, a herd of cattle was difficult to deliver. In addition, as a store of value, cattle were only as good as their life expectancy.

To overcome all these weaknesses cattle were first supplemented and later replaced by articles of common use such as cloth, axes, hoes, and fish hooks. The virtual disappearance of the use of cattle as money did not occur without leaving a lasting reminder. The word "pecuniary" is derived from *pecus*, the Latin word for cattle, and "fee" comes from the Old English *feoh* (cognate of the German *vieh*), also meaning cattle. Today cattle and goats are still used as a measure of value by the Dinka people of the southern Sudan.

The use of copper, iron, silver, and gold can be traced back as far as 5000 B.C. Metals gained preference over other commodities because of certain essential characteristics: they were relatively homogeneous, easily recognizable, highly durable, readily portable, and divisible into any size. Metals had the additional advantage that a high intrinsic value could be placed on them. A few ounces of gold or silver could be exchanged for large units of other goods.

As a medium of exchange, metals had disadvantages relating to both their quality and their quantity. It was difficult to determine the fineness or purity of metals, and each transaction involved the inconvenience of weighing the metal. It is believed that in the seventh century B.C., a merchant in Lydia started to punch an identifying mark on each metal ingot after he had assayed it. If the metal again passed through his hands, he would recognize his symbol and escape the task of doing another assay. This practice marked the beginning of rudimentary coinage.

The final step in the evolution of money was the issuing of paper money, which in its later stages of sophistication is associated with the establishment of banks and banking. Paper money, banks, and banking as we know them today were predated by a long period in which the sole purpose of paper instruments was to provide facilities for the transfer of money and the extension of credit. Because bullion and coin were difficult to transport and were easily stolen, merchants carried with them in their travels written evidence of their command over money. These claims against money were similar to what we know today as warehouse receipts—receipts issued by a warehouse in which goods are left. The ownership of goods can be transferred by simply transferring the ownership of a warehouse receipt. Paper receipts or claims against coin were issued by the Chinese emperors and circulated as money in the middle of the seventh century. The Mongols, following their invasion of China, were quick to learn about the use of paper money. The Mongol chief, Kublai Khan, issued paper money to pay his army when bronze coin was scarce. Then, with the decline of the Mongols' fortunes in China, their paper money became worthless. This fate for paper money became a familiar one throughout history. At first, because of either need or greed, paper money was issued in amounts that made it impossible to redeem the paper into coin or promised commodities. Later, when it was issued with no promise of redemption, the paper frequently passed out of circulation as people lost confidence in its general acceptability for payment at its face value.

BOX 2–2 BACKGROUNDER (*continued*)

In the Western world, monastic orders during the ninth, tenth, and eleventh centuries and the Knights Templar during the following three centuries used paper claims for the same purpose: to transfer the ownership of money deposited with the abbeys and temples located in the important centres of the then-known world. Although these religious and semi-religious groups concentrated on the safekeeping of money and its transfer from one place to another, they also made loans. Hence, they employed money claims to transfer money over time; such claims are now known as credit instruments. The Jews, not subject to canon law prohibiting usury, gradually replaced the monasteries and the religious orders as the chief lenders of money. However, in the thirteenth century they lost favour, partly because of their great financial success, and were plundered and persecuted. Their place was taken by the Lombards, a group of merchant bankers from Venice and Genoa, who were very successful as moneylenders because they enjoyed papal indulgences on the charging of interest.

Before the seventeenth century, paper claims served the prime purpose of transferring credit and the ownership of money from one place or person to another. Although these claims also served the incidental function of a medium of exchange, it was not until the beginning of the seventeenth century that they became generally accepted as money, rather than as a substitute for money. As we shall see later, the goldsmiths of London issued certificates of deposit and the government of New France issued "cards" that were accepted as money and served as a medium of exchange. This practice marked the beginning of paper money and the establishment of banks for its creation.

vertibility under metallic standards, especially under the pressure of major wars. Having the government issue paper to finance wars was an easy solution to the problem of metal shortages. Paper was employed for other reasons as well. Sweden and other nonbelligerent countries adopted a paper standard during the First World War to avoid inflation resulting from the inflow of gold sent there for safekeeping. Today, countries operate under a paper standard mainly because it allows the monetary authorities discretionary power to manage the country's money supply. How the money supply is managed, and to what purpose, will be our chief concerns in the chapters that follow.

Paper standards have the following three characteristics:

1. The unit of account is not defined in terms of a commodity. In other words, the unit of account is abstract.

2. The commodity value of the circulating media is zero. The various kinds of money in circulation, government notes, bank notes, cheques drawn on deposit accounts, as well as token-coin are usually maintained at parity with one another. A large proportion of the circulating money is usually also the standard money.

3. The purchasing power of the monetary unit is not kept at par with any commodity.

Proponents of paper money have argued that the quantity of money required by any country depends on such factors as the organization of business, the volume of business activity, the means of transportation and communication, and the state of development of the banking and financial system. None of these factors is directly related to the volume of commodities used under commodity standards. Only paper money provides the kind of flexibility required to adapt the money supply to the nation's capacity to produce and consume. A fiat system makes the social control of money, prices, and credit possible, and it can be used to provide a source of tax revenue.

Critics of paper money point to the disastrous experience of nearly every country that has adopted it. With almost no exceptions, most governments at one time or another have succumbed to the temptation to overissue. As we have noted earlier, one of the alleged strong points of a commodity standard is that it imposes a certain discipline on the monetary authorities. No such discipline exists under a paper standard.

Because paper standards are completely divorced from commodities, they have no fixed links with the monetary systems of other countries. Under an international commodity standard where each country defines its monetary unit of account in terms of gold, the relationship among the various countries' currencies is fixed. It is argued that this relationship fosters international trade. For example, a Canadian manufacturer is willing to sell her wares in Britain when she knows that for each British pound she receives in payment, she can get a specified amount of Canadian dollars. If she were uncertain of what the exchange rate between pounds and dollars would be when payment was made, she would be less willing to deal with Britain.

Today, most countries employ a paper standard. Citizens presenting their national money for redemption receive only paper and subsidiary coin from their monetary authorities. Between the Second World War and 1973, countries that were members of the **International Monetary Fund (IMF)** defined their monetary units in terms of gold or another country's monetary unit so defined. This practice served to maintain a fixed relationship between the monetary units of the different countries. After 1973, however, most foreign exchange rates—that is, the exchange rates between national monetary units— were no longer based on a relationship to gold but on the market forces of supply and demand in foreign exchange markets. Periodically, monetary authorities intervened in the foreign exchange market to modify the market rate of their national monetary units in relation to others.

www.

International Monetary Fund (IMF) an international body created after the Second World War to assist nations experiencing balance-of-payments difficulties

The Composition of the Canadian Money Supply

Although "money" is an everyday word, it does not have a definition accepted by everyone. Disagreement has existed about which financial assets should be encompassed by the term "money." When the IOUs of individuals, merchants, institutions, and governments were accepted in payment and had a limited or wide circulation, it became more difficult to specify what constituted the money supply. For example, during Britain's famous currency and banking controversy of the late 1830s, the **currency school** insisted that only bank notes and coin made up the money supply because only changes in their amounts

currency school a view that only bank notes and coin make up the money supply

banking school
a view that bank deposits and circulating bills of exchange should be included in the definition of the money supply

monetary aggregates
money stock or money supply measures the sum of the values of financial assets in a specific definition of money, such as M1 and M2

caused fluctuations in the general level of commodity prices. In contrast, the **banking school**, whose most vocal proponent was Thomas Tooke, argued on similar grounds that bank deposits and circulating bills of exchange should be included in the definition of the money supply.

Anything that served all the functions we outlined would be classified as money without question. It is impossible, however, to specify any one asset, or even a small subset of assets, that ideally satisfies all these functions simultaneously. Hence, it has become customary to define money narrowly or broadly. Narrow definitions include only those assets that the public holds as generally acceptable and as immediately available media of exchange. These assets may be said to be the public's transaction balances, which can be transferred at little or no cost. Broad definitions of money include assets that are held as stores of value but that may, with some inconvenience and at some cost, also be used as media of exchange.

Various measures of the Canadian money supply and their corresponding values at the end of March 2000 are presented in Table 2.1. The values of these measures—M1, M1+, M1++, M2, M3, adjusted M2+, and M2++—are regularly reported by the Bank of Canada in its *Weekly Financial Statistics* and the monthly *Bank of Canada Banking and Financial Statistics*. However, the Bank identifies these measures as **monetary aggregates** rather than money supply. Some economists prefer the term "money stock" rather than "money supply."

M1 is the official measure of narrow money in Canada. It consists of currency outside the chartered banks and demand deposits held by the public at the chartered banks. These demand deposits and currency are used primarily as a medium of exchange. Currency, which includes coin and Bank of Canada notes (dollar bills), is readily transferable by hand, while demand deposits, which include current accounts held by businesses and personal chequing accounts, are readily withdrawn and transferable by cheque or other payment orders.

Three measures of the Canadian money supply reported by the Bank of Canada and shown in Table 2.1—M2, M2+, and M3 —are broader measures. They add to the M1 measure the monetary assets that are used both as a medium of exchange and as a store of value or only as a liquid store of value.

M2 is derived by adding to M1 nonpersonal notice deposits and personal savings deposits held by the public at chartered banks. Although the banks reserve the right of notice of withdrawal of personal savings deposits, in practice they have waived this right. Hence, most personal savings deposits serve as a medium of exchange; almost one-quarter of them are chequable accounts. The M3 measure adds to M2 chartered bank nonpersonal term deposits that are available in large denominations, plus foreign currency deposits of residents booked in Canada. The M2+ measure includes, in addition to the M2 components, deposits at trust and mortgage loan companies and at the Province of Ontario Savings Offices, personal deposits at Alberta Treasury branches, and deposits and shares of caisses populaires and credit unions. The M2+ measure also includes money market mutual funds and individual annuities. Money market mutual funds are mutual funds invested in treasury bills and other short-term money market instruments denominated in Canadian dollars with terms to maturity of less than one year. They are marketed by deposit-taking institutions, life insurance companies, and independent fund

TABLE 2.1	**MEASURES OF MONEY IN CANADA** Millions of Dollars, Not Seasonally Adjusted, March 2000		
MEASURE	COMPONENTS	AMOUNTS	
	(1) Currency outside banks	32 455	
	(2) Personal chequing accounts	17 935	
	(3) Current accounts	46 966	
	(4) Adjustments to M1	–306	
Gross M1	= (1) + (2) + (3) + (4)		97 050
	(5) Chartered bank net demand deposits	66 786	
Total M1			98 936
M1+	Gross M1 plus chequable notice deposits at chartered banks plus all chequable notice deposits at trust and mortgage loan companies, credit unions, and caisses populaires		218 466
M1++	M1+ plus nonchequable notice deposits at chartered banks plus all chequable notice deposits at trust and mortgage loan companies, credit unions, and caisses populaires		274 904
	(6) Chartered banks nonpersonal notice deposits	42 936	
	(7) Personal savings deposits	334 554	
	(8) Adjustments to M2	–49	
Total M2	= Total M1 + (6) + (7) + (8)		476 377
	(9) Chartered bank nonpersonal term deposits plus foreign currency deposits of residents booked in Canada	176 618	
	(10) Adjustments to M3	–4 138	
Total M3	= Total M2 + (9) + (10)		648 857
M2 Unadjusted			476 377
	(11) Trust and mortgage loan companies	6 369	
	(12) Credit unions and caisses populaires	103 976	
	(13) Life insurance company individual annuities	38 011	
	(14) Personal deposits at government owned savings institutions	8 374	
	(15) Money market mutual funds	44 805	
	(16) Adjustments to M2+	732	
Total M2+	(M2+) + (11) + (12) + (13) + (14) + (15) + (16)		678 645
	(17) Canada Savings Bonds	27 056	
	(18) Non–money market mutual funds	357 339	
M2++	(M2+) + (17) + (18)		1 063 040

SOURCE: Bank of Canada, *Weekly Financial Statistics*, June 9, 2000.

managers. Money market mutual funds can typically be cashed within one to two business days, and some are even chequable. Individual annuities included in the M2+ money measure are similar to term deposits.

currency in public circulation
currency outside banks and other financial institutions

float *the term used to refer to the value of funds in the process of being transferred from one deposit account to another*

The currency included in all money supply measures excludes currency held in the tills, automated banking machines, and vaults of the banking system. Only currency outside the banks, referred to as **currency in public circulation**, is counted as part of the money supply. When currency is taken out of public circulation and deposited with a chartered bank, it becomes a bank deposit. If our measure of money were to count both the currency held by a bank and bank deposits, we would be double counting.

In addition, to avoid double-counting chequable deposits, an adjustment is made for float. **Float** is the term commonly used to refer to the value of funds in the process of being transferred from one deposit account to another. Debit float occurs when cheques in the process of collection are credited to one account before being debited to another account. Alternatively, credit float occurs whenever one account is debited before another is credited. This situations occurs when a bank certifies a cheque drawn against a deposit held with it. Although large amounts of both debit and credit float are always outstanding, on balance, debit float in Canada tends to exceed credit float, and this results in double-counting chequable deposits. To avoid double counting, the Bank of Canada estimates the amount of float and adjusts the values of chequable deposits in its money measures accordingly.

All the money measures shown in Table 2.1 exclude interbank and other interinstitution deposits as well as federal government deposits. Interbank and interinstitution deposits are not included to avoid double counting. Federal government deposits are usually omitted from money supply measures because they are not available for spending by the public. On the same grounds we should expect deposits held by other levels of government to be omitted as well, but they are not. This practice suggests that the choice of deposits to be included in money supply measures is somewhat arbitrary.

Two other examples can be cited to indicate the arbitrary way in which assets are chosen to be included in money supply measures. First, on November 10, 1969, a nonbank deposit institution in Quebec, whose deposits were not included in money supply measures, became a chartered bank. On that date, with the stroke of a pen, $88 million of nonbank deposits were classified as bank deposits and increased the money supply by an equivalent amount. In the second example, chartered banks, after 1980, were required to include in their consolidated balance sheets the operations of their wholly owned mortgage loan company subsidiaries. When this change took effect, the public deposits held with these subsidiaries were transformed into bank deposits and included in money supply measures. At the same time, deposits held with similar institutions that were not subsidiaries of the chartered banks remained excluded from the narrow money supply measure.

You will note that we have not yet discussed some of the other measures of money contained in Table 2.1. These measures are relatively new: M1+, M1++, adjusted M2+, and finally M2++ were introduced in the late 1990s in response to changes in financial markets that made it difficult to classify certain types of deposit accounts as being purely transactions or savings related. M1+ is the sum of currency and all chequable (demand or notice) deposits at chartered banks, credit unions and caisses populaires, and trust and mortgage loan companies. M1++ is the sum of M1+ and all nonchequable notice deposits at chartered banks, credit unions and caisses populaires, and trust and mortgage loan companies. Joseph Atta-Mensah and Loretta Nott (1999) have shown that both of these aggregates appear to have a much closer association with real GDP and inflation than the traditional definition of narrow balances, M1, does.

Throughout the 1990s, many households shifted their savings from traditional deposit instruments to bond and equity mutual funds, and in response the Bank of Canada has created two new measures of broadly defined money. Adjusted M2+ adds Canada Savings Bonds and nonmoney market mutual funds at deposit-taking institutions to M2, while the aggregate M2++ adds other nonmoney market mutual funds to adjusted M2+. These wider definitions of money "internalize" the substitution between savings deposits and mutual funds and are a better measure of "money" when we look at how households plan to spend their income over time (to which we will return in the next chapter). Recent developments in the monetary aggregates suggest they are growing at a rate that is consistent with the Bank of Canada's objective of a low and stable rate of inflation, as reported by Atta-Mensah (2000).

Other Approaches to Defining and Measuring Money

In the 1950s two U.S. economists, John Gurley and Edward Shaw, argued that economists should consider the liquid store of value function to be the essential characteristic of money. According to this point of view, the choice of assets to be included in the money measure should be based primarily on their superior liquidity. An asset is said to be perfectly liquid if it can be used or transferred at any time for making payments equal in value to the nominal value at which it was initially acquired by its holder. Currency is a perfectly liquid asset. For example, a $10 Bank of Canada note can always be passed with no transaction costs to make a payment amounting to $10. We can also make payment by writing a cheque. The deposit against which the cheque is written is not as liquid as currency, however, because a fee is usually charged for transferring deposits by cheque, and not everyone is willing to accept a cheque in payment. Nonchequable deposits, as well as Canada Savings Bonds, rank still lower in liquidity because they have to be converted into currency or chequable deposits to be used for making payments. They can be considered to have superior liquidity, however, because their conversion costs are relatively small and because they can be converted into a medium of exchange at their nominal value. The same is not true for marketable bonds and other debt instruments, whose conversion value into a medium of exchange can be uncertain and whose conversion cost can sometimes be quite high.

Economists can agree that money is an asset distinguishable from other assets by its superior liquidity. However, they cannot agree on the degree of liquidity money should possess for inclusion in the money supply measure. Some economists have tackled the question of an appropriate measure of money by assessing the "moneyness" of assets. They start by accepting currency and demand deposits as money and then employ various statistical techniques to calculate the degree of substitution between these and other potential money assets. The latter are then classified in terms of their "moneyness" according to the degree of their substitution with currency and demand deposits. The difficulty of this approach to defining money is similar to that of the liquidity approach: What degree of substitution should be required to give an asset "moneyness"?

John Gurley has suggested that the money supply be defined as a weighted sum of currency, demand deposits, and their substitutes, with weights assigned based on the degree of substitutability or "moneyness." For example, currency and chequable deposits might be assigned a weight of unity, other deposits and similar assets a weight between zero and one, and all other assets completely unrelated to currency and chequable deposits a weight of zero. While this appears to be the ideal way of specifying a money aggregate, its formulation awaits an acceptable method for assigning appropriate weights.

A somewhat different approach to defining and measuring the money supply has been advocated by the U.S. economist, Milton Friedman. Friedman believes the money supply measure should include financial assets whose aggregate amount the monetary authorities can control and that best describe the course of economic activity or important variables that directly influence that activity. From 1975 to 1982, when the Bank of Canada set money supply growth targets, it used the narrow M1 money measure. At the time, some economists were critical of the Bank's use of the M1 measure because they considered a broader measure of the Canadian money supply to be much more closely related to the course of economic activity and to be more readily controllable by the Bank.

The debate over what assets should be included in our money measure is by no means a sterile academic exercise. As we shall see in later chapters, the debate is associated with a long-standing controversy over the quantity of money as a determinant of economic activity. The conclusion we draw about the latter depends in large part on how we define, and therefore measure, the money supply. Moreover, governments have assumed responsibility for the level and rate of change of economic activity. If money is an important determinant, they will, therefore, want to know which financial assets, and therefore financial institutions, they should be able to exercise control over. These issues are closely related to monetary policy, one of the major themes of this book.

The Canadian Payments System

The payments system consists of social or institutional arrangements for expressing value using a generally acceptable unit of account, and for exchanging value using a generally acceptable medium of exchange. In this section we trace the evolution of payments systems in Canada, starting from the time before the arrival of the Europeans and ending with a glimpse into the twenty-first century and beyond.

THE NATIVE PEOPLES   Before the arrival of European colonists in North America, the native peoples had developed a form of money known as *wampum*. Wampum consisted of white and purple or blue beads that the people on the eastern part of the continent made into strings and belts as a medium of exchange. The people of the west coast used strings of dentalium shells and necklaces made of dentalium and abalone shells. When the French arrived, the native peoples used wampum in their trade with them. Wampum made of white beads was valued at about one French sou, while that made of blue beads was worth about two sous. Later, with the introduction of glass counterfeits, wampum became almost worthless. It enjoyed legal tender status until 1690 but continued to circulate among the colonists until 1704 and among the native peoples until about 1825.

The Hudson's Bay Company had at various times used porcupine quills, shell beads, ivory discs, and oak tally sticks as units of account in its fur trade with the native peoples. About 1870 it introduced round brass coins denominated as "One Made Beaver." This unit of account was equal to the value of one adult beaver pelt in prime condition. The beaver coins were still being used in the 1930s. The company had issued its own £1 and £5 notes for trade with the settlers on the Red River, but these were not used after the 1840s except in the west. Much later, when the company started to purchase white fox pelts from the people of the eastern Arctic, it replaced the traditional Made Beaver coin with its own coin denominated as "One Arctic White Fox," which was equivalent to the dollar value of one arctic white fox pelt.

NEW FRANCE AND THE FRENCH REGIME   Like the English colonies to the south, the French colony in Canada used commodities of various kinds to serve as a unit of account or as a medium of exchange, or both. A list of such commodities includes wheat, Indian corn, salt pork, moose hides, beaver skins, wildcat skins, and even liquor. Also, like the English, colonists in New France employed coin, which continually remained scarce. Coin was originally brought to New France by the colonists. The supply was augmented by the funds the French government sent out to maintain its military establishment and the machinery of civil government, and by subscriptions raised throughout France by religious orders to establish and support missionaries. The export trade, mostly in furs, brought coin to the colony, but this was usually returned to France immediately as payment for essential commodities imported from there.

In an attempt to overcome the shortage of coins and the chronic shortage of a medium of exchange in general, the colonial government gave coins legal values above those assigned to them in France. The higher-valued coins became known as *monnoye du pays* to distinguish them from the *monnoye de france*. By overrating coins, the colonies hoped to attract them and to hold them there for circulation. However, when prices in the colonies rose in proportion to increases in the ratings assigned to the coins, the attraction of higher ratings was lost.

In 1685, Intendant Jacques de Meulles turned to another expedient to provide a more adequate medium of exchange and to prevent financial embarrassment to the local administration. When funds did not arrive from France to support the colony, and all local resources had been exhausted, he issued card money. Since there were no printing presses or suitable paper, the seal of the Treasurer and the signatures of the Governor and the Intendant were affixed to the backs of ordinary playing cards. Although "card money" began as a short-term financial expedient, it was not long before the cards began to circulate as a medium of common exchange. Later issues of cards in whole, half, quarter, and other sizes were provided with this specific purpose in mind.

The issue of card money was backed by the credit of the local administration and the anticipated arrival of coins from France each autumn. It became common to issue card money on the security of bills of exchange drawn on the annual appropriation of the French government to the colony. Since these bills were redeemed in silver coin in France, the colony was really on a silver exchange standard.

An important feature of card money was that it remained within the colonial territories, since it was of no use in trade with France or elsewhere. It was frequently accepted in payment, though with some reluctance, in place of the overrated coins. Another feature of card money, which recommended it in the eyes of the colonial authorities, was that quantities could be issued on the spot whenever the Intendant was hard-pressed for money and was unable to obtain funds from the continental French authorities. The King consistently opposed the issue of card money because it implied a loss of financial control over the colony. Only reluctantly was authorization for issue granted when the need apparently could not be satisfied in other ways. Card money provided the most important medium of exchange, but it was supplemented periodically by other types of paper. IOUs or notes in the form of *acquits de depense* and *ordinances de paiement* were issued by the local authorities in denominations sufficiently small to encourage their circulation as money.

www.

BRITISH NORTH AMERICA In 1710 British troops from New England captured Port Royal and took over the French colony in the Annapolis Valley of present-day Nova Scotia. The Acadians had engaged in very little trade up to this time, partly because trade between them and the English colonies had been forbidden. The existing currency requirements had been met by a short experiment with card money and by a few coins from outside. In their dealings with the Acadians, the English continued the French basis of value, the livre. Their accounts with the British government were kept using the pound sterling. Transactions within the garrison at Port Royal (renamed Annapolis Royal), as well as trade with New England to the south, were conducted in terms of the dollar, also known as Boston money. Thus, rating or value systems were based on the livre, the pound, or, at times, the dollar. An agitation for standardization in the system of valuation was only natural. This agitation resulted in a system of valuation known as Halifax money (shortly after Chebucto was renamed Halifax in 1749). Halifax money, similar to that used in New England, was another system for rating coin. It exerted an influence on monetary affairs in Canada almost up to the time of Confederation.

When the British took over Quebec in 1759, they inherited the chaotic paper issues of the French, most of which were now all but worthless. While peace was being negotiated, rumours began to circulate that the British would redeem the outstanding paper. The demand by speculators did add some value to the paper, which the British eventually redeemed at one-quarter of its face value. Under the British regime, specie (coined money) gradually returned to circulation. The odd assortment of gold and silver coins that appeared included many that had previously been hoarded, those sent by Britain to maintain troops and pay for civil administration, and some acquired in trade.

The most abundant coins were the Spanish silver dollars earned in trade with the American colonies along the Atlantic seaboard. The value of the silver content of the average Spanish dollar was four shillings and sixpence, but its monetary value depended on the rating it was given. East of Quebec it circulated at five shillings, being rated in terms of Halifax currency; west of Quebec it was rated at eight shillings and was known as York currency because that was the rating current in New York.

The disastrous paper issues of the French regime left a lasting prejudice against paper money in Lower and Upper Canada. In 1794 John McGill was appointed by Lieutenant-Governor John Graves Simcoe to the new office of Agent of Purchases. McGill started to pay for supplies, which he bought directly from the settlers rather than by contract from merchants, with transferable certificates. Although limited and not legal tender, these certificates did pass into circulation and marked the beginning of a successful paper issue in Upper Canada. In Lower Canada, especially Montreal, merchants issued their own paper notes, or *bons*, to their customers. These bons were redeemed in goods at the store of issue and circulated fairly widely. Although both these early issues helped to break down the prejudice against paper money in the Canadas, the most important influence toward this end was the fortunate experience with army bills issued during the War of 1812.

After the United States had declared war on Great Britain, Sir Isaac Brock was instructed to prepare for the attack. To pay for the goods and services he requisitioned, he issued paper money known as "army bills." These bills had face values of 4, 25, 100, and 400 dollars. Those of 25 dollars or more bore interest. The bills were to be accepted as specie in payment at all public offices. When the initial issue proved insufficient, an additional issue of 1-, 2-, 8-, 10-, 12-, and 16-dollar bills was made. In 1813 the bills were made legal tender in both Upper and Lower Canada, where they circulated freely throughout the war. The complete redemption of all bills outstanding after the war went a long way toward wiping out unhappy memories of earlier and less satisfactory paper money. The new confidence in paper money also helped to prepare the way for the establishment of commercial banks and the issue of bank notes soon after the war.

In the Maritimes, where the stigma of the paper issues of New France remained relatively unknown, the provincial governments resorted to paper issues quite early to provide a medium of exchange. In 1763 Nova Scotia issued transferable interest-bearing certificates or notes to solve the colony's coin shortage as well as to pay off its debts. In 1790 Prince Edward Island issued treasury bills designed to serve as currency. New Brunswick started to issue notes denominated in dollars in 1805. To finance its commitments in the War of 1812, Nova Scotia issued treasury notes, which circulated successfully. Further issues followed in an attempt to offset the continuing scarcity of coins in the postwar period. Their amount was not adequately controlled, however, and as a result they suffered severe depreciation. In 1834 the government passed legislation that, in effect, gave it a monopoly on small-denomination notes.

The shortage of coins or "hard money" in circulation was a continuing problem in British North America, as it had been earlier in New France. The Halifax currency system rated coins above their sterling value in much the same way that *monnoye du pays* coins had been rated above their value in New France. However, with price inflation, frequently the result of the overissue of paper money, much of the advantage of holding coin was lost. Poor coin as a result of sweating and clipping also tended to drive good coin out of circulation. Gresham's Law also came into play when the legal ratings assigned to coins did not reflect the changes in the market values of their metal content.

In 1813, when Lieutenant-Governor Smith arrived in Prince Edward Island, he believed that although the island was almost entirely without a circulating medium, substantial amounts of British and Spanish coins were being hoarded. To bring them into circulation as well as to attract others to the island, Smith established higher currency ratings. In so doing, however, he gave a higher currency value to the Bank of England dollar than to the Spanish dollar coins. Realizing that Gresham's Law would not allow the Spanish dollar to circulate in competition with its British counterpart, Smith directed that 1000 Spanish dollars should have a hole punched out of them. The resulting "holey" dollar was given a currency value of five shillings, and the plug a value of one shilling. The two parts together were worth six shillings, the same value as the Bank of England dollar. Thus Smith ensured that Gresham's Law would no longer apply, and that the holey dollar would find little acceptability off the island.

After 1800, much of the small change in circulation consisted of merchants' tokens. Many were copper penny or halfpenny tokens of good quality imported from Britain, but these were gradually replaced by lighter tokens of copper or brass. Then, after 1838, bank issues of copper tokens replaced those of the merchants. At various times between 1817 and 1923 some of the provinces put their own tokens into circulation. Prince Edward Island, for example, imported lightweight tokens that bore patriotic slogans like "Success to the Fisheries" and "Speed the Plough."

With the union of Upper and Lower Canada, providing a common national currency became a high priority. For a long time the British government had resisted all suggestions for a distinctive Canadian coinage based on the U.S. decimal system. It feared that such a decimal system would increase the dangers for Canada of political annexation by the United States. Moreover, the hope remained, however faint, that the British sterling currency standard of value and medium of exchange might be introduced throughout the Empire.

The *Currency Act* of 1841, passed by the new Union Parliament of Upper and Lower Canada, retained the Halifax standard, but there were still no coins corresponding to it. The American eagle and the British sovereign, both gold coins, were given the status of full legal tender. Silver coins given the same status were the U.S. dollar and half-dollar, and the new French five-franc piece. Other coins, including British silver coins, were accorded a limited legal tender status. An act passed in 1850 providing for the issue of Canadian silver coins, denominated in pounds sterling but corresponding to the value of the United States' coinage, was immediately disallowed by the British government.

In June 1851, representatives of the provinces of Canada, Nova Scotia, and New Brunswick met in Toronto and agreed to work toward a common unit of account based on the decimal system. The imperial authorities were still pressing for pound currency and proposed that it be represented by an actual gold coin to be called a royal, with subsidiary gold and copper coins in decimal ratios. Finally, in 1857, an act was passed in the Province of Canada providing that all accounts submitted to the government, as well as accounts kept by it, should be in dollars and cents. At about the same time the home government granted permission to issue a special colonial coinage. The new coins, silver 5-, 10-, and 20-cent pieces and bronze cents, were made legal tender on December 10, 1858. By Confederation, in 1867, Prince Edward Island was the only British North American colony not to have adopted decimal currency.

CONFEDERATION AND THEREAFTER   By Confederation in 1867, the new nation's standard unit of account had been settled. Subsequently confirmed by the *Uniform Currency Act* of 1871, it was the dollar, equal to 100 cents, with a fixed exchange value in terms of a specified amount of gold. The medium of exchange was currency—coin and notes. Canadian coin was supplied by the Royal Mint in England until 1908, when the Ottawa Mint was established as a branch operation. The Ottawa Mint was taken over by the Dominion Government in 1931 and became the Royal Canadian Mint, which to this day retains the mandate of producing and supplying coinage for Canada. In 1910, the Canadian dollar, whose gold content was still defined in terms of the British sovereign, was given its own identity. It was now defined as containing 23.22 grains of pure gold, which was equivalent to the gold content of the U.S. dollar. After Canada abandoned the gold standard in 1933, our dollar was no longer defined in terms of a legally specified amount of gold.

With the establishment of commercial banks in the 1820s, bank notes started to supplement coin as a medium of exchange. Problems involving the quality and supply of coin during the early colonial period now repeated themselves in terms of notes for circulation. For example, before Confederation, 21 of the 58 banks that had commenced operations failed. Not only was the note circulation reduced with the failure of each bank, but also the exchange value of the notes of any bank could become virtually worthless if the bank's soundness were questioned. Periodically, provincial governments attempted to overcome these difficulties by issuing their own notes for circulation.

At Confederation, the *British North America Act* allocated to the new federal government exclusive jurisdiction over currency and coinage, banking, the incorporation of banks, and the issue of notes for circulation. Under the *Dominion Notes Act*, passed as a temporary measure, the federal government took over all notes previously issued by the provinces. Another *Dominion Notes Act*, passed two years later, restricted the chartered banks to issuing notes of a minimum denomination of $5, whereupon the government began to issue Dominion notes of 25¢ and $1 and $2. The government was required to hold a gold reserve of 20 percent against the first $9 million of notes issued by it, and each additional dollar in excess of this amount had to be covered dollar for dollar by gold. The 25-cent paper notes, later known as "shinplasters" following the U.S. name for small notes, were issued as a temporary expedient because it was thought that it would take some time to provide Canadian silver coins in sufficient quantity to meet the initial need. Twenty-five-cent paper notes remained in use until 1935, long after the reason for their introduction had disappeared. By way of contrast, in 1896 the Dominion government started to issue notes in denominations of $500, $1000, and $5000. These notes, known as "bank legals," were used for the transfer of large sums of money between banks. It was illegal for private individuals to hold them.

Despite the new federal government's legislative authority to print notes for circulation, the notes issued by the chartered banks were the currency most frequently used for making payments. However, with another 28 bank failures before the founding of the **Bank of Canada** in 1935, the exchange value and the adequacy of supply of bank notes were recurring themes in *Bank Act* revisions. In fact, these very events eventually led to the establishment of the central bank. With the establishment of the Bank of Canada, the chartered banks were required to gradually reduce their notes in circulation. In 1950, the liability of bank notes still outstanding was assumed by the Bank of Canada, which exchanged them for its own notes.

Table 2.2 presents information on the composition of paper money outstanding. Did you know Canada once had a $25 dollar bill? It was issued in 1935 as a special commemorative note in honour of the Silver Jubilee of King George V. You might also be interested to know that the $1000 bill is going to be discontinued in an attempt to discourage illicit activities in which large sums are traded. Money laundering, according to the Royal Canadian Mounted Police, involves a disproportionately large number of $1000 notes. With the assistance of financial institutions and a change to the regulations that cover Bank of Canada notes, all $1000 banknotes will be withdrawn from circulation, making it somewhat more difficult to conceal large sums of money.[2]

Bank of Canada
Canada's central bank

www.

TABLE 2.2	**BANKNOTES AND COIN IN CANADA, 1998**

	($000)
Total banknotes and coin issued	36 048 976
Coinages	3 411 475
Denomination of banknotes (approximate time to replacement)	
1 000 (13 years)	3 409 390
500	23
100 (11 years)	13 252 651
50 (8 years)	4 210 957
25	46
20 (4 years)	9 569 673
10 (1 year)	1 014 074
5 (1 year)	774 833
2	232 613
1	160 370
Other	12 871
Banknotes and coin held by chartered banks	4 313 339
Banknotes and coin held outside chartered banks	31 735 637

SOURCE: Bank for International Settlements, *Statistics on the Payments Systems in the Group of Ten Countries*: December 1998, March 2000; and Bank of Canada.

2. See Finance Canada, News Release 2000-011, February 17, 2000.

BOX 2–3 BACKGROUNDER

Y2K and the Demand for Banknotes

Today, people use many methods of payment to settle their transactions, including bank notes and coins, credit cards, cheques, debit cards, and electronic transfers. In recent years, with new telecommunications and information technology, the last two options—debit cards and electronic funds transfers—have become increasingly popular. While this has reduced the use of cash, the demand for currency remains significant—in excess of $1000 for every man, woman, and child in Canada. These notes are held primarily by businesses, particularly retailers, rather than by individuals. The demand for notes also exhibits marked seasonal variations and tends to rise sharply near the end of the year during the holiday period.

Toward the end of 1999, with public concern about year 2000 computer problems and their possible effect on electronic payment services, there was a risk that the demand for cash would rise. The Bank of Canada and financial institutions therefore stockpiled bank notes. Having increased its stock of notes fourfold to $23 billion, the Bank was easily able to accommodate the demand from financial institutions and the public. As of 31 December 1999, the Bank of Canada had placed an additional $5.5 billion in notes into circulation. The bulk of this (some $4 billion), was in the hands of financial institutions. There was, in fact, only a relatively small increase in demand from Canadian households compared with the amount they normally hold at year-end. With the arrival of the year 2000, it was soon apparent that all was well, and Y2K fears faded. The surplus notes in circulation were quickly returned to the Bank of Canada.

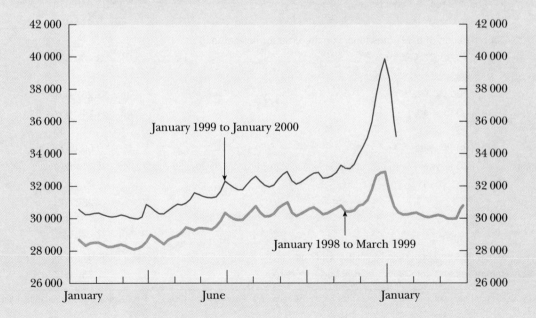

January 1999 to January 2000

January 1998 to March 1999

SOURCE: *Bank of Canada Review,* Winter 1999–2000, p. 12

The use of cheques for making payments developed slowly during the latter part of the nineteenth century. This system called for an arrangement among the banks for the exchange of cheques and the resulting settlement of cash balances between them. At first, when a bank cashed a cheque drawn on a deposit held in another bank, it sent its messenger to that bank to exchange the cheque for currency. With the regular use of cheques for payment, this procedure became cumbersome, if not risky. In 1887, the banks in Halifax, and within a few years in Montreal, Toronto, Hamilton, and Winnipeg, set up clearinghouses. A **clearinghouse** was an agreed-on place, usually the branch or office of a bank, where the messengers of all the banks in a community gathered each day at the same time to exchange cheques and to settle interbank cash claims. In 1900 the Canadian Bankers' Association assumed the responsibility for establishing and supervising the operations of clearinghouses. Following the founding of the Bank of Canada in 1935, the Bank was represented at regional clearing points; interbank clearing balances were settled there with the transfer of deposits that the chartered banks were required to hold with the Bank of Canada.

clearinghouse
an arrangement among depository institutions for settling balances that result from accepting one another's cheques and payments orders issued by their respective depositors

As we shall learn later, central to our payment system are institutional arrangements for the clearing and settlement of money transfers between financial institutions. Such arrangements are necessary because during each business day, deposit-taking institutions accept thousands of cheques and other payment orders, each representing a cash claim. Because an institution accepts a cheque drawn against a deposit account held at another institution, cash claims between deposit-taking institutions arise. Clearing refers to the process of setting these claims against each other in a manner that increases the efficiency of the clearing process by reducing the number of settlements that have to be made.

In 1980 the federal government established the Canadian Payments Association (CPA) as a regulated public-purpose organization to establish and operate a national clearing and settlements system and to plan the evolution of the national payments system. In 1999 the CPA handled 3.8 billion transactions requiring settlement worth about $16.9 trillion. Some 37 percent of all these payment items were cleared via electronic rather than paper media.

Today's Payments Instruments

As we shall learn, a variety of instruments is available in Canada today to facilitate payments. Indeed, it is hardly unusual when making a payment to be asked, "would that be by cash, cheque, or card?" Consider Figure 2–1. The left panel demonstrates the distribution of noncash payments in Canada in 1990, while the right panel illustrates how noncash payments were made in 1997. The use of credit cards has remained stable over this period, while cheques have been replaced, in large part, by debit cards and direct debits. Let us look at this more closely.

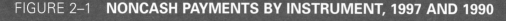

FIGURE 2–1   **NONCASH PAYMENTS BY INSTRUMENT, 1997 AND 1990**

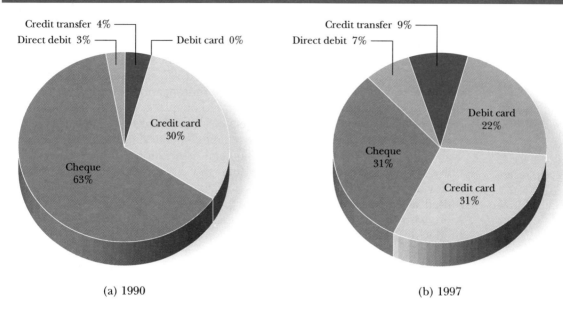

Credit transfer 4%
Direct debit 3%
Debit card 0%
Credit card 30%
Cheque 63%

(a) 1990

Credit transfer 9%
Direct debit 7%
Debit card 22%
Cheque 31%
Credit card 31%

(b) 1997

SOURCE: *Retail Payments in Selected Countries: A Comparative Study*, Bank for International Settlements, September 1999.

CASH AND CHEQUES The majority of payments are still settled by hand-to-hand exchange of cash, that is, currency consisting of coin and Bank of Canada notes. Early in 2000 the authorities announced plans to examine whether a $5 coin should be added to the Canadian "loonie" and "toonie" (and become a "foonie"?). In terms of the total value of all transactions, however, cheques and other paper payments issued against transferable deposits held at deposit-taking institutions are the most important payment media. As is shown in Table 2.3, cheques and other paper payments also dominate in both volume and value.

PAYMENTS CARDS Four major types of payment cards are issued or sponsored by deposit-taking institutions to facilitate payments: credit cards, bank cards, debit cards, and prepaid payment cards. Many of these institutions have replaced their credit and bank cards with one card called a convenience card. Cards are not money, but like cheques are a means of transferring money, typically from an individual's deposit account to the accounts of the sellers of goods and services.

CREDIT CARDS The most widely used multipurpose credit cards are issued by the Visa and MasterCard companies and are sponsored by banks and near-banks. The issuing companies guarantee payment and at the same time give cardholders a specified line of credit, which is drawn down as cards are used to make payment for purchases. In effect, cardholders receive an interest-free loan from card companies until the month-end billing date.

| TABLE 2.3 | INDICATORS OF VARIOUS PAYMENTS INSTRUMENTS, 1998 | |

| | TRANSACTIONS | |
| | Volume | Value |
Instruments	*($ Millions)*	*($ Billions)*
Cheques issued	1 690.0	19 250.5
Payments by credit cards	1 008.8	98.6
Payments by debit card	1 355.4	58.5
Paper based credit transfers	89.2	17.2
Paperless credit transfers	374.6	397.6
Direct debits	361.9	132.6
Total	4 879.9	19 955.0

SOURCE: Bank for International Settlements, Statistics on the Payments Systems in the Group of Ten Countries: December 1998, March 2000.

Credit cards have a magnetic strip on their plastic surfaces, used for cardholder identification and payment authorization. When a merchant accepts a credit card for payment, the card may be used to imprint sales vouchers mechanically. These sales vouchers, which include all the relevant sales information, are then taken by the merchants to their own banks for payment (at a discount of 2 of 3 percent). The merchants' banks, in turn, send the sales vouchers to the appropriate card company's clearing centre for clearing and ultimate settlement. The card companies pay the banks for the sales vouchers submitted to them and, at the end of the reporting period, bill cardholders.

Alternatively, many merchants now have special terminals attached to their cash registers. Once the credit card passes through the terminal, identification is confirmed, and authorization is approved, all relevant sales information passes automatically to a card company's clearing centre for processing. The sales slip signed by the cardholder is retained for the merchant's records, with a copy given to the cardholder. The payment process involving cardholders, merchants, credit card companies, and financial institutions is accomplished electronically with little need for paper transactions. Advances in technology have also allowed cardholders to use their cards in many countries outside Canada.

ABMs Automated bank machines (ABMs) provide individuals with banking services traditionally supplied by tellers working at the counters of the deposit-taking institutions. Hence, they are commonly referred to as ATMs (automated teller machines). By 1999 more than 20 000 ABMs were in service in Canada. Most are in convenient locations allowing access around the clock. The left frame of Figure 2–2 shows that most ABMs were located in chartered banks, while the right frame demonstrates that the vast majority of machines are located in Ontario and Quebec.

www.

Individuals access ABMs with a plastic bank card and the cardholder's PIN (personal identification number). Among other uses, the machines are used for making deposits and withdrawals, for interaccount transfers, and for deposit balance enquiries.

FIGURE 2–2 THE DISTRIBUTION OF ABMs IN CANADA, 1999

(a) By Type of Institution

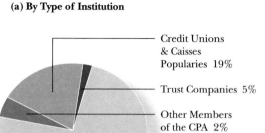

Credit Unions & Caisses Popularies 19%

Trust Companies 5%

Other Members of the CPA 2%

Banks 74%

(b) By Province

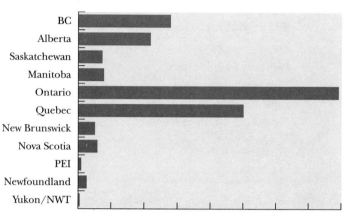

Number of ABMs

SOURCE: Canadian Payments Association, 2000.

Interac Association a group of financial institutions that created an electronic switching network to connect ABMs

convenience cards cards that can be used to access accounts

cash back when debit cards are used to withdraw cash

In 1986 the **Interac Association**, formed two years earlier by major depository institutions, established an electronic switching network to connect ABMs.[3] As a result of this shared network, cardholders of one institution's ABM can use their cards at the ABM of other member and associated institutions. ABMs are increasingly being used as an alternative to in-branch tellers for obtaining regular banking services.

CONVENIENCE CARDS   In 1994 the Interac Association's electronic switching network allowed for the national introduction of debit cards and an EFTPOS (electronic funds transfer point of sale) payment system. With a **convenience card** and a cardholder's PIN, access is granted to a retailer's EFTPOS terminal attached to a cash register. With access, the total amount of a purchase shown on a retailer's cash register is automatically transmitted via the Interac network to the retailer's depository institution for credit, and simultaneously to the cardholder's institution for debit. Convenience cards may also be used to get cash directly from participating retailers who then use the Interac Direct Payment System to debit the cardholder's account. This service is called **cash back.** Indeed, since many financial institutions charge a fee for the use of ABM machines each time they are used, consumers have become more interested in using their convenience cards to obtain cash back rather than use the ABM machine.

3. As a result of a ruling on a settlement reached in December 1996 between the Interac Association and the Competition Bureau, the Association has expanded its members from the original nine financial institutions to include nondepository institutions and third-party processors of debit and credit card transactions. Fees assessed for transactions based on cost recovery and a portion of the direct investment in the shared network software have replaced the original high front-end fee for membership.

Convenience cards have become a substitute for the use of cheques and cash. As is indicated in Table 2.3, debit cards are now a major payment instrument. First placed in grocery stores, direct debit terminals can now be found in a variety of retail outlets including clothing, liquor, and drug stores, as well as at many gas stations. Table 2.4 shows that more than $44 billion worth of transactions were undertaken using debit cards in 1997. There were more than 330 000 direct payment terminals in Canada in 1997.

TABLE 2.4   ABM AND EFTPOS TRANSACTIONS, 1998

	TRANSACTIONS	
ABMs	**Volume** ($ Millions)	**Value** ($ Billions)
Withdrawals	1 120.0	103.4
Deposits	304.5	NA
Bill payments	88.1	6.6
Interaccount transfers	97.0	NA
Balance inquiries	NA	NA
Total	1 609.6	NA
EFTPOS	1 355.4	58.5

Some values were not reported and denoted by NA.

SOURCE: Bank for International Settlements, *Statistics on the Payments Systems in the Group of Ten Countries*: December 1998, March 2000.

www.

smart cards
cards that have computer chips capable of storing and transferring money used for transaction purposes

PREPAID PAYMENT CARDS A common characteristic of prepaid payment cards, also referred to as **smart cards**, is that they have a microcomputer chip embedded in them. Cash in electronic form can be transferred onto the chip and stored there until it is electronically loaded for making payments. These stored-value multipurpose cards can be reloaded or disposed of after all their stored value has been exhausted. In regional pilot projects undertaken in Canada, the card has been used for multiple small-value retail transactions, vending machines, parking meters, and pay phones. In all these uses the cards substitute for cash, so such electronic purses or wallets may well be the harbinger of the often-predicted "cashless society." Because of the high costs associated with using coinage and bank notes, a strong incentive exists to develop the infrastructure necessary for the wider implementation of prepaid general purpose payment cards.

In 1997 Mondex Canada tested a cash-card in Guelph, Ontario. It was used for vending machines, buses, parking meters, and other small transactions. Mondex has recently revised its card, and the new version is being tested in Sherbrooke, Quebec. Late in 1999, Visa began testing its VisaCash card in Barrie, Ontario. In the United States, there are pilot projects involving wristbands containing computer chips that act just like a convenience card. Just swipe your wrist across a scanner, and presto, you have paid for your groceries. In which state are they testing this new gadget? You guessed it, California. Once the industry establishes a common framework for the use of smart-cards, and people become more secure in using them to transact, we'll probably hold even less cash in our pockets than we do now.

OTHER PAPERLESS PAYMENTS INSTRUMENTS   It is not unusual for individuals to receive their salaries or wages, pensions, social insurance benefits, or other incomes by electronic credit transfers, that is, direct deposit, to their bank accounts. Many individuals also pay their monthly utility and other bills with preauthorized deposits (PADs), whereby electronic debit transfers are made directly out of their deposit accounts. The accompanying box provides some additional information on "electronic money."

For many individuals, home-banking substitutes for in-branch teller services or the use of ABMs. Using their touch-tone telephones or their computers with modems, they can pay bills, make interaccount transfers, and make balance enquiries.

BOX 2–4   BACKGROUNDER

Electronic Money

Electronic money (e-money) has the potential, over time, to significantly reduce the use of other methods of payments (particularly coins and notes) in small-value transactions.

E-money is a way of storing purchasing power electronically. It can take the form of a card (something referred to as a "smart" or "stored-value" card or an "electronic purse"), or it can be software on a computer network (sometimes referred to as "digital cash"). The consumer obtains a certain value from an e-money "provider," and the value of purchases is subtracted from this balance.

Promoters of various e-money schemes are currently conducting pilot projects in cities across Canada. While predicting the commercial success of e-money is very difficult, its acceptance will ultimately depend on its attractiveness to consumers, merchants, and providers. Governments and central banks in a number of countries have begun to consider the policy issues raised by e-money. Of particular interest to central banks are the implications for central bank revenues, monetary

policy, and the payments system in general. Among the questions being raised are: Who should provide e-money? Should the providers be regulated and, if so, how? What is the appropriate form of consumer protection? Are existing laws sufficiently clear on the legal rights and obligations of e-money users and providers? What are the implications for criminal activities, particularly counterfeiting, fraud, and money laundering? Finally, what are the consequences of serious technical malfunctions?

During 1996 the central banks in the Group of Ten (G-10) countries (including the Bank of Canada) actively studied and discussed many of these issues. Much of this work was carried out under the auspices of the Bank for International Settlements and led to the publication of two reports.

Further studies by governments are under way in the areas of consumer protection, law enforcement, and the possible supervision and regulation of e-money products and providers.

SOURCE: Bank of Canada, *Annual Report*, 1996, p. 29.

Electronic data interchange (EDI) enables businesses to exchange electronic messages that include funds transfers as well as remittance data such as purchase orders. These funds transfers can be likened to electronic cheques with the cheque stubs included. Commercial cash management payments (CCMPs) are similar to PADs, but are designed for electronic debit transfers between businesses. In 1997 the Canadian Payments Association introduced the Large Value Transfer System (LVTS). Under this system, payment orders of at least $50 000 are transferred electronically, with payees given same-day value for any payments received. The LVTS system became operational in 1999.

www.

THE PAYMENTS SYSTEM OF THE FUTURE   Predictions abound over the payments system of the twenty-first century. Imagine every person or organization with a payment card having access to a nationwide or an international system. In such a comprehensive funds transfer system, computer networks linked by satellite would record transactions electronically. Debit and credit deposit accounts would be updated instantaneously throughout the world. With terminals to access the system at our fingertips, physical currency would be unnecessary.

Before a full-scale electronic funds transfer system becomes a reality, many issues must first be resolved. These include the equitable sharing of the system's costs and benefits, the ownership and control of computer communications networks, the possible invasion of privacy, the documentation of transactions and the ability to reverse them, the need for security and the prevention of fraudulent transactions, and the provision of a backup mechanism in the event of computer failure or a system's breakdown.

KEY TERMS

absolute price
Bank of Canada
banking school
barter economy
bimetallic standard
brassage
cash back
clearinghouse
commodity reserve standard
commodity standard
convenience cards

currency in public circulation
currency school
double coincidence of wants
fiat money
float
Gresham's Law
Interac Association
International Monetary Fund (IMF)
liquid
liquidity
metallic coin standard

metallic exchange standard
monetary aggregates
money
monometallic bullion standard
paper standards
quantity theory of money
relative prices
smart cards
symmetallism

REVIEW QUESTIONS

1. What is a monetary standard, and why does each nation have one?
2. What are the key features of a gold coin, gold bullion, and a gold exchange standard?
3. What are the major advantages and disadvantages of a commodity standard?
4. What are the characteristics of a bimetallic standard? Explain how Gresham's Law comes into play in the operation of such a standard.
5. What is a commodity reserve standard, and what is its major strength?
6. What is meant by a paper standard? What are its major advantages and disadvantages?
7. What major difficulties were experienced with providing a medium of exchange during the colonial period? What expedients were introduced to overcome these difficulties?
8. What is the Canadian Payments Association?
9. Consider two ways in which the Canadian payments system might develop and how these developments could benefit Canadians.
10. Define money in terms of its functions.
11. Price is nothing more than a ratio of exchange. How many prices are there in a barter economy where there are 200 commodities to be exchanged for each other? How many prices are there when one of these commodities serves as money?
12. Without money, direct exchanges of goods and services require that the double coincidence of wants be satisfied. What do we mean by a double coincidence of wants?
13. Money is referred to as a "bearer of options" whose introduction provided individuals with new-found freedoms and society with a more efficient allocation

of resources. Describe these freedoms and efficiencies.
14. Why did metals satisfy the functions of money better than other commodities?
15. What are the strengths and weaknesses of each of the following for use as commodity money: oysters, diamonds, wine, sand?
16. Differentiate between narrow and broad money measures in Canada.
What criteria, other than its functions, might be used to determine a money measure?
17. What criteria, other than its functions, might be useful to determine a money measure?
18. This question involves research. Plot the last 20 years of annual data on M1 and M3 in Canada, using the year-end value for your measure of "money." Now plot nominal income over the same period. What do you observe, and can you suggest a possible explanation?
19. Many financial institutions charge for cash withdrawals at automatic bank machines. Call at least three institutions in your community and ask them about their least-expensive account plans. How many withdrawals are individuals allowed a month? Why would a limit be placed on the number of times you can make a withdrawal? Is there a way for you to obtain cash from your account without making a withdrawal at an automated bank machine? How?
20. In April 2000, the Royal Canadian Mint began to study whether a new $5 coin should be introduced in Canada. Suppose they invited you to provide an economic analysis of the proposal. How would you structure your investigation? What are the important issues to consider?

SELECTED READINGS

Alchian, Armen. "Why Money?" *Journal of Money, Credit and Banking* 9 (February 1977), pp. 133–41.

Atta-Mensah, J., and L. Nott. "Recent Developments in the Monetary Aggregates and their Implications." *Bank of Canada Review* (Spring 1999), pp. 5–19.

Atta-Mensah, J. "Recent Developments in the Monetary Aggregates and their Implications." *Bank of Canada Review* (Spring 2000), pp. 3–10.

Bank of Canada. *The Story of Canada's Currency.* Ottawa: Bank of Canada, 1953.

Bank for International Settlements. *Statistics on Payment Systems in the Group of Ten Countries* (various issues). Basel, Switzerland.

Breckinridge, S.P. *Legal Tender.* Chicago: University of Chicago Press, 1903.

Brunner, Karl, and Allan Meltzer. "The Uses of Money in the Theory of an Exchange Economy." *American Economic Review* 61 (December 1971), pp. 784–806.

Canadian Bankers' Association. *Adam Shortt's History of Canadian Currency and Banking 1600–1880.* Toronto: Canadian Bankers Association, 1987.

Canadian Payments Association. *Annual Review.*

Carlisle, W.W. *The Evolution of Modern Money.* London: Macmillan, 1901

Eichengreen, Barry, ed. *The Gold Standard in Theory and History.* New York: Methuen, 1985.

Friedman, Milton. "Commodity Reserve Currency," in *Essays in Positive Economics.* Chicago: University of Chicago Press, 1953.

Galbraith, J.K. *Money: When It Came, Where It Went.* Boston: Houghton Mifflin, 1975.

Graham, Frank D. *World Commodities and World Currency.* New York: McGraw-Hill, 1944.

Hawtrey, R.G. *Currency and Credit*, 3rd ed. London: Longmans, Green, 1928.

Jevon, W. Stanley. *Money and the Mechanism of Exchange.* New York: D. Appleton, 1896.

Kemmerer, Edwin W. *Gold and the Gold Standard.* New York: McGraw-Hill, 1944.

Keynes, John Maynard. *A Treatise on Money*, 2nd ed. London: Macmillan, 1930, Vol. 1, Ch. 1.

Laidler, David. "The Definition of Money." *Journal of Money, Credit and Banking* 1 (August 1969), pp. 508–25.

Lloyd, T.H. "Early Elizabethan Investigations into Exchange and the Value of Sterling, 1558–1568." *Economic History Review* 53 (1, 2000).

Mann, F.A. *The Legal Aspects of Money*, 2nd ed. London: Oxford University Press, 1953.

McCullough, A.B. *Money and Exchange in Canada to 1900.* Toronto and Charlottetown: Dundwin Press Limited, 1984.

McPhail, K. *Broad Money: A Guide to Monetary Policy.* Paper prepared for the Annual Bank of Canada Conference, November 1999, Bank of Canada.

Powell, James. *A History of the Canadian Dollar.* Ottawa: Bank of Canada, 1999.

Quiggin, A. Hingston. *A Survey of Primitive Money.* London: Methuen, 1963.

Radford, R.A. "The Economic Organization of a P.O.W. Camp." *Economica* 12 (November 1945), pp. 189–201.

Schumpeter, J.A. "Money and the Social Product," in *International Economic Papers*, No. 6. London: Macmillan, 1956, pp. 148–211.

Stuber, Gerald. *The Electronic Purse: An Overview of Recent Developments and Policy Issues.* Bank of Canada Technical Report No. 74, Ottawa, January 1996.

Walker, Francis A. *International Bimetallism.* New York: Henry Holt, 1896.

CHAPTER THREE

THE FLOW OF FUNDS AND INTERTEMPORAL CONSUMPTION

After reading this chapter you should be able to
1. *Demonstrate how the flow of funds works for one sector of the economy*
2. *Explain the flow of funds for the entire economy*
3. *Demonstrate the process of intermediation*
4. *Use the intertemporal consumption model to explain decisions to save and borrow*
5. *Show how changes in income and interest rates affect borrowing and lending decisions*

National Income and Expenditure Accounts *the accounts that show Gross Domestic Product (GDP) and that record the saving and investment of each of four main sectors in the economy*

Anything that influences the stream of money and credit in the economy affects some part of the financial markets. In turn, this influence has an impact on total spending on goods and services by changing the cost and availability of various types of financing as well as the liquidity of borrowers and lenders. In this chapter we begin by outlining a framework that expresses the interrelationships between financial markets and the markets for goods and services in terms of some fundamental equalities. For analytical purposes, we can divide the economy into homogeneous groupings or sectors composed of economic units similar in behaviour, function, and institutional structure. For example, the **National Income and Expenditure Accounts,** familiar to most students as the accounts that show Gross Domestic Product (GDP), record the saving and investment of each of four main sectors: (1) personal and unincorporated business, (2) corporate and business enterprises, (3) government, and (4) the rest of the world. As another example, the Financial Flow Accounts, which we discuss in this chapter, are divided into 13 major sectors and 29 subsectors that are thought to be homogeneous in terms of basic economic behaviour.

After reviewing the sources and uses of funds, we briefly touch on the process of intermediation—the means by which savers and dissavers come together through an intermediary. Then, once we are satisfied that we know some of the basics about how borrowers and lenders interact, we will delve into an intertemporal consumption model that can be used to explain borrowing and saving decisions over time. We will see that the interest rate is a key component of this model. The implications for monetary policy are significant. Through this intertemporal consumption model, we will begin to appreciate "the big picture" of Figure 1.6.

A Sector's Income Statement

For each sector of the economy we can draw up an income statement similar to the one in Table 3.1. The income statement shows a sector's current income, current expenditures, and saving. As indicated by the summation signs at the bottom of the table, over a given period, usually a year or a quarter of a year, current income is equal to current expenditures plus saving. The statement expresses the following fundamental equality:

$$\text{Saving} = \text{Current Income} - \text{Current Expenditures}$$

For the government sector saving is usually called a budget surplus; for a business sector it is usually referred to as either retained earnings or addition to net worth.

TABLE 3.1	INCOME STATEMENT FOR A SINGLE SECTOR
Current Expenditures	Current Income
Saving	
$\Sigma = \Sigma$	

A Sector's Balance Sheet

For each sector of the economy, we can also draw up a balance sheet similar to the one in Table 3.2. The balance sheet lists a sector's assets, liabilities, and net worth at a particular point in time. These elements are arranged to produce the following balance sheet equality:

$$\text{Real Assets} + \text{Financial Assets} = \text{Liabilities} + \text{Net Worth}$$

For a particular sector, its real assets need not equal its net worth, and its financial assets need not equal its total liabilities. As we will see later, however, for the economy as a whole (all sectors taken together) real assets are equal to net worth and financial assets are equal to liabilities.

A sector has three types of assets: real assets, financial assets, and human assets. The last, commonly referred to by economists as human capital, includes the education, skill, and experience embodied in the sector's work-

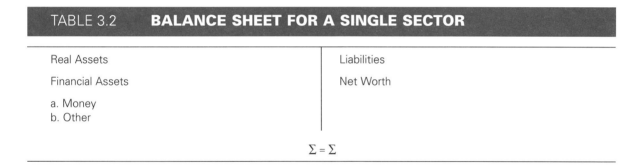

TABLE 3.2	**BALANCE SHEET FOR A SINGLE SECTOR**	
Real Assets		Liabilities
Financial Assets		Net Worth
a. Money		
b. Other		

$$\Sigma = \Sigma$$

force. Because we have no adequate measures for human capital, it is not included on balance sheets. Real assets are land, buildings, and equipment. Financial assets include money, debt claims such as bonds and mortgages, and equities or shares of stocks that represent ownership rights to corporations.

Whereas a sector's financial assets are its claims on other sectors, its liabilities or debts are other sectors' claims on it. In other words, the liabilities of one sector are the financial assets of some other sectors. Net worth is the difference between the values of a sector's assets and its liabilities. For business firms net worth is usually referred to as book value.

A Sector's Sources and Uses of Funds

A sector's income statement is a flow statement in that it shows the volume of transactions over some period. A balance sheet, in contrast, is a stock statement in that it measures the level of its components at a particular point in time. However, if we take the difference between two balance sheets drawn up for a sector at two different points in time, we end up with a flow statement. Such a statement, presented in Table 3.3, shows a sector's real and financial sources and uses of funds. The Δ symbol in the table indicates change.

A distinction is made in the table between the real and the financial uses and sources of funds. An increase in real assets represents investment spending. So as not to confuse investment spending with the purchase of financial assets, we shall always refer to the latter as financial investment. An increase in net worth is the same as saving. We assume that the change in the sector's balance sheet covers the same period as that in the income statement in Table 3.1, and therefore the saving shown in that table corresponds to the sector's saving identified as a change in net worth in Table 3.3.

A sector whose saving exceeds its investment (that is, whose current income exceeds its current consumption expenditures plus investment expenditures) is called a **surplus sector** (or surplus spending unit). A surplus sector must dispose of its surplus by lending, repaying debts, or hoarding (building up its cash holdings). Alternatively, a sector whose investment exceeds its saving (spends more than its current income on current consumption and investment) is called a **deficit sector** (or deficit spending unit). A deficit sector has to finance its deficit by borrowing, selling off financial assets, or dishoarding (running down its cash holdings in an amount equal to its deficit).

surplus sector
a sector whose current income exceeds its current consumption expenditures plus investment expenditures

deficit sector
a sector whose current income falls short of its current consumption expenditures plus investment expenditures

TABLE 3.3	CHANGE IN A SECTOR'S BALANCE SHEET

Real Uses	Real Sources
Δ Real Assets (Investments)	Δ Net Worth (Saving)
Financial Uses	**Financial Sources**
Δ Financial Assets	Δ Liabilities (Borrowing)
a. Money (Hoarding)	
b. Other (Lending)	

$$\Sigma = \Sigma$$

In summary, a sector can increase its sources of funds in the following ways:

1. increases in net worth (saving)
2. increases in liabilities (borrowing)
3. decreases in assets
   a. decrease in cash holdings (dishoarding)
   b. recall of loans

and use its funds by

1. increases in real assets (investment)
2. increases in financial assets
   a. increase in cash holdings (hoarding)
   b. increase in lending
3. decreases in liabilities (repaying debts)

The Flow of Funds for the Whole Economy

When we put together individual sector statements similar to the one shown in Table 3.3, we get a flow of funds matrix for the economy as a whole that shows the financial interrelationships among the sectors and the aggregate totals of saving, investment, borrowing, and lending. Table 3.4 presents a summary of the Canadian Financial Flow of Funds Matrix for 1999. For convenience of presentation, we have aggregated the data reported by Statistics Canada for 42 sectors and subsectors into five sectors.

Table 3.4 is divided into two parts. The upper portion summarizes the net outcome of current transactions in real goods and services. It shows gross saving generated by each of four domestic sectors and the contribution to gross domestic saving by nonresidents. The difference between a sector's gross saving and its gross capital formation (investment) identifies it as a net borrower or net lender. A "residual error" column is included in the table to reconcile the estimates of total gross saving and gross capital formation reported by Statistics Canada in its **Financial Flow Accounts** with those reported in its National Income and Expenditure Accounts.

www.

Financial Flow Accounts estimates of total gross saving and gross capital formation reported by Statistics Canada

TABLE 3.4   SUMMARY OF CANADIAN FINANCIAL FLOW MATRIX FOR 1999
Millions of Dollars

SECTORS	I	II	III	IV	V		
Transactions Category	Persons and Unincorporated Businesses	Public and Private Corporations	Financial Sector	Government*	Rest of the World	Residual Error	Total
I. NONFINANCIAL USES AND SOURCES OF FUNDS							
Gross Saving	41 538	107 448	13 357	42 720	–4 097	–202	187 407
Nonfinancial Capital Acquisition	62 829	107 773	5 607	16 603	0	202	187 407
Net Lending (+) or Net Borrowing (–)	–21 291	–325	7 750	26 117	–4 097	–404	0
II. FINANCIAL USES AND SOURCES OF FUNDS							
Net Increase in Financial Assets	22 777	251 896	193 042	39 368	27 168	—	341 209
Net Increase in Liabilities	38 634	246 502	181 054	12 228	43 845	—	341 209
Discrepancy	–5 434	–5 719	–4 238	–1 023	–404	—	0

Note: Errors are due to rounding.
* Includes federal and other levels of government, hospitals, and social security funds.

SOURCE: Statistics Canada, CANSIM Database Matrices 701, 740, 741, 742, 743, 744, 749, March 2000.

It is important to observe that what is true for any one sector is not true for the economy as a whole. For example, for any one sector, saving can be larger or smaller than its investment (nonfinancial capital acquisition). But for the economy as a whole (all sectors taken together), saving must equal investment. This relationship can be shown as follows:

$$\text{Investment} + \text{Lending} + \text{Hoarding} = \text{Saving} + \text{Borrowing}$$

But since one sector's financial assets is another sector's liability:

$$\text{Lending} + \text{Hoarding} = \text{Borrowing}$$

Therefore for the whole economy:

$$\text{Investment} = \text{Saving}$$

Net lending must equal net borrowing, as shown in the table. The lower portion of Table 3.4 presents the estimates for 1999 of the net financial behaviour for each of our five sectors. (The corresponding financial uses and sources of funds are shown in detail for the Persons and Unincorporated Businesses sector in Table 3.5). A "discrepancy" item is included at the bottom of Table 3.4 to reconcile each sector's net change in financial assets and liabilities with its net lending or net borrowing position, as estimated in the upper portion of the table. Since for every lender there is a borrower, for the economy as a whole the net increase in financial assets must be equal to the net increase in liabilities.

During any year, some households, business firms, and governments spend less than their current income for consumption and real investment, while others spend more. In 1999, households were deficit spenders while the government and the financial sector were surplus spenders. The surpluses that were provided by these latter two sectors were absorbed primarily by the rest of the world and by the household sector.

At any given time, the flow of funds through financial markets exceeds the flow that arises from the matching of deficit and surplus sectors because each sector is simultaneously both a lender and a borrower. For example, as shown in the bottom portion of Table 3.4, during 1999 persons and unincorporated businesses lent almost $22.8 billion, while at the same time they borrowed more than $38.6 billion, as indicated by their net increase in liabilities. For instance, the typical household, as reflected in Table 3.5, borrows using residential mortgage loans, bank loans, and consumer credit, while at the same time lends by the acquisition of financial assets such as deposits, money market securities, stock, life insurance, and pensions.

Net lending or borrowing also does not show the entire flow of funds through financial markets. The total flow of funds generated by a sector exceeds its net acquisition of assets by the amount of financial assets it gives up, while the amount of funds it provides to financial markets exceeds the net increase in its liabilities by the amount of debts that it retires.

TABLE 3.5	FINANCIAL TRANSACTIONS OF PERSONS AND UNINCORPORATED BUSINESSES, 1999 Millions of Dollars		
	NET ACQUISITION OF FINANCIAL ASSETS	NET INCREASE IN LIABILITIES	NET USE (–) OR NET SOURCE (+) OF FUNDS
Financial Instrument			
Currency and deposits	30 196		–30 196
Consumer credit, trade payables		12 484	+12 484
Money market securities	11 362		–11 362
Bonds:			
Canada Savings	– 783		+ 783
Other	– 5 822		+ 5 82
Life insurance and pensions	17 919		–17 919
Stocks	23 513		–23 513
Foreign investment	– 1 699		+ 1 699
Loans:			
Bank		2 153	+ 2 153
Other		5 919	+ 5 919
Mortgages	– 256	18 078	+18 334
Other financial assets	–51 653		+51 653
Total	22 777	38 634	+15 857
Discrepancy			5 434
Net lending position			21 291

SOURCE: Statistics Canada, CANSIM Database, Matrix 701, March 2000.

Financial Market Activity

A perspective on the total flow of funds via financial markets (organized markets for security issues and negotiated loans) to final borrowers is provided by the financial market summary in Table 3.6. This table shows the original suppliers and final demanders of funds without the double counting that would occur if borrowing and simultaneous relending of financial intermediaries were included. The table also shows the type of financial instrument used by domestic nonfinancial sectors to raise funds. The characteristics of these various financial instruments are described in the next few chapters of the text.

TABLE 3.6	FINANCIAL MARKET SUMMARY TABLE, 1999	
Borrowing	**$Millions**	**%**
Persons and unincorporated businesses	36 581	18.5
Nonfinancial private corporations	52 868	27.0
Nonfinancial government enterprises	–3 381	–2.0
General government	9 669	5.0
Domestic financial institutions	77 873	39.5
Rest of the world	23 536	12.0
Total funds raised	197 146	100.0
Lending		**%**
Persons and unincorporated businesses	26 315	13.0
Nonfinancial private enterprises	4 368	2.0
Government, general	10 215	5.0
Domestic financial institutions	133 191	68.0
Shares purchased by affiliated corporations	10 088	5.0
Nonresidents	12 969	7.0
	197 146	100.0

SOURCE: Statistics Canada, CANSIM Database, Matrix 750, March 2000.

Intermediation

As we have said, each sector possesses a balance sheet and an income statement. Changes in the balance sheet provide us with flow data, as does the income statement. When we look at a particular sector, we can determine how its sources of funds match its uses of funds; the same is true for the entire economy. But how do firms, households, and governments interact in financial markets? When your consumption is less than your income, and you want to save, how do you go about it? You have several choices. If you knew something about which households, firms, or governments wanted to borrow funds, you might directly lend your funds to the borrower. But if you think about it, that is a tough task. You might have very little information about the credit-worthiness of the borrower, and it takes time (so there is a cost involved) for you to do an exhaustive search and gather all the information you might want to have before making a loan.

Suppose, however, your firm has $1 million after taxes and must decide what to do with the funds. Should it reinvest in the firm itself? Buy out a competitor? Lend the money to another firm? How does the firm come up with a plan to put that $1 million to the best use possible? Again, if the company had detailed information on all the firms, households, or governments that wanted to borrow, the decision would be easy. But who has time to gather and maintain this kind of database?

intermediation
the process of bringing surplus and deficit economic units together

The solution to both these problems is for the household or the firm to take its surplus funds to an intermediary that is able to specialize in the process of **intermediation**—bringing surplus and deficit economic units together. The

intermediary
*an institution
bringing surplus
and deficit eco-
nomic units
together*

intermediary—be it a chartered bank, an investment dealer, or a financial institution—can, because of economies of scale and economies of scope, gather and process huge amounts of data on credit risk and capital requirements. In return for offering these services, the intermediary charges a fee. If this fee is lower than the costs of securing the specialized knowledge the intermediary possesses, individuals will be willing to pay it.

One way to visualize this function is to consider Figure 3–1. The process of economic activity generates income, which can be saved or spent. If the income is directly saved or reinvested, no intermediation is required. Of course, individuals and firms might reinvest directly by becoming primary lenders, lending to primary borrowers. But, as we have said, this endeavour requires detailed information on the firms or households or governments wanting to secure funds—and reliable data on risk and credit history are sometimes difficult to secure. Failing that specialized knowledge, indirect investment through an intermediary offers the saver an opportunity to earn a return on her investment. The cycle continues: borrowers increase economic activity, thereby generating more saving, and so on. Intermediaries provide the lubrication necessary for economic growth and prosperity.

FIGURE 3–1 **INTERMEDIATION**

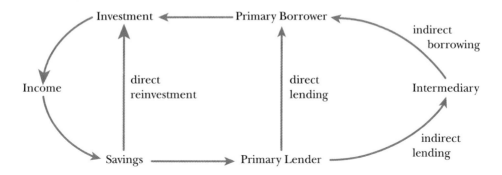

Financial intermediaries "lubricate" the flow of savings to investment.

Intertemporal Consumption

We think we have convinced you that households, firms, and governments borrow and lend—they have sources and uses of funds. We think, too, that you see the benefits of using an intermediary to lubricate that process. Just as money eliminates the double coincidence of wants, so too does intermediation eliminate the specialized knowledge that we would all have to possess if we were to distribute our savings directly to borrowers. It is now time to show you some of the determinants of the borrowing and lending decision.

Let us start by asking a simple question. Why do people, firms, and governments borrow? Obviously, it's because they want to consume in excess of

lifecycle model of consumption
a theory attempting to describe consumption behaviour over an individual's lifetime

their income. Indeed, Franco Modigliani received a Nobel Prize in economics in part for suggesting that people face periods of prolonged "overconsumption," followed by "underconsumption." For example, consider Figure 3–2, which plots a hypothetical individual's lifetime consumption and income streams. Early in life, consumption exceeds income—so the individual is borrowing. Debts are repaid during periods in which income exceeds consumption—so savings are being used to pay down debt. This **lifecycle model of consumption** makes much intuitive sense (at least to economists).

It would seem that this idea explains why we borrow and lend. During different periods of our lives, we choose to consume more than we earn. We finance this consumption by borrowing and agreeing to consume less than we earn in the future, when the loan has to be repaid. Additionally, if we plan to retire, we'll need to build a nest egg to finance our consumption in retirement, suggesting that after we have repaid the funds we borrowed, we will want to save even more to create the pool of funds from which to draw during retirement.

intertemporal consumption decision
the decision to smooth consumption over time

One of the ways economists try to explain the borrowing and lending decision is in terms of individuals maximizing their welfare, given the constraints they face and their tastes for present and future consumption. This explanation leads to a tractable model that answers questions about how changes in income and interest rates affect the **intertemporal consumption decision**. If we think of monetary policy in terms of its influence (or lack of influence) over interest rates, we can see how monetary policy might affect decision making over time. Conditional on a host of assumptions, we can begin to build a model of how monetary policy affects the economy. That construction is our next objective.

FIGURE 3–2 **LIFETIME CONSUMPTION AND INCOME STREAMS**

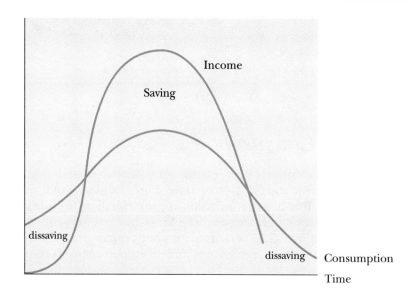

INDIFFERENCE CURVES   Consider Figure 3–3. It plots an **indifference curve**, demonstrating an individual's preferences for current and future consumption. On the horizontal axis we plot the current level of consumption, while on the vertical axis we plot the future level of consumption. An indifference curve shows combinations of current consumption and future consumption that provide the same level of satisfaction. That means this individual is indifferent between a current level of consumption of C_0 and a future level of consumption of C_1—point *A* on the curve—and point *B* on the curve, where future consumption is lower than C_1 and current consumption is greater than C_0. Points *A* and *B* both provide the same level of utility or satisfaction.

Where does this information come from? Individuals have preferences for future and current consumption. Those preferences, or tastes, determine the rates at which future consumption must rise (and current consumption must fall) to maintain a constant level of satisfaction. What would an indifference curve look like for an individual who did not care about future consumption, only about present consumption? If you said a vertical line, you've got it! Any level of future consumption would provide the same level of utility for a given level of current consumption. What if an individual cared only about future consumption? Any level of current consumption would provide the same level of satisfaction for a given level of future consumption, so the indifference curve would now be horizontal. The slope of the indifference curve thus tells us something about an individual's tastes for current and future consumption. A steeper indifference curve reflects relatively strong preferences for present consumption. A flat indifference curve tells us the preference is in favour of future consumption.

FIGURE 3–3   INDIFFERENCE CURVES

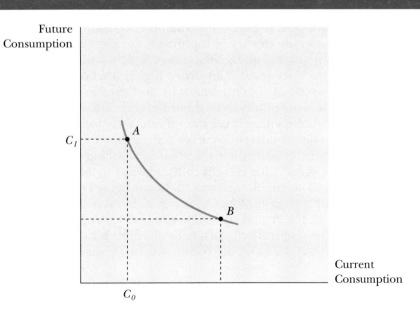

FIGURE 3–4   **INDIFFERENCE CURVES AND UTILITY**

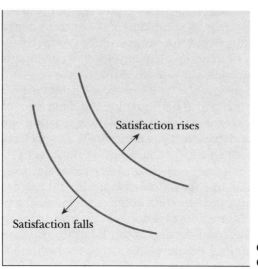

Many indifference curves are found everywhere in the "space" between the axes. These indifference curves must meet several conditions. The first is that people always prefer more to less, so higher levels of consumption always lead to higher levels of utility. In Figure 3–4 the indifference curve on the left has a lower level of satisfaction associated with it than that on the right. The individual can enjoy higher levels of both future and current consumption on the right-hand indifference curve, so his or her utility must be higher. The second condition is that indifference curves never intersect (otherwise decisions wouldn't be transitive). For example, consider Figure 3–5. Since point A is common to both curves, it provides the same degree of satisfaction. Yet, A is indifferent to B along IC_0, and A is also indifferent to point C along IC_1. However, since point B involves a higher level of current and future consumption than point C, point B must be preferred to point C. But that's not what we infer from the intersecting indifference curves, so they don't make sense. Thus, indifference curves cannot intersect (for the same tastes).

Finally, indifference curves reflect the fact that to get more of one good (like future consumption), one must be willing to give up increasingly more of another good (like current consumption) to maintain a constant level of satisfaction. This condition shows up in our figures in the "bow" of the indifference curve. Figure 3–6 plots a series of indifference curves demonstrating similar tastes for future and current consumption, with utility rising as we move away from the origin. The individual's objective is to get to the highest indifference curve possible, given the constraints he or she faces. Let us look at this more closely.

CONSTRAINTS FACING INDIVIDUALS   Individuals try to maximize their utility by choosing the "right" mix of future and current levels of consumption,

FIGURE 3–5 INDIFFERENCE CURVES NEVER INTERSECT

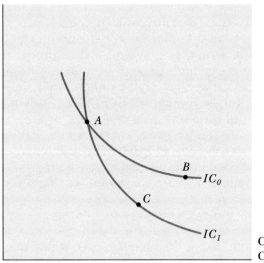

but we all face limitations. Even if you won that $5 million lottery, you wouldn't be able to buy that $7 million airplane. Similarly, when you choose to consume today and tomorrow, you'll be making decisions about whether to save or borrow. How? When you determine current and future levels of consumption, they are relative to your current and future income. If you choose to consume

FIGURE 3–6 MANY INDIFFERENCE CURVES

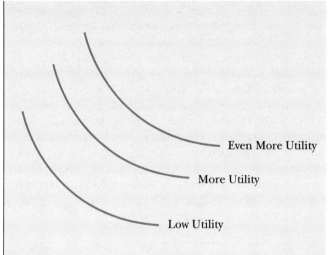

in excess of your income, you are **overconsuming**. Conversely, if your consumption is less than your income, you are **underconsuming**.

None of us knows what our income will be in the future, so there's quite a bit of guessing involved when we try to maximize our utility over time. We're going to assume that income is completely exogenous (determined outside the model) and fully known, both in the present and in the future. This concept is most easily accepted if you think about farming apples. Forget about fire, pests, and changes in apple prices over time. Just assume so many apples will fall on your head each year, and that you can trade those apples for dollars today and tomorrow at known apple prices. Your incomes today and tomorrow are thus known with certainty.

Now for the fun part. There's a financial institution in this make-believe world that will allow you to borrow and lend at the same interest rate. If you choose to underconsume today, your savings will return principal plus interest in the future. This system allows your future consumption to exceed your future income. If you choose to overconsume today, you must repay in the future by underconsuming—your future consumption will be less than your future income. Let's suppose the rate of interest is denoted by r (the **real rate of interest**; that is, the nominal interest rate that we see in the market, less an adjustment for what people believe inflation will be during the same period—we'll return to this concept in upcoming chapters). Let us also assume your current income is Y_0 while your future income is Y_1.

Consider Figure 3–7. On that curve we plot the endowment point E given by the current level of income Y_0 and the future level of income Y_1. Note that we've also extended a straight line through this point to both axes. Why? Suppose you save one dollar in current income. What would that do to the total funds you have available for future consumption? Well, in one period (this is a two-period model, the present and the future), you'd have that $1 plus interest at a rate of $r\%$, so you'd have $Y_1 + \$1(1 + r)$ for future consumption. If you saved $2 today instead of $1, you'd have $Y_1 + \$2(1 + r)$ in the future. And if you saved all your current income (Y_0), your future consumption could be as high as $Y_1 + Y_0(1 + r)$. That point is labelled on the vertical axis.

Now, instead of saving a dollar, what if you were to borrow a dollar today against your future income? How much would the bank lend you? The present value of $1, or the amount that, invested at an interest rate of $r\%$, would just equal one dollar in the future—given by $\$1/(1 + r)$. How so? Well, {$\$1/(1 + r)$} invested at a rate of $\{1 + r\}$ would just equal $1 after one period. If you borrowed the present value of $2 instead of $1, you'd be able to increase your current consumption by $\$2/(1 + r)$. Extending this to all your future income, you could, at a maximum, consume all your current income (Y_0) plus the present value of your future income $\{Y_1/(1 + r)\}$. That extension gives us the point labelled on the horizontal axis, $Y_0 + Y_1/(1 + r)$. This straight line tells us how individuals are able to trade off their consumption across time, given their incomes and the interest rate. The maximum value for future consumption is $Y_1 + Y_0(1 + r)$, while the maximum value for present consumption is $Y_0 + Y_1/(1 + r)$.

OPTIMIZATION   The individual's problem is now simple. Given income and the interest rate, each individual will try to get to the highest indifference

FIGURE 3–7   **HOW YOU TRADE CONSUMPTION ACROSS TIME**

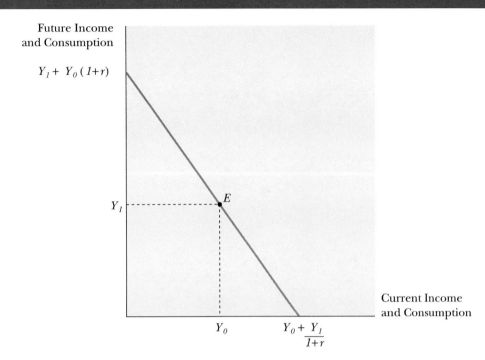

curve possible. In Figure 3–8, that is at point *A*. How about point *B*? No, since by reducing future consumption and raising current consumption, total utility will rise (we move to a higher indifference curve). How about point *C*? No, since by reducing current consumption and raising future consumption, total utility will rise (we move to a higher indifference curve). In short, individuals maximize their utility when the indifference curve is just tangent to the "budget constraint" that tells us how people are able to trade off consumption across time. Indeed, the slope of the consumption function tells us the rate at which people are willing to trade consumption across time. When the rate at which they are *able* to trade consumption across time equals the rate at which they are *willing* to trade consumption across time, individuals have maximized their welfare.

Note that the optimum need not be coincident with the endowment point. People can choose to save or to borrow today. Consider Figure 3–8 again. Current income is Y_0, while current consumption is C_0—greater than Y_0. How is this overconsumption achieved? It is achieved by borrowing against future income. Note that C_1 is below Y_1. The difference reflects the future underconsumption required to finance current overconsumption. In Figure 3–9 we demonstrate the opposite case: an individual choosing to save today. This antecedent allows future consumption to rise above future income.

CHANGES IN INCOME AND THE INTEREST RATE   We can now ask questions about how changes in current income and the interest rate affect the bor-

FIGURE 3–8 **OPTIMIZATION**

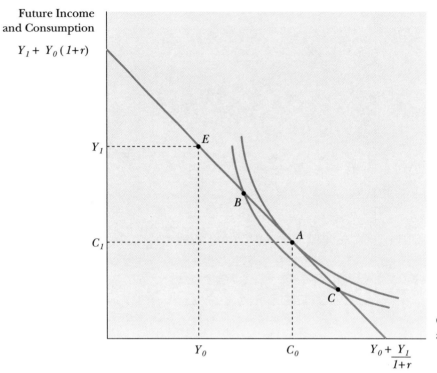

FIGURE 3–9 **CONSUMING AND SAVING OVER TIME**

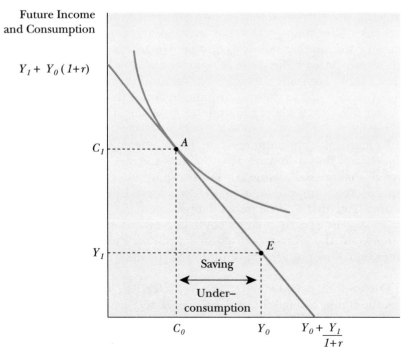

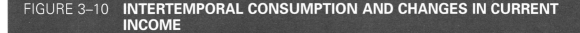

FIGURE 3–10 **INTERTEMPORAL CONSUMPTION AND CHANGES IN CURRENT INCOME**

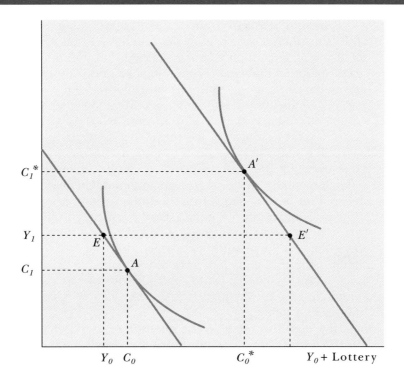

An increase in current income shifts the endowment point to E^1 from E. The individual maximizes her welfare by raising both current and future consumption to C_0^* and C_1^* from C_0 and C_1, respectively. The equilibrium moves from point A to point A'.

rowing and lending decision. Suppose the individual in Figure 3–10 wins the lottery today. What will happen to current saving and consumption? A lottery win shifts current income to Y_0 plus the lottery win, leaving future income unchanged (the usual number of apples will still fall on your head tomorrow). This win shifts out the "budget constraint," allowing for a greater range of possible consumption patterns. Maximizing utility leads to an increase in both current and future consumption, as the figure is drawn. You'll note that the individual who was at first a borrower (consumption exceeded income) is now a lender (since present consumption is below present income plus the lottery win).

How about changes in the interest rate? Suppose the interest rate rises. Would this increase affect indifference curves? No. Their shape is given by an individual's tastes for current and future consumption, and they are assumed to be independent of the interest rate. The interest rate does affect the rate at which an individual can trade off consumption across time, so the budget line rotates through the endowment point (a change in the interest rate doesn't change the number of apples falling on your head today and tomorrow). Higher interest rates mean the maximum your future consumption could be would be greater; the present value of your future income would be lower at a higher interest rate. Maximizing utility leads to a new equilibrium, where current consumption could be higher or lower than before the change in the interest rate.

income effect captures the change in consumption that results from a change in the interest rate due solely to the ability to move to a different indifference curve

substitution effect captures the change in consumption that results from a change in the interest rate, when we restrict movement to be along the original indifference curve

This result stems from the fact that there are two effects: an **income effect** and a **substitution effect.** You will recall these terms if you have taken an intermediate microeconomics course. The substitution effect captures the change in consumption that results from a change in the interest rate, when we restrict movement to be along the original indifference curve (so we are "adjusting for," or "compensating for," changes in the individual's ability to move to a different indifference curve). The income effect captures the change in consumption that results from an individual's ability to move to a new indifference curve. For many goods, the substitution and income effects operate in the same direction, but in some cases they work in opposition. For example, a reduction in the price of peanut butter might lead to an increase in the demand for peanut butter from both the substitution and income effects, but if the price of an inferior good falls, the same result might not apply. Suppose the price of a low-quality product falls. The substitution effect will always lead to an increase in quantity demanded, but the income effect might actually reduce quantity demanded, since the reduction in price has increased the individual's real income (income controlled for price changes), leading this consumer to substitute a higher-quality product in place of the less-expensive low-quality good.

How does this relate to the question of how a change in the interest rate affects consumption decisions over time? When the interest rate rises, the cost of current consumption rises because we are giving up the interest that could be earned on saving current income rather than consuming it today. This rise leads us to reduce current consumption (as long as our tastes for future and current consumption are "normal"), independently of whether we currently borrow or save. Consider Figures 3–11 and 3–12. In Figure 3–11, the individual is borrowing today to finance current consumption in excess of current income. An increase in the rate of interest rotates the budget line through the endowment point, with the new equilibrium at point B. Clearly, current consumption has fallen and future consumption has risen. Note that since the equilibrium moves to a lower indifference curve, the borrower is worse off as a result of an increase in the rate of interest. In Figure 3–12, the individual is currently saving to finance future consumption in excess of future income; the higher interest rate raises utility and future consumption, while current consumption falls.

You should be able to draw the diagrams for the case of a reduction in interest rates. If you find that a fall in interest rates raises the welfare of borrowers and reduces the welfare of lenders, you've drawn the figures correctly. If not, review the last few pages and try again!

ECONOMIC POLICY   Now we're equipped to answer some important questions about economic policy. Suppose the government wanted to stimulate the economy. Consider Figure 3–13, the aggregate demand/aggregate supply model of Chapter 1. The current equilibrium is at point *A*, but the authorities want income to rise to be consistent with point *B*. They want to achieve this

FIGURE 3–11   **RAISE THE INTEREST RATE: A BORROWER**

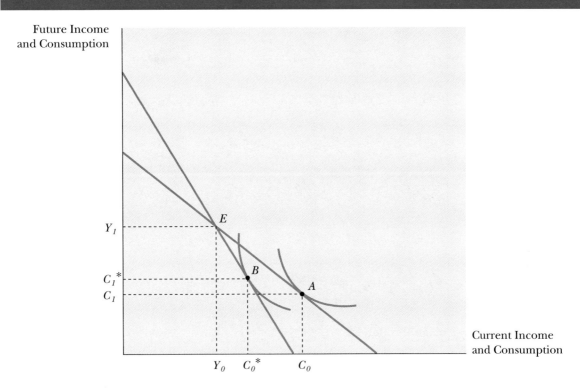

An increase in the interest rate rotates the budget line through the endowment point. The equilibrium moves from A to B, with current consumption falling and future consumption rising.

objective by shifting the aggregate demand curve right, to AD'. One way this task can be accomplished is to raise the current level of consumption expenditures made by households. What would lead to a higher level of current consumption, independently of whether individuals are current lenders or borrowers? If you said a reduction in interest rates, you're on the mark. A reduction in the interest rate will stimulate current consumption, whether or not we currently borrow or lend.

Now for the tricky part: The interest rate in our model of intertemporal consumption is the real interest rate—the nominal interest rate adjusted for expected inflation. Typically, economists believe that the real interest rate is independent of many policy initiatives, with the nominal interest rate more likely to be sensitive to economic policy shifts. However, since we never observe the real interest rate in the market (because we never see those inflationary expectations), there is scope for economic policy to affect real interest rates and, thereby, intertemporal consumption—so long as the nominal interest rate does not move perfectly in tandem with inflationary expectations. The empirical evidence as to whether this happens or not is relatively mixed, with no clear consensus emerging on whether changes in inflationary expectations lead to one-for-one changes in nominal interest rates. Hence, it is relatively safe to say

FIGURE 3–12   **RAISE THE INTEREST RATE: A LENDER**

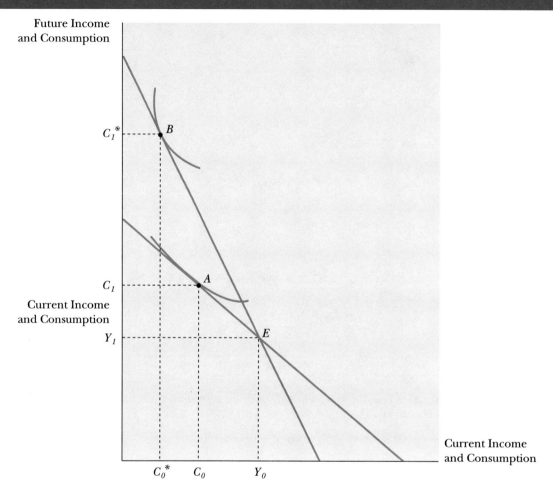

An increase in the interest rate rotates the budget line through the endowment point. Utility rises from points A to B. Current consumption falls as its cost—the interest rate—rises.

that economic policy affects consumption decisions over time by affecting interest rates.[1]

1. For some recent empirical evidence of the issue see M. Evans, and K. Lewis, "Do Inflation Expectations Affect the Real Rate?" *Journal of Finance* 50 (1995), pp. 225–53; S. Kandel, A. Ofer, and O. Sarig, "Real Interest Rates and Inflation," *Journal of Finance* 51 (1996), pp. 205–25; and W. Crowder, and D. Hoffman, "The Long-Run Relationship Between Nominal Interest Rates and Inflation: The Fisher Equation Revisited," *Journal of Money, Credit and Banking* 287 (1996), pp. 102–18. Espinosa-Vega and Russell demonstrate that the real interest rate might fall permanently as a result of an expansionary monetary policy in M. Espinosa-Vega, and S. Russell, "Can Higher Inflation Reduce Real Interest Rates in the Long Run?" *Canadian Journal of Economics* 31 (1998), pp. 92–103. The article may be a little difficult for students in an introductory course, but it offers a theoretical treatment of the issue.

FIGURE 3–13   **RAISING AGGREGATE DEMAND**

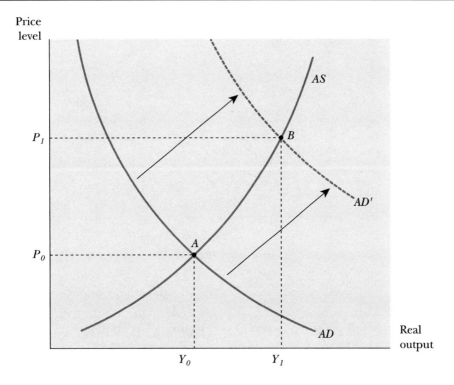

A reduction in interest rates may raise aggregate demand and take the economy from point *A* to point *B*.

Next, we look at financial assets and interest rates in detail to see why and how this effect takes place.

BOX 3–1 PERSONAL SAVINGS RATES AND HOUSEHOLD BALANCE SHEETS

Personal Savings and Increase in Net Worth as a Percentage of Disposable Income

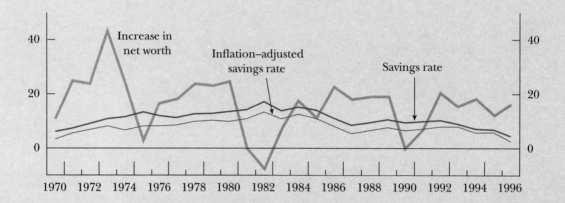

Some commentators have voiced concerns that low personal savings rates and high household debt levels will prevent the household sector from contributing significantly to the economic expansion. A closer look shows that this should not be the case.

The conventional measure of the personal savings rate, even after adjustment for inflation,* declined steadily from 1982 to 1996. As household spending expanded strongly in the fourth quarter of 1996, the savings rate fell to 3.2 percent. However, there is no reason why it should not remain at this level for a time or go even lower temporarily while interest rates are low and the economy is expanding. The increase in personal net worth, an alternative measure of savings,** which shows a much higher savings rate in recent years, lends credence to this possibility.

Although the ratio of household debt to personal disposable income continues to rise, the ratio of this debt to household assets has been stable at around 18 percent, after declining substantially in the 1980s. Viewed another way, the net worth of the household sector, boosted by capital gains on securities, has grown rapidly in the past few years. While debts and assets may not be equally distributed across households, the fact that three-quarters of household debt is in the form of mortgages on residential properties suggests that most of the indebted households have offsetting assets.

What is most important, however, is that the burden of servicing household debt has diminished considerably since the early 1990s because of the large decline in interest rates. Together with the increase in net worth, this lower debt-service cost should help to sustain Canada's economic recovery.

* For more detail on the inflation adjustment to the personal savings rate, see Lau (1993).

** Net worth is the value of assets (at current prices) minus liabilities. Assets include financial assets and real estate but exclude stocks of consumer durables.

SOURCE: Bank of Canada, *Monetary Policy Report*, May 1997, p. 7.

KEY TERMS

deficit sector
Financial Flow Accounts
income effect
indifference curve
intermediary

intermediation
intertemporal consumption decision
lifecycle model of consumption
National Income and Expenditure
   Accounts

overconsuming
real rate of interest
substitution effect
surplus sector
underconsuming

REVIEW QUESTIONS

1. What are the three types of assets accumulated by most wealth holders? What are they composed of?
2. What is a surplus sector? A deficit sector?
3. How can a sector increase its sources of funds? How can it increase its uses of funds?
4. Show that, for an economy as a whole, investment must be equal to saving.
5. Why does Table 3.6 not show the entire flow of funds through the market?
6. Explain the relation between each individual sector and the economy as a whole.
7. Why is it that society's wealth is the sum of its real assets and not of its financial assets?
8. What is the difference between a flow statement and a stock statement?
9. If individuals only care about the future, will a reduction in interest rates reduce current consumption? Draw a graph to support your answer.
10. If interest rates rise, future consumption will fall. True or false?

11. If the government introduces a tax on current but not on future income, saving will fall. True or false?
12. "Nations have been overconsuming for decades and now face prolonged periods of underconsumption to finance the overconsumption." Support this statement using properly labelled diagrams.
13. "Money serves as both a medium of exchange and as a store of value." Demonstrate how the intertemporal consumption model can be used to illustrate this statement.
14. Suppose that the authorities want a lower level of output and that individuals are currently overconsuming. How might the authorities accomplish this objective? Use the intertemporal consumption model to illustrate your argument.
15. If the central bank wants to lower both the current level of consumption and the future level of consumption, under what conditions would an increase in the interest rate lead to these objectives? Why?

SELECTED READINGS

Attanasio, O., J. Banks, C. Meghir, and G. Weber. "Humps and Bumps in Lifetime Consumption." *Journal of Business and Economic Statistics* 17 (1, 1999).

Berk, J.M. "Measuring Inflation Expectations: A Survey Data Approach." *Applied Economics* 31 (11, 1999).

Bérubé G., and D. Côté. "Long-Term Determinants of the Personal Savings Rate: Literature Review and Some Empirical Results for Canada." Bank of Canada Working Paper 2000-3, 2000.

Coulombe, S. "A Non-Paradoxical Interpretation of the Gibson Paradox." Bank of Canada Working Paper 98-22, 1998.

Crowder, W., and D. Hoffman. "The Long-Run Relationship between Nominal Interest Rates and Inflation: The Fisher Equation Revisited." *Journal of Money, Credit and Banking* 28 (1996), pp. 102–18.

Duffy, J., and J. Ochs. "Emergence of Money as a Medium of Exchange: An Experimental Study." *American Economic Review* 89 (4, 1999).

Espinosa-Vega, M., and S. Russell. "Can Higher Inflation Reduce Real Interest Rates in the Long Run?" *Canadian Journal of Economics* 31 (1998), pp. 92–103.

Evans, M., and K. Lewis. "Do Inflation Expectations Affect the Real Rate." *Journal of Finance* 50 (1995), pp. 225–53.

Kandel, S., A. Ofer, and O. Sarig. "Real Interest Rates and Inflation." *Journal of Finance* 51 (1996), pp. 205–25.

Lau, Hung-Hay. "Behaviour of the Personal Saving Rate in Canada in Recent Years: A Note." *Bank of Canada Review* (Spring 1993), pp. 31–44.

Modigliani, F., and R. Brumberg. "Utility Analysis and the Consumption Function: An Interpretation of Cross-section Data," in *Post-Keynesian Economics*, K. Kurihana (ed.), New Jersey, Rutgers University Press, 1957, pp. 388–436.

Muscatelli, V., and F. Spinelli. "Fisher, Barro, and the Italian Interest Rate, 1845–93." *Journal of Policy Modeling* 22 (2, 2000), pp. 149–69.

Ricketts, N. 1996. "Real Short-Term Interest Rates and Expected Inflation: Measurement and Interpretation." *Bank of Canada Review* (Summer), pp. 23–39.

Statistics Canada. *A Guide to the Financial Flow and National Balance Sheet Accounts*, Catalogue 13-585E, Ottawa.

———. *Financial Flow Accounts*, Catalogue 13-014, Ottawa.

Thomas, L.B. "Survey Measures of Expected U.S. Inflation." *Journal of Economic Perspectives* 13 (4, 1999), pp. 125–44.

CHAPTER FOUR

FINANCIAL ASSETS: THEIR NATURE, PRICE, AND YIELD

After reading this chapter you should be able to
1. Describe several characteristics of financial assets
2. Calculate present values and future values and relate them to asset prices
3. Define and apply four different measures of interest rates
4. Explain why bonds trade at par, at a discount, or at a premium
5. Use an annuity formula to determine the value of a flow of payments
6. Explain two ways in which bond prices and yields are related
7. Demonstrate how exchange rate risk affects yields on securities denominated in different currencies

The Nature of Financial Assets

debt securities
securities such as bonds that represent a legally enforceable promise by the borrower to pay, in some future period, a stated amount of interest and the principal amount lent

equity securities
securities, such as stock, that represent shares in the ownership of an enterprise and entitle the owners to a pro rata share of any distributed profits of the enterprise

Although many types of financial assets exist, they may be divided into two main categories according to whether they represent a contractual or a residual claim to future income. **Debt securities**, such as bonds, represent a legally enforceable promise by the borrower to pay, in some future period, a stated amount of interest and the principal amount borrowed. **Equity securities**, or simply equities, such as common stock, represent shares in the ownership of an enterprise and entitle the owners to a pro rata share of the distributed profits, if any, of the enterprise.

Financial assets are also differentiated in terms of maturity, liquidity, risk, yield, and taxability. By maturity, we mean the time that can elapse before the borrower is obliged to repay the debt in full. For example, a bond issued in 2000 and due to be repaid in 2020 would have a 20-year maturity when issued, but a 10-year maturity in 2010. When issued, most debt securities have a well-defined maturity that may range from a single day to many years. Bonds can be issued with retractable or extendable provisions that allow the issuer to advance or delay the maturity date. In other instances bonds may be callable, which means lenders can redeem or retire the bond before maturity. Consols or perpetual bonds, as well as demand deposits and common stock, have no specific maturity.

Liquidity refers to the ease and the cost of converting a particular asset into money. As we noted in Chapter 2, money is perfectly liquid: It can be used immediately to pay debts or to spend, and has a constant nominal value. An asset is illiquid to the extent that its conversion into money requires time and entails loss of value, either through a decline in its market value or through transaction costs such as inconvenience, fees, and commission payments.

Liquidity is closely associated with an asset's redeemability and marketability. For example, a Canada Savings Bond has a high degree of liquidity: It can be redeemed at any time for what was paid for it, with little or no cost beyond that of inconvenience. A demand deposit also has a high degree of liquidity because at any time it can be redeemed for currency for its nominal amount, or can be transferred by cheque to make payment (with relatively little cost). Most other assets are not redeemable, and thus their liquidity depends on their marketability. An asset is said to possess **marketability** if readily available markets for its sale exist. As a rule, the more marketable the asset, the higher its degree of liquidity, because of the greater ease with which it can be turned into money. Also, the more competitive the market for an asset, the lower the transaction costs will be for its purchase and sale.

The risks inherent in holding financial assets derive from the probability of not recovering the value of funds originally invested together with the contractual or expected return on these funds. There are two major types of risk: **default risk** and **market risk**. Default risk, also known as credit risk, is the probability that the borrower will be unable or unwilling to make agreed-on payments on time. Default occurs when the borrower does not make a contractual payment or when this payment is late. In either case the lender suffers a loss. An asset's default risk varies directly with the borrower's creditworthiness. Market risk is the probability that the market price of an asset may decline for reasons other than default by the borrower. Whereas default risk is specific to the borrower, market risk depends on market conditions such as the outlook for business earnings and market interest rates. For investors concerned with the real value of their investment, the probability of changes in the rate of inflation is an important market risk attribute.

In Canada, two private organizations, the Dominion Bond Rating Service and the Canadian Bond Rating Service, assess the creditworthiness of debt issuers and provide, for a fee, a default-risk rating of corporate and government securities. Even Government of Canada securities, once thought to have no default risk, are rated. As shown in Table 4.1, bond ratings range from the highest-quality issues with little or no credit risk, to those that have some speculative characteristics and therefore some credit risk, to those that are principally speculative and extremely risky, to those that are in default and undoubtedly risky.

A financial asset's **yield** is the total rate of return received by its holder; that is, the total dollar amount received on resale or redemption (including both interest payments and capital gain or loss on its acquisition cost). In the case of deposit instruments whose nominal value remains fixed, their yield is always the same as the interest rate received, and their rate of return is commonly called the **interest rate** rather than the yield. With other debt instruments

---

www.

marketability *an asset is said to possess marketability if there are readily available markets for its sale*

default (credit) risk *the probability that the borrower will be unable or unwilling to make agreed-on payments on time*

market risk *the probability that the market price of an asset may decline for reasons other than default by the borrower*

www.

yield *the total rate of return on an asset*

interest rate *the stated rate of return on an asset*

TABLE 4.1	**BOND RATING DESIGNATION**		
DOMINION BOND RATING SERVICE		**CANADIAN BOND RATING SERVICE**	
AAA	Highest investment quality (near perfection)	A++	Highest quality
AA	Superior investment quality (well above average)	A+	Very good quality (above average)
A	Upper medium grade (up to high average)	A	Good quality
BBB	Medium grade (up to low average)	B++	Medium quality (average)
BB	Lower medium grade (mildly speculative)	B+	Lower medium quality
B	Middle speculative	B	Poor quality
CCC	Highly speculative (in danger of default)	C	Speculative quality
CC	In default	D	Default
C	In default (lowest rating, second tier of debt)	**Rating Suspended**	Uncertainty about future of company
NR	Not rated		

In addition, both services may give a high or low rating to indicate the company's relative position within a class.

effective interest rate *the rate of return on an asset after capital gains and losses are considered*

market rate *when the yield on a debt instrument is equal to the contractual rate of interest*

whose yield may include a capital gain or loss, the rate of return is often called the **effective interest rate**. Reference is also frequently made to a debt security's **market rate**. This term implies that its yield is equal to the contractual rate of interest paid.

The rate of return earned on an asset can cause much confusion because, as is shown below, we can calculate yields and interest rates in many different ways. Lenders and investors are usually interested in the after-tax yield they can earn. Hence, it is common to differentiate among financial assets according to how their returns are taxed. Calculating the effects of taxes on yields need not concern us here and should be left to a tax consultant—much as you'd probably not ask your dentist to set your broken arm.

Future Value and Present Value

time value of money *the increase in the value of an investment over time*

Given the choice, we prefer to be paid now rather than later because money can be invested, earn interest, and grow in value. The increase in the value of an investment is called the **time value of money**. We saw that in the last chapter, when we considered the intertemporal consumption model. Remember the "intercepts" of the budget constraint? They were, in part, a function of the future value of present income (for the *Y*-axis intercept), and the present value of future income (for the *X*-axis intercept). Flip back a few pages if you need to refresh your memory about the intertemporal consumption model.

FUTURE VALUE   To illustrate the time value of money, suppose that a surplus spending unit lends $100 for one year, and the borrower agrees to pay interest of 5 percent per annum on this amount. At the end of the year, the lender will receive back the principal of $100 plus $5, representing the amount of interest accrued at the agreed 5 percent rate. The time value of money in our example is the additional $5 returned at the end of the year; the $100 has literally grown to become $105. Let us refer to the amount of an investment made today as its present value and the amount to be received back at the end of a year as its future value. The relationship between the two can be shown to be

(4.1)
$$FV = PV + PV \times i$$
$$= PV(1 + i)$$

where *FV* is future value, *PV* is present value, and *i* is the annual rate of interest earned. In terms of our numerical example

$$\$105 = \$100 \, (1 + 0.05)$$

Now suppose that the initial $100 together with the $5 of interest it earned is invested at 5 percent for an additional year. The equation to calculate the future value at the end of two years is

(4.2)
$$FV = PV(1 + i) + PV(1 + i)(1 + i)$$
$$= PV(1 + i)^2$$
$$= \$100(1 + 0.05)(1 + 0.05)$$
$$= \$110.25$$

In general, the equation that calculates future value is

(4.3)
$$FV = PV(1 + i)^n$$

where *n* is the number of years the asset is held, or its maturity, and we assume the interest rate remains fixed at *i* % in each year.

The process of adding interest payments on which, in turn, interest is earned is called **compounding**. Equation 4.3 above is the standard formula for calculating the future value of an amount earning interest compounded annually. The formula where interest is added twice a year, that is, compounded semi-annually, is

compounding *when an asset earns interest that is reinvested, generating additional income on both the principal and interest earned*

(4.4)
$$FV = PV\left[1 + \left(\frac{i}{2}\right)\right]^{2n}$$

and where it is compounded quarterly is

(4.5)
$$FV = PV\left[1 + \left(\frac{i}{4}\right)\right]^{4n}$$

Banks, trust companies, and credit unions offer the public daily interest deposit accounts. If interest earned is credited to an account at the end of each day, and if we assume a 365-day year, the compound interest formula is

(4.6)
$$FV = PV\left[1 + \left(\frac{i}{365}\right)\right]^{365n}$$

PRESENT VALUE   The present value of an amount of money to be received in the future is calculated by reversing the compound interest process. By rearranging equation 4.3, we obtain the standard present value formula:

(4.7)
$$PV = \frac{FV}{(1 + i)^n} = FV(1 + i)^{-n}$$

To arrive at the present value, *PV*, the future value, *FV*, is discounted at a rate *i*. Using the data from our earlier numerical example, the present value of $110.25 received two years from now, discounted at 5 percent per year, is

$$PV = \frac{\$110.25}{(1 + 0.05)^2} = \$100$$

Figure 4–1 illustrates how the present value of a fixed future claim of one dollar depends both on which year in the future the dollar is receivable and on the rate of interest used to discount the claim. The figure shows, for example, that the present value of one dollar to be received in 10 years drops from 61 cents to 38 cents to 25 cents as the interest rate rises from 5 percent to 10 percent to 15 percent. The figure also shows how the present value of one dollar declines (at the given rates of interest) as the length of time to its receipt increases.

Another way to express the relationship between present value, future value, and the rate of interest is in terms of solving for the interest rate, given both present value and future value. If we reconsider equation 4.7 and solve for the interest rate, we obtain

(4.7′)
$$i = \left(\frac{FV}{PV}\right)^{\frac{1}{n}} - 1$$

For example, if we know the current selling price for a three-year bond with a face value of $10 000 is $8655, we can use equation 4.7′ to determine the rate of interest one would earn if the bond were held to maturity. Plugging *FV* = $10 000 and *PV* = $8655 into Equation 4.7′, we arrive at an interest rate of about 4.93 percent

$$i = \left(\frac{\$10\ 000}{\$8655}\right)^{\frac{1}{3}} - 1 = 0.04933$$

where we have also used the fact that, in our example, *n* = 3. What would happen to the rate of interest if *n* = 4? Use your calculator (or computer) to find that the rate of interest would be 3.677 percent. See? Interest calculations really are simple (even though they involve a little bit of math).

FIGURE 4–1   **PRESENT VALUE OF ONE DOLLAR TO BE RECEIVED IN *N* YEARS**

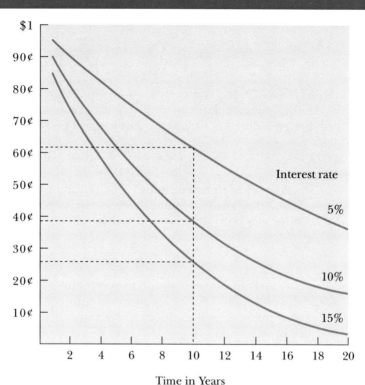

The present value of one dollar payable in the future depends both on the number of years in the future that the dollar is payable and on the interest rate used to discount the future claim. For example, the present value of one dollar to be received in ten years drops from 61¢ to 38¢ to 25¢ as the interest rate rises from 5 percent to 10 percent to 15 percent. On the other hand, as shown on the bottom curve, the present value of one dollar earning 15 percent decreases from some 80¢ to less than 10¢ as the number of years into the future increases from 2 years to 20 years.

Understanding Interest Rate Calculations

Interest rates can be calculated and expressed in different ways. Hence, you have to be clear exactly which interest rate you are talking about. The four commonly used rates are (1) the coupon rate or simple interest, (2) the current yield, (3) the yield to maturity, and (4) the discount yield.

THE COUPON RATE OR SIMPLE INTEREST   In the past, bonds had coupons attached that indicated the amount of interest to be received on cashing the coupons at a specified time in the future. Today the practice is to print a statement on the face of a bond to the effect that its holder will receive an interest payment each year. That payment is stated as a given amount or a percentage of the face value. The **face value**, also known as the bond's **par value**, is the principal amount promised at maturity.

face value (par value) *the principal amount promised at maturity*

BOX 4–1   UNDERSTANDING INTEREST RATES

Effective Annual Rate of Interest

Have you ever read the fine print on those advertisements you see in the newspaper that offer interest rates that appear to be too low to be true? By law, in most provinces, the advertiser has to provide you with an explicit description of the effective annual interest rate associated with the "great deal" you have coming if you buy their product. How do they calculate this effective annual interest rate, and why is it so different from the rate that's in bold print in the ad?

The answer rests in compounding and in the difference between the annual percentage interest rate and the effective annual interest rate. The annual percentage interest rate is the rate of interest on which your periodic payments are based. For example, an advertisement might offer an annual interest rate of 15 percent, which is a mere 1.25 percent per month (obtained as $15\% \div 12$). This rate is the periodic interest rate. The fine print, however, might tell you that interest is compounded monthly, meaning that on $1000, the total payment over 12 months would amount to over 16 percent, obtained as

$$\frac{\$1000(1.0125)^{12} - \$1000}{\$1000} = 0.16075$$

This rate is the effective annual rate of interest. It is greater than the annual interest rate because of compounding. The general relationship between the periodic interest rate and the effective annual rate of interest can be expressed as:

Effective Annual Interest Rate =
$$(1 + \text{Periodic Interest Rate})^n - 1$$

The difference between the annual and effective interest rates can be seen very clearly if you look at some credit cards and the interest rates they charge. Some department store cards charge interest at a rate of 2 percent a month—or what you think is an annual rate of 24 percent. However, if you calculate the effective annual rate of interest, you will see it is a whopping 26.82 percent. Remember that the next time you want to pay the minimum balance on your credit card bill.

---

coupon rate *the yearly interest payment on a debt instrument divided by its face amount*

Suppose the annual amount of interest earned on a bond with a $1000 face value is $50. Further, assume that the bond's face value was paid when the bond was purchased by its holder. The bond's **coupon rate** is calculated by dividing the amount of the annual coupon revenue by the bond's face value. The coupon rate is therefore

(4.8) $$\text{Current Rate} = \frac{\text{Coupon}}{\text{Face Value}} = \frac{\$50}{\$1000} = 5\%$$

When a bank makes a $1000 loan and the borrower agrees to make an annual interest payment of $50 at the end of each year, the annual interest rate is calculated in a similar way. In this case, the rate is known as simple interest.

current yield *the annual interest payment divided by the price paid*

THE CURRENT YIELD   Bonds and other debt securities are not necessarily purchased at their face, or par, value. To calculate the **current yield**, divide the annual dollar interest received by the price paid for the bond. If the annual interest is $50 and you paid $900 for the bond, the current yield is

$$(4.9) \qquad \text{Current Yield} = \frac{\text{Coupon}}{\text{Price}} = \frac{\$50}{\$900} = 5.56\%$$

THE YIELD TO MATURITY This rate is the most widely used interest rate in securities markets. Unlike the current yield, it takes into account interest receipts beyond a one-year time horizon, and it includes any capital gains or losses from holding a security until its maturity. The calculation of the **yield to maturity** uses the present value formula already introduced. The yield to maturity is the particular interest rate (also called the rate of discount) that equates the present value of all expected future cash receipts from a debt instrument with its present value (or cost).

yield to maturity the interest rate that equates the present value of all expected future cash receipts from a debt instrument with its present value

Suppose you pay $987.67 for a three-year bond today that will give you annual interest revenue of $100 in each year, and return its face value of $1000 at the end of three years. The present value of all these cash receipts (assuming a constant interest rate of $i\%$) is obtained by discounting them as follows:

$$(4.10) \qquad PV = \frac{\$100}{(1+i)} + \frac{\$100}{(1+i)^2} + \frac{\$100}{(1+i)^3} + \frac{\$1000}{(1+i)^3} = \$987.67$$

The first term to the right of the equal sign constructs the present value of the interest payment after one year. The second captures the present value of the interest payment in the second year, and the third term captures the present value of interest in the third year. The fourth term calculates the present value of the principal, to be returned after three years. If you paid $987.67 today for your bond purchase, the discount factor i, which equates all received monies with the bond's price or present value, is the yield to maturity. Although you could figure out the numerical value for i by trying out different rates until you found the one that makes the sum of the above terms equal to $987.67, this job could take some time. Fortunately, bond yield tables exist in which the calculation has already been made for you. By consulting such tables, we discover that i is 10.5 percent. This amount can be verified as follows:

$$\$987.67 = \frac{\$100}{(1+0.105)} + \frac{\$100}{(1+0.105)^2} + \frac{\$100}{(1+0.105)^3} + \frac{\$1000}{(1+0.105)^3}$$

Had you paid the bond's face value, $1000, for its acquisition, the yield to maturity would have been 10 percent, which in this case is also the coupon rate and the simple interest rate.

If bond yield tables are not readily available, a short-cut approximation of the yield to maturity can be made by using the formula

$$(4.11) \qquad i = \frac{\text{Coupon Amount} + \left(\dfrac{\text{Face Value} - \text{Purchase Price)}}{\text{(Number of Years to Maturity}} \right)}{(\text{Face Value} + \text{Purchase Price})/2}$$

THE DISCOUNT YIELD The return on money market instruments such as Treasury bills is called a **discount yield**. These instruments do not pay a stated amount of interest. Instead, the return received for holding them is represented by the difference between their purchase price and their par or face

discount yield the return for holding an instrument that is always sold at a discount

value. Although money market securities typically have maturities in terms of days rather than years, their discount yield is given on an annual basis. Canada uses 365 days and the United States uses 360 days in the calculation. The formula for deriving the discount yield is

$$i = \frac{\text{Par} - \text{Price}}{\text{Price}} \times \frac{365}{\text{Time}}$$

where time is measured in days.

Suppose you purchase a 91-day Government of Canada Treasury bill with a $1000 par value for $988.78. The discount yield you will earn is 4.55 percent, calculated as follows

$$\frac{\$1000 - \$988.78}{\$988.78} \times \frac{365}{91} = 4.55\%$$

Note that when calculating the yield on Treasury bills it is usual to consider the par value to be $100. Treasury bills always trade at a discount (but that's not true for all financial instruments).

TRADING AT PAR, DISCOUNT, OR PREMIUM When the market price of a bond equals its face value, we say it is trading at par. This indicates that the coupon rate on the bond equals the current market interest rate. We can see

www.

BOX 4-2 UNDERSTANDING INTEREST RATES

Semi-Annual Interest

Many financial instruments offer semi-annual interest payments. For example, a two-year bond with a face value of $1000 may offer a coupon rate of 8 percent, paid semi-annually, when the current market yield on two-year bonds is 6 percent. What would you be willing to pay for this two-year bond? Well, the coupon rate is paid on the face value of the bond, so you'd receive two $40 payments each year for two years. The value of the bond is the present value of this stream of interest payments, plus repayment of principal in two years. To calculate the present value, we need to convert the 6 percent market yield (the effective annual interest rate) on two-year bonds to a periodic rate (remember, you'll receive two interest payments a year, so there are two periods every year). We do this using a formula you first encountered in the previous box on calculating effective annual interest rates:

Periodic Interest Rate = $(1 + \text{Effective Annual Interest Rate})^{1/n} - 1$

where n is the number of periods in the year (in this case, two). Plugging an effective rate of 6 percent into the formula, we arrive at a periodic interest rate of 2.9563 percent. We then use this to calculate the present values as:

$$PV = \frac{\$40}{1.029563} + \frac{\$40}{1.029563^2} + \frac{\$40}{1.029563^3}$$
$$+ \frac{\$40}{1.029563^4} + \frac{\$1000}{1.029563^4} = \$1038.83$$

That's the present value of $1000 in two years with a semi-annual coupon of 8 percent when the effective market yield is 6 percent. Try plugging other values into the formula, and make up your own examples to see if you follow the logic. It really is simple once you get the hang of it.

this readily if we use the approximate formula for the yield to maturity in Equation 4.11:

$$(4.11) \quad i \approx \frac{\text{Coupon Amount} + \left(\dfrac{\text{Face Value} - \text{Purchase Price)}}{\text{(Number of Years to Maturity}}\right)}{(\text{Face Value} + \text{Purchase Price})/2}$$

Suppose a 10-year bond with a face value of $1000 offering a coupon rate of 6 percent trades at $1000. What is the approximate yield to maturity? Using Equation 4.11

$$i \approx \frac{\$60 + \left(\dfrac{\$1000 - \$1000}{10}\right)}{\$1000} = 0.06$$

In this case the yield to maturity is equal to the coupon rate.

Now suppose this same bond trades at a current price that exceeds its face value. Let's say the current price is $1067. In this case the bond trades at a **premium**. Equation 4.11 suggests the coupon rate on the bond exceeds the yield to maturity (the market yield):

premium *when the market price of a bond is below its face value*

$$i \approx \frac{\$60 + \left(\dfrac{\$1000 - \$1067}{10}\right)}{(\$1000 + \$1067)/2} = 0.05157$$

Thus, bonds trade at a premium—the current market price of the bond exceeds its face value—when the market yield is below the coupon rate.

discount *when the market price of a bond is below its face value*

Bonds trade at a **discount** when the market yield exceeds the coupon rate. Suppose a 10-year bond trades at a current price of $950. In this case the approximate yield to maturity from Equation 4.11 is

$$i \approx \frac{\$60 + \left(\dfrac{\$1000 - \$950}{10}\right)}{(\$1000 + \$950)/2} = 0.06667$$

Hence, bonds can trade at par, at a premium, or at a discount depending on whether the market yield is equal to, below, or above the coupon rate, respectively.

The Valuation of Financial Assets

Over the past three decades, very sophisticated financial asset pricing models have been developed, among them the capital asset pricing model (CAPM) and its generalized arbitrage pricing theory (APT). We will leave these theories for a later chapter and consider here the traditional basic model that explains the market valuation of financial assets.

The basic model assumes that in competitive markets, the current prices of financial assets reflect the discounted values of the expected cash flows generated by them. In the case of a debt security such as a coupon bond, the cash flow consists of annual interest revenue $(C_1, C_2, ..., C_n)$ and the receipt at maturity of the principal amount, F. By using the present value formula and discounting the expected cash flow by a market rate of i, we approximate the price of the coupon bond as follows:

(4.13)
$$P = \frac{C_1}{(1 + i)} + \frac{C_2}{(1 + i)^2} \cdots + \frac{C_n}{(1 + i)^n} + \frac{F}{(1 + i)^n}$$

perpetual bonds
called perpetuities or consols, bonds that have no maturity date

Perpetual bonds, also called perpetuities or consols, once popular in the United Kingdom, have no maturity date. They promise to pay their holders a fixed amount of interest each year—literally forever. Where there is an infinite number of fixed amount annual interest receipts and no repayment of a principal amount, the above equation reduces to

(4.14)
$$P = \frac{C}{i}$$

where C is the fixed annual cash flow and i is the market rate of interest.

annuities *bonds that promise to make equal annual payments until maturity*

Bonds that promise to make equal annual payments until maturity are known as **annuities**. These instruments do not return principal on maturity. Rather, they offer a stream of payments made up of both interest and principal repayment over time. The market price of an annuity that offers to pay $\$C$ every year for n years is given by

(4.15)
$$P = \frac{C_1}{(1 + i)} + \frac{C_2}{(1 + i)^2} \cdots + \frac{C_n}{(1 + i)^n} = C\left(\frac{1}{i}\right)\left[1 - \left(\frac{1}{(1 + i)^n}\right)\right]$$

annuity factor
used to calculate the value of an annuity

where we have assumed that the interest rate remains the same in each year. The term in "square brackets" is the **annuity factor**. When Canadians cash in their RRSPs on retirement, many opt for an annuity payout—a guaranteed series of payments over a specified period. We can use equation 4.15 to determine an approximate price of an annuity that one could receive from a pool of savings. For example, suppose you decided you needed $\$20\ 000$ a year for 10 years after you retire, and use an interest rate of 7 percent. What would that annuity cost? Using equation 4.15

$$P = \frac{\$20\ 000}{(1 + 0.07)} + \frac{\$20\ 000}{(1 + 0.07)^2} + \cdots + \frac{\$20\ 000}{(1 + 0.07)^{10}}$$
$$= \$20\ 000\left(\frac{1}{0.07}\right)\left[1 - \left(\frac{1}{(1 + 0.07)^{10}}\right)\right]$$
$$= \$140\ 471.63$$

You had better start saving now for retirement!

zero-coupon bonds *bonds that promise to pay the principal amount at a specified maturity date*

Zero-coupon bonds do not entitle their holders to any interest revenue whatsoever. They only promise to pay the principal amount at a specified maturity date. As with Treasury bills, the revenue earned on holding zero-coupon bonds is represented by the difference between their face value (principal value at maturity) and the price at which they are acquired. The approximate market price of these securities can be estimated using the formula

(4.16)
$$P = \frac{F}{(1 + i)^n}$$

where F is the bond's face value and i is a market rate of interest.

Treasury bills are usually quoted in terms of their yield rather than their price. The market price corresponding to a given yield can be derived by

(4.17)
$$\text{Price} = \frac{\$100}{1 + \left(\dfrac{\text{Yield} \times \text{term}}{365}\right)}$$

where the yield is expressed as a decimal and the term in days. Again, the price is typically calculated for a $100 par value.

The same basic model for approximating the value of debt securities can be used to approximate the market value of equities such as shares of common stock. A dividend valuation model is used, the assumption being that the expected cash flow from holding common stock is future dividends. By assuming that a given dividend amount will be paid in perpetuity, we express the present value of these expected dividends; hence, the market price of common stock can be approximated as

(4.18)
$$P \approx \sum_{t=1}^{\infty} \frac{D_t}{(1 + i)^t}$$

where D_t are expected cash dividends and i is some average of long-term market yields or interest rates.

The above equation tells us that the price of common stocks tends to increase with an expectation that larger annual dividends will be paid, and that the price tends to decline when market interest rates rise. These tendencies reflect what normally happens to shares of common stock traded regularly in stock markets.

The Relationship between Yields and Bond Prices

Two fundamental relationships exist between yields and bond prices:

1. Higher bond prices are accompanied by lower interest rates and market yields, and lower bond prices by higher interest rates and yields.
2. Prices of bonds with longer maturities experience a greater price change for a given change in market yields than do bonds with shorter maturities.

The inverse relationships between the market price and the yield of bonds can be demonstrated with the use of bond-pricing equations. Suppose that when 10-year market yields were 8 percent you purchased a 10-year zero-coupon bond with a $1000 face value. Since this bond was priced according to equation 4.16, you paid

$$\$463.19 = \frac{\$1000}{(1 + 0.08)^{10}}$$

After one year, during which market yields declined from 8 percent to 6 percent, you offer your bond for sale. You can expect to receive

$$\$591.90 = \frac{\$1000}{(1 + 0.06)^{9}}$$

With the decrease in market yields, you will receive more for the bond than you paid for it. However, if market yields had increased, your fortunes would have been reversed. Assuming a market yield increase say to 10 percent, the best you could expect for your bond would be

$$\$424.09 = \frac{\$1000}{(1.10)^{9}}$$

As you can see, a two-percentage-point decline in market yields (from 8 percent to 6 percent) changed the price of the 10-year coupon bond by 28 percent, while a two-percentage-point increase in market yields (from 8 percent to 10 percent) changed the price of the 10-year coupon bond by about 9 percent. The price effects of a 2 percent increase in market yields are different from a 5 percent decrease in market yields—that is, they are asymmetric—because of the effects of compounding: relative to $(1.08)^{10}$, $(1.06)^{9}$ is much different from $(1.10)^{9}$.

If we consider the same kind of changes in market yields on a bond with a shorter term to maturity, we will find that bond prices are much less responsive to changes in interest rates. Suppose we consider a five-year zero-coupon bond, where the initial market yield was 8 percent. Now let market yields rise or fall by 2 percent, after one year. The price changes that arise are

2% Decline:	$\$792.09 = \$1000/(1 + 0.06)^{4}$
Initial Purchase:	$\$680.58 = \$1000/(1 + 0.08)^{5}$
2% Increase:	$\$683.01 = \$1000/(1 + 0.10)^{4}$

Here, a two-percentage-point increase in yield from 8 percent to 10 percent results in a less than 1 percent increase in the price of a five-year bond, while a similar decline in yield would result in a 16 percent increase in the bond's price—again demonstrating the asymmetric effects of changes in market yields on bond prices. These results, summarized in Table 4.2, demonstrate that the prices of bonds with longer maturities are more sensitive to changes in market

TABLE 4.2	**YIELDS, BOND, AND TERM TO MATURITY**				
	FIVE-YEAR TERM			TEN-YEAR TERM	
Market Yield	**Price**	**% Change**		**Price**	**% Change**
6%	792.09	+16		591.90	+ 28
8%	680.58	–		463.19	–
10%	683.01	+0.4		424.09	–9

yields than bonds with shorter maturities, and that changes in bond prices are asymmetric with respect to changes in market yields.

Exchange Rates and Interest Rates

Canada is a trading nation and depends heavily on foreign sources of capital for economic activity. How do exchange rates affect interest rates? This question will be addressed in detail in a later chapter, but we want you to start thinking now about these international effects, since they are so important to Canada. Let us make up an example to illustrate what is involved.

Suppose you have $1 million and have the option to invest in a Canadian-dollar-denominated one-year bond offering 5 percent interest, or a one-year bond denominated in French francs that offers 7 percent interest. How can you compare what appear to be "apples and oranges"? If you invest in the dollar-denominated bond, at the end of the year you'll have principal plus 5 percent interest, in Canadian dollars. If you invest in the franc-denominated bond, at the end of the year you'll have principal plus 7 percent interest, but in francs, not dollars. To determine the yield from holding the franc-denominated asset, you'll first need to determine how many francs can be bought for $1 million. Then you'll have to form an estimate of how many dollars a franc will buy in a year, so that you can express the franc investment in dollar terms.

exchange rate
the domestic currency price of foreign exchange

For the sake of argument, suppose the current **exchange rate**—the domestic currency price of foreign exchange (in this case, francs)—is 0.50. This means it takes $0.50 to buy a franc. With $1 million, you could buy 2 million francs and invest them at 7 percent, and at the end of the year you will have 2.14 million francs. What's this worth in dollars? You don't know what the exchange rate is going to be in a year. It could remain fixed (not likely, but strange things happen in currency markets), in which case 2.14 million francs would buy $1.07 million. This figure exceeds what you would have earned had you invested in the dollar-denominated bond. However, the exchange rate could change and lead to a lower return on your franc investment. Suppose the exchange rate moved to 0.25. Now, each franc costs $0.25, or alternatively it takes four francs to buy a dollar. Your 2.14 million francs is worth a measly $535 000. You should have invested in the dollar-denominated asset. At the other extreme, the exchange rate could have jumped to 0.75, in which case your 2.14 million francs buys $1.605 million, much more than you'd have earned from the dollar-denominated investment.

Changes in exchange rates play a critical role in determining the benefits to investing in foreign-currency-denominated—or, indeed, domestic-currency-denominated—securities. Exchange-rate risk is an important factor in explaining differences in interest rates on securities denominated in different currencies. How firms and individuals can shelter themselves from this risk is something that we shall deal with later in the book.

www.

KEY TERMS

annuities

annuity factor

compounding

coupon rate

current yield

debt securities

default (credit) risk

discount

discount yield

effective interest rate

equity securities

exchange rate

face value (par value)

interest rate

market rate

market risk

marketability

perpetual bonds

premium

time value of money

yield

yield to maturity

zero-coupon bonds

REVIEW QUESTIONS

1. What is the difference between a debt security and an equity?

2. What are the characteristics of a financial instrument that is said to be liquid?

3. Explain the difference between credit risk and market risk.

4. Your grandmother suddenly remembers a deposit certificate purchased five years ago. She remembers being promised interest compounded at 9 percent per year. A phone call informs her that her certificate is now worth $7693.12. What amount did she originally deposit?

5. You deposited $1500 in a savings account on January 1, 1995. You were promised interest at 8 percent per year. What is your deposit account balance on December 31, 2000, if interest is calculated and compounded monthly, quarterly, and annually?

6. What is the value of an annuity that promises to pay $25 000 per year for 20 years when the interest rate is 10 percent? What if the interest rate fell to 5 percent?

7. Does an increase in the frequency of compounding from monthly to weekly increase or decrease the future value of $100 at an interest rate of 10 percent? What about quarterly to monthly?

8. Does an increase in the exchange rate increase or decrease the domestic currency value of an invest-

ment in foreign-currency-denominated securities? Make up an example to illustrate your answer.

9. Find an advertisement in a local newspaper in which the annual percentage interest rate and the effective annual interest rate are quoted. Which is higher, and why?

10. Using Equation 4.18, demonstrate why the announcement of new oil reserves increases the stock prices of oil companies long before any oil is pumped out of the ground.

11. How much are you willing to pay for a two-year bond that has one year left until maturity if the bond pays 5% interest, has a face value of $5000, and market interest rates are currently 7%? Why?

12. Is the yield to maturity always greater than the simple yield? Are they related?

13. When the interest rate is currently 10 percent, what is the present value of 10 years of income of $50 000 a year?

14. An investor paid $14 090 for a $15 000 bond that matures in a year. What return did she receive?

15. Suppose the value of the Canadian dollar falls. Does this make investing in Canadian-dollar-denominated assets more attractive? Why?

16. An investor buys a four-year bond for $50 302. It promises to pay $500 in interest each year, plus $53 000 at maturity. Did the investor pay too much for the bond?

SELECTED READINGS

Conrad, J.W. *An Introduction to the Theory of Interest.* Berkeley: University of California Press, 1959, pp. 287–367.

———. *The Behavior of Interest Rates.* New York: Columbia University Press, 1966.

Homer, Sidney, and Martin Leibowitz. *Inside the Yield Book.* Englewood Cliffs, N.J.: Prentice-Hall, 1972.

Kolb, Robert W. *Principles of Finance.* Glenview, Ill.: Scott, Foresman, 1988.

Van Horne, James C. *Financial Market Rates and Flows*, 2nd ed. Englewood Cliffs, N.J.: Prentice-Hall, 1984.

CHAPTER FIVE

THE LEVEL AND STRUCTURE OF INTEREST RATES

After reading this chapter you should be able to
1. *Explain how interest rates are set using the loanable funds and liquidity preference theories*
2. *Explain the difference between real and nominal interest rates*
3. *Describe, in detail, four theories of the term structure of interest rates*
4. *Demonstrate how interest rate differentials can be used to predict economic growth*
5. *Explain the implications of the term structure for monetary policy and portfolio optimization*

In subsequent chapters we will learn that the level and structure of interest rates are of great importance to the functioning of the economy. Changes in interest rates act to equilibrate the total demand for, and supply of, financial resources. The structure of interest rates directs the allocation of financial resources and, thereby, that of real resources in the economy. In this chapter we consider some of the factors that determine interest rates and examine the difference between the nominal interest rate and the real interest rate. The link between the nominal rate of interest and the expected rate of inflation, known as the Fisher effect, is also introduced. Finally, we describe the term structure of interest rates and its implications for portfolio choice and monetary policy, and even show you how to use the term structure to forecast economic growth. Who needs those big economic consulting companies? You can forecast growth all by yourself!

The Level of Interest Rates

Let us assume that all the interest rates in the financial system can be averaged together and represented by one interest rate. What determines this interest rate at any particular point in time? At this stage of our analysis, we can provide only a partial answer to this question, because the interest rate depends on both the financial system and the real sector of the economy. The latter refers to the flow of spending on goods and services and the resulting real income or output that is generated. For now we'll assume away those real factors and concentrate on how interest rates are determined in the financial system.

Two approaches are used to explain how the interest rate is determined in the financial system: the loanable funds theory and the liquidity preference theory. Both are partial equilibrium theories: They assume that the level of real income is constant and that the short-run equilibrium level of the interest rate is determined primarily by forces in the financial sector of the economy.

According to the liquidity preference theory, in the short run the equilibrium level of the interest rate is determined by the stock of money demanded and supplied in the financial system. This theory is associated with John Maynard Keynes, who assumed that individuals demand money because of its superior liquidity and that their choice to hold money rather than other financial assets depends on the opportunity cost of money. A more complete discussion of the liquidity preference theory will be provided later in the book when we consider the determinants of the demand for money.

The **loanable funds theory** of interest rate determination underlies much of the flow of funds framework outlined in Chapter 3. According to the loanable funds theory, the short-run equilibrium level of the interest rate is determined by the supply of and demand for loanable funds. The supply of loanable funds provided to the financial marketplace comes from saving by households, businesses, and governments; the creation of money by the banking system; and net hoarding of money. When interest rates are low, individuals are inclined to hang on to money—that is, to hoard it, rather than to supply it to the loanable funds market. In contrast, at higher interest rates individuals will be induced to supply the market with previously hoarded money—that is, to dishoard.

The overall demand for loanable funds consists of the separate demands by consumers, businesses, and governments. Individuals borrow essentially to acquire homes, automobiles, and durable consumer goods. Businesses use loanable funds to finance investment expenditures in inventories, plant, and equipment. Governments demand loanable funds to finance their overall budget deficits.

The supply of and demand for loanable funds jointly determine the short-run equilibrium rate of interest at given levels of real income and prices. This relationship is illustrated by the intersection of the supply and demand curves of loanable funds in Figure 5–1. The supply curve is drawn to slope upward, assuming that as interest rates rise, the banking system creates more money and individuals dishoard. The demand curve slopes downward, assuming that economic agents' desire for loanable funds increases as the rate of interest decreases.

The short-run equilibrium rate of interest changes with a shift in one or both of the curves. For example, with an increase in saving for reasons other than changes in interest rates, the supply of loanable funds curve shifts to the right, and as a result the rate of interest declines. Conversely, the interest rate will rise if governments finance larger deficits, because the demand for loanable funds curve shifts to the right.

loanable funds theory a theory that suggests the short-run equilibrium interest rate is determined by the supply of and demand for loanable funds

FIGURE 5–1   **SUPPLY OF AND DEMAND FOR LOANABLE FUNDS**

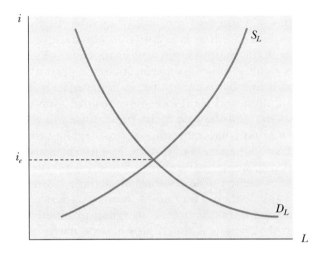

The demand for loanable funds curve (D_L) slopes downward because as the rate of interest (i) declines, the lower cost of borrowing will cause consumers, businesses, and the government to demand more loanable funds (L). The supply of loanable funds curve (S_L) slopes upward because as i increases, the banking system creates more money and individuals dishoard to take advantage of the higher returns to saving. The intersection of D_L and S_L determines the short-run equilibrium rate of interest (i_e).

Real and Nominal Interest Rates

Gibson Paradox
*a positive corre-
lation between
the price level
and the interest
rate*

Fisher equation
*an equation
linking the nom-
inal interest rate
to the real
interest rate and
the expected
rate of inflation*

A central proposition of classical monetary theory was that the interest rate is independent of the price level. This belief was questioned in the 1920s by A.H. Gibson, an Englishman who found a positive correlation between the price level and the long-term interest rate. Keynes referred to this relationship as the **Gibson Paradox**. In the 1930s, Irving Fisher, a prominent U.S. economist at Yale University, observed a close relationship, now known as the Fisher effect, between the nominal rate of interest (the actual market rate) and the expected rate of inflation. This relationship is expressed by the **Fisher equation**:[1]

(5.1) $$i = r + \pi^e$$

---

1. The Fisher equation is an approximation derived from:
    $$(1 + i) = (1 + \pi^e)(1 + r)$$
    $$= 1 + r + r\pi^e + \pi^e$$

    The term $r\pi^e$ maintains the real value of the interest payment and is usually ignored because it is very small for the range of expected inflation rates historically observed for many developed economies. Rearranging leads to the familiar Fisher equation, $i = r + \pi^e$.

**nominal rate of
interest** *the
interest rate we
see in the
market*

where *i* represents the **nominal rate of interest**, and *r* the real rate of interest, and where the expected rate of inflation (the expected percentage change in the price level) is denoted by π^e.

The real interest rate, not observable in the marketplace, is a long-run equilibrium rate that is assumed to equate individuals' marginal time preference with the marginal physical productivity of capital. Time preference refers to individuals' subjective preferences for present, relative to future, consumption. It is usually assumed that, in general, individuals prefer present to future consumption and therefore have positive time preference. This relationship implies that, on the one hand, individuals will want a reward to forgo present consumption (that is, to save), at least equal to their marginal time preference. Owners and managers of productive enterprises, on the other hand, are willing to pay a reward, in the form of interest payments, to induce individuals to release present resources that allow these owners and managers to increase their capital stock. The rate of interest owners and managers are prepared to offer savers depends on the **marginal productivity of capital** (the additional output that results from employing one more unit of physical capital). Since postponing current consumption is defined as saving and an increase in the capital stock implies investment expenditures, in the long run the real rate of interest equates saving and investment.

**marginal
productivity of
capital** *the
additional output
that results from
using one or
more units of
physical capital*

The implicit real interest rate embedded in the nominal interest rate can be estimated by rearranging equation 5.1 as follows

$$(5.2) \qquad\qquad\qquad r = i - \pi^e$$

For example, if the inflation rate is expected to be 4 percent over the next year, the real interest rate on a one-year security with an annual nominal interest rate of 7 percent is 3 percent. Real interest rates can be estimated using the expected rate of inflation (as in equation 5.2), in which case they are called *ex ante* (before the fact) real interest rates. They can be estimated also using actual inflation rates, in which case they are called *ex post* (after the fact) real interest rates.

Historically, a fairly close relationship has existed between the rate of inflation and nominal interest rates. This relationship is illustrated in Figure 5–2. Comparisons of *ex ante* and *ex post* real rates are illustrated in Figure 5–3. While it is usually assumed that longer-term real rates remain relatively constant, quite substantial deviations have occurred in recent decades.

We introduced you to the real interest rate when we considered the intertemporal consumption model in Chapter 3. We said it was the real interest rate that determined consumption decisions across time: The nominal rate contains "compensation" for expected inflation, so it is the real return to saving or borrowing that determines how you will smooth your consumption over time.

Let's make up an example—albeit unreal—to illustrate this point. Suppose you are paid $100 every period, and immediately after being paid, you scurry to the store to buy your usual bundle of goods, whose price is $100. You repeat this process period after period (which might be year after year, month after month, and so on). Today you've received your $100 and are about to head to the store when your friend asks for a loan of $100. Since you have a pantry full

FIGURE 5–2 **THE NOMINAL INTEREST RATE AND THE INFLATION RATE**

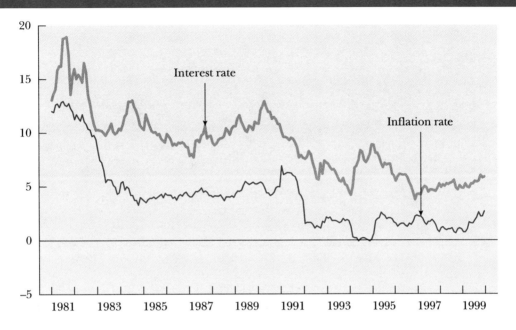

Nominal interest rates and inflation rates move closely together over time.

SOURCE: Statistics Canada, CANSIM Database, Series P200000 and B14013, March 2000.

of goodies, you don't really have to go to the store today—you have a spare bundle at home you could consume. You agree to lend your friend $100. After one period, she promises to pay you $100 plus interest (she isn't *that* close a friend). What interest rate are you going to charge? Well, suppose you expect the price of your bundle to rise by 5 percent over the period (the central bank just announced it is going to allow 5 percent inflation this period). This rise means the price of your bundle is going to rise to $105 in one period, so you want your friend to pay you at least 5 percent interest to maintain the purchasing power of your $100—to be able to buy the bundle next period. However, you'd also like to be somewhat better off for postponing your purchases today; you do, after all, have to dip into your pantry and exhaust your backup stores for the period. As compensation, you'd like to be able to increase your consumption next period above the usual bundle—perhaps buying yourself a small treat. So you require your friend to pay you 7 percent interest—that is, she must pay you $107 next week. Five dollars, or 5 percent, was to compensate you for what you expect inflation to be over the period; and two dollars, or 2 percent, was to compensate you for making the loan.

What we have just described is exactly what's behind the Fisher equation. The nominal rate of interest contains two components: compensation for expected inflation during the period we're looking at, plus a real return—compensation for postponing current consumption. Of course, you don't know what the actual inflation rate is going to be. You have to form an expectation—

FIGURE 5–3   *EX ANTE* AND *EX* POST REAL INTEREST RATES

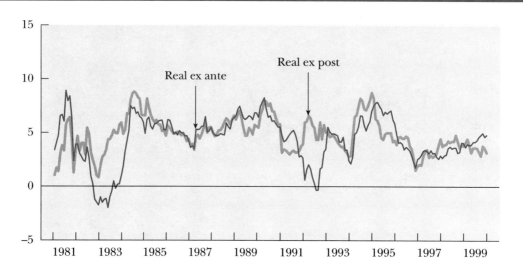

Real interest rates have been calculated for the average yields on Government of Canada one-year to three-year bonds. The *ex ante* real rate is based on an expected inflation rate computed by lagging inflation one year.

SOURCE: Statistics Canada, CANSIM Database, Matrices 2566 and 9957, March 2000.

and, if your expectations are incorrect, you could end up being worse off (or better off) than you thought. Consider the example above. What if the inflation rate turns out to be 10 percent instead of 5 percent? To continue to allow you to receive a 2 percent real return, your friend should pay you 12 percent interest. Unfortunately, you've agreed to accept 7 percent, which doesn't even allow you to buy the original bundle next period. You are worse off (your friend is better off). Therefore, *unanticipated inflation benefits debtors,* since the interest they end up paying won't fully compensate lenders for the effects of inflation.

Alternatively, if inflation turned out to be 3 percent rather than 5 percent as expected, your friend only had to pay you 5 percent to provide you with a 2 percent real return, but she is paying more than that when she agreed to pay 7 percent. In this case you, the creditor, are better off, since the borrower is paying you much more than what was required to compensate for the effects of inflation and provide a 2 percent real return. As we shall see, monetary policy operates on nominal interest rates directly and indirectly by means of the effects of expected inflation on nominal interest rates. If nominal interest rates don't fully reflect changes in expected inflation, real interest rates could change because of policy. This relationship, as we saw in Chapter 3, provides a role for monetary policy in that it alters real rates of interest and intertemporal consumption decisions.

The Term Structure of Interest Rates

In Chapter 4 we observed that an inverse relationship exists between bond prices and their yields. We also saw that a given change in the yield of a marketable bond will produce a larger fluctuation in its price, the longer its term to maturity. We now will explore the relationship between bond yields and their maturities. This relationship, viewed at a particular time for bonds with identical characteristics, is referred to as the **term structure of interest rates** and is usually presented graphically as a **yield curve**.

term structure of interest rates *the relationship between yields on securities of similar characteristics across different terms*

yield curve *a graph describing yields across different terms to maturity*

The yield curves for Government of Canada bonds are drawn in Figure 5–4. Yield curves that have an ascending slope, such as the one for February 1995, are usually referred to as normal yield curves because it is assumed that historically they have been more common. Downward-sloping yield curves, such as the one for February 1990, are referred to as inverted yield curves because the normal relationship between yield to maturity and time has been turned over or inverted. When a yield curve combines both ascending and descending portions, as did the one for Government of Canada bonds in February 2000, it is said to be humped. Not shown in Figure 5–4 is a flat yield curve, where yields remain constant across different maturities.

FIGURE 5–4 YIELD CURVES, GOVERNMENT OF CANADA SECURITIES

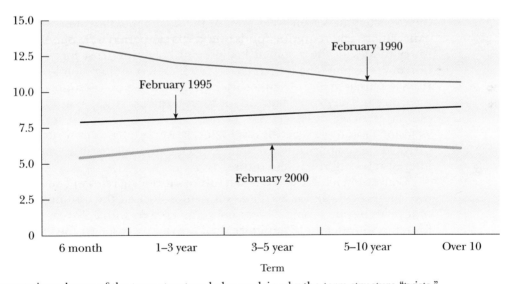

The expectations theory of the term structure helps explain why the term structure "twists."

SOURCE: Statistics Canada, CANSIM Database, Matrix 2566, March 2000.

Economists have put forward four hypotheses to explain the term structure of interest rates: (1) the expectations theory, (2) the liquidity preference theory, (3) the preferred habitat theory, and (4) the market segmentation theory.

The Expectations Theory

The **expectations theory** views the term structure of interest rates as determined by expectations of future interest rate movements. According to this theory, the yield on any long-term debt security will adjust to a level equal to the average of short-term yields expected to prevail over the life of the long-term security. These conclusions are based on the assumptions that lenders and borrowers have no reason to prefer long-term over short-term securities (or vice versa), and that lenders are only interested in maximizing their yields and borrowers in minimizing their cost of borrowing. In addition, the theory assumes that both lenders and borrowers have identical expectations about future short-term interest rates. Given these assumptions, the expectations theory concludes that, with expectations of higher future short-term yields, the yield curve for default-free securities will slope upward. Alternatively, with expectations of lower future short-term yields, the yield curve will slope downward. If future short-term yields are expected to remain at their current levels, the yield curve will be flat.

Suppose that surplus spending units have funds that can remain invested in financial assets over a 20-year period. Currently, these funds can be invested either in 20-year bonds yielding 10 percent or in one-year bonds yielding 5 percent. Suppose further that lenders expect that the yield of one-year bonds will increase over the next 20 years. Given this expectation, lenders will try to maximize their yield over the 20-year period by investing their funds in one-year bonds, and reinvesting both principal and interest at the end of each year at the expected higher one-year rate. At the same time, borrowers with the same expectations and requiring funds over a 20-year period will issue 20-year bonds to try to lock in the assumed low present borrowing cost for years to come. Borrowers issuing long-term securities and lenders selling their long-term securities to purchase short-term securities will create an excess supply of long-term securities and an excess demand for short-term securities. As a result, the price of short-term securities will rise relative to that of long-term securities, and the yields of short-term securities will fall relative to long-term securities. Hence, the yield curve slopes upward when expectations in general are that short-term interest rates will rise in the future.

Conversely, if it is expected that future short-term rates will decline, lenders with funds available for 20 years will want to lock in the assumed higher current yields by purchasing 20-year bonds. Borrowers with a 20-year requirement for funds will attempt to minimize their borrowing cost over the 20-year period by successively issuing one-year bonds at the end of each year at the expected lower rates. The financial market transactions by lenders and borrowers will now create excess demand for long-term securities and excess supply for short-term securities. The price of long-term securities will rise relative to that of short-term securities, and the yields of short-term securities will rise relative to those of long-term securities. Therefore, with expectations of lower short-term rates in the future, the yield curve slopes downward.

A flat yield curve, according to the expectations theory, implies that both lenders and borrowers perceive that the current level of yields conforms to the level expected to prevail on average in the near future.

geometric average *a means of calculating an average when compounding is involved; values are multiplied, and the appropriate root is taken to determine an average*

THE ALGEBRA OF THE EXPECTATIONS THEORY   According to the pure expectations theory, long-term interest rates are the **geometric average** of the current and the expected short-term rates.

The pure expectations theory of the term structure of interest rates is based on the following assumptions: (1) All investors have the same expectations about future one-year interest rates, (2) the bonds they hold have no default risk and are differentiated only according to their maturities, (3) bonds of different maturities are substitutable without transactions costs, (4) investors have no maturity preferences aside from a given holding period.

Investors with an n-year holding period can keep their funds invested for n years using one of two strategies. They can purchase an n-year bond at the long-term spot rate of i_n, or they can purchase a sequence of one-year bonds for n years. The latter involves first buying a one-year bond at the current, known, one-year spot rate i_{11}, and then, at the end of the year, reinvesting principal plus interest for another year. This reinvestment would be at the expected one-year rate, i^e_{12}, where the superscript e reflects the fact that this one-year rate for year two is unknown; the investor must form an expectation of the future rate. (The first subscript tells us the term to maturity and the second tells us the year in which the asset is held.) This investment strategy is continued at one-year rates for n years.

The expectations theory posits that arbitrage—the process of simultaneous buying and selling in different markets—will make investors indifferent between investing in one n-year bond, or in a series of one-year bonds over n years at the current and expected future one-year rates. Either investment strategy produces an identical expected outcome. Otherwise, investors would substitute out of long-term or short-term bonds, thereby changing bond prices and hence their interest rates until no further arbitrage opportunities existed. The relationship between long-term bonds and short-term bonds is given by:

$$(5.3) \qquad i_n = \{(1 + i_{11})(1 + i^e_{12})(1 + i^e_{13})(1 + i^e_{14}) \dots (1 + i^e_{1n})\}^{1/n} - 1$$

That is, the average annual return (where we have calculated a geometric average, since we are compounding) on an n-period bond will equal the average annual return on a series of one-year bonds over n years. Otherwise, arbitrage will force the relationship back into equality.

Equation 5.3 can be used to explain the slope of the yield curve at any point in time. For example, suppose the current long-term rate is greater than the current short-term rate, so that the yield curve is upward sloping. When would this occur? The expectations theory suggests that the long rate will be above the current short rate as long as the market expects future short-term rates to rise. Similarly, if the market expects future short-term rates to fall, the current long-term rate will be below the current short-term rate. Hence, expectations of future short-term rates are critically important in determining long-term rates of interest. The yield curve would be flat when—you guessed it—the market expected future short-term rates to remain at current levels.

arbitrage *the simultaneous purchase (sale) in one market and sale (purchase) in another to profit from price differences across markets*

The process of **arbitrage** is central to the expectations theory of the term structure, as is the implicit assumption that investors see short-term securities as being substitutable with long-term securities in their portfolios. Otherwise, there would not be any arbitrage (as we shall see in the market segmentation theory of the term structure). To see this, suppose the current return on a long-term bond were greater than the average expected from a series of one-term bonds. In this case, the relationship could be expressed by

$$(5.4) \qquad i_n > \{(1 + i_{11})(1 + i^e_{12})(1 + i^e_{13})(1 + i^e_{14}) \ ... \ (1 + i^e_{1n})\}^{1/n} - 1$$

What will investors do? Call their brokers and demand fewer short-term instruments in favour of more long-term instruments. This response will increase the demand for long-term bonds, thereby raising their prices and reducing their yields (since the two are inversely related). At the same time, the reduction in the demand for short-term bonds will reduce the price of short-term bonds, thereby raising their yields. The left side of equation 5.4 will fall while the right side will rise, with the process continuing until the equality is re-established. Arbitrage forces investors to be indifferent between holding a long-term bond or a series of short-term bonds under the expectations theory of the term structure.

The Liquidity Preference Theory

Issuers and purchasers of debt instruments are subject to capital risk and income risk because of a change in market interest rates. Capital risk refers to the possibility of capital gains or losses; income risk refers to the possibility of a decrease or increase in income resulting from a change in interest rates. The **liquidity preference theory** assumes that lenders have a preference for capital certainty and borrowers for income certainty. Because a change in market interest rates has a greater effect on the price of long-term securities than on short-term ones, a relatively smaller capital risk is associated with short-term securities. Hence, we can presume lenders prefer to hold securities with short-term rather than long-term maturities. Conversely, borrowers with a preference for income certainty (that is, certainty of a constant interest cost over the period for which they require financing), will want to borrow for the long term rather than the short term.

Capital and income risks can be reduced or eliminated if the maturities of securities are identical to the periods over which lenders' funds are available and the periods over which borrowers require funds. Borrowers are usually more certain of the period for which they require funds than lenders are of the period for which their funds may be available. Lenders are therefore more likely to underestimate the period for which their funds are available than are borrowers to overestimate the period for which they require funds. As a result, lenders usually prefer to lend for shorter periods than borrowers want to borrow for. To induce lenders to make their funds available for longer periods, borrowers have to "bribe" them by offering a premium called a **liquidity premium**. This premium is paid to compensate lenders for capital risks. Since capital risks increase as the maturity of debt securities increases, it follows that liquidity premiums incorporated into interest rates are higher for long-term than for short-term securities. Therefore, according to the liquidity preference theory of the term structure of interest rates, we should expect that the yield curve normally slopes upward.

liquidity preference theory a theory that suggests the equilibrium interest rate is determined by the stock of money in the economy in the short run

liquidity premium a premium paid to compensate lenders for capital risks

Whether the yield curve normally has a positive slope depends on the critical assumption that borrowers want funds for longer periods than lenders want to commit funds for. There may be times when most lenders prefer stability of yield (income certainty) to capital certainty, while the majority of borrowers need short-term financing. Under these circumstances it is possible for short-term rates to exceed long-term rates, in which case the yield curve would slope downward.

A variant of the liquidity preference theory of the term structure of interest rates is the **risk premium theory**. This theory accepts the expectations theory—with one major qualification. Since long-term securities are less liquid and have greater capital risk than short-term securities, market forces normally produce a risk premium in longer-term securities in the form of a higher yield, denoted by rp_n in equation 5.5. If investors are risk-averse—that is, they do not like risk—they must be compensated for the greater risk inherent in the price volatility of longer-term debt securities. The risk premium theory asserts that the normal yield curve has a positive slope. Only if financial market participants hold a very strong view that interest rates will come down in the future will the normal ascending yield curve give way to a descending one.

$$(5.5) \quad i_n = \{(1 + i_{11})(1 + i^e_{12})(1 + i^e_{13})(1 + i^e_{14}) \ldots (1 + i^e_{1n})\}^{1/n} - 1 + rp_n$$

Gravelle, Muller, and Streliski (1998) examined the expectations theory of the term structure using Canadian data. They were able to reject the pure expectations theory and the risk premium theory (assuming the risk premium was constant over their observations). They did report evidence suggesting that the risk premium varies over time and rises with the term to maturity. They also found that these premia increase during periods of excessive interest rate volatility. If we assume this volatility measures uncertainty in the market, then their results suggest that the risk premium depends on both the term to maturity and the level of uncertainty in the market. This conclusion satisfies our intuition.

risk premium theory a theory of the term structure based on expectations of future interest rates and a risk premium that rises with the term to maturity

The Preferred Habitat Theory

preferred habitat theory a theory of the term structure based on expectations of future interest rates and a risk premium that rises as investors move away from their preferred term to maturity

The **preferred habitat theory** of the term structure is a variant of the liquidity premium theory. It relies on the fact that investors prefer securities of a certain maturity, and that while there is arbitrage across short-term and long-term markets, the risk premium required for investors to move out of their preferred habitat rises, but not necessarily with the term to maturity. The preferred habitat theory says that the risk premium in equation 5.5 is not a monotonic function of the term to maturity. Consider Figure 5–5. Investors whose preferred habitat is long-term require a liquidity or risk premium that rises if they move out of their preferred habitat to either longer or shorter maturities, as do investors with a medium-term or a short-term preferred habitat. This theory allows for a certain degree of market segmentation without assuming away opportunities for arbitrage across markets.

FIGURE 5–5   LIQUIDITY AND PREFERRED HABITAT

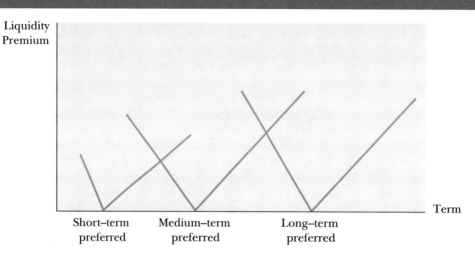

Under the preferred habitat theory of the term structure, the liquidity premium rises as investors move out of the preferred habitat of the maturity spectrum.

The Market Segmentation Theory

market segmentation theory a theory of the term structure that assumes that rates of return across different terms to maturity are unrelated

Our final theory of the term structure is the **market segmentation theory**. It is based on the assumption that the major financial market participants have different maturity needs. Accordingly, they confine their security purchases to different segments of the maturity spectrum. This suggests that, unlike in the other three theories of the term structure that we have considered, short-term securities and long-term securities are not substitutable in an investor's portfolio, so there are no opportunities for arbitrage across markets. Changes in the short-term market have no effect on the long-term market.

For example, the liabilities of the chartered banks are primarily deposits subject to withdrawal on demand or short notice. As a result, the banks' preferred habitat for their assets is in relatively liquid short-term securities. In contrast, the liabilities of life insurance companies and pension funds are long term. To avoid the transaction costs and uncertainty of a variable return associated with constant reinvestment in short-term securities, they prefer to match their liabilities with longer-term securities. The preferences of institutional investors are usually reinforced by legal restrictions on their investment behaviour.

If the major market participants prefer, or are legally required, to hold most of their financial assets in either short-term or long-term securities, security markets may be segmented into separate markets, each corresponding to a certain maturity. If this is the case, the term structure of interest rates should reflect the relative demand and supply conditions in the respective maturity sectors of the economy.

The market segmentation theory is consistent with any shape of the yield curve. Changes in its shape reflect the market dominance, at any particular time, of institutions with a preference for either short-term or long-term maturities. The recent behaviour of major financial institutions and the removal of legal restrictions on the composition of their assets make the market segmentation theory less plausible as an explanation of the term structure of interest rates. It's hard to believe that short-term interest rates and long-term interest rates are independent.

Using the Term Structure to Forecast Output Growth

Economists have found a quick and dirty method of forecasting real output growth using information in the term structure. We feel somewhat like magicians going public on how they actually pull that rabbit from the hat, but here goes. Take the interest rate on long-term Government of Canada bonds (say the 10-year and longer bond interest rate) and subtract from it a short-term interest rate (let's use the 91-day Treasury bill rate). Now plot the interest rate differential data along with the rate of growth of real output. We do that in Figure 5–6 for 1962 through 1999.

The interest rate differential appears to "lead" economic growth by about two years. A strong correlation exists between changes in real economic activity and changes in the term structure. When short-term interest rates are above long-term interest rates (the yield curve is downward sloping), real output falls.

FIGURE 5–6 OUTPUT GROWTH AND THE TERM STRUCTURE

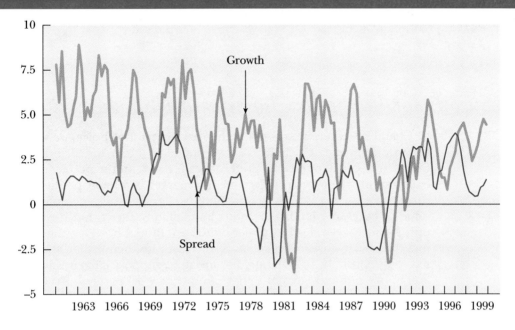

Information in the term structure appears to predict output growth fairly well over the last 40 years.

SOURCE: Statistics Canada, CANSIM Database, Matrices 6549 and 2560, March 2000.

When long-term interest rates exceed short-term interest rates (the yield curve is upward sloping), real output growth rises. Why?

Conventional wisdom is that short-term interest rates reflect the cost of current consumption—either because that consumption is financed short-term, or because you give up short-term interest if you spend your savings rather than save them. If the yield curve is downward sloping, so that the market expects short-term interest rates to fall in the future, you'll wait for those short-term rates to fall before you finance higher levels of consumption (or you'll save now, since the interest rate you'll be able to get in the future will be lower than what you can currently get). This lower level of consumption reduces aggregate demand, and output growth declines. When the yield curve is upward sloping, the market expects future short-term interest rates to rise above their current levels, so people consume now rather than later (when the cost of borrowing will be higher than it is today, or when the interest they'll receive on their savings will be higher than it is currently).

What is the empirical evidence for Canada? Harvey (1997) reported that the information in both the American and the Canadian term structures helped explain Canadian business cycles. He demonstrated that the Canadian term structure was particularly useful at explaining the part of the Canadian business cycle that was unrelated to fluctuations in U.S. economic activity.

www.

Before you run out and open your own economic consulting firm, remember that this relationship isn't always flawless—sometimes the interest rate differential does not truly reflect future changes in output growth, particularly since Canadian interest rates frequently respond to exchange rate pressures that may persist for months at a time. However, on average, over the past 25 years or so, the information in the term structure has been useful to economists when they are trying to get a ballpark estimate of impending changes in output growth.

Implications for Portfolio Choice and Monetary Policy

In Chapter 8, where we present a theory of portfolio choice, we will learn that a portfolio manager's choice of investments to be included in a portfolio of financial assets depends on preferences for risk and expected return. If the expectations theory is correct and the market is a good predictor of future short-term interest rates, the portfolio manager's expected return will be the same whether she lends her funds immediately over a long-term period, or only for successive short-term periods. If she thinks, however, that she can predict the course of future short-term interest rates better than the market, she may try to profit by speculating. For instance, suppose current short-term rates are 10 percent and current long-term rates are 15 percent. According to the expectations theory, this scenario indicates that most market participants expect future short-term rates to increase. If, however, our portfolio manager thinks that she is a better predictor of future short-term rates and believes they will fall rather than rise, she will lend long and borrow short. If her prediction of future short-term interest rates turns out to be correct, she will profit; if her prediction is wrong and that of the market is correct, she will lose.

The liquidity preference theory, in contrast, tells the portfolio manager that she can always get a larger expected return by acquiring long-term rather than short-term securities. However, higher yields come at the expense of more risk.

The market segmentation theory leads to the conclusion that our portfolio manager can, at any time, maximize her expected return by concentrating her asset holdings in the segment of the market in which an excess supply of securities currently exists.

In later chapters we will learn that there are times when the central bank may desire a certain pattern of interest rates. For example, the central bank may want high short-term rates to attract an inflow of foreign capital into Canada and at the same time low long-term rates to stimulate domestic investment expenditures. In other words, it may want to twist an upward-sloping yield curve into a downward-sloping one. According to the market segmentation theory, this twist can be accomplished if the central bank becomes a heavy seller of short-term securities and at the same time a heavy buyer of long-term securities. In addition, according to this theory, if the central bank wants to shift rather than twist existing yield curves, it should become a heavy purchaser, or seller, in all maturity segments of the financial markets.

In direct contrast to the market segmentation theory, the expectations theory tells us that the only way the central bank can produce a change in the current structure of interest rates is by changing the market's expectations with respect to future short-term rates. If, for example, the central bank becomes a heavy buyer of short-term securities and the market expects that this trend will continue, it may be led to expect that future short-term rates will be lower. As a result, current long-term rates may fall to reflect the expected, lower future short-term rates, and the yield curve may twist to take on a downward slope.

There are times when the central bank may want to concentrate its market transactions in the short-term end of the market without affecting the long-term end. From our discussion of the various theories of the term structure of the market, we have learned that this route is possible only if the central bank's activities in short maturities do not affect market expectations concerning the level of future short-term rates, or if financial markets are indeed severely segmented.

According to the pure expectations theory, the market's expectations of future interest rates can be computed from the yield curve. How this computation is done is shown in Box 5–1. Unfortunately, interest rate forecasts based on the expectations theory have usually turned out to be biased—they deviate in a systematic way from actual interest rates observed later. This bias probably is explained by the presence of liquidity preference and, in some cases, market segmentation.

BOX 5–1   YIELD CURVES AND MARKET EXPECTATIONS OF FUTURE YIELDS

The pure expectations theory of the term structure can be used to calculate expected future interest rates. Suppose an investor has a two-year holding period during which he wants to keep his funds invested. Assume that he has two investment strategies, each giving the same yield. He can buy a two-year security, or can first buy a one-year security and then reinvest the funds he receives at maturity for a further year. He is indifferent about the investment strategy to be used because the current average return on the two-year bond i_2, equals the average annual return from a one-year bond (paying i_{11} interest) and a one-year bond (paying the expected rate of i^e_{12}):

$$i_2 = \{(1 + i_{11})(1 + i^e_{12})\}^{1/2} - 1$$

The prevailing two-year and one-year bond rates are 10 percent and 9 percent, so that

$$0.1 = \{(1 + 0.09)(1 + i^e_{12})\}^{1/2} - 1$$

The implicit or expected one-year rate beginning one year from the present is calculated as follows:

$$i^e_{12} = \{(1.1)^2 \div 1.09\} - 1$$
$$= 0.110917$$

Try to make up your own example to see if you can predict future short-term rates.

KEY TERMS

arbitrage
expectations theory
Fisher equation
geometric average
Gibson Paradox

liquidity preference theory
liquidity premium
loanable funds theory
marginal productivity of capital
market segmentation theory

nominal rate of interest
preferred habitat theory
risk premium theory
term structure of interest rates
yield curve

REVIEW QUESTIONS

1. Why is the supply of loanable funds curve upward sloping? Where does this supply come from? Why is the demand for loanable funds curve downward sloping? Where does this demand come from? What does it mean when an individual dishoards? How is the short-run level of interest determined according to this theory?

2. What is the Fisher equation? What is time preference, and what are its implications for a positive interest rate? What determines the real interest rate?
3. Explain the three theories of term structure and their relation to yield curves.
4. What does "twisting the yield curve" mean? How can it be brought about according to the market segmentation theory? the expectations theory?

5. Using the generalized equation of the pure expectations theory in Box 5–1, calculate today's four-year bond interest rate; assume that the spot one-year rate is 8 percent but that in each of the next three years, the one-year rate is expected to rise by one percentage point each year.

6. You have purchased a one-year bond at 8 percent and you expect the rate of inflation to be 3 percent during the year. What is the real interest rate that you expect to earn? The after-tax real interest rate may be expressed as

$$r = i\,(1 - t) - \pi^e$$

where t is the income tax rate. What is the after-tax real rate if the applicable tax rate is 20 percent?

7. What is the expected future one-year interest rate if the current one-year rate is 5 percent and the current two-year rate is 8 percent?

8. This question will require a trip to the library. Consult the latest summer issue of the *Bank of Canada Review* for data on the preceding June. Look at the yields on two-year, three-year, and five-year Government of Canada bonds (CANSIM numbers B14067, B14068, and B14069). Suppose you expect the three-year bond rate to be equal to its current value in two years, when the two-year bond matures. Does the expectations theory work? (That is, is the yield on a five-year bond equal to the average yield you would expect to receive from a two-year bond, followed by a three-year bond? Hint: remember to adjust the expectations theory for the fact that you are holding a two-year bond for two years and then a three-year bond for three years.)

9. This question will require a trip to the library. Consult the latest spring issue of the *Bank of Canada Review* for data on the preceding January. Collect annual data for the past five years on real output growth and the difference between the Government of Canada 91-day Treasury bill rate and the average yield on Government of Canada bonds of 10 years' duration or longer. Plot the data on a graph. Is real output going to grow over the near term, or will it fall? Why?

10. Suppose the return from a six-year bond is currently below the expected average annual return from a series of one-year bonds over six years. Using both words and graphs, explain the process by which arbitrage will adjust the term structure. Under which theory of the term structure would this inequality persist? Why?

11. Explain how an investor may demand a higher risk premium to move out of her preferred habitat. Can you think of examples where this premium rises as the term to maturity falls? Explain.

SELECTED READINGS

Booth, P. "Interest Parity, Cointegration, and the Term Structure in Canada and the United States." *Canadian Journal of Economics* 24 (August 1991), pp. 595–603.

Campbell, John Y. "A Defense of Traditional Hypotheses about the Term Structure of Interest Rates." *Journal of Finance* (March 1986), pp. 123–93.

Dobson, Stephen W. "The Term Structure of Interest Rates and the Maturity Composition of the Government Debt: The Canadian Case." *Canadian Journal of Economics* 6 (August 1973), pp. 319–31.

Fisher, Irving. T*he Theory of Interest Rates*. New York: Macmillan, 1930. Reprinted by Augustus M. Kelley, 1955, 1961.

Gravelle, T., P. Muller, and D. Streliski. "Towards a New Measure of Interest Rate Expectations in Canada: Estimating a Time-Varying Term Premium." Information in Financial Asset Prices: Proceedings of a conference held by the Bank of Canada, Ottawa, May 1998.

Harvey, C. "The Relation between the Term Structure of Interest Rates and Canadian Economic Growth." *Canadian Journal of Economics* 30 (February 1997), pp. 169–93.

Hejazi, Walid, H. Lai, and X. Yang. "The Expectations Hypothesis, Term Premia, and the Canadian Term Structure of Interest Rates." *Canadian Journal of Economics* 33 (February 2000), pp. 133–48.

Hicks, J.R. *Value and Capital*, 2nd ed. Oxford: Oxford University Press, 1946, Ch. 11–13.

Jondeau, E., and R. Ricart. "The Expectations Hypothesis of the Term Structure: Tests on U.S., German, French, and U.K. Euro-rates." *Journal of International Money and Finance* 18 (5, 1999).

Lutz, F.A. *The Theory of Interest*. Chicago: Aldine, 1968.

Malkiel, Burton Gordon. *The Term Structure of Interest Rates: Expectations and Behavior Patterns*. Princeton, N.J.: Princeton University Press, 1966.

———. *The Term Structure of Interest Rates: Empirical Evidence and Applications*. New York: General Learning Corp., 1970.

Melino, A. "The Term Structure of Interest Rates: Evidence and Theory." *Journal of Economic Surveys* 2 (4, 1988), pp. 335–66.

Pesando, James E. *The Impact of Inflation on Financial Markets in Canada*. Montreal: C.D. Howe Institute, 1977.

Shiller, R.J. "The Term Structure of Interest Rates," in B. Friedman and F. Hahn (eds.), *The Handbook of Monetary Economics*. Amsterdam: North-Holland, 1990.

Van Horne, James C. *Financial Market Rates and Flows*, 2nd ed. Englewood Cliffs, N.J.: Prentice-Hall, 1984.

Wallace, M. and J. Warner. "The Fisher Effect and the Term Structure of Interest Rates: Test of Cointegration." *Review of Economics and Statistics* (1993), pp. 320–24.

Wicksell, Knut. "Lectures on Political Economy." Trans. E. Classen. *Money,* Vol. 2. London: Macmillan, 1934.

———. *Interest and Prices*. London: Macmillan, 1936.

*C*HAPTER SIX

*F*INANCIAL *M*ARKETS

After reading this chapter you should be able to

1. *List seven different classifications of financial markets*
2. *Discuss the characteristics of 14 money market instruments*
3. *Compare and contrast the properties of capital market and money market securities*
4. *Explain the manner in which different securities are traded in Canada*
5. *Outline different types of financial derivatives—futures, options, and swaps—and briefly describe how they are used to reduce risk*
6. *Summarize three variants of the efficient markets hypothesis and show that security prices should be a random walk if markets are efficient*

Financial markets are the places in which financial instruments are created and traded. Financial markets provide an arena in which funds are transferred and the prices and yields of financial instruments are determined. It is in financial markets that the flow of funds (discussed in Chapter 3) is facilitated between surplus and deficit spending units. Financial markets play an important role in the allocation of resources, especially because they accommodate individual differences among economic agents' preferences with respect to risk, expected return, and the time pattern of consumption.

In this chapter we begin with a classification of the various types of financial markets. We go on to describe the characteristics of the major financial instruments created and traded in these markets, and conclude with a brief description of market efficiency.

Types of Financial Markets

Debt Markets versus Equity Markets

debt *a legal obligation to pay a specified amount at a specified time*

Financial markets are frequently classified in terms of the legal obligation of the issuer of a security; the fundamental difference is between debt and equity securities. **Debt** represents a legal obligation to pay a specified amount at a specified time. Equity represents an ownership interest in a business.

Primary Markets versus Secondary Markets

New issues of securities are sold in **primary markets**. It is in these markets that funds are transferred from surplus spending units to deficit spending units. A new issue of securities offered to the investing public for the first time is referred to as an **IPO (initial public offering)**.

Previously issued securities are traded in **secondary markets**. These markets facilitate the change of ownership of existing securities. The liquidity of financial assets, which cannot be redeemed on demand or short notice, depends on secondary markets.

Auction Markets versus Over-the-Counter Markets

In **auction markets**, financial assets trade by open bidding in a central trading facility. Secondary markets for equities are mostly auction markets. The best examples of auction markets are the stock exchanges, whose operations are described later in this chapter. When there is no central trading facility, such as the floor of a stock exchange, trades are arranged through dealers and brokers. This market is called an **over-the-counter market**; in practice it is an over-the-telephone or electronic communication market. Unlike brokers, who act as agents for buyers and sellers, dealers also hold inventories of securities for sale. Brokers and dealers may prearrange to sell new issues of securities directly to surplus spending units in a practice known as direct placement.

Money Markets versus Capital Markets

The most common classification of financial markets makes a distinction between money markets and capital markets. This distinction is based arbitrarily on the maturity of financial assets. Short-term assets, usually with maturities of one year or less and seldom with maturities of more than three years, are bought and sold in **money markets**. In addition, money market instruments are all debt securities. **Capital markets**, however, deal in long-term debt and equity securities.

Intermediated Markets versus Nonintermediated Markets

Nonintermediated markets deal in the primary issues, called **direct securities**, of nonfinancial institutions and firms. For example, bonds issued by manufacturing firms are direct issues and therefore nonintermediated. Intermediated markets deal in the financial instruments, called **indirect securities**, issued by financial institutions called intermediaries. The most important financial intermediaries are the chartered banks; the most important indirect securities are deposits. As we will learn, the distinguishing feature of financial intermediaries is the transformation of direct securities into indirect securities.

Cash Markets versus Futures Markets

spot markets
markets in which financial assets are bought and sold for immediate delivery

In cash markets, also frequently called **spot markets** (an outgrowth of the phrase "on the spot"), financial assets are bought and sold for immediate delivery. In financial **futures markets**, as we will describe in detail later in this chapter, financial assets are bought and sold for future delivery. In our discussion of financial markets, we assume that they are spot markets unless they are specifically identified as futures markets.

futures markets
markets in which financial assets are bought and sold for future delivery

Regulated Markets versus Unregulated or Exempt Markets

regulated markets
markets in which securities trading is restricted to investment dealers and brokers who are registered to conduct business by a regulatory agency

In **regulated markets**, securities trading is restricted to investment dealers and brokers who are registered to conduct business by a regulatory agency. Furthermore, all new issues must be accompanied by a prospectus that, among other things, provides potential investors with a history of the issuer's operations, the issuer's financial statements, and the terms and conditions under which the issue is offered. Stock exchange trading is restricted to registered dealers and brokers. In unregulated markets, certain classes of securities, such as government bonds and "high quality" instruments, can be issued without a prospectus. This exemption is made either because the issuers themselves are regulated institutions or because the public is generally well informed about their operations. In addition, certain types of trades can be made by unregistered dealers and brokers and without the use of a prospectus. These trades are with institutions whose activities are already regulated, or who are assumed to have the expertise or sophistication to determine for themselves the underlying risks involved. For example, **private placements**, in which securities issues are sold (or "placed") directly with buyers, are exempt if the total value of an issue exceeds a defined minimum value. In recent years the unregulated segment of the Canadian securities market has been increasing.

private placements *securities sold (placed) directly with buyers*

The Money Market

Financial instruments with typical maturities of less than one year and as short as overnight are issued and traded in the money market. It is a wholesale market insofar as the minimum amount of each transaction is $100 000 and usual trades are in the millions. The annual turnover in the Canadian money market now exceeds $1 trillion.

Corporations invest their temporary excess cash, securities dealers borrow to finance their inventories of securities, businesses and governments finance their short-term cash requirements, and the depository institutions adjust their daily cash positions in the money market. However, most important, as we will learn later, the money market is at the heart of the process by which the Bank of Canada implements monetary policy.

Government of Canada Treasury Bills

Treasury bills
*short-term, nego-
tiable promissory
notes issued by
the federal gov-
ernment*

Government of Canada **Treasury bills** are short-term, negotiable promissory notes issued by the federal government. They were first issued in 1934. In 1937 fortnightly auctions were introduced, but the amount of Treasury bills outstanding remained small until the Second World War, when the government increased its issues as part of its war financing. In 1953, the federal government, in an effort to develop a Canadian money market, changed from a fortnightly to a weekly auction and substantially increased the amount of its bills outstanding. Until recently, these bills had become a significant source of government financing and a major financial instrument in the money market.

Weekly auctions of Treasury bills took place until September 1997. Since then, biweekly auctions have been conducted by the Bank of Canada on behalf of the federal government for bills with terms of three months, six months, and one year. The federal government also issues bills with terms as short as a few days to cover low points in its cash balances with the directly clearing members of the **Canadian Payments Association (CPA)**. The change to a biweekly framework was a result of several steps taken to enhance the liquidity and the efficiency of the bond and money markets. Box 6–1 shows how a reduction in government financing requirements has affected these markets.

**Canadian
Payments
Association
(CPA)** *an associ-
ation charged
with clearing
cheques for all
financial institu-
tions in Canada*

www.

Bids for regular federal government Treasury bills are accepted by the Bank of Canada until 12:30 p.m. every other Tuesday, except when holidays intervene.[1] Bills are allotted to successful bidders, starting with the highest price submitted, until the total amount of each maturity is taken up. If the amount of bids at the lowest successful price exceeds the amount of bills available, the remainder are divided on a pro rata basis among those submitting bids at that price. Bids are made in multiples of $1000 par value with the bid price per $100 expressed to no more than three decimal points. Hence, a bid could be for $97.730. The difference between a successful bid and a bill's par value represents the amount of interest earned.

**government
securities
distributors**
*entities eligible
to participate
directly in the
tender process
for government
securities; once
called primary
distributors*

All financial institutions and investment dealers on the Bank of Canada's list of **government securities distributors** for Government of Canada securities are eligible to submit sealed tenders for bills. Two weeks before each tender, the Bank of Canada announces the amounts and maturities of bills to be offered. Shortly after the auction, the Bank of Canada announces information on the yields and associated prices accepted by the Bank of Canada on behalf of the minister of finance.

The Bank of Canada usually submits one bid for the bills it wants to purchase for its own account and another as a reserve bid for the entire issue being offered. The reserve bid is made to guarantee that the entire issue will be taken up so as not to embarrass the government. Although the minister of finance reserves the right to accept or reject any tender in whole or in part, this has been done infrequently and with much reluctance. The Bank of Canada also submits a reserve bid to prevent bidders from forming an agreement in an attempt to manipulate the price.

---

1. As we will learn later, the Bank of Canada also auctions Treasury bills as part of its cash management operations. These auctions are open to bids until 10:30 am.

BOX 6–1 BACKGROUNDER

Fiscal Surpluses Mean Less Debt

In the late 1990s the federal government found that its tax revenues exceeded its program spending. In other words, the government didn't need to borrow as much money as it had been borrowing. You might think this change is a good thing, but consider it from the perspective of an investor looking for a safe haven for her cash. The government debt market offers a relatively safe environment in which to hold surplus funds. If the government isn't borrowing as heavily, the supply of these instruments will be relatively small. Although the government will always be financing some of its spending (to bridge the gap between the timing of its payments and its receipts), it wants to maintain sufficiently liquid markets to ensure that a market will exist from which it can secure funds from surplus units if its budgetary position changes. Of course, the federal government also wants

to encourage the flow of funds between surplus and deficit units.

At the same time that the federal surpluses were growing, the federal government decided to move much of its debt operations to the long-term end of the market to shelter its financing from unexpected increases in interest rates. It had been relying on relatively short-term debt to finance its expenditures. When interest rates rise, the cost of servicing the government's debt can rise considerably. The following table demonstrates that the number of Treasury bills outstanding has fallen over the past decade, while the number of long-term bonds has risen. In 1988 the average term to maturity of federal debt was just over four years. Early in 2000 the average term had risen to just over six years.

Government of Canada Direct Securities Outstanding ($ Billions)

Securities	February 1988	February 1993	February 1998	February 2000
Treasury bills	77.5	158.0	109.2	91.6
Bonds: 3 Years and Under	27.3	57.5	107.0	117.5
Bonds: 3–5 Years	20.6	27.6	61.5	60.0
Bonds: 5–10 Years	31.7	44.7	72.6	75.9
Bonds: 10 Years and Over	32.8	50.0	72.0	74.4
Canada Savings Bonds	53.1	34.3	30.7	27.5

SOURCE: Statistics Canada, CANSIM database, Matrix 923, March 2000.

Bank Rate *the rate of interest at which members of the Canadian Payments Association may borrow from the Bank of Canada*

overnight financing rate *the rate of interest on overnight (one-day) securities*

In 1996 the Bank of Canada changed the mechanism for setting the **Bank Rate** (which had been one of the instruments of monetary policy, as we will see in a later chapter). The Rate had been set as one-quarter of a percent above the average weekly Treasury bill rate, but was moved to the upper band of the **overnight financing rate**—the rate of interest on overnight (one-day) securities. Again, as we'll see in a later chapter, the overnight financing rate is the rate of interest most sensitive to monetary policy, and indeed, the Bank of Canada has set a 0.5 percent band in which it would like to see this interest rate fluctuate. With the Treasury bill market playing less and less of a role in the daily operation of monetary policy, the Bank of Canada in 1996 reduced its holdings of Treasury bills in favour of other Government of Canada financial instruments (bonds). In 1996, the borrowing requirements of the federal government fell below what was expected for that year, leading to a reduction in both the supply of and the demand for Treasury bills (because the federal government did not have to borrow as much as in the past). The fact that the Bank of Canada had reduced its demand for Treasury bills actually helped the private sector adjust to the changing structure of the Treasury bill market.

when-issued Treasury bill *a Treasury bill that is to be auctioned at the next weekly tender*

Even so, a "when-issued" market for Treasury bills has developed. A **when-issued Treasury bill** is a contract to purchase or sell bills that are to be auctioned at the next tender. These contracts allow investors to take a position in Treasury bills before the bills are auctioned for assured amounts and rates. Contracts are settled on the business day following the auction, when new bills are delivered. Later in this chapter we will discuss recent evidence on whether yields on when-issued Treasury bills were accurate predictors of the actual yields on Treasury bills.

Short-Term and Short-Dated Government of Canada Bonds

Short-term marketable government bonds are issued with maturities of three years and under. Initially, short-dated bonds were issued with long maturities but within three years of maturing. At the end of 1999, bonds outstanding with three years and under to maturity accounted for about 28 percent of the federal government's marketable direct and guaranteed securities outstanding (excluding Canada Savings Bonds and perpetuals).

Other Government Paper

Provincial and municipal governments and their agencies offer Treasury bills and other short-term notes through regular tender or through arrangements with investment dealers who act as their fiscal agents. The larger municipalities, for example, borrow periodically by offering short-term paper in anticipation of tax receipts or to provide funds until longer-term financing is arranged. While terms of this paper vary considerably, most is issued for 90 days in denominations of $100 000 or more. Some municipalities also issue notes on demand or call.

Day-to-Day Loans, PRAs, and SRAs

Day-to-day or simply day loans are overnight loans made by the chartered banks to primary dealers (until recently, known as money market jobbers) to assist them to finance their inventories of Government of Canada securities. Day loans may be called by the banks before noon the next day; if not called they are automatically renewed for another day. These loans are made in minimum denominations of $100 000 and are secured by Government of Canada Treasury bills and short-term bonds.

primary dealers *those government securities distributors that maintain a high level of activity on primary and secondary markets*

The **primary dealers** are a small group of investment dealers who regularly are primary distributors of Government of Canada securities and, as such, hold

Purchase and Resale Agreements (PRAs) primary dealers can arrange to sell the securities to the Bank of Canada with an agreement (a PRA) to repurchase them at an agreed-on price and future date

inventories of them. In 1953, the Bank of Canada instituted **Purchase and Resale Agreements (PRAs)** to encourage the primary dealers to hold larger inventories of government securities to help develop a broader market for the securities. Under these agreements, primary dealers who are unable to find the necessary financing for their inventories of securities elsewhere can arrange to sell the securities to the Bank of Canada with an agreement to repurchase them at an agreed-on price and future date. Each primary dealer has a line of credit with the Bank that specifies the total dollar amount of funds available to that dealer under PRA. In 1954, the chartered banks, as part of their contribution toward the development of a Canadian money market, introduced day-to-day loans to the primary dealers. These loans provide primary dealers with an alternative source of funds for financing their inventories of Treasury bills and other short-term Government of Canada securities. The amount of chartered bank day-to-day loans is limited to the unused portion of a primary dealer's line of credit with the Bank of Canada for PRA.

Special PRAs (SPRAs) used when the central bank wants to increase liquidity in the financial system and put an upper bound on the overnight financing rate

Special PRAs (SPRAs) are used when the central bank wants to increase liquidity in the financial system and put an upper bound on the overnight financing rate. Through a SPRA the central bank is increasing cash in the banking system, thereby limiting the extent to which the demand for overnight funds will increase the cost of borrowing. PRAs and SPRAs are also known as "repos" (since they involve repurchase).

Sale and Repurchase Agreements (SRAs) the central bank sells securities to a chartered bank and agrees to repurchase them later at its own initiative

The Bank of Canada also enters into **Sale and Repurchase Agreements (SRAs)**, which are the opposite of Purchase and Resale Agreements, when it wants to reduce liquidity in the banking system or put upward pressure on very short-term interest rates. The central bank sells securities to a chartered bank and agrees to repurchase them later at the initiative of the Bank of Canada. This process reduces liquidity in the banking system.

Special SRAs used when the central bank wants to reduce liquidity in the financial system and put a lower "bound" on the overnight financing rate

Special SRAs (SSRAs) are used to put a "floor" on the overnight financing rate, since they involve a transfer of liquidity from the banking system to the central bank. (There is too much cash in the banking system.) The central bank uses an SSRA to eliminate the excess, which might bid the overnight interest rate down as borrowers demand lower loan rates from surplus units). SSRAs and SRAs are known as "reverse repos." (We will return to this term, which applies generally and isn't always specific to central bank transactions.) The Bank of Canada exerts influence over the overnight financing rate, using SSRAs and SPRAs, if the rate begins to move from where the Bank thought it would be.

Call and Short Loans

call loans loans to securities brokers and dealers to finance their inventories of securities

In addition to day loans, the chartered banks make **call loans** to finance the inventories of securities of brokers and dealers. Call loans, collateralized primarily with Government of Canada securities, are now referred to as ordinary call loans. They can, in principle, be called by the banks on short notice, but in practice they are viewed as longer-term collateral loans. The interest rate charged on these loans is closely related to the major banks' prime rate (the rate they charge their best commercial customers).

In 1967 the chartered banks introduced special call loans. Unlike ordinary call loans, these loans are used by the securities brokers and dealers to finance their inventories of money market securities other than those issued by the federal government. As such, they can be secured with collateral not eligible for day loans and ordinary call loans. Special call loans may be renewed or called, in whole or in part, by either party on any business day provided notice is given before noon. Loans not called before noon are typically automatically renewed for another day.

Chartered Bank Deposits

term notes
a fixed-term deposit liability issued by a financial intermediary

deposit certificates
fixed-term deposit liabilities, usually in large denominations

swapped deposits
Canadian-dollar term deposits that a bank converts into foreign currency for investment in foreign money markets

forward contract *in the foreign exchange market, a contract to convert a foreign currency investment back into Canadian dollars at maturity, at a set rate of exchange*

interbank deposits *loans from one chartered bank to another*

In addition to their role as major lenders to money market participants, the chartered banks are also borrowers in the market. They purchase funds by issuing bearer **term notes** and other fixed-term deposits. Bearer term deposit notes are issued in multiples of $100 000 and are sold at a discount with maturities from 30 days to one year. They are transferable but not redeemable before maturity. Other fixed-term deposits include deposit receipts and **deposit certificates** (also known as CDs.) Because these are issued in blocks of $100 000, they are frequently referred to as wholesale deposits to differentiate them from the banks' other term and notice deposits, which are offered in much smaller denominations to their retail (branch) customers. Wholesale deposits are placed with the banks by corporations, institutions, and provincial and municipal governments. They are not transferable, but they may be redeemed after notice before maturity, subject to a reduced interest rate. Maturities may be as short as one day and as long as several years.

The chartered banks have also offered **swapped deposits** to take advantage of relatively higher money market rates outside Canada and of conditions in foreign exchange markets. Swapped deposits are Canadian-dollar term deposits that a bank converts into foreign currency, usually U.S. dollars, for investment in foreign money markets. At the same time the bank undertakes, through a **forward contract** in the foreign exchange market, to convert the foreign currency investment back into Canadian dollars at maturity. The Canadian depositor's return consists of the yield earned on the foreign investment and the profit or loss on the foreign exchange transactions.

Interbank Funds

In 1973 the chartered banks introduced an overnight lending market to allow banks with excess cash reserves to lend them to other banks short of cash reserves. The interbank market remained relatively small until after the establishment of foreign-bank subsidiaries in Canada. Today **interbank deposits** provide most Canadian banks, not just the foreign-bank subsidiaries, with an important source or use of funds in their daily cash management.

Transactions in interbank deposits are in multiples of $100 000. The banks arrange them directly with each other or through the intermediation of deposit brokers. Interbank deposits grew from some $80 million at the end of 1968 to more than $15 billion at the end of 1999; most of this growth came after 1980.

Finance Company Paper

**instalment debt
contracts**
*promissory notes
signed by
purchasers of
durable
consumer, com-
mercial, and
industrial goods*

finance paper
*promissory
notes issued by
sales finance
companies*

The earliest nongovernment and nonbank participants in the money market
were the sales finance companies, whose activities are described later in the
book. They purchase **instalment debt contracts** (promissory notes signed by
purchasers of durable consumer, commercial, and industrial goods) from
wholesalers and retailers. They then "package" these contracts by maturity and
default risk and use them as collateral for the notes and certificates they issue
and sell in the money market. These notes and certificates are called **finance
paper**, or, more colloquially, "acceptance paper." This paper is sold at a discount in minimum denominations of $50 000, usually with terms from 30 to
365 days. Not all paper offered is specifically secured; paper issued by Canadian
subsidiaries of foreign companies is usually guaranteed by parent organizations.

Corporate Paper

**commercial
paper** *notes
issued by nonfi-
nancial corpora-
tions to borrow
funds for short
periods*

Nonfinancial corporations borrow funds for short periods to offset seasonal
cash flows, to finance inventories, or to extend trade credit to their customers.
They issue notes, referred to as corporate paper or **commercial paper**, through
investment dealers who may act as agents or as principals purchasing the notes
for subsequent resale.

Unlike finance company paper, which is usually specifically secured, corporate paper is backed by the general credit of its issuer. Corporate paper is
usually also supported by a corporation's stand-by or unused line of credit with
its bankers or by guarantees from a parent corporation. Most borrowers issue
notes with minimum denominations of $50 000 for terms of one year or less
but usually with an original term of 30 or 90 days. Some paper issues have a call
feature that allows lenders to demand repayment on 24 hours' notice.
Corporate notes may be interest-bearing or sold at a discount and may be fully
registered to the lender or in bearer form.

Although most commercial paper is issued by large, well-established corporations, smaller companies also use this source of financing, usually after
first gaining market recognition by issuing bankers' acceptances.

Bankers' Acceptances

**bankers'
acceptances**
*time drafts
drawn on banks
by borrowers
that order the
banks to pay cer-
tain amounts on
specified future
dates*

Bankers' acceptances are time drafts drawn on banks by borrowers that order
the banks to pay certain amounts on specified future dates. The bank on which
the draft (also known as a bill of exchange or, simply, a bill) is drawn acknowl-
edges its acceptance of the conditions stated in the draft by applying its stamp.
When stamped, for which the bank is paid a fee, the draft becomes an acceptance that is returned to the borrower for sale in the money market. In practice,
investment dealers market bankers' acceptances for borrowers.

Bankers' acceptances trade in the money market at a discount from their
face value, which is denominated in multiples of $100 000. Acceptances have
maturities from a few days to one year, but normally are for 30 to 90 days.

The major role of the bank in an acceptance transaction is to guarantee the creditworthiness of the borrower rather than to lend money to the individual. Most acceptances are drawn against a borrower's bank line of credit. At maturity, the bank pays the face value of the acceptance to its then holder, and then the bank usually receives payment by drawing down the borrower's line of credit.

Bankers' acceptances were first introduced into the Canadian money market in 1962. Since then their use has expanded in response to the growth of the money market, a reduction in the banks' stamping fees, and revisions in the *Bank Act* that removed restrictions on their issuance. As we will see later in the chapter, Canada now has a derivatives market in bankers' acceptances.

Trust and Mortgage Loan Company Instruments

guaranteed trust and investment certificates (GICs) *term deposits offering a guaranteed rate of return*

Trust and mortgage loan companies compete with the chartered banks for wholesale deposits by offering term deposits, deposit receipts, and **guaranteed trust and investment certificates (GICs)**. These deposits are placed directly with lenders by the institutions or are intermediated by deposit brokers. The terms of these deposits vary from 24 hours to several years. GICs are not transferable, but are usually redeemable before maturity with an interest rate penalty. In 1981 some of the trust companies started to offer term deposits with variable-rate interest—the interest rate is adjusted periodically before maturity to reflect changing market rates.

Repurchase Agreements or Buy-Backs

repurchase agreements (repos) *the immediate sale of securities and the simultaneous agreement to repurchase these securities at a specified future price and date*

reverse repo *the immediate purchase of securities and a simultaneous agreement to resell the securities later*

short sale *selling an asset that you don't currently own in anticipation of a decline in its price*

Repurchase agreements, or **repos**, are the immediate sale of securities and the simultaneous agreement to repurchase these securities at a specified future price and date. The seller of the securities typically continues to receive any dividend or interest payment on the underlying securities during the life of the transaction. In the money market, security dealers use repos to finance their inventories of financial assets, making repos an important alternative to call loans from the banks. Banks, insurance companies, pension funds, and other financial corporations now regularly also transact in repos. Repos are similar to the Purchase and Resale Agreements (discussed earlier) the Bank of Canada has arranged with primary dealers.

A **reverse repo**, the opposite of a repo, is the immediate purchase of securities and a simultaneous agreement to resell the securities later. A reverse repo is typically conducted between a party that needs to borrow a particular security, usually for a **short sale** (the sale of an asset that you don't currently own in anticipation of a decline in its price) and a counterparty that wants to augment the returns on its security portfolio. (If the market price of the asset is falling, its yield should be rising.) Any two or more parties may engage in repos and reverse repos. These terms apply generally, and they are not specific to central bank intervention in security markets.

The Dimensions of the Money Market

Since its inception in the mid-1950s, the Canadian money market has experienced continual growth. As a result it now has depth (a large number of different types of financial instruments) and breadth (a large number of debt instruments) outstanding at any one time. Table 6.1 shows the major short-term securities outstanding in the Canadian money market.

TABLE 6.1	ESTIMATED MAJOR MONEY MARKET INSTRUMENTS OUTSTANDING December 1999, $ Millions		
Short-term paper			
Paper issued by financial corporations		94 300	
Paper issued by nonfinancial corporations		22 094	
Canadian-dollar bankers' acceptances		47 063	
Total corporate short-term paper		163 457	163 457
Government Treasury bills and other short-term paper			
Municipal and provincial governments and their enterprises		16 882	
Government of Canada Treasury bills		93 450	110 332
		110 332	273 789

SOURCE: Statistics Canada, CANSIM Database, Matrices 923 and 2550, March 2000.

Capital Markets

We have already indicated that markets in which funds are lent or borrowed for periods longer than one year are called capital markets. Capital markets encompass both primary and secondary markets and both debt and equity securities. The three major capital markets are the bond market, the residential mortgage market, and the stock market.

The Bond Market

bond *a promise by its issuer to pay a principal amount of money at a specified maturity date and usually to make regular interest payments in the interim*

A **bond** is a promise by its issuer to pay a principal amount of money at a specified maturity date and usually to make regular interest payments in the interim. Coupon bonds pay both principal and interest, while zero-coupon bonds, as their name implies, are issued without interest-bearing coupons or statements declaring the amount or rate of interest to be paid. Zero-coupon bonds also originate by "stripping" interest coupons from the bonds and trading the principal value and interest payments as separate securities.

Bonds are issued with a trust deed that sets out all the provisions related to them. These provisions may include a restrictive covenant limiting the borrower's ability to buy and dispose of assets or to issue more securities.

Bonds are classified by type of borrower, by type of asset pledged as security, and by special features attached to them. As shown in Table 6.2, the six major borrowers in the domestic bond market are the Government of Canada, provincial and municipal governments, financial and nonfinancial corporations, and institutions.

TABLE 6.2	BONDS OUTSTANDING: GOVERNMENT OF CANADA, PROVINCIAL, MUNICIPAL, CORPORATE AND OTHER BONDS Millions of Canadian Dollars, December 1998	
	Canadian Dollars	**Other Currencies[1]**
Government of Canada	333 632	27 679
Provincial, direct and guaranteed	200 757	166 690
Municipal, direct and guaranteed	33 205	4 126
Corporate: financial	46 460	55 992
nonfinancial	64 807	101 918
Institutions	1 001	165
Foreign debtors[2]	550	
Total	680 412	356 570

1. Foreign currency values have been converted into Canadian dollars.
2. These are issues payable in Canadian dollars by the World Bank and certain foreign government and corporations

SOURCE: *Bank of Canada Review*, October 1999, Table K8.

debentures
bonds secured by a claim on the general creditworthiness of the issuer

convertible bonds *these allow their holders to exchange them for another financial instrument, generally common stock*

warrants
attached to bonds, they can be used to purchase the issuer's common stock at stated prices

junk bonds *high-yield bond usually rated as risky*

Mortgage bonds are secured by a pledge of property and equipment, and collateral trust bonds are secured by financial assets. Debenture bonds, or simply **debentures**, are secured by a claim on the general creditworthiness of the issuer and, as such, represent a general charge against borrowers. Except in the case of municipal bonds, a distinction is usually not made between bonds and debentures. Bonds whose claims on issuers in case of default are subordinated (comes next) to those of others are said to be subordinated, or junior, bonds. In some cases the bond indenture (the contract) requires the issuer to establish a sinking fund in which funds are accumulated to retire (redeem) a certain proportion of the bond's principal value each year. Callable bonds allow the issuer to retire a portion of an issue before its maturity, while **convertible bonds** allow their holders to exchange them for another financial instrument, generally common stock. Bonds with retractable or extendable provisions give their holders the option to shorten or lengthen their maturity. Some bonds have **warrants** attached to them that can be used to purchase the issuer's common stock at stated prices. Warrants are frequently detachable so that they can trade separately from bonds.

Historically bonds were issued to finance projects with long productive lives such as railroads, industrial plants, and electrical generating stations. Recently an active market for high-yield bonds, colloquially known as **junk bonds**, has developed. These bonds are issued to finance high-risk activity and corporate restructuring. They usually are very risky, which is reflected in their high yield.

New issues of bonds are sold in primary markets by public offerings and private placements. The process by which new issues are sold to the public is known as underwriting. For the public's protection, new offerings usually require the preparation of a prospectus, a document that provides information about the borrower, how the borrowed funds are to be used, and other provisions pertaining to the issue itself. Security underwriters acquire issues for resale to the public from the borrower through competitive bids or by negotiations. A more recent innovation is the **bought deal**, an arrangement whereby one or more securities dealers buy an entire issue of new bonds from borrowers at a fixed price, and accept the risk of reselling them. With a private placement, a borrower, usually with the assistance of security dealers, places (sells) an entire issue directly with large institutional investors such as life insurance companies and pension funds. This arrangement usually eliminates the cost of preparing a prospectus and other costs associated with securities underwriting.

Once bonds have been issued, they are subsequently traded in secondary markets. Most outstanding bonds are bought and sold in the over-the-counter market. In this market, securities dealers hold inventories of bonds and are prepared to trade at regularly posted "bid" and "ask" quotes. In this way dealers are said to make a market for bonds. This market does not have a specific location such as a stock exchange. Instead, market participants exchange information and conduct trades using a network of telephone lines, fax machines, and computers.

In its role as the federal government's fiscal agent, the Bank of Canada also is the government's debt manager. We have already described the regular auctions of federal government Treasury bills. Traditionally, new federal government bonds were allotted at specified prices to primary distributors consisting of security dealers and chartered banks. The portion of a new issue allotted to any one distributor was based on the distributor's contribution to maintaining an efficient secondary market for federal government debt. In recent years the federal government has tended to use auctions more often, whereby dealers and institutions bid for a portion of any new issue to be resold by them in the secondary market.

Canada Savings Bonds, unlike other government bonds, are not traded in secondary markets. These bonds are sold and redeemed at their face value by the government through securities dealers, banks, and other financial institutions that, for a fee, act as the government's agents.

REAL RETURN BONDS **Real return bonds** were first issued in Canada by the federal government in late 1991. These bonds differ from conventional bonds in two main ways. Their principal amount is increased at maturity or, when sold, by the full increase in the Consumer Price Index. The coupon rate is a fixed real rate because the amount of the interest payments is a fixed percentage of the principal adjusted to include any increases in the inflation rate. The real return bonds issued in 1991 were for 30 years with a 4.5 percent annual real coupon rate.

STRIPPED ZERO-COUPON BONDS **Stripped zero-coupon bonds** are created when an investment dealer separates a conventional bond into its two constituent parts: coupons, consisting of all future coupon payments; and the

---

bought deal whereby one or more securities dealers buy an entire issue of new bonds at a fixed price, and accept the risk of reselling them

real return bonds bonds whose principal amount is increased at maturity, or when sold by the full increase in the Consumer Price Index

stripped zero-coupon bonds created when an investment dealer separates a conventional bond into its two constituent parts

bond residual, consisting of the principal. Each of these two parts is then sold separately to investors at a discount from its face value. Each bond residual component and each coupon is a stripped zero-coupon bond. Often all the coupons from the same conventional bond are sold together as a package of strips. Stripped bonds have been created from Government of Canada bonds, corporate bonds, provincial government bonds, and other bonds such as those issued by provincial crown corporations and municipalities.

The Dimensions of the Bond Market

The par value of Canadian-dollar bonds outstanding at the end of 1998, as shown in Table 6.2, was more than $678 billion. In addition, Canadian borrowers had $356 billion outstanding in bonds payable in foreign currencies. Provincial governments and their agencies, such as Ontario Hydro (now called Ontario Power Generation) and Hydro Quebec, have tended to dominate Canadian-dollar bond issues. In recent years Canadian corporate bond issues outstanding and payable in foreign currencies exceeded outstanding Canadian dollar issues.

The Mortgage Market

A **mortgage** is a debt contract in which real property, usually land and buildings, serves as security for the contract. Claims by mortgage lenders on the borrower's property vary widely in case of default. With a first mortgage the lender has first claim on the property pledged to secure the loan. With junior mortgages, such as second, third, or lower, the lender's claim on the property is subordinated according to rank.

There are two major types of residential mortgage loans: NHA mortgages and conventional mortgages. **NHA mortgages** are insured under the *National Housing Act* by the Canada Mortgage and Housing Corporation (CMHC). Although these mortgage loans are now mostly made by financial institutions approved by the CMHC, their terms are subject to government regulations. **Conventional mortgages** are not insured by the CMHC but may be insured by a private insurer. They are not subject to the same regulations as are NHA mortgages.

Most residential mortgage loans are **amortized**, which means that the principal amount borrowed is gradually repaid, along with interest, during the life of the mortgage. The life of a mortgage can be as long as 30 years. In Canada, residential mortgage borrowers have the legal right to repay part or all of their conventional mortgages after five years and their NHA mortgages after three years.

In the 1980s various innovations were made to residential mortgage contracts to cope with escalating property values and interest rates. These innovations included graduated-payments mortgages, whereby monthly payments by borrowers were initially low but thereafter increased at a predetermined rate; renewable-term mortgages with terms as short as six months; and variable-rate mortgages with fixed monthly payments and regular adjustments to the principal outstanding based on variations in market interest rates. During this same

mortgage *a debt contract in which real property, usually land and buildings, serves as security for the contract*

NHA mortgages *mortgages insured under the National Housing Act by the CMHC*

conventional mortgages *mortgages not insured by the CMHC but that may be insured by a private insurer*

amortized *when the principal amount borrowed is gradually repaid, along with interest during the life of the financial claim*

www.

period, the CMHC introduced a mortgage-rate protection plan. Under the plan, mortgagers can purchase insurance that reimburses them for a portion of specified increases in their mortgage interest rate.

The primary residential mortgage market where new loans are originated is dominated by the chartered banks, trust and mortgage loan companies, life insurance companies, and credit unions. In addition, mortgage brokers originate mortgages for sale to lenders. Because the financial institutions that originate residential mortgages have tended to hold these mortgages as an investment, either directly or through affiliated mortgage loan companies, a well-developed secondary residential mortgage market does not exist in Canada. However, a secondary market for NHA mortgage-backed securities, although still small, has developed. In this market, NHA mortgages are acquired from their originators and repackaged into pools (bundles) of mortgage loans with similar qualities. A distinction is usually made between prepayable and nonprepayable mortgage pools. The former contains only **open mortgages**, which allow unscheduled principal payments; the latter contains only **closed mortgages**, on which unscheduled payments are not permitted. Pass-through securities are issued against these pools. Monthly interest and principal repayments on mortgage loans in the pools are "passed through" to the holders of these securities. The CMHC has provided a "timely payment guarantee" to ensure that holders of these securities receive regular payments in the event that mortgages default. These securities are commonly known as "Cannie Maes," a name taken from their more popular U.S. counterparts.

A more recent innovation in the residential mortgage market has been the introduction of **reverse mortgages**. These mortgages are designed to allow homeowners, typically senior citizens, to continue to live in their homes while releasing their equity in them for some income. Today, the trust companies that offer these mortgages on a proportion of a homeowner's equity pay out part of the mortgage loan in a lump sum and use the remainder to purchase a guaranteed annuity. The annuity provides the homeowner with a monthly income and it also makes principal and interest payments on the loan.

open mortgages mortgages that allow unscheduled principal payments

closed mortgages mortgages that do not allow unscheduled payments

reverse mortgages mortgages designed to allow homeowners to borrow against their equity in the home

The Dimensions of Residential Mortgage Credit

Table 6.3 shows outstanding balances of the major private lending institutions on their residential mortgage credit. At the end of 1999 private institutional lenders held $420 billion in residential mortgage loans. Next to the chartered banks, the credit unions and caisses populaires were the largest holders of residential mortgage loans.

Stock Markets

common stock a class of shares that represents ownership or equity in a business

preferred stock a class of shares having privileges attached to it, usually a claim on dividends before the common stock

As their name implies, stock markets facilitate the sale and purchase of the stock of incorporated companies. While bonds denote borrowing, stocks represent ownership. Companies issue two main types of stock: **common stock** and **preferred stock**. They are frequently referred to as equities or shares. Common stock may also be divided into classes that differ according to the right to participate in corporate control. Preferred stockholders receive a specified dividend to which they are entitled before the common stockholders get anything. In some cases these dividends need not be paid every year, but can be cumulative and paid later before common stockholders receive dividends. Common stockholders receive a residual or variable dividend depending on the company's profitability. Preferred stock may be convertible, in which case it can be converted into common stock at a predetermined price. It may also be callable, which gives its issuer the right to redeem it during a specified period and at a stated call price.

www.

TABLE 6.3	**RESIDENTIAL MORTGAGE CREDIT: OUTSTANDING BALANCES OF MAJOR PRIVATE INSTITUTIONAL LENDERS** Millions of Canadian Dollars, December 1999
Chartered banks*	242 236
Trust and mortgage loan companies	20 097
Credit unions and caisses populaires	56 521
Life insurance companies	18 325
Pension funds	7 728
Other financial institutions	28 726
NHA mortgage backed securities	27 372
Special purpose corporations	46 434
Total	420 067

* Includes mortgage loan companies associated with the chartered banks.

Note: Some series are estimated so figures may not add to total.

SOURCE: Statistics Canada, CANSIM Database, Matrix 2570, March 2000.

Corporations that want their stock to be traded on organized stock exchanges list their stock with these exchanges. A stock is said to be interlisted if it is listed on more than one exchange. Some companies have their stock listed in both domestic and foreign exchanges. Until late 1999, Canada had five stock exchanges, located in Montreal, Toronto, Winnipeg, Calgary, and Vancouver.

In late 1999 a major realignment of stock market operations in Canada took place. The Toronto Stock Exchange remains the exchange in which senior equities (stocks of companies that have been in business for some time, or those that have shown themselves to be profitable) are traded, while all trading in options and futures moved to the Montreal Exchange. The Alberta and Vancouver Exchanges merged to become the Canadian Venture Exchange (CNDX), whose goal is to provide venture corporations with access to capital markets while still protecting investors. Early in 2000 the Winnipeg Stock Exchange agreed to join the Canadian Venture Exchange. In February 2000, the CDNX reported an average daily volume of 78 million shares, with an average value of $106 million.

Stock exchanges are private organizations whose trading facilities are available only to members. These members, primarily securities dealers and brokers and other financial institutions, have purchased seats on the exchange that entitle them to have a certain number of traders there. Each exchange sets its own rules with respect to eligibility requirements for listing a company's stock, trading procedures, and the disclosure of information. Of particular concern is the prevention of insider trading, which sees trades made on information before it is made available to all potential traders.

Small-cap stocks are shares of companies with low capitalization—the number of outstanding shares multiplied by the share price. Small-cap firms are sometime defined as having capitalization of $100 million or less.

A **stock split** is a subdivision of each company share into two or more shares. Companies usually prefer for the price of their stock to be in a reasonable range of its average trading price on the stock exchanges where it is listed. If the price moves well above this average and remains there for some time, the price is usually split to reduce the per share price on the market.

Traditionally, trading on most of the major exchanges has been by auction through **open outcry**, whereby traders confront each other directly to bargain over price. Auctions of individual stocks take place at specific locations, called pits, on the floor of the exchange. In these pits, "specialist" traders, designated by the exchange, act as auctioneers and make a market in the stocks assigned to them. Making a market involves the specialists matching buyers and sellers and quoting bid and offer prices at which they are prepared to trade. These functions require them to buy for their own accounts (at their bid price) and to sell from their inventory of stocks (at their offer price), thereby maintaining orderly market conditions.

In recent years, the traditional open-outcry floor-trading system of the exchange has been supplemented, and in many cases replaced, by computer systems called **electronic order books**. Orders are automatically matched, executed, and reported in these books. Securities dealers and brokers can enter their orders in an exchange's electronic order book directly from terminals in their own offices, based on information on their computer screens.

Stock trading in over-the-counter (OTC) markets is conducted by brokerage firms and investment dealers who make markets in certain stocks by matching buyers and sellers and by quoting bid and offer prices at which they stand prepared to trade. The dealers' inventories of stock serve as buffers against volatile price movements when temporary order imbalances occur. Many of the stocks traded in OTC markets are stocks of companies that, because of their small size, do not qualify for listing on the exchanges. Some companies prefer to have their stocks traded in OTC markets to avoid the exchanges' listing fees.

The Canadian Dealing Network, formerly the Canadian Over-the-Counter Trading System, organized in 1986, is an electronic quotation- and trade-reporting system for OTC stocks. In late 1999 it joined the Canadian Venture Exchange. In the United States, the National Association of Securities Dealers Automated Quotation service (NASDAQ) is a computerized system for displaying bid and asked prices for OTC stocks. The values of transactions on Canadian stock exchanges in 1998 are shown in Table 6.4. The Toronto Stock Exchange overshadowed the other Canadian markets.

small-cap stocks shares of companies with low capitalization

stock split the division of a share into two or more shares

open outcry an auction whereby traders confront one another directly to bargain over price

electronic order books a computerized facility that encourages trading

TABLE 6.4	TRADING VALUE OF TRANSACTIONS ON CANADIAN STOCK EXCHANGES IN 1998 VALUE
	$Billions
Montreal	55.70
Toronto	493.20
Vancouver	8.90
Alberta	1.80
Winnipeg	0.01
Total	559.61

SOURCE: Annual Reports of various stock exchanges.

www.

stock indexes
weighted averages of the prices of shares trading on stock exchanges

Overall stock prices are measured by **stock indexes**. The Toronto Stock Exchange 300 Composite Industrial Index is based on 300 individual stocks and the number of outstanding shares of each stock. The TSE 35 Index is based on 35 stocks actively traded on the Toronto Stock Exchange. In the United States, the two leading stock market indicators are Dow Jones Industrial Average and Standard & Poor's 500 Stock Index. Figure 6–1 plots the value of the TSE 300 over the past 50 years, with the value of the index in 1975 set equal to 100 so we can compare stock prices to this base period.

FIGURE 6–1   **THE TSE 300 INDEX**

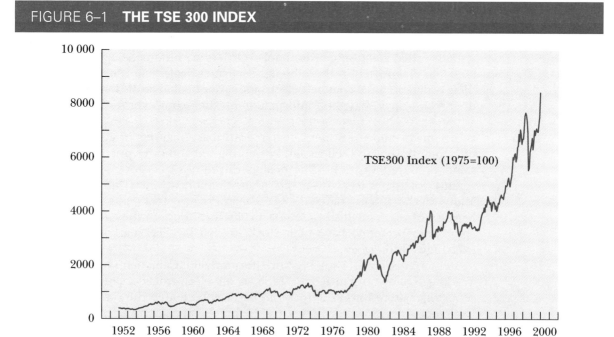

SOURCE: Statistics Canada, CANSIM Database, Matrix 191, March 2000.

BOX 6–2 **BACKGROUNDER**

Discount Brokers

Many investors are tired of paying hefty commissions to brokers for stock trading. The financial industry has responded by creating discount brokerages, with lower commissions and fewer services offered to investors. The *Financial Post* examined how quickly discount brokerages were able to process a stock purchase in the morning, and the sale of the stock later that afternoon. They were surprised to find the results reported in the following table.

Peak trading hours are reported to be between 9 and 10 in the morning, and 3 and 4 in the afternoon (Eastern time zone). Industry experts suggest you trade during midday, away from the peak hours around market opening and closing times.

Discount Brokerage	Waiting Time to Buy	Waiting Time to Sell
Scotia Discount Brokerage	23 minutes	32 minutes
BMO InvestorLine	35 minutes	16 minutes
TD Waterhouse Canada	30 minutes	15 minutes
Royal Bank Action Direct	67 minutes	13 minutes
CBIC Investor's Edge	50 minutes	35 minutes
National Bank InvesTel	12 minutes	18 minutes
Charles Schwab Canada	5 minutes	2.5 minutes

SOURCE: Adapted from "Discount Brokerages Put to the Stopwatch Test," *Financial Post*, February 19, 2000, pp. C1 and C5.

In February 1990, the Toronto Stock Exchange introduced Toronto 35 Index Participation Units (TIPs). TIPs were units of a trust created by the TSE. The underlying assets of the trust were shares of the 35 companies that make up the Toronto 35 Index. The value of each unit approximated one-tenth of the index level plus dividends that had accrued since the last quarterly payment. Dividends received by the trust were distributed to unit holders quarterly in April, July, October, and December. TIPs were traded on the Toronto Stock Exchange. Investors holding a prescribed minimum amount of TIPs could redeem them for the underlying basket of assets at any time.

In early 2000, the Toronto Stock Exchange and Barclays Global Investors Canada Limited announced an agreement to merge the TIPS 35 Fund (and a TIPS 100 Fund, based on the 100 shares making up the Toronto 100 Index) with the iUnits S&P/TSE 60 Index Participation Fund (i60s Fund). The S&P/TSE 60 Index was developed in 1998 and consists of 60 of the largest stocks traded on the TSE. The S&P/TSE 60 Index will eventually replace both the Toronto 35 Index and the TSE 100 Index.

www.

Financial Futures and Options

derivative
financial instruments whose existence and value are derived from some other underlying financial asset

futures contract
a transferable written agreement to buy or sell a specified amount of a financial asset at a stated price for delivery at a given future date

long position
buying the asset

short position
selling the asset

Financial futures and options are **derivative** financial instruments in that their existence and value are derived from some other underlying financial asset.

Financial Futures Contracts and Markets

A financial **futures contract** is a transferable written agreement to buy or sell a specified amount of a financial asset at a stated price for delivery at a given date in the future. The buyer (holder) of a futures contract agrees to accept future delivery of an asset, while the seller (writer) of the contract agrees to deliver the asset at the contract price and date. Purchasers of futures contracts are said to be taking a **long position** and writers a **short position** in futures markets.

Currency futures are contracts for delivery of a foreign currency; stock futures for delivery of shares; and interest rate futures for delivery of debt securities such as long-term government bonds, Treasury bills, commercial paper, bankers' acceptances, and certificates of deposit. Stock-index futures provide their holders with a cash payment based on the future level of a stock index, such as the Toronto 60 Index.

Financial futures contracts are traded in organized futures exchanges. In late 1999 and early 2000 all derivatives trading in Canada was moved to the Montreal Exchange. Although trading in future contracts on agricultural commodities dates from the middle of the nineteenth century, exchange arrangements for trading financial futures contracts only started in the 1980s. Each futures exchange specifies standard contract size, delivery dates, and trading rules. Stock futures contracts generally consist of 100 shares. Long-term government bond contracts are for $100 000, and Treasury bills and other money market instruments are for $1 million. The trading unit for a stock-index future is the current value of the index multiplied by a set dollar amount. For example, with TSE 35 Index futures, this amount was $500, so that if the index were 170.15, the futures contract would be worth $85 075.

Delivery dates are usually standardized in terms of a monthly cycle. For example, the Montreal Exchange's delivery months for Canadian government bond futures are March, June, September, and December. At any one time, contracts for eight different delivery dates may be traded. Trading for each delivery date on a new contract can begin two years in advance.

Each futures exchange operates or is associated with a clearinghouse. The clearinghouse guarantees that all traders in the futures market will honour their contractual obligations. It serves this role by taking the position of buyer to every seller and seller to every buyer. In this way, the clearinghouse substitutes its own credibility for the promise of each trader in the market. As a result, traders need not check one another's creditworthiness, and anonymity between contracting parties can be maintained. To protect themselves against nonperformance by traders, futures exchanges and their clearinghouses set margin requirements. There are two types of margin requirements: initial margin and mark-to-market margin. Initial margin represents a security deposit all traders must make when they open a new contract. It is returned when the transaction is completed. Mark-to-market margin is computed at the end of each day's trading session. When futures contract prices rise, investors with long positions experience a theoretical gain and those with short positions undergo a theoretical loss. The opposite is the case when futures contract prices fall. At the end of each day's trading session, the clearinghouse collects all losses and transfers them to the gainers in what is known as mark-to-market settlement. Traders have to maintain margin accounts to settle each day's losses. To facilitate the collection process, the futures exchanges impose price limits on the amount that contract prices can change each day.

The price of a futures contract is established by auction on the floor of futures exchanges. However, arbitrage trading produces a close relationship between the spot market price of an asset and its futures market price. The amount by which the futures market price exceeds the spot market price of the underlying asset is called the **basis**. With arbitrage trading, basis equals the **cost of carry**—the cost of holding the underlying asset until its delivery.

Arbitrage profits can be realized whenever the basis does not equal the cost of carry. When the basis exceeds the cost of carry, arbitragers gain from purchasing the asset in the spot market and simultaneously selling a futures contract against it. These arbitrage transactions cause spot market prices to rise and futures market prices to fall, restoring the basis at the cost of carry. Conversely, when the basis is less than the cost of carry, arbitragers gain from selling the asset in the spot market and simultaneously buying a futures contract against it. These arbitrage activities restore equality between the basis and the cost of carry by causing spot prices to fall and futures prices to rise. Since carrying costs decline as the settlement dates of futures contracts approach, futures prices converge to the underlying assets' spot prices at the settlement dates. On the final day of trading in a futures contract, its price should equal the spot price of the underlying asset.

Except for arbitrage trading, participants in the financial futures market usually do not plan to take or make delivery of financial assets as specified in futures contracts. Speculators purchase financial futures only to sell them later at a profit before the settlement date. Contracts are settled with offsetting sales or purchases of identical contracts. Financial institutions, as we will learn, use financial futures contracts to reduce their exposure to risk by **hedging**. Hedging involves taking a position in the financial futures market to offset an existing spot market position.

Financial Options and Their Markets

The holder of a **financial option** has the right, but not the obligation, to buy or sell a financial asset at a specified price (the exercise or **strike price**) on or before a specified expiry date. A U.S.-type option may be exercised at any time before the expiry date, while a European-type option may be exercised only at its expiry date.

Two types of options exist: call options and put options. A **call option** gives its holder the right to buy financial assets from, and a **put option** gives its holder the right to sell financial assets to, the writers of these options at specified prices in the future. To obtain these rights, option holders (the buyers of options) pay option writers (the sellers of options) a premium whether the

---

basis *the cash price or spot price, less the futures price*

cost of carry *the cost of holding an asset until its delivery*

hedging *the act of matching one risk with a counterbalancing risk to reduce the overall risk of loss*

financial option *a right, but not an obligation, to buy or sell a financial asset at a specified price*

strike price *the price at which an option may be exercised*

call option *an option giving its holder the right to buy financial assets*

put option *an option giving its holder the right to sell financial assets*

BOX 6-3 BACKGROUNDER

Borrow to Invest

Many investors borrow funds to invest. Aside from the tax advantages (you are allowed to write off the cost of borrowing the funds from your profits when calculating your income tax), it encourages investors to leverage their investments. That is, an investor does not have to have sufficient funds to cover the entire cost of their investment. She can open a margin account with her broker and borrow the difference between the total cost of her investment and the margin deposit. In Canada, most margin trades in the stock market require a 50 percent margin. If you were to buy $100 000 worth of shares on a company traded on the Toronto Stock Exchange, you would have to deposit $50 000 with your broker. You would borrow the balance from your broker. If the share price rises, you can make a profit by selling your shares; if the price falls, you may end up facing a margin call. This situation occurs when the margin account has insufficient funds to cover the required margin. You would have to deposit additional funds into your margin account or face immediate liquidation of your position to cover the loan you received from your broker. Suppose the value of your shares fell to $70 000. You still owe the broker $50 000, but your margin account is now $20 000 (the $30 000 loss came from your margin account). Your would have to deposit an additional $15 000 to maintain the 50 percent margin!

In 1999, Canadians had more than $7 billion in margin debt, an increase of $2 billion from the year before. Much of this was used to finance purchases of technology stocks, which exhibited extraordinary growth during the year.

SOURCE: Adapted from Garry Marr, "Canadians Take On Extra $2B in Margin Debt," *Financial Post*, March 17, 2000, pp. C1, C8.

---

option premium
the price of an option

www.

option contract is exercised or not. This **option premium** constitutes the option's price.

Financial options are traded in over-the-counter markets and on option exchanges. The Chicago Board Options Exchange (CBOE), opened in 1973, was the first exchange for financial options trading. In September 1975 the Montreal Exchange started to trade call options, and in November 1979 to trade put options on a small number of Canadian stocks. The Toronto Stock Exchange introduced option trading in 1976. Both exchanges added options trading in other financial assets in the early 1980s.

As with futures exchanges, clearinghouses are associated with options markets. Trans Canada Options Inc., established in 1977, serves as the clearinghouse for all options traded on the Toronto, Montreal, and CDNX exchanges. As with futures contracts, the exchanges standardize option contracts with respect to size and monthly expiration cycles. However, unlike trading in futures, exchanges do not require daily mark-to-market settlement for trading in options.

The price of an option before its expiration date combines an intrinsic value and a time value. The intrinsic value is the difference between the option's strike price and the market price of the underlying asset. The time value is the difference between the option's market price and its intrinsic value. The more time the holder of an option has to wait for the underlying assets'

BOX 6–4   THE RELATIVE PAYOFFS TO FUTURES AND OPTIONS

Put-Call Parity

Let's remove ourselves from the costs of paying for options and futures and use simple graphs to look at the payoffs that they might offer. Suppose we consider a call option with a strike price of $100. As long as the underlying security price is below $100, the option will expire worthless. As soon as the security price rises above $100 (remember, we're ignoring the option premium—or the price of the option—for now), the option will be exercised, since you could buy the security at the $100 strike price rather than at the higher market price of $100. Similarly, for a put option with a strike price of $100, the option will expire worthless if the underlying security price is above $100, since you would sell the security at the higher market price. You will exercise the put (again, ignoring the option premium) only if the underlying security price falls below the strike price. The pay-off structure to these call and put options is graphically described below.

Note that aside from the option premium (which we're ignoring for now), the worst you could do is allow the option to expire, in which case your loss is simply the price of the option (which we have ignored). That's not the case for the payoff to futures contracts, since futures oblige you to buy or sell the underlying asset. Options carry the right, but not the obligation, to buy or sell. Suppose, for example, you had a long future with a contract price of $100 (you must buy the asset at maturity for a price of $100). If the market price of the asset is above $100 at maturity, you gain; but if it is below, you lose. For example, if the market price at maturity is $125, you've "gained" $25.

A short future works the same way. Suppose it, too, had a contract price of $100 (so you must sell at $100 on maturity). If the market price is above $100 at maturity, you've lost (since you could have sold for a higher price, but used the futures contract to "lock in" a price of $100). Of course, if the market price is below $100, you gain. The following figure plots this payoff information.

What do we see from these graphs? Payoffs from options are asymmetrical, whereas payments from futures are symmetrical. This

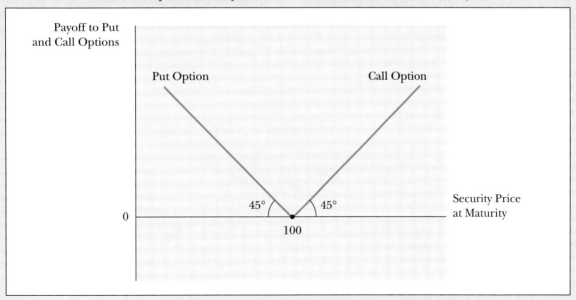

BOX 6–4   THE RELATIVE PAYOFFS TO FUTURES AND OPTIONS *(continued)*

finding led financial economists to realize that arbitrage between options and futures links the two markets—by put–call parity—since you could create a portfolio of options that would "mimic" the positive payoffs to futures. Consider options and futures on the same underlying security, with identical maturity dates and where the contract prices equal the strike prices. An investor who purchases a call option (duplicating the payoff to a long futures contract if the market price at maturity exceeds the strike price), and sells a put option (duplicating the payoff to a short futures if the market price at maturity falls short of the strike price), has replicated the gains to holding a short and long futures contract. Arbitrage will force put–call parity to reign

Value of a call – value of a put = value of a long future

or

Value of a put – value of a call = value of a short future

This concept might be easier to grasp if we create a table listing the gains and losses from the two options and the futures contract. Let's consider buying a call and writing a put, both with identical maturity dates and strike prices of $50, and a long futures with a contract price of $50. If the security price at maturity is below the strike price, the call option will be allowed to expire (since you could buy on the spot market for less than the strike price of $50). When the security price is above the strike price, you will exercise the call option and buy at $50, with the value of the call equal to the difference between the maturity security price and the strike price. The put you wrote will expire worthless if the market price at maturity is above the strike price (since the

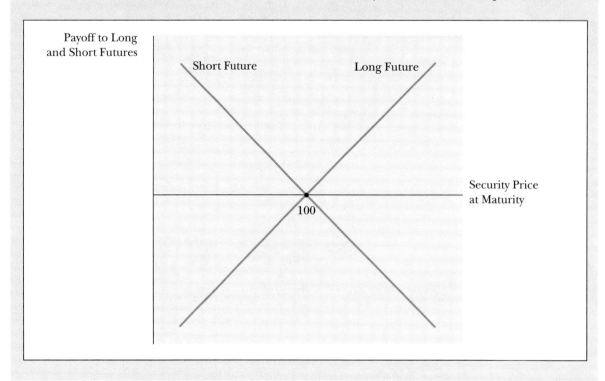

BOX 6–4 **THE RELATIVE PAYOFFS TO FUTURES AND OPTIONS** *(continued)*

holder of the put will sell on the spot market for the higher-than-strike price). If, however, the market price at maturity is below the strike price, the holder of the put will exercise the option and you will lose the difference between the strike price and the market price.

The long futures locks you into buying the security at the contract price of $50. If the market price at maturity exceeds the contract price, you gain. If it is less than the contract price, you lose. The following table demonstrates that put–call parity works. Try to make up an example for a short futures.

Security Price at Maturity	Value of Call	Value of Put	Value of Long Futures
$70	$20	$0	$20
$60	$10	$0	$10
$50	$0	$0	$0
$40	$0	–$10	–$10
$20	$0	–$20	–$20

Options and futures markets—more generally, all derivatives markets—are inextricably linked through arbitrage.

price to change (and thus allow the holder to realize a profit), the more valuable the option. Thus, the longer the time to the expiration date, the greater the time value.

in-the-money denotes when an option has intrinsic value and, hence, can be exercised profitably

An option is said to be **in-the-money** when it has intrinsic value and, hence, can be exercised profitably. A call option is in-the-money if the underlying asset is selling at a price greater than the strike price. A put option is in-the-money when the asset is trading below the strike price. An option has no intrinsic value if the underlying asset's market price is equal to the strike price. An option is out-of-the-money if exercising it would result in a loss. This is the case with a call option when the underlying asset's price is lower than the strike price, and a put option when the strike price is lower than the asset's market price. Option holders need not take a loss on out-of-the-money options because they do not have an obligation to exercise them. If an option is not exercised, it becomes worthless. This result is the reason options are referred to as "wasting assets." A person who writes an option does so to earn the option premium, in the hope that the option will stay out-of-the money and expire worthless. Option holders, on the other hand, hope to make a gain when option prices move into-the-money. Financial institutions use financial options to hedge their interest rate risk.

Financial Swaps

swaps transactions in which two parties agree to exchange streams of payments over time

Financial **swaps** are transactions in which two parties, referred to as swap counterparties, agree to exchange streams of payments over time. Two basic types of swaps exist: currency swaps and interest rate swaps.

currency swap
the exchange of debt or assets denominated in one currency for debt or assets denominated in another currency

A **currency swap** is the exchange of debt or assets denominated in one currency for the debt or assets denominated in another currency. For example, suppose a Canadian firm has borrowed Canadian dollars in Edmonton and a U.S. firm has borrowed U.S. dollars in New York. Each borrower's debt has the same maturity date and is at fixed interest. A swap intermediary, usually a banker, arranges a currency swap whereby the two firms exchange the funds they have borrowed at the existing foreign exchange rate. As a result, the Canadian firm has U.S. dollars immediately available, and the U.S. firm has Canadian dollars. The Canadian firm pays the U.S. dollar interest obligation of the funds borrowed by the U.S. firm, while the U.S. firm makes the interest payments on the Canadian firm's debt. The swap agreement can also provide for the currencies to be swapped back at the maturity of each firm's debt, or for the firms to make each other's principal repayments. The swap intermediary may guarantee part or all payments to be received by the swap counterparties.

interest rate swap *two borrowers exchange interest rate payments for a specified length of time*

An **interest rate swap** is a financial transaction in which two borrowers exchange interest rate payments for a specified time on a notional principal amount of money. No actual principal amount is exchanged either initially or at maturity. Only interest payment streams with different characteristics are swapped. In a so-called coupon swap, fixed-rate interest payments are exchanged for floating-rate interest payments. The exchange of floating-rate payments with different characteristics is called a basis swap. Floating-rate interest is tied to (that is, it "floats with") a reference rate. Commonly used reference rates are LIBOR (London Interbank Offer Rate), the banks' prime lending rate, and treasury-bill and commercial paper rates. A basis swap, for instance, could call for the exchange of interest payments based on one-month LIBOR for payments based on 91-day treasury-bill rates.

Loan Securitization

loan securitization *involves the transformation of bank loans into marketable securities*

Loan securitization is a relatively recent innovation in financial markets involving the transformation of bank loans into marketable securities. Securities dealers and trust companies buy bank loans and repackage them into pools that are similar in terms of quality, interest rate, and maturity. These pools of loans are then used for the creation of pass-through and asset-backed securities.

A pass-through security gives direct ownership in the pool of loans from which it is created. Interest and loan repayments are "passed through" to the holders of the securities. The most popular pass-through securities have been the Cannie Maes. These securities, as explained earlier, pass through interest and repayments on pools of *National Housing Act*-insured mortgages. The Canada Mortgage and Housing Corporation guarantees the holders of these securities the timely payments of mortgage loan interest and principal.

An asset-backed security differs from a pass-through in that its holders do not assume ownership in a pool of loans, and the interest and repayment of loans are not directly passed through to security holders. The issuer of asset-backed securities uses the pool of loans as collateral, makes interest payments at the stated rate, and repays the principal at maturity.

In the United States, credit card and automobile loans, computer leases, and various types of trade credit have been securitized. To improve the marketability of the securities created, so-called **credit enhancement** techniques have been used. For example, banks have issued letters of credit committing them to cover possible shortfalls in stated payment flows to security holders. Another credit enhancement method has been overcollateralization, whereby the value of the pool of loans exceeds the principal amount of the securities issued.

The originators of loans used for securitization usually continue to service the loans by collecting all payments made by the borrowers. Fees received for servicing these loans have become an important new source of income for many financial intermediaries. Moreover, as we will learn later, securitization has made it easier for intermediaries to manage their risk exposure by getting rid of loans with undesirable characteristics.

credit enhancement used to improve the marketability of the securities created through loan securitization

Financial Market Efficiency

Financial markets maximize their contribution to the efficient allocation of resources in an economy when financial assets are priced to reflect their level of expected return and risk. How quickly security prices adjust to reflect the "proper" risk–return relationship is a function of market efficiency. Financial markets are said to be **efficient** when financial asset prices continually reflect all available information that bears on their evaluation.

Implicit in this **efficient market hypothesis** are two assumptions: that the market price of individual securities adjusts very quickly to new information because no market imperfections exist to impede the rapid diffusion of information; and that market participants react rapidly to any new information.

Stock market efficiency has been characterized in terms of randomness. It is assumed that information flows occur randomly, and that if security prices continually reflect new information as it becomes available, the path of stock prices will be a random walk.

The degree to which financial markets achieve efficiency depends in large part on the depth, breadth, and resiliency of the assets traded in them. Depth refers to the range of viable trading orders above and below the prevailing market price. If such buy-and-sell orders exist in large volume and stem from diverse trading groups, the market is said to have breadth. The market possesses resiliency when asset price changes trigger a wave of new trading orders. Broad, deep, and resilient markets are, necessarily, highly competitive ones in which transactions costs are small. These traits allow a ready response to any new information about assets traded in these markets.

Three variants of the efficient market hypothesis, which is the idea that no one can profit from forecasting security prices since these prices are formed using all available information, exist. (Hence, no one can use personal information and consistently profit from it.) **Weak-form efficiency** says that stock

efficient markets are efficient when financial asset prices continually reflect all available information that bears on their evaluation

efficient market hypothesis the idea that no one can profit from forecasting security prices, since these prices are formed using all available information

weak-form efficiency security prices should not be "predictable" using past price data

prices should not be "predictable" using past price data. For example, if we denote stock prices at time t by P_t, then the expected value (as based on an analysis of historical probabilities) of the stock price at time $t + 1$ should not be a function of stock prices for times before date t. That is, nothing in the history of stock prices can be used to forecast future stock prices. This implies that the best "guess" or expectation of future stock prices is the current stock price. Mathematically we denote this by

(6.1) $$E(P_{t+1}) = P_t$$

The actual stock price at time $t + 1$ will deviate from the expectation because of randomness, so if we define a random stock at time $t + 1$ to be ε_{t+1} then the actual stock price at time $t + 1$ can be expressed as

(6.2) $$P_{t+1} = E(P_{t+1}) + \varepsilon_{t+1}$$

If you look at this closely, you will recognize something we said earlier: Stock prices should be random over time. This relationship is easy to understand if you plug equation 6.1 into equation 6.2 and rearrange

(6.3) $$P_{t+1} - P_t = \varepsilon_{t+1}$$

The left side of the equation tells us how stock prices are changing over time. The right side of the equation is a random variable (resembling a car weaving down a road). This fact suggests there is no merit in trying to forecast stock prices. The implication bodes ill for investment professionals; they can't guess any better than you can.

A wide variety of empirical studies can be used to argue either in favour of or against this theory. Two other versions of the efficient markets hypothesis are somewhat more interesting. The first is the **semi-strong efficiency** version, which widens the information base on which predictions, or expectations, are formed. It suggests that economywide information (data on inflation and unemployment rates, for example) is of no use in forecasting stock prices. The **strong-form efficiency** version of the efficient markets hypothesis extends this information set to all public and private information. Both variants imply that market participants enjoy access to a wider information set than under the weak form of market efficiency, and it is assumed that none of this specialized information is of use in predicting future stock prices (for example, by persons operating the firm). Financial economists have difficulty believing these assertions because insider-trading legislation exists to preclude business operators and investment professionals from unduly benefiting from their specialized knowledge. Indeed, when trying to create an investment strategy, investment professionals look to the portfolios of the owners and operators of a firm to determine their expectations of future stock prices.

One interesting study on market efficiency, published by the Bank of Canada (Pugh, 1994), examined whether the when-issued market for Treasury bills provided unbiased estimates of actual Treasury bill yields. The results were at odds with market efficiency, in that yield changes tended to be followed by future yield changes in the same direction, and there were profits to be made

semi-strong efficiency
economywide information is of no use in forecasting stock prices

strong-form efficiency
neither public nor private information can be used to forecast stock prices

from hedging. In addition, the yields on the when-issued Treasury bills consistently underpredicted the actual yields.

Financial asset prices also contain information that may be of use to the central bank in its conduct of monetary policy. Indeed, a recent conference at the Bank of Canada examined this issue. A number of authors reported that information on yield curves as well as the prices of financial derivatives provided useful estimates of market expectations. Others tested the expectations theory of the term structure of interest rates to determine whether expected future short-term interest rates were consistent with the central bank's desired path for short-term interest rates. The results suggested the presence of time-varying risk premia that rise with the term to maturity (the pure expectations theory was rejected by the data). These premia need to be taken into account when the authorities respond to unanticipated shocks to the financial system. The papers presented at the conference demonstrated that financial asset prices contain information of critical importance to the design and implementation of monetary policy. We will return to some of the reasons these results may have been expected, when we examine the tools of monetary policy in a later chapter.

www.

KEY TERMS

amortized
auction market
Bank Rate
bankers' acceptances
basis
bond
bought deal
call loans
call option
Canadian Payments Associations (CPA)
capital markets
closed mortgages
commercial paper
common stock
conventional mortgages
convertible bonds
cost of carry
credit enhancement
currency swap
debentures
debt
deposit certificates
derivative
direct securities
efficient
efficient market hypothesis
electronic order books
finance paper
financial option

forward contract
futures markets
futures contract
government securities distributors
guaranteed trust and investment certificates (GICs)
hedging
indirect securities
initial public offering (IPO)
instalment debt contracts
interbank deposits
interest rate swap
in-the-money
junk bonds
loan securitization
long position
money markets
mortgage
NHA mortgages
open mortgages
open outcry
option premium
overnight financing rate
over-the-counter (OTC) market
preferred stock
primary dealers
primary markets
private placements
Purchase and Resale Agreements (PRAs)

put option
real return bonds
regulated markets
repurchase agreements (repos)
reverse mortgages
reverse repo
Sale and Repurchase Agreements (SRAs)
secondary markets
semi-strong efficiency
short position
short sale
small-cap stocks
Special PRAs
Special SRAs
spot markets
stock indexes
stock split
strike price
stripped zero-coupon bonds
strong-form efficiency
swapped deposits
swaps
term notes
Treasury bills
warrants
weak-form efficiency
when-issued Treasury bill

REVIEW QUESTIONS

1. What is the money market? Describe and compare the various financial instruments used in this market.
2. Describe the following bond provisions: callable, extendable, retractable, convertible, and sinking fund.
3. Differentiate between common and preferred stock.
4. What is the difference between an NHA mortgage and a conventional residential mortgage?
5. What is the difference between a financial future and an option?
6. How does the cost of carry explain the pricing of financial futures?
7. When are call and put options in-the-money?
8. Why are options said to be a "wasting asset"?
9. Describe an interest rate swap and a currency swap.
10. Explain loan securitization and swaps.
11. Graphically describe the payoff to a portfolio composed of (a) a put option with a strike price of $75, and (b) a call option on the same security with the same maturity date with a strike price of $65.
12. Put–call parity, through arbitrage, links options markets to futures markets. Demonstrate the link using an example. Include a graph in your response.
13. Why do people use investment dealers if markets are efficient?

SELECTED READINGS

Bank of Canada. Information in Financial Asset Prices: Proceedings of a conference held by the Bank of Canada, Ottawa, May 1998.

Gravelle, Toni. "Markets for Government of Canada Securities in the 1990s: Liquidity and Cross-Country Comparisons." *Bank of Canada Review* (Autumn 1999): Ottawa, pp. 9–18.

Harvey, Nancy. "Recent Initiatives in the Canadian Market for Government of Canada Securities." *Bank of Canada Review* (Summer 1999), Ottawa, pp. 27–36.

Hirschmann, Thomas. "Discount Brokerages Put to the Stopwatch Test." *Financial Post*, February 19, 2000, pp. C1, C5.

Kolb, Robert W. *Understanding Futures Markets*, 3rd ed. Miami, Fl.: Kolb Publishing Company, 1991.

———. *Financial Derivatives*, 2nd ed. Cambridge, Mass.: Blackwell Business, 1996.

Marr, Garry. "Canadians Take On Extra $2B in Margin Debt." *Financial Post*, March 17, 2000, pp. C1 and C8.

Miville, Martin, and Andre Bernier. "The Corporate Bond Market in Canada." *Bank of Canada Review* (Autumn 1999): Ottawa, pp. 3–8.

O'Connor, S. "The Development of Financial Derivatives Markets: The Canadian Evidence." *Bank of Canada Technical Report* 62, June 1993.

Powers, Mark, and David Vogel. *Inside the Financial Futures Markets*, 2nd ed. New York: Wiley, 1984.

Pugh, G. "Tests of Market Efficiency in the One-Week When-Issued Market for Government of Canada Treasury Bills." *Bank of Canada Technical Report* 65, 1994.

Smith, Lawrence. *The Postwar Canadian Housing and Residential Mortgage Markets and the Role of Government.* Toronto: University of Toronto Press, 1974.

Toronto Stock Exchange. TSE Fact Book, 1997. Toronto: Toronto Stock Exchange, Annual.

CHAPTER SEVEN

EXCHANGE RATES AND INTERNATIONAL PAYMENTS TRANSACTIONS

After reading this chapter you should be able to

1. Differentiate between the nominal exchange rate, the effective exchange rate, and the real exchange rate
2. Show how spatial and cross-rate arbitrage can be used to profit from price disparities across markets
3. Explain how covered and uncovered interest rate arbitrage link interest rates and exchange rates across countries
4. Show how expected changes in exchange rates affect interest rate differentials
5. Argue why exchange markets are expected to be efficient
6. Show how swaps and futures can be used to hedge exchange rate risk
7. Explain how call and put options can be combined to manage exchange rate risk

So far we have been concerned primarily with a closed economy—one without foreign trade or payments. Canada, however, is one of the most open economies in the world. More than 25 percent of all goods and services produced in Canada are sold to nonresidents, while a similar proportion of all goods and services consumed in Canada are produced by nonresidents. Our trade with other countries is of great benefit not only to us, but also to our trading partners. Through specialization, international trade leads to the more efficient allocation of resources in the same way as internal trade does. In Chapter 2 we pointed out that specialization is facilitated by the presence of a commonly acceptable unit of account and medium of exchange. The absence of an international monetary unit is probably the most important reason international specialization is less intensive than that found within most countries, especially industrialized nations. Without a common unit of account, international trade is more cumbersome than internal trade and is less willingly undertaken. The degree of possible international specialization, therefore, is limited.

The lack of a common international monetary unit introduces a complication into trade between countries. Whereas in internal trade transactions are finalized by the exchange of goods for the country's monetary unit, in international trade an additional exchange is required—the money of one country must be exchanged for that of another country. Moreover, the seller of a good in Canada must know not only the price of the good in terms of Canadian dollars, but also the price of the foreign currency in terms of Canadian dollars. One prime concern of any nation is the rate at which a unit of a foreign currency can be exchanged for units of its domestic currency. This is known as the exchange rate. In this chapter we dive headlong into an analysis of exchange rates, how they are determined, and how derivatives can be used to manage exchange rate risk. For some background on the causes of international indebtedness (the types of transactions that result in payments between residents of different countries), see the appendix to this chapter, where we discuss the balance of payments.

The Market for Foreign Exchange

Unlike stock markets, foreign exchange markets are not housed in separate physical locations. When the London money market was at its zenith before the First World War, English merchants and bankers met twice a week on the floor of the Royal Exchange in the heart of London to buy and sell bills of exchange, which were commonly used to make payments denominated in foreign currencies. At the Royal Exchange after the war, however, trading of foreign bills of exchange was replaced by the interbank foreign exchange market, where foreign payments are made between banks by the transfer of deposits denominated in foreign currencies.

The major banks throughout the world maintain foreign currency trading departments that are in almost constant contact with one another, with foreign exchange brokers, and with central banks, using telephone, cable, and electronic information channels. The most important communications network for international financial transactions is the Society for World Wide Interbank Financial Telecommunication (SWIFT), a Belgian nonprofit cooperative. In 1999, SWIFT carried more than one billion messages with an average daily value of payments estimated at more than five trillion U.S. dollars.

The world foreign exchange market is a 24-hour market, since as one foreign exchange centre closes down for the day, others, in other time zones, are still trading. Box 7–1 gives you an idea of the dimensions of the global market.

From 1950 to 1986, the Canadian Bankers Association hired its own foreign exchange brokers to facilitate foreign exchange trading among its members. Today, most foreign exchange transactions between financial institutions in Canada are intermediated by a small group of independent foreign exchange brokerage firms.

Foreign Exchange Markets

Five types of foreign exchange markets exist: spot, forward, swap, futures, and options. In the spot market, currencies are bought and sold for immediate

BOX 7–1 TIME IS MONEY: TRADING IN CURRENCIES

Trading in exchange rates takes place during every second of every day, as you can see from the following map. That's why many currency traders have home offices equipped with the latest technology—and perhaps one reason why they have trouble sleeping!

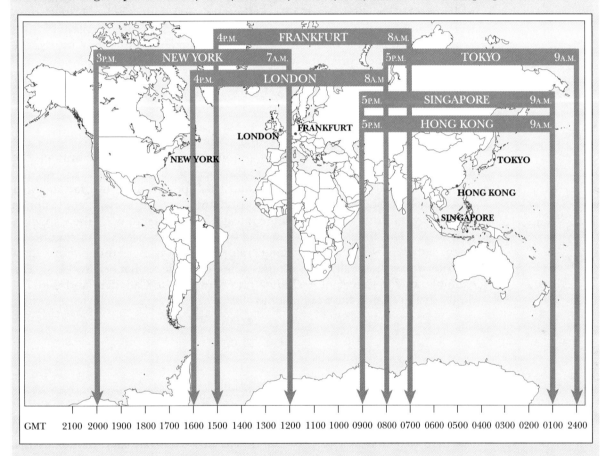

delivery. When a transaction takes place between parties in the same time zone, delivery usually takes place on the same day; when more than one time zone is crossed, delivery occurs within two days. In forward markets currencies are sold at exchange rates negotiated now, but delivery takes place at some specified future date. Unlike the spot, forward, and swap currency markets, which are over-the-counter markets, currency futures and options markets are centred in futures exchanges, sometimes associated with stock exchanges. These exchanges establish their own rules, which standardize the minimum amounts of each contract and the future delivery dates. In swap markets, the seller of a foreign currency simultaneously agrees to repurchase it at some date in the future.

The Exchange Rate

The exchange rate is the relative price of two national monies or currencies. The exchange rate expresses the number of units of one nation's currency that can be exchanged for a unit of another nation's currency. This relative price can be expressed in two ways, and therefore you must be careful to indicate which method is being used. The method we shall follow, unless noted otherwise, is to define the exchange rate as the number of domestic currency units required to purchase one unit of a foreign currency. (In other words, the domestic currency price of one foreign currency unit.) We identify the exchange rate as *E*. For example, it can be expressed as the Canadian dollar price of one U.S. dollar (Can. \$/U.S. \$), as the Canadian dollar price of a British pound (Can. \$/£), or as Canadian dollars per Deutschemark (Can. \$/DM).

The other method for expressing a foreign exchange rate shows the number of foreign currency units required to purchase one unit of the domestic currency. For example, it can be the U.S. dollar price of one Canadian dollar (U.S. \$/Can. \$) or the British pound price of the Canadian dollar (£/Can. \$). When defining the exchange rate in this way, confusion is avoided by referring to the exchange rate as the external value of the Canadian dollar (*S*). The financial press in Canada commonly uses this terminology. Note that expressing the exchange rate in this way is nothing more than showing it as the reciprocal of the other definition; that is, $S = 1/E$. For example, the average spot exchange rate between the Canadian and the U.S. dollar in 1999 could have been shown as:

www.

$$E = \frac{\text{Can. \$1.49}}{\text{U.S. \$1.00}} = 1.49$$

or

$$S = \frac{\text{U.S. \$1.00}}{\text{Can. \$1.49}} = 0.67$$

Figure 7–1 plots the value of the Canadian dollar against the U.S. dollar for the past 40 years. You can see there has been substantial variation in the exchange rate. One of our objectives is to try to explain this variation.

bid *the price at which someone is willing to buy*

asked *the price at which someone is willing to sell*

bid–asked spread *the difference between the price at which someone is willing to buy and the price at which someone is willing to sell*

The major financial institutions and foreign exchange brokerage firms that make markets in foreign currencies regularly quote **bid** or buying prices, and **asked** (offered) or selling prices. However, the exchange rates reported in the financial pages of national newspapers are not the ones individuals pay when purchasing foreign currencies from a financial institution or foreign exchange broker. The published rates are those that apply on transactions of \$1 million or more in the interbank or wholesale market.

The market for currency notes and travellers cheques (the retail market) is quite separate from the interbank market. Since the amounts of most personal transactions are relatively small, the **bid–asked spread** in retail markets is usually quite large to compensate for the higher transactions costs involved in handling the smaller currency exchanges.

As is shown in Table 7.1, prices on forward exchange agreements for the major currencies—U.S. dollar, British pound, German mark, and Japanese

FIGURE 7–1 **THE VALUE OF THE CANADIAN DOLLAR IN U.S. DOLLARS**

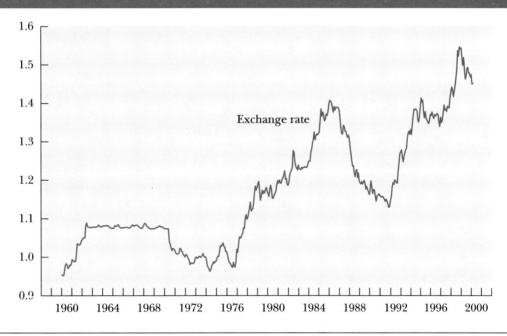

SOURCE: Statistics Canada, CANSIM Database, Series B3400, March 22, 2000.

forward premium
when a currency's forward value is greater than its spot value

forward discount
when a currency's forward value is less than its spot value

swap rate *the difference between the sale price of a currency and its repurchase price*

C-6 index *the value of the Canadian dollar relative to the currencies of the G-10 nations as well as those in the European Monetary Union*

yen—are reported regularly in the financial press for maturities of up to 12 months. For U.S. dollars, forward prices are quoted for up to 10 years.

The percentage difference between a currency's forward value and its spot value is called the **forward premium** if positive, and the **forward discount** if negative. For any two currencies, a forward premium (discount) on one currency is equivalent to a forward discount (premium) on the other. Hence, when reference is made to a forward premium or discount it is important to specify the currency to which it applies.

In a swap transaction, the **swap rate** is the difference between the sale price of a currency and its repurchase price. It is estimated that of the total daily foreign exchange transactions by the Canadian chartered banks and other financial institutions, 41 percent were spot, 5 percent were forward, and 54 percent were swaps.

The foreign exchange rate may also be expressed in terms of a group of currencies rather than bilaterally for just two countries. For example, the Bank of Canada calculates and reports a trade-weighted exchange rate index of the Canadian dollar, illustrated in Figure 7–2. The Canadian dollar **C-6 index** is constructed against six major industrial countries as well as those members of the European Monetary Union.[1] The weight assigned to each country's cur-

---

1. The G-10 countries include Belgium, Canada, France, Germany, Italy, Japan, the Netherlands, Sweden, Switzerland, the United Kingdom, and the United States. The members of the European Monetary Union are Austria, Belgium, Finland, France, Germany, Ireland, Italy, Luxembourg, the Netherlands, Portugal, and Spain.

TABLE 7.1   FOREIGN EXCHANGE

Cross rates

	Canadian dollar	U.S. dollar	British pound	German mark	Japanese yen	Swiss franc	French franc	Dutch Euro	Italian lira
Canada dollar	–	1.4773	2.2199	0.6985	0.013480	0.8824	0.2083	1.3661	0.000706
U.S. dollar	0.6769	–	1.5027	0.4728	0.009125	0.5973	0.1410	0.9247	0.000478
British pound	0.4505	0.6655	–	0.3146	0.006072	0.3975	0.0938	0.6154	0.000318
German mark	1.4317	2.1150	3.1782	–	0.019299	1.2633	0.2982	1.9558	0.001010
Japanese yen	74.18	109.59	164.68	51.82	–	65.46	15.45	101.34	0.052339
Swiss franc	1.1333	1.6742	2.5158	0.7916	0.015277	–	0.2360	1.5482	0.000800
French franc	4.8017	7.0935	10.6592	3.3539	0.064727	4.2370	–	6.5596	0.003388
Euro	0.7320	1.0814	1.6250	0.5113	0.009868	0.6459	0.1524	–	0.000516
Italian lira	1417.37	2093.88	3146.42	989.9996	19.106167	1250.6885	295.1826	1936.2710	–

Country	Cdn. E Currency	U.S. $ per unit	per unit	Country	Cdn. E Currency	U.S. $ per unit	per unit
Algeria	dinar	49.08	72.51	Burundi	franc	476.44	703.85
Andorra	French franc	4.8017	7.0935	Cameroon	CFA franc	480.17	709.35
Span.	peseta	121.80	179.93	Canary Islands	peseta	121.80	179.93
Angola	kwanza	6.4587	9.5415	Cape Verde Is	escudo	79.56	117.54
Antigua	E. Carib	1.8277	2.7000	Cayman Islands	dollar	0.5641	0.8333
Argentina	peso	0.6765	0.9994	Central Afr. Rep	CFA franc	480.17	709.35
Aruba	florin	1.2117	1.7900	Chad	CFA franc	480.17	709.35
Australia	dollar	1.1516	1.7013	Chile	peso	377.28	557.35
Austria	schilling	10.0727	14.8804	China	renminbi	5.6044	8.2794
Azores	escudo	146.76	216.80	Colombia	peso	1469.57	2171.00
Bahamas	dollar	0.6769	1.0000	Comoros	franc	360.13	532.01
Bahrain	dinar	0.2552	0.3770	Congo	CFA franc	480.17	709.35
Balearic Islands	peseta	121.80	179.93	Congo (DemRep)	franc	15.1120	22.3250
Bangladesh	taka	34.42	50.85	Costa Rica	colon	207.34	306.30
Barbados	dollar	1.3538	2.0000	Croatia	kuna	5.5551	8.2066
Belgium	franc	29.5293	43.6236	Cuba	peso	14.2151	21.0000
Belize	dollar	1.3538	2.0000	Cyprus	pound	0.4208	0.6216
Benin	CFA franc	480.17	709.35	Czech Rep	koruna	26.0042	38.4160
Bermuda	dollar	0.6769	1.0000	Denmark	krone	5.4573	8.0621
Bhutan	rupee	30.33	44.81	Djibouti	franc	105.87	156.40
Bolivia	boliviano	4.1968	6.2000	Dominica	E. Carib. $	1.8277	2.7000
Botswana	pula	3.5164	5.1948	Dominican Rep	peso	10.6613	15.7500
Brazil	real	1.2076	1.7840	Ecuador	sucre	16855.07	24900.00
Brunei	dollar	1.1738	1.7340	Egypt	pound	2.3523	3.4750
Bulgaria	lev	1.4243	2.1041	El Salvador	colon	5.8756	8.6800
Burkina Faso	CFA franc	480.17	709.35	Guinea	CFA franc	480.17	709.35
Burma	kyat	4.2318	6.2517	Estonia	kroon	11.45	16.91

Country	Cdn. E Currency	U.S. $ per unit	per unit	Country	Cdn. E Currency	U.S. $ per unit	per unit
Ethiopia	birr	5.4627	8.0700	Liechtenstein	Swiss franc	1.1333	1.6742
Faeroe Islands	krone	5.4573	8.0621	Luxembourg	franc	29.53	43.62
Falkland Is	pound	0.4505	0.6655	Macao	pataca	5.4090	7.9907
Fiji	dollar	1.4236	2.1030	Madagascar	franc	4321.4	6384.0
Finland	markka	4.3523	6.4297	Madeira	escudo	146.76	216.80
French Guiana	franc	4.8017	7.0935	Malawi	kwacha	38.25	56.50
French Pacific Is	CFP franc	87.30	128.97	Malaysia	ringgit	2.5721	3.7998
Gabon	CFA franc	480.17	709.35	Maldive Islands	rufiyaa	7.97	11.77
Gambia	dalasi	8.5629	12.6500	Mali	CFA franc	480.17	709.35
Ghana	cedi	4044.54	5975.00	Malta	lira	0.2976	0.4396
Gibraltar	pound	0.4505	0.6655	Martinique	French franc	4.8017	7.0935
Greece	drachma	246.84	364.66	Mauritania	ouguiya	162.93	240.69
Greenland	krone	5.4573	8.0621	Mauritius	rupee	17.13	25.30
Grenada	E. Carib $	1.8277	2.7000	Mexico	peso	6.3372	9.3620
Guadeloupe	franc	4.8017	7.0935	Monaco	French franc	4.8017	7.0935
Guam	U.S. dollar	0.6769	1.0000	Mongolia	togrog	699.05	1032.70
Guatemala	quetzal	5.2691	7.7840	Montserrat	E. Carib. $	1.8277	2.7000
Guinea Bissau	CFA franc	480.2	709.4	Morocco	dirham	7.1901	10.6220
Guinea	franc	1096.60	1620.00	Mozambique	metica	10302.6	15220.0
Guyana	dollar	122.18	180.50	Namibia	dollar	4.7130	6.9625
Haiti	gourde	13.88	20.50	Nauru	Australian $	1.1516	1.7013
Honduras	lempira	10.0657	14.8700	Nepal	rupee	47.89	70.75
Hong Kong	dollar	5.2784	7.7978	Netherlands	guilder	1.6131	2.3831
Hungary	forint	190.53	281.47	Neth. Antilles	guilder	1.1981	1.7700
Iceland	krona	53.16	78.53	New Zealand	dollar	1.4783	2.1839
India	rupee	30.33	44.81	Nicaragua	cordoba	8.6025	12.7085
Indonesia	rupiah	6021.1	8895.0	Niger	CFA franc	480.17	709.35
Iran	rial	1174.4	1735.0	Nigeria	naira	71.41	105.50
Iraq	dinar	0.2105	0.3109	Norway	krone	5.9893	8.8480
Ireland	punt	0.5765	0.8516	Oman	sul rial	0.2606	0.3850
Israel	new shekel	2.7625	4.0810	Pakistan	rupee	36.13	53.37
Ivory Coast	CFA franc	480.17	709.35	Panama	balboa	0.6769	1.0000
Jamaica	dollar	28.43	42.00	Papua New G	kina	1.7814	2.6316
Jordan	dinar	0.4793	0.7080	Paraguay	guarani	2371.2	3503.0
Kenya	shilling	50.09	74.00	Peru	new sol	2.3512	3.4735
Kiribati	Australian $	1.1516	1.7013	Philippines	peso	30.36	44.85
Korea (North)	won	1.4892	2.2000	Pitcairn Island	N.Z. dollar	1.4783	2.1839
Korea (South)	won	755.77	1116.50	Poland	zloty	2.9378	4.3400
Kuwait	dinar	0.2083	0.3077	Portugal	escudo	146.76	216.80
Laos	kip	5144.52	7600.00	Puerto Rico	U.S. dollar	0.6769	1.0000
Lebanon	pound	1023.5	1512.0	Qatar	riyal	2.4631	3.6388
Lesotho	loti	4.7130	6.9625	Reunion, Ile de la	French franc	4.8017	7.0935
Liberia	dollar	0.6769	1.0000	Romania	leu	14800.6	21865.0
Libya	dinar	0.3399	0.5022	Russia	ruble	18.8249	27.8100

Country	Cdn. E Currency	U.S. $ per unit	per unit	Country	Cdn. E Currency	U.S. $ per unit	per unit
Rwanda	franc	243.04	359.05	Syria	pound	31.14	46.00
St. Christopher	E. Carib. $	1.8277	2.7000	Taiwan	dollar	20.96	30.97
St. Helena	pound	0.4505	0.6655	Tanzania	shilling	538.14	795.00
St. Lucia	E. Carib. $	1.8277	2.7000	Thailand	baht	28.00	41.37
St. Pierre, Miq	French franc	4.8017	7.0935	Togo	CFA franc	480.17	709.35
St. Vincent	E. Carib. $	1.8277	2.7000	Tonga	pa'ange	1.1534	1.7039
Samoa (West.)	tala	2.1703	3.2062	Trinidad, Tobago	dollar	4.2168	6.2295
Samoa (Amer.)	U.S. dollar	0.6769	1.0000	Tunisia	dinar	0.9273	1.3699
San Marino	Ital. lira	1417.4	2093.9	Turkey	lira	429980.4	635210.0
Sao Tome	dobra	1617.82	2390.00	Turks and Caicos	U.S. dollar	0.6769	1.0000
Saudi Arabia	riyal	2.5388	3.7506	Tuvalu	Australian $	1.1516	1.7013
Senegal	CFA franc	480.17	709.35	Uganda	shilling 1st	1086.4	1605.0
Seychelles	rupee	3.8245	5.6500	Ukraine	Hryvnia	3.6816	5.4388
Sierra Leone	leone	1187.98	1755.00	United Arab Em	dirham	2.4860	3.6726
Singapore	dollar	1.1738	1.7340	Uruguay	peso	8.2651	12.2100
Slovakia	koruna	31.01	45.82	Vanuatu	vatu	92.91	137.26
Slovenia	tolar	152.33	225.03	Vatican	lira	1417.4	2093.9
Solomon Is	dollar	3.4101	5.0378	Venezuela	bolivar	465.21	687.25
Somalia	shilling	1773.5	2620.0	Vietnam	dong	9537.7	14090.0
South Africa	rand	4.7130	6.9625	Virgin Is. (Brit.)	U.S. dollar	0.6769	1.0000
Spain	peseta	121.80	179.93	Virgin Is. (U.S.)	U.S. dollar	0.6769	1.0000
Sri Lanka	rupee	53.00	78.30	Yemen North	rial	105.39	155.70
Sudan	dinar	173.8306	256.8000	Zambia	kwacha	2210.1	3265.0
Suriname	guilder	547.96	809.50	Zimbabwe	dollar	25.9257	38.3000
Swaziland	lilangeni	4.7130	6.9625	Spec Drawing Right	SDR	0.5143	0.7597
Sweden	krona	6.1937	9.1499				

CANADIAN DOLLAR FORWARDS

$ to buy one	1 month	2 months	3 months	6 months	1 year
U.S dollar	1.4762	1.4751	1.4740	1.4704	1.4639
British pound	2.2194	2.2188	2.2182	2.2167	2.2132
German mark	0.6992	0.7000	0.7005	0.7021	0.7048
Japanese yen	0.013545	0.013609	0.013674	0.013873	0.014276
Swiss franc	0.8845	0.8860	0.8877	0.8921	0.9009
French franc	0.2085	0.2087	0.2089	0.2093	0.2101
Euro	1.3676	1.3691	1.3701	1.3731	1.3784
Italian lira	0.000706	0.000707	0.000708	0.000709	0.000712

FIGURE 7–2   **THE C-6 INDEX**

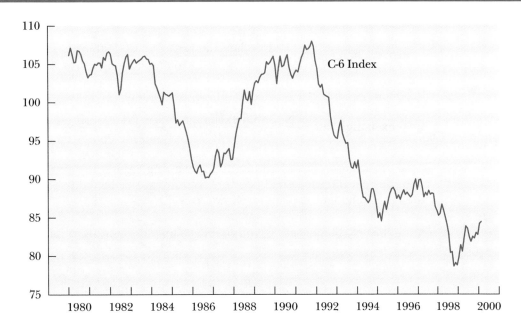

SOURCE: Statistics Canada, CANSIM Database, Series B3431, March 22, 2000.

www.

***effective
exchange rate*** *a
weighted-average
exchange rate
based on mer-
chandise trade*

rency reflects its share of merchandise trade with Canada. A weighted-average exchange rate based on merchandise trade is commonly referred to as an **effective exchange rate**. The International Monetary Fund calculates the effective exchange rate for the Canadian dollar as well as for many other currencies.

Nominal and Real Exchange Rates

***nominal
exchange rate***
*the value of one
currency in terms
of another*

***real exchange
rate*** *the relative
price of the goods
and services of
two countries*

A distinction is also made between nominal and real exchange rates. The exchange rate quoted in foreign exchange markets, which we have defined as the relative price of the currencies of two countries, is the **nominal exchange rate**. In contrast, the **real exchange rate** is the relative price of the goods and services of two countries. It is the rate of exchange at which the goods and services of one country are exchanged for those of another country. The real exchange rate is also known as the terms of trade—the number of units of a foreign good that can be obtained for one unit of the domestic good.

Suppose the price of a Canadian dollar is 120 Japanese yen. Let us further suppose that a Canadian car costs $10 000 and that the equivalent Japanese car costs 1.2 million yen. To compare the prices of these two cars, we convert them into a common currency. Since we know the Canadian dollar is worth 120 yen, the Canadian car costs 1.2 million yen (120 ¥/$ × $10 000). Comparing the yen prices of the two cars, we discover that the Canadian car costs the same as the Japanese car; at current prices, we can trade one Canadian car for one Japanese car, which is the real exchange rate. The real exchange rate is calculated as follows:

$$\text{Real exchange rate} = \frac{(1 \text{ dollar}/120 \text{ yen}) \times (1\ 200\ 000 \text{ yen}/\text{Japanese car})}{\$10\ 000/\text{Canadian car}}$$

More generally, this calculation can be written:

$$\text{Real exchange rate} = \frac{\text{Nominal exchange rate} \times \text{Price of foreign good}}{\text{Price of domestic good}}$$

Furthermore, if we include not only a single good in our calculation, but also the general price of all goods of a country as reflected by their price level, the real exchange rate can be shown as

Real exchange rate = Nominal exchange rate × ratio of price levels

$$\varepsilon = E \times \left(\frac{P^*}{P} \right)$$

where ε is the real exchange rate, E is the nominal exchange rate (domestic currency price of foreign currency), P is the domestic price level, and P^* is the foreign price level. When the real exchange rate is above 1, foreign goods are expensive relative to domestic goods. When the real exchange rate is below 1, domestic goods are expensive relative to foreign goods.

Exchange Rate Arbitrage

Arbitrage is the simultaneous purchase and resale, or lending and borrowing, of an asset (in this case, foreign currency) in two different markets, or two segments of the same market, to profit from a price disparity.

bilateral arbitrage arbitrage between two markets

SPATIAL ARBITRAGE   Spatial arbitrage, also known as two-point or **bilateral arbitrage**, integrates two financial centres into a single market for exchanging two different national currencies. For example, suppose the Swiss franc trades for Can. $0.25 in Montreal and for Can. $0.24937 in Zurich. An exchange arbitrager can make a quick profit without assuming any risk by purchasing Swiss francs with Canadian dollars in Zurich and simultaneously selling the Swiss francs in Montreal for Canadian dollars. Although only one-sixteenth of a cent gross profit is realized on each franc trade, by employing Can. $1 million, within a few seconds the arbitrager will realize a gross profit of Can. $2526.[2] The purchase of and resulting increase in demand for francs will increase their Canadian dollar price in Zurich, while their simultaneous sale and resulting increase in supply will depress their dollar price in Montreal. These two oppo-

---

2. How did we get this? In Zurich, $1 million would buy 4 010 105.5 Swiss francs. Sold in Montreal, this would bring $1 002 526.40. The profit is about $2526.

site price movements will continue until all potential arbitrage profits have been exploited and the only difference in the franc/dollar exchange rate between Montreal and Zurich is the arbitrager's transactions cost.

CROSS RATE ARBITRAGE   Cross-rate arbitrage links all financial centres and foreign exchange markets. It involves the simultaneous trading of more than two currencies. Since three currencies are usually traded, it is also known as **triangular arbitrage**. Suppose that the Canadian dollar price of sterling (a British pound) is Can. $2.00 and the Canadian dollar price of Deutschemark is Can. $0.40. This situation implies a third rate, called a cross rate, between the mark and the pound, that is, 5 DM/£. If the cross rate is consistent, cross-rate equality exists and no arbitrage profits can be made. In the example, cross-rate equality exists since (Can. $2.00/£)/(Can. $0.40/DM) = (5 DM/£). Now suppose that dollar/sterling rate increases to Can. $2.40/£. This rate is now inconsistent with the other two rates and a profit can be made by simultaneously buying and selling all three currencies. For example, given (Can. $0.40/DM), the arbitrager can buy 5 DM with Can. $2.00. With a 5 DM/£ rate, the arbitrager can use these 5 marks to buy £1. This £1 can now be sold at its higher price for Can. $2.40. Hence, the arbitrager has made a profit of 40 cents. However, the potential for such profit will be short lived because arbitrage activity quickly re-establishes consistent rates between the three currencies as arbitragers exploit this profit opportunity. Arbitrage transactions will drive up the dollar price of the mark and the mark price of the pound while driving down the Canadian dollar price of the pound. The mark price of dollars and the pound price of marks decline, while the pound price of dollars increases. A new consistent equilibrium, for example, can emerge with (Can. $2.25/£)/(Can. $0.35/DM) = 6.43 DM/£.

triangular arbitrage
arbitrage between three markets for three assets

Interest Rate Arbitrage

interest arbitrage
arbitrage based on deviations between international interest rate differentials and expected changes in spot exchange rates

uncovered interest arbitrage *arbitrage positions in which futures or forward markets have not been used to set a price for delivery of an asset in the future*

covered interest arbitrage *arbitrage position in which markets have been used to set a price for delivery of an asset in the future*

Interest arbitrage is somewhat different from spatial and cross-currency arbitrage, but the basic motive of finding and exploiting profitable opportunities still applies. Interest arbitragers seek to profit from deviations between international interest rate differentials and expected changes in spot exchange rates, or the interest equivalent of the spread between forward and spot exchange rates. The decision to hold funds either in domestic or foreign currency assets depends on interest differentials between countries and on whether the person is willing to bear risk. If you are a risk taker, you can engage in **uncovered interest arbitrage** and base the decision about the currency denomination of the assets to be held on international interest rate differentials and your expectations about future spot exchange rates. On the other hand, if you do not want to take risk, you can engage in **covered interest arbitrage**, where the international interest rate differentials and the differential between the spot and forward exchange rates are important determinants of the currency denomination of the assets to be held.

Uncovered Interest Arbitrage

The incentive to hold your funds in foreign-denominated assets rather than in domestic currency assets is based on the interest rate differential between domestic and foreign assets and your expectations about changes in the spot exchange rate.

Suppose that you can hold $1 for a year in a Canadian money market asset that pays an annual rate of interest of i. The amount accumulated at the end of the year in domestic currency will be $1 + i$ (the return of capital plus the accrued interest). Alternatively, you can convert your dollar into a foreign currency at its spot exchange rate (E_t) in terms of the Canadian dollar at time t, $1/E_t$, for investment at a rate of i^* in a foreign currency asset. At the end of the year, your accumulated foreign currency funds will be $(1/E_t)(1 + i^*)$. At that time, you convert the accumulated foreign currency funds into dollars at what you expect will be the spot dollar price of the foreign currency, E^e_{t+1}. Hence, by investing in foreign currency assets you expect to retrieve an amount, $(E^e_{t+1}/E_t)(1 + i^*)$, denominated in Canadian dollars at the end of the year.

You will have an incentive to hold foreign rather than domestic (dollar) denominated assets when

$$(7.1) \qquad (E^e_{t+1}/E_t)(1 + i^*) > 1 + i$$

On the other hand, you will want to hold assets denominated in the domestic currency when

$$(7.2) \qquad (1 + i) > (E^e_{t+1}/E_t)(1 + i^*)$$

However, you will be indifferent as to the currency denomination of the assets held when

$$(7.3) \qquad (1 + i) = (E^e_{t+1}/E_t)(1 + i^*)$$

uncovered interest parity a relationship linking interest rates, exchange rates, and expected changes in exchange rates across nations

This equilibrium condition is known as **uncovered interest parity**. Equation 7.3 can be rewritten as

$$(7.4) \qquad E^e_{t+1}/E_t = (1 + i)/(1 + i^*)$$

which can be expressed as

$$(7.5) \qquad \frac{E^e_{t+1} - E_t}{E_t} = \frac{i - i^*}{1 + i^*}$$

which can be approximated as

$$(7.6) \qquad i - i^* = (E^e_{t+1} - E_t)/E_t$$

In this form, uncovered interest parity tells us that in equilibrium, the differential between domestic and foreign interest rates is equal to the expected change in the spot exchange rate. If the interest rate differential is in favour of domestic-currency-denominated assets, $(i - i^*) > 0$, but if this differential is less than the expected percentage increase in the spot exchange rate, arbitragers will switch to foreign-currency-denominated assets. This switch will cause $(E^e_{t+1} - E_t)/E_t$ to rise until uncovered interest parity is restored. A numerical example of an uncovered interest arbitrage transaction is shown in Box 7–2.

Covered Interest Arbitrage

As we have seen with uncovered interest arbitrage, an interest arbitrager assumes risk because when holding foreign-currency-denominated assets, the arbitrager does not know the future spot exchange rate at which these assets can be converted back into domestic currency. With covered interest arbitrage, this risk is removed (covered) with a forward exchange transaction.

As in the previous interest arbitrage examples, if you hold $1 in a Canadian-dollar-denominated asset, you can accumulate $1 + i$ dollars by the end of the year. Alternatively, you can convert your dollar into foreign currency at the current spot exchange rate and invest the proceeds in foreign-currency-denominated assets at an interest rate i^*. Remember, Can. $1 buys $1/E_t$ foreign currency assets. By the end of the year these assets will return an amount of for-

---

BOX 7–2   BACKGROUNDER

Uncovered Interest Arbitrage

You have Can. $1000 to invest. The interest rate in Canada is $i = 0.10$, and in the United States $i \doteq 0.05$. You expect that the Canadian dollar price of the U.S. dollar will rise by the end of the year from $E =$ Can. $1.15 to Can. $1.25.

If you invest your funds in Canada you will accumulate by the end of the year.

$$\$1000 \ (1 + 0.10) = \text{Can. } \$1100$$

If you convert your Can. $1000 into U.S. dollars at the current spot foreign exchange rate, you will have $[(1/1.15)(\text{Can. } \$1000]$, or U.S. $869.57, for investment in the United States. At the end of the year you will have accumulated

$$\text{U.S. } \$869.57(1 + 0.05) = \text{U.S. } \$913.05$$

However, since you expect that by the end of the year the Canadian dollar price of U.S. currency will rise to Can. $1.25, the accumulated U.S. dollars are expected to be worth

$$\text{U.S. } \$913.05 \times 1.25 = \text{Can. } \$1141.31$$

Hence, despite higher interest rates in Canada, you expect to maximize your return by investing in the United States because you anticipate the gain from the foreign exchange transaction to more than offset the interest rate differential in favour of Canada. The example assumes that transactions costs do not offset the expected higher return from investing in the United States.

eign currency funds equal to $(1 + i^*)(1/E_t)$. Since you do not want to assume any risk on your foreign exchange transactions, you fix the domestic currency equivalent of the amount of foreign currency available to you at the end of the year by selling it today in the forward exchange market. If F_t^{t+1} is the forward exchange rate at time t (the Canadian dollar price of one foreign currency unit for delivery at time $t + 1$), your initial dollar investment in foreign currency assets will return to you an amount of $(F_t^{t+1}/E_t)(1 + i^*)$ Canadian dollars. This return is known as the **covered** or **hedged return** on foreign-currency-denominated assets. If this return is larger than what you can earn by investing in Canadian dollar assets, you will have the incentive to hold foreign, rather than domestic currency assets. In other words, when

covered (hedged) return the return from an investment strategy in which futures or forward contracts have been employed to manage risk

$$(7.7) \qquad (F_t^{t+1}/E_t)(1 + i^*) > 1 + i$$

interest arbitragers can profit without assuming any risk by switching from domestic to foreign currency assets. Over time, however, covered interest arbitrage activities will tend to eliminate the potential for profit because of the following effects:

- The initial increase in Canadian-dollar borrowing for the purchase of foreign-currency assets can put upward pressure on domestic interest rates, i (since domestic security prices fall).
- The purchase of foreign currency for the acquisition of foreign currency assets places upward pressure on the price of the spot exchange rate, E_t (the Canadian dollar loses value).
- The increase in the demand for foreign currency assets can put downward pressure on foreign interest rates, i^* (foreign security prices rise as Canadians increase their demand).
- The forward sale of foreign currency places downward pressure on the forward exchange rate, F_t^{t+1}.

These effects will tend to produce the following equilibrium condition, known as **covered interest rate parity**:

covered interest rate parity a relationship linking interest rates, exchange rates, and futures or forward exchange rates across nations

$$(7.8) \qquad (F_t^{t+1}/E_t)(1 + i^*) = 1 + i$$

A numerical example of covered interest arbitrage is shown in Box 7.3. Equation 7.8 can be rewritten as

$$(7.9) \qquad (F_t^{t+1}/E_t) = (1 + i)/(1 + i^*)$$

which can be expressed as

$$(7.10) \qquad \frac{F_t^{t+1} - E_t}{E_t} = \frac{i - i^*}{1 + i^*}$$

which can be approximated as

$$(7.11) \qquad \frac{F_t^{t+1} - E_t}{E_t} = i - i^*$$

BOX 7–3   BACKGROUNDER

Covered Interest Arbitrage

The following rates are quoted in the financial markets:

Foreign exchange rates
Spot rate	$2.00/£
One-year forward rate	$1.98/£

Interest rates
United Kingdom (£)	10%
Canada ($)	8%

An arbitrager could profit by the following sequence of actions:
1. Borrow $200 000 for one year at 8 percent and convert loan proceeds to £100 000 at spot rate of $2.00.
2. Invest £100 000 at 10 percent for one year in the United Kingdom.
3. Undertake a one-year forward contract for delivery of £110 000 (principal of £100 000 and interest of £10 000 on the above investment at the forward rate of $1.98/£ or $217 800).
4. One year later, collect principal and interest totalling £110 000, deliver the £110 000, and collect $217 800 on the forward contract.
5. Pay the principal ($200 000) and interest ($16 000) on the loan, realizing a profit of $1800.

In this form, covered interest rate parity tells us that in equilibrium, the differential between domestic and foreign interest rates determines whether a currency trades at a forward discount or a forward premium. When the forward exchange rate exceeds the spot exchange rate, the foreign currency is said to be trading at a forward premium (since it will take more domestic currency to buy the foreign currency in the future). When the forward exchange rate is less than the spot exchange rate, the foreign currency trades at a forward discount (since it will take less domestic currency to buy a unit of the foreign currency in the future).[3] This fact suggests that when domestic interest rates exceed foreign interest rates ($i - i^* > 0$), the foreign currency trades at a forward premium, while if the interest rate differential is in favour of the foreign country, the foreign currency trades at a forward discount. In the absence of any transactions costs, the exploitation of all interest rate arbitrage opportunities should result in covered interest parity holding exactly. In the real world, deviations from parity exist owing to a variety of costs and barriers, including differential taxation, government controls, and political risk, as well as exchange rate speculation.

---

3. Of course, when the foreign currency trades at a forward discount, the domestic currency trades at a forward premium, and vice versa.

Exchange Rate Expectations and Interest Rates

With international financial market integrations and international capital mobility, nominal interest rate differentials between countries are closely related to expectations about changes in spot foreign exchange rates. This relationship is implicit in the uncovered interest parity equation 7.6:

(7.6) $$i - i^* = (E^e_{t+1} - E_t)/E_t$$

where i and i^* are the domestic and foreign interest rates respectively, and $(E^e_{t+1} - E_t)/E_t$ is the expected percentage change of the exchange rate. If the exchange rate is expected to rise, this is equivalent to expecting the domestic currency to depreciate. To highlight this point, we shall assume $(E^e_{t+1} - E_t)/E_t = \Delta E^e_{t+1}$, where ΔE^e_{t+1}, when positive, is the expected rate of depreciation of the domestic currency and when negative, the expected rate of appreciation of the domestic currency. By substituting and rearranging equation 7.6 we obtain:

(7.12) $$i = i^* + \Delta E^e_{t+1}$$

which says that domestic interest rates are equal to foreign interest rates plus the expected rate of depreciation (appreciation) of the domestic currency.

In the Canadian–U.S. context, equation 7.12 tells us that Canadian interest rates can only exceed those of their U.S. counterparts to the extent that investors expect the Canadian dollar to depreciate. In practice, this relationship appears to hold fairly closely. Disparities can be explained, among other things, by small transactions costs, some nonsubstitutability of financial assets internationally because of investors' portfolio preferences, and risk premiums.

Suppose that the interest rate on a one-year government bond in the United States is 8 percent, while in Canada it is 10 percent. An American who purchases Canadian government bonds for a year will, at the beginning of the year, exchange his U.S. dollars for Canadian dollars, and at the end of the year exchange the Canadian dollars (principal plus interest) for U.S. dollars. If, however, he expects that the Canadian dollar will depreciate relative to the U.S. dollar over the year, say by 5 percentage points, he will expect to earn only 5 percent (10 percent minus 5 percent) by investing in Canadian government bonds. In this case he will prefer to invest in his own government's bonds, on which he can earn 8 percent. Thus, if the Canadian government wants to sell its bonds to U.S. investors, it will have to offer them interest rates that are at least 5 percentage points higher than those offered in the United States.

Consider, as an example, the early 1990s, when the Bank of Canada changed its monetary policy stance by lowering short-term interest rates by one-third of a percentage point (30 basis points). The immediate response was a drop in the U.S.-dollar price of the Canadian dollar by 1.7 percentage points. This sharp drop reflected not only the narrowing of the interest differential between Canada and the United States, but also investors' expectations that an easing of monetary policy in Canada would be followed by a depreciation of the Canadian dollar. Despite a quick reversal in the Bank's interest rate policy, the Canadian dollar dropped further before investors became convinced that the Canadian authorities would not allow the Canadian dollar to depreciate.

This incident underscored the reality that Canada cannot chart an independent interest rate policy without affecting the exchange rate. When interest rates rise in the United States, the Canadian choice can be to follow the United States, or to resist the transmission of higher U.S. interest rates to Canada by allowing the Canadian dollar to depreciate against the U.S. dollar.

Efficiency of Foreign Exchange Markets

Markets are said to be efficient if prices established in these markets fully reflect all available information. We discussed the efficient markets hypothesis in Chapter 6. In the foreign exchange market this hypothesis implies that the forward rate is a good predictor of the future spot rate and that forward rates adjust quickly to any new information. In an efficient foreign exchange market, no profit opportunities remain to be exploited by arbitragers. Any remaining difference between the forward rate and the expected future spot rate is equal to an unpredictable risk premium that investors may demand as compensation for bearing risk. Equations 7.13 and 7.14 capture this idea. At time t, the forward exchange rate for delivery at time $t + 1$, F_t^{t+1} is simply the expected future spot exchange rate (E_{t+1}) based on current information (Ω_t) in equation 7.13.

(7.13) $$F_t^{t+1} = E(E_{t+1} \mid \Omega_t)$$

(7.14) $$E_{t+1} = F_t^{t+1} + \zeta_{t+1}$$

The actual spot exchange rate at time $t + 1$ will be equal to its expected value (denoted by the $E(\cdot)$ term), plus a random, unpredictable component, ζ_{t+1}. The efficient markets hypothesis is really a joint hypothesis that markets are efficient and that people form their expectations rationally; that is, they form their expectations using all available information. Another way of looking at this is to say that expectations embody all relevant information—there is no way to make abnormal profits by using additional information in forming expectations of future spot exchange rates.

Most of the empirical evidence suggests that forward exchange rates are poor predictors of future spot exchange rates. Typically, this result is not interpreted as evidence that exchange markets are inefficient; rather, there are perhaps time-varying risk premiums incorporated into exchange rates in the real world that simple tests (based on simple economic models) of efficiency cannot identify. Much of current empirical research in international finance addresses these issues. Pick up any macrofinance or international finance journal at your library. You're bound to find at least one article on the topic.[4]

---

4. To understand some of these journal articles, you'll require a working knowledge of regression and statistics.

Hedging Foreign Exchange Risk

hedge *when a trader takes a position in one asset to offset the risk of a position in another asset*

Given the variability of foreign exchange rates, it is important for financial institutions and firms operating in foreign currencies to reduce exchange risks whenever possible. Canadian manufacturing firms that export abroad and that are paid in foreign currency claims are often reluctant to assume the risks involved. They can **hedge** their foreign exchange risks when they render their invoices to foreign importers by forward selling their expected currency receipts to the banks. In this way exporters can fix their Canadian dollar receipts from anticipated or actual sales to foreigners. Alternatively, Canadian importers can fix their Canadian dollar payments by forward buying the foreign exchange they require to finalize a foreign purchase. For example, Exxon may have a scheduled payment of £25 million in six months and may buy that amount of British pounds forward today. No money will change hands now. The forward contract will simply lock in the amount of dollars Exxon will have to pay six months from now to obtain the required £25 million.

As a rule, financial institutions and businesses that have to hold both assets and liabilities denominated in foreign currencies attempt to reduce their exchange risk by matching their assets and liabilities in each respective currency denomination. For example, a bank that has sold a large amount of sterling forward may buy sterling forward to reduce or remove its risk exposure.

Swaps

A bank or firm can also reduce its foreign exchange risk exposure with a swap transaction. For example, the Bank of Montreal may consider itself to be temporarily overexposed in Deutschemarks. It might reduce its risk exposure, by selling DM 10 million to the Deutsche Bank for Can. $7 million, with a simultaneous agreement to buy the Deutschemarks back in six months. The Bank of Montreal may also find that it has an undesirable gap in the maturity structure of its assets and liabilities in British pounds. It can use a swap transaction to close this gap with the simultaneous purchase and sale of pounds for different maturity dates. The Bank of Canada uses swap transactions on behalf of the government to temporarily replenish the country's official foreign exchange reserves used to intervene in the foreign exchange market.

Futures

Tables 7.2 and 7.3 illustrate the use of foreign currency futures markets to protect against risk associated with fluctuations in the value of currencies. In Table 7.3, we show a short (selling) hedge. We assume that in June an investor has $200 000 with which to buy £100 000 in the spot (or cash) foreign exchange market, to immediately purchase 90-day British government securities. At the same time she hedges her exchange risk by selling £100 000 in the futures market for September delivery. By September the spot price of the pound has declined from $2 to $1.90. If our investor had not hedged against the value of the pound, she would have incurred a loss of $10 000 when the British securi-

TABLE 7.2	**SHORT HEDGE IN FOREIGN CURRENCIES FUTURES MARKET**

Cash Market	Futures Market
	June 1
Buy £100 000 sterling at $2/£ = $200 000	Sell £100 000 sterling (September delivery) at $1.95/£ = $195 000
	September 1
Sell £100 000 sterling at $1.90/£ = $190 000	Buy £100 000 sterling (September delivery) at $1.85/£ = $185 000
Loss = $10 000	Gain = $10 000

TABLE 7.3	**LONG HEDGE IN FOREIGN CURRENCIES FUTURES MARKET**

Spot (Cash) Market	Futures Market
	June 1
Sell £100 000 sterling at $2/£ = $200 000	Buy £100 000 (October delivery) at $2.05/£ = $205 000
	September 1
Buy £100 000 sterling at $2.05/£ = $205 000	Sell £100 000 sterling (October delivery) at $2.10/£ = $210 000
Loss = $5 000	Gain = $5 000

ties matured and the pounds were converted at the then spot price into dollars. The hedge, however, allows her to offset this loss. In September she buys £100 000 in the futures market for September delivery at $1.85. This transaction, together with the June transaction in the futures market, provides the investor with a $10 000 gain, thus offsetting her spot market transactions loss. If the investor had hedged her position, and the pound had appreciated, rather than depreciated as expected, the potential gain in spot exchange would have been offset by a potential loss in the futures exchange.

In Table 7.3, we summarize the possible effect of a long (buying) hedge. In this case we assume that a British multinational firm wants to transfer funds to its Toronto plant for three months and is concerned about its foreign currency risk. To make the transfer in June, the firm sells £100 000 at $2.00/£ in the spot foreign exchange market for a total of $200 000. At the same time the firm buys a futures contract of £100 000 for October delivery at $2.05 per pound. In September, when the firm's subsidiary has to transfer the funds back to Britain, it buys £100 000 in the spot market at the higher price of $2.05/£. It thus takes a loss of $5000 on the spot transactions, but it can sell £100 000 in the futures market for October delivery at $2.10/£, thus realizing a gain of $5000 on the futures transactions. The gain and loss offset each other, thus having allowed the British firm to make a temporary transfer of funds to its Canadian subsidiary without experiencing any loss other than transactions costs.

Options

www.

The two examples of currency risk hedging show the results of perfect hedges. In the real world such results are fortuitous, and at best one can expect a substantial reduction in risk exposure.

Financial options, described in Chapter 6, provide another method for hedging foreign currency risks. Foreign currency options limit the risk of adverse changes in the exchange rate by "locking in" the exchange rate given by the foreign currency price at which the option can be exercised. At the same time, unlike currency futures, options give their holders the right to take advantage of beneficial changes in the spot or forward exchange rate because options resulting in negative consequences need not be exercised. Regardless of how the exchange rate moves, option holders cannot lose more than the premiums paid for the options, because no obligation binds them to exercise their options. Foreign currency options also are ideally suited to protect against contingency exposure. For example, if a firm submits a bid to produce an item for export, but is uncertain whether the bid will be accepted, the potential foreign currency receivable can be hedged with a put option. If the bid is not accepted, the option does not have to be exercised, and the cost of hedging is limited to the premium. If the bid is accepted, the put option ensures that the firm can sell the foreign exchange received at the striking price, and the firm is thus protected against the risk of an adverse movement in the exchange rate. Furthermore, since the premium is known at the time the option is purchased, the firm can incorporate this hedging cost into its bid offer. Let's look at options in more detail.

TERMINOLOGY You'll recall from our brief discussion of options in Chapter 6 that the derivatives markets have their own lingo. It's important for you to be comfortable with this vocabulary, so remember that to *write* an option means you are selling the option—whether it be a *put* (giving someone the right to sell) or a *call* (giving someone the write to buy). To *buy* the option, you are buying the option—be it a put or a call. In Chapter 6 we said the price at which you can exercise the option is its *strike price*, or exercise price, and that whether an option is exercised or not depends on the strike price relative to the price of the underlying security at maturity. We did not discuss the price you paid (or received) when you bought (or wrote) the option. It is known as the *option premium*.

PAYOFFS TO OPTIONS Suppose the option premium is 0.0 DM for both a put and a call and that we're looking at an option on buying and selling dollars (for Deutschemarks). If the strike price is at an exchange rate of 1.00 DM/$1, then the call (the right to buy dollars) will be exercised if, at maturity, the price of the dollars is above the strike price of 1.00 DM/$1. Why? Suppose at maturity the spot rate is 1.50 DM/$1. This rate tells you that it costs 1.50 DM to buy $1. But your option gives you the right to buy those dollars at a lower cost (only 1 DM), so you exercise the option. Your gain is the difference between the market price of the dollar at maturity, and the strike price (in this case, 0.5 DM). Panel (a) in Figure 7–3 demonstrates the payoff to the call option.

FIGURE 7–3   **PAYOFFS TO CALL AND PUT OPTIONS**

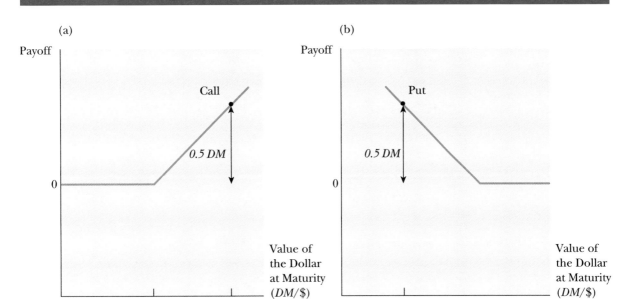

(a) In panel (a) we demonstrate the payoff to a call option on the dollar. It generates profits if the value of the dollar at maturity exceeds the strike price (assuming a zero option premium).

(b) In panel (b) we demonstrate the payoff to a put option on the dollar. It generates profits if the value of the dollar at maturity is less than the strike price (assuming a zero option premium).

Panel (b) of Figure 7–3 captures the payoff to the put option. It will be exercised if the market price of the dollar at maturity is below the strike price (since you can sell the dollar and receive more Deutschemarks at the strike price than the market price at maturity). Again, the payoff to the put is a function of the difference between the market price at maturity and the strike price. Suppose the market price at maturity were 0.5 DM/$1. Then the gain to exercising the put is 0.5 DM (since you can sell it for 1 DM rather than the 0.8 DM).

PAYOFFS REVISITED   Now let's try to work the option premium into the analysis. Suppose we consider both a call option and a put option on dollars with identical strike prices (of 1 DM/$1) and maturity dates, and assume they each cost 0.05 DM. What does the payoff structure now look like? First, consider buying a call option (referred to as a **long call**, since we are looking at the buyer of the call option), which gives you the right to buy dollars at the rate of 1 DM/$1 and costs 0.05 DM. When will you exercise the option? Well, if the market price of a dollar at maturity is less than 1 DM/$1, the option will expire worthless (since an option holder could buy dollars at the cheaper market rate). At a market price at maturity of 1 DM/$1 or more, the option will be exercised. For example, at a market price of 1 DM/$1, by exercising the call you will end up losing the option premium (0.05 DM). If the market price at maturity were 1.01 DM/$1, you would exercise the option and buy at the rate

long call when someone buys a call option

FIGURE 7–4   **LONG AND SHORT CALLS**

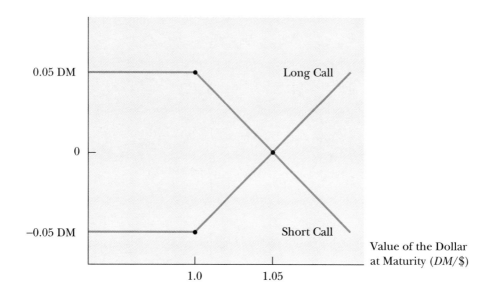

With an option premium of 0.05 DM on the long call and the short call, you can see that any gains to the short call are offset by losses on the long call and vice versa. This figure illustrates the zero-sum-game feature of the options market for calls.

of 1 DM per dollar, saving 0.01 DM over the market rate. But recall, you had paid 0.05 DM for the option, so you would end up losing 0.04 DM. Similarly, if the market price at maturity were 1.04 DM/$1, you would gain 0.04 DM by exercising the option (relative to the market price), yet with the outlay of 0.05 DM for the option, you would be down 0.01 DM. If the market price of the dollar went to 1.05 DM, the long call would just break even, and, if the price rose above 1.05 DM/$1, the net gain would be the difference between the market price of the dollar at maturity and the sum of the option premium and the strike price. Figure 7–4 plots the net gain to the long call on dollars.

short call   *when someone sells a call option*

Note that Figure 7–4 also plots the payoff to the **short call** (the seller of the call option). The seller earns the option premium up to the point at which it is exercised by the person holding the call, after which the seller's net gain falls steadily. For example, at a market price of 1.03 DM/$1, the short call earns the option premium of 0.05 DM. The seller of the short call must sell dollars to the holder of the long call at the rate 1 DM/$1, but it costs him 1.03 DM/$1 to buy dollars on the market to close out the call. The seller of the call's net gain is 0.02 DM. When the price of the dollar at maturity rises above 1.05 DM, the short call ends up making a loss (given by the difference between the market price of the dollar at maturity and the sum of the option premium and the strike price of the dollar).

Figure 7–4 demonstrates the concept of a zero-sum game. In a zero-sum game, what one party gains, the other loses. No net benefit is secured by trading "on both sides" on call options (with the same strike price and matu-

FIGURE 7–5 LONG AND SHORT PUTS

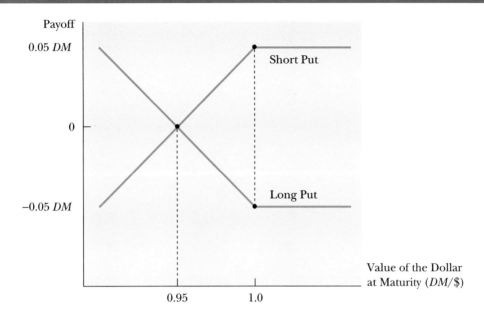

With an option premium of 0.05 DM on both the long put and the short put, you can see that any gains to the long put are offset by losses on the short put, and vice versa. This figure demonstrates the zero-sum-game feature of the options market for puts.

long put *when someone buys a put option*

short put *when someone sells a put option*

straddle *a put and a call on the same currency, with identical strike prices and maturity dates*

rity date). Figure 7–5, which you should work through carefully (since there's an assignment question based on the figure), demonstrates the same is true for **long puts** and **short puts**.

USING OPTIONS TO HEDGE: STRADDLES   Options can be incorporated in a hedging strategy in several ways, and we'll briefly touch on only one (you'll get much more exposure to this material in a course on financial derivatives). It is known as a **straddle**—a put and a call on the same currency, with identical strike prices and maturity dates. The option premium on the call is assumed to be above that on the put. For example, suppose we continue our dollar–Deutschemark analysis and examine the case of a strike price of 1 DM/$1, with an option premium on the call at 0.1 DM and the option premium on the put of 0.07 DM. What's the payoff to a long straddle (the person buying the straddle), and what's the payoff to the short straddle (the person selling the straddle)? Consider Table 7.4. It presents information on the payoff to the put, the call, and the long straddle. The call will expire worthless until the market price of the dollar at maturity reaches the strike price. Thereafter it will be exercised, and the net loss will turn into a net gain as the market price of the dollar rises above the strike price (plus the option premium). The put will be exercised until the market price reaches the strike price, with the gain to the put falling until it reaches its minimum value (the option premium of 0.07 DM) at a market price of 1 DM/$1.

FIGURE 7–6 LONG AND SHORT STRADDLES

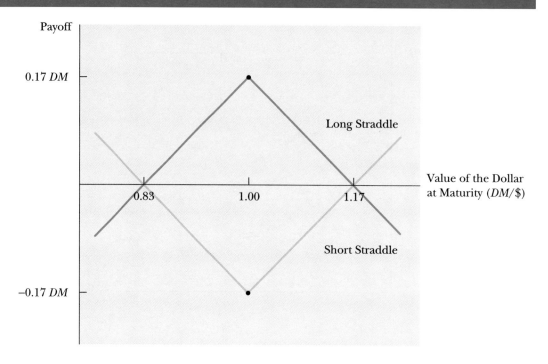

A straddle consists of a put and a call on the same currency with identical strike prices and maturity dates. For a straddle the option premium on the call is greater than the option premium on the put.

A long straddle creates profits when a currency is expected to face substantial volatility, whereas a short straddle generates profits when the underlying currency is expected to trade within a narrow range.

Figure 7–6 plots the payoff structure to the long straddle. For dollar prices that lie outside the range 0.83 DM/$1 to 1.17 DM/$1, the long straddle provides a positive payoff. For values of the dollar in that range, the long straddle offers a net loss. Hence, a long straddle would be used if the investor believed the value of the dollar would be much higher or much lower than the range 0.83 DM to 1.17 DM (which is essentially the strike price plus or minus the sum of the option premiums).

The opposite result is shown for the case of the short straddle in Table 7.5. Here the short straddle generates profits if the value of the dollar lies within the range 0.83 DM to 1.17 DM. It too is plotted on Figure 7–6. Hence, investors will prefer to use long or short straddles depending on where they believe the value of the dollar will lie when the option matures. If the dollar is expected to appreciate greatly or depreciate greatly, the long straddle offers profits. If the dollar is expected to remain in a relatively stable trading zone, the short straddle is the way to go.

So, there you have it. Options, futures, swaps, and forward contracts are essential components of managing exposure to exchange rate risk.

TABLE 7.4 PAYOFFS TO CALL, PUT, AND LONG STRADDLE

Value of the dollar at maturity	Value of call	Value of put	Value of long straddle
0.50	−0.10DM	0.43DM	0.33DM
0.80	−0.10DM	0.13DM	0.33DM
0.83	−0.10DM	0.08DM	0.00DM
0.85	−0.10DM	0.03DM	−0.02DM
0.90	−0.10DM	−0.02DM	−0.07DM
0.95	−0.10DM	−0.07DM	−0.12DM
1.00	−0.10DM	−0.07DM	−0.13DM
1.05	−0.10DM	−0.07DM	−0.12DM
1.10	0.00DM	−0.07DM	−0.07DM
1.15	0.05DM	−0.07DM	−0.02DM
1.17	0.07DM	−0.07DM	0.00DM
1.20	0.10DM	−0.07DM	0.03DM
1.50	0.40DM	−0.07DM	0.33DM

TABLE 7.5 PAYOFFS TO CALL, PUT, AND SHORT STRADDLE

Value of the dollar at maturity	Value of call	Value of put	Value of short straddle
0.50	0.10DM	−0.43DM	−0.33DM
0.80	0.10DM	−0.13DM	−0.33DM
0.83	0.10DM	−0.10DM	0.00DM
0.85	0.10DM	−0.08DM	0.02DM
0.90	0.10DM	−0.03DM	0.07DM
0.95	0.10DM	0.02DM	0.12DM
1.00	0.10DM	0.07DM	0.13DM
1.05	0.10DM	0.07DM	0.12DM
1.10	0.00DM	0.07DM	0.07DM
1.15	−0.05DM	0.07DM	0.02DM
1.17	−0.07DM	0.07DM	0.00DM
1.20	−0.10DM	0.07DM	−0.03DM
1.50	−0.40DM	0.07DM	−0.33DM

Now that we have a good understanding of financial assets and financial markets, we turn to a discussion of financial intermediation. What is a financial intermediary? What services do intermediaries provide, and how does the process of intermediation work? Knowing the answers to these questions helps us understand how money and banking affect our lives.

KEY TERMS

asked	current account	nonmerchandise trade
balance of payments	debit transactions	real exchange rate
bid	effective exchange rate	services
bid–asked spread	financial account	short call
bilateral arbitrage	forward discount	short put
C-6 index	forward premium	statistical discrepancy
capital account	hedge	straddle
capital inflows	interest arbitrage	swap rate
capital outflows	investment income	transfers
covered (hedged) return	long call	triangular arbitrage
covered interest arbitrage	long put	uncovered interest arbitrage
covered interest rate parity	merchandise trade	uncovered interest parity
credit transactions	nominal exchange rate	

REVIEW QUESTIONS

1. What are the differences between spot, forward, swap, and future currency markets?
2. Define the foreign exchange rate of the Canadian dollar. What is an effective exchange rate of the Canadian dollar?
3. What is a cross rate? When is it said to be consistent? How is consistency of cross rates achieved in the market?
4. Suppose that the following exchange rates are observed:
   Montreal: Can. $2.00 = £1
   New York: U.S. $0.80 = Can. $1.00
   London: U.S. $2.00 = £1
   Given these exchange rates, is there a potential for arbitrage profits for a Canadian arbitrager with Can. $1 million?
5. Explain why you might expect the profit incentives of international interest rate arbitragers to produce interest parity.
6. How is the relationship between a currency's spot and forward rate explained by covered interest arbitrage?
7. How does the uncovered interest parity condition explain the relationship between Canadian and foreign interest rates?
8. How can exporters hedge their currency risks?
9. Using Figure 7–5, demonstrate the gains and losses to a short put and a long put on dollars with identical maturity dates, where the strike price is 0.50 DM/$1 and the option premiums are identical at 0.05 DM. Is there a net gain to short and long puts in this example? Why?
10. Will a short put be exercised if the market price at maturity is greater than the strike price? Will a long call be exercised if the market price at maturity is lower than the strike price? Why? Use properly labelled diagrams and assume the strike price on each option is 4.2 DM/$1 and that the option premiums are identical at 1.1 DM/$1.
11. Explain the motives of the seller and the buyer of a straddle. Use properly labelled diagrams to support your answer. Assume the strike prices are 0.50 DM/$1, that the option premium on the call is 0.05 DM/$1, and that the option premium on the put is 0.035 DM/$1.
12. Why would an investor use options rather than futures when hedging? Make up an example to illustrate your answer.
13. Suppose you produce peanut butter and import peanuts from the Jimmy Carter Peanut Company for U.S. $100 000. They give you 30 days to pay. The current spot exchange rate is U.S. $1.4 = Can. $1.00, while the current futures rate for delivery in 30 days is U.S. $1.45 = Can. $1.00. You produce your peanut butter, and by day 14, have it shipped to Harry's Grocery Store, along with a bill for Can. $165 000. You give the grocery store 14 days to pay your invoice. Is there any reason for you to hedge? Under what conditions would it make sense for you to hedge?

14. This question requires some research. Using interest rates on three-month Treasury bills, does covered interest arbitrage explain the relationship between U.S. and Canadian interest rates in June 2000? Why?

15. This question requires some research, for which you should use data for July 2000. Using interest rates on one-month Treasury bills and the spot exchange rate, construct an estimate of the expected exchange rate on August 2, 2000. Compare that to the one-month forward rate reported on July 2, 2000. Explain your result.

16. Explain the differences between covered interest arbitrage and uncovered interest arbitrage using data for the last trading day of October 2000 and interest rates on three-month Treasury bills in Canada and the United States.

SELECTED READINGS

Anker, P. "Uncovered Interest Parity, Monetary Policy and Time-Varying Risk Premia." *Journal of International Money and Finance* 18 (6, 1999).

Canada. *Canada's Balance of International Payments.* Statistics Canada, Catalogue 67-001 (Quarterly).

———. *Canada's International Investment Position, 1991.* Statistics Canada, Catalogue 67-202 (Annual).

———. *Canada's International Transactions in Securities.* Statistics Canada, Catalogue 67-002 (Quarterly).

Christoffersen, P.F., and L. Giorgianni. "Interest Rate Arbitrage in Currency Baskets—Forecasting Weights and Measuring Risk." IMF Working Paper WP/99/16, 1999.

Chrystal, K. Alec. "A Guide to Foreign Exchange Markets." *Federal Reserve Bank of St. Louis Review* (March 1984), pp. 5–18.

Grabbe, J. Orlen. *International Financial Markets*, 2nd ed. New York: Elsevier, 1991.

Gregory, Allan W. "Testing Interest Rate Parity and Rational Expectations for Canada and the United States." *Canadian Journal of Economics* (May 1987), pp. 289–305.

Kim, S. "Do Macro-Economic News Announcements Affect the Volatility of Foreign Exchange Rates? Some

Evidence from Australia." *Applied Economics* 31 (12, 1999).

Levich, Richard M. "Empirical Studies of Exchange Rates: Price Behaviour, Rate Determination and Market Efficiency," in Ronald W. Jones and Peter B. Kennen (eds.), *Handbook of International Economics*, Vol. II. Amsterdam: North Holland, 1985, pp. 979–1040.

McCallum, B.T. "A Reconsideration of the Uncovered Interest Parity Relationship." *Journal of Monetary Economics* 33 (1994).

———. "Monetary Policy and the Term Structure of Interest Rates." NBER Working Paper No. 4938, 1994.

Murray, J. "International Financial Crises and Flexible Exchange Rates: Some Policy Lessons from Canada." *Bank of Canada Technical Report* 88, 2000.

Stern, J., and D. Chew (eds.). *New Developments in International Finance.* Oxford: Basil Blackwell, 1988.

Thornton, Daniel L. "Tests of Covered Interest Rate Parity." *Federal Reserve Bank of St. Louis Review* (July–August 1989), pp. 55–66.

$\mathscr{A}$PPENDIX 7A

The Balance of International Payments Accounts

balance of payments *a summary of all economic transactions between a country's residents and nonresidents during a given period*

The statement of a country's **balance of payments** is a summary of all economic transactions between its residents and nonresidents during a given period. It records the money value of the flow of merchandise, services, and assets bought or sold, as well as the value of gifts and other transfers between residents and nonresidents. A transaction is included in the balance of payments whether or not it involves a money payment, as long as a resident of one country is dealing with someone in another country.

Transactions are recorded in the balance of payments statement following the system of double-entry bookkeeping. For every transaction two entries are made: a debit and a credit. Since for each debit there is a corresponding and equal credit, the total balance of payments statement must always add up to zero. But how do we decide what is a credit transaction (indicated by a plus sign) and what is a debit transaction (indicated by a minus sign)? **Credit transactions** involve receiving payments from nonresidents; **debit transactions** involve making payments to nonresidents. Hence, exports of goods and services, which give rise to the receipt of payments from nonresidents, are recorded as credits, while imports of goods and services, which give rise to the making of payments to nonresidents, are recorded as debits.

credit transactions *receiving payments from nonresidents*

debit transactions *making payments to nonresidents*

Since exports of goods and services are recorded as credits, corresponding debit entries must be made on the balance of payments statement. The debit entries record the monetary arrangements by nonresidents for the payment of Canadian exports. Nonresidents can pay Canadians with foreign monetary claims (for example, U.S. dollar deposits with New York banks), or with Canadian monetary claims (for example, Canadian dollar deposits held by the nonresidents with banks in Calgary). In the first case, Canadians acquire foreign assets and thereby increase their claims on nonresidents. In the second, Canadians reduce their liabilities to nonresidents. Either way, the transaction is recorded as a debit to offset the credit transaction that initiated it.

Since imports of goods and services are recorded as debits, offsetting credit entries must be made in the balance of payments. The credit entry records the monetary arrangements by Canadians to pay nonresidents for the imports. Canadians can pay nonresidents with Canadian monetary claims, such as Canadian dollar deposits, or with foreign monetary claims, such as U.S. dollar deposits. In the first case, Canadians increase their liabilities to nonresidents; in the second, they reduce their claims on foreigners by giving up foreign assets.

capital inflows *an increase in Canadian liabilities to nonresidents, or a decrease in Canadian claims on nonresidents*

When Canadians borrow from nonresidents, the transaction can be viewed as the export of Canadian debt instruments such as government or corporate bonds. The issue of Canadian securities to nonresidents requires payment from nonresidents, just as the export of goods and services does, and is therefore recorded as a credit transaction in the balance of payments. These credit transactions are called **capital inflows.** A capital inflow can take the form of either

capital outflows
a decrease in Canadian liabilities held by nonresidents, or an increase in Canadian claims on nonresidents

current account *the values of the flow of goods and services and other current receipts and payments between residents of Canada and residents of the rest of the world*

capital account
capital transfers of migrants' assets, inheritances, federal government superannuation and debt forgiveness, as well as the acquisition or disposal of intangible assets such as patents and leases

financial account
net flows, both private and official (government), resulting from changes in Canadian claims on nonresidents and of changes in Canadian liabilities to nonresidents

an increase in Canadian liabilities to nonresidents or a decrease in Canadian claims on nonresidents. Conversely, **capital outflows**, which involve payments to nonresidents, can take the form of either a decrease in Canadian liabilities, such as the retirement of Canadian bonds held by nonresidents, or an increase in Canadian claims on nonresidents, such as the acquisition of foreign assets by Canadians.

The rules for deciding whether a transaction is recorded as a debit or a credit in the balance of payments statement are summarized in Box 7A–1.

Table 7A.1 presents Canada's international balance of payments for 1999. The table is divided into two major parts: the **current account** and the **financial account**. In a double-entry bookkeeping system of accounting, the balance on the current account should be exactly offset by an opposite balance in the financial account. In practice, however, because of the estimating procedures available, equality between these two major accounts is not achieved. The net difference between the current and financial accounts is identified as the statistical discrepancy.

BOX 7A–1 BALANCE OF PAYMENTS ACCOUNTING

Recording Credit Transactions and Debit Transactions

Debit Transactions
- imports of goods and services
- gifts and unilateral transfers to nonresidents
- increase in Canadian claims on nonresidents } capital
- decrease in Canadian liabilities to nonresidents } outflows

Credit Transactions
- exports of goods and services
- gifts and unilateral transfers from nonresidents
- decrease in Canadian claims on nonresidents } capital
- increase in Canadian liabilities to nonresidents } inflows

TABLE 7A.1   CANADA'S INTERNATIONAL BALANCE OF PAYMENTS, 1999
Millions of Dollars

	Credits	Debits	Balance
Current account			
Merchandise trade			
Exports	360 600		
Imports		326 662	33 938
Nonmerchandise trade			
Services	49 158	55 790	−6 631
Investment income	31 166	63 903	−32 737
Transfers	5 501	4 408	1 092
Balance on nonmerchandise trade			−38 277
Current account balance			**−4 339**
Capital account			**5 090**
Financial account			
Canadian assets (net flows)			
Direct investment abroad	25 795		
Portfolio investment	22 947		
Loans and deposits		17 420	
Official international reserves	8 818		
Other claims		239	
Total Canadian assets			39 901
Canadian liabilities to nonresidents (net flows)			
Direct investment in Canada	36 057		
Canadian stocks	14 164		
Canadian bonds			
Trade in outstanding issues	7 789		
New issues	31 793		
Retirements		36 450	
Money market investments		13 438	
Loans and deposits		14 226	
Total liabilities to nonresidents			26 591
Total capital and financial accounts			−8 219
Statistical discrepancy			12 559
Grand total, balance of payments			0

Note: Errors due to rounding

SOURCE: Statistics Canada, CANSIM Database, March 2000, Matrix 2369.

The Current Account

merchandise trade *the value of all physical goods sold to nonresidents (exports) or purchased from them (imports)*

nonmerchandise trade *the value of all services, investment income, and transfers sold to nonresidents less those purchased from nonresidents*

services *travel, freight, shipping, and a broad range of professional and managerial services*

investment income *interest, dividends, and miscellaneous investment income*

transfers *inheritances and migrants' funds, personal and institutional remittances, official contributions, and withholding taxes*

The current account of the balance of payments records the values of the flow of goods and services and other current receipts and payments between residents of Canada and residents of the rest of the world. Transactions shown in the current account directly affect the level of Canada's national income. The current account comprises four major types of transactions: merchandise trade, services, investment income, and unilateral transfers.

Merchandise trade is the value of all physical goods sold to nonresidents (exports) or purchased from them (imports). As shown in Table 7A.1, in 1999 Canada had a favourable balance in merchandise trade insofar as the value of its merchandise exports exceeded the value of merchandise imports by almost $34 billion.

Nonmerchandise trade captures exports and imports relating to services, investment income, and transfers. **Services** consist of travel, freight, shipping, and a broad range of professional and managerial services. In 1999, Canadians had to pay substantially more to foreigners than they received from them for these services.

Investment income comprises interest, dividends, and miscellaneous investment income. Investment income is primarily income derived from the ownership of assets. As indicated in Table 7A.1 (and as has been the case throughout Canada's history), in 1999 Canadians paid more investment income to nonresidents than they received from them (nearly $33 billion more). This figure reflects Canada's position as a net borrower abroad and indicates that foreigners hold more income-earning Canadian assets than Canadians hold income-earning foreign assets.

Transfers differ from all other items in the balance of payments statement in that they are not associated with a direct economic quid pro quo. Transfers comprise inheritances and migrants' funds, personal and institutional remittances, official contributions, and withholding taxes. Remittances include government pension payments to nonresidents and charitable, educational, and interpersonal gifts. Official contributions consist of food aid and technical, economic, and educational assistance given by the Canadian government to developing countries. In 1999, Canadians transferred more than $1 billion less to nonresidents than they received in transfers from them.

Finally, by adding up all the items we have described, we derive the current account balance. The current account is said to be in surplus when foreign payments to Canadians exceed Canadian payments to foreigners, and in deficit when Canadian payments exceed those received from foreigners. In 1999, Canada had a current account deficit of just less than $4.4 billion. Current account deficits are financed by the sale of assets owned by Canadians and by Canadians borrowing from foreigners. The latter involves an increase in Canadian liabilities to nonresidents.

The Capital and Financial Accounts

While every transaction in the current account is an income-related flow, every transaction in the capital account is an asset-related flow. The financial account in Table 7A.1 records net flows, both private and official (government), resulting from changes in Canadian claims on nonresidents and of changes in Canadian liabilities to nonresidents. These claims arise from the financing of the current account balance and from the investment activities between residents of Canada and residents of the rest of the world.

Canadian claims on nonresidents increase when Canadians acquire foreign assets. A net increase in foreign assets held by Canadians, as already explained, constitutes a capital outflow, which is shown in the balance of payments statement as a debit. In 1999, Canada's claims on nonresidents increased to just less than $40 billion. This net capital outflow was the result of direct foreign investment abroad, the net acquisition of foreign portfolio stocks and bonds, and other claims abroad. A distinction is made between direct and portfolio investments: with direct investment the investor acquires an ownership claim that involves control of the asset.

Changes in claims on nonresidents by the government of Canada are referred to as official transactions. These transactions record changes in the government's holdings of international reserve assets and net capital flows resulting from its export loans and its subscriptions, loans, and advances to international institutions and foreign governments. In 1999, Canada's official international reserves fell and resulted in about a $9 billion capital outflow. Canada's official international reserve assets include its gold and foreign currency holdings, and its reserve position and Special Drawing Rights (SDRS) with the International Monetary Fund. SDRS are international reserves created on the books of the International Monetary Fund (IMF) and distributed to member nations according to their importance in international trade. Canada's reserve position is its automatic right to borrow from the IMF in case of need.

Canadian liabilities to nonresidents (that is, nonresident claims on Canadians) increased because of foreign direct investment in Canada and the net acquisition by nonresidents of Canadian portfolio stocks and bonds and other Canadian assets. As shown in Table 7A.1, in 1999 the net acquisition of Canadian assets by nonresidents resulted in a $26.6 billion capital inflow.

statistical discrepancy a data adjustment required to set the balance of payments equal to zero

Since the overall debit total in 1999 exceeded the overall credit total, there is a credit entry of almost $12.6 billion in Table 7A.1, shown as the **statistical discrepancy**. This entry is required to make the total debits (including the statistical discrepancy) equal to the total credits, as required by double-entry bookkeeping. The statistical discrepancy results from transactions (or payments) that are incorrectly valued or not reported at all, especially international capital flows.

CHAPTER EIGHT

FINANCIAL INTERMEDIATION

After reading this chapter you should be able to

1. *Describe six methods by which financial intermediaries provide services to financial markets*
2. *Explain how the expected return and the risk of a portfolio are measured*
3. *Demonstrate that diversification reduces unsystematic risk*
4. *Show how an optimal portfolio is selected*
5. *Use the capital asset pricing model to price assets and determine their rates of return*

Financial institutions provide services that facilitate the flow of funds between ultimate lenders (surplus spending units) and ultimate borrowers (deficit spending units). As is illustrated in Figure 8–1, funds may be channelled either directly or indirectly from ultimate lenders to ultimate borrowers.

The direct flow of funds takes place when ultimate lenders acquire the primary (or direct) securities that are claims issued by ultimate borrowers against themselves. Such direct transactions have major shortcomings. For the lenders, they may involve unacceptable risks. For example, in the case of personal loans, even if the borrowers are the epitome of honesty, the risk always exists that they may have to default on repayment due to circumstances beyond their immediate control. For instance, default may be due to involuntary unemployment because of poor health or an accident.

Direct lending and borrowing usually also require relatively high search and information costs for the participants. Time, inconvenience, and other transactions costs are incurred by lenders and borrowers in their search to find each other. Lenders have the additional cost of collecting information on the creditworthiness of potential borrowers, and on the economic viability of projects to be financed. There is also the cost of monitoring the behaviour of borrowers during the period that loans remain outstanding.

Direct lending and borrowing requires a double coincidence of wants with respect to the amount, or denomination, and period, or maturity, of each transaction. For example, ultimate lenders must make their savings available for the period required by ultimate borrowers, or else borrowers must accom-

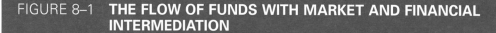

FIGURE 8–1 **THE FLOW OF FUNDS WITH MARKET AND FINANCIAL INTERMEDIATION**

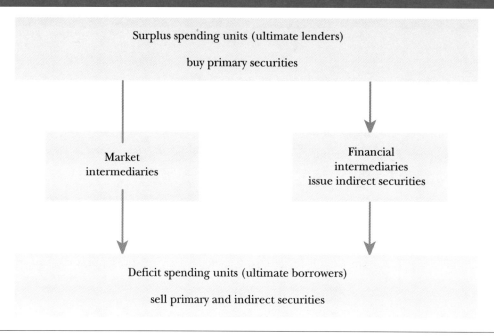

modate their needs to the availability period of lenders. The average small saver usually has limited information about the availability of borrowers and little expertise in evaluating the risk and return characteristics of primary securities offered by them. Market intermediaries, such as brokers and security dealers, sell search and information services to both lenders and borrowers and thereby assist the direct flow of funds through money and capital markets.

The indirect flow of funds takes place when financial intermediaries acquire the primary securities issued by deficit spending units, while offering their own secondary (or indirect) securities to surplus spending units. Indirect securities, which are claims that financial intermediaries issue on themselves, can take various forms, such as contracts to pay annuities and pensions, shares in the variable value and net income of asset portfolios, and deposits or debt instruments with fixed nominal (money) values. Financial intermediaries purchase securities from, and lend to, deficit spending units with the funds they obtain from selling their indirect securities to surplus spending units. Economists call financial intermediation **asset transformation** because it can be viewed as transforming claims on ultimate borrowers into claims on intermediaries. This process allows ultimate borrowers to issue claims with characteristics that best meet their needs, and at the same time provides savers with financial assets whose characteristics best satisfy their preferences.

asset transformation transforming claims on borrowers into claims on intermediaries

Financial Intermediation Services

Payments intermediation refers to the transformation of financial assets into media of exchange. It is undertaken by the government's central bank and the private depository institutions, of which the chartered banks are the largest. Since **payments intermediation** is the primary function of the banks, it can also be called banking. The central bank engages in payments intermediation when it issues currency for public circulation against its asset portfolio of government securities. The depository institutions, which include the chartered banks and the near-banks such as the trust companies, the mortgage loan companies, the caisses populaires, and the credit unions, undertake payments intermediation by holding portfolios of financial assets against which they issue their own claims in the form of deposits with fixed nominal (money) values that serve as a medium of exchange.

payments intermediation the transformation of financial assets into media of exchange

Denomination Intermediation

Deficit spending units usually issue their primary securities in denominations too large for the small saver, and larger than those preferred by most ultimate lenders. Primary securities are usually issued in relatively large denominations to minimize the borrower's transactions costs. Financial institutions engage in denomination intermediation when they purchase primary securities and in turn offer the public their own liabilities in smaller denominations. **Denomination intermediation** can be viewed as dividing primary securities into smaller pieces, another aspect of asset transformation. Payments intermediation, described above, also involves denomination intermediation. Mutual funds resolve the indivisibility shortcomings of primary securities for the average saver by offering the public shares or units in small denominations.

denomination intermediation the transformation of financial assets into media of exchange or relatively small denominations

Default-Risk Intermediation

The financial intermediaries' indirect securities held by the public are to various degrees insulated from loss through default. As we will demonstrate later, to the extent that the probabilities of losses through default on loans and securities are independent of each other, the intermediaries' risk of incurring large proportionate losses through default on their asset portfolios is less than the default risk on the individual loans and securities in these portfolios. An indirect security issued by an intermediary represents a claim on the intermediary's asset portfolio rather than on the individual components of the portfolio. Hence, by holding indirect securities rather than primary securities, that is, by **default-risk intermediation**, savers can reduce their exposure to default risk.

default-risk intermediation the reduction in default risk resulting from holding indirect securities rather than primary securities

Maturity-Risk Intermediation

When borrowing short-term to meet long-term requirements, borrowers expose themselves to the risk of being unable to replace or extend the term to maturity of their short-term borrowing. Lenders, by making their funds available for long periods, expose themselves to the risk of requiring their funds before their long-term loans mature. Hence, the maturity preferences of ultimate borrowers are usually longer than those of ultimate lenders. Financial institutions attempt to resolve this conflict between borrowers and lenders by engaging in **maturity-risk intermediation**.

Financial institutions undertake maturity-risk intermediation by holding portfolios of assets with long-term maturities and financing these portfolios with the issue and creation of short-term liabilities. This practice exposes them to funding risk—the probability that at any given time the public will not want to hold a sufficient amount of the short-term liabilities that were issued by the financial intermediaries to fund their asset portfolios. The intermediaries try to minimize their funding risk by pooling (distributing) their liabilities over a large number of diversified savers.

maturity-risk intermediation
holding portfolios of assets with long-term maturities and financing these portfolios with the issue and creation of short-term liabilities

Interest Rate Intermediation

interest rate intermediation
when financial intermediaries provide fixed interest rates to lenders but not to borrowers, or vice versa

Financial institutions engage in **interest rate intermediation** when they provide fixed interest rates to lenders but not to borrowers, or vice versa. When market interest rates are expected to rise, borrowers will want to borrow for a long term at fixed rates to minimize their cost of funds, while lenders will want to make their funds available at various rates for short terms to maximize their expected returns. Financial intermediaries resolve this conflict between borrowers and lenders with fixed-rate long-term lending, which in turn is funded by variable-rate short-term borrowing. Interest rate intermediation shifts the risk of adverse interest rate movements from borrowers or lenders to the financial intermediaries. During periods of extreme interest rate volatility, intermediaries have reduced the risk inherent in interest rate intermediation with the use of financial futures and options as well as interest rate swaps.

Capital-Value Intermediation

capital-value intermediation
when the market value of the liabilities an intermediary issues against itself fluctuates less than the market value of the public's liabilities held by the institutions in their portfolios

Financial institutions engage in **capital-value intermediation** when the market value of the liabilities they issue against themselves fluctuates less than the market value of the public's liabilities held by the institutions in their asset portfolios. Depository institutions undertake pure capital-value intermediation by providing the public with assets in the form of deposits that have fixed nominal (money) values. The redemption value of shares held by the public in a mutual fund is based on a portfolio of assets whose market value fluctuates less than the market value of the individual components of the portfolio. Capital-value intermediation allows the public to hold financial assets whose value is to varying degrees insulated from loss due to market conditions.

Liquidity-Risk Intermediation

Most of the real assets held by the public, such as buildings, equipment, land, and the claims issued against these physical assets are illiquid in that they

liquidity-risk intermediation involves financial institutions transforming the public's illiquid claims into liquid claims on the institutions themselves

cannot be immediately used as a medium of exchange to obtain consumable goods. Holding illiquid assets exposes the public to the risk of not being able to satisfy the desired timing of its consumption efficiently. The public can be said, in this respect, to be exposed to liquidity risk. **Liquidity-risk intermediation** involves financial institutions, particularly the banks and the near-banks, transforming the public's illiquid claims into liquid claims on the institutions themselves. In this way the financial institutions share some of the public's liquidity risk. Unlike individuals' other risks, their liquidity risks are private and not publicly verifiable. Hence, individuals cannot be as readily insured for liquidity risk as they can be for other kinds of risks. Liquidity-risk intermediation, therefore, serves as an alternative solution for providing direct liquidity insurance.

Principles of Portfolio Management

Most financial intermediaries are private enterprises, and, as such, one of their main objectives is to generate a profit for their shareholders. This objective implies maximizing the rate of return on the funds that are collected from the public and utilized for lending and for purchasing securities. In a world of perfect certainty, the principles governing the choice of loans and securities to create an investment portfolio would be straightforward. All that would be required, once the inflows and outflows of funds from deposits and other liabilities were determined, would be the selection of those assets having the highest yield and that were not subject to default. Assets would also be selected so that cash inflows were gainfully employed immediately on receipt, and cash outflows were readily accommodated when they occurred. We do not, however, live in a world of perfect certainty. A financial intermediary generally cannot predict with certainty when it will experience large cash inflows or outflows. Nor can it predict with certainty the return it will receive on its investment portfolio. It can, at best, measure the expected return and risk on each individual asset it holds as well as on its total portfolio.

In this section we describe the Tobin–Markowitz mean-variance approach to measuring the expected rate of return and risk of individual financial assets and of asset portfolios. We show how the risk of a portfolio can be reduced with appropriate asset **diversification** and how a financial intermediary may decide on the type of portfolio of assets to hold. The mean-variance approach to portfolio management was introduced by James Tobin and Harry Markowitz in the 1950s.

diversification an investment strategy designed to avoid widespread portfolio losses by holding a variety of assets whose prices are not tied to one another

Measuring Expected Return of a Financial Asset

In an uncertain world, each financial asset has a number of different rates of return that could arise given different "states" or situations occurring in the world. For instance, as shown in Table 8.1, Asset *A* has four possible outcomes: It could give no return (a 0 percent rate of return) or a 10, 15, or 30 percent rate of return. Associated with each possible rate of return is a probability that the rate will occur. In our example in Table 8.1 Asset *A* has a 30 percent chance

TABLE 8.1	**CALCULATION OF EXPECTED RETURN**

ASSET A

Possible Rate of Return		Probability of Possible Rate of Return		
0%	×	.3	=	0.0%
10%	×	.2	=	2.0%
15%	×	.4	=	6.0%
30%	×	.1	=	3.0%
		Expected rate of return	=	11.0%

ASSET B

Possible Rate of Return		Probability of Possible Rate of Return		
5%	×	.3	=	1.5%
7%	×	.4	=	2.8%
10%	×	.3	=	3.0%
		Expected rate of return	=	7.3%

of no return, a 20 percent chance of a 10 percent return, a 40 percent chance of a 15 percent return, and a 10 percent chance of a 30 percent return. Note that for a given asset, the sum of the probabilities of the different possible rates of return must equal one. (After all, something has to happen.) If we assume that only four stated rates of return are possible and that the probabilities given for 0, 10, and 15 percent rates of return are correct, the 30 percent return must have a 10 percent chance of occurring.

www.

Calculation of Expected Return

expected rate of return the weighted average of all possible rates of return, where the weights are the probability of each rate of return occurring

The **expected rate of return** of a financial asset is simply the weighted average of all the possible rates of return, where the weights are the probability of each rate of return occurring. The probability of a rate occurring gives that rate's contribution to the total expected return. Thus, in general

(8.1)
$$E(R^A) = p_1 R_1^A + p_2 R_2^A + p_3 R_3^A + \ldots + p_n R_n^A$$
$$= \sum_{i=1}^{n} p_i R_i^A$$

where $E(R^A)$ is Asset A's expected rate of return; $R_1^A, R_2^A, \ldots, R_n^A$ are the possible rates of return for each of n possible states of the world; and $p_1, p_2, \ldots, p_n$ are the associated probabilities that these states will occur.

In our example of Asset A

$$E(R^A) = p_1 R_1^A + p_2 R_2^A + p_3 R_3^A + p_3 R_4^A$$
$$= .3(0.0) + .2(0.10) + .4(0.15) + .1(0.30)$$
$$= 0.11$$

Thus, the expected rate of return to Asset *A* is 11 percent. Similarly, as is shown in Table 8.1, the expected rate of return to Asset *B* is 7.3 percent. Note, as is pointed out by these examples, that the expected rate of return of an asset is not a possible rate of return, but rather a weighted average of the possible rates of return—useful information for comparing assets with different rates of return across different possible states of the world.

Measuring Risk of an Asset

risk a measure of the degree of certainty with which investors can predict that actual rates of return will be close to the expected rate of return

Unless only one rate of return is possible, each financial asset has a certain amount of risk attached to it. The **risk** of a financial asset is a measure of the degree of certainty with which an investor can predict that actual rates of return will be close to the expected rate of return, because risk measures the spread or dispersion of the possible rates of return around the expected rate of return. The greater the spread, the greater the risk, because with a wider spread there is a greater chance of getting rates of return far from the expected rate of return.

Figure 8–2 shows an investor's subjective assessment of the probability distribution of outcomes or yields on two financial assets, A and B. The horizontal axis measures the yield; the vertical axis measures the probability of attaining this yield. As drawn here, the average yield, known as the expected yield, is the same for both assets and equal to $E(Y)$. In the case of a bell-shaped curve, the expected yield is under the highest point of the probability distribution. The dispersion of probable outcomes, as shown, is greater for Asset B than for Asset A. Since the probable yields on Asset A are dispersed more closely about its expected yield, it is considered less risky than Asset B. Dispersion of possible yields about an asset's expected yield indicates the risk associated with an asset and is measured by a concept you may be familiar with if you've taken a statistics course.

variance a measure of dispersion about the mean used to measure risk

The spread between the various possible rates of return and the expected return is usually measured by the **variance** or **standard deviation** (the square root of the variance) of the probability distribution of expected returns. The variance of a probability distribution is found by weighting the relative deviation of the possible rates of return (in state *i*) from the expected rate of return. The deviation of a possible rate of return on Asset A, R_i^A, from the expected rate of return, $E(R^A)$, is $\{ R_i^A - E(R^A) \}$. To compute the variance, each deviation is squared and weighted by its respective probability.[1] Hence the variance, σ_A^2, is

standard deviation a measure of dispersion about the mean used to measure risk; it is the square root of the variance

(8.2)
$$\sigma_A^2 = \left[\sum_{i=1}^{n} P_i \{R_i^A - E(R^A)\}^2 \right]$$

and the standard deviation, σ_A, is simply the square root of the variance

(8.3)
$$\sigma_A = \left(\sum_{i=1}^{n} P_i \{R_i^A - E(R^A)\}^2 \right)^{\frac{1}{2}}$$

---

1. In calculating an estimate of the variance, you have the choice of dividing by the number of possible states, *n*, or as you might have learned in a statistics class, $(n-1)$. For our purposes, we will perform calculations by dividing by *n*.

FIGURE 8–2   THE CONCEPT OF RISK

The diagram below shows an investor's subjective assessment of the probability distribution of outcomes or yields on two financial assets, A and B. The horizontal axis measures the yield; the vertical axis measures the probability of attaining this yield. As drawn here, the average yield, known as the expected yield, is the same for both assets and equal to $E(Y)$. (In the case of a bell-shaped curve, the expected yield is under the highest point of a probability distribution.) The dispersion of probable outcomes, as shown, is greater for Asset B than for Asset A. Because the probable yields on Asset A are dispersed more closely about its expected yield, it is considered less risky than Asset B. Dispersion of possible yields about an asset's expected yield indicates the risk associated with an asset and is measured by the standard deviation of returns, as explained in the text.

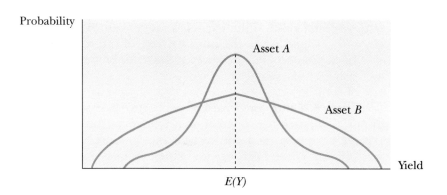

If the possible rates of return are normally distributed (that is, if they have a bell-shaped probability distribution), then roughly two-thirds of all returns will fall within one standard deviation on either side of the expected rate of return, and 95 percent of all returns will fall within two standard deviations on either side. Therefore, the smaller the dispersion, the smaller the standard deviation, and the greater the chance of getting a rate of return close to the expected rate of return. In addition, the smaller the standard deviation, the smaller the risk associated with a financial asset.

From our example in Table 8.1, the variance of Asset A is

$$\sigma_A^2 = [.3(0.0 - .11)^2 + .2(0.1 - .11)^2 + .4(0.15 - .11)^2 + .1(0.3 - .11)^2]$$
$$= 0.0079$$

with $\sigma_A = 0.089$ (the square root of 0.0079). The variance of Asset A as shown by the calculation is 0.79 percent, and its standard deviation is 8.9 percent. With a similar calculation we find that Asset B has a variance of 0.038 percent and a standard deviation of 1.95 percent. Although Asset A has a higher expected rate of return than Asset B (11 percent as compared to 7.3 percent), it carries with it a greater amount of risk, indicated by its higher variance and standard deviation. We cannot tell which asset an investor will choose (or how much of each asset will be chosen) without knowing the investor's preferences toward risk and return and the trade-off between them. It is normally taken for granted that investors are **risk-averse**—that is, they will only accept a greater amount of risk if it comes with a larger expected return. We can visualize that

risk-averse *when investors will only accept a greater amount of risk if it comes with a larger expected return*

FIGURE 8–3 THE TRADE-OFF BETWEEN EXPECTED RETURN AND RISK

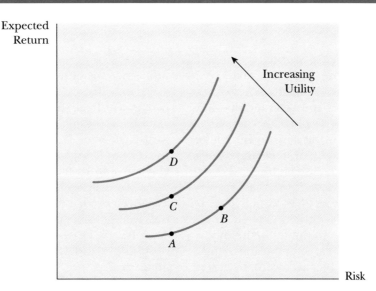

Investors require increasing levels of expected return to take on more risk and maintain a constant level of utility (moving from *A* to *B*). Utility rises as one moves to the left to "higher" indifference curves. At points *A*, *C*, and *D* risk is constant, yet *D* and *C* provide a greater expected return than at *A*.

assumption if we consider an investor's indifference curves for risk and expected return. (Recall that indifference curves in Chapter 3 were introduced when we covered the intertemporal consumption model.) Figure 8–3 demonstrates that to maintain a constant level of utility or satisfaction, the investor must receive an increasing expected rate of return to take on additional risk. In practice, the degree of risk aversion varies among investors.

Measuring Expected Return and Risk of a Portfolio

In our discussion of the various types of intermediation, we noted that a financial intermediary could use portfolio diversification to reduce its overall risk without reducing its expected return. To understand why this is so, we must first derive the expected return and risk for a portfolio (a collection of assets). We already have obtained measures of these concepts for individual assets.

The expected rate of return on a portfolio depends on the expected rates of return on the assets making up the portfolio. More specifically, a portfolio's expected rate of return is the weighted sum of the expected rates of return on the individual assets, where the weights are the proportionate values of the assets making up the portfolio. The expected rate of return on a portfolio of *Z* assets is defined as follows:

(8.4) $$E(R) = w_A R^A + w_B R^B + w_C R^C + \dots + w_Z R^Z$$

BOX 8–1 RISK AND VARIANCE

An Example

To give you a better feel for using variance to measure risk, suppose you can take your Money and Banking course from either of two instructors, whose past course grade distributions are publicly available. Instructor A's most probable grade is the same as Instructor B's; that is, their averages, or expected values, are identical. However, Instructor A is known to give exams that are either very easy or very hard. Instructor B always gives exams that are of the same degree of difficulty. Their grade distributions are given in the figure below.

Whom would you rather take the course from if your only objective were to get a passing grade? If there aren't any quality differences between instructors, you might not want to risk enrolling in Instructor A's section, since the odds of getting a very low grade are much higher than the odds of getting a bad grade from Instructor B. Although the chance of getting a high grade is more likely with Instructor A, there is "downside" risk, too. Other things being equal, you will probably enrol in Instructor B's section.

As you can see from this simple example, variance, or the degree of dispersion about the average or expected value, captures risk. That is why we use variance (and its square root, the standard deviation) to provide a measure of the variability of an asset's expected return—its risk.

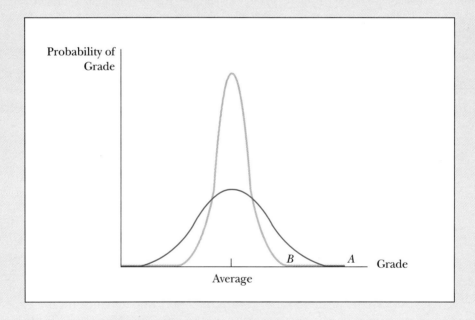

where $E(R)$ is the expected rate of return on the portfolio, R^A is the expected rate of return on Asset A, and w_A is the proportion invested in Asset A, where the w must sum to one.

Measuring the risk, in terms of the variance or standard deviation of a portfolio's expected return, is somewhat more complicated than calculating the risk of an individual asset. For a multi-asset portfolio, we need to know the *covariance* a measure of the degree to which two or more data series are linearly related

covariance of the respective assets' expected returns. Covariance is a measure of the degree to which the returns on two assets change together. A positive covariance means their returns tend to change in the same direction, while a negative covariance means their returns tend to change in the opposite direction. The covariance between two assets, A and B, is given by

$$(8.5) \qquad COV_{AB} = \rho_{AB}\sigma_A\sigma_B$$

where ρ_{AB} is the correlation coefficient of expected returns on the two assets, and σ_A and σ_B are the standard deviations of Assets A and B, respectively. The **correlation coefficient**, ρ_{AB}, the most frequently used measure of linear association, can have values ranging from 1.0, denoting perfect comovement in the same direction, to –1.0, denoting perfect comovement in the opposite direction. Note that if we know the standard deviations and either the covariance or the correlation coefficient, we can determine the "unknown" variable. In equation 8.5 we assumed the correlation coefficient was known, and solved for the covariance. Alternatively, we might know the covariance and the standard deviations and solve for the correlation coefficient:

correlation coefficient a measure of linear association; positive values suggest a direct relationship between two or more series, while negative values indicate that when one series rises, the other falls

$$(8.6) \qquad \rho_{AB} = COV_{AB}/\sigma_A\sigma_B$$

The risk of a portfolio of two assets, as given by its variance, is derived from the following equation:

$$(8.7) \qquad \sigma^2 = w_A^2\sigma_A^2 + w_B^2\sigma_B^2 + 2w_Aw_B\rho_{AB}\sigma_A\sigma_B$$

This equation tells us that the variance of the expected rates of return of the portfolio, σ^2, is a weighted sum of the variances of the expected rate of return on the individual assets, σ_A^2 and σ_B^2, where the weights are the squares of the proportion each asset makes up of the portfolio (that is, the squares of the proportion of the total portfolio value invested in each asset). There is also a weighted covariance term, $2w_Aw_B\rho_{AB}\sigma_A\sigma_B$, which measures how the expected returns of the two assets moving together affect the variance. The correlation coefficient is ρ_{AB}, and σ_A, and σ_B are the standard deviations of Assets A and B, respectively.[2] The correlation coefficient can vary between +1 (perfect positive correlation) and –1 (perfect negative correlation). If there is no relationship between the two expected returns, ρ_{AB} is zero. If an increase in the expected return on Asset A is accompanied by an increase in the expected return on Asset B and vice versa, ρ_{AB} will be positive. If an increase in the expected return on Asset A is accompanied by a reduction in the expected return on Asset B, ρ_{AB} will be negative. The coefficient of correlation is very important to the concept of portfolio diversification.

2. Equation 8.7 can be expanded to include three assets in the portfolio by adding components that take into account the variance of the third asset as well as the degree to which its expected return is correlated with the expected return on the other two assets in the portfolio. Suppose we label this third asset *C*, then the risk of the portfolio will be:

$$\sigma^2 = w_A^2\sigma_A^2 + w_B^2\sigma_B^2 + w_C^2\sigma_C^2 + 2w_Aw_B\rho_{AB}\sigma_A\sigma_B + 2w_Aw_C\rho_{AC}\sigma_A\sigma_C + 2w_Bw_C\rho_{BC}\sigma_B\sigma_C$$

If all assets are uncorrelated, the variance of the expected return on the portfolio will be

$$\sigma^2 = w_A^2\sigma_A^2 + w_B^2\sigma_B^2 + w_C^2\sigma_C^2$$

Portfolio Diversification

We are all familiar with the saying "Don't put all your eggs in one basket." Applying this to portfolio selection, investors should be able to reduce a portfolio's risk of expected return by including a large number of different assets in its composition. The Tobin–Markowitz mean-variance analysis can be used to show that the inclusion of additional assets in a portfolio does not necessarily reduce its risk. However, the risk of a portfolio can be reduced without simultaneously reducing its expected return by combining assets with expected returns that are less than perfectly correlated.

Consider Figure 8–4, where we provide the expected returns to two different assets for five different states of the world: a very weak economy, a weak economy, a normal economy, a strong economy, and a very strong economy. Now suppose you are considering which assets to hold in your portfolio. Do you pick assets that pay off similarly across the different states of the world? Probably not. You will choose to hold securities that shelter your portfolio from fluctuations in the state of the economy: You won't put all your eggs in one basket. Asset A, for example, might be shares of stock in a luxury car company. If the economy is in the doldrums, the demand for luxury cars will wane and the return on these shares will be low. When times get better, the demand will pick up, leading to a more positive investment outlook for these shares. Asset B, on the other hand, might be stock in a firm dealing with bankruptcies. When the economy is doing poorly, this firm may earn high returns; when economic times are good, this firm might not do so well. By holding shares in both companies you shelter your overall portfolio from the business cycle; any gains you might make on one share will be offset by losses on the other. The two shares provide a "floor" to your expected return since they are **negatively correlated**.

negatively correlated two series are negatively correlated when one falls as the other rises

We can illustrate this concept numerically by taking a simple example of a portfolio with only two assets. Suppose Asset A and Asset B each make up 50 percent of the total value of a portfolio. The expected return and standard deviation for Asset A are 10 percent and 0.30, and for Asset B, 25 percent and 0.60, respectively. The expected return of the portfolio is calculated by using equation 8.4 as follows:

$$E(R) = w_A R^A + w_B R^B$$
$$= 0.5(0.1) + 0.5(0.25)$$
$$= 0.175$$

The risk of the portfolio (using its standard deviation) is derived from equation 8.7, where we have not yet plugged in values for the correlation coefficient:

$$\sigma = [w_A^2 \sigma_A^2 + w_B^2 \sigma_B^2 + 2w_A w_B \rho_{AB} \sigma_A \sigma_B]^{1/2}$$
$$= [.5^2(.3)^2 + .5^2(.6)^2 + 2(.5)(.5)\rho_{AB}(.3)(.6)]^{1/2}$$
$$= [.1125 + 0.09\rho_{AB}]^{1/2}$$

FIGURE 8–4   DIFFERENT PAYOFFS IN DIFFERENT STATES OF THE ECONOMY

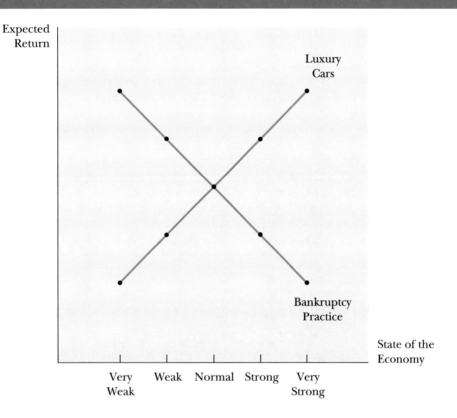

Diversification through holding assets with different payoff structures shelters a portfolio from fluctuations in economic activity.

Now, using the values $\rho_{AB} = +1$, 0, and −1 in the correlation coefficient, we get the risk of returns figures shown in column four below.

Case	$\rho_{AB,BC}$	Expected Return $_{AB}$	Risk of Return $_{AB}$	Risk of Returns with Replacement Asset C
I	+ 1.0	17.5%	45%	50%
II	0.0	17.5%	33%	36%
III	−1.0	17.5%	15%	10%

This table clearly shows the "magic" of Tobin–Markowitz diversification. The risk of return of the portfolio is shown to decline as the degree of positive correlation between the assets in the portfolio is reduced. Furthermore, the expected rate of return on the portfolio is not affected. While we use a negative correlation coefficient in Case III, in the real world very few assets have negative correlations.

Another lesson can be learned from diversification. You can increase the expected return of a portfolio, and at the same time reduce the risk of the expected return, by substituting a riskier asset for a less risky asset—if the expected return of the replacement asset is correlated much less with the other assets than was the case of the asset it replaced.

Suppose that, in the above example, Asset A is replaced by Asset C with an expected return of 20 percent and a standard deviation of 0.40. The expected return of the portfolio is now 22.5 percent rather than 17.5 percent:

$$22.5\% = (0.50)(0.20) + (0.50)(0.25)$$

and the risk of returns with the replacement asset is now $[0.13 + 0.12\rho_{AC}]^{1/2}$. If we assume that in the original portfolio containing Assets A and B, the relevant correlation between these two assets was -1.0, then as shown in the table, when replacing Asset A with the riskier Asset C, the risk of return of the portfolio is smaller when the correlation of returns between Asset C and Asset B is less than zero. Hence, the risk of a portfolio can be reduced by replacing one asset with another as long as the replacement asset is correlated much less with the other assets than was the case with the asset replaced.

Portfolio Selection

Later, when we explain the operations of the various types of financial intermediaries, we will observe that they can be broadly categorized according to the respective characteristics of their asset portfolios. These characteristics can be defined in terms of the concepts of expected return and risk that we have described.

Each financial intermediary is one among many in financial markets competing for the financial claims of deficit spending units. At any given time, each intermediary is confronted with an array of financial assets with a given expected return and risk associated with each one. The intermediary can combine these assets into many different types of portfolios, each different from the others with respect to expected return and risk. How does an intermediary choose among this wide array of possible portfolios?

To demonstrate how a financial intermediary decides on the type of portfolio to hold, let us assume that there are only two assets available on the market. One is a government security with an expected return of R^G and a zero risk. The other is a corporate security with a relatively higher expected return, R^C, and a relatively high degree of risk, σ_C^2. The expected return and risk of the various portfolios containing these two securities depend on the proportion of each security included in the respective portfolio. Let us denote the proportion of government securities by a and corporate securities by $(1 - a)$. The total expected return on a portfolio, $E(R)$, is therefore

(8.8) $$E(R) = aR^G + (1 - a)R^C$$

Since we have assumed the risk of the government security to be zero, the risk of a portfolio, σ^2, is entirely dependent on the portion of the portfolio devoted to the corporate security and the risk attached to it; that is

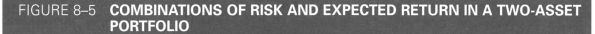

FIGURE 8–5 **COMBINATIONS OF RISK AND EXPECTED RETURN IN A TWO-ASSET PORTFOLIO**

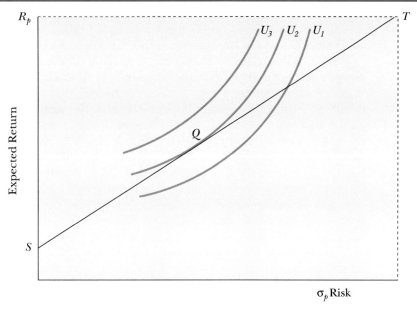

The line *ST* represents the combinations of expected return and risk available to the financial intermediary by varying the proportion of government and corporate securities it holds in its portfolio. Point *S* represents a portfolio consisting of only government securities while point *T* consists entirely of corporate securities. Each indifference curve (U_1, U_2, and U_3) shows the combinations of risk and expected return needed to give the financial intermediary a certain level of utility. (This level is higher on U_3 than U_2 and on U_2 than U_1.) The financial intermediary will hold that portfolio which maximizes its utility: the point of tangency of line *ST* and indifference curve U_2 (point *Q*).

(8.9)
$$\sigma^2 = (1 - a)^2 \sigma_C^2$$

In Figure 8–5, the line *ST* describes the combinations of expected return and risk available to the financial intermediary by varying the proportion in which it divides its portfolio between the government security and the corporate security. Each point on line *ST* represents a particular portfolio with a given amount of expected return and risk. Point *S* on line *ST* represents a portfolio of only the government security (so the return on the portfolio is R^G). As we move to the right of *S*, points along line *ST* represent increasingly larger proportions of the corporate security; at *T* the portfolio consists entirely of the corporate security (so the *expected return on the portfolio*—expected because this asset offers an uncertain return—is R^C). Portfolios to the right of portfolio *S* along line *ST* also have successively higher expected returns and risk.

Which portfolio of those available along line *ST* does a financial intermediary choose? It will choose the portfolio that represents a combination of expected return and risk giving the owners of the intermediary the highest possible level of utility, or satisfaction. Curves U_1, U_2, and U_3 in Figure 8–5 are indifference curves that describe the financial intermediary's preference between expected return and risk. Each indifference curve connects combinations of risk and expected return for which the intermediary receives the same level of utility. It is "indifferent" between portfolios lying along an indifference curve. Its utility level is higher on curve U_2 than on U_1, and higher on U_3 than on U_2. The utility level on U_2, for example, is higher than on U_1 because for a given portfolio risk a higher expected return is received.

As noted above, the shape of an indifference curve tells us something about the intermediary's preference for risk. Intermediaries are risk averters, which means that they must be compensated through increasingly higher expected returns for accepting additional risk. We have drawn the indifference curves in Figure 8–5 convex from below; that is, their slope increases as risk increases. This shape means that as more risk is undertaken, an even larger increment in expected return is needed for our intermediary to accept a little more risk and remain at the same level of utility. The more risk-averse the intermediary, the more the slope of its indifference curve increases as risk increases. A financial intermediary assesses its preference for risk based on what it believes its depositors and liability holders, government regulators, and stockholders feel about the appropriate trade-off between expected return and risk.

The financial intermediary will hold the portfolio that maximizes its utility. Its optimum portfolio is shown in Figure 8–5 at point Q. At this tangency point that portfolio is on the highest possible indifference curve between risk and expected return, given the risk and expected return on the financial securities available in the market as shown by line ST.

www.

The Capital Asset Pricing Model (CAPM)

Capital Asset Pricing Model (CAPM) *a model that shows how the rate of return (or the price of an asset) is determined in an efficient market*

The **Capital Asset Pricing Model (CAPM)** builds on our earlier analysis to show how the rate of return, or the price of an asset, is determined in efficient markets.

Underlying Assumptions

The conclusions of the CAPM critically depend on the following underlying assumptions:

1. All investors prefer the highest expected return for any given level of risk.
2. Capital markets are efficient in that asset prices and yields reflect all information.
3. All investors have the same expectations about each asset's return and risk. This condition is called **homogeneous expectations**. It does not imply that all investors have identical risk–return preference, but that they assess each asset in the same way. Moreover, this assessment is not affected by a change in an investor's income and wealth.

homogeneous expectations *when all market participants hold identical expectations*

4. Investors can both borrow and lend at a risk-free rate of interest.

Efficient Portfolios

efficient portfolio
portfolios that offer the highest expected return, given a constant level of risk

An **efficient portfolio** is a collection of assets that offers the highest possible expected return at a given level of portfolio risk, or the lowest risk for a given expected return. Investors who are risk-averse and utility maximizers will want to hold only efficient portfolios.

In Figure 8–6, points lying in the shaded area give all possible (feasible) portfolios that can be constructed with a given number of risky assets. However, only points lying along the broken line *AD* represent efficient portfolios. Line *AD* is referred to as the efficient frontier. Feasible portfolios to the right of the efficient frontier are not efficient since other portfolios exist that provide a higher expected return at the same level of risk or, alternatively, a lower level of risk at the same expected return. Efficient portfolios are said to dominate all other feasible ones.

Combined Portfolios of Risk-Free and Risky Assets

Suppose that investors want to hold a portfolio of assets that combines a risk-free asset with an efficient portfolio of risky assets found on an efficient frontier. The question now becomes: Which portfolio among those along the efficient frontier should be included in the combined portfolio? The question can be answered with the assistance of Figure 8–7. The curve *AD* is an efficient frontier of portfolios of risky assets similar to that drawn earlier in Figure 8–6. We now draw a straight line from R^S, the risk-free rate of return for the risk-free asset, to intersect the efficient frontier at *V*. The line $R^S V$ shows combinations

FIGURE 8–6   **FEASIBLE AND EFFICIENT PORTFOLIOS**

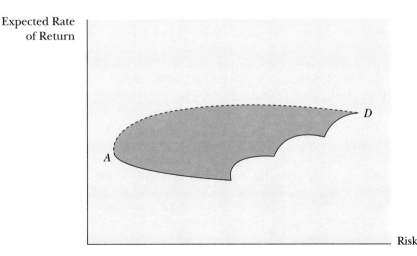

Points lying in the shaded area represent all feasible portfolios of risky assets. However, only points lying along the broken *AD* line represent efficient portfolios. Line *AD* is the efficient frontier.

FIGURE 8–7   **THE CAPITAL MARKET LINE**

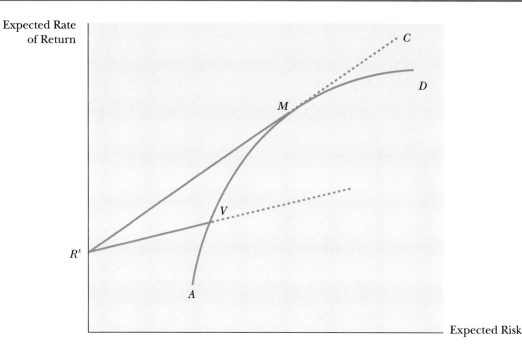

The capital market line, R^SMC, is tangent to the efficient frontier, at M. It represents the efficient frontier of portfolios that combine the market portfolio of risky assets as given at M with borrowing or lending at the risk-free rate of interest.

market portfolio
the optimum portfolio of risky assets

capital market line (CML) *the efficient frontier of combined portfolios given the four underlying assumptions of the CAPM*

of the risk-free asset with the V portfolio of risky assets on the efficient frontier. At R^S on this line only the risk-free asset is held, while at V only the V portfolio of risky assets is held. In between, as we move along the line from R^S to V, increasingly less of the investor's given funds are held in the risk-free asset and more are held in the V portfolio of risky assets. An investor can go beyond point V on the broken portion of the line by borrowing at the risk-free rate.

Combined portfolios along the straight line running from R^S through V are inefficient portfolios relative to those lying on a similar line drawn through R^S but intersecting the efficient frontier above V, because higher expected returns can be obtained at the same risk. Rotating the RSV line upward until it is just tangent to the efficient frontier produces the optimum portfolio of risky assets to be combined with the riskless asset. This optimum portfolio is shown in Figure 8–7 at the tangency point M. The optimum portfolio of risky assets at M is called the market portfolio of risky assets, or simply the **market portfolio**. The straight line R^SMC is called the **capital market line** (**CML**). The CML is now the efficient frontier of combined portfolios, given the four underlying assumptions of the CAPM. The compositions of these efficient portfolios only differ as to the amount of the risk-free asset (or of borrowing at the risk-free rate of interest) that is combined with the market portfolio.

BOX 8–2   DON'T BE LIMITED ON FOREIGN CONTENT

BY GORDON POWERS
Special to *The Globe and Mail*

With RRSP season fast approaching, investors are already receiving reminders about maximizing the 20 percent foreign content in their retirement funds. Good advice—except that most analysts suggest the optimum international component in a well-balanced growth portfolio could be three times that amount.

"The 20 percent limit on RRSPs is a regulatory, not an investment, issue," says Wilfred Hahn, senior vice-president of Royal Bank of Canada's global private banking group. "Canadian investors, even if they're quite conservative, would be wise not to let themselves be constrained by it."

Diversifying among markets to get ahead has long been one of investing's favourite rubrics. But don't Canadians investors going abroad to bump up their returns have to shoulder more risk?

Actually, it's the other way around, says Patrick Forrett, an analyst with Global Strategy Financial Inc. in Toronto. Investing internationally both reduces risk and boosts returns, as the accompanying chart shows.

The chart's vertical axis represents the average return of varying mixes of stock portfolios over time. The portfolios go from having all of your money invested in Canada to having it all outside the country.

The horizontal axis reflects risk, here measured by standard deviation—the degree to which returns fluctuate around their average. The higher the number, the greater the volatility.

Looking back over the 25 years ended September 30, one can see that the return-to-risk ratio is highest somewhere around the point where foreign stocks make up roughly 35 percent of the portfolio. That means you're getting the most return for the least risk.

The Globe and Mail, December 10, 1996, p. C1.

[In early 2000 the federal government raised the foreign content limit to 25 percent in 2000 and to 30 percent in 2001.]

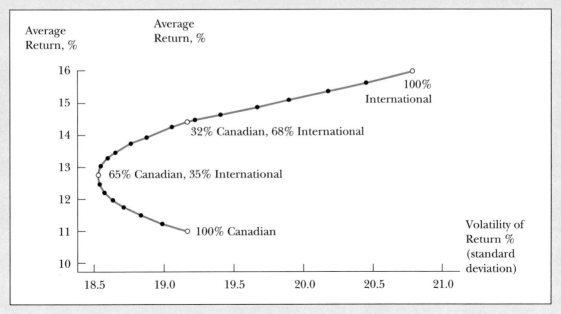

SOURCE: Global Strategy Financial Inc., Ibbotson and Associates.

If all investors have the same expectations about asset returns and risk, each will want to hold a combined portfolio lying along the capital market line. The combination of the risk-free asset and the market portfolio will vary among investors according to their different risk-return preferences. However, no investor will want to hold any portfolio of risky assets other than the market portfolio. If all investors hold identical portfolios of risky assets, then in equilibrium their total holding of any particular risky asset must be equal to the total supply of that asset. It follows that, if all investors hold the market portfolio, then not only must it contain each available asset, but it must do so in the proportion that the value of each asset bears to the market value of all assets in aggregate.

Systematic and Unsystematic Risks

systematic risk
that part in the variability of an asset's return that is attributable to economywide trends and events

unsystematic risk
the variability in the return on an asset that is specific to that asset

The total risk of an individual asset or portfolio of assets may be broken into two components: **systematic risk** (or market risk) and **unsystematic risk** (or specific risk). Systematic risk is that part in the variability of an asset's return that is attributable to economywide trends and events. For example, a change in monetary policy affects the yields on all marketable securities, but not necessarily to the same degree. Unsystematic risk is the variability in the return on an asset that is specific to that asset. For example, the yield on a firm's stock is affected if that firm suffers severe mismanagement or introduces a new product, while the yields of the stocks of other firms remain unaffected. The CAPM assumes that in efficient market portfolios, unsystematic risk is diversified away, leaving only systematic risk.

Measuring Systematic Risk

beta *a measure of the systematic risk of an asset*

How can we measure the systematic risk of an individual asset in a market portfolio? A measure first suggested by William Sharpe is an asset's beta coefficient or, simply, **beta**. Beta is derived by comparing the historical returns of an asset to those of a market portfolio. Earlier we defined the market portfolio as containing every asset in the market. To calculate an asset's beta using all assets in existence would be a horrendous task. Fortunately, this is not necessary because the major characteristic of a market portfolio is that it has no systematic risk. Furthermore, we can construct portfolios in which most, if not all, unsystematic risk is diversified away, leaving only systematic risk, with the inclusion of only a small percentage of all assets in the market. In practice, securities included in a stock index, such as the TSE 300 Index, serve as a surrogate for a market portfolio.

In Figure 8–8, the Xs show the relationship over time between actual yields on Asset A and the market portfolio (or its surrogate). A linear regression (a line that in some sense "best" describes the relationship between these vari-

---

BOX 8–3 BACKGROUNDER

Prospect Theory Comes of Age

Two researchers in behavioural finance published a groundbreaking paper in 1979. They posed the following questions:

- Suppose you have $1000 and need to choose between making a $500 gain without any risk, or face a 50–50 chance to gain either nothing or $1000.

- Suppose you have $1000 and need to choose between making a $500 loss without any risk, or face a 50–50 chance to lose either nothing or $1000.

They found that many people facing the first question chose the $500 gain that did not involve any risk, while most of the people responding to the second question chose the uncertain 50–50 option of either losing $1000, or nothing. If you think about it, both questions offer the same net benefits to an investor. However, the researchers found that people generally put more emphasis on avoiding risk rather than maximizing benefits, and they called this Prospect Theory.

Their results help to explain why many people would rather hold relatively safe, low interest bearing assets (like a GIC) in their portfolios rather than stocks. Over the long haul, stocks will return a higher average net benefit (if history is any guide), but investors tend to be shortsighted and concerned with risk. Suppose you bought a commodity-based mutual fund back in the early 1990s to hold in your RRSP. Its value is probably much lower today, since commodity prices have fallen considerably over the last decade. Should you hold on to the fund, or sell it and take the proceeds and invest in some other fund? Many people will hold on, hoping that the fund will return to its previous value. Others will see that it's probably time to bail out and dump the fund.

We need to remember that psychological factors are sometimes as important as economic factors when determining investment decisions.

SOURCE: Amos Tversky, and Daniel Kahneman, "Prospect Theory: An Analysis of Decision under Risk," *Econometrica* 47 (March 1979), pp. 263–91.

---

ables) of these data is shown by the line AB.[3] The slope of this line is the beta of Asset A. (Statistically, the beta of an individual asset is the covariance between its returns and those of the market portfolio, divided by the variance of the market portfolio's returns.) If an asset has a zero beta, this indicates that it has no systematic risk; if its beta is unity, its systematic risk is equal to market risk; if its beta is larger or smaller than unity, its systematic risk is respectively larger or smaller than market risk.

---

3. The equation of the regression line is $R^A = \alpha + \beta_A R^M + \varepsilon^A$, where R^A and R^M are the rates of return on Asset A and the market portfolio, respectively, and ε^A is a random component capturing other factors left unexplained. The beta of Asset A is given by β_A, a measure of its systematic risk. The total risk, or variance of the return to Asset A is given by $\beta_A{}^2 \sigma_M{}^2 \sigma_e{}^2$, where $\sigma_M{}^2$ is the variance of the return to the market portfolio and $\sigma_e{}^2$ is the variance of the random component ε^A. The first term captures the systematic component of the variance of the expected return to Asset A, while the second captures the unsystematic component. Investors who are well diversified should care only about systematic risk, since they have already reduced unsystematic risk as much as possible.

FIGURE 8–8   YIELDS ON ASSETS A, AND THE MARKET PORTFOLIO

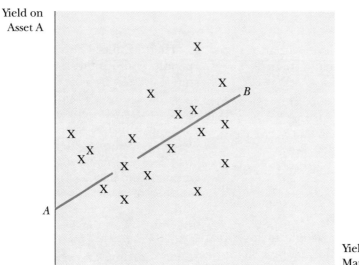

The Xs show the historical relationship between Asset A's yields and those on a market portfolio. A linear regression line of best fit of these data is shown by *AB*. The slope of this line is the beta of Asset A.

The CAPM for Market Pricing

security market line (SML) *the relationship between an asset's expected rate of return and the systematic risk of the asset, the risk-free rate of interest, and the market price of risk*

risk premium *the difference between the expected rate of return on an asset and the risk-free rate of interest*

According to the CAPM or pricing equation, when all investors hold the market portfolio, the price (and thereby the rate of return) of every asset in the market is determined by three factors: (1) the systematic risk of the asset as indicated by its beta, (2) the risk-free rate of interest, and (3) the market price of risk.[4] The relationship between an asset's expected rate of return and these three factors is shown by the **security market line** (**SML**) in Figure 8–9.

The security market line in Figure 8–9 shows the expected rate of return on an asset and the market portfolio as a function of their respective betas. The intercept of this line is the risk-free rate and the slope of this line equals the market price of a unit of risk (or simply the market price of risk). The *SML* slopes upward from left to right, indicating that the expected rate of return on an asset, given the market price of risk, is higher the larger its beta. The market price of a unit of risk is the **risk premium** demanded on the market portfolio, which is the difference between the expected rate of return on the market portfolio and the risk-free rate of interest.

The equation of the security market line, commonly referred to as the CAPM, is

$$(8.10) \qquad E(R^A) = R^F + [E(R^M) - R^F]\beta_A$$

---

4. The CAPM can be expressed in terms of security prices or their rates of return. We have chosen an exposition that relies on rates of return rather than on price. You may see this material presented the other way in a finance course.

BOX 8–4 SYSTEMATIC AND UNSYSTEMATIC RISK

We can graphically describe the difference between systematic and unsystematic risk by considering the following figure. The vertical axis measures the risk of a portfolio, while the horizontal axis measures the number of assets in the portfolio.

If we hold the market portfolio, there is no unsystematic risk. By definition, we have diversified as much as possible and, hence, the only risk left is systematic risk—risk that cannot be eliminated through diversification. If we hold only one asset in our portfolio, the degree of unsystematic risk is high. As we add assets to the portfolio, this component of total risk

falls, since diversification reduces unsystematic risk. In the limit, if we construct a portfolio of all assets in the market (the market portfolio), we have gone as far as we can to reduce unsystematic risk, leaving only systematic risk. You can see in the figure that the total risk of the portfolio approaches the systematic risk as we add more and more assets to the portfolio—that is, as we diversify.

The implication is that investors who create well-diversified portfolios should ignore unsystematic risk and care solely about systematic risks that cannot be diversified out of their portfolios.

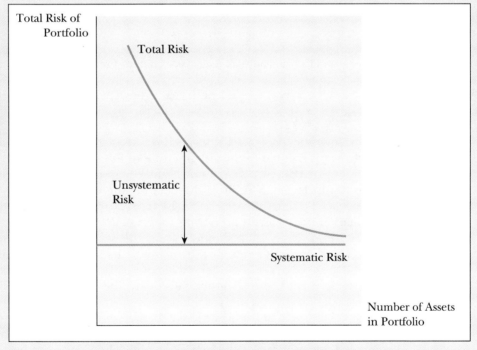

Risk that cannot be eliminated through diversification is systematic risk. As the number of assets in a portfolio rises, unsystematic risk is diversified away.

FIGURE 8–9   THE SECURITY MARKET LINE

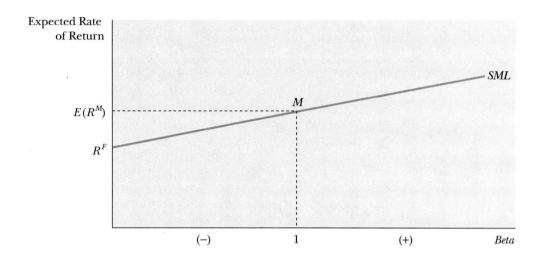

According to the Capital Asset Pricing Model (CAPM), the security market line, *SML*, gives the equilibrium relationship between a risky asset's yield and its systematic risk. The expected rate of return on an asset should be equal to the risk-free rate R^F, plus the product of the market price of risk given by the slope of the *SML* and an asset's risk as indicated by its beta.

This equation says that the expected rate of return on each asset in the market, $E(R^A)$, is equal to the risk-free rate of interest, R^F, plus the product of the market price of risk, $[E(R^M) - R^F]$, and the systematic risk, β_A, of the asset. As is shown in Figure 8–9, since the beta for the market portfolio is equal to one, its expected rate of return is the risk-free rate plus the market price of risk. If the market prices assets according to the CAPM equation 8.10, the rate of return on every risky asset should fall on the security market line shown in Figure 8–9. If an asset's rate of return (given its beta) is above this line, this means that the market is underpricing it relative to the prediction of the CAPM. If the asset's rate of return falls below the line, the asset is overpriced relative to the prediction of the CAPM.

The CAPM is a normative theory. It does not necessarily describe what investors do, but rather what they should do if their behaviour reflects the underlying assumptions of the market model. The CAPM has been subject to extensive empirical testing, but there has been little evidence to support it. This result is not surprising given its assumptions of investor behaviour. It is unlikely that all investors have the same expectations concerning the future rate of return and risk of every asset in the market, and even less likely that the lending rate equals the borrowing rate (which equals the "risk-free" rate of interest).

Arbitrage Pricing Theory (APT) an alternative to the CAPM that assumes multiple sources (factors)

An alternative to the CAPM, which attempts to avoid its shortcomings, is the **Arbitrage Pricing Theory (APT)**. Unlike the CAPM, it is not based on unre-

factors the *underlying determinants of the expected return, or price of an asset; examples include the inflation rate, the term structure of interest rates, and industrial production*

alistic assumptions of investor behaviour or on a common market portfolio of risky assets that is held by all of them when market equilibrium is achieved. However, like the CAPM, the APT states that the expected return, or the price of an asset, depends on its systematic risk. Whereas the CAPM defines only one source of systematic risk—market conditions[5]—the APT assumes multiple sources referred to as **factors**. The APT can be expressed by the following linear relationship:

$$(8.11) \qquad E(R^A) = R^F + \beta_1 F_1 + \beta_2 F_2 + \beta_3 F_3 + \dots + \beta_K F_K$$

where $E(R^A)$ is the expected return on an individual asset; $F_1, F_2, F_3, \dots, F_K$ are systematic risk factors (candidates like the inflation rate, the term structure of interest rates, and industrial production have been suggested as useful factors to consider); $\beta_1, \beta_2, \beta_3, \dots, \beta_K$ indicate the sensitivity of the asset's expected return to the respective factors; and R^F is the risk-free rate of return. The APT is a relatively new theory, and hence the identification of factors that generate systematic risk awaits conclusive evidence. Preliminary findings suggest the APT is better at explaining the historical data than the CAPM, but that may be the result of the empirical methods and tests employed by different researchers.

We will return to issues concerning portfolio models in Chapter 10, when we examine the degree to which options and futures can be used to reduce risk. At that point, we should be able to determine an intermediary's "optimal" hedge ratio—the optimal proportion of its cash position it should hedge by entering into offsetting futures transactions. We will also touch on the links between futures prices and cash prices, as well as the manner in which options are priced.

KEY TERMS

Arbitrage Pricing Theory (APT)	diversification	payments intermediation
asset transformation	efficient portfolio	risk
beta	expected rate of return	risk premium
Capital Asset Pricing Model (CAPM)	factors	risk-averse
capital market line (CML)	homogenous expectations	security market line (SML)
capital-value intermediation	interest rate intermediation	standard deviation
correlation coefficient	liquidity-risk intermediation	systematic risk
covariance	market portfolio	unsystematic risk
default-risk intermediation	maturity-risk intermediation	variance
denomination intermediation	negatively correlated	

---

5. For this reason the CAPM is sometimes called a single-factor model.

REVIEW QUESTIONS

1. What is the difference between the direct and indirect flow of funds in an economy?
2. Describe the various types of financial intermediation.
3. How can an investor measure expected returns and their risks for an asset and a portfolio of assets?
4. How does the slope of an indifference curve explain risk aversion?
5. Under what conditions can diversification reduce the overall risk associated with a portfolio of assets?
6. What is the difference between systematic and unsystematic risk? How is systematic risk measured in the CAPM?
7. What is an efficient portfolio? What is a market portfolio of risky assets? Will investors ever hold assets that fall along the efficient frontier?
8. Suppose you have the following information:

Probability of State %	Expected Asset A	Rate of Asset B	Return Asset C
.10	1%	–2%	3%
.25	3%	–4%	4%
.15	8%	5%	–5%
.25	4%	7%	4%
.10	–2%	9%	–3%
.15	0%	4%	–2%

You are also told that the variance of Asset A is 3.3, the variance of Asset B is 5.5, and the variance of Asset C is 4.3; and that the correlation coefficient between Assets A and B is 0.7, between Assets A and C is –0.8, and between Assets B and C is 0.5.

a. Using a figure similar to that of Figure 8–4, plot the expected return data against each state of the economy for all three assets.
b. Calculate the expected return and risk to a portfolio composed of equal shares of Assets A and B.
c. Calculate the expected return and risk to a portfolio composed of equal shares of Assets A and C.
d. Calculate the expected return and risk to a portfolio composed of equal shares of Assets B and C.
e. Calculate the expected return and risk to a portfolio composed of equal shares of Assets A and B and C. Of the four portfolios you have examined, which one leads to the lowest risk? to the highest expected return?

9. If an investor holds two securities, the expected return on the portfolio is

$$R^P = w_A R^A + w_B R^B$$

where w_i is the share of total funds invested in asset i, and R^i is the expected return on security i. Assume the expected returns are equal at 10 percent, and that the standard deviations of the expected returns are equal at 2.0.

a. Assuming that the securities are perfectly positively correlated, what are expected portfolio return and risk if
   i) only Asset A is held?
   ii) only Asset B is held?
   iii) Assets A and B are held in equal proportions?
b. With respect to (iii), does diversification reduce risk? Why?
c. If the securities are assumed to be perfectly negatively correlated, what are expected portfolio return and risk if
   i) only Asset A is held?
   ii) only Asset B is held?
   iii) Assets A and B are held in equal proportions?
d. With respect to part (iii), does diversification reduce risk? Why?

10. This question relies on information in Question 9. Suppose you have no idea how the returns on Assets A and B are related. If both assets are held in equal proportions, what would be necessary for portfolio risk to be zero? Why?

11. Can unsystematic risk be eliminated through diversification? Explain your answer using properly labelled diagrams.

12. Suppose you have the following information:

Probability of State %	Expected Asset A	Rate of Asset B	Return Asset C
.10	15%	9%	13%
.25	–1%	4%	–2%
.15	2%	2%	4%
.25	–3%	3%	–8%
.10	6%	1%	2%
.15	3%	–14%	3%

You are also told that the variance of Asset A is 10.5, the variance of Asset B is 3.2, and the variance of Asset C is twice as large as that of Asset A. The correlation coefficient between Assets A and B is –0.3, between Assets A and C is 0.1, and between Assets B and C is 0.9.

a. What are the expected return and risk to a portfolio composed of equal shares of Assets A and B and C?
b. What are the expected return and expected risk to a portfolio composed of 10 percent in Asset A, 30 percent in Asset B, and the balance in Asset C?

c. What are the expected return and risk to a portfolio composed only of Asset C?

d. Is the risk of the portfolio in your answer to (b) greater than the portfolio in (c)? Why?

13. Congratulations. You've just inherited a portfolio composed of equal shares of Pete's Pizza Parlour and Fred's Vacuum Supply Shop. The following table describes the payoffs to each share under three different possible states of the world.

Probability of State %	Expected Rate of Return	
	Pete's Pizza Parlour	Fred's Vacuum Supply Shop
.5	15%	9%
.15	–1%	4%
.35	2%	–12%

You know that the variance of Pete's Pizza Parlour shares is 15.5 and that of Fred's Vacuum Supply Shop is 12.5. You also know that the correlation coefficient is –0.5.

a. What is the expected return to your portfolio? What is the risk of the portfolio?

b. Your friend tells you that you should be holding 2/3 of your portfolio in shares of Pete's Pizza Parlour. Is he right? Why?

c. Your sister tells you she thinks you need to hold 90 percent of your portfolio in Fred's Vacuum Supply Shop shares. She says it will reduce the risk of your portfolio and raise your expected return. Is she correct? Why?

14. You are about to decide how to allocate $100 000 across three different stockbrokers, whose expected returns are described by the following table:

Probability of of State%	Expected Rate of Return		
	Boris	Sally	Natasha
.50	–5%	2%	6%
.15	1%	–4%	4%
.35	8%	6%	–6%

You are told that the variance of Boris's returns is 15, that of Sally's is 10, while Natasha's returns have a variance of 8. The correlation between Boris's returns and Sally's returns is 0.4 while that between Boris and Natasha is –0.8. The correlation between Sally's returns and Natasha's returns is –0.4.

a. Using a figure similar to that of Figure 8–4, plot the expected return data against each state of the economy for all three stockbrokers.

b. Calculate the expected return and risk to a portfolio split evenly between the three stockbrokers.

c. Calculate the expected returns and risks to a portfolio if you give all your money to Boris to invest. Repeat this for Sally and Natasha.

d. Calculate the expected return and risk to a portfolio split evenly between Natasha and Boris.

e. Calculate the expected return and risk to a portfolio split evenly between Sally and Boris.

f. Calculate the expected return and risk to a portfolio split evenly between Sally and Natasha.

g. Given your answers to (c), (d), (e), and (f), will you invest all your money with one stockbroker or will you split the portfolio evenly across two of the brokers? Why?

SELECTED READINGS

Black, Richard, and C. Telmer. "Liability Management Using Dynamic Portfolio Strategies." Department of Finance Working Paper 2000-1, Ottawa.

Buckley, A. "An Introduction to Security Returns." *European Journal of Finance* 5 (3, 1999).

Cochrane, John H. "New Facts in Finance," *Economic Perspectives*. Federal Reserve Bank of Chicago (Third Quarter 1999), pp. 36–58

———. "Portfolio Advice for a Multifactor World." *Economic Perspectives*, Federal Reserve Bank of Chicago (Third Quarter 1999), pp. 59–78.

Cromwell, N., W. Taylor, and J. Yoder. "Diversification Across Mutual Funds in a Three-Moment World." *Applied Economics Letters* 7 (4, 2000).

Fama, Eugene. *Foundations of Finance: Portfolio Decisions and Securities Prices*. New York: Basic Books, 1976.

Fama, Eugene, and Kenneth French. "Common Risk Factors in the Returns on Stocks and Bonds." *Journal of Financial Economics* 33 (1, February 1993), pp. 3–56.

Huang, Y. "An Empirical Test of the Risk–Return Relationship on the Taiwan Stock Exchange." *Applied Financial Economics* 7 (3, 1997).

Jacoby, G., D. Fowler, and A. Gottesman. "The Capital Asset Pricing Model and the Liquidity Effect: A Theoretical Approach." *Journal of Financial Markets* 3 (1), pp. 69–81.

Markowitz, Harry. *Portfolio Selection: Efficient Diversification of Investments*. New York: Wiley, 1959.

Morelli, D. "Tests of Structural Change Using Factor Analysis in Equity Returns." *Applied Economics Letters* 6 (4, 1999).

Robinson, M.J. "Univariate Canadian CAPM Tests," in M.J. Robinson and B.F. Smith (eds.), *Canadian Capital Markets*. London, Ont.: Western Business School, 1993.

Shaken, Jay. "The Current State of Arbitrage Pricing Theory." *Journal of Finance* 47 (September 1992), pp. 1569–74.

Sharpe, William F. "A Simplified Model for Portfolio Analysis." *Management Science* 9 (January 1963), pp. 277–93.

———. *Portfolio Theory and Capital Markets*. New York: McGraw-Hill, 1970.

Tobin, James. "Money, Capital and Other Stores of Value." *American Economic Review* (May 1961), pp. 26–37.

———. "A General Equilibrium Approach to Monetary Theory." *Journal of Money, Credit and Banking* (February 1969), pp. 15–29.

Tversky, Amos, and Daniel Kahneman. "Prospect Theory: An Analysis of Decision under Risk." *Econometrica* 47 (March 1979), pp. 263–91.

CHAPTER NINE

PAYMENTS INTERMEDIATION AND THE CREATION OF MONEY

After reading this chapter you should be able to

1. Explain what is meant by "debt monetization"

2. Differentiate between primary and secondary deposits

3. Demonstrate the deposit creation process by an individual bank

4. Show how clearing drain and currency drain affect the deposit creation process

5. Extend the logic of the deposit creation process beyond demand deposits to the creation of other deposit liabilities

6. Use reserve positions to show how a banking system can multiply its deposits

7. Incorporate near-banks into the deposit creation mechanism and demonstrate how this is related to the supply of money in the economy

In Chapter 8 we referred to payments intermediation as the transformation of financial assets into a medium of exchange and noted that it is undertaken by the government's central bank and by depository institutions. Since payments intermediation was traditionally the primary function of commercial banks, it has also come to be known as banking. Today, it is not only the commercial banks, which in Canada are the chartered banks or simply "the banks," that engage in payments intermediation, but also other depository institutions such as trust companies, mortgage loan companies, caisses populaires, and credit unions. Depository institutions other than the banks are referred to as the **near-banks**.

near-banks
depository institutions other than the banks

In earlier years the banks were unique in that they were the only institutions that transformed commercial loans into notes and deposits that served as the medium of exchange. The issue of notes for circulation has become the sole prerogative of the government's central bank. While lending and the associated creation of deposits that serve as a medium of exchange remain the primary role of the Canadian chartered banks, they now share this payments intermediation role with the near-banks. However, because of their relative size, and therefore the predominance of their deposits in the payments system, the banks retain much of their former uniqueness.

In this chapter we learn the mechanics of how depository institutions create deposits and the limitations imposed on the them, showing us how these institutions can create and destroy money. The discussion, which begins with deposit creation, and hence money creation, by the chartered banks, is later extended to include the near-banks.

Debt Monetization and the Money Supply

debt monetization the transformation of financial assets into money

The transformation of financial assets into money is also known as **debt monetization**. In Canada debt is monetized by the Bank of Canada and the chartered banks. The Bank of Canada monetizes the government's debt when, for example, it purchases government bonds and pays for them with its own liabilities, which include Bank of Canada notes. In other words, Bank of Canada notes (that is, paper money in our pockets) are the result of government debt monetization by the central bank. The chartered banks monetize debt whenever they purchase securities and pay for them with their own liabilities in the form of deposits, or extend loans by exchanging the borrowers' promissory notes for bank deposits.

www.

legal tender financial assets that by law must be accepted for all payments

Notes issued by the Bank of Canada because of government debt monetization are **legal tender**, which means that by law they must be accepted for all payments. Certain coins also have legal tender status. However, deposits held with the chartered banks and the near-banks are not legal tender. Hence, the ability of these institutions to monetize debt depends on the public's acceptance of their deposits as payment. This acceptance, in turn, depends on the public's confidence in the ability of depository institutions to convert their deposit liabilities into Bank of Canada notes and coins, which are legal tender.

Bank Deposits and the Money Supply

demand liabilities deposits that must be paid or transferred on demand

Funds held on deposit at a bank are shown on its balance sheet as a liability because they represent an amount owed by the bank that it must ultimately pay or transfer to someone else. Deposits that must be paid or transferred on demand by a bank are commonly called its **demand liabilities**. For analytical purposes they are classified as primary deposits and derivative or secondary deposits. The essential difference between the two is that only derivative or secondary deposits add to or subtract from the total money supply.

Primary Deposits

Let us assume that an individual deposits currency with a bank, which credits his or her account accordingly. In the following example, $100 in the form of currency has been deposited with Bank A. The bank's demand deposits have increased by $100, and at the same time its assets in the form of currency have

reserve asset *an asset held to allow a bank to convert the public's deposits into cash on demand or short notice*

increased by an equivalent amount. For a bank, currency is a **reserve asset** because it is held to allow the bank to convert the public's deposits held with it into cash on demand or short notice.

BALANCE SHEET CHANGES FOR BANK A

Assets		Liabilities	
Reserves (currency)	+$100	Primary deposit	+$100

An increase in a bank's deposits that increases its currency holdings, or reserves, by an equivalent amount is called a **primary deposit**. Primary deposits may result not only from the deposit of currency (cash), but also from the deposit of cheques drawn on other banks.[1] These cheques will increase the cash reserves of the receiving bank, since cheques may be converted into currency on demand through clearinghouse operations, which will be discussed later.

primary deposit *a deposit that may result not only from the deposit of currency (cash), but also from the deposit of cheques drawn on other banks*

While a demand deposit is part of the money supply, changes in a bank's primary deposits do not result in a net addition to or subtraction from the money supply. All that occurs is a change in the composition of the money supply. In the case where currency is deposited in Bank A and the depositor chooses to hold money in the form of bank deposits rather than currency, the decrease in the amount of currency in the hands of the public equals the increase in bank deposits. Therefore, the total money supply remains unaffected.

In the next example, in which the depositor chooses to transfer a bank deposit by means of a cheque from Bank B to Bank A, the total money supply also remains unaffected. The only change, as shown in the balance sheets of the two banks, is a transfer of deposits (and reserves) from one bank to another.

BALANCE SHEET CHANGES FOR BANK A

Assets		Liabilities	
Reserves	+$100	Primary deposits	+$100

BALANCE SHEET CHANGES FOR BANK B

Assets		Liabilities	
Reserves	−$100	Primary deposit	−$100

Derivative Deposits

When an individual obtains a loan from a bank, he or she usually receives the proceeds of the loan in the form of a demand deposit. The bank's balance sheet will show an increase in deposits and a corresponding increase in loans.

derivative (secondary) deposits *newly created deposits that do not increase the reserves of a bank*

BALANCE SHEET CHANGES FOR BANK A

Assets		Liabilities	
Loans	+$100	Primary deposits	+$100

The newly created deposits are called **derivative** or **secondary deposits**. They differ from primary deposits in that they do not increase the reserves of

1. As we will see, these cheques may include a cheque on the central bank.

promissory notes
promises to repay a loan with principal and interest

the lending bank. In return for a borrower's **promissory note** (debt, which is not money), the bank creates a deposit (its own debt, which is money). Thus, when the bank extends a loan, it makes a net addition to the money supply; the borrower's debt is monetized. The money supply is also increased when a bank buys a bond or other financial security in the market.

Assume Bank A buys a security for $1000 and pays for it by writing a cheque against itself.[2] The seller deposits this cheque in his or her account, which happens to be in Bank A. The following change will be recorded in Bank A's balance sheet:

BALANCE SHEET CHANGES FOR BANK A

Assets		Liabilities	
Securities	+$1000	Demand (derived) deposits	+$1000

In return for the public's debt in the form of a security, the bank has created its own debt in the form of a derivative deposit (a demand deposit, but we mark it as derived since it is a derivative deposit). The significant difference between these two types of debts is that only the bank's debt is money.

In the above case we assumed that the seller of the financial security deposited the proceeds in the bank that purchased the security. Let us now assume that the seller of the security has no account in Bank A but has one in Bank B, where the seller deposits the proceeds of his or her sale of the security to Bank A. This will transfer cash reserves from Bank A to Bank B, as shown below.

BALANCE SHEET CHANGES FOR BANK A

Assets		Liabilities
Reserves	−$1000	
Securities	+$1000	

BALANCE SHEET CHANGES FOR BANK B

Assets		Liabilities	
Reserves	+$1000	Deposits	+$1000

For the banking system as a whole, deposits and security holdings have increased, but reserves have remained unchanged. From the point of view of Bank B, the new deposits are primary because the bank's reserves have been increased by an amount equal to the increase of deposit liabilities. In terms of the whole banking system, however, they are derivative deposits because there has been no corresponding change in the total volume of the banking system's reserves.

credit *savings available to be lent to deficit economic units*

We have shown that a bank can increase the money supply by creating **credit**. Credit is created when a bank extends loans and when it buys securities. Similarly, when a bank sells securities or retires loans without extending new ones, credit is destroyed and the money supply is decreased.

---

2. A cheque drawn by a bank on itself it referred to as a draft in Canada and a cashier's *cheque* in the United States.

We must now answer a critical question. Is there a limit to the amount of credit a bank or banking system can create or destroy? In answering we must beware of what is called the "fallacy of composition." We must remember that what is true for the individual bank is not true for the banking system as a whole, nor is it true for a monopoly bank that also constitutes the entire banking system.

Deposit Creation by an Individual Bank in a Banking System

Reserve Requirements

cash reserves *cash held by financial institutions to meet the demand for cash*

desired cash reserve ratio *the ratio of total deposits that financial institutions want to hold as cash to meet the demand for cash*

The public will regularly use bank deposits as money if it is confident that the banks can convert these deposits on demand into currency and that cheques written against these deposits will be generally accepted in payment of debt. The fact that a bank can convert its deposits to currency does not mean that it has to hold an equivalent amount of currency against each deposit. From experience the banks know what amount of their deposits will be converted into currency under normal circumstances. They know, therefore, how much currency must be held in their vaults, cash tills, and automated banking machines against a given amount of deposits. The absolute amount of currency held by a bank is called the bank's **cash reserves**; the percentage of deposits held in the form of currency is known as the bank's **desired cash reserve ratio**.[3] During the early history of banking, banks determined the reserve ratio through custom and experience. Later, to ensure a sound monetary and banking system and to protect the interests of depositors, governments imposed a legal minimum cash reserve ratio. In the early 1990s the requirement for chartered banks to hold reserves was phased out, so that Canadian intermediaries are no longer legally required to hold a minimum cash reserve against their deposit liabilities.[4]

We noted earlier that a bank has two types of deposits: primary and derivative. Primary deposits can increase without limit because with each change in them, the bank's currency and reserves change by a corresponding amount. However, since this is not the case with a change in derivative deposits, the ability of an individual bank in a banking system to create deposits is limited. Let us illustrate this proposition.

Suppose that a bank wants to hold an amount of currency in its vaults and cash tills equal to 5 percent of its deposits.[5] This amount is assumed to be

---

3. At this stage of our discussion, we assume that the bank's cash reserves consist entirely of currency. At a later stage we will learn that, in practice, the cash reserves of the banks consist of their currency holdings and their deposits with the central bank. Because the banks can draw down these deposits at any time, they may be considered currency.

4. Until July 1994 the chartered banks had to hold a declining level of required reserves based on historical averages (using July 1991 to June 1992 data). Today, chartered banks are not required to hold a minimum reserve against their deposit liabilities, although they are required to satisfy other conditions (that we will discuss in a later chapter).

5. We assume here and in the discussion that follows that all of the banks' deposits are demand deposits. Later, we will consider time, or notice, deposits.

sufficient to meet all of the bank's normal demands to convert deposits into currency.

Now suppose an individual deposits $1000 in currency in Bank A, which makes the following entry in its books:

BALANCE SHEET CHANGES FOR BANK A

Assets		Liabilities	
Reserves (currency)	+$1000	Demand (primary) deposits	+$1000

The bank's balance sheet shows that its currency holdings have increased by an amount equal to the increase in its deposits. As a result, its increase in reserves equals 100 percent of the increase in deposits. With a desired reserve ratio of 5 percent, Banks A's desired reserves against the increase in deposits are only $50.

Banks are in business to make profit. They have to produce a reasonable return for their shareholders; otherwise, the shareholders will employ their funds elsewhere. The banks do not earn a penny on currency that sits idle in their own vaults, cash tills, and automated bank machines. It is, therefore, in the best interests of a bank to hold only sufficient currency to meet the day-to-day demands of its customers. There may be times, especially in periods of economic depression, when the banks hold more currency (and therefore larger reserves) than is needed to meet the normal demands of their customers. This increase may be the result of the banks' inability to put their currency holdings into earning assets, or of their desire to avoid the risks of lending and purchasing securities at low prevailing interest rates.

In our example, under normal conditions Bank A holds only $50 of the $1000 in currency as desired reserves. The remaining $950, which is not required for cash reserve purposes, can be considered excess reserves (excess reserves = actual reserves – desired reserves). To maximize its profit potential, the bank will put its excess reserves to work earning returns for its shareholders by using them to extend loans and to buy securities.

When a bank makes a loan or purchases a security, it can make payment by using currency directly from its vaults and cash tills, by issuing a bank draft, or by establishing a deposit account. If the bank employs the first method of settlement, it will immediately lose currency in an amount equal to its loans or purchases of securities. The amount of currency paid out must not exceed its excess reserves. As a first approximation, we can therefore conclude that *an individual bank must restrict any net increase in its loans and purchase of securities to an amount equal to its excess reserves.*

More usually a bank will make settlement by issuing a bank draft (a cheque on itself) or by creating a deposit account. If a cheque is issued, the bank can lose cash through the clearinghouse operations (to be discussed below). Alternatively, if settlement is made by creation of a deposit, currency will be lost only if the holder of the deposit writes a cheque against it that is deposited with another financial institution, or withdraws it in cash. If the deposit were held indefinitely, the bank would lose no currency. Then the only restriction on a bank's ability to expand its loans and security holdings would be its desired reserve requirements against its deposits. In practice, such a situation is conceivable for an individual bank only if it is a monopoly bank and if bank deposits are the only form of money.

A borrower of funds will not usually leave them in his or her account with the lending bank indefinitely. The borrower will probably withdraw currency from an account in the lending bank or write cheques against it to meet obligations to individuals, businesses, or governments. The individual's cheques may be taken to other banks, which will then demand currency from the lending bank. As a result, borrowed funds in the form of demand deposits will be lost by the lending bank to other banks and to nonbank currency holdings. The individual bank, therefore, cannot assume that any of the funds transferred when it makes loans will remain with it. This situation is also true when it transfers funds in payment of security purchases. Our initial conclusion remains: An individual bank cannot safely expand its loans and investments beyond its excess reserves.

Clearinghouse Operations and the Clearing Drain

clearing drain the loss of cash reserves by one bank to another

The loss of cash reserves by one bank to another is called a **clearing drain**. Depositors of a bank write cheques against their accounts in payment for goods, services, and debts. Many of the recipients of these cheques will take them to other banks, where they will demand currency or place them on deposit. (For simplicity, we assume away the existence of near-banks.) Suppose, for example, that a cheque is written against a deposit held in Bank A and that this cheque is cashed by Bank B or deposited with it. Bank B now holds a cheque written against an account in Bank A. In the early days of banking, Bank B would send its messenger with the cheque to Bank A and demand cash. As a result, cash drained from Bank A to Bank B. If the two banks were close to each other, Bank A could expect this drain to follow quickly. Of course, at the same time that Bank B's messengers went to Bank A, the latter's messengers went to Bank B for the same reason. In time, instead of the banks' messengers going from one bank to another to redeem each others' cheques into cash, they met in a common place that became known as a clearinghouse. Here all the cheques would be gathered up and a tabulation (similar to that shown in Table 9.1) would be prepared before settlement was made.

Table 9.1 shows the clearing drains in a banking system composed of four banks. Bank A experiences no drain since the claims by it for cash reserves are equal to the claims on it. Banks C and D, however, have net claims against them and therefore lose cash. This loss is a net gain to Bank B. While the principles of clearinghouse operations illustrated by the simple example in our table still apply today, they have become much more sophisticated and are now accomplished electronically. In addition, instead of physically moving cash from one bank to another, settlement is made by debiting or crediting a bank's settlement account with the central bank.

A bank that expands its lending, and therefore its derivative deposits, faster than the rest of the banking system can expect to have an adverse clearing drain. A bank with a large number of branches relative to the rest of the banking system can expect to experience a favourable clearing drain. If a bank anticipates an adverse clearing drain it must limit its expansion (lending and creation of deposits) to an amount less than the volume of its excess reserves.

TABLE 9.1	**CLEARING OPERATIONS**				
	In Dollars				

Claims by	Cheques Drawn against Deposits in				Total Claims by
	A	B	C	D	
A	–	5	6	7	18
B	6	–	7	9	22
C	8	4	–	2	14
D	4	6	4	–	14
Total Claims against	18	15	17	18	68

Bank	Total Claims by	Total Claims against	Net
A	18	18	0
B	22	15	+7
C	14	17	–3
D	14	18	–4

However, a bank that expects a favourable clearing drain can safely expand its lending beyond its initial excess reserves.[6]

Table 9.2 shows the net effect on the balance sheet of Bank A following an increase in primary deposits of $1000. The table is divided into two parts. In Part I Bank A maintains a 5 percent desired reserve ratio and expands its loans and deposits by $950. All of these deposits and an equivalent amount of reserves are lost by the bank in subsequent clearinghouse operations. Therefore, the net effect of the initial increase in primary deposits is a net increase of $1000 in deposits, $950 in loans, and $50 in reserves.

In Part II we assume that Bank A has a consistently favourable clearing balance equal to 2 percent of its newly created deposits. With a clearing balance of zero, our bank can create $950 in loans and deposits, the amount of its excess reserves. With a favourable clearing balance, the bank can create more than $950 in deposits and still meet all the demands on it for cash. It can create deposits of 1/0.981 times the volume of its excess reserves.[7] With excess reserves equal to $950 following an initial increase in primary deposits of $1000 and a desired reserve ratio of 5 percent, the bank can create deposits equal to $968.40. The cheques presented by other banks for collection are 2 percent less than the amount of these newly created deposits. The bank's

---

6. A favourable clearing balance over a period provides a bank with excess reserves. Thus, while during any given day a banker may expand the bank's investments and deposits beyond the bank's excess reserves, in the long run the expansion must be equal to the increase in reserves (its excess reserves).

7. The ratio 1/0.981 is based on the formula

$$x = 1/[(1 - q) + rq]$$

where r is the reserve ratio, q is the percentage of new deposits that return to the bank, and x is the multiple of its excess reserves by which the bank may expand its deposits. In the formula, r acts as the contractionary force, while q has the opposite effect.

TABLE 9.2   BALANCE SHEET CHANGES FOR BANK A

PART I: 5 PERCENT RESERVE RATIO (IN DOLLARS)

	Assets			Liabilities		
Stage 1						
Primary Deposit	Reserves:	+	1 000	Deposits	+	1 000
State 2						
Credit Expansions	Loans:	+	950	Deposits:	+	950
Stage 3						
Clearing Drain	Reserves:	–	950	Deposits:	–	950
Net Effect	Reserves:	+	50	Deposits:	+	1 000
	Loans:	+	950			000
		+	1 000		+	1 000

PART II: 5 PERCENT RESERVE RATION AND FAVOURABLE CLEARING DRAIN (IN DOLLARS)

	Assets			Liabilities		
Stage 1						
Primary Deposit	Reserves:	+	1 000.00	Deposits	+	1 000.00
Stage 2						
Credit Expansions	Loans:	+	968.40	Deposits	+	968.40
Stage 3						
Cleaning Drain	Reserves:	–	949.04	Deposits	–	949.04
Net Effect	Reserves:	+	50.96	Deposits	+	1 019.36
	Loans:	+	968.40			
		+	1 019.36		+	1 019.36

reserves therefore decline by only $949.04. The net effect, as shown in the table, is a $1019.36 increase in deposits, a $50.96 increase in reserves, and a $968.40 increase in loans. A favourable clearing balance equal in value to 2 percent of its newly created deposits allowed our bank to expand its loans and its deposits by $19.36 more than it could without such a favourable clearing balance.

If one bank in a banking system has a favourable clearing balance, other banks in the system must have unfavourable balances. The bank or banks in the system that have adverse clearing balances cannot expand their investments and deposits to the full extent of their excess reserves. But for the banking system as a whole, there can be neither a favourable nor an unfavourable clearing position.

Currency Drain

We have seen that the ability of an individual bank to create deposit money depends principally on its reserve position. A proportion of its reserves (which we have called desired reserves), specified by custom, by experience (and sometimes by law), has to be held in the bank's vaults, cash tills, and bank machines, and usually also with an agency of the government such as a central bank. The remainder, which we have called excess reserves, is available for the creation of deposits. However, the amount of excess reserves, and therefore a bank's potential ability to expand its deposits, is subject to fluctuation resulting from favourable or adverse clearing balances. Other factors also affect a bank's excess reserves. Some of the more important of these are the nonbank public's propensity to change the amount of its currency holdings, the relative preferences of the nonbank public for time and demand deposits, the willingness of a bank to lend and of borrowers to borrow, and government monetary policy. We will consider the last factor in later chapters dealing with central banking and the policies of the federal government.

Suppose that the total money holdings of the nonbank public consist of currency and commercial bank deposits. When people decide to hold more currency as part of their given money holdings, they exchange bank deposits for currency. The cash reserves and deposits of the individual bank and of the entire banking system are reduced by an amount equal to the withdrawal of currency into public circulation. In Table 9.3 we present three examples of currency withdrawal from Bank A. In the first example the bank supplies $100 of currency demanded for circulation by reducing its deposits by this amount, and by reducing its desired reserves by $5 and its excess reserves by $95. In the second example the bank does not initially hold any excess reserves. As in the first case, it supplies $5 in currency to the public by reducing its desired reserves by this amount. But to supply the remaining $95 of currency, it liquidates $95 in loans for cash, which it pays out to the public.

In the third example the bank's initial deposits are $10 000, against which it holds desired reserves of $500. It meets the demand for currency by reducing its deposits and reserves by the $100 the public withdraws. With a 5 percent desired reserve requirement, $400 of reserves will support only $8000 of deposits, so that $1900 in loans must be liquidated. In the second example the loans are repaid in cash. In the third example they are paid with the reduction in customers' deposit accounts.

The three examples in Table 9.3 show how the withdrawal of currency from a bank may affect its potential deposit-creating ability. We refer to the withdrawal of currency from the banking system into public circulation as **currency drain**.

currency drain
the withdrawal of currency from the banking system into public circulation

Currency drain may be defined in various ways. Currency held outside the banking system may be expressed as a proportion of the total money supply, or total deposits, or only demand deposits. Changes in the size of the currency ratio over time are influenced by such factors as income levels, the utilization of credit cards and other cash substitutes, the use of automatic bank machines, and uncertainties regarding general economic conditions and seasonal requirements. For instance, during the Christmas season when people make more cash purchases and make cash gifts, banks usually increase their currency holdings.

There are also times when the public reduces its currency holdings relative to its bank deposits, thereby increasing excess reserves and deposits in the banks. This situation often occurs following holiday seasons. The banks as a

TABLE 9.3 BALANCE SHEET CHANGES FOR COMMERCIAL BANK A
5 Percent Reserve Ratio; In Dollars

EXAMPLE 1

	Assets			Liabilities		
Stage 1 Initial position with excess reserves	Reserves:			Deposits:	+	1 000
	(Desired)	+	50			
	(Excess)	+	95			
	Loans:	+	855			
		+	1 000		+	1 000
Stage 2 Currency withdrawal	Reserves:			Deposits	–	100
	(Desired)	–	5			
	(Excess)	–	95			
Net Effect	Reserves:	+	45	Deposits	+	900
	Loans	+	855			
		+	900		+	900

EXAMPLE 2

	Assets			Liabilities		
Stage 1 Initial position with no excess reserves	Reserves:			Deposits:	+	1 000
	(Desired)	+	50			
	Loans:	+	950			
		+	1 000		+	1 000
Stage 2 Currency withdrawal	Reserves:	–	5	Deposits:	+	900
	Loans:	–	95			
Net Effect	Reserves:	+	45	Deposits:	+	900
	Loans:	+	855			
		+	900		+	900

EXAMPLE 3

	Assets			Liabilities		
Stage 1 Initial position no excess reserves	Reserves:			Deposits:	+	10 000
	(Desired)	+	500			
	Loans:	+	9 500			
		+	10 000		+	10 000
Stage 2 Currency withdrawal	Reserves:	–	100	Deposits:	–	100
Stage 3 Reductions in loans and deposits	Loans:	–	1 900	Deposits	–	1 900
Net Effect	Reserves:	+	400	Deposits:	+	8 000
	Loans:	+	7 600			
		+	8 000		+	8 000

rule do not respond with an immediate increase in their loans. If they do, central banks can prevent such an increase by reducing the reserves of commercial banks. However, because the demand for loans tends to fall off when there is a sudden seasonal influx of currency, central bank restrictions are generally unnecessary.

The Demand for Time Deposits

So far, our analysis has assumed that the banks only hold demand deposits. Now let us assume that they hold both demand and time deposits and that a different cash reserve ratio applies to each. If the desired reserve requirement is the same for each type of deposit, we need not make a distinction about the type of deposits held for formulating the banking system's deposit multiplier. In practice, intermediaries may want to hold different proportions of each type of deposit as cash reserves. A smaller cash reserve ratio would probably apply against time deposits than against demand deposits, since time deposits exhibit greater stability over time, partly because they may not be chequable and cash withdrawals may be subject to prior notice.

The difference in desired reserve ratios weakens the reserve position of a bank when the public shifts its bank accounts from time deposits to demand deposits. Table 9.4 illustrates this point. Bank A initially holds $20 000 in deposits divided equally between time and demand deposits. The desired reserve ratio on demand deposits is 10 percent (or $1000); for time deposits it is 4 percent (or $400). The public now shifts $5000 from time deposits to demand deposits. As a result, the reserve requirement for time deposits is reduced by $200, while that for demand deposits is increased by $500. The total reserve requirement has increased by $300 to $1700, so that with no change in its total reserves, Bank A now has a reserve deficiency of $300 and will have to decrease its loans and deposits accordingly. If the shift had been from demand

| TABLE 9.4 | **BALANCE SHEET CHANGES FOR BANK A** | | | | | | |
| | In Dollars | | | | | | |

	Assets			**Liabilities**		
Initial Position	Reserves (10%)	+	1 000	Demand Deposits	+	10 000
	Reserves (4%)	+	400	Time Deposits	+	10 000
		+	1 400		+	20 000
Shift in Deposits	Desired Reserves	+	500	Demand Deposits	+	5 000
and Change in						
Desired Reserves	Desired Reserves	–	200	Time Deposits	–	5 000
Net Effect	Desired Reserves:					
	Demand Deposits		1 500	Demand Deposits		15 000
	Time Deposits		200	Time Deposits		5 000
			1 700			20 000
	Actual Reserves		1 400			
	RESERVE DEFICIENCY		300			

deposits to time deposits, the bank would have acquired excess reserves, allowing it to expand loans and deposits.

The Willingness to Lend and Borrow

A bank's ability to expand its deposits and therefore to create money is in no way automatic. A bank must be willing to extend loans and purchase securities. Nonetheless, even if a bank wants to expand, it cannot do so unless the non-banking public is willing to sell securities or to seek loans. Thus, while excess reserves are a necessary condition for bank expansion, they are not a sufficient condition.

Deposit Creation by a Banking System with No Currency Drain

The ability of an entire banking system to create (and destroy) deposits, and therefore money, depends—like that of an individual bank—on reserve positions. However, unlike an individual bank, whose potential to create deposits is limited by the volume of its own excess reserves, a banking system has the potential to expand deposits by a multiple of the entire system's excess reserves.

To illustrate the multiple money-creating ability of a commercial banking system, let us begin by assuming that each bank's desired reserve ratio is 10 percent. Let us further assume that a primary deposit of $1000 is made in Bank A, which allocates $100 of this sum to its desired reserves, leaving $900 in excess reserves.

It is important to keep in mind just how the banking system initially receives excess reserves. In our example we assume that a $1000 primary deposit is made by the federal government in Bank A.[8] Later, we will see that an increase in the reserves of a banking system can take place without a change in primary deposits, and that the way in which a banking system gains reserves has important implications for the expansionary potential of the system.

Now let us return to Bank A. Based on its excess reserves of $900, Bank A attempts to maximize its profits by extending its loans and secondary deposits by this amount. Since bank borrowers do not usually borrow funds to let them sit idle in a bank, we will assume that all of the secondary deposits are withdrawn in cash and by cheque. The recipients are all customers of another bank, say Bank B, where the funds are placed on deposit. After all the cheques have been cleared through the clearinghouse process, Bank A will have lost secondary deposits and reserves equal to $900, and Bank B will have new primary deposits and a net addition to its reserves of an equal amount.

---

8. This primary deposit may be a result of a shift in government deposits from the central bank to the commercial banks. We need not now concern ourselves with the mechanics involved. The precise nature of such a shift is described later in the book.

When Bank B has allowed for its 10 percent desired reserve ratio against the new primary deposits of $900, it will have $810 (90 percent of $900) in new excess reserves and will be in a position to expand its loans and purchases of securities. Suppose Bank B lends the whole $810. Again, as was the case with Bank A, borrowers pay debts to individuals and firms who deposit this money with yet another bank in the banking system, this one Bank C.

Now Bank C will hold the desired reserve of $81 (10 percent of $810) and put its excess reserves of $729 ($810 less $81) to work by extending its loans and its purchases of securities. Bank C, therefore, has created secondary deposits of $729. The expansion of loans and secondary deposits is outlined in Table 9.5.

As a result of an initial deposit of $1000 in currency in Bank A, Banks A, B, and C are able, on the basis of a 10 percent desired reserve ratio and with no cash drains, to expand their loans and create secondary deposits in the total amount of $2439 ($900 + $810 + $729). In addition, Banks D, E, F, and G (and the rest of the banking system) increase their secondary deposits by an aggregate of $6561, so that the total increase in secondary deposits for all the banks in the banking system is $9000. The banking system must stop expanding its deposits when all the reserves that were excess at the beginning ($900 in our example) have come to be required to support the additional deposits. With a 10 percent desired reserve ratio and with no cash drains, this point is reached when the banking system has created secondary deposits of $9000. Total additional deposits of all the banks are then equal to $10 000, against which a desired reserve of $1000 is held.

An alternative way of showing the process of deposit expansion by the banking system is presented in Table 9.6. Here, too, it is assumed that each bank holds a desired reserve of 10 percent and that each bank expands its deposits to the full potential of its excess reserves. The expansionary process follows an initial deposit of currency in Bank A, which is fully loaned up before it receives this deposit. Again we assume that not a penny of the initial deposit of currency is drained out of the banking system.

When there are no currency drains, we can summarize the expansionary process of the banking system as a whole as follows:

$$(9.1) \qquad \Delta D = \Delta R_0 + (1 - r) \, \Delta R_0 + (1 - r)^2 \, \Delta R_0 + \dots + (1 - r)^n \, \Delta R_0 + \dots$$

where ΔD is the change in total deposits as a result of an increase in cash reserves, ΔR_0, given a cash reserve ratio of r (the Greek letter Δ identifies a change). This series may be written:

$$(9.2) \qquad \Delta D = \Delta R_0 \, [1 + (1 - r) + (1 - r)^2 + \dots + (1 - r)^n + \dots]$$

and as n (which captures each iteration of the process) approaches infinity (and given r is less than one):

$$(9.3) \qquad \Delta D = \left(\frac{1}{r}\right) \Delta R_0$$

We refer to $1/r$ as the deposit multiplier. Note that $\Delta R_0 = r\Delta D$. This notation tells us that the banking system will stop the expansion of deposits when

TABLE 9.5	MULTIPLE EXPANSION OF LENDING AND DEPOSITS THROUGH THE BANKING SYSTEM
	Desired Reserves 10 Percent, No Other Drains; In Dollars

Assets			Liabilities		
Bank A					
Reserves:		+ 1 000	Deposits:		
Desired Reserves	+ 100		Initial Primary Deposit	+	1 000
Excess Reserves	+ 900		Secondary Deposits	+	900
Loans		+ 900			
Total Assets		+ 1 900	Total Liabilities	+	1 900
Bank B					
Reserves:		+ 900	Deposits:		
Desired Reserves	+ 90		Primary Deposits	+	900
Excess Reserves	+ 810		Secondary Deposits	+	810
Loans		+ 810			
Total Assets		+ 1 710	Total Liabilities	+	1 710
Bank C					
Reserves:		+ 810	Deposits:		
Desired Reserves	+ 81		Primary Deposits	+	810
Excess Reserves	+ 729		Secondary Deposits	+	729
Loans		+ 729			
Total Assets		+ 1 539	Total Liabilities	+	1 539
Additional banks D, E, F, G ...					
Reserves:		+ 729	Deposits:		
Desired Reserves	+ 729		Primary Deposits	+	729
Excess Reserves	+ 0		Secondary Deposits	+	6 561
Loans		+ 6 561			
Total Assets		+ 7 290	Total Liabilities	+	7 290
All Banks					
Reserves:		+ 1 000	Deposits:		
			Initial Primary Deposit	+	1 000
Desired Reserves	1 000		Secondary Deposits	+	9 000
Excess Reserves	0				
Loans		+ 9 000			
Total Assets		+ 10 000	Total Liabilities	+	10 000

all the newly acquired reserves are absorbed as desired reserves to support the additional deposits.

As can be seen in Tables 9.5 and 9.6, the expansion in secondary deposits is less than that in total deposits of the system. In our example, the initial increase in reserves of Bank A is the result of a primary deposit of $1000 against which the bank has to hold desired reserves amounting to 10 percent

TABLE 9.6	MULTIPLE EXPANSION OF LENDING AND DEPOSITS THROUGH THE BANKING SYSTEM Desired Reserves 10%				
Banks	**Primary Deposits**	**Desired Reserves**	**Excess Reserves**	**Loans**	**Secondary Deposits**
Bank A	$1 000.00	$100.00	$900.00	$900.00	$900.00
Bank B	900.00	90.00	810.00	810.00	810.00
Bank C	810.00	81.00	729.00	729.00	729.00
Bank D	729.00	72.90	656.10	656.10	656.10
Bank E	656.10	65.61	590.49	590.49	590.49
Bank F	590.49	59.05	531.44	531.44	531.44
Bank G	531.44	53.14	478.30	478.30	478.30
Bank H	478.30	47.83	430.47	430.47	430.47
Bank I	430.47	43.05	387.42	387.42	387.42
Bank J	387.42	38.74	348.68	348.68	348.68
Still other banks	3 486.78	348.68	3 138.10	3 138.12	3 138.10
Total all banks	10 000.00	1 000.00	0	9 000.00	9 000.00

or $100. Hence only $(1 - r)\Delta R_0$, or $900, is available as excess reserves for the expansion of secondary deposits. If ΔD_S represents the change in secondary deposits, their total expansion by the banking system following an initial increase in reserves, ΔR_0, can be expressed as

$$(9.4) \qquad \Delta D_S = \left(\frac{1}{r}\right)\Delta R_0(1 - r)$$

When the banking system acquires reserves without a corresponding change in primary deposits, the $(1 - r)$ expression in the above equation is omitted. As a result, the expansion of secondary deposits is identical to that of total deposits as shown in equation 9.3.

With Currency Drain

So far we have assumed that the initial increase in bank reserves remains within the banking system and is ultimately employed as desired reserves. In our earlier discussion of an individual bank, we observed that it is subject to two cash drains that use up its reserves: the clearing drain and the currency drain. We will assume that the banking system is not subject to a clearing drain, but, as with the individual bank, experiences a currency drain as its deposits expand.[9]

---

9. An international clearing drain can exist among banking systems of different countries. Any clearing drains from the commercial banking system to other financial institutions are included in our definition of clearing drain.

The currency drain from the banking system is the result of the public's desire to hold a proportion of its money in the form of currency at all times. In the following analysis we assume that the public has a desired ratio of currency holdings to bank deposits, $c = C/D$, where D represents bank deposits and C is the actual amount of currency held by the public. Assume that this ratio is 10 percent; that is, people want to hold 10 cents in currency for every dollar held in deposits. Although this ratio is assumed to remain constant, its size is influenced by such factors as income levels, credit card use, and uncertainties regarding general economic stability, all of which, for simplicity, we disregard.

With a currency drain, not all of the initial increase in the bank's reserve is available for desired reserves to support additional deposits. As deposits increase, the public will want to increase its currency holdings to maintain its desired currency ratio. The increase in the public's currency holdings has to come from the banking system, which in turn loses an equivalent amount of cash reserves. An initial increase in the bank's cash reserves, ΔR_0, is ultimately distributed such that

$$(9.5) \qquad\qquad \Delta R_0 = \Delta C + \Delta R$$

where ΔC represents the increase in the public's currency holdings and ΔR the increase in the banking system's desired reserves. As we have already noted, ΔC depends on the public's desired currency ratio, $c = C/D$. ΔR depends on the banking system's desired reserve ratio, $r = R/D$. Hence, we can rewrite equation 9.5 as follows:

$$(9.6) \qquad\qquad \begin{aligned} \Delta R_0 &= c\Delta D + r\Delta D \\ &= (c + r)\Delta D \end{aligned}$$

which we can rearrange to obtain

$$(9.7) \qquad\qquad \Delta D = \left(\frac{1}{c + r}\right)\Delta R_0$$

where $[1/(c + r)]$ is now the deposit multiplier, allowing for a currency drain.

If we substitute our assumed values for c, r, and ΔR_0, then ΔD becomes

$$[1/(0.10 + 0.10)]\$1000 = \$5000$$

If we compare this result with the results shown in Table 9.5, we note that the currency drain has reduced the banking system's ability to expand its deposits. On the other hand, the reduction in bank deposits following a decrease in the banks' reserves will also be smaller when account is taken of the currency drain.

In our example, deposit expansion by the banking system halts when the public's currency holdings have increased by $500 and the banking system's desired reserves have increased by $500; the two together absorb the entire initial increase of $1000 in the banks' reserves. The banks' loans have increased

TABLE 9.7	CHANGES IN BANKING SYSTEM					
	When $r = 0.10$ and $c = 0.10$					

Assets				Liabilities		
Reserves	+	$ 500		Deposits	+	$5 000
Loans	+	$4 500				
		$5 000				$5 000

by $4500.[10] The final equilibrium change in the banking system's balance sheet is shown in Table 9.7. This result may be compared with the bottom portion of Table 9.5.

Excess Reserves

The two deposit multipliers contained in equations 9.3 and 9.7 assume that banks are willing and able to expand their loans (including security purchases) by the full amount of their excess reserves. This assumption is usually not true. Because of their inability to predict their clearing and currency drains accurately, banks maintain precautionary and working balances of excess reserves as a "buffer stock."

Let us assume that the banks hold idle excess reserves, E, equal to a constant fraction, $E/D = e$, of their deposits. An initial increase in reserves will now ultimately be absorbed in desired reserves, currency outside the banks, and idle excess reserves. That is,

$$(9.8) \qquad \Delta R_0 = \Delta R + \Delta C + \Delta E$$

which can be expressed as

$$(9.9) \qquad \Delta R_0 = r \Delta D + c \Delta D + e \Delta D$$
$$= (r + c + e)\Delta D$$

and the formula for the change in demand deposits that can be supported by an initial change in reserves is now

$$(9.10) \qquad \Delta D = \left[\frac{1}{(r + e + c)} \right] \Delta R_0$$

---

10. The increase in loans can be calculated directly as follows: as shown in Table 9.7, the increase in loans, ΔL, is equal to the increase in deposits, ΔD, less the increase in desired reserves, ΔR_0, which are equal to $r\Delta D$. That is, $L = \Delta D - r\Delta D$. Substituting, we obtain

$$\Delta L = [1/(c + r)]\Delta R_0 - [r/(r + c)]\Delta R_0$$
$$= [(1 - r)/(c + r)]\Delta R_0$$

The expression $[(1 - r)/(c + r)]$ is referred to as the credit multiplier.

TABLE 9.8	**CHANGES IN BANKING SYSTEM** When $r = 0.10$, $c = 0.10$, and $e = 0.04$		
Assets		**Liabilities**	
Desired Reserves	$ 416.67	Deposits	$4 166.67
Excess Reserves	166.67		
Loans	3 583.33		
	$4 166.67		$4 166.67

Again, in terms of our numerical example, if $e = 0.04$ and c, r, and ΔR_0 equal their earlier values, then

$$\Delta D = [1/(0.10 + 0.10 + 0.04)]\$1000 = \$ 4166.67$$

The balance sheet changes in the banking system are shown in Table 9.8. Comparing Table 9.8 with 9.7 shows that when the banks hold idle excess reserves, their ability to expand their deposits and to increase their loans is decreased.

Time Deposits

Assume that the banks hold demand deposits, D_d, for which they have to maintain a desired reserve ratio $R_d/D_d = r_d$, or $R_d = r_d D_d$, and time deposits, D_t, with a desired reserve ratio $R_t/D_t = r_t$, or $R_t = r_t D_t$. R_d and R_t are the amount of reserves held against demand deposits and time deposits, respectively. The banks also hold excess reserves that we can express as a fixed proportion of their demand deposits: $E/D_d = e$ or $E = e D_d$. Assume that the public's desired amount of time deposits is a constant proportion of demand deposits; $t = D_t/D_d$ or $D_t = t D_d$; and that the currency drain is also a constant proportion of demand deposits; $c = C/D_d$ or $C = c D_d$.

The initial increase in reserves may now be held in four ways: currency outside the banking system; desired reserves against demand deposits; idle excess reserves; and desired reserves against time deposits. This can be expressed as follows:

(9.11) $$\Delta R_0 = \Delta C + \Delta R_d + \Delta E + \Delta R_t$$

and with the appropriate substitutions

(9.12) $$\Delta R_0 = c \, \Delta D_d + r_d \Delta D_d + e \, \Delta D_d + r_t \, t\Delta D_d$$
$$= (c + r_d + e + r_t \, t)\Delta D_d$$

and

$$(9.13) \qquad \Delta D_d = \left(\frac{1}{c + r_d + e + r_t t} \right) \Delta R_0$$

The above expression defines only the expansion in demand deposits following an increase in reserves. We can readily derive the expression for the increase in total deposits. Total deposits, D, are the sum of demand deposits, D_d, and time deposits, tD_d, expressed as a proportion of demand deposits. The change in total deposits is therefore

$$(9.14) \qquad \Delta D = \Delta D_d + t \Delta D_d$$
$$= (1 + t) \Delta D_d$$

If we now substitute for ΔD_d from equation 9.13, we have an expression for the increase in total deposits following an increase in initial reserves:

$$(9.15) \qquad \Delta D = \left[\frac{(1 + t)}{(c + r_d + e + r_t t)} \right] \Delta R_0$$

Deposit Creation in a System of Banks and Near-Banks

We now want to extend our analysis of deposit creation to include the near-banks. We assume that the public's demand for currency is a constant fraction of total deposits, which now include those held with both the banks, D^B, and the near-banks, D^N. This is expressed as $c(D^B + D^N)$, where c is the currency ratio. The banks' and near-banks' demand for cash reserves are given by $r_B D^B$ and $r_N D_B^N$, respectively, where r_B and r_N are their respective desired reserve ratios. We assume that no legal minimum reserve ratios apply (as is the case currently in Canada), and therefore these reserve ratios reflect the minimum cash reserves these depository institutions normally hold consistent with their perceived needs for cash. We will also assume that the deposits at the near-banks are a constant proportion, d, of those at the banks, so that $D^N = dD^B$.

If we now increase the available amount of cash in the economy, ΔR_0, in equilibrium it will be held as follows:

$$(9.16) \qquad \Delta R_0 = c \Delta D^B + cd \Delta D^B + r_B \Delta D^B + r_N d \Delta D^B$$
$$= (c + cd + r_B + r_N d) \Delta D^B$$

After rearranging the above equation we derive the following expressions for the expansions of the banks and the near-banks deposits as a result of an increase in the availability of cash reserves.

$$(9.17) \qquad \Delta D^B = \left[\frac{1}{(c(1 + d) + r_B + r_N d)} \right] \Delta R_0$$

and

$$(9.18) \qquad \Delta D^N = \left[\frac{1}{c(1 + 1/d) + r_B + r_N + 1/d} \right] \Delta R_0$$

Furthermore, the change in total deposits, ΔD^T, following an increase in cash reserves is as follows:

$$(9.19) \qquad \Delta D^T = \Delta D^B + d\Delta D^B$$
$$= (1 + d)\Delta D^B$$

and after substituting from equation 9.17

$$(9.20) \qquad \Delta D^T = [(1 + d)/\{c(1 + d) + r_B + r_B d\}]\Delta R_0$$

The Creation of Deposits and the Money Supply

Finally, we want to show the relationship between changes in the availability of reserve assets, the creation of deposits by the banks and the near-banks, and changes in the money supply.

As we will learn, the total amount of "high-powered money" in the economy, which we call the monetary base, is controlled by the central bank. At any given time the total supply of cash is held by the depository institutions as cash reserves, and by the public as currency. The relationship between the monetary base and the money supply may be expressed by

$$(9.21) \qquad M_S = mB$$

where M_S is the money supply variously defined, m is the money multiplier or base multiplier associated with the money supply measure used, and B is the monetary base.

Suppose that the money supply is broadly defined as $M_3 = C + D^B + D^N$, where C is currency held by the public and D^B and D^N are deposits with the banks and the near-banks, respectively. Using our previous analysis, M_3 can be expressed as

$$(9.22) \qquad M_3 = cD^B + cdD^B + D^B + d\,D^B$$
$$= [1 + d + c(1 + d)]D^B$$

Substituting from equation 9.17 for D^B, after replacing ΔR_0 with B and rearranging the terms, we obtain an expression for the money multiplier (which shows the competing demands for cash) and the relationship between the monetary base and M_3:

$$(9.23) \qquad M_3 = \left[\frac{(1 + d)\ (1 + c)}{c\ (1 + d) + r_B + r_N d} \right] B$$

A similar relationship can be shown between M_1 and B, where $M_1 = C + D$ and D represents demand deposits held with the banks. We assume that demand deposits are a given fraction, s, of the banks' total deposits ($D = sD^B$). The equation for M_1, similar to the one for M_3 shown in equation 9.22, is

(9.24)
$$M_1 = cD^B + sD^B$$
$$= (c + s)\, D^B$$

After similar substitutions and rearrangement of terms to obtain equation 9.23, we have the following relationships between the monetary base and M_1:

(9.25)
$$M_1 = \left[\frac{(c+s)}{c(1+d) + r_B + r_N d}\right] B$$

When we explain the process of monetary control later in the book, we will return to equation 9.25 to describe the techniques used by the monetary authorities to manage the total amount of cash available in the monetary system. In some sense, equation 9.25 is the "holy grail" (or at least a pretty fundamental component) in our study of how the central bank ultimately affects the quantity of money in the economy.

KEY TERMS

cash reserves
clearing drain
credit
currency drain
debt monetization

demand liabilities
derivative (secondary) deposits
desired cash reserve ratio
legal tender
near-banks

primary deposit
promissory notes
reserve asset

REVIEW QUESTIONS

1. What is debt monetization? What are the necessary conditions for an institution to successfully engage in debt monetization?
2. Why is the ability of an individual bank in a banking system to create deposits limited? Would it make a difference if this bank were the only bank in a banking system?
3. What limits the banking system (all banks taken together) from creating deposits?
4. Why would you expect that an increase in the availability of cash to the financial system will not necessarily result in an immediate increase in bank deposits?

5. Did the elimination of legal cash reserve requirements affect our deposit creation multipliers?
6. Suppose $c = 0.3$, $s = 0.7$, $d = 0.5$, $r_B = 0.2$, and $r_N = 0.15$. What is the effect of a $100 million increase in the monetary base on M_1? M_3? Explain your answers.
7. Does clearing drain increase or decrease the degree to which an intermediary can expand its deposits? Why?
8. "Cash drain reduces the deposit expansion multiplier." Explain whether this statement is true or false, using an example to demonstrate your answer.

9. How are primary deposits different from secondary deposits?

10. Suppose there is no currency in circulation and the desired reserve ratio is 5 percent. How will an increase in the monetary base of $40 million affect demand deposits? Must they change? Why?

11. "When there is currency in circulation, the money supply and deposit expansion multipliers fall relative to the model without currency in circulation." Explain whether this statement is true, false, or uncertain.

12. This question requires some library research. Obtain monthly data on chartered bank Canadian dollar liquid assets from January 1994 to December 2000, using CANSIM series B603 and B670 (Bank of Canada deposits, notes, and coin; and total Canadian dollar assets). Plot the ratio of notes, coin, and Bank of Canada deposits to total Canadian dollar assets. Has this ratio been stable over the 1994–2000 period? What might explain the result?

13. This question requires the data from Question 12, and monthly data on the one-month Treasury bill rate, CANSIM number B14059. Plot the interest rate and the ratio you calculated in Question 12. Does there appear to be a link between the two series? What might explain what you found?

SELECTED READINGS

Angell, J.W., and K.F. Ficek. "The Expansion of Bank Credit." *Journal of Political Economy* (1933), pp. 1–32, 152–93.

Crick, W.E. "The Genesis of Bank Deposits." *Economica* 7 (1927), pp. 191–202. Reprinted in American Economic Association. *Readings in Monetary Theory*. Philadelphia: Blakiston, 1951.

Freedman, C. "The Canadian Banking System," *Bank of Canada Technical Report* 81, 1998.

Galbraith, J.A. "A Table of Banking System Multipliers." *Canadian Journal of Economics* 1 (November 1968), pp. 763–71.

Keynes, J.M. *A Treatise on Money*, Vol. 2. New York: Harcourt Brace, 1930, Ch. 25.

Orr, Daniel, and W.J. Mellon. "Stochastic Reserve Losses and Bank Credit." *American Economic Review* 51 (September 1961), pp. 614–23.

Vining, R. "A Process Analysis of Bank Credit Expansion." *Quarterly Journal of Economics* 54 (August 1940), pp. 599–623.

Winker, P. "Sluggish Adjustment of Interest Rates and Credit Rationing: An Application of Unit Root Testing and Error Correction Modelling." *Applied Economics* 31 (3, 1999).

$\mathscr{A}$PPENDIX 9A

Incorporating Other Deposits

In the past, Canadian banks were required to hold reserves against Canadian residents' foreign currency deposits in Canada. If we take account of these deposits, D_f we have yet another use to which ΔR_0 can be put and our equation for the demand for reserve funds becomes

(9A.1) $$\Delta R_0 = \Delta C + \Delta R_d + \Delta E + \Delta R_t + \Delta R_f$$

where R_f represents cash reserves held against foreign currency deposits. We will assume that these deposits also tend to equal a certain fraction, f, of public demand deposits so that $D_f/D_d = f$, or $D_f = fD_d$. The desired reserve ratio is $R_f/D_f = r_f$. Equation 9A.1 can now be expressed as follows:

(9A.2) $$\Delta R_0 = c\,\Delta D_d + r_d\,\Delta D_d + e\Delta D_d + r_t\,t\,\Delta D_d + r_f f\Delta D_d$$
$$= (c + r_d + e + r_t t + r_f f)\Delta D_d$$

and

(9A.3) $$\Delta D_d = \left[\frac{1 + t}{(c + r_d + e + r_t t + r_f f)}\right]\Delta R_0$$

Total deposits are now $D_d + D_t + D_f$, and the change following a decrease or increase in the banks' cash reserves can be expressed as follows:

(9A.4) $$\Delta D = \left[\frac{1 + t + f}{c + r_d + e + r_t t + r_f f}\right]\Delta R_0$$

You should begin to see a pattern in how we have dealt with the different types of deposits against which an intermediary wants to hold reserves. If we can express the new type of deposit as a constant fraction of demand deposits, then it is relatively simple to extend the analysis to determine how a change in reserves is multiplied throughout the financial system.

CHAPTER TEN

PAYMENTS INTERMEDIATION, RISK, AND RISK MANAGEMENT

After reading this chapter you should be able to

1. Discuss the role of asset management by financial institutions
2. Show how liability management plays a central role in the operation of a financial institution
3. Demonstrate how the management of maturity gap and duration gap are vital components of asset-liability management
4. Examine the benefits of using the value-at-risk methodology for risk management
5. Explain how interest rate risk can be managed using financial derivatives
6. Explain why capital funds are viewed as a cushion against insolvency
7. Show that value-at-risk methods can be used to manage risk
8. Outline the development of deposit insurance in Canada and provide evidence of its efficacy
9. Discuss the pros and cons of various suggestions for reforming the deposit insurance system in Canada

We have already observed that financial intermediation occurs when financial institutions hold a portfolio of assets and issue their own liabilities to finance these assets. This role exposes them to risk, which if not properly managed results in failure. By engaging in what we have defined as payments intermediation, depository intermediaries expose themselves to considerable risk. You will recall that most of their liabilities are liquid, have a fixed nominal value, and may be transferred or withdrawn in cash on demand or short notice. A large proportion of the loans and investments in their asset portfolios are illiquid, since their value is uncertain and may not be realizable until some time in the future. Hence, these intermediaries expose themselves to risk of loss with respect to the value of their assets and their ability to fund these assets. However, risk goes hand-in-hand with the business of financial intermediation. In this chapter we describe how the depository intermediaries manage their assets and their liabilities to control their exposure to risk and remain profitable and viable financial institutions.

The major risks faced by depository institutions that can result in a loss for others are liquidity risk, interest rate risk, market risk, and foreign exchange risk. All financial institutions are exposed to operating risk, which among other factors, is caused by the breakdown in information processing and by procedural failures, human error, and outright fraud.

Asset Management

risk of insolvency *the risk of not being able to make payments to creditors and depositors*

liquidity risk *the risk of not having sufficient cash on hand to meet cash drain and clearing drain*

primary reserves *currency held by financial institutions and deposits at the central bank*

secondary reserves *very liquid assets held by financial institutions to ensure they meet their desired ratio of reserves to deposits*

real bills doctrine (commercial loans theory) *if loans made by banks were based on "real bills" (promises backed by goods in the process of production or marketing), an optimum quantity of money would always be supplied*

The first principle of asset management by financial institutions is to control the **risk of insolvency** by ensuring that the market value of their asset portfolios remains equal to the value of their liabilities. For payment intermediaries, the additional important principle of asset management exists: To control the **liquidity risk**, they must hold a sufficient amount of cash to meet their clearing and currency drains (described in Chapter 9). To accomplish this, these institutions hold part of their assets in the form of **primary reserve**s consisting of currency and deposits with the Bank of Canada. In addition, they hold **secondary reserves** in the form of money market securities.

In the early days of banking it was thought that banks could remain sufficiently liquid to meet their clearing and currency drains if all their assets other than their primary reserves were held in short-term, self-liquidating loans. When banks issued their own notes, as does the Bank of Canada today, and these notes provided the most important medium of exchange, it was also thought that as long as the banks met the legitimate credit needs of commerce and industry, they would at the same time supply the appropriate amount of money for circulation. This theory, known in the United Kingdom as the **real bills doctrine** and in North America as the **commercial loans theory**, subsequently proved inadequate as a basis both for achieving a sufficiently elastic money supply and for maintaining a satisfactory degree of bank liquidity.

On the one hand, creating money primarily for the needs of business at times resulted in a scarcity of the medium of exchange, since money is required for many purposes aside from those of business. On the other hand, allowing businesses to expand without limit, based on commercial loans for the production of goods and services, could result in price inflation and the depreciation of the currency. Thus, following the commercial loans theory failed to provide the "proper" amount of the medium of exchange.

Commercial loans did not provide the banks with adequate liquidity to meet the demands for cash at all times, especially during periods of financial crisis. Commercial loans were, as a rule, repaid out of income generated by the project they financed. In many cases, the ability to purchase the goods produced by a firm that was financed by a bank also depended on the availability of bank loans to the purchasers of these goods. In other words, the repayment of one bank loan depended on the acquisition of yet another. Hence, the liquidity of any one bank was closely related to that of all other banks. During periods of financial crisis when there was a general scramble for cash, a bank could find itself in difficulty if it had to depend on calling in its commercial loans to meet the demands for cash.

shiftability doctrine of liquidity *the idea that banks could protect themselves against large deposit withdrawals by holding government securities*

After the First World War, when a market for government securities developed in the United States and subsequently in Canada, the commercial loans theory gave way to a new **shiftability doctrine of liquidity**. The gist of this theory was that the banks could better protect themselves against large deposit withdrawals by holding government securities. These securities could be readily shifted into cash without incurring a heavy loss. With the development of the money market, the banks, and today the near-banks as well, have come to rely more on the money market to manage their liquidity risk.

Aside from liquidity risk, financial intermediaries are exposed to default risk, also known as credit risk. This risk refers to the possibility that a loan or an investment will not be recovered in full with interest—because the undertaking being financed generates insufficient income, or the borrower's financial circumstances change, or the borrower is actually dishonest. Intermediaries are able to limit their default risk in a variety of ways. They manage default risk by using their expertise to scrutinize the creditworthiness of borrowers and the financial viability of the projects to be financed. Carefully screening information about borrowers, monitoring loans on their books, and enforcing loan contracts are among the most important financial services that intermediaries provide to their depositors and other creditors. Where it is difficult to assess the underlying risks, as is frequently the case because of incomplete information, lending intermediaries ask borrowers to pledge collateral and to provide additional guarantees to secure the loans. Furthermore, to preserve the value of the collateral pledged against loans and investments, borrowers may have to agree to restrictive covenants on their activities. In some cases, loan agreements allow the lender to take part in management decisions or even to replace management personnel should the borrower encounter difficulty in making interest and principal payments.

Some default risk will always be associated with intermediaries' lending and investment, but, as we learned in Chapter 8, by appropriately diversifying their asset portfolios to ensure the independence of most individual risks undertaken, intermediaries can reduce their credit risk exposure.

In managing their credit risks the banks make both specific and general provisions. When there is no longer reasonable assurance of timely collection of principal and interest on loans outstanding, these loans are classified as impaired. A specific provision is then made by reducing their carrying amount to their estimated realizable amount, measured by discounting their expected future cash flows at the effective interest rates inherent in the loans. Similarly, general provisions are made for risks of losses inherent in loans but that have not been specifically identified.

Liability Management

The public's willingness to hold the deposit liabilities of banks and near-banks depends on its confidence in their ability to convert its deposit accounts into cash. When an institution loses this trust, perhaps because of default on a large proportion of its assets, the public will want to withdraw its deposits. Since individuals will usually rush to their depository institution to get there before others have depleted the institution's available cash, large and persistent cash withdrawals, referred to as *runs*, take place. When one institution experiences a run, the public frequently becomes suspicious about the soundness of similar types of institutions. Hence, it has not been uncommon for the failure of one bank to set off runs on other banks even though these banks were sound. This phenomenon is called **contagion** because, as with a contagious disease, it can spread from the sick to the healthy. Once a run starts, the suspicion of instability can become a self-fulfilling prophecy with the potential to rock the entire financial system. To prevent contagion, central banks are authorized to make cash advances to specified depository institutions, and **deposit insurance** has been introduced to provide guarantees for specified amounts of individual deposits.

The possibility of a depository institution not retaining or attracting a sufficient amount of primary deposits to fund its assets is called **funding risk**. The larger the number of deposit accounts and the smaller the dollar amount of each account, the smaller the probability of unpredictable large cash withdrawals at any one time. By pooling its funding requirement over a larger number of diversified depositors, an intermediary reduces its funding risk.

The large Canadian banks, with their extensive national branch networks through which they accept deposits from a large cross-section of individuals, businesses, and institutions, have successfully reduced their funding risks. In contrast, smaller and regional depository institutions, which have had to depend on relatively large wholesale deposits to meet their funding requirements, have experienced large funding risks that have resulted in failure and insolvency, or in mergers with sounder institutions. For example, following the failure of the Canadian Commercial Bank in 1985, the public lost confidence in the liquidity and soundness of other regional banks that depended on funding their asset portfolios with wholesale deposits. Because of continuing large deposit withdrawals, the Northland Bank also failed, the Bank of British Columbia had to be restructured to survive, and the Mercantile Bank of Canada and the Continental Bank of Canada were merged with other banks.

Asset-Liability Management

In the 1970s, when interest rates became more volatile and climbed to historically unprecedented high levels, depository institutions became increasingly exposed to **interest rate risk.** This risk has two components. The first, **income risk**, is the risk of loss in net interest income when the rates paid on deposits are not synchronized with the rates earned on assets. The second, called **investment risk**, is the risk of loss in net worth due to unexpected interest rate changes. Net worth is the difference in the market value of assets and liabilities.

To facilitate control of interest rate risk, measures have been developed to gauge an intermediary's exposure to it. Two measures that serve this purpose are maturity gap and duration gap.

Margin notes:

contagion the failure of one bank sets off runs on other banks

deposit insurance insurance that provides a guarantee for specified amounts of individual deposits

funding risk denotes when a depository institution does not retain sufficient primary deposits to fund its assets

www.

interest rate risk risk due to volatility in interest rates

income risk the risk of loss in net interest income when the rates paid on deposits are not synchronized with rates earned on assets

investment risk the risk of loss in net worth due to unexpected changes in interest rates

Maturity Gap Management

maturity gap management *the management of risks due to differences in maturities of assets*

maturity gap (GAP) *the difference between the volume of an intermediary's interest-rate-sensitive assets and its interest-rate-sensitive liabilities*

Maturity gap management can be used by payments intermediaries to insulate their net interest income from changes in market interest rates. To measure an intermediary's maturity gap, the assets and liabilities on its balance sheet are grouped according to their interest rate sensitivity. Financial instruments that mature, or can be renegotiated or repriced within a short-term interval, usually less than a year, are said to be interest sensitive. An institution's **maturity gap (GAP)** is the difference between the volume of its rate-sensitive assets (*RSA*) and that of its rate-sensitive liabilities (*RSL*). That is,

(10.1) $GAP = RSA - RSL$

Where the value of *RSA* exceeds that of *RSL*, an asset-sensitive positive gap exists; where *RSL* exceeds *RSA*, a liability-sensitive negative gap exists; and when the two are equal there is a neutral or zero gap.

Financial intermediaries with a positive maturity gap (*RSA > RSL*) experience a reduction in their net interest income when interest rates fall, because the decline in total revenue generated by their assets exceeds the decline in the total interest cost of their liabilities. Intermediaries with a negative gap (*RSL > RSA*) suffer a decline in their net interest income when market interest rates rise. With a rise in interest rates, the total interest costs associated with their liabilities rise faster than the total revenue earned on their assets. Only a neutral or zero gap (*RSA = RSL*) insulates net interest income from interest rate risk—regardless of the direction in which interest rates move. However, even in this case, the extent to which the insulation provides protection depends on the extent to which the change in interest rates earned on assets parallels the change in interest rates paid on liabilities.

Traditionally, depository institutions, particularly the chartered banks, have exposed themselves to interest rate risk by relying on interest-sensitive deposit liabilities to fund their fixed-rate longer-term loans and investments. Because of their negative maturity gap, their net interest income tends to decline with rising market interest rates because interest-sensitive deposits have to be repriced or replaced with deposits paying higher rates. To insulate themselves against the possibility of large reductions in their net interest income, these institutions have used neutral gap management. This management involves increasing the maturity of their liabilities by encouraging their depositors to shift more of their funds from demand accounts to time accounts, and by decreasing the maturity of their assets by lending at shorter-term and variable interest rates. However, since the latter change transfers interest rate risk to the borrower, institutional lenders may be increasing the default risk of their asset portfolios.

duration gap management *the management of risks due to the amount and timing of cash flows*

Duration Gap Management

To remain solvent, the total dollar amount of a financial intermediary's assets must exceed the total dollar amount of its liabilities; that is, it must have a positive net worth. **Duration gap management** can be used by payments intermediaries to insulate the present value of their net worth from changes in market interest rates. Duration, as illustrated in Box 10–1, is a present-value, time-weighted measure of maturity that considers the amount and timing of all cash flows. It is a measure of how long it takes a security to pay back its purchase price in present value terms. Since it measures the average amount of time it takes for all cash flows from a security to be paid out, it is a measure of the average maturity of an expected stream of cash payments.

duration gap *the difference between the durations of an institution's assets and its liabilities, weighted by their total dollar amounts*

A **duration gap** is the difference between the durations of an institution's assets weighted by their total dollar amounts, and its liabilities weighted by their total dollar amounts. A duration gap is expressed as:

$$(10.2) \qquad Duration\ Gap = D_A - D_L (L/A)$$

where D_A and D_L are the respective durations of its assets and liabilities held by an intermediary, and L and A are the total dollar amounts of its liabilities and assets.

If a payments intermediary has a positive duration gap, that is,

$$(10.3) \qquad Duration\ Gap = D_A - D_L(L/A) > 0$$

a change in market interest rates will result in the value of its liabilities changing by less, up or down, than the value of its assets. Hence, a rise in interest rates will lower the present value of its net worth as its asset values fall further than the value of liabilities.[1] The institution can insulate the present value of its net worth from declining as a result of a rise in interest rates by closing its duration gap accordingly. This solution could present difficulties if the institution cannot readily find assets and liabilities with appropriate durations. Even if the institution can make the required duration match, insulation requires that when market interest rates change there is a parallel change in the rates of both its assets and its liabilities. Given recent changes in the slope of the yield curve, this parallel is by no means assured.

Managing Interest Rate Risk

For financial intermediaries, assessing their interest rate risk with gap analysis is only the first step; the more difficult second step is deciding how it is to be managed. Various strategies can be used to control their interest rate risk exposure, including: (1) adjusting the composition of their assets and liabilities, (2) changing the characteristics of their cash flows with interest rate swaps, (3) hedging with financial futures and options, and (4) entering into interest rate agreements.

---

1. The sensitivity of a financial intermediary's net worth (*NW*) to changes in the market interest rates (Δr) is approximated by the following equation, where the left side of the equation is the percentage change in net worth and *DG* is the duration gap:

$$\frac{\Delta NW}{NW} = (-DG)\Delta r$$

BOX 10–1   **BACKGROUNDER**

Calculating the Duration of a Financial Instrument

While there are different measures of duration, the principal one is the so-called *Macaulay duration,** which is calculated as follows:

$$D = \frac{\sum_{t=1}^{N} \dfrac{C_t t}{(1 + r)^t}}{\sum_{t=1}^{N} \dfrac{C_t t}{(1 + r)^t}}$$

where C_t is the cash flow of interest and principal payments over n periods to maturity, t is the length of time (number of days, months, years, etc.) from present to when cash flow is received, and r is the yield to maturity.

The duration of a $1000 bond with an 8 percent coupon, maturing in three years, is calculated as follows:

$$D = \frac{\dfrac{80(1)}{1 + .08} + \dfrac{80(2)}{(1 + .08)^2} + \dfrac{80(3)}{(1 + .08)^3} + \dfrac{1000(3)}{(1 + .08)^3}}{\dfrac{80}{1 + .08} + \dfrac{80}{(1 + .08)^2} + \dfrac{80}{(1 + .08)^3} + \dfrac{1000}{(1 + .08)^3}} = 2.8 \text{ years}$$

This bond will pay itself out in present value terms in 2.8 years, which is the *average* maturity, considering the timing of its expected cash flows of principal and interest.

---

* See Frederick R. Macaulay, *The Movement of Interest Rates, Bonds, Yields, and Stock Prices in the United States since 1865* (New York: Columbia University Press, 1938).

Adjusting the Composition of Assets and Liabilities

Financial intermediaries can reduce positive maturity gaps by increasing the proportion of their liabilities that are interest sensitive and by reducing the proportion of their assets that are interest sensitive. Negative maturity gaps can be reduced with a smaller proportion of interest-sensitive liabilities and a larger proportion of interest-sensitive assets.

The chartered banks traditionally had negative maturity gaps because they funded their customer loans with deposits that were chequable and withdrawable on demand and short notice. More recently chartered banks have attempted to reduce these gaps by changing the characteristics of the financial instruments they offer to the public and by introducing new instruments. For example, banks have lengthened the maturity of their liabilities by offering longer-term certificates of deposit and imposing higher early withdrawal penalties on these deposits. At the same time, they have made their assets more interest sensitive by shortening the maturity of their loans and by extending loans at variable interest rates.

Other methods of reducing maturity gaps have included the outright sale of loans, especially loans to third-world countries. This practice has been associated with the banks' desire to reduce their credit risk as well. Loan securitization is yet another technique used to remove assets with inappropriate interest rate risk or credit risk characteristics.

When changing the composition and characteristics of their assets and liabilities to reduce their interest rate risk, financial intermediaries shift this risk to their customers and to other institutions. If interest rate risk is shifted from an intermediary to a borrower who is unable to absorb a loss, the intermediary's credit risk increases. As a result its overall risk may be increased rather than reduced.

Rebalancing the match between assets and liabilities according to predicted interest rate changes can be both expensive and difficult for financial intermediaries. Rebalancing can be expensive because of the transactions costs it involves. It can be difficult because it may require financial institutions to offer financial instruments with characteristics that do not satisfy their regular customers. To avoid these difficulties, the institutions have increasingly turned to using interest rate swaps and to hedging their interest rate risks with financial futures and options.

Changing the Characteristics of Cash Flows with Interest Rate Swaps

In Chapter 6 we learned that with an interest rate swap, two borrowers exchange their interest rate payments on a notional principal amount of money. Interest rate swaps can be used by financial intermediaries to convert fixed-rate into variable-rate interest payment flows and vice versa, to reduce their interest rate risk.

The maturity gap positions of two banks are shown in Figure 10–1. Bank A has a positive maturity gap as a result of financing its variable-rate customer loans (on which it earns on average the 91-day Treasury bill rate plus 1 percent) with fixed-rate certificates of deposit (for which it pays 12 percent). At the same time, Bank B has a negative maturity gap because it has funded fixed-rate customer loans (for which it receives a 12 percent rate) with the sale of variable-rate money market instruments (on which it pays on average the 91-day Treasury bill rate plus 1 percent). Each bank can remove its undesirable gap, which we assume to be $50 million, by arranging an interest rate swap with the other. Bank B, as shown in Figure 10–1, swaps its variable-rate interest obligations for Bank A's fixed-rate obligations. Both banks remove their maturity gaps and, hence, their exposure to interest rate risk as a result of unexpected changes in market interest rates. All of Bank B's cash flows are based on fixed-rate interest, and all of Bank A's cash flows are based on variable-rate interest.

Hedging with Financial Futures and Options

Hedging refers to matching one risk with a counter-balancing risk to reduce the overall risk of loss. Financial institutions can use a variety of hedge strategies, some extremely complex, with financial futures and options.

FIGURE 10–1   INTEREST RATE SWAP TO REDUCE INTEREST RATE RISK

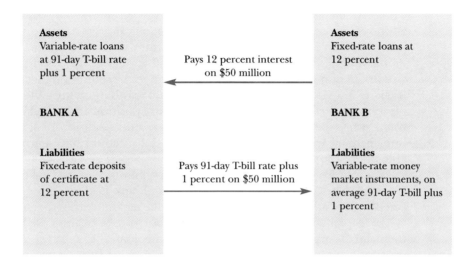

A Short or Selling Financial Futures Hedge against Rising Interest Rates

Suppose that a financial intermediary has a liability-sensitive, negative maturity gap and a positive duration gap. Hence, it is subject to a loss if interest rates rise. It can avoid these losses by writing (selling) financial futures contracts. If interest rates rise and, therefore, security prices fall, the short futures position can be closed out at a profit by purchasing financial futures contracts at a lower price than the one at which the same contracts were initially purchased. With a perfect hedge, the profit made on futures trading will offset the loss in the value of the intermediary's assets and the higher interest cost on its liabilities due to the rise in interest rates.

A Long or Buying Financial Futures Hedge against Falling Interest Rates

Suppose that a financial intermediary has an asset-sensitive, positive maturity gap and a negative duration gap. In this situation it faces a loss if interest rates fall. It can avoid these losses by buying financial futures contracts. If interest rates fall and, therefore, security prices rise, it can close out its long futures position at a profit by selling its futures contracts at a higher price than it paid for their initial purchase. With a perfect hedge, the profits made on futures trading will offset the loss in revenue due to the lower yields on its assets.

Synthetic Loans

synthetic loans
*when the nature
of a loan is
charged by com-
bining it with a
futures contract*

Financial intermediaries can use futures contracts to construct **synthetic loans**. This term means that the nature of a loan can be changed by combining it with a futures contract. Assume that an intermediary prefers to make adjustable-rate loans because it expects market interest rates to rise. However, its clients are demanding fixed-rate loans. The intermediary can satisfy its clients' demands and at the same time meet its own preferences by selling financial futures contracts to transform its fixed-rate loans into synthetic adjustable-rate loans. If interest rates rise, the profit from the short position in financial futures contracts, when combined with the interest from fixed-rate loans, provides the intermediary with an income similar to what it could have earned from variable-interest loans.

Alternatively, a financial intermediary may prefer to make variable-rate loans while borrowers prefer only fixed-rate loans. Both preferences can be satisfied with synthetic fixed-rate loans. While making variable-rate loans, these are transformed into fixed-rate loans for borrowers. In this case borrowers sell financial futures against their variable-rate loans. If interest rates rise, the profits that can be earned by the borrowers' short futures position cancel the intermediary's higher loan rate. In effect, the borrowers' lending rate reflects that on a fixed-rate loan.

The Risks of Hedging with Interest Rate Futures

basis risk *risk due
to the fact that
changes in the
prices of futures
contracts do not
perfectly offset
changes in the
prices of the
assets being
hedged*

**marking-to-
market risk** *refers
to undesirable
cash flows
resulting from
futures positions*

www.

Although hedging with interest rate futures allows investors to reduce interest rate risk, constructing a perfect hedge whereby all risk is eliminated is the exception rather than the rule. All hedges generally contain some residual or **basis risk** because the change in the price of futures contracts does not perfectly offset the change in the price of the asset being hedged. This happens when factors other than interest rates are an important source of the changes in the price of the asset. The price of the futures contract also may not move parallel to that of its underlying asset if, at the time of its initial purchase, its price already reflected expected changes in interest rates. To the extent that differences in price movements can be predicted by hedgers, they can offset for changes in basis with the number of futures contracts used to hedge interest rate risk.

Marking-to-market risk is also associated with futures contracts. As we observed earlier, at the end of each trading day funds are transferred from futures traders who lose on their contracts to traders who gain on their contracts, so that buyers and sellers actually realize the gains and losses from daily price changes as they occur. The marking-to-market risk refers to undesirable cash flows resulting from futures positions.

Put Options to Protect against Rising Interest Rates

Suppose that a financial intermediary is exposed to loss if interest rates rise because it holds a large portfolio of fixed-rate government bonds. The intermediary can insulate itself against such a loss with a protective put option hedge. This option involves the intermediary purchasing put options contracts. If interest rates rise and bond and options prices fall before the expiration date of the put options purchased, the intermediary can make a profit by exercising its options contracts. The profit results because the strike price of the options at which it has to deliver the underlying bonds is higher than the market price at which bonds can be purchased for delivery. The gain from the options transactions offsets the loss in the value of the intermediary's bond portfolio. The use of protective put option contracts is similar to buying insurance. The cost of this insurance is the premium for the option contracts purchased.

Call Options to Protect against Falling Interest Rates

While put options can be used to offset losses from a negative maturity gap (*RSL* > *RSA*) when interest rates rise, call options can be used to offset losses from a positive maturity gap (*RSA* > *RSL*) should interest rates fall. The intermediary can insulate itself from loss due to a decline in interest rates with a covered call option hedge. Suppose the intermediary has a positive maturity gap because it holds a large proportion of its assets in money market securities. It protects itself from falling interest rates by purchasing, say, call option contracts on Treasury bills. Should interest rates fall and Treasury bill prices rise before expiration of the call options, the options can be exercised at a profit because their market price will exceed their strike price. The profits from the call options contracts will offset the loss in net interest income because of the decline in revenue from interest-sensitive assets.

Hedging interest rate risk with options rather than with futures has a significant advantage. With a hedge using futures, the intermediary gives up potential gains should interest rates move in the opposite direction from that for which protection was arranged. However, with an options hedge, protection is provided against an adverse movement in interest rates without necessarily sacrificing the potential for gain should interest rates move in the opposite direction.

Forward Rate Agreements

Forward rate agreements are yet another technique used by financial intermediaries to manage their interest rate risk. Three such types of agreements are commonly referred to as caps, floors, and collars.

interest rate cap
the ceiling or "cap" rate specified in an agreement

With an **interest rate cap** agreement, the writer (seller) agrees to pay the purchaser of the cap, in return for a one-time fee in advance, the difference between a rise in the market interest rate and a ceiling or "cap" rate specified in the agreement. The effect of the cap is to set a maximum cost on an intermediary's outstanding debt. Suppose, for instance, that a financial intermediary has borrowed funds with an interest rate of LIBOR (London Interbank Offered Rate) and buys a LIBOR cap of 10 percent with the notional principal of the cap equal to its borrowing. As long as the LIBOR rate remains below 10 percent, the intermediary will pay that rate on its debt and receives nothing from its cap. However, should the LIBOR rate exceed 10 percent, the intermediary would receive a payment from the cap partner to the agreement equal to the difference between the cap rate and the higher market price.

A floor is an interest rate risk management technique similar to a cap, except that a floor sets a minimum rather than a maximum rate. In a floor agreement, should the market rate drop below the floor, the writer (seller) of the agreement pays the purchaser an amount equal to the floor minus the market rate. Floor agreements are used by financial intermediaries to control their interest rate risk resulting from fixed-rate liabilities matched by floating-rate assets.

collar agreements agreements that combine buying a cap and writing a floor in which the cap rate differs from the floor rate

Collar agreements (collars) combine buying a cap and writing a floor in which the cap rate differs from the floor rate. A collar is used to contain the effective cost of floating-rate borrowing within a narrow band. Suppose an intermediary borrows by issuing debt with an interest rate of LIBOR and enters into a collar, with the floor rate set at 9 percent and the cap rate set at 11 percent. If LIBOR rates drop below 9 percent, the intermediary will pay 9 percent; the debt holders will receive LIBOR, and the other party to the collar will receive 9 percent minus LIBOR. The intermediary will pay LIBOR, and no payments will be made under the collar agreement if LIBOR stands between 9 percent and 11 percent. If LIBOR exceeds 11 percent, the intermediary's net cost will be 11 percent; the debt holders will receive LIBOR, and the writer of the collar will pay the intermediary LIBOR minus 11 percent.

Market Risk and Value-at-Risk Methodology

value-at-risk (VaR) an estimate of the largest loss that a portfolio is likely to suffer during all but truly exceptional periods

Market risk is the risk of loss that results from changes in interest rates, foreign exchange rates, equity, and commodity prices. In recent years financial intermediaries have used a new methodology called **value-at-risk** (**VAR** or **VaR**) to estimate their potential losses from market risk exposure. VaR is an estimate of the largest loss that a portfolio is likely to suffer during all but truly exceptional periods. More precisely, it is a risk measurement that uses statistical models to calculate with a given confidence level (probability) the maximum loss in market value over a specified period (holding period) as a result of an adverse change in market rates and prices.[2] For example, a one-day holding period and a 99 percent confidence level imply that actual changes in the market value of a portfolio may exceed the VaR dollar loss estimate approximately 1 percent of the time.

One major advantage of using VaR is that it aggregates the various components of market risk into one number that expresses potential loss in terms of dollars.

The Canadian banks routinely estimate the daily VaR of their trading portfolios, including derivatives, foreign exchange, fixed income, and equity

---

2. The concept may be easier to understand when we calculate the VaR of a single stock over a one-day horizon and with a 98 percent confidence level. We estimate the variance of the stock's price volatility and multiply its square root by the product of today's stock price and the confidence factor of 98 percent. Calculating the VaR for a portfolio of stocks is a little more difficult, since it involves the use of covariance and correlations.

trading on a global scale. These portfolios are managed with the intent to buy and sell financial instruments over a short period rather than to hold positions for investment purposes. The Bank of Nova Scotia, for example, reported in its 1999 annual report that its average daily VaR was $26.1 million. The Canadian Imperial Bank of Commerce reported an average daily VaR for 1999 of $24.96 million. The difference in these VaR amounts reflects the different sizes of these two banks' assets and the different assumptions used to construct the estimates.

In addition to gap analysis and value-at-risk methodology, financial institutions have moved toward simulation-based evaluation systems. These systems use Monte Carlo simulations to project interest rates, exchange rates, commodity and equity prices, and implied volatilities.

BOX 10–2 BACKGROUNDER

Value-at-Risk Analysis

Value-at-risk is a measure of the estimated value that may be lost when the market experiences an unusual decline. VaR can be constructed for a portfolio consisting of a single asset, or one consisting of a large number of assets. To calculate VaR we need information on the returns generated by the portfolio as well as on the measure of the volatility of those returns. We use the volatility figures to establish a value below which we would infrequently expect to see returns. For example, if the returns on a portfolio were normally distributed, elementary statistics tells us that 95 percent of the observations will lie within 1.96 standard deviations of the mean return, while 98 percent of the values will lie within 2.33 standard deviations of the mean return. If we

measure volatility as the standard deviation of the portfolio's return, we can establish the limits beyond which the returns would lie a small percentage of the time.

Suppose the daily return on a portfolio consisting of one stock had a variance of 0.6 percent. Using the above rule and the 98 percent value, we would expect to see 98 percent of the returns between –1.398 (–1.96 × 0.6%) percent and +1.398 (+1.96 × 0.6%) percent. One percent would lie above +1.398 percent and 1 percent would lie below –1.398 percent. So, 99 percent of the time we would expect to see returns above –1.398 percent. One percent of the time, the daily return would be below –1.398 percent.

On the off chance that a daily return were below –1.398 percent, how much could we lose? That's easy! If the shares were valued at $100 000, the most we could lose in one day would be 1.398% × $100 000 = $1398.00. That's a measure of the risk of holding the stock: The daily loss on holding the shares will exceed $1398 on one day out of 100.

If we have two assets in our portfolio, our measure of the variance of the portfolio would need to take into account the covariance or correlation between the returns on the assets, as we learned in Chapter 8. Suppose my shares of Apple Computer are

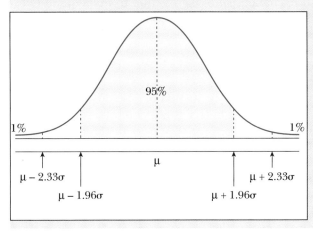

BOX 10–2   **BACKGROUNDER** *(continued)*

worth $10 000 while my shares of IBM Computer are worth $5000. The volatility of the daily returns to Apple shares is 0.99 percent while the volatility of daily returns to IBM shares is 0.90 percent. Let's also assume that the correlation between the returns is –0.80. Assuming both returns are normally distributed, and using the 98 percent level of confidence, I expect to see Apple returns below –2.3067 percent (2.33 × 0.99 percent) only 1 percent of the time, while I expect to see IBM returns below –2.097 percent only 1 percent of the time. My risk on Apple shares is $10 000 × 0.99 % = $99 while my risk on IBM shares is $5000 × 0.9 % = $45. However, the risk of the portfolio containing shares in both companies needs to take into account the correlation between the returns. If we denote the dollar value of risk due to Apple shares by σ^2_A and that of IBM shares by σ^2_{IBM} and the corre-

lation of the returns by ρ, then the VaR of the portfolio is

$$\text{VaR} = [\sigma^2_A + \sigma^2_{IBM} + 2\rho\sigma_A\sigma_{IBM}]^{1/2}$$

$$= [\$90 + \$45 + 2(-0.8)(\$90)^{1/2}(\$45)^{1/2}]^{1/2}$$

$$= (33.176)^{1/2}$$

$$= \$5.76$$

You can see the benefits to diversification from VaR. If Apple and IBM shares were uncorrelated ($\rho = 0$), the VaR would be the square root of the sum of the individual risks, or $11.62. Compare this amount to the diversified risk of $5.76 and you will see that, through diversification, I can reduce the risk by $5.86. That is, if the Apple and IBM shares were uncorrelated, one day out of 100 I could expect to lose as much as $11.62. By choosing stocks that are negatively correlated, I can reduce this amount to $5.76.

For more on VaR, and some of its limitations, see Simons (1996) or visit the Riskmetrics Website at <http://www.riskmetrics.com>.

Capital Funds Management

An important function of financial intermediation is the assumption of risk, which inevitably results in losses, regardless of how well intermediaries manage their assets and liabilities. We already have referred to credit risk, liquidity risk, funding risk, interest rate risk, and market risk. Other risks include exchange risk from dealings in foreign exchange, *operating risk* due to inadequate management, and *crime risk* as a result of fraud and embezzlement.

Financial intermediaries hold capital funds to absorb losses that can result in failure and, ultimately, insolvency. An institution becomes insolvent when the value that can be realized from selling its assets is less than the value of its liabilities.

Capital funds are viewed as a cushion against failure because they can be used to absorb losses. They also act as a buffer that protects an institution's depositors and creditors from losing funds entrusted to the intermediaries. While the depositors have first claim on a payments intermediary's assets in case of insolvency, they have incomplete information on the quality and, consequently, the value of these assets. Capital funds compensate for this lack of information since they are available to meet any shortfall between depositors' claims and the value of the assets that are supposed to support them. With depositors' confidence bolstered by the intermediaries' ability to satisfy their claims, runs that can threaten the stability of the entire financial system may be avoided. Capital funds also limit the losses of deposit insurers, arising from insurance claims by depositors of failed institutions.

The capital funds of financial intermediaries consist of equity and borrowed funds. Equity includes the amount invested by shareholders in common shares (and, in the case of credit unions and caisses populaires, members' contributions), together with retained earnings and reserves set aside for known and anticipated losses on loans and other assets. Borrowed funds are obtained from the sale of securities issues. In the case of payment intermediaries, outstanding securities are their subordinated debt because, in case of failure, depositors have a prior claim on any remaining assets.

Disagreement exists about what should constitute a financial institution's capital and what amount should be considered adequate. Traditionally, capital adequacy has been measured in terms of the proportionate amount of shareholders' equity or capital to assets—the equity to asset and capital to asset ratios; or their inverse, the leverage ratios. When minimum leverage ratios are specified by government regulators, they are frequently called borrowing ratios or multiples, since they set the multiple by which assets are allowed to grow relative to the amount of funds borrowed.

While higher equity or capital to asset ratios may increase the safety of deposits, payment intermediaries have an incentive to maintain lower ratios because, by so doing, they improve their stockholders' potential for higher returns. Hence, a conflict of interests exists between an intermediary's stockholders and its depositors. This conflict is referred to in the financial literature as the agency problem. The conflict has been resolved with the introduction of deposit insurance and the setting of minimum capital to asset ratios by government regulators.

REGULATORY CAPITAL   The primary measures of regulatory capital strength for Canadian banks are risk-adjusted capital ratios specified in guidelines issued by the Office of the Superintendent of Financial Institutions. These guidelines are based on international capital standards established under the auspices of the Bank for International Settlements (BIS). The BIS, an international clearing bank for central banks located in Basel, Switzerland, has assumed an important role in resolving issues concerning the soundness and stability of the international financial system.

Total regulatory capital is divided into two tiers. Tier 1 is made up of primary capital, also known as core or permanent capital, which consists essentially of shareholders' equity. Tier 2 is made up of secondary capital or supplementary capital, which includes subordinated debt and a limited amount of reserves for loan and lease losses.[3]

Regulatory minimum capital to asset ratios are calculated by dividing tier 1 and total capital by "risk adjusted assets." Assets are assigned to different cate-

www.

---

3. Regulatory capital differs from capital recorded on the banks' balance sheets in that goodwill and investments in associated companies are excluded from regulatory capital, while noncontrolling interests in subsidiaries are included in regulatory capital. As well, subordinated debentures for regulatory capital are amortized by 20 percent per year in the final five years to maturity.

gories, each with a different weight reflecting its credit risk. Off-balance-sheet financial transactions, described in Chapter 13, are converted into credit-equivalent values and assigned a weight for inclusion in risk-adjusted assets.

Since the end of 1992, Canadian banks have been required to maintain a minimum total capital ratio of 8 percent and a minimum tier 1 capital ratio of 4 percent. In practice, they have maintained their ratios well above the minimum regulatory requirement.

In 1996, the BIS amended its 1988 Capital Accord to incorporate market risk. These amendments, requiring Canadian banks to report under new guidelines, were adopted by the Superintendent of Financial Institutions in January 1998.

Deposit Insurance

The Goals of Deposit Insurance

Deposit insurance has at least two major goals. One is to protect small, unsophisticated depositors who are unable to assess the soundness of the payment intermediaries to whom they entrust their funds. The other goal is to enhance the public's confidence in the soundness of these institutions and the safety of their deposits. If depositors' confidence in an institution is shaken, they have the incentive to be among the first to withdraw their funds from that institution before it runs out of money. As noted earlier, as more and more depositors rush to retrieve their funds, a situation known as a bank run takes place. Loss of confidence in one institution can quickly spread to others, even though the others may be quite sound. Because of this so-called contagion effect, the stability of the entire payments system can be threatened. Deposit insurance is one way to avoid contagious runs and promote the stability of the payments system.

Deposit insurance may also promote competition and efficiency in payments intermediation. New institutions should find it easier to start up because with deposit insurance, they can more readily compete for deposits. It is also argued that by eliminating the competitive advantage of large institutions over small ones, deposit insurance provides a level playing field and creates competitive fairness.

Deposit insurers are usually mandated by their respective governments, as is the case in Canada, to promote standards of sound business and financial practices. This mandate reduces the vulnerability of depository institutions to failure, protects the safety of deposits, and, thereby promotes the stability of the payments system.

www.

BOX 10–2 BACKGROUNDER

Deposit Insurance around the World

Almost all industrialized nations have one form of deposit insurance or another. Many are run by government, while in some cases the banking industry administers the program. The following table provides a summary of deposit insurance programs for the G-10 and members of the European Union.

Deposit Insurance Schemes of the G-10 Countries and the European Union

Country	Extent of Coverage	Administration of System	Government Guarantee or Other Backup	Base for Premiums	Prefunding
Belgium	ECU 15 000 until Dec. 1999; ECU 20 000 thereafter	Joint government/industry	Yes	0.2% covered deposits in ECU or any EU currency	No
Canada	$60 000	Government	Yes	1/6 of 1% of insured deposits	Yes
France	FF 400 000 per deposit	Industry	Significant government ownership and involvement in deposit-taking system	1. 0.1% of claims settled in max. of FF 200 000 2. Proportional contribution based on formula	No
Germany	100% up to a limit of 30% of the bank's liable capital per depositor	Industry (commercial banks—25% of deposits)	Majority of deposits with credit unions and 100% of deposits in government-guaranteed savings and postal savings banks	0.03% of balance sheet item "liabilities to customers"	Yes + extra assessment if needed
Italy	100% of first 200 million lira and 75% of next 800 million lira per deposit	Industry (with input from central bank)	Significant government ownership and involvement in deposit-taking system	Maximum limit for fund: 4000 billion lira; contributions according to formula	No; but banks commit *ex ante*
Japan	10 million yen per depositor	Joint government / industry	Large share of small retail deposits in postal savings banks with 100% government guarantees	0.012% of insured deposits	Yes
Netherlands	ECU 20 000 per depositor	Government	Bridge financing	Compensation apportioned among institutions; maximum of 5% of institution's own funds; maximum of 5% of all institutions' own funds	No
Sweden	SEK 250 000 per depositor	Government	Yes	0.25% of covered deposits	Yes
Switzerland	SF 30 000 per depositor	Industry	No	1. Fixed fee based on gross profit 2. Variable fee based on share of protected deposits	No
United Kingdom	90% of protected deposits (maximum amount of protected deposits per depositor is £20 000, so maximum is £18 000)	Government	Yes	0.01% of deposits in European Economic Area currency less certain deposits by financial institutions and others	Yes; £10,000 at start-up; additional amount if fund below £3 million
United States	US$100 000 per depositor	Government	Yes	0% to 0.27% of domestic deposits; flat minimum of $2000 for highest-rated banks	Yes
European Union	Aggregate deposits of each depositor up to a maximum of ECU 20 000	Must be at least one officially recognized deposit insurance scheme in each territory	Determined by each member	Determined by each member	Determined by each member

SOURCES: Department of Finance, "Improving the Regulatory Framework," Background Paper #5, Task Force on the Future of the Canadian Financial Services Sector, September 1998; A.W. Moysey, "Deposit Insurance and Other Compensation Arrangements," Task Force on the Future of the Canadian Financial Services Sector, Department of Finance, 1998.

The Canadian Deposit Insurance System

Canada Deposit Insurance Corporation (CDIC) *the body that provides deposit insurance in all provinces except Quebec*

Quebec Deposit Insurance Board *the body that provides deposit insurance in Quebec*

In Canada, deposit insurance is provided by the **Canada Deposit Insurance Corporation (CDIC)** and the **Quebec Deposit Insurance Board** (Régie de l'assurance dépôts du Québec). In addition, the credit union and caisses populaires movements outside Quebec have their own provincial systems that protect members' deposits. In Quebec, deposits and shares of members of credit unions and caisses populaires are protected by the Quebec Deposit Insurance Board.

Deposit insurance was first introduced in Canada in 1967. The first law was passed in Ontario, but when the federal government introduced its own legislation only a week later, Ontario elected to come under the federal program. Quebec set up its own scheme, while the other provinces followed Ontario by also requiring their institutions to be insured under the federal program.

The CDIC insures the deposits at all the chartered banks and at federally incorporated trust and mortgage loan companies. By agreement with the provinces, the CDIC also insures deposits (outside Quebec) at provincially incorporated trust and loan companies. The Quebec Deposit Insurance Board insures all deposits of depository institutions, including credit unions and caisses populaires, in Quebec, excluding the deposits held by the chartered banks in the province. The federal and Quebec insurance systems are similar. The CDIC is empowered to make short-term secured loans to the Quebec board to enable it to meet emergency liquidity needs that may arise from its insurance operations. The CDIC can also provide lender of last resort facilities to Canadian-controlled sales finance companies, and to national and provincial central credit unions that in turn provide lender of last resort facilities to credit unions.

The CDIC protects deposits in institutions insured by it in four ways: (1) it provides a cash settlement to depositors of a failed institution, (2) it requires insured institutions to follow standards of sound business and financial practices, (3) it extends loans to and acquires assets from institutions in distress, and (4) it provides assistance to enable institutions with severe difficulties to be merged with or acquired by healthy ones.

When an insolvent institution has to be liquidated, the CDIC settles a depositor's claim for up to $60 000 (increased from $20 000 in 1983) either with a cash payment or by way of a $60 000 deposit with another insured institution. Deposits insured generally include all deposit-like instruments accepted on demand or those that can be claimed within five years. Recent legislative changes allow banks that accept only wholesale deposits (defined as $150 000 or more) to operate without deposit insurance. In March 2000, J.P. Morgan Canada and Rabobank were the first to opt out of CDIC membership under the legislation.

CDIC RESOURCES   The CDIC has financed its operations and paid insurance claims primarily with premium income and earnings on investments, and through borrowing against the federal government. Since 1996, the CDIC has been authorized to borrow in private capital markets through the issuance and sale of bonds, debentures, and notes. Total borrowing (public and private) may not exceed $6 billion or greater amounts as may be authorized by Parliament under an appropriation Act.

INSURANCE PREMIUMS   Member institutions of the CDIC pay an annual insurance premium set at a standard rate per dollar of insured deposits. Until recently, the CDIC charged the same premium (one-sixth of a percent) to all member institutions. In 1996 the CDIC proposed the development of a system of varying premia based on a risk rating of the institutions. In 1999 the legislation was adopted. Today, premia are based on the prudence with which members conduct their business, with four categories as demonstrated in Table 10.1.

TABLE 10.1	CDIC PREMIUM CLASSIFICATIONS	
PREMIUM CATEGORY	RATE	RESULT
1	12.5% × 0.33%*	0.0417% or 1/24 of 1%
2	25% × 0.33%	0.0833% or 1/12 of 1%
3	50% × 0.33%	0.1667% or 1/6 of 1%
4	a) 50% × 0.33% for the first two years of the by-law	0.1667% or 1/6 of 1%
	b) 100% × 0.33% thereafter	0.3333% or 1/3 of 1%

* The maximum rate permitted under the *CDIC Act* is one-third of one percent of insured deposits.

SOURCE: The Canada Deposit Insurance Corporation, *Annual Report 1998–1999*, p. 21.

CDIC Loss Experience

During its first 14 years, up to the end of 1980, aside from providing financial assistance to struggling member institutions, the CDIC had to deal with only three institutional failures, which involved paying depositors' claims. In the 1980s, however, 21 member institutions failed, 3 of which were banks and the others trust and loan companies. Of the 21 failures, 7 occurred in each of the years 1983 and 1985. During the 1990s, up to March 1996, another 12 institutions failed; all except one of them, a foreign bank subsidiary, were trust and loan companies. As of early 2000, there have been no failures since June 1996 when the Security Home Mortgage Corporation was liquidated.

The number of failures in a year is determined by a variety of factors, which include a deterioration of economic conditions and a deterioration in the quality of an institution's management. The large number of failures during the 1980s can be attributed largely to the quality of management, if not to the deposit insurance system itself, which encouraged managers to run more risky operations while attracting deposits by paying higher interest rates. The failures during the early 1990s, in contrast, were in large part due to economic conditions that resulted in a deterioration in the institutions' commercial real estate loans.

In 1992 the CDIC's borrowing from the federal government to finance its costs of deposit insurance peaked at $3.7 billion. However, its accumulated deficit continued to increase until 1995, when it peaked at $1.7 billion. By the end of 1999 the deficit and the debt had been completely eliminated, allowing the CDIC to reduce the premia it charges its three best classifications of member institutions by as much as 75 percent.

Failure Resolution Methods

The CDIC handles failures of member institutions in one of four ways.

DEPOSIT PAYOUT   When a member institution is insolvent and subsequently placed into liquidation, the CDIC pays depositors up to the limit of their insured deposits and becomes a creditor up to the amount it paid out.

AGENCY AGREEMENT   Another institution acting as an agent of the CDIC takes over the running of a failed member, for which it is paid a fee by the CDIC. This method was used in the 1980s in place of immediate liquidation of insolvent institutions to minimize CDIC costs and the amount of funds it had to borrow from the federal government to cover its losses. A shortcoming of agency agreements was that not only insured deposits, but also uninsured ones were paid by the CDIC. This shortcoming gave the public the perception that, in effect, all their deposits were insured. This perception was reinforced in 1985, when a bailout was arranged for all depositors of the failed Canadian Commercial Bank and the Northland Bank.

FINANCIAL ASSISTANCE   The CDIC provides financial assistance to failing member institutions with the intention to rehabilitate them and have them survive. Assistance may take the form of loans and advances, loan guarantees, the acquisition of assets, or deposits made at the troubled institution.

PURCHASE AGREEMENTS   To facilitate the sale of a troubled member institution, the CDIC provides loans and may guarantee to pay the purchaser a portion of the principal and income losses that may occur. These guarantees are also referred to as deficiency coverage agreements.

Reducing the Cost of Failure

In the early 1990s, following a review of all its policies and procedures, the CDIC introduced new systems in an attempt to reduce the high incidence of failure among its member institutions and thereby control the high costs of deposit insurance. In cooperation with the Office of the Superintendent of Financial Institutions (OSFI), it developed Standards of Sound Business and Financial Practices that were made into law in 1993. These standards relate to a member institution's liquidity management, interest rate risk management, credit-risk management, securities portfolio management, capital management, real estate appraisals, and internal control. Institutions that fail these standards may be subject to a premium surcharge. If corrections still are not made, the CDIC can cancel the institution's deposit insurance, which would in effect close it down; without insurance it would be legally prevented from accepting deposits from the public. These two sanctions available to the CDIC provide a strong incentive for institutions to meet the standards and thereby reduce their risk of failure.

In January 2000, the CDIC released a consultation paper relating to a revision of the 1993 Standards of Sound Business and Financial Practices. Aside from updating the standards, the paper put forward a number of changes to the way in which the CDIC administers deposit insurance, including the following:[4]

- the Standards will be reviewed to align more closely with current concepts of risk management;
- the frequency and detail with which compliance must be reported will be reduced in many cases. Institutions that are highly rated for supervisory and deposit insurance purposes will generally not be required to file comprehensive reports every year. For all institutions, it will be made clear that compliance is to be assessed relative to the broad principles in the standards by-laws, and that the booklets are intended to be a source of commentary and guidance, not a detailed code;
- CDIC's opinion on whether an institution is following the standards should take into account the significance of any deficiencies, and nonmaterial deficiencies should not necessarily be viewed as non-compliance. The statutory requirement imposed on examiners (OSFI for federal companies) to provide CDIC with standards compliance reports (section 29 of the *CDIC Act*) will be amended to address this materiality concept; and
- CDIC and OSFI will enhance their coordination and information-sharing in order to reduce the reporting burden on institutions.

The CDIC does not regulate the affairs of its member institutions; this is the primary responsibility of either the OSFI or the provincial regulators, depending on whether an institution is federally or provincially incorporated.

Early intervention to restore the health of a failing institution or to have it taken over by a healthy one is a major way that the CDIC can manage its own costs. To facilitate its timely intervention and to make the corporation more efficient, the CDIC has developed a system of risk assessment and rating. Among other factors, risk assessment takes into consideration a member's corporate structure, the quality and diversification of its assets, its financial strength as reflected in its capital-to-asset ratio, its financial performance and profitability, its access to new capital injections if required, the quality of its management, and its regulatory compliance.

The CDIC rates its members according to their overall assessed risks and places those with poor ratings on a watch list for early intervention. While the CDIC must depend on its members' primary regulators to examine and supervise them on an ongoing basis, more recently the CDIC has conducted its own special examination of members that appear to be in critical condition. These examinations focus primarily on asset quality and loss provisions.

---

4. Canada Deposit Insurance Corporation. *Standards of Sound Business and Financial Practices: Consultation Paper* (January 2000), p. 26.

Reforming the Deposit Insurance System

With the large number of failures of deposit-taking institutions in the 1980s in both Canada and the United States, attention focused on the possible causes and on the role of deposit insurance. In 1985 the federal government appointed the Wyman Committee to study the structure and operations of the CDIC. Issues relating to deposit insurance were also considered by the Ontario Task Force on Financial Institutions and by federal parliamentary and Senate committees.

Studies have found that, rather than enhancing the soundness of depository institutions, deposit insurance may have unwittingly made the institutions less sound because deposit insurance has given them an incentive for excessive risk taking. It is well known that insurance coverage can alter the behaviour of the insured and thereby increase the probability that the event underwritten by insurance will happen. This phenomenon is called the "moral hazard problem" of insurance. For example, with fire insurance on a home, one may take less care to prevent fires, and with theft insurance, less care to lock doors. Similarly, with government deposit insurance, depositors have little incentive to monitor the risk-taking activities of insured institutions. As a result, these institutions are able to obtain deposits to finance risky operations without paying the higher interest rates that would reflect these higher risks. Nor are these higher risks reflected in higher insurance premiums, since premiums are a uniform percentage of the amount of insurable deposits. Furthermore, with all institutions paying the same premium rate for insurance, irrespective of their different risk exposures, the less risky institutions end up subsidizing the additional risk that the more aggressive institutions take on. Insured institutions also have the incentive to assume more risk because their shareholders benefit from favourable outcomes, while the cost of unfavourable outcomes is borne by the insurer and, with government bailouts, by the taxpayer.

When institutions themselves do not bear the cost of the risks they undertake, it is known as risk not being internalized—risk bearing is incorrectly priced and, hence, inefficient. The socially optimum degree of risk taking occurs when an institution's risk is completely internalized—that is, its marginal costs and marginal benefits of risk are equated.

www.

Risk-Based Insurance Premiums

Historically, the premium rate charged to institutions for insuring deposits held with them has been the same for all institutions regardless of their behaviour toward risk. With flat-rate insurance premiums, riskier institutions indeed subsidize less risky ones. It is argued that if riskier institutions were to pay higher insurance premiums they would have less incentive to expose themselves to excessive risk. Two difficulties had prevented the implementation of risk-based insurance premiums. One was finding an acceptable way to measure the risk exposure of different institutions; the other was deciding on the appropriate level of risk taking to be allowed from society's point of view, in a system with risk-based insurance premiums.

Amendments in 1996 to the *CDIC Act* required the CDIC to develop a system to vary premia to member institutions based on a risk rating of institutions. As we noted above, the CDIC has now designed a system for classifying members into risk categories and has set out a method for calculating the annual premium applicable to each category.

The CDIC will retain its ability to levy a premium surcharge, which can be any amount up to one-sixth of 1 percent of insurable deposits, on member institutions that do not conform to the CDIC Standards of Sound Business and Financial Practices. The premium surcharge will be in addition to the risk-rated premium levied on a member.

Coinsurance with Depositors

With the safety of their deposits protected by deposit insurance, depositors have little or no incentive to discipline depository institutions known to be operating in an unsound manner. Under a system of coinsurance, depositors would have such an incentive because a fraction of their deposits would remain at risk. They would discipline risky institutions by withdrawing their funds from them or by demanding higher interest rates for deposits with them. Risky institutions would be forced to absorb the higher interest cost or become less risky.

The extent to which depositors can be counted on to exercise discipline over risky institutions depends on the information they have to assess the relative riskiness of different deposit-taking institutions. It also raises the question whether the degree to which depositors have to be put at risk to provide an appropriate incentive would sacrifice the goal of deposit insurance, which is to protect small, unsophisticated depositors.

Various suggestions for coinsurance have been made. The Wyman Committee, for example, proposed in 1985 that following a transition period, all insured depositors be at risk for 10 percent of the amount of their deposits. The Canadian Bankers' Association proposed that depositors remain at risk for 25 percent of their deposits in excess of $20 000. In 1994 the Senate Standing Committee on Banking, Trade, and Commerce proposed that depositors be fully protected for the first $30 000 of deposits and only 90 percent for the next $35 000. More recently, a research paper written by Moysey (1998) for the Task Force on the Future of the Canadian Financial System recommended coinsurance because it reduces costs and encourages depositors to take more responsibility for their actions.

www.

Subordinated Debt and Capital Adequacy

Issuing subordinated debt has been proposed as a means of imposing market discipline on the risk-taking activities of financial intermediaries. It has been argued that institutions should be required to issue a specified amount of debt that is subordinate to all other creditors in the event of insolvency. Since holders of this debt would be at risk, they would have the incentive to monitor and discipline risk-taking institutions. Restrictive covenants accompanying subordinate debt issues would serve to control risky activities, as would the higher returns demanded by debt holders for incurring additional risk. The higher returns that would have to be paid on the subordinated debt of the risky institutions would internalize their cost of risk-taking and thereby discourage such activities.

Higher capital to asset ratios achieved by issuing subordinated debt would also serve to internalize the cost of risk-taking. With higher ratios, owners and managers would have more at stake when risky undertakings end in institutional failure. The Wyman Committee in its report on reforming the Canadian deposit insurance system, proposed not only higher capital requirements, but also capital ratios based on the risk profile of each insured institution.

Private Insurance and Reinsurance

Proponents of replacing government deposit protection with private insurers argue that profit-motivated private insurers are more skillful at measuring and pricing risks, and thereby controlling moral hazard problems. It is questionable, however, whether depositors would have sufficient confidence in the ability of private insurance companies to pay their claims in the event of large failures. It is also doubtful whether private firms would want to insure deposits on a large scale, because failure of depository institutions can be systemic—that is, economywide. In other words, private insurance companies cannot sufficiently diversify individual risks to make their overall risk acceptable. It has been suggested that this difficulty could be overcome with reinsurance.

Reinsurance is a risk-transfer technique whereby either the primary insurer sells a portion of the insurance contract to other parties or other insurers insure a portion of the risks underwritten by the primary insurer. It has been proposed that either government deposit insurers reinsure some portion of deposit insurance with private insurers, or that in a system of private deposit insurance the government reinsure claims above a certain level. Either method of reinsurance would allow private sector market discipline to contain moral hazard.

Tighter Regulation and Supervision

The alternative to risk-based insurance premia and other reforms that would impose market discipline on insured institutions' risk-taking activity is to impose discipline by government through tighter controls and more careful supervision. This action would equalize risk across insured institutions and remove the incentive toward excessive risk-taking that results from a flat insurance premium structure. It assumes that the insurer does not underprice the risks that remain after tighter regulation and more supervision have been imposed.

KEY TERMS

basis risk
Canada Deposit Insurance Corporation (CDIC)
collar agreements
contagion
deposit insurance
duration gap
duration gap management
funding risk

income risk
interest rate cap
interest rate risk
investment risk
liquidity risk
marking-to-market risk
maturity gap (GAP)
maturity gap management
primary reserves

Quebec Deposit Insurance Board
real bills doctrine (commercial loans theory)
risk of insolvency
secondary reserves
shiftability doctrine of liquidity
synthetic loans
value-at-risk (VAR or VaR)

REVIEW QUESTIONS

1. Outline the various risks that may threaten a financial intermediary's solvency.
2. What is the commercial loans theory and what are its shortcomings?
3. What is the difference between maturity gap and duration gap?
4. Give examples of the use of financial futures and options to hedge interest rate risk.
5. How are caps, floors, and collars used to control interest rate risk?
6. How do financial intermediaries use swaps?
7. What constitutes an intermediary's capital funds? What are the major purposes served by capital funds?
8. How does the Canada Deposit Insurance Corporation provide a safety net for depositors?
9. What are the shortcomings of deposit insurance? What reforms have been proposed?
10. Suppose your shares of Peter's Pizzeria are worth $230 000 while your shares of Mary's Diner are worth $500 000. The volatility of the daily returns to Pizzeria shares is 0.76 percent while the volatility of daily returns to Diner shares is 0.81 percent. Also assume that the correlation between the returns is –0.75 and that the returns are normally distributed.

a. Using a 1 percent confidence level, what is the most you could be expected to lose on your portfolio on any day?
b. If you only held Pizzeria shares, what is your VaR using the 1 percent level? What if you only held Diner shares?
c. What is the benefit of diversifying your portfolio and holding shares in both firms?

11. Suppose your shares of Suzie's Socks are worth $560 000 while my shares of Bill's Shoes are worth $2 500 000. The volatility of the daily returns to Socks shares is 0.4 percent while the volatility of daily returns to Shoes shares is 0.99 percent. Assume that the correlation between the returns is –0.1 and that the returns are normally distributed.

a. What is the most you could expect to lose on your portfolio, 2.5 days out of 100?
b. If your only held Socks shares, what is your VaR using the 1 percent level? What if you held only Shoes shares?
c. What is the benefit of diversifying your portfolio and holding shares in both firms? Use the 1 percent level.

SELECTED READINGS

Abken, Peter A. "Interest Rate Caps, Collars and Floors." *Federal Reserve Bank of Atlanta, Economic Review* (November/December 1989), pp. 2–24.

Bank for International Settlements. *Recent Innovations in International Banking.* Basel: BIS, 1986.

Binhammer, H.H. "Depository Institutions: Risks and Insolvencies." Discussion Paper No. 333, Economic Council of Canada. Ottawa: Economic Council of Canada, 1987.

———. Department of Finance. *Enhancing the Safety and Soundness of the Canadian Financial System.* Ottawa, 4 February 1995.

———. Senate of Canada. *Deposit Insurance.* Tenth Report of the Senate Standing Committee on Banking, Trade and Commerce. Ottawa, December 1985.

Canada Deposit Insurance Corporation. *Annual Report,* various issues.

———. *Standards of Sound Business and Financial Practices: Consultation Paper,* January 2000.

Carr, John, G.F. Mathewson ,and N.C. Quigley. *Insuring Failure: Financial System Stability and Deposit Insurance in Canada.* Toronto, C.D. Howe Institute, 1994.

Department of Finance. "Improving the Regulatory Framework." Background Paper #5, Task Force on the Future of the Canadian Financial Services Sector, September 1998.

———. "Enhancing the Safety and Soundness of the Canadian Financial System." White Paper, February 1995.

Drabenstott, Mark, and Anne O'Mara McDonley. "Futures Markets: A Primer for Financial Institutions." *Federal Reserve Bank of Kansas City, Economic Review* (November 1984), pp. 17–33.

Eftekhari, B., and C. Pedersen. "On the Volatility of Measures of Financial Risk: An Investigation Using Returns from European Markets." *European Journal of Finance* (1, 2000).

Fallon, William. "Calculating Value-at-Risk." Wharton Financial Institutions, Working Paper No. 96–49, 1996.

Final Report of the Working Committee on the Canada Deposit Insurance Corporation (CDIC) (Wyman Report). Ottawa, April 1985.

Hopper, Gregory. "Value at Risk: A New Methodology for Measuring Portfolio Risk." B*usiness Review, Federal Reserve Bank of Philadelphia* (July/August 1996), pp. 19–29.

Koppenhauer, Gary D. "Futures Options and Their Use by Financial Intermediaries." *Federal Reserve Bank of Chicago, Economic Perspectives* (January/February 1986), pp. 18–31.

Morris, Charles S. "Managing Interest Rate Risk with Interest Rate Futures." *Federal Reserve Bank of Kansas City, Economic Review* (March 1989), pp. 3–20.

Moysey, A.W. "Deposit Insurance and Other Compensation Arrangements." Task Force on the Future of the Canadian Financial Services Sector, Department of Finance, 1998.

Murton, Arthur J. "A Survey of the Issues and the Literature Concerning Risk-Related Deposit Insurance." *Banking and Economic Review* (September/October 1986), pp. 11–86.

Pastor, A.A.J. "Efficiency and Risk Management in Spanish Banking: A Method to Decompose Risk." *Applied Financial Economics* 9 (4, 1999).

Pesando, James E. "Deposit Insurance and the Incentive for Excessive Risk-Taking: Alternative Strategies for Reform." Ontario Economic Council, Discussion Paper Series. Toronto: Ontario Economic Council, 1985.

Simons, K. "Value at Risk—New Approaches to Risk Management." *New England Economic Review, Federal Reserve Bank of Boston* (September/October 1996).

Smith, B., and R.W. White. "The Deposit Insurance System in Canada: Problems and Proposals for Change." *Canadian Public Policy* (December 1988), pp. 331–46.

CHAPTER ELEVEN

The Regulation of Financial Intermediaries and Regulatory reform

After reading this chapter you should be able to
1. *Describe the goals of financial regulation*
2. *Outline the various approaches to the regulation of financial institutions*
3. *Explain the regulatory reforms to foster competition and diversification in the financial sector*
4. *Explain the regulatory reforms to ensure soundness and stability in the financial sector*

Between 1980 and 1985, Canada experienced an unprecedented number of failures of financial institutions. The cause of these failures was seen by many to have been an antiquated regulatory and supervisory system that could no longer cope with the changing practices of financial institutions. In this chapter we start by presenting goals for financial regulation. We go on to describe regulatory jurisdiction, regulatory approaches, the reform process, and the legislative response.

Goals of Financial Regulation

market conduct regulation *regulations designed to protect consumers*

prudential regulation *regulations designed to maintain a stable financial system and sound financial institutions*

The two major goals of public policy with respect to the regulation of financial intermediaries are **market conduct regulation** and **prudential regulation**. Market conduct regulation is designed for consumer protection while prudential regulation is designed to maintain the soundness of financial institutions and the financial system as a whole. Additional reasons for the regulation of financial intermediaries are to achieve monetary control, to achieve certain social goals, and to prevent excessive concentration of economic power.

Safety and Soundness

The safety and soundness goal is the traditional reason for government regulation of payment intermediaries. A peculiar aspect of the payments system is that, as with the telephone system, any one user's benefit from it depends on its use by others. The extent to which the use of the payments system is optimized and its benefits enjoyed by all depends critically on the public's confidence in the safety of their deposits. This confidence in turn is reflected in the public's perception of the soundness of the payments intermediaries. These perceptions can be weak—or wrong—if the public does not have sufficient information about an institution's risk exposure. Adequate information about the risk behaviour of institutions is usually costly and not readily available to most depositors. Government regulation of institutions' risk behaviour serves as a substitute for information and, as such, supports the public's confidence in the safety of their deposits.

Most of the difficulties in financial intermediation that give rise to the need for regulation to ensure safety and soundness stem from the existence of asymmetric information and principal–agent relationships. **Asymmetric information** refers to the imperfect distribution of information that allows one party to a transaction to take unfair advantage of, and in the extreme, to expropriate wealth from, the other party to the transaction. Information asymmetries exist because of the cost to individuals of acquiring sufficient information to monitor the behaviour of intermediaries. Individuals could pool their interests to generate sufficient information, but they are not likely to do so. Information is a public good from which individuals can benefit without paying. This situation is known as the free-rider problem.

Because of asymmetric information, financial markets can fail. As we have already observed, inadequate information on the part of depositors can result in runs on depository institutions that can threaten the stability of the entire payments system. To avoid this possibility, governments have put in place so-called safety nets. These safety nets consist of central bank lender-of-last-resort facilities, deposit insurance, and prudential regulations and supervision.

Most financial services are provided within a **principal–agent relationship**, where a principal delegates an agent to take some action on the principal's behalf.[1] Payments intermediaries, for example, act as agents for their depositors. When depositors place their money with these institutions, they are delegating to them the responsibility to monitor the performance of the firms to which they lend depositors' funds and to enforce loan contracts. Managers of financial intermediaries act as agents of their owners in the everyday operations of the intermediaries.

Problems can arise in the principal–agent relationship that lead to market failure when the goals of the agent differ from those of the principal, especially if the agent and principal have different information related to the decisions

asymmetric information
refers to imperfect distribution of information, allowing one party to a transaction to take unfair advantage of the other party

principal–agent relationship
when a principal delegates an agent to take some action on the principal's behalf

---

1. For a discussion of the agency theory of the firm, see John W. Pratt, and Richard J. Zeckhauser (eds.). *Principals and Agents: The Structure of Business* (Boston: Harvard Business School Press, 1985); Michael C. Jensen, and William H. Meckling. "Theory of the Firm: Managerial Behavior, Agency Costs and Ownership Structure," *Journal of Financial Economics* (1976), pp. 305–60; and Joseph E. Stiglitz, "Credit Markets and the Control of Capital," *Journal of Money, Credit and Banking* (May 1985), pp. 133–52.

the agent is supposed to make on the principal's behalf. Abusive conflicts of interest and self-dealing, described below, can result in the expropriation of wealth by agents from their principals. Managers of financial intermediaries, for instance, may expropriate funds from legitimate claimants by the excess consumption of prerequisites. Owners and managers might expropriate funds from depositors and other creditors by investing them in the risky enterprises of firms in which they hold a proprietary interest and by paying excess dividends. Regulations directed toward preventing such problems of misappropriation specify the allowable organizational form of ownership and cover the relationship of intermediaries with associated firms, as well as the type of activities that intermediaries can undertake. Intermediaries, for instance, have been severely limited in engaging in real sector commercial activities.

Financial intermediaries can also expropriate wealth by means of the types of contracts they write for their customers. Governments regulate allowable terms of contracts and require the disclosure of information to minimize chances of such expropriation. Institutions, for example, cannot make personal loan contracts that prohibit prepayment before the due date of money advanced. Loans by depository institutions cannot be subject to the condition that borrowers maintain a minimum credit balance in a deposit account. At one time, usury laws set ceilings on interest rates that could be charged because rates above a certain level were considered unconscionable. Today, regulations require disclosure of the manner of calculating the cost of borrowing in respect of loans.

The Enhancement of Competition

The ultimate role of financial intermediaries is to transfer funds efficiently between surplus and deficit spending units. Efficiency implies that goods and services are produced at the lowest attainable cost and that all resources are allocated to their most valuable use. Competition encourages efficiency and forces firms to be innovative in responding to technological change and market demand. As a result, the convenience and options available to consumers of financial services are increased, as are the sources of credit available to individuals and firms. The internationalization of financial markets also requires that Canadian financial intermediaries provide services, in terms of quality and price, that are at least as good as those offered by their competitors in other countries.

For markets to be competitive, firms must be allowed to enter into them freely, while weak and inefficient firms must be allowed to fail or otherwise withdraw. As we have already observed, with payments intermediaries, the failure of an institution can threaten the stability of the entire payments system. For this reason, regulations that are directed toward greater competition must be carefully balanced with regulations that preserve the safety and soundness of the entire system of payments intermediation.

Regulation and Monetary Control

As we will learn in later chapters, because of their important role in the payments system, the depository institutions, and particularly the chartered banks, also play a pivotal role in the implementation of monetary policy. To assist the central bank in controlling the money supply or credit conditions, regulations specify the way in which depository institutions can manage their cash reserves. In some countries, where the volume of credit is also considered an important element of monetary policy, control over lending is an additional argument for regulating financial intermediaries.

Social Goals

Financial intermediaries may be regulated to achieve certain social goals. Three such goals are a desired allocation of credit, a high degree of Canadian ownership, and the prevention of an excessive concentration of power. With respect to the allocation of credit, some governments have required intermediaries to allocate a certain proportion of their funds to housing, exports, small businesses, or low-income groups. It can be argued that, because money is highly fungible, regulation of a particular flow of funds tends to direct credit through other channels, often less efficiently. Rather than imposing regulations to achieve a particular allocation of credit, the Canadian government has used loan guarantee programs to induce intermediaries to enter socially desirable lending fields. Both the federal and the provincial governments have also established their own financial institutions to serve particular sectors of the economy.

Before the 1960s foreign ownership of Canadian financial institutions was not a major public policy concern, and no specific regulations governing foreign ownership of these institutions existed. In the *Bank Act* revisions of 1967, however, the federal government imposed, for the first time, restrictions on foreign ownership of any chartered banks. Revisions to legislation governing other financial institutions, at both the federal and the provincial levels, subsequently also included provisions limiting foreign ownership.

More recently, concern over foreign ownership of Canadian financial institutions has been tempered by the recognition that foreign participation can be an important stimulus to competition in domestic markets. In addition, restrictions on the activities of foreign-owned financial institutions in Canada can result in reciprocal restrictions on the operations of Canadian financial institutions abroad.

Excessive Concentration of Power

www.

The control of concentration of power in a regulatory context relates to the excessive concentration in individual markets and the concentration of ownership of financial institutions, both of which may result in noncompetitive behaviour. The concentration of economic power also has the potential for undesirable social power. To avoid excessive concentration of power, the ownership and control of financial institutions has mostly been kept separate from the ownership and control of nonfinancial firms. For example, the banks have been prevented from engaging in nonfinancial activities, and business firms from controlling banks, although as we will see, recent proposals suggest these restrictions will be loosened soon.

Regulatory Jurisdiction

Jurisdiction over the regulation and supervision of financial intermediaries in Canada has been divided between the federal and provincial governments in what has been described as a rather "mixed" and "confused" fashion. The Canadian Constitution expressly gives the federal government the exclusive authority to legislate banks and banking. The word "banks" has come to mean nothing more than institutions that the federal government chooses to call banks, and "banking" refers to the activities carried on by those institutions. However, in practice, many of the same activities engaged in by banks are carried out by institutions that do not fall within the exclusive jurisdiction of the federal government.

Securities regulation is wholly within provincial jurisdiction, not strictly as a constitutional prerogative, but more as a matter of practice and convention, reinforced by decisions of the courts. Federally chartered banks, empowered by federal legislation to engage in certain securities activities, observe provincial regulations in most aspects of their dealings in the provincially regulated securities markets.[2] Uniform securities statutes and policies have been developed through cooperative efforts among the provinces to avoid unnecessary regulatory duplication. Administration of securities regulation is through independent regulatory agencies, such as the Ontario Securities Commission, and not through government departments.

www.

Trust, mortgage loan, and insurance companies may be either federally or provincially chartered. Although each financial institution is governed by the jurisdiction of its incorporation and is regulated by its incorporating statute, some activities undertaken by federally incorporated institutions may fall within provincial jurisdiction. For example, the authority to regulate trust activities, whether performed by a trust company or by an individual trustee, falls exclusively within provincial jurisdiction.

Federally chartered trust, mortgage loan, and insurance companies are licensed by each province in which they operate. Consequently many institutions are subject to several different regulatory authorities in their business dealings. All mortgage loan companies and trust companies that are members of the Canada Deposit Insurance Corporation are subject to its standards of sound business and financial practices to qualify for deposit insurance.

Local credit unions and caisses populaires are in practice incorporated and supervised by provincial governments. Provincially incorporated centrals (the second level of associations) that choose to be members of the Canadian Cooperative Credit Society, which is federally incorporated, also come within federal jurisdiction.

---

2. In 1983, the right of the Toronto-Dominion Bank to offer a discount brokerage access service to its customers was challenged by members of the investment community before the Ontario Securities Commission as an encroachment on the exclusive territory of the securities industry. The Commission concluded that banks and other financial institutions should be permitted to offer access to discount brokerage services, but only under controlled conditions. See Ontario Securities Commission, *Report on Implications for Canadian Capital Markets for the Provision by Financial Institution of Access to Discount Brokerage Service* (Toronto: Dataline Inc., 1983).

Regulatory Approaches

corporate governance *refers to rules, procedures, and standards of behaviour specified by each firm*

self-regulation *enforcement of standards and rules by industry and associations*

government regulations *rules and regulations governing behaviour of institutions as set out in laws, regulations, and guidelines*

four-pillar concept *separate legislation applying to four types of institutions: chartered banks, insurance companies, trust companies, and security dealers*

Three basic approaches to the regulation of financial institutions exist: corporate governance, self-regulation, and direct government regulation. In practice the Canadian approach has been a blend of all three, with an emphasis on one depending on the type of institution being regulated. All institutions must rely on some degree of **corporate governance**, and as a rule their management and directorate formulate rules and regulations and establish administrative mechanisms to see that the rules and regulations are being followed. In the case of **self-regulation**, financial institutions form associations, such as members of the various stock exchanges, and by common agreement set down and enforce rules and regulations for their members. Under direct **government regulations**, rules and regulations governing the behaviour of financial institutions are set down in law and government agencies or officials are responsible for ensuring compliance with them.

Regulation by Institution versus Regulation by Function

In Canada the direct government regulatory approach has been by institution. Institutions have been grouped by type according to a primary or core function, with separate legislation applying to each type of institution. Since traditionally only four distinct types of institutions were identified, this approach to regulation has been referred to as the **four-pillar concept**. Until the 1950s the core functions performed by each pillar remained quite separate and distinct. For example, the banks were identified with taking demand deposits and extending commercial loans, the trust companies with fiduciary services, the insurance companies with insurance underwriting, and the investment dealers with securities underwriting. These distinctions between the four pillars became progressively more blurred.

One reason for this blurring was that legislative changes allowed institutions to expand their activities beyond their original core functions. For example, revisions to the *Bank Act* in 1967 allowed the banks to supplement their traditional core functions of commercial lending and demand deposits with residential mortgage lending, consumer credit, and term deposits. In addition, factors such as technological change, inflation rate and interest rate volatility, greater financial sophistication of individuals and businesses, the internationalization of financial services, and deregulation of financial institutions in other countries encouraged the institutions to innovate within their regulatory constraints. For example, in the field of deposit taking, it became difficult to distinguish between the banks, the trust and mortgage loan companies, and the credit unions and caisses populaires. Moreover, short-term deferred annuities introduced by life insurance companies and interest-earning balances in customer accounts with securities dealers offered services similar to deposits held with other institutions.[3]

---

3. For a more complete description of these and other innovations that have blurred the distinction between financial institutions and the services that they provide, see Canada, Department of Finance, *The Regulation of Canadian Financial Institutions: Proposals for Discussion*, Green Paper (Ottawa, April 1985), pp. 77–83.

The expansion of their services beyond their traditional core functions resulted in different types of institutions being subject to different regulations for the similar services that they provided. This difference in regulations led to demands for a level playing field whereby institutions providing the same or similar financial services are similarly regulated to maintain competitive equity.

In contrast to regulating institutions, the functional approach is to regulate financial activities regardless of the type of financial institution that provides them. Only functions are regulated, and financial institutions are allowed to engage in similar functions as long as they observe the regulations that apply to each function that they undertake. In 1969 Quebec's Parizeau Report proposed regulation by function rather than by type of institution.[4] Subsequent legislative changes in Quebec allowed some institutions to expand their cross-pillar activities. In 1976, and again 10 years later, the Economic Council of Canada recommended that the government adopt a regulation-by-function approach to the reform of the Canadian financial system.[5] In its 1986 statement the council recognized that regulation by function cannot be a complete substitute for regulation by institution, because institutions rather than functions are subject to insolvency. It therefore proposed a "one-function/one-institution" approach, whereby functions are regulated separately, with each institution performing a single function and being subject to the regulator responsible for the particular function. In this way, institutions performing the same function would fall under the same regulator and thus benefit from a level playing field. Cross-function diversification would be allowed through cross-ownership of financial institutions in a financial holding company.

The one-function/one-institution approach proposed by the Economic Council of Canada requires that the major functions be well defined. The council suggested that the range of permissible activities that encompass a major function be determined "by what is considered prudent for each function." With changing technology and financial innovation, the concept of what constitutes prudent activities for any one function may change over time. Although the activities of life and casualty insurance, or securities underwriting and trading, now are readily identifiable, those for banking call for definition. The council recommended that the banking function be defined as "the provision of a means of payments," and that all institutions undertaking this function come under the umbrella of the *Bank Act*.

www.

Regulatory Reform: The Reform Process

The Canadian financial system and its regulatory framework were studied in 1964 by the Royal Commission on Banking and Finance (the Porter Commission).[6] A major recommendation of the commission was to liberalize

4. Government of Quebec, *Report of the Study Committee on Financial Institutions* (Parizeau Report) (Quebec, 1969).
5. Economic Council of Canada, *Efficiency and Regulation: A Study of Deposit Institutions* (Ottawa: Ministry of Supply and Services Canada, 1976); *Framework For Financial Regulation* (Ottawa: Minister of Supply and Services Canada, 1986).
6. *Report of the Royal Commission on Banking and Finance* (Ottawa: Queen's Printer, 1964).

regulatory controls and to allow financial institutions to diversify their activities. A similar conclusion was contained in 1969, in a report by a Quebec government task force (the Parizeau Report). In 1976, the Economic Council of Canada in its study *Efficiency and Regulation* also proposed financial deregulation, and, in particular, regulation by function.

When the federal government presented the 1980 decennial revisions to the *Bank Act*, it promised major revisions (none had been made for some 60 years) to the federal legislation of insurance, trust, and mortgage loan companies. In early 1980, following the failure of a number of trust and mortgage loan companies, the government of Ontario started to review its legislation and later appointed a task force that produced the Dupré Report in 1984 and 1985.[7]

In October 1987 the Quebec government released a document setting out guiding principles of reform for financial institutions under its jurisdiction. Those principles in large part anticipated federal reforms in that they allowed institutions to expand their range of financial services far beyond their traditional perimeters.[8]

For its part, the federal government released a Green Paper in 1985 that presented proposals for discussion on the regulation of financial institutions.[9] This paper was followed by a federal task force study, known as the Wyman Report, that made proposals for possible reforms to the deposit insurance system.[10] The various reform proposals in the Green Paper and the Wyman Report were subsequently examined both by the House of Commons Standing Committee on Finance, Trade, and Economic Affairs, and by the Senate Standing Committee on Banking, Trade, and Commerce.[11] In addition the Estey Commission reported on the failure of the Canadian Commercial Bank and the Northland Bank, and the Economic Council of Canada issued a statement on competition and solvency.[12]

7. Ontario Ministry of Consumer and Commercial Relations, *Proposals for Revisions of the Loan and Trust Corporation Legislation and Administration in Ontario* (Toronto, December 1984); and *The Ontario Task Force of Financial Institutions—Final Report* (Toronto, December 1985).
8. Government of Quebec, *Reform of Financial Institutions in Quebec: Guiding Principles and Action Plan* (Quebec, 1987).
9. Department of Finance, *The Regulation of Canadian Financial Institutions: Proposals for Discussion* (Ottawa, 1985).
10. *Final Report of the Working Committee on the Canada Deposit Insurance Corporation (CDIC)* (Ottawa: Minister of Supply and Services, Canada, 1985).
11. *Canadian Financial Institutions,* the Eleventh Report of the House of Commons Standing Committee on Finance, Trade and Economic Affairs (Blenkarn Report) (Ottawa, November 1985); *Towards a More Competitive Financial Environment,* Sixteenth Report of the Senate Standing Committee on Banking, Trade and Commerce (Ottawa, May 1986); and *Canada 1992: Toward a National Market in Financial Services,* Eighth Report of the Senate Standing Committee on Banking, Trade and Commerce (Ottawa, May 1990).
12. *Report of the Inquiry into the Collapse of the CCB and Northland Bank* by the Honourable Willard, Z. Estey, Commissioner (Ottawa: Minister of Supply and Services Canada, August 1986); Economic Council of Canada, *Competition and Solvency: A Framework for Financial Regulation* (Ottawa: Minister of Supply and Services Canada, 1986).
13. *New Directions for the Financial Sector,* House of Commons (Ottawa, December 18, 1986).

Regulatory Reform: The 1992 Legislative Response

In December 1986 in the House of Commons, the federal government tabled a Blue Paper setting out the directions the new reform legislation was to take.[13] This paper was followed in December 1987 by a discussion draft of proposed legislation to revise the *Trust and Loan Companies Act*, and in autumn 1990 by the document *Reform of the Federal Financial Institutions Legislation: Overview of Legislative Proposals*. This last report provided the basis for the new financial institutions legislation, passed by the federal Parliament in December 1991, which came into effect in June 1992.

Under the revised financial legislation, all financial institutions continued to be separate and identifiable according to their major functions. The primary purpose for such separation was to facilitate prudential regulation and control. Aside from specific restrictions on the retailing of insurance, fiduciary activities, and the leasing of personal property, little separation remained between institutions regarding the financial products and services that they could offer to the public.

Fostering Competition and Diversification

Before 1967, the only federal government policy directly concerned with competition in the financial system was a restriction on mergers of banks with insurance, mortgage loan, and trust companies. However, both the 1967 and 1980 revisions to the *Bank Act*, as we will learn in Chapter 13, made specific provisions to introduce more competition among the banks and between the banks and other financial institutions.

In the discussions about reforming the regulatory system, three major methods by which to enhance competition were considered. Regulators could allow the financial intermediaries to diversify their activities by expanding the institutions' in-house powers, by permitting diversification through subsidiaries, or holding companies, and by granting networking powers.

Expanded In-House Powers

Under the reformed legislation, federally incorporated trust, loan, and insurance companies that had a minimum of $25 million in capital, and that had received supervisory approval, were no longer restricted in the amount of commercial loans that they could make. Companies that did not meet these criteria were required to limit their commercial loans to 5 percent of their assets. All former restrictions on the ability of trust, loan, and insurance companies to make consumer loans were removed.

The banks and loan companies were given in-house powers to offer management and investment advice services. Formerly, these services could be offered only by trust and insurance companies and securities dealers.

Federally incorporated financial institutions were prohibited from engaging in car leasing and from owning car-leasing institutions. All except

---

13. *New Directions for the Financial Sector,* House of Commons (Ottawa, December 18, 1986).

trust companies could not provide in-house trust services, but they could engage in a full range of fiduciary activities through a trust company subsidiary and by networking. Specific rules prevented all institutions except insurance companies from retailing insurance. The depository institutions, for instance, were not allowed to act as an agent in the placing of insurance, nor could they provide space in a branch to an insurance agent or broker.

Traditionally, the power of financial intermediaries to lend and invest was restricted by investment rules. Under these rules only those assets that satisfied certain quality tests were eligible for acquisition, and the total quantity of certain assets that could be held was restricted to a specified proportion of an institution's total assets or capital. Most of the existing investment rules were replaced by the **prudent portfolio approach** to investment. With this approach, boards of directors of institutions were required to establish standards and procedures governing their lending and investment activities. These standards and procedures should be those followed by a prudent person who holds a well-diversified portfolio of assets to match liabilities.

prudent portfolio approach *portfolio investment standards followed by a prudent person who holds a well-diversified portfolio*

Some quantitative portfolio limits were set out in the legislation. For example, neither the value of real estate investments nor the value of equity investments held by a deposit-taking institution, including those held by prescribed subsidiaries, was permitted to exceed 70 percent of the institution's regulatory capital. Moreover, an institution's aggregate investment in real estate and equities could not exceed 100 percent of its regulatory capital.

Expansion with Subsidiaries

The 1980 revisions to the *Bank Act* allowed the banks to expand some of their activities, such as residential mortgage lending and factoring, by establishing separate subsidiaries for the conduct of these and other functions. In December 1986, the Ontario Securities Commission announced that, beginning June 30, 1987, Canadian financial institutions would be allowed 100 percent ownership of securities dealers while foreign institutions would be allowed 50 percent ownership, to be increased to 100 percent after June 1988. The federal government revised its legislation in 1987 (Bill C-56) to allow federal financial institutions to acquire wholly owned subsidiaries engaged in all aspects of the securities business. Thus ended the long-established public policy of keeping market intermediation separate from financial intermediation.

Under the 1992 legislation, cross-ownership via subsidiaries between financial institutions was allowed with ministerial approval. For example, the banks could own one or more of trust, loan, and insurance subsidiaries as well as wholly owned securities firms.

The legislation permitted financial institutions to own not only other financial institutions as subsidiaries, but also corporations engaged in activities that were specifically set out in the legislation. Such activities included factoring, mutual fund distribution, information services, and other ancillary businesses. The ownership of commercial corporations by financial institutions was generally limited to a maximum of 10 percent of the voting shares, or 25 percent of the shareholders' equity of a commercial corporation.

Networking

Networking is a term used to describe arrangements between financial institutions whereby one institution provides the public with access to products or services supplied by another. This type of arrangement can exist between affiliated or independent institutions. It provides an opportunity for independent and smaller institutions to offer a broader range of financial services than they could offer on their own.

With the exception of retailing insurance, full networking powers were granted to all federally regulated financial institutions, allowing financial institutions to provide a broader range of financial services to their customers.

tied selling *when one purchase is conditional on another purchase*

A major policy concern with networking is **tied selling**. This situation occurs when the sale of a good or service is conditional on the purchase of other related goods or services. An example of tied selling is a borrower being required to take a specified credit insurance contract as a condition for receiving a loan.

www.

Ensuring Soundness and Stability

Thirteen financial institutions failed between 1980 and 1984 and were declared insolvent, while others avoided insolvency through mergers with other institutions. In 1985 two banks failed—the first bank failures since 1923—and two banks probably avoided failure by merging with others. In the same year, five trust and mortgage loan companies and two general insurance companies failed. The historically high incidence of failure by financial institutions focused reform proposals on the goal of public policy with respect to the soundness of financial institutions and the stability of the financial system. Deposit insurance, as we observed in Chapter 10, came under scrutiny. In addition, issues involving self-dealing, conflict of interest, inspection and supervision, and ownership entered the regulatory reform debates.

Conflicts of Interest

conflict of interest *when a financial institution must choose between its own interests and those of a client on whose behalf it is acting or whom it is advising*

Whenever an intermediary has to choose between its interests and those of a client on whose behalf it is acting as agent, it finds itself in a **conflict of interest** situation. When financial institutions offer a wide variety of services, either in-house or through subsidiaries, and customer information is shared, the potential exists for abuses that can financially damage a customer. For example, potential conflicts exist when an institution engages in both commercial lending and securities marketing. As a commercial lender, the institution acts on its own behalf; as a marketer of securities, it acts on behalf of the investing public to whom it provides advice on the selection of securities to purchase. The institution trades off the interests of its securities clients for its own if, for example, it advises them to purchase the securities of a corporation in financial difficulty to allow that corporation to repay outstanding loans to the institution.

Legislative reforms set out rules requiring officers and directors of federally regulated financial institutions to make timely disclosures of transactions in which they may have an interest. Institutions also must make clear their role as either agents or principals in transactions with their customers. As well, procedures must be put in place to restrict the flow of "inside" information; a conduct review committee of an institution's board of directors is charged with reviewing compliance. Procedures used to prevent the flow of information that gives rise to undesirable conflicts of interest are frequently referred to as Chinese walls.

Self-Dealing

self-dealing

engaging in a nonarm's length transaction that benefits those undertaking it

Self-dealing refers to transactions between a financial institution and persons who are in a position of influence over, or control of, that institution. Such transactions are said to be at nonarm's length. Abusive self-dealing was an important cause of insolvencies of trust and mortgage loan companies during the 1980s. For example, senior officers of some of these companies sold assets to their institutions at artificially high prices and obtained loans from them at terms that did not reflect underlying risks.

The legislation placed a general ban on the banks and on federal loan, trust, and insurance companies regarding transactions with related parties. These transactions included the purchase of services and assets, including real estate from related parties as well as loans to related parties and investments in corporations that were substantial shareholders of the financial institutions. Related parties primarily include those persons or entities who, directly or indirectly, are significant shareholders of the financial institutions, or who are in a position of influence or control over the institution. The legislation set out classes of persons considered to be related. The superintendent of financial institutions may further designate individuals and corporations as being related parties or as being exempt from such designations.

Exemptions to the general ban on transactions with related parties include the sale or purchase of business services at market terms and conditions, transactions between affiliated regulated financial institutions, and interaffiliated loans secured by provincial or federal government securities. Each institution is required to establish internal controls to screen transactions permitted under exemptions to the general ban. This screening is to be achieved by enhanced corporate governance, which among other things requires each institution to set up a conduct review committee. All related-party transactions require prior approval from this committee. Certain nonarm's length transactions are allowed with pre-clearance of the superintendent of financial institutions.

Ownership Policy

Before the 1960s few rules regarding the forms and degree of ownership of financial institutions in Canada were used to implement public policy. In the 1950s, mutualization of insurance companies was facilitated to protect that industry from nonresident takeovers. For similar reasons, the 1967 *Bank Act* revisions mandated widely held ownership for banks for which the shareholding of any one individual or group of associated individuals is limited to 10 percent of any class of shares of a bank. However, to encourage more compe-

BOX 11–1   BACKGROUNDER

A Tale of Two Mergers

December 14, 1998, News Release

Finance Minister Paul Martin today announced that the bank mergers proposed by the Royal Bank of Canada and the Bank of Montreal, and by the Toronto-Dominion Bank and the Canadian Imperial Bank of Commerce will not be allowed.

The minister based his decision, in part, on information the government received from the Competition Bureau and the Office of the Superintendent of Financial Institutions (OSFI), as well as the MacKay Task Force report recommendations and input from parliamentarians and public consultations.

The minister said the mergers were not in the best interests of Canadians and will not be allowed to proceed because they would lead to:

• an unacceptable concentration of economic power in the hands of fewer, very large banks

• a significant reduction of competition

• reduced policy flexibility for the government to address potential future prudential concerns

"This is a decision," the minister said, "that reflects the government's commitment to ensuring strong competition in the financial services sector.

"Quite simply, allowing the mergers would further concentrate a very high level of economic power in the hands of an even smaller number of very large institutions.

"Looking forward, we believe that our immediate priority must now be to focus on establishing an appropriate policy framework for the financial sector for the twenty-first century.

"Whereas the merger proponents wanted the mergers to be allowed in order to change the status quo, we believe the status quo must be changed before any merger can be considered.

"The government will not consider any merger among major banks until the new policy framework is in place.

"But even then, new proposals will first have to demonstrate, in the light of the circumstances of the day, that they do not unduly concentrate economic power, significantly reduce competition or restrict our flexibility to address prudential concerns," Martin said.

January 31, 2000, News Release

Finance Minister Paul Martin and Secretary of State (International Financial Institutions) Jim Peterson today announced the government's decision to permit the acquisition of CT Financial Services Inc. by The Toronto-Dominion Bank, subject to certain terms and conditions.

"The government has decided to accept the recommendations of both the commissioner of competition and the superintendent of financial institutions and approve this transaction with certain conditions," Minister Martin said.

The conditions necessary for approval were largely identified by the commissioner of competition. In his analysis, he advised that the Canada Trust MasterCard business and a certain number of branches be divested to address competition concerns. TD has agreed to meet these conditions.

The government also took into account a number of public interest considerations, particularly *service standards for consumers* and issues surrounding employment.

"The government is pleased that TD has agreed to adopt the Canada Trust service model," Secretary of State Jim Peterson stated. Among other things, this will mean that TD customers will enjoy longer and more flexible bank branch service hours in keeping with Canada Trust practice.

The government also welcomed the commitment by TD to establish for affected employees severance and personal assistance packages that meet or exceed private sector best practices. TD will be providing complete details of the employment adjustment measures.

Under the *Bank Act*, the *Trust and Loan Companies Act*, and the *Insurance Companies Act*, the minister of finance must provide final approval for such acquisitions to proceed.

SOURCES: Department of Finance. "Minister of Finance Announces Decision on Bank Merger Proposals," News Release, December 14, 1998; Department of Finance. "Federal Government Approves Acquisition of Canada Trust by the Toronto-Dominion Bank," News Release, January 31, 2000.

tition in banking, the 1980 amendments to the *Bank Act* (to be discussed in Chapter 13) provided for the establishment of narrowly held Schedule II domestic banks as well as foreign bank subsidiaries.

In the debates on financial reform during the 1980s, it was argued that widespread ownership of financial institutions reduces the incentive to self-deal because the potential for gains is smaller for each shareholder. In addition, it was argued that widespread ownership was necessary to avoid a concentration of power and foreign control of the financial sector and to preserve the integrity of the credit allocation process. However, it was thought that narrow ownership would encourage the entry of new institutions and thereby enhance competition and efficiency.

The ownership question during the 1980s also focused on the form and degree of ownership of regulated financial institutions by nonfinancial enterprises. The traditional policy of separating commercial from financial activities already had been eroding as provincial trust, loan, and insurance companies came under the ownership of groups with commercial links. Furthermore, the announcement by the federal government to allow American Express (AMEX) to establish a foreign bank subsidiary was seen as an invitation to others with commercial links to gain direct access to banking and the Canadian payments system.

Under the ownership rules contained in the 1992 legislation, all significant changes in the ownership of federal financial institutions have to be approved by the minister of finance. A significant change implies the acquisition by any person (or persons acting in concert) of more than 10 percent of any class of shares of an institution, or an increase in an existing significant interest in the institution's shares.

Federal trust, loan, and life insurance companies can continue to be started, held, and sold on a closely held basis. The 1992 legislation, however, established the "35 percent rule," whereby a federal institution whose consolidated capital reached $750 million is required, within five years of reaching this level, to have at least 35 percent of its voting shares widely held and publicly traded on a Canadian stock exchange. This 35 percent rule may be satisfied by a financial holding company, or by a regulated financial institution on behalf of its trust, loan, or insurance company subsidiaries.

Schedule I banks, which include all the large domestic banks, have to be widely held. Schedule II domestic banks may be narrowly held for only the first 10 years of their existence. However, if during these 10 years their assets exceed the $750 million threshold, they too will need to have 35 percent of their shares widely held and publicly traded.

Corporate Governance

Mismanagement of financial institutions, which has resulted in their failures, can be traced to inadequate self-governance. To overcome such deficiencies, legislative changes have been made to improve the quality of information flowing to auditors. This information bolsters the auditors' independence from the management of the institutions, and it enhances their communication with directors and government supervisors.

At least one-third of the members of each board of directors must be independent of the financial institution. An independent, or outside, director is neither an officer nor an employee of the institution and has no other significant associations with it. Each institution is required to have an audit committee and a conduct review committee, and the committees must be composed of a majority of independent directors. The remainder of the directors of these committees cannot be officers or employees of the institution.

Prudential Safeguards

www.

In 1987 the two federal supervisory bodies, the Office of the Inspector General of Banks and the Department of Insurance (which was responsible for supervising federal trust, loan, and insurance companies), were merged into the new Office of the Superintendent of Financial Institutions (OSFI).

As we will explain in Chapter 13, the OSFI is responsible, among other things, for regulating and supervising the banks and federally incorporated trust, loan, and insurance companies. The superintendent monitors these institutions using information obtained from statutory filings and financial-reporting requirements by the institutions, as well as by making periodic onsite examinations. The OSFI, as we will learn later, has broad powers of intervention in the affairs of the institutions subject to its regulation and supervision.

As we saw in Chapter 10, the deposit-taking institutions have to satisfy the Canada Deposit Insurance Corporation's (CDIC) Standards of Sound Business and Financial Practices to qualify for deposit insurance, which is mandatory.

Although it has been proposed that the OSFI and the CDIC might best be merged into one institution, their two functions of regulator and insurer have been kept separate to preserve beneficial checks and balances in the regulatory and supervisory system.

The Changing Nature of Regulation and Prudential Supervision

The increasing multiservice activities of Canadian financial intermediaries and the growing use of derivative instruments, together with the globalization of financial intermediation, have brought with them new risks. These risks, if not appropriately managed and controlled, can threaten institutional and market stability on both a national and an international scale. The changes have called for new regulatory and supervisory approaches. As we have seen, corporate governance of Canadian financial institutions has been strengthened to better identify and manage institutional risks. Government regulators are now placing more emphasis on risk management in their prudential supervision.

Capital requirements following newly established international standards have been raised and adjusted to incorporate new risks. At the same time, guidelines on sound practices for derivatives have been jointly issued by the Basel Committee on Bank Supervision and the International Organization of

Securities Commissions. These are two examples of international approaches to regulation and prudential supervision of institutions operating in global markets.

Further Legislative Reform

More failures of financial institutions had to be resolved in the early 1990s through liquidation or through merger with healthy financial institutions, with financial assistance provided by the Canada Deposit Insurance Corporation. These failures, particularly that of one of Canada's larger life insurance companies, refocused public attention on the prudential supervisory system and the system of deposit insurance. In February 1995, the federal government released a White Paper entitled *Enhancing the Safety and Soundness of the Canadian Financial System.* The White Paper reflected many of the observations contained in *Regulation and Consumer Protection, Striking a Balance,* a report by the Senate Standing Committee on Banking, Trade, and Commerce.

The government's White Paper included proposals for strengthening the regulatory and supervisory framework for federal financial institutions and for changes to the federal deposit insurance system. These proposals were subsequently contained in legislation enacted by the federal Parliament in April 1996. Both the White Paper proposals and the legislation were based on three principles:

1. Ownership of a financial institution is a privilege, not a right. This principle implies that protection of the interests of policyholders, depositors, and creditors come before the interest of shareholders.
2. Sufficient regulatory incentives should exist for institutions to solve their own problems on a timely basis.
3. When institutions experience financial difficulty, regulatory intervention and resolution should occur at an early point.

The so-called sunset clause in the 1992 financial reform legislation required Parliament to enact new legislation in 1997. Toward this end, the federal government released in June 1996 a discussion paper entitled *1997 Review of Financial Sector Legislation: Proposals for Changes.* The government's 1997 legislative review process focused on two questions. The first was whether the 1992 reform legislation was functioning as intended. The second was whether the reform legislative framework remained adequate in view of evolving trends in the financial sector.

With respect to the first question, the government's answer was that the legislative framework of 1992 was generally working well, and at best required only some fine tuning. A similar conclusion had been recorded by the Senate Standing Committee on Banking, Trade, and Commerce.[14] Hence, the 1997 legislative revisions to satisfy the 1992 sunset clause concerned themselves primarily with strengthening consumer protection and lessening the regulatory

---

14. See proceedings of the Senate Standing Committee, Thursday, August 3, 1995.

burden on financial institutions. The government announced in the 1996 budget speech that it would not accede to the banks' request for permission to market insurance products through their branches.

As for the second question relating to its 1997 review of financial legislation, the government recognized that technological advances, competitive intensity, and the ongoing globalization of financial service markets required a more comprehensive review. To this end, it appointed a Task Force on the Future of the Canadian Financial Services Sector to provide advice to government on the appropriate legislative framework for the Canadian financial sector in the twenty-first century.

The Task Force Recommendations and Regulatory Reforms for the Twenty-First Century

The Task Force on the Future of the Canadian Financial Services Sector submitted its report in 1998. Two parliamentary committees then studied the report until early 1999. In June 1999 the minister of finance reported his intention to implement many of the 124 recommendations contained within the report, with four general areas in which changes could be expected: (1) promoting efficiency and growth, (2) fostering domestic competition, (3) empowering and protecting consumers of financial services, and (4) improving the regulatory environment.

www.

PROMOTING EFFICIENCY AND GROWTH   We know that the process of financial intermediation brings savers and borrowers together. This process encourages economic activity and stimulates growth. The Task Force recommended that financial services legislation should be flexible enough to respond to changes in the structure of financial markets. The information age has led to fast-paced changes to markets, and policymakers appear to continually respond to, rather than accommodate, these structural shifts. This change in regime requires a move away from a heavily regulated structure to one that is dynamic and capable of allowing strategic partnerships between financial institutions. This shift is accomplished through a change in legislation regarding holding companies and the types of activities they may undertake. It is also achieved through changing the existing structures associated with reviewing bank merger proposals. A transparent process with an opportunity for public input will make the decision-making process fair, and appear to be fair, to all parties involved. Finally, the issue of capital taxation will be examined to ensure that Canadian financial institutions are not severely disadvantaged by the Canadian tax system.

FOSTER DOMESTIC COMPETITION   The federal government see a competitive marketplace as essential to a well-functioning financial sector. Toward this end, they have changed ownership rules and reduced the minimum capital requirements necessary for incorporation as a chartered bank. The federal

BOX 11–2   **BACKGROUNDER**

A Guide to Mergers

Canada's review process for allowing financial intermediaries to merge is now transparent and follows a set protocol as exhibited in the following figure.

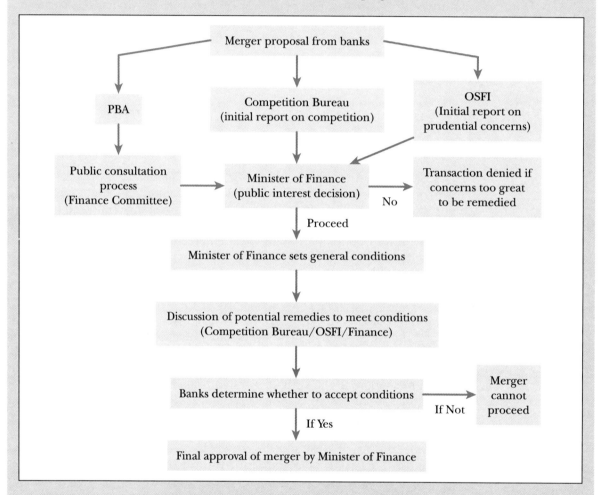

SOURCE: Department of Finance. *Reforming Canada's Financial Services Sector—A Framework for the Future*, Ottawa, June 1999, Chart 2.2, <http://www.fin.gc.ca/finserv/docs/finserv2e.html>.

government have also given credit unions the opportunity to change their structure and merge into bank entities. They have also expanded access to the payments system to nonbank intermediaries to encourage deposit-taking activities. Finally, the government have allowed and encouraged foreign banks to undertake activities in Canada, both with and without having a physical presence in Canada (for example, virtual banks). Table 11.1 illustrates some of the planned changes to the ownership rules.

TABLE 11.1   PROPOSALS FOR CHANGES TO OWNERSHIP RULES
Millions of Dollars

Equity	Banks	Life Insurers — Demutualized Stock Company[1]	Life Insurers — Other Stock Company	Trust Companies	P&C Insurers
Large (greater than $5 billion)	Widely held[2] Raises current ownership limit from 10% of shares to 20% voting and 30% nonvoting	Widely held[2] Raises current ownership limit from 10% of shares to 20% voting and 30% nonvoting	35% public float No change	35% public float No change	35% public float No change
Medium (between $1 billion and $5 billion)	35% public float[3] Threshold raised from $750 million to $1 billion	35% public float[3] May become closely held after transition period, with 35% float requirement at $1 billion	35% public float Threshold raised from $750 million to $1 billion	35% public float Threshold raised from $750 million to $1 billion	35% public float Threshold raised from $750 million to $1 billion
Small (less than $1 billion)	No restrictions[3] Removes all ownership restrictions for small banks	No restrictions[3] No ownership restrictions for small demutualized insurers after transition period	No restrictions No change	No restrictions No change	No restrictions No change

1. A transition period of two years has been established for demutualized life insurance companies. During the transition period, the companies cannot merge or be acquired.
2. Banks and demutualized life insurers held by an eligible financial institution will not be required to meet the widely held requirement if they grow over $5 billion in equity.
3. Existing banks and demutualized insurance companies below $5 billion in equity will remain widely held. The Minister of Finance will have the discretion to allow them to become closely held.

SOURCE: Table 3.2 of *Reforming Canada's Financial Services Sector—A Framework for the Future*, Ottawa, June 1999, <http://www.fin.gc.ca/finserv/docs/finserv3e.html>.

EMPOWERING AND PROTECTING CONSUMERS   Many banks have been criticized for not providing services to some Canadians—perhaps those without employment or a regular residence. A Financial Consumer Agency is to oversee consumer protection and education activities, and all institutions will be required to provide a low-fee account to depositors. The Canadian Financial Services Ombudsman will help oversee and mediate disputes, many of which have already been launched against online discount brokerages. Allegations of poor service leading to financial loss abound; the role of the ombudsman is to provide a nonlegal forum for mediation of these types of disputes.

www.

Institutions will be required to provide greater public accountability for their actions, particularly with respect to closing branches in areas of population decline. For example, when a branch is the only one in a rural community within a 10 km radius, the institution will be required to provide six months notice of the planned closure, if it is a federally regulated institution. Institutions will also be required to demonstrate a greater understanding and sensitivity to the needs of small businesses, and to their role in the economy.

IMPROVING THE REGULATORY ENVIRONMENT   Finally, the federal government plans to provide the superintendent of financial institutions with greater powers to deal with the risks created through changes to the existing legislation. Regulatory approval processes will be streamlined, with greater coordination between consumer compensation plans, such as the CDIC and others aimed at protecting insurance policyholders. Indeed, the CDIC's standards will be updated to enhance risk management activities in the CDIC and the OSFI.

The *Bank Act* should be updated within the next two years to incorporate many, if not all, of these proposals.

Concluding Observation

Three major elements ensure the soundness of financial institutions and, thereby, the financial system: internal corporate governance, official oversight by government, and market discipline. Over time the weight given to each of these has changed. More recently market discipline has been given far more weight than it formerly had. In part, this emphasis has been the result of better information, which has allowed markets to perform more efficiently. The challenge for policymakers is to strike the appropriate balance among the three key elements.

KEY TERMS

asymmetric information	government regulations	prudent regulation
conflict of interest	market conduct regulation	self-dealing
corporate governance	principal–agent relationship	self-regulation
four pillar concept	prudent portfolio approach	tied selling

REVIEW QUESTIONS

1. What do we mean by asymmetric information? Why does its existence give rise to the need for regulation?
2. Define the principal–agent relationship and explain how it gives rise to conflicts of interest.
3. Why should expropriation concern regulators of financial institutions?
4. How do the reforms to financial legislation address public policy issues relating to safety and soundness?
5. How do these reforms address issues with respect to competition, diversification, and ownership?
6. Provide a two-page rationale for allowing two or more financial institutions to merge. Now write a two-page argument against the merger. What are the important issues to consider?
7. Many critics of Canadian financial policy argue that domestic banks will be left by the wayside if not allowed to merge. Explain the salient features of their argument, making sure to describe the relative sizes of Canadian and international banks.
8. How will proposals to change ownership rules affect the Canadian financial sector?
9. Why would the Canadian authorities allow foreign banks to operate in Canada? Is this harmful to domestic banks? Explain.
10. Take any five of the Task Force recommendations from 1998 and discuss the reasons they were included in the final report. Did the federal government address these issues in its 1999 policy statement? Explain.

SELECTED READINGS

Canada. *Enhancing the Safety and Soundness of the Canadian Financial System.* Department of Finance. Ottawa, February 1995.

———. *1997 Review of Financial Sector Legislation: Proposals for Changes.* Department of Finance. Ottawa, June 1996.

———. *The Regulation of Financial Institutions: Proposals for Discussion.* Technical Report. Ottawa, June 1985.

———. *Reforming Canada's Financial Services Sector—A Framework for the Future.* Ottawa, June 1999.

———. *Report of the Task Force on the Future of the Canadian Financial Service Sector* (MacKay Report). Ottawa 1998.

———. *Competition, Competitiveness and the Public Interest.* Task Force on the Future of the Canadian Financial Services Sector, Background Paper # 1, Ottawa, September 1998.

———. House of Commons. *Canadian Financial Institutions.* Report of the Standing Committee on Finance, Trade and Economic Affairs (Blenkarn Report). Ottawa, November 1985.

———. Ministry of State for Finance. *New Directions for the Financial Sector.* Ottawa, December 18, 1986.

———. Senate. *Towards a More Competitive Financial Environment.* Sixteenth Report of the Senate Standing Committee on Banking, Trade and Commerce. Ottawa, May 1986.

———. *Canada 1992: Toward a National Market in Financial Services.* Eighth Report of the Senate Standing Committee on Banking, Trade and Commerce. Ottawa, May 1990.

———. *Regulations and Consumer Protections: Striking a Balance.* Senate Standing Committee on Banking, Trade and Commerce. Ottawa, November 1994.

———. *1997 Financial Institution Reform: Lowering Barriers to Foreign Banks.* Ottawa, October 1996.

Chant, John. *Regulation of Financial Institutions: A Functional Analysis.* Bank of Canada Technical Reports, No. 45. Ottawa: Bank of Canada, January 1987.

Courchene, Thomas, and Edwin Neave (eds.). *Reforming the Canadian Financial Sector: Canada in a Global Perspective.* John Deutsch Institute for the Study of Economic Policy. Kingston: Queen's University, 1997.

Daniel, Fred, Charles Freedman, and Clyde Goodlet. "Restructuring The Canadian Financial Industry." *Bank of Canada Review* (Winter 1992–93), pp. 21–45.

Economic Council of Canada. *Efficiency and Regulation: A Study of Deposit Institutions.* Ottawa: Minister of Supply and Services Canada, 1976.

———. *Competition and Solvency: A Statement by the Economic Council 1986.* Ottawa: Minister of Supply and Services Canada, 1986.

———. *A Framework for Financial Regulation: A Research Report Prepared for the Economic Council of Canada 1987.* Ottawa: Minister of Supply and Services Canada, 1987.

Government of Quebec. *Report of the Study Committee on Financial Institutions* (Parizeau Report). Quebec, June 1969.

Interim Report of the Ontario Task Force on Financial Institutions. A Report to the Honourable Robert G. Elgie, M.D., Minister of Consumer and Commercial Relations. Toronto, December 1984.

Neave, Edwin. "Canadian Financial Regulation: A System in Transition." C.D. Howe Commentary, No. 78, March 1996.

Ontario Task Force on Financial Institutions—Final Report. A Report to the Honourable Monte Kwinter, Minister of Consumer and Commercial Relations. Toronto, December 1985.

Report of the Inquiry into the Collapse of the CCB and Northland Bank (Estey Commission). Ottawa: Minister of Supply and Services Canada, 1986.

Report of the Royal Commission on Banking and Finance. Ottawa: Queen's Printer, 1964.

Théoret, Raymond. "Stages of Deregulation." *Canadian Banker* (November–December 1988), pp. 40–43.

Summary of Key Legislative Measures and Statements of Government Policy

This legislation is the culmination of a process that began in 1996 with the establishment of the Task Force on the Future of the Canadian Financial Services Sector and the Payments Advisory Committee. In September 1998, the Task Force presented the government with its report entitled *Change, Challenge, Opportunity,* which was subsequently reviewed by two parliamentary committees. The committees, in turn, conducted extensive public consultations and presented the government with their own recommendations. This extensive consultation process led to the emergence of a broad consensus on measures to improve the sector.

That consensus provided a solid foundation for *Reforming Canada's Financial Services Sector: A Framework for the Future,* the policy paper released by the government in June 1999. The policy paper contained 57 measures to promote the efficiency and growth of the sector, foster domestic competition, empower and protect consumers and improve the regulatory environment.

An overview of the new policy framework can be found at the website for this textbook, <http://money.nelson.com>. It summarizes both the measures contained in the bill and the measures being implemented by non-legislative means such as guidelines. In addition, the document contains a number of statements of government policy that complement the legislation. Together these implement the policy framework.

CHAPTER TWELVE

THE DEVELOPMENT OF CANADIAN BANKING

> After reading this chapter you should be able to
> 1. Explain the origin of modern banking
> 2. Outline the evolutionary forces in Canadian banking
> 3. Describe some of the characteristics of early bank charters
> 4. Describe early attempts to introduce government note issues for circulation
> 5. Discuss the free banking experiment of the 1850s
> 6. Explain how early Bank Acts restricted the chartered banks' note issues
> 7. Explain how the Finance Act handled the note issue problem
> 8. Describe events leading up to the founding of the Bank of Canada

The Origin of Modern Banking

goldsmiths *the activities of the London goldsmiths*

The origin of modern banking can be traced to the operations of the **goldsmiths** of seventeenth-century England. The goldsmiths had strongrooms for the safekeeping of the materials of their trade. Extra space in these rooms was often rented to merchants and others to safe keep valuables, including large sums of money. At first the money was accepted in locked and sealed boxes that were returned to their owners in the same condition they had been left for safekeeping. Later, it became common for customers to deposit coin in return for a receipt or certificate of deposit. In time the goldsmiths observed that their depositors did not demand the identical coin initially left with them, but only coin equal to the value shown on the certificates of deposit. In practice, if not in law, the goldsmiths assumed ownership of the coin deposited with them and employed the coin as required, being careful that they always held an amount sufficient to convert certificates of deposit into coin on demand. This practice was the beginning of deposit taking, a characteristic of commercial banking as distinct from the function of safekeeping.

The goldsmiths also observed that a predictable quantity of coin was always left with them. They could gauge the quantity by observing the activities of the merchants, many of whom deposited their coin with the same goldsmith. When one merchant wanted to make payment to another, he would simply write an order to his goldsmith requesting the transfer of coin from his own account to that of his creditor without converting his deposit certificate into coin. This process was the beginning of chequing or clearing, another characteristic of commercial banking.

To facilitate more efficient clearing services, the goldsmiths, instead of issuing one certificate of deposit to cover a customer's entire deposit of coin, started to issue notes in small denominations, usually of standard value. The total amount of these notes added up to the value of all deposits. When these notes became generally accepted for payment, the goldsmiths made them payable to the bearer. This system marked the beginning of note issue, a characteristic of early commercial banking that later became the prerogative of central banks.

As a rule, the goldsmiths were men of wealth, and it was not uncommon for them to lend to customers from their own resources. When it became a common practice for their notes to circulate as a medium of exchange, the goldsmiths began to make loans not by using their own coin or coin deposited with them, but their notes. These notes were the same as the notes given to the depositors of coin, with one important exception: They were not issued in return for a deposit of coin, but in return for a promissory note left by the borrower with the goldsmith. The distinction is important. As long as all the notes issued by the goldsmiths were not turned in at one time for conversion into coin, the goldsmiths could issue notes to a greater value than the value of the coin they held. This process marked the beginning of **fractional reserve banking**. The goldsmith assumed the role of a commercial banker, who, through his lending operations, creates money out of his customers' promises to pay.

fractional reserve banking *where banks hold cash reserves equal to only a fraction of their deposits and formerly their note liabilities*

The total quantity of notes that the goldsmiths could issue against a given reserve base of coin depended on the note holders' propensity to redeem them in coin. The goldsmiths soon learned from experience how much coin would remain with them during any given period and learned that this amount fluctuated. When they miscalculated, as was the case when the British fleet was destroyed by the Dutch at Chatham (1667), they met certain doom. On hearing of the disaster at Chatham, Englishmen did what people were to do repeatedly during periods of social or political uncertainty: They hurried to convert their paper money holdings into as intrinsic a form as possible. They ran to the goldsmiths and demanded coin for their notes, precipitating what we now call a run on the bank. Since the goldsmiths' notes were only partially secured by **specie** (gold and silver coin and bullion), not all note holders could be satisfied and the goldsmiths had to declare bankruptcy.

specie *gold and silver coin and bullion*

Although fractional reserve banking is usually traced to the operations of the goldsmiths, it was by no means confined to them. Soon after the goldsmiths began the practice, if not simultaneously, merchants began to issue notes that were only fractionally secured by specie and served as a medium of exchange. Governments started to grant charters incorporating companies authorized to conduct banking operations that included accepting deposits, clearing or transferring money, and issuing notes only fractionally secured by reserves of specie. Among the first chartered banks were the Bank of Sweden (1656), the

Bank of England (1694), and the Banque Générale (John Law's Bank) in France (1716).

Evolutionary Forces in Canadian Banking

Early banking developments in the colonies that were to become the Dominion of Canada were determined by three main evolutionary forces. The strongest of these was the British connection. The British government made its views known through memoranda, minutes, circulars, and letters issued by the colonial office in London, and by disallowing bills passed by the colonial legislatures. The British influence was further emphasized by the early bankers themselves, most of whom had come from the United Kingdom, particularly Scotland, and who heavily stressed the virtues of prudent banking.

The second of these forces was the U.S. experience. Because the Canadian money and banking system developed later than the U.S. system, its Canadian founders had the opportunity to observe and avoid many of the difficulties encountered by their neighbours.

branch banking *when banks serve the public in different locations through branches*

unit bank *a bank limited to a single office*

Finally, the actual experience of operating in Canada gave Canadian banking characteristics that were neither American nor British. Overbanking did not become a problem in Canada, partly because Canadians, not having the intense individualism of their American cousins, were not so concerned with "democratic" banking and were prepared to accept **branch banking** rather than a **unit bank** in every community. Charters were very difficult to obtain in Canada because of the close connection between the legislatures and the early banking interests. Both government and banking in the two Canadas were controlled by select groups—in Lower Canada by the Rouge, and in Upper Canada by the Family Compact.

Early Attempts to Establish Banks

The initiative to establish a bank in Lower Canada was taken by merchants in Montreal in 1792. They proposed to form the Canadian Banking Company to receive deposits in cash, to issue notes for circulation, and to discount bills. Their proposals resulted in a private bank that took deposits but did not issue notes. In 1808 another attempt was made to establish a bank, this time in Quebec City, but the legislature of Lower Canada refused to grant it a charter.

Further efforts to establish banks were interrupted by the War of 1812, but after the war the situation was favourable for the promotion of banking. Early redemption of the wartime army bills did much to create confidence in paper issues, a precondition for successful banking. The genuine shortage of currency, the nuisance created by the circulating paper originated by merchants and others, and the shortage of capital all served to point out the urgent need for a sound paper circulation. The successful operation of the First Bank of the

United States provided an example of how sound banking could furnish such paper.

The First Chartered Banks

In 1817 nine Montreal merchants signed Articles of Association to establish the Bank of Montreal without statutory authority. Their second petition for a charter was approved by the legislature of Lower Canada, but it was not until 1822 that the charter was finally confirmed by royal assent. In rank of precedence, the Bank of New Brunswick is the first chartered bank in British North America. Its act of incorporation passed in the legislature of New Brunswick in 1820 and received royal assent the same year.[1]

charters *statutory authority to operate a bank requires a charter obtained by a special Act of Parliament*

Although many similarities exist between the **charters** of these two banks, the differences reflect their independent evolution. The 20-year charter of the Bank of New Brunswick followed the banking traditions of New England, partly because its founders included a Loyalist from Virginia and a Harvard graduate, and partly because most of the commerce of the Maritimes was carried on with the New England states. The terms of the 10-year Bank of Montreal charter, on the other hand, duplicated almost exactly the terms governing Alexander Hamilton's First Bank of the United States.

The charter of the Bank of New Brunswick reflected the traditionally conservative banking practices of New England. The debts of the bank were limited to twice its paid-up capital. By contrast, the Bank of Montreal's charter limited its total debts to three times the amount of its paid-up capital stock, plus an amount equal to monies deposited for safekeeping. The New Brunswick bank was also more restricted in its note issue. While both banks were allowed to issue notes up to the amount of their paid-up capital, plus holdings of gold and silver, and debentures or other securities issued or guaranteed by the respective legislatures, the directors of the New Brunswick bank were held personally liable for an overissue of notes. Arrangements for paying capital were also stricter. The capital of £50 000 of the Bank of New Brunswick had to be fully paid "in current Gold and Silver coins of the Province," a year and a half after incorporation. The charter of the Bank of Montreal authorized capital of £250 000 that had to be paid by instalments of 10 percent within nine years in the money then current in Lower Canada. While the Bank of New Brunswick had to make regular yearly statements to the government, the Bank of Montreal had to provide statements only on request. Finally, the former was not allowed to open branches, while the latter was permitted to establish branches in any part of Upper or Lower Canada.

The two charters had some similarities. Both limited the number of votes any one stockholder might cast: A Bank of New Brunswick stockholder was limited to a maximum of 10 votes and a Bank of Montreal stockholder to 20 votes, regardless of the number of shares held. Neither bank was allowed to lend money on mortgages, land, or real property. Both banks were permitted to

---

1. For more on the development of banking in Canada, see Powell (1999).

receive deposits, to deal in gold and silver bullion, to issue notes redeemable in specie on demand, and to discount bills.[2]

The return of prosperity in the early 1820s and the economic expansion in the 1830s up to the crisis of 1837 encouraged the establishment of a few more banks. Their number remained small, however, because of the monopoly position held by a few banks and because of restraining rules issued in 1830 by the British government on colonial bank charters.

The legislature of Upper Canada granted its first charter in 1817 to the Bank of Upper Canada in Kingston, but since royal assent was delayed for about two years, the charter lapsed and the bank failed almost immediately. Its place was taken by the Chartered Bank of Upper Canada established in York (Toronto). This bank was chartered by the legislature in 1819 and received royal assent in 1821. Its charter differed from others of the time in that the government of Upper Canada was authorized to subscribe to the bank's stock.

Because of the close political alliances of those associated with these banks, the Chartered Bank of Upper Canada and the Bank of Montreal in Lower Canada were able to exert an effective restricting influence on the number of banks their respective legislatures chartered. The same was true in Nova Scotia, where the Halifax Banking Company (organized in 1825), though a private bank, was able to maintain its monopoly position until the formation of the Bank of Nova Scotia in 1832. Another reason for the relatively late chartering of banks in Nova Scotia was that most of the applications stipulated a franchise of monopoly, which the legislature was unwilling to grant.

The Commercial Crisis of 1837–38

The period of rapid economic expansion after the mid-1820s came to an end a decade later with a commercial crisis that started in the United Kingdom. In Lower Canada the banks, following the trend in the United States, suspended specie payments on their notes. This action was given legal sanction in 1838, but at the same time each bank was required to restrict the total amount of notes issued during the period of suspension to its paid-up capital. In Upper Canada the Lieutenant Governor was opposed to suspension primarily on the grounds that it meant copying the United States. At first he promised assistance to the Bank of Upper Canada from the military chest, but when other banks demanded equal treatment, the government announced that it would receive at par the notes of all banks. In a special session of the legislature, specie suspension was finally authorized, but the banks' note issue was limited at first to twice and later to three times their paid-up capital. Maritime banks also suspended specie redemption during this period.

As a result of the suspensions between 1837 and 1840, private individuals and institutions, including the Toronto city council, issued paper money

---

2. The discount procedure of the Bank of New Brunswick, followed by other banks, is recounted in *The Bank of Nova Scotia, Monthly Review* (Toronto, May 1956): "The Directors were to vote by ballot on the discounts, three negative votes being sufficient to reject a note or bill. Voting was by black beans and white beans. According to evidence later produced in a public inquiry, a Director interested in a particular discount would sometimes threaten his brother Directors with the Black Beans on discounts in which *they* were interested."

payable at some future date. While the principle that financial crisis must be fed rather than starved appears to have been understood at the time, the method of providing paper money during such periods remained undiscovered.

The provision of sufficient notes in times of stress became a public issue following the crisis of 1837. Bank notes tended to increase in number during the prosperous times as discounting by the banks increased, and to decline during the depressed times when the public reduced its bank borrowing. Low prices, therefore, were blamed on an insufficiency of circulating money. This situation could be remedied, it was felt, by allowing the banks to issue their notes against government bonds, rather than against a fluctuating amount of commercial paper.

Bond-Backed Notes

Following the union of Upper and Lower Canada to form the Province of Canada in 1841, the first Governor General, Lord Sydenham, exerted his influence to have legislation passed that would provide for a more stable money supply. Lord Sydenham had been an active participant in the English currency school, so it is not surprising that the new Union government's proposals for reform closely followed those in England. All the existing banks were to forfeit their privilege of note issue. A new government bank of issue was to be created. This new bank, to be named the Bank of the Province of Canada, was to be allowed to issue notes to a maximum amount of £1 million redeemable in specie, and against gold equal to 25 percent and government securities equal to 75 percent of the notes issued. Any amount of notes in excess of £1 million was to be backed by a 100 percent specie reserve.

To put these notes into circulation, the government was to use them to pay its expenses and issue them to the chartered banks in return for gold or government securities. The banks were also asked to buy government securities and exchange them for notes, but unlike legislation current in the United States, the banks were to receive no interest on the bonds turned over to the government bank for new notes.

The government's proposed scheme was designed to kill two birds with one stone. On the one hand, it would provide a market for the bonds of the government, which was in financial difficulty, and on the other, it would provide a money supply that could be controlled during both prosperity and depression. The chartered banks openly opposed the government's proposals. Since deposit banking was as yet little developed, the banks would deprive themselves of their single most important source of revenue by giving up their right to issue notes. Moreover, as was later pointed out, the government's plan would have stabilized the money supply by sacrificing its essential elasticity. The plan was never enacted, and the government sought an alternative way to control the note issue.

The new bank charters imposed double liability on shareholders and limited note issue to an amount equal to a bank's paid-up capital. An annual tax of 1 percent was levied on the amount of circulating bank notes in excess of the amount of specie, legal tender, and government securities held by a bank. In this way the government intended to compensate itself for the interest it would have received had its earlier proposal been accepted. Moreover, when the charter of the Bank of Montreal came up for renewal in 1841, the government assured a market for its own bonds by amending the charter to require the bank, by this time the largest, to hold a certain percentage of its assets in government bonds. This clause was made a general provision of all chartered banks in 1854.

The Free Banking Act, *1850*

Depressed economic conditions returned in 1847 and remained until 1850. Although no banks failed, the banks' capital was substantially impaired by business failures. As a result of reduced bank capital and the reduced demand for credit, bank notes tended to become scarce. At first, the Canadian government issued government debentures in the form of ordinary notes payable one year after date of issue with interest at 6 percent. Later, debentures issued were payable either on demand or at some future date, and either with or without interest. This situation, as one commentator of the times noted, "laid the foundation for a permanent element of government paper in the currency of the country."[3]

With the return of economic prosperity in the early 1850s, the government stopped issuing its own notes for circulation. However, the apparent success of these notes revived interest in establishing a government bank of issue. The system of **free banking** introduced in New York State also attracted considerable attention because it appeared to contain the principles, earlier advocated by Lord Sydenham, of a sound basis for note issue and a market for government securities. This system permitted free entry into banking without a state charter, provided that the new bank would purchase a specific amount of state bonds, which, in turn, served as an upper limit on the bank's note issue. Free banking had an additional attraction for populists, who saw it as a way to break the monopoly of existing bankers and allow the establishment of small local banks oriented to local, particularly rural, needs.

The *Free Banking Act*, modelled on New York State legislation, was passed in 1850. The Act allowed individuals, partnerships, or incorporated companies to organize a bank with a minimum capital of $100 000. This amount was small relative to chartered bank practices at the time. The banks to be formed under the *Act* were not allowed to open branches. While they were not subject to the 1 percent tax on their notes as were the chartered banks, their note issue was limited to the amount of government debt held by them. Bank notes were to be printed for them by the government and were available from the inspector general on depositing with him an equivalent amount of government securities.

The *Free Banking Act* met with little success. Only five new banks were established, and the Bank of British North America, which had been operating under a royal charter, took advantage of the provisions of the *Act* to issue small-

free banking
allowing banks to be formed without separate legislation in each case

3. Adam Shortt, "Currency and Banking, 1840–1867," reprinted by E.P. Neufeld, *Money and Banking in Canada* (Toronto: McClelland and Stewart, 1964), p. 134.

denomination notes. Two of the five new banks soon failed, and the others converted to legislative charters. The restriction on branching and the issue of bank notes based on government securities rather than commercial lending made banking under the *Free Banking Act* less attractive than under legislative charters.

Private unit banks (with no branches) operated in Canada before and after the experiment with free banking legislation. Because they were not chartered, they were not allowed to issue their own notes for circulation. They were set up to accept deposits from the public and to make loans to farmers and small manufacturing and processing firms. Their inability to issue their own notes forced them to become affiliated with chartered banks, which eventually absorbed them to build their branch networks.

Bank Expansion

Except for a short period after 1857, the Canadian provinces experienced an economic boom that lasted from 1850 until Confederation in 1867. The Reciprocity Treaty with the United States in 1854 assured Canadians of a market for their growing extractive industries, while the Crimean War created a demand for agricultural products. Railway construction opened the frontiers, providing the opportunity for land speculation. During these years the number of banks in Canada increased rapidly, an experience that was to recur in the early 1870s.[4]

In this era of economic expansion, the banks held 10 percent of their funds in government securities, with the rest almost entirely committed to loans. Very little was held in the form of coin or bullion. Consequently, the banks were in a vulnerable position when caught by the crisis of 1857, which originated in England, as had the crisis of a decade earlier. In Canada, the crisis of 1857 coincided with poor harvests and the collapse of the real estate boom. The banks, which had invested heavily in real estate and depreciated railway stock, were unable to feed the crisis by meeting the demands for credit.

In 1859 the government appointed a committee to investigate the banking and currency system. The ***Act Granting Additional Facilities in Commercial Transactions***, passed in the same year, introduced provisions that became a distinctive feature of Canadian banking. The *Act* and subsequent amendments in 1861 and 1865 allowed the banks to make loans secured by bills of lading or warehouse receipts. Thus, a farmer could have a warehouse receipt issued for grain stored in his granary and could use this receipt as collateral for a bank loan. This principle, modified and expanded, is distinctive to Canadian banking in that it transgresses the strict definition of commercial banking based on commercial or self-liquidating loans. As a result of this feature, the

Act Granting Additional Facilities in Commercial Transactions *a distinctive feature of Canadian banking that allowed banks to make loans secured by warehouse receipts*

---

4. Included in the number of banks that made an appearance during the 1850s were the following: the Bank of Toronto, St. Francis Bank, the Eastern Townships Bank, the Bank of Brantford, the Bank of Western Canada, the Bank of the County of Elgin, the Ontario Bank, La Banque Nationale, the International Bank, and the Chartered Bank of Canada, which later became the Canadian Bank of Commerce.

banks have played an important role in the development of the nation's agricultural and mineral resources.

The Provincial Notes Act, *1866*

Provincial government notes had been in circulation in Nova Scotia since 1812. Although provincial notes circulated periodically in the central provinces, all proposals for a permanent issue were turned down. Both Lord Sydenham's proposal in 1841 and its revival by Alexander Galt in 1860 were rejected. In 1866, however, the proponents of a government currency finally achieved the enactment of the *Provincial Notes Act*. Three factors contributed to their success: the government's financial requirements; the final collapse of the Bank of Upper Canada, the first chartered bank failure in Canadian history; and, following the suspension of specie payments by the U.S. banks during the Civil War, the recognition of the need for greater soundness in the currency.

The *Act* of 1866 authorized a provincial note issue of $8 million redeemable in gold. The first $5 million of this issue was to be 20 percent secured by specie and the next $3 million 25 percent secured by specie, with government bonds providing the remaining security. By way of compromise, the government agreed that if $5 million could be obtained from the banks as a government loan, it would not use the note-issue powers provided in the *Act*. The banks failed to provide the government with the loan, and it proceeded to issue its own notes. To discourage the banks from issuing their own notes, the *Act* further authorized the provincial government to pay a subsidy of 5 percent per annum on the value of any notes the banks should retire before their charters expired, and to pay them a commission of one-quarter of 1 percent for handling and servicing provincial notes. The banks, except the Bank of Montreal, continued to issue notes in spite of the provisions of the *Act*.[5] However, they gradually began to hold small quantities of the new currency, which, because of its legal reserve status, could be substituted for specie. Thus began the shift from the banks to the government of the responsibility for maintaining the national specie reserves.

Banking Following Confederation

The *British North America Act* granted the new Dominion government exclusive jurisdiction over all matters pertaining to currency and coinage, banking, the incorporation of banks, and the issue of paper money. In the first session of the new Parliament, an interim *Act Respecting Banking* extended the existing charters of all banks until a general revision of banking legislation could be made.

The failure in 1867 of the second large chartered bank, the Chartered Bank of Canada, again raised the need for a sound currency. Alexander Galt, the first Minister of Finance, introduced a bill (later withdrawn) for a bond-

---

5. The Bank of Montreal had become the government's banker in 1864 and was therefore in a position to benefit by following the government's wishes.

secured currency similar to the United States' National Bank notes. The bill was replaced by a temporary currency measure, the *Dominion Notes Act* of 1868, which extended the provisions of the *Provincial Notes Act* of 1866 to all the provinces. Two years later the ***Dominion Notes Act* of 1870** was passed as the first step toward a strictly government note issue. The chartered banks were restricted to issuing their notes in minimum denominations of $5, thus giving the Dominion government a monopoly on $1 and $2 issues. The *Act* also authorized the government to increase its fiduciary note issue to $9 million against which a gold reserve of 20 percent was to be held. Any issue in excess of $9 million had to be covered dollar for dollar by gold. These authorized amounts were raised to $20 million in 1880, to $30 million in 1903, and to $50 million in 1914. Although the required gold backing had increased from 20 percent to 25 percent, by 1914 the actual amount of gold held against the total issue outstanding had grown to such an extent that the Dominion notes had practically become gold certificates.

Dominion Notes Act of 1870 *the Act gave the federal government a monopoly on the issue of $1 and $2 notes for circulation*

The Bank Act, *1871*

The *Bank Act* of 1871 was preceded in 1870 by a temporary act that included the provisions of the *Dominion Notes Act* of that year and required the banks to hold from one-third to one-half of their cash reserves in the form of Dominion notes. The temporary act also repealed the earlier provisions that banks pay a 1 percent annual tax on their notes and invest 10 percent of their paid-up capital in government securities.

www.

The ***Bank Act* of 1871** was the first permanent legislation governing banking passed by the new federal government. It consolidated into a general statute the provisions contained in the charters of the individual banks granted before Confederation. The *Act*, the more important features of which are outlined below, served as a blueprint not only for all future banking legislation, but also for the development of Canadian banking practices generally.

Bank Act of 1871 *the first permanent legislation governing Canadian commercial banks*

NEW BANKS   All new banks were to be chartered by a special Act of Parliament. All new charters were to conform to the general provisions of the *Bank Act*, and all existing charters were extended until July 1, 1881. This common date for the expiry of all charters became a feature of the Canadian system. Since charters are granted for 10 years, a periodic revision of the *Bank Act* is automatic, while annual tinkering is minimized.

The capital requirement for new banks remained large. Subscribed capital was set at $500 000. Of this, $100 000 had to be paid up before a bank could open for business, and a further sum of $100 000 had to be paid within two years. The high capital requirement, together with permission to open branches, preserved the Canadian branch banking structure.

NOTE ISSUE   The banks were to restrict their circulation to notes of $4 and upward, the government being given a monopoly on small note issues. The banks' note issue was limited to the amount of their paid-up capital. Bank notes were made redeemable at certain designated places, and suspension of payment by a bank for 90 days would result in the forfeiture of its charter.

RESERVES   The banks were required to hold in Dominion notes at least one-third of whatever cash reserves they chose to carry.

DIVIDENDS   Dividends or bonuses by a bank were limited to 8 percent until it accumulated a rest or surplus fund equal to 20 percent of its paid-up capital stock, after allowing for all bad or doubtful debts.

LIABILITY   Directors were individually liable for the impairment of paid-up capital. Shareholders, on the other hand, were liable for double the amount of their subscription.

ACCOUNTABILITY   Each bank was required to make a monthly statement to the government.

BANK LENDING   Loans against real estate or with a bank's own stock as security were prohibited. The "pledge" provision allowing banks to make loans on certain bills of lading and warehouse receipts was continued and extended.

Revisions Strengthening Bank Note Issues

The revisions made to the *Bank Act* in the period before the First World War were intended to provide greater safety for holders of bank notes, to ensure that these notes would circulate at par throughout the country, and to provide a means whereby they could be increased beyond the limits set in the *Act*.

Six years of prosperity following Confederation came to an end with a depression that lasted from 1873 to 1879. The banks were hard hit; during the preceding years of prosperity and optimism, they had become involved to an undesirable degree in the financing of the lumber industry and of ship-building. As the depression had its origin in Canada's main export markets, these industries, together with agriculture, suffered. Many of the small and weaker banks were doomed to failure; four failed in 1878, five in 1887, and another four by 1890. The consequent loss to note holders created a public demand for greater security of bank notes.

In the *Bank Act* revisions of 1880, bank notes were made a first charge against a bank's assets in the event of liquidation. It was argued at the time that, in contrast to depositors, note holders were involuntary creditors of the banks and should therefore be given preferential treatment. The revisions to the *Act* also gave the government a further monopoly on note issue by restricting the chartered banks' issues to denominations in multiples of $5. Moreover, the cash reserves that the banks were required to hold in Dominion notes were raised to 40 percent.

Because bank notes could be redeemed only at the head offices of the issuing banks, they did not circulate at par throughout the country. To overcome this fault, the *Bank Act* revision of 1890 required the banks to maintain a redemption office in each province. A Bank Circulation Redemption Fund for failed banks, into which the banks had to deposit 5 percent of their average annual circulation, was established to provide a mutual guarantee of notes in circulation. The fund was supervised by the minister of finance, whose department paid 3 percent interest on such deposits. To protect the fund, notes were made a first lien on the assets of a failed bank. In addition, to ensure that note holders would not lose after a bank was liquidated, its notes were to bear interest at 6 percent (later reduced to 5 percent) until paid, and the Bank Circulation Redemption Fund was to redeem the notes of a failed bank within 60 days of suspension if the liquidator were unable to do so.

Revisions Increasing Bank Note Issues

The period after mid-1890 was one of unprecedented economic development, in which the banks played an important role. Expansion, especially after 1900, caused bank note issues to reach the ceiling that the *Bank Act* had fixed at paid-up capital. (The maximum allowable amount of note issue by a bank was the amount of its paid-up capital.) The demand for additional credit was especially strong in the autumn, when farmers were paid for their crops. In 1907, a low-quality wheat crop that had to be moved to market quickly lest it deteriorate precipitated an unprecedented demand for extra notes. Since the banks showed no intention of increasing their capital stock (and thus their note issues), the government provided for an emergency issue by lending Dominion notes to the banks. In the following year, a special amendment to the *Bank Act* permitted the banks to exceed their capital stock limit of note issue during the months of October, November, December, and January. By a further revision in 1912, the period of permitted excess issue was extended to six months beginning in September of each year. In both cases the permitted excess was limited to 15 percent of a bank's paid-up capital and surplus, and a penalty tax of 5 percent per annum was imposed to ensure withdrawal of the excess issue as quickly as possible.

In 1913, the decennial revision of the *Bank Act* (postponed since 1911) provided for a more elastic note issue system. Being subject to a special 5 percent tax, the excess issue provided for in 1908 and 1912 was not very profitable to the banks. They therefore generally paid out cash in the form of Dominion notes rather than avail themselves of the excess issue privilege. The amendment of 1913 permitted the banks to issue notes beyond the capital stock limit without tax after depositing dollar for dollar gold or Dominion notes in a fund known as the Central Gold Reserve. This fund was not in fact a central reserve, but only a depository for a certain form of collateral against excess bank note issues.

The Finance Act *and the Money Supply*

With the approach of war, the future of the Canadian dollar became uncertain. Some depositors began converting their funds to gold for hoarding, whereupon the banks became anxious about their gold reserves. Customarily, relatively small cash reserves were retained in the banks' vaults, most of their cash being held in the form of secondary reserves invested in New York. With war looming, the banks feared that it might become impossible to repatriate their reserves, particularly in gold. They consulted the minister of finance, and the government responded by passing an order-in-council on August 3, 1914, ending the convertibility of Dominion notes and bank notes into gold. In addition, the Department of Finance was authorized to make advances of Dominion notes to chartered banks on the pledge of securities as well as the banks' own promissory notes as approved by the Treasury Board.

Finance Act *of 1914* *the act allowed the federal Department of Finance to function as a pseudo-central bank*

The abandonment of gold payments and advances from the Department of Finance became the essential features of the ***Finance Act* of 1914**, passed at a special autumn session of Parliament in 1914. This legislation, which was to have been a temporary wartime expedient, was re-enacted each year until 1923, when it was made a permanent feature of the Canadian financial system. Under the terms of the *Finance Act*, the Department of Finance was allowed to function as a pseudo-central bank until the establishment of the Bank of Canada in 1935.

Toward a Central Bank

During the war, the expansion of bank notes and deposits became the prime source of government and business borrowing. The government borrowed from the banks through the sale of its Treasury bills, floated war loans to repay these bills at maturity, and immediately began to borrow from the banks again to finance current expenditures. The banks used their holdings of government securities to obtain advances of Dominion notes from the Department of Finance. These notes, in turn, were deposited with the Central Gold Reserve to allow the banks to expand their own note issue. The banks were able to expand their cash positions not only as a result of the advances of Dominion notes from the Department of Finance, but also as a result of the direct issues by the government of unsecured Dominion notes and of an increase in their foreign balances that could be repatriated in the form of gold.

Toward the end of the war the first serious attempt was made to establish a central bank in Canada. The Canadian Bankers' Association, at the instigation of its president, E.L. Pease, formed a committee to investigate the possibilities of founding a "bank of rediscount." Pease himself proposed the establishment of such a bank, which would take over the Dominion note issue, the Central Gold Reserves, and the operations under the *Finance Act*. At the same time the chartered banks were to retain their note issue. While the proposed bank was to be controlled directly by the government, its capitalization would be shared between it and the chartered banks. The banking community, which was quite satisfied with the operations of the *Finance Act*, considered a bank of rediscount quite unnecessary and therefore turned down the proposals by Pease. Instead, they recommended that the *Finance Act* be renewed.

Wartime monetary expansion carried over into the postwar period. Except for a short downturn in economic activity after the latter part of 1920, Canada experienced almost unprecedented boom conditions until the end of 1929. Although the banks continued to take advances from the Department of Finance, during most of this period they were able to reduce their dependence on such advances for cash and rely on Canada's favourable balance of payments to provide cash resources from abroad.

On July 1, 1926, Dominion notes were again made convertible into gold at a specified price, and Canada was back on the gold standard.[6] However, about this time imports began to rise sharply, and by 1928, with the decrease in the inflow of long-term investment capital, large deficits occurred in the balance of payments. The country's gold and foreign exchange reserves had to be called on to finance this imbalance. The banks were able to meet the demands made on them for gold and foreign exchange and at the same time maintain their cash reserves at a level that permitted monetary expansion. They accomplished this by taking advances of Dominion notes from the Department of Finance, which in turn was obliged to redeem these notes in gold as requested. Hence, the gold drain was transferred from the banks to the government. Because the Department of Finance was not prepared to exercise discretionary powers in limiting its advances to the banks, the government, at the beginning of 1929, terminated the unrestricted convertibility of Dominion notes to avoid depletion of its gold holdings. This de facto departure from the gold standard was not officially recognized by the government until 1931.

By late 1929 Canada was in the midst of the worldwide depression. While other countries responded by depreciating their currencies and by putting up tariff barriers, the Canadian government continued what it considered to be a sound monetary policy. It refused to depreciate the Canadian dollar, largely because of the extra burden this would have placed on Canada as a result of its large external debt. For a short time at least, it was aided in maintaining the external value of the dollar by the inflow of capital as the confidence of foreign investors in the Canadian economy persisted. As the depression deepened, however, the Canadian dollar began to slide and assumed an intermediate position above sterling and below the U.S. dollar. Despite this limited depreciation, Canada suffered an adverse balance of payments that had to be financed by a reduction in the banks' monetary gold and their external assets. The banks, however, did not have to obtain additional cash by taking advances of Dominion notes, because the depressed economic conditions led to an internal flow of cash into the banks from businesses retiring their bank loans. The banks, not cognizant of the connection between monetary contraction and business conditions, used the extra cash to reduce their advances from the Department of Finance, rather than to encourage bank lending.

As economic conditions deteriorated and the money supply contracted, more voices were heard on the subject of monetary reform. In November 1932, in an attempt to increase the money supply and ease credit conditions, the government forced the banks to borrow $35 million in Dominion notes under the *Finance Act.* At the same time the banks loaned an equal amount to the government by purchasing a two-year issue of Treasury bills. The banks took advantage of these bills to obtain advances of Dominion notes, but instead of

---

6. Dominion notes were unofficially convertible into gold before 1926. After 1922, in its transactions with the chartered banks the government accepted gold in exchange for Dominion notes and redeemed Dominion notes in gold.

Royal Commission on Banking and Currency in 1934 the commission proposed the formation of a central bank

expanding their loans with this cash, they used it as well to reduce their indebtedness to the government. In 1934, in another attempt to achieve monetary expansion, the government made a direct issue of Dominion notes to finance public works.

As none of these attempts improved economic conditions, criticism of monetary policy at last led the government to appoint a **Royal Commission on Banking and Currency**. In 1934 the recommendations of the Commission were written into the *Bank of Canada Act*, giving Canada a central bank.[7]

KEY TERMS

Act Granting Additional Facilities in Commercial Transactions
Bank Act of 1871
branch banking
charters

Dominion Notes Act of 1870
Finance Act of 1914
fractional reserve banking
free banking
goldsmiths

Royal Commission on Banking and Currency
specie
unit bank

REVIEW QUESTIONS

1. What are the common characteristics of the operations of the goldsmiths of seventeenth-century London and those of modern banking?
2. How did Lord Sydenham propose to change the banking system to provide revenue for the government and at the same time to stabilize the money supply?
3. Describe the free banking experiment of the 1850s.
4. What are the major provisions contained in the first bank charters? How did early revisions to the *Bank Act* attempt to make bank notes safer?

5. How did the early *Bank Act*s limit the chartered banks' ability to expand their note issue? What expedients did the government introduce to permit the banks to exceed these limitations?
6. Provide a short (two typed pages) summary of Powell's description of the evolution of Canadian banking (see the selected readings). What events were most important in the development of the Canadian dollar?

SELECTED READINGS

Breckenridge, R. M. *The History of Banking in Canada.* Washington: National Monetary Commission, 1910.

Canadian Bankers' Association. *Adam Shortt's History of Canadian Currency and Banking 1600–1880.* Toronto: Canadian Bankers' Association, 1987.

McIvor, R. Craig. *Canadian Monetary, Banking and Fiscal Development.* Toronto: Macmillan, 1961.

Neufeld, E.P. *Money and Banking in Canada.* Toronto: McClelland and Stewart, 1964.

Powell, J. *A History of the Canadian Dollar.* Ottawa: Bank of Canada, 1999.

---

7. The Bank of Canada is discussed later in the book.

CHAPTER THIRTEEN

THE CHARTERED BANKS

After reading this chapter you should be able to
1. Explain the structure of the Canadian banking system
2. Differentiate between Schedule I and Schedule II banks
3. Explain the chartered banks' sources of funds
4. Explain the chartered banks' uses of funds
5. Outline the foreign currency operations of banks in Canada
6. Discuss how the banks have become multiservice institutions
7. Describe electronic and virtual banking
8. Explain bank failures in Canada during the 1980s

The traditional role of banks was to extend commercial loans, financed at first by the issue of their own notes and later by the acceptance and creation of deposits. Commercial loans usually were for no longer than a year, and were extended to traders and merchants to finance the inventories of goods until their sale to retail customers. Because the banks were the only institutions to provide this service, they came to be known as the commercial banks.[1] Today the lending activities of most of the commercial banks throughout the world extend far beyond the former confines of commercial lending.

The commercial banks in Canada, unlike those in other countries, are commonly called the chartered banks. This terminology dates from before 1980, when a bank in Canada could be established only by charter granted in a special Act of the federal Parliament.

Banking Structure

Over the years, Canada moved from a banking structure with a large number of locally based banks to one with a relatively few large banks with nationwide branch networks. In 1867, the year of Confederation, there were 35 banks in

---

1. The word "bank" is of German origin but came into English usage from French and Italian. At first it referred to the bench or counter used by moneychangers and dealers. Later, it assumed its more general meaning of the place of business of money dealers. Akin to the early English use of the word "bank" is the use of the French word *banque* and the Italian word *banca*.

Canada. By 1874, this number had grown to 51, a nineteenth-century peak. From Confederation to 1900, 24 banks disappeared; seven were merged with other banks while 17 failed or had their charters repealed. By 1925 another 35 banks had disappeared, 27 by merger. (An amendment to the *Bank Act* of 1900, allowed mergers to take place following approval of the Governor in Council rather than requiring the more cumbersome method of a special Act of Parliament.) Over the next three decades only one new bank was established, the Mercantile Bank of Canada in 1953. Because of further mergers and amalgamation, however, the number of banks was reduced to its historical low of eight in 1961.

In 1967 Parliament chartered the Bank of Western Canada and the Bank of British Columbia. Because of disagreement among its founders, the Bank of Western Canada never opened for business. In 1972 the Unity Bank of Canada was founded, but in 1977, to avert failure, it merged with the Provincial Bank, which two years later merged with the National Bank of Canada. In the early 1970s dissatisfaction with the major banks in Western Canada, whose head offices were all in central Canada, was expressed in demands for the establishment of regional banks more responsive to Western needs. The Canadian Commercial Bank (initially the Canadian Commercial and Industrial Bank) and the Northland Bank were chartered in 1975, with head offices in Western Canada. Both banks failed and were liquidated in the mid-1980s. Four other banks in Western Canada did not survive. The Morguard Bank, chartered in 1982, was merged three years later with the Security Pacific Bank of Canada, an American foreign subsidiary bank. The Western and Pacific Bank of Canada and the Bank of Alberta, chartered in 1983 and 1984, respectively, were amalgamated and became the Canadian Western Bank in 1988. When the Bank of British Columbia experienced difficulties, its assets were acquired by the Hongkong Bank of Canada.

The Continental Bank of Canada, established in 1977 and headquartered in Ontario, ran into difficulties in 1986 and was taken over by Lloyd's Bank International Canada. It was subsequently taken over by the Hongkong Bank of Canada, which together with its purchase of the assets of the Bank of British Columbia became the largest foreign bank subsidiary in Canada.

The Laurentian Bank was established in 1988 with the transformation of The Montreal City and District Bank. The Désjardin Group in the Province of Quebec became its dominant shareholder.

The Manulife Bank of Canada was formed in 1993 by the Manufactures Life Insurance Company with the merger of the Regional Trust, Cabot Trust, and Huronia Trust companies.

In 1996 the Toronto-Dominion Bank launched the First Nations Bank of Canada jointly with the Saskatchewan Indian Equity Foundation Inc. and the Federation of Saskatchewan Indian Nations Inc.

In 1997, the Vancouver City Savings Credit Union converted its federally chartered Citizens Trust into the Citizens Bank of Canada. This bank was Canada's first branchless one; its clients do all the banking by telephone, personal computer and ABM, 24 hours a day, seven days a week.

In January 2000, 11 Canadian-owned chartered banks were operating in Canada. Eight of these were Schedule I banks, whose shares, as explained below, are widely held by Canadians. The other three, the Manulife Bank of

Canada, the Citizens Bank of Canada, and the First Nations Bank of Canada, have closely held shares, where a shareholder may, under specified conditions, hold more than 10 percent of a bank's outstanding shares.

Table 13.1 identifies the major Canadian banks (according to assets) as of January 31, 2000. The three largest banks, each with total assets over $230 billion, held 58 percent of the total assets of the Canadian domestic banks. The five largest Canadian banks held 93 percent of the total assets of all domestic banks and 87 percent of all bank assets in Canada. The assets of the foreign bank subsidiaries represented only 7 percent of all bank assets held in Canada.

www.

TABLE 13.1 **THE DOMESTIC BANKS IN CANADA** January 31, 2000		
	DATE OF ESTABLISHMENT	ASSETS (MILLIONS OF DOLLARS)
Royal Bank of Canada	1869	270 909
Canadian Imperial Bank of Commerce	1961[1]	257 060
Bank of Montreal	1822	228 525
The Bank of Nova Scotia	1832	232 421
The Toronto-Dominion Bank	1955[2]	233 915
National Bank of Canada	1980[3]	73 500
Laurentian Bank of Canada	1987[4]	13 831
Canadian Western Bank	1988[5]	2 666
		1 103 647
Other domestic banks[6]		1 599
		1 105 246
Foreign banks		89 530
		1 194 776

1. Amalgamation of the Canadian Bank of Commerce and the Imperial Bank of Canada, established in 1867 and 1873, respectively.
2. Amalgamation of the Bank of Toronto and the Dominion Bank, founded in 1855 and 1869, respectively.
3. Amalgamation of the Banque Canadienne Nationale and La Banque Provinciale du Canada, which, through mergers, trace their lineage to 1873 and 1962, respectively.
4. Conversion of the Montreal City and District Savings Bank, founded in 1846, into a domestically owned Schedule II chartered bank.
5. Amalgamation of Western and Pacific Bank and Bank of Alberta, chartered in 1983 and 1984, respectively.
6. Including Manulife Bank of Canada, Citizens Bank of Canada, and First Nations Bank of Canada. As of April 2000, these were the only domestic Schedule II banks operating in Canada.

SOURCE: Office of the Superintendent of Financial Institutions, January 2000.

The Canadian banks have more than 8000 branches in communities in all provinces and territories. These branches together offer access to more than 16 000 automated banking machines in the Canadian-shared ABM network, providing Canadians with exceptional access to banking facilities. For example, at the end of 1999, there were 2.5 bank branches and 5.3 ABM per 10 000 inhabitants in Canada. Canada's per capita branch coverage is among the best in the world.

Foreign Banks in Canada

Until the 1980s the presence of foreign banks in Canada had remained insignificant. Before 1928, only three foreign banks, all of them British, had been chartered: the Bank of British North America in 1859, the Bank of British Columbia in 1862, and Barclay's Bank of Canada in 1928. Then in 1953 the Mercantile Bank of Canada was chartered by Dutch interests. In 1963 it was taken over by First National City Bank of New York. This takeover was viewed unfavourably by the then Liberal government, which in the 1967 revisions to the *Bank Act* specifically prohibited foreign banks from operating agencies, branches, or bank subsidiaries in Canada.[2] The Mercantile Bank, at the time the only foreign-controlled bank in Canada, had the size of its assets frozen and was required to reduce its foreign ownership to 25 percent over a certain period.

Despite the 1967 prohibitions, foreign banks penetrated Canadian financial markets by establishing some 100 nonbank financial affiliates as ordinary corporations, mostly under provincial legislation. While these companies were not allowed to call themselves banks, most of their operations were similar to those of the banks. They typically extended loans with funds raised in the money market, often with guarantees from their foreign parent institutions. In the 1980 *Bank Act* revisions, the government made provision to bring these "back-door" Canadian banking activities of foreign banks under the umbrella of the federal regulatory authorities. Most of the nonbank financial affiliates took advantage of the revisions to the *Bank Act* that allowed them to convert to foreign bank subsidiaries. Although nonbank affiliates of foreign banks were allowed to continue after 1980, restrictions were placed on their operations to induce them to convert to banks. They were, for example, no longer allowed to engage both in lending money and in accepting deposits transferable by order. Nor were they allowed to use the guarantees of their parent institutions when borrowing funds. In addition, they were required to regularly provide the superintendent of financial institutions with financial statements and other information.

After 1980 the incorporation of foreign bank subsidiaries became the major route of foreign bank entry into Canadian banking. Before granting a bank licence, the minister of finance must be satisfied that the proposed foreign bank subsidiary will be capable of making a contribution to the financial system in Canada, and that treatment favourable to Canadian banks exists or will be provided in the home jurisdiction of the parent bank. In addition, evidence must be shown that the foreign parent is sound, well supervised, and in good standing in its home jurisdiction. Toward this end the foreign parent must provide a "letter of comfort" stating that it undertakes ultimate responsibility to support its Canadian subsidiary.

A stampede for charters followed approval of the legislation in 1980, allowing foreign banks to establish subsidiaries in Canada. Because the government had placed a ceiling of 8 percent of the total domestic assets of all Canadian banks on aggregate foreign bank Canadian assets, charters were

---

2. For an interesting discussion of the politics of foreign banks, see Robert MacIntosh. *Different Drummers: Banking and Politics in Canada*, Toronto: Macmillan, 1991, Ch. 11.

aggressively sought before the ceiling would be achieved. In total, some 65 foreign bank subsidiaries were incorporated during the 1980s.

Foreign banks that did not want to conduct business in Canada, either through subsidiaries or nonbank affiliates, could nevertheless maintain representative offices. In March 1996 Canada had 36 such offices. These were opened after registration and the payment of a fee. The offices could not, however, conduct any business in Canada other than that of promoting the services of the foreign bank they represented.

In February 1997 there were 41 active foreign bank subsidiaries operating in Canada. Although more had been incorporated after 1980, their number declined by withdrawal and amalgamation. The largest was the Hongkong Bank of Canada with some $22 billion in assets and more than 115 branches. This bank had achieved its size by acquiring the assets of the Bank of British Columbia in 1986, and in 1990 those of Lloyd's Bank of Canada, which previously had absorbed the Continental Bank of Canada. Other foreign bank subsidiaries with assets over $3 billion were Citibank Canada from the United States, Credit Suisse Canada, the Netherlands ABN AMRO Bank Canada, the German Deutsche Bank Canada, and the French Société Générale (Canada). Most of the foreign bank subsidiaries had few branches and usually only a head office that also served as a branch.

Foreign ownership of banks again became an issue in 1988 when American Express Company (AMEX) made application to establish a foreign bank subsidiary in Canada. The Canadian Banker's Association strongly lobbied the government not to grant AMEX a Canadian bank licence. The CBA argued that AMEX was not itself a regulated bank in the United States, a criterion that the government had used for incorporating foreign bank subsidiaries. By granting AMEX a banking licence, a precedent would be set whereby other unregulated foreign companies would demand similar treatment. It was also argued that AMEX wanted to gain access to the Canadian payments system and the automated teller machine network, and thereby, indirectly, to similar national networks in the United States that had been denied to it. Finally, the Canadian banks also protested because a Canadian banking licence would allow AMEX to provide nonbank services that the Canadian banks could not offer under existing legislation. While AMEX was issued letters patent for a foreign bank subsidiary, the government promised to meet some of the demands of the Canadian bankers in revisions to the *Bank Act* under consideration at the time.

When the 1997 revisions to the *Bank Act* were being considered, some foreign banks complained that the requirement to set up a Canadian subsidiary with a minimum capital base of $10 million was too costly. They argued that if they were able to lend to Canadians from the large capital base of the parent companies, they would be able to lend more money and in turn increase competition for loans in Canada. In response to the appeal, the federal government introduced legislation to allow foreign branches to do business in Canada by establishing branches. However such branches would not be allowed to take consumer deposits.

In 1999 42 foreign bank subsidiaries operated in Canada, sharing about 10 percent of total banking sector assets. The Task Force on the Future of the Canadian Financial Services Sector recommended that the government ease the entry requirements to allow a larger number of foreign banks to enter the industry. This easement should provide greater access to funds for businesses and increase the degree of competition in the marketplace.

Early in 2000, foreign banks were allowed to restructure their activities either as full-service branches or as lending branches. While neither type of branch could engage in retail deposit taking (those deposits under $150 000), full-service branches could take deposits above the $150 000 limit and did not have to be covered by deposit insurance. Lending branches were forced to borrow from other financial intermediaries to provide their source of funds. While most foreign bank subsidiaries offer commercial banking services, some are involved in providing consumer credit through their credit card and personal line of credit activities. In June 1999 the minister of finance announced that impending legislative changes would include a new entry regime for foreign banks in Canada.

Schedule I and II Banks

The 1980 revisions to the *Bank Act* (the *Banks and Banking Law Revisions Act* 1980) specifically focused on introducing more competition into Canadian banking by making it easier to charter a bank and by allowing the establishment of foreign bank subsidiaries. Banks became classified as either Schedule A or Schedule B, which was subsequently changed to Schedule I and Schedule II. Both types of banks may be chartered by the traditional, and more cumbersome, method of a special Act of the federal Parliament, or by the new and easier method of letters patent issued by the minister of finance. Before issuing letters patent to incorporate a bank, the minister must pay particular attention to the nature and sufficiency of the financial resources of the applicants, their business record and experience, the soundness and feasibility of their plans for the future conduct and development of the proposed bank, their character and competence, as well as the best interests of the financial system in Canada. When a bank has paid-in capital of at least $10 million, or such greater amount as may be specified by the minister, the superintendent of financial institutions may make an order approving the commencement and carrying on of the business of banking.

The 1992 revisions to the *Bank Act* for the first time defined the business of banking. According to the *Act* such business generally appertains to providing financial services; acting as a financial agent; providing investment counselling services and portfolio management services; and issuing payment, credit, and charge cards.

As we saw in Chapter 11, the major difference between Schedule I and II banks is their ownership and some of their powers. Schedule I banks must be widely held (no person alone or with associates may own more than 10 percent of any class of a bank's shares), and a bank's nonresident shareholding is limited to 25 percent of its outstanding shares. In addition, at least three-quarters of a Schedule I bank's board of directors must be Canadian residents, and more than half of its initial capital ($2 billion or any larger amount that may be designated by the minister of finance) must be paid in before it can start business.

www.

A Schedule II bank is incorporated either as a closely held Canadian bank or as a foreign bank subsidiary. In a closely held Schedule II Canadian bank, a Canadian resident or a U.S. resident, as provided by the Canada–U.S. free trade agreement, may have a significant shareholding (more than 10 percent) for the first 10 years. A Canadian financial institution, other than a bank, that is widely held may own a domestic Schedule II bank, and with ministerial approval can continue its ownership after the first 10 years. When the equity of a Schedule II bank reaches $750 million, within five years it has to have at least 35 percent of its voting shares widely held; these shares have to be listed and posted for trading on a recognized stock exchange in Canada.

The powers of foreign bank subsidiaries, with the exception of U.S. parent banks according to the Canada–U.S. free trade agreement, differ in two ways from those of domestic banks. Foreign bank subsidiaries can add branches to their initial branch only with ministerial approval. A ceiling applies to the total Canadian banking assets that all foreign subsidiaries may hold. In 1984 the initial ceiling of 8 percent of domestic assets of all banks (both domestic and foreign) was increased to 16 percent. After U.S. banks received an exclusion from the asset ceiling under the free trade agreement, the percentage for the other foreign subsidiaries was reduced to 12 percent.

Proposals for the reform of the financial sector released in 1999 included a significant change in the way in which the government defines the term "widely held" and the ownership rules. A single investor will be allowed to hold as much as 20 percent of any class of voting shares (30 percent of nonvoting shares) in a widely held bank subject to a "fit and proper" test. (The current rules for a Schedule I bank limit ownership to 10 percent.) Widely held will apply to banks whose equity is above $5 billion, where the fit and proper test examines the suitability of the prospective owners. This test examines the past business record of the owners, their business plan, and the reasons why they want to enter the business of banking. Integrity and fitness of character are also part of the review process.

On June 13, 2000, the government introduced its proposed changes to the financial services sector, Bill C-38. Ownership restrictions will be based on the size of the firm, with different rules for small (less than $1 billion), medium ($1 billion to $5 billion), and large (greater than $5 billion) banks. Large banks will continue to be widely held, with the minister of finance having the discretion to change the status of any bank to closely held. Medium-sized banks will be allowed to have individual shareholdings of as much as 65 percent. Small banks have no ownership restrictions other than the "fit and proper" test. Any recategorization must be approved by a special vote of the institution's shareholders, along with the approval of the majority of the directors of the bank.

Regulation and Supervision

The chartered banks are among the most severely regulated business enterprises in the country. Although they are privately owned firms, a presumption exists that because of their pivotal role in the country's payments system, they must be treated as quasi-public institutions.

The *Bank Act*, which historically had a statutory life of 10 years and as a result was reviewed and usually revised within a 10-year time frame, prescribes the conditions under which a bank may be chartered, the range of activities in which it may engage, the general conduct of its operations, and its relationship with the federal government and the Bank of Canada. In the 1992 revisions of the *Bank Act*, a "sunset clause" of five years replaced the 10-year period.

The system of control and supervision of the soundness and safety of chartered banks, which was already in existence before the 1992 legislative revision, was put in place during the first three decades of the twentieth century. The system consisted of each bank's internal audit and inspection system, two external shareholders' auditors, and the inspector general of banks. The Office of the Inspector General of Banks (OIGB) was established in 1924, following the failure of the Home Loan Bank of Canada in 1923. The OIGB was made responsible to the minister of finance for the administration of the *Bank Act*, and on the minister's behalf was required to inquire into the affairs of each bank at least once a year to be satisfied that the provisions of the *Act* with respect to the safety and soundness of each bank were observed. The costs of the inspector's office were shared by the banks. In practice the OIGB did not employ a staff for extensive on-site inspections; for this supervision it relied on the information the banks were required to disclose on a regular basis, the reports from the external auditors, and on discussions with the banks' managers. In the 1986 Estey Inquiry into the collapse of the Canadian Commercial Bank and the Northland Bank, this was described as a "wink and nod system." In response to the difficulties experienced by these two banks, the OIGB engaged bankers to make on-site inspections of banks and in particular to examine the quality of their loan portfolios. In 1984 the OIGB introduced an early warning system that rates banks on a scale from one to five with respect to capital adequacy, asset quality, management quality, earnings, and liquidity. This rating system, used by regulators in the United States, is known by its acronym, CAMEL.

Office of the Superintendent of Financial Institutions, Canada

In 1987 the OIGB was replaced by the Office of the Superintendent of Financial Institutions (OSFI), which became the federal government's agency for regulating and supervising all federally chartered, licensed, or registered banks; insurance, trust, loans, and investment companies; cooperative credit associations; and fraternal benefit societies. The OSFI also monitors federally regulated pension plans.

Institutions are examined by the OSFI with respect to their liquidity, their solvency, and their compliance with legislation, regulation, and guidelines issued by the OSFI. The costs of supervision are assessed to the institutions that are supervised. The superintendent has broad powers to control the activities of institutions subject to federal prudential supervision. For example, if in the superintendent's opinion, any assets on the books or records of a bank are not satisfactorily accounted for, or if a bank is unable to pay its liabilities as they become payable, or if there exists any practice that is materially prejudicial to the interests of the depositors or creditors of a bank, the superintendent may immediately take control of the bank.

www.

Revisions to the *Office of the Superintendent of Financial Institutions Act* in 1997 made it clear that the OSFI's prime responsibilities are to help to minimize losses to depositors and insurance policy holders and to contribute to public confidence in the Canadian financial system. The legislation introduced in June 2000 gave the superintendent even more power to exercise control over the financial system.

Despite government regulation and supervision, financial institutions do fail. Preventing failure in the first place is the responsibility of their boards and management. When institutions do fail, it is the responsibility of the OSFI to try to minimize the cost of failure. This minimization of cost requires early intervention to ensure that problems are resolved through (1) a management–director turnabout of the affairs of the failing institution, (2) a sale of all or part of the institution's business, or (3) the closure of the institution while it still has some positive net worth that can be used to reduce the cost of failure.

In addition to the prudential oversight of the OSFI, the banks also have to satisfy the standards of sound business and financial practices set out as a requirement for deposit insurance by the Canada Deposit Insurance Corporation (CDIC). The CDIC also becomes directly involved in the supervision of a bank whose solvency is severely threatened. Because of the need for close cooperation between the OSFI and the CDIC, a liaison committee chaired jointly by their respective heads meets regularly. The Financial Institutions Supervisory Committee, composed of the heads of the OSFI and the CDIC, the governor of the Bank of Canada, and the deputy minister of finance, has the responsibility to ensure the coordination of the activities of the various financial regulators and supervisors.

The Chartered Banks' Sources and Uses of Funds

The sources of funds for chartered banks and their employment are reflected in their balance sheets. A balance sheet provides a snapshot of liabilities and capital accounts, identifying sources of funds and of assets, showing their use at a particular time. Tables 13.2 and 13.3 show the consolidated balance sheet items of all the chartered banks in January 2000. Note, however, that the tables conceal differences among the balance sheets of individual banks and, hence, also many of the interesting relationships between the banks' sources and uses of funds.

Sources of Funds

Canadian Dollar Deposit Liabilities

The major source of funds to the chartered banks is their deposit liabilities. As shown in Table 13.2, in January 2000 their Canadian dollar deposits amounted to $523 billion. In addition, they held $433 billion in foreign currency-denominated deposits. The banks' foreign currency operations are discussed separately, later in this chapter.

A characteristic feature of the Canadian banking system is the large national or regional branch networks maintained by most of the Canadian-owned banks. This enables them to accept deposits from a wide cross-section of businesses and institutions, and in particular from persons representing every walk of life.

TABLE 13.2	**CANADIAN CHARTERED BANK LIABILITIES**
	Millions of Dollars, January 2000

Canadian dollar deposits		
Government of Canada	4 888	
Gross demand deposits	68 443	
Personal savings deposits	300 331	
Nonpersonal term and notice deposits	149 746	
		523 408
Advances from Bank of Canada	169	
Bankers' acceptances	48 902	
Subordinated debt	16 287	
Other liabilities1	159 069	
Capital funds		
Shareholders' equity	69 055	293 482
Total Canadian dollar liabilities		816 890
Foreign currency liabilities[2]		584 886
Total of all liabilities		1 401 776

Note: Errors due to rounding
1. Includes liabilities of subsidiaries other than deposits and noncontrolling interest in subsidiaries.
2. See Table 13.4 for details.

SOURCE: Statistics Canada, CANSIM Database, Matrix 00914, April 2000.

Gross Demand Deposits

current accounts
chequable bank accounts used by businesses for transactions purposes

Demand deposits are interest-bearing and noninterest-bearing deposits that have chequing privileges and are redeemable on demand. The banks normally charge a fee for servicing demand deposits accounts and for handling cheques.

Most demand deposits are **current accounts**. These accounts are the standard deposit accounts used by businesses for their day-to-day transactions.

Until the early 1990s, the majority of these accounts paid no interest. Corporations, therefore, had an incentive to economize on their balances in these accounts, particularly after the banks offered cash management services. These services included the electronic transfer of a corporation's current account balances held at any of a bank's branches across the country to a central account. Company treasurers, in turn, would distribute the balances in the central account to interest-bearing accounts. This transfer allowed them to hold zero balances in their non-interest-earning current accounts, except for relatively brief periods when balances were required to cover cheques written. As businesses came to manage their demand deposits more carefully, these deposits became a much smaller proportion of the banks' total deposits.

More recently the major banks have introduced a tiering feature to their current accounts whereby interest is paid on a scale that is a rising function of the average balance size. Account balances in the higher tiers now tend to earn a market-oriented interest rate.

The banks also offer demand deposits to individuals in the form of personal chequing accounts.

Personal Savings Deposits

Personal savings deposits are the single most important source of funds for the Canadian-owned chartered banks with large branch networks. The banks offer three types of personal savings accounts: chequable, nonchequable, and fixed term. Banks can require 5 to 15 days' notice for withdrawal from personal savings accounts, but rarely do so.

Personal savings accounts also are differentiated in terms of how interest is calculated and when it is paid; the service charges for writing cheques and for withdrawals; the issue of regular statements or passbook accounting; the return of cheques; and automatic overdraft protection.

Since the early 1980s daily-interest (interest calculated on the average daily closing balance and paid monthly), chequable, and nonchequable savings accounts have increased in popularity. For many individuals the daily-interest chequable account serves as an "all in one" universal bank account. The interest rate paid on these accounts is now usually tiered; that is, the interest earned depends on minimum balances, with higher interest rates paid on higher balances or only on the balance above the minimum amount for the particular tier.

Personal fixed-term deposits, which can only be withdrawn after a specified term, are the largest source of personal savings funds for the banks. The terms of these deposits can be from 30 days to as long as five years. Interest rates paid may be fixed or may change during the term of the deposit to reflect changes in market rates. Term deposits, usually those with larger terms, take the form of guaranteed investment certificates (GICs). In some cases term deposits may be withdrawn before the expiration date but at a penalty in the form of a reduced interest rate.

In their competition for deposit funds, the banks offer registered savings plans that allow individuals to shelter part of their interest income from current income taxes. Deposits held under the federal government's Registered

Retirement Savings Plan, and its Registered Home Ownership Savings Plan, before it was terminated, qualify for tax deferral shelter.

Nonpersonal Term and Notice Deposits

Nonpersonal deposits, including deposits held by one bank with another bank (these are called interbank deposits), are held by provincial and municipal governments, corporations, and institutions. Three classes of nonpersonal deposits exist: chequable and nonchequable notice deposits, bearer term notes, and other fixed-term deposits.

Nonpersonal chequable and nonchequable notice deposits are typically held by small business firms and are similar to personal chequable and nonchequable deposits. Bearer term notes, first introduced in 1964, are issued by the banks in multiples of $100 000 with maturities from 30 days to one year, and in bearer form (requiring no official registration when ownership changes). They are issued at a discount and mature at par so that the discount at which they are purchased determines the interest yield. Bearer term notes are bought by investment dealers and resold in the money market. Other fixed-term deposits, often referred to as Certificates of Deposit or CDs, are usually issued by the banks in multiples of $100 000. They bear interest at a specified rate and mature at a specified time, which may be anywhere from a few days to a year. Provision may be made for repayment upon call by the issuer, or after notice at the option of the registered owner, subject to an interest penalty.

Bearer term notes and Certificates of Deposit are referred to as the chartered bank "purchased" money or wholesale deposits. They were the most important source of funds for the small domestic chartered banks before their demise, and still are for the foreign bank subsidiaries that do not have large branch networks for the acceptance of retail deposits. Banks may use agents and brokers who are paid fees to solicit wholesale deposits for them. In this case the deposits purchased are referred to as **brokered deposits.**

brokered deposits *deposits placed by money brokers*

Government of Canada Deposits

The federal government holds its cash balances in the name of the receiver general with the Bank of Canada and the direct clearers of the Canadian Payments Association. As we will learn in a later chapter, the federal government does not use its deposits held at the direct clearers for chequing purposes. All its cheques are written against its deposits at the Bank of Canada, from which deposits to the direct clearers are transferred and retrieved.

In 1986 the Bank of Canada started to auction off to the direct clearers the federal government's cash balances in excess of daily requirements for fixed terms of one or more days, offering yields more attractive than those on demand deposits. In 1989 the Bank also started to auction off to direct clearers a share of the government's demand deposits held with it and the direct clearers. Direct clearers submit bids expressed in terms of an interest differential below the banks' prime rate for the share of government's demand deposits they want to receive each day over the next bimonthly reserve-averaging period.

As the federal government's banker, the Bank of Canada, through its regular auctions of these balances, attempts to minimize the cost to the government of holding cash balances. The Bank regularly conducts auctions of these federal government demand deposits so that the excess cash it holds for the receiver general gains interest.

Other Funding Transactions

In the mid-1990s, when interest rates began to fall and stabilize at lower levels, investors started to place more of their savings directly into capital markets, particularly in the form of mutual funds. As a result the banks experienced a process of **disintermediation**, whereby their customers' deposits declined or grew at a much smaller rate as investors and savers sought higher returns in capital markets.

disintermediation
loss of deposits by financial intermediaries because of higher returns in alternative capital market instruments

To fund their assets over the very short run as well as to generate trading revenue, the banks, as an alternative, sell securities short and sell securities under resale agreements (repos). The obligations by the banks related to these transactions are recorded as liabilities on their balance sheets. A short sale implies that the seller of a security does not own the security being sold but undertakes the obligation to acquire it before delivery has to be made to the purchaser. In a repo, a bank sells a security that it owns and undertakes a commitment to buy it back from the purchaser at a specified price in the future. A repo is a form of short-term funding.

Asset securitization is another relatively new form of funding employed by the banks. With securitization, the banks' illiquid loans, such as personal auto loans, are packaged in various ways for sale in securities markets. In addition to obtaining funds for new lending, securitization has an additional attraction for the banks in that in most instances, they receive management fees for continuing to service these loans.

Advances from the Bank of Canada

As we will learn in more detail when we discuss central banking, the Bank of Canada, in its role as lender of last resort, makes loans or advances to the chartered banks and other members of the Canadian Payments Association. These advances are made to meet unexpected cash deficiencies resulting from adverse clearing balances or a sudden withdrawal of deposits. Advances by the Bank of Canada usually remain outstanding to any one bank or other direct clearer for less than two weeks, and normally only for a day, at the end of a cash reserve averaging period. The Bank of Canada is allowed to make advances with initial terms of six months. After 1982, when some of the smaller regional banks experienced difficulties, and a loss of public confidence in them resulted in their inability to retain and attract wholesale deposits, the Bank made advances to them on a continuing basis.

Bankers' Acceptances

Unlike the other liabilities on the banks' balance sheets, bankers' acceptances are not a source of funds to finance their operations. As we learned previously, bankers' acceptances are commercial drafts drawn by corporate borrowers against their lines of credit with the banks and "accepted" by borrowers' banks. By accepting a commercial draft, a bank guarantees its payment and thereby has a contingent liability recorded on its balance sheet. However, because the customer or client on whose behalf the bank assumes a liability arranges with the bank to make payment in case the Bank actually has to pay a third party, an offsetting entry is recorded as an asset, as shown in Table 13.3.

Subordinated Debt

Subordinated debt is unsecured bank debt that ranks behind the claims of depositors and certain other creditors in the event of liquidation. The banks were given permission for the first time in the *Bank Act* revisions of 1967 to raise additional funds with the sale of their own debentures. However, certain restrictions apply: They may only be issued with a stated term of at least five years, during which time they may not be called, and the amount of debentures a bank has outstanding may not exceed one-half its equity.

Other Liabilities

This item, shown as part of the banks' consolidated liabilities in Table 13.2, includes the liabilities of the chartered banks' subsidiaries other than deposits, noncontrolling interest in subsidiaries, and all other liabilities not otherwise identified on the banks' balance sheets.

The Banks' Capital Funds

While a bank's capital funds are used to finance its operations, what is more important is that they provide a cushion of safety for depositors and other creditors in case the bank becomes insolvent. A bank is said to be insolvent when the value of its assets falls short of that of its liabilities. When a bank is first formed, the cushion of safety consists entirely of its paid-up capital (cash received from purchasers of its shares). For this reason, successive *Bank Act*s have specified the minimum amount of capital that must be contributed by shareholders before a bank can open its doors for business. It has been argued that an initial high capital requirement not only keeps out "fly-by-night" would-be bankers, but also encourages shareholders to take a personal interest and make sure that the bank is operated prudently. Before the 1967 revision to the *Bank Act*, bank directors were required to hold a substantial proportion of a bank's total shares outstanding. This requirement was dropped in 1967 because, as pointed out by the Porter Commission, it could prevent capable persons from serving as directors of a bank.

double liability *denotes that in case of bank failure, shareholders pay an additional amount equal to par value of shares*

www.

BIS Capital Accord *international agreement for minimum capital requirements for banks*

master netting agreements *agreement to sum all positive and negative values together to arrive at a net amount legally owed to or from a counterparty*

At one time stockholders of banks in both Canada and the United States were subject to **double liability;** in Canada this provision in the *Bank Act* expired in 1950. With the double-liability provision, if a bank failed, its stockholders lost not only their initial payment for the stock but, in addition, an amount equal to the stock's par value. The par value of a share is the value at which it is brought on the books of a bank at the time of its issue. The double-liability requirement was dropped because it discouraged the holding of bank shares, and because of the difficulty, if not the impossibility, of collecting the additional amounts from stockholders of a failed bank.

A bank's capital funds consist of shareholders' equity and subordinated debentures. Shareholders' equity includes capital stock (common and preferred shares), contributed surplus, which arises from the sale of shares above the value recorded in the bank's stock registers, and retained earnings.

The banks are required to include a provision for specific and expected credit losses each year in the calculation of their net income, which, in turn, is transferred to their retained earnings. The value of assets against which allowances for credit losses are made is marked down accordingly. Retained earnings after dividends have been paid constitute the banks' general reserves. When the reserves grow in excess of what is considered necessary to meet future contingencies, the excess may be transferred to contributed surplus.

As explained in Chapter 10, the superintendent of financial institutions has specified regulatory ratios of capital to risk-adjusted assets based on the guidelines developed by the Bank of International Settlements (BIS). By international agreements among regulators (the so-called **BIS Capital Accord**), the banks were required to have a Tier 1 ratio of at least 4 percent and a total capital ratio of at least 8 percent by the end of 1992. The Canadian banks satisfied these requirements well before the 1992 deadline and subsequently remained well above it.

In 1996 the BIS Capital Accord was amended to incorporate market risk. Beginning in 1998, Canadian banks were required to have minimum levels of capital for market risk inherent in their securities trading activities and the foreign exchange and commodity risks arising from their entire operations. A main feature of the Capital Accord amendment was to allow banks the use of proprietary in-house models to measure market risk for regulatory supervisory purposes.

Bank capital adequacy guidelines by the superintendent of financial institutions now also include certain standards for measuring capital required to support the credit risk exposure arising from derivatives. These standards recognize the risk-reducing benefits of legally enforceable **master netting agreements**. Under such agreements, if a counter-party defaults, a bank has the right to terminate all transactions with the counter-party at their current market value and then to sum all positive and negative current market values together to arrive at a single ("net") amount owed either to or from the counter-party. The banks' total assets also may not exceed 20 times their capital. This relative amount is referred to as the leverage ratio.

Uses of Funds

The way in which the banks employ their funds is reflected by the composition of the assets on their balance sheets. Remember, however, that a balance sheet is a snapshot of financial affairs at a given time. Although the overall composition of the banks' assets changes little from day to day, significant changes do take place in response to macroeconomic changes and in particular to conditions in money and capital markets. Financial innovation and competition, as well as government regulations, also affect the way the banks employ their funds. Finally, while we present a snapshot of the banks' assets in the consolidated balance sheet in Table 13.3, it does not show the differences among individual banks, and in particular among the large banks, the small banks, and the foreign bank subsidiaries.

Canadian Chartered Bank Assets

Canadian Dollar Liquid Assets

We have observed that a characteristic feature of the chartered banks' liabilities is the large proportion of money held in deposits that can be redeemed in cash on demand or on relatively short notice. The banks maintain two lines of defence to satisfy this requirement. The first is their cash reserves, also known as their primary reserves. These reserves consist of coin and Bank of Canada notes held in their vaults, tills, and automated bank machines, together with deposits at the Bank of Canada. The traditional legal minimum cash reserve requirement was completely phased out by the end of 1994. We'll touch on some of the history behind this decision later in the book. The amount of cash the banks actually hold has increased with the increase in the use of automated banking machines.

The chartered banks' second, and in practice most important, line of defence for paying on demand or short notice is their secondary reserves. These reserves consist primarily of money market instruments, which we have already described in a previous chapter. Included in their secondary reserves are Treasury bills and other government of Canada securities, day-to-day loans, and call and short loans.

In November 1955, the banks agreed to a request by the governor of the Bank of Canada that after June 1956, in addition to the legal cash reserve, each bank would maintain a minimum secondary reserve of Treasury bills and day-to-day loans equal to 7 percent of its Canadian dollar deposits. In 1967 the Bank of Canada was given statutory authority to require the banks to hold a minimum amount of secondary reserves, and in the 1980 revisions to the *Bank of Canada Act*, provision was made for the minister of finance to issue directives with respect to the adequacy of the chartered banks' liquidity. Existing legal secondary reserve requirements were abolished in 1992.

TABLE 13.3	**CANADIAN CHARTERED BANK ASSETS**
	Millions of Dollars, January 2000

Canadian Dollar Liquid Assets

Bank of Canada deposits, notes, and coin	4 545	
Treasury bills	18 049	
Other Government of Canada securities	56 789	
Call and short loans	578	
		79 961

Less Liquid Canadian Dollar Assets

Loans to federal government, provinces, and municipalities	2 653	
General loans		
Personal loans	105 782	
Business loans[1]	179 630	
		285 412
Leasing receivables	4 013	
Mortgage loans:		
Residential	245 073	
Nonresidential	13 904	
		258 977
Canadian securities	85 593	716 609

Other Assets

Canadian dollar deposits with other regulated financial institutions	17 660
Customer liability under acceptances	48 902
Canadian dollar items in transit (net)	–850
All other Canadian dollar assets	60 503
TOTAL Canadian dollar assets	842 824
TOTAL Foreign currency assets	558 952
TOTAL ASSETS	1 401 776

1. Of which 49 231 were reverse repos.

SOURCE: *Statistics Canada*, CANSIM Database, Matrix 00914, April 2000.

Bank Lending

As lenders, bankers traditionally took the view that they did not employ their own funds, but acted as custodians of funds entrusted to them by their creditors, especially their depositors. This placed on them a special responsibility to act prudently and to take care in assessing the creditworthiness of their borrowers. In general, creditworthiness was determined by the borrower's character, the quality and amount of collateral that was pledged as security, and the borrower's financial capacity as revealed by his or her past record and future prospects. While all these factors are still important determinants for placing a loan, today the banks also rely on the expected cash flow generated by the business or the project being financed for the repayment of their loans. During the 1980s, the banks got increasingly involved in so-called highly leveraged lending, where their loans were secured by the prospective cash flow of borrowers and by real estate that, typically, was in the process of being developed. Subsequently, when the economy and particularly real estate markets faltered, some of the banks experienced large losses.

commercial loan theory banks should make short-term self-liquidating loans

The lending activities of the chartered banks traditionally have been closely regulated by the government and as a rule have been restricted to those specifically authorized by the *Bank Act*. Early versions of this *Act* were based on the **commercial loan theory** of banking, also known as the real bills doctrine. As explained, the commercial loans theory held that banks should only make short-term, self-liquidating loans to commerce to finance the purchase of real goods. Although commercial lending is still the major activity of the chartered banks, successive revisions to the *Bank Act*, as we will learn, have authorized banks to enter many different lending fields.

pledge provisions historically a section in the Bank Act specifying assets the banks can accept to secure certain loans

Bank lending in Canada acquired some distinctive features because of the sections in the *Bank Act* known as the **pledge provisions**. These features trace their origin to the 1859 *Act Granting Additional Facilities to Commercial Transactions*. These pledge provisions were originally designed to enable banks to make loans to small businesses and farmers who could not provide traditionally acceptable collateral to secure loans.

The pledge provisions of the *Bank Act* set out the procedures by which a bank may lend on the security of goods in the process of being prepared for market, or on the security of a warehouse receipt or bill of lading. Under these provisions a bank is able to make loans on the security of natural products and goods, wares, and merchandise that remain in the borrower's possession. For example, section 426 of the *Bank Act* allows banks to lend money on the security of "hydrocarbons or minerals under or in the ground, in place or in storage," while section 427 allows the banks to make loans "to any farmer on the security of crops growing or produced on the farm…to any fisherman on the security of fishing vessels, fishing equipment and supplies, or products of the sea, lakes, and rivers.…" Without the pledge provisions of the *Bank Act*, prudent banking practices probably would have prevented the banks from assisting in the development of primary products to the extent that they have.

Periodically, the federal government has sponsored guaranteed loan plans to induce the banks to make loans to certain sectors or groups without charging higher interest rates to compensate them for what they considered to be higher risks. From 1867 to 1944 the banks were prohibited from charging more than 7 percent on their loans; in 1944 the ceiling was lowered to 6 percent; and in 1967 provision was made for its complete removal, which happened in January 1968.

The federal government's lending program, first introduced in 1937, includes Farm Improvement Loans, Fisheries Improvement Loans, Home Improvement Loans, Small Business Loans, Veterans' Business and Professional Loans, and Canada Student Loans. Under each program the government has provided the banks with guarantees against a certain proportion

BOX 13–1   BACKGROUNDER

Buddy, Can You Spare a Dime for an Economics Course?

Ottawa Resumes Control of Student Loan Program—Will Cost $155M More

BY ALAN TOULIN

OTTAWA: The federal government—facing the imminent collapse of the $1.5 billion annual Canada Student Loan Program—stepped in yesterday to take over direct financing of the program from banks and other lenders after an attempt to renegotiate a new five-year contract faltered.

Thomas Townsend, director general of Human Resources and Development Canada (HRDC), assured students there will be funds in place by August 1 when they start to apply for loans for the coming school year. It will cost taxpayers at least $155 million more for Ottawa to once again assume financial responsibility for the program, he added.

The federal government financed and administered the loan program from its inception in 1964 to 1995, when the government contracted with a group of financial institutions as partners in operating the program as a cost-saving measure.

About 450 000 students each year use student loans for university, college, and private vocational school education. Students don't start to repay the loans until six months after they graduate or leave an educational institution.

"We want to ensure there will be a student loans program in place on August 1," Mr. Townsend said at a news conference. "The service [students] have come to expect from the Canada Student Loans Program (CSLP) will be unaltered and, from a student's perspective, they won't see any change."

The federal government will borrow the $1.5 billion to finance student loans and will ask private sector bidders to take over the administration, record-keeping, and collections involved in the loan program.

Mr. Townsend said there are a number of financial service companies that could take on this business, including companies from the United States that specialize in student loan programs.

Assuming financial responsibility for the program isn't the best solution, Mr. Townsend said, but Ottawa had no choice since "there are insufficient financial institutions willing to participate in the program in its current form."

Over the past five years, the default rate on loans has soared, climbing to more than 30% in 1996 and hitting 27% in 1997. The higher-than-expected default rate prompted the financial institutions to ask for a better deal than the 5% risk premium in the contract. In negotiations, Ottawa and the lenders settled on a 9.75% premium rate to cover the expected future default rate and also built in additional protection should the loan loss rate be higher, Mr. Townsend said.

Three major banks—the Royal Bank, the Canadian Imperial Bank of Commerce, and the Bank of Nova Scotia—anchored the program during the past five years. A number of smaller financial institutions such as regional credit unions also participated. But sources said the Bank of Nova Scotia did not even respond in February when the Human Resources Department asked for bidders to renew the five-year deal.

HRDC, which is currently under pressure because of the ongoing grants scandal, attempted to find another financial institution to replace Scotiabank, but was unsuccessful, sources said.

Yesterday, officials from the Bank of Nova Scotia didn't respond to questions about their withdrawal from the program.

A Royal Bank representative said there weren't enough large banks participating in the program to share the risks of financing student loans.

Michael Conlon, chairman of the Canadian Federation of Students, welcomed Ottawa's return to direct financing as a positive change in policy.

SOURCE: *National Post*, March 10, 2000.

of their losses. In April 1997, the banks had $8 billion outstanding under the guaranteed loan programs still in existence at that time. Under the new Student Loan Plan of 1995, participating lenders faced the risk associated with loan repayment but received a 5 percent premium to cover possible losses. In March 2000, the federal government took control of the Canada Student Loan program. The banks found these loans too risky and decided to pull out of the program.

Business Loans

line of credit
commitment by a financial intermediary to stand ready to lend up to a specified amount to a customer

revolving credit
a contractual line of credit for longer periods than under a standard line of credit

Lending by the banks to businesses is usually facilitated by loan agreements. A business's credit needs are essentially recurrent and often unpredictable. To satisfy their ongoing needs for credit, businesses arrange a **line of credit** with their bankers, which is an expression of willingness by a bank to lend up to a specified maximum for agreed purposes. Under normal circumstances, lines of credit are extended for a period of one year and renewed from year to year. To avoid the necessity of frequent renegotiations, many businesses arrange revolving credits that are normally for longer periods and are used to obtain long-term working capital. Under a **revolving credit**, which is usually expressed in a formal contractual agreement, the borrower may pay a commitment fee on the unused portion of his or her line of credit in addition to the agreed-on rate of interest on the amount actually used.

The maturities of bank loans vary widely. Most loans made under lines of credit can be classified as demand loans, which remain outstanding for periods of less than five years and usually for no longer than one year. In addition to these loans, the banks make term loans, frequently to finance fixed investment. Loan agreements for term loans specify a fixed maturity and usually impose certain restrictions on the borrower, such as limiting the amount of other debt that can be incurred. Another requirement imposed on borrowers, which applies to most business loans, is to provide the bank with collateral so that if a loan is not repaid, the bank can sell the collateral to pay it off. The value of the collateral accepted usually exceeds the amount of the loan it secures. This additional value protects the bank in case the collateral's market value declines.

impaired *denotes when there is no reasonable assurance of repayment*

loan loss provision *the provision reducing the outstanding value of a loan in the books of a bank to its estimated realizable value*

When in the opinion of the bank it no longer has reasonable assurance of the timely collection of the full amount of principal and interest, a loan is classified as being **impaired**. When a loan becomes impaired bankers usually make a **loan loss provision** on their balance sheet and enter into a loan restructuring arrangement with the delinquent borrower.[3] This arrangement, frequently referred to as a workout, may require the borrower to pledge additional collateral and to observe limitations on his or her activities. To make it easier for the borrower to meet his or her obligations, the bank may also reschedule the loan by changing its terms with respect to the payment of interest and repayment of the principal amount.

The major Canadian banks have diversified loan portfolios that include loans to agriculture, fishing, and trapping; mines, quarries, and oil wells; manufacturing; construction; transportation, communications, and other utilities;

---

3. The book value of the loan is reduced to its estimated realizable amount. To estimate, the expected future cash flows are discounted using the interest rate inherent in the loan.

wholesale and retail trade; service industries; financial institutions including banks; and governments. The 1980 *Bank Act* for the first time authorized the banks to engage in financial leasing and factoring, but this has to be done through wholly owned subsidiaries. The banks' leasing subsidiaries borrow money in the market, or from the parent bank, to purchase capital equipment that they lease to their corporate and government clients.

While most of the banks established subsidiaries after 1980 to engage in factoring, by 1986 the majority of them had abandoned this type of activity. **Factoring** is a specialized financial service that involves the purchase or discounting of business accounts receivable and lending against receivables with an understanding to collect them. Although factoring has a long history, particularly in the textile industry, the banks did not find it profitable when they tried to extend its use to a broad range of commercial and industrial firms.

The interest rate that banks charge their borrowers traditionally was based on their **prime rate**, which was the interest rate that they typically charged their lowest-risk (prime) borrowers for short-term loans. In the 1980s, with the introduction of floating-rate loans, the prime rate lost much of its former importance. It is now used as a reference rate that is determined by money market conditions. The rate charged customers can be prime, a discount from prime, or "prime plus," depending on the degree of risk the bank associates with a loan. Loans are also frequently made on a cost-of-funds basis. Here, banks lend funds for a fixed period at a set markup over the rate they pay to raise the funds in the money market.

Banks and Small Business

In 1995, in response to public criticism, all of the major banks implemented codes of conduct that govern their relationship with small-business customers. These customers typically have loan authorizations of less than $500 000 and annual revenues of less than $5 million. The codes of conduct establish the minimum level of service that small and medium-sized business customers can expect from their bank. The codes of conduct have been accompanied by an alternative dispute-resolution mechanism for small-business customers who have complaints about the loss or reduction of credit or about a bank calling its security. To further enhance the effectiveness of the dispute resolution process, the banking industry in 1996 created the Office of Canadian Banking Ombudsman, which serves as an avenue of appeal for decisions made by the banks' own internal banking ombudsmen.

The banks have entered into strategic alliances with the federal government's Business Development Bank to help small knowledge-based and high-growth firms enter export markets. Knowledge-based firms depend on technology and innovation to produce competitive products. To service these businesses, each of the major banks has established specialized lending units with access to venture capital.

The banks have also worked with the governments' Export Development Corporation to develop risk-sharing programs to help small- and medium-sized businesses export their products. One such framework provides smaller exporters with a secure operating line of credit of up to $500 000 against the value of their foreign receivables.

factoring the purchase of receivables at a discount and the lending against receivables with an understanding to collect them

prime rate the interest rate the banks traditionally charged their most creditworthy borrowers

www.

Personal Loans

Before the 1950s, because the Canadian chartered banks considered themselves guardians of the savings of individuals and households, they reluctantly extended loans to them. In fact, many bankers looked on loans for consumer purchases with suspicion and felt that it was somewhat immoral for a person to buy something before the money was earned and saved. Since then both the bankers' and the public's views have changed, and consumer credit has become an important way of life. The authority to take chattel mortgages in 1954 and the removal of the 6 percent ceiling on bank charges in 1967 opened the doors for the banks to engage in consumer lending.

Today the banks are the most important lenders to individuals and households; almost 60 percent of all consumer credit outstanding is being provided by the banks. Loans to individuals for nonbusiness purposes are used to purchase or carry securities and to purchase goods and services. Some 50 percent of all personal loans are made under a **personal loan plan**. These loans usually have a fixed interest rate and fixed term and are fully repaid in instalments over a period of six months to five years. They are usually secured by marketable securities, motor vehicles, or other household property.

personal loan plan *an arrangement under which a bank provides loans to individuals*

A major form of loans to individuals is through bank credit cards; such loans now account for almost 14 percent of the banks' personal loans. Each month credit card purchasers receive a statement for payment within 25 days, during which time no interest is charged. Cardholders are permitted to defer payment under a specified line of credit, and are thereby offered a flexible and informal method of obtaining bank loans on a broad range of purchases and on cash advances. Government regulations specify how the banks must disclose information with respect to borrowing costs to their customers.

Another form of loan to individuals is a variable-rate personal line of credit plan. Individuals can arrange for a line of credit similar to that for a credit card, but usually for much higher amounts.

Residential Mortgage Loans

Early disastrous experiences of banks lending on the security of real estate, particularly in the United States, induced governments, almost without exception, to prohibit banks from making loans with mortgage security, save as subsequent security. Following the revisions to the *National Housing Act* (NHA) and the *Bank Act* in 1954, Canadian banks were allowed to acquire mortgages to secure loans made under NHA terms. After some initial reluctance the banks became major mortgage lenders for a short period, until the maximum rates permitted on NHA mortgages were raised above the rates the banks were allowed to charge under the *Bank Act*. The banks could have taken mortgages at less than the maximum rate set under the *National Housing Act,* but this would have created such a rush for loans that they would have been unable to ration their funds equitably. As a result they virtually withdrew from the direct financing of residential construction.

In 1967 the banks' authority to make residential mortgage loans was extended to include conventional mortgages, with two limitations: (1) the total amount of any such loans a bank could have outstanding was restricted to 10 percent of its Canadian dollar deposits and outstanding debentures, and (2) mortgage loans were limited to a maximum of 75 percent of the mortgaged property's value, unless repayment was otherwise guaranteed or insured. The latter limitation still applies today. After the banks were freed from legal interest rate ceilings on their loans and were allowed to make conventional loans, they rapidly became the most important lenders for new residential construction. To prevent themselves from being locked into illiquid mortgage loans, and to be able to expand their mortgage origination beyond the amounts they were allowed to hold in their own asset portfolios, the banks formed affiliated mortgage loan companies. These companies, which after 1980 had to become wholly owned by their parent bank, are passive mortgage lenders in that they usually purchase all of their mortgages from the parent bank.

The chartered banks have become significant originators of residential mortgage loans; mortgages held by them represent some 55 percent of the total outstanding balances of the major private institutional lenders. The banks originate mortgages for their own portfolio, for their mortgage loan company affiliates, and for other financial institutions. Residential mortgage loans originated by the banks are also used for the issue of mortgage-backed securities.

Investments

Since the banks consider lending to be one of their primary functions, holding securities for other than liquidity purposes has been generally considered residual to their lending activities. Their security holdings include medium-term Government of Canada direct and guaranteed bonds, and provincial, municipal, and corporate securities. Although all these securities are usually acquired to obtain good yields, they are used sometimes to assist in underwriting and marketing, and more recently as a competitive alternative to bank lending.

The 1991 revisions to the *Bank Act* have allowed the banks to hold a substantial investment (defined generally as more than 10 percent of the voting shares or greater than 25 percent of equity) in permitted subsidiaries. The banks, however, are limited as to the total amount of real property and common shares in which they may invest. Investments in either real property or common shares (not including those of permitted subsidiaries) may not exceed 70 percent of a bank's capital, while the total of both may not exceed 100 percent. In addition to these limits, banks are restricted in their investments to what is referred to as a prudential portfolio approach. This approach requires them to pursue an approved plan of investment encompassing a well-diversified and risk-minimizing strategy. This investment plan is judged based on what a reasonable person would do in similar circumstances.

The banks make a distinction between investment account securities and trading account securities. Investment account securities are held with the original intention to hold the securities to maturity or until market conditions render alternative investments more attractive. Trading account securities, on the other hand, are held for resale over a short period. Securities for trading are generally held to meet short-term liquidity risk management requirements and are part of the banks' Canadian dollar liquid assets shown in Table 13.3.

In 1999 the government announced it would allow financial institutions to organize within holding company structures. A **holding company** is usually a firm that does not produce any output but simply owns other firms that do operate and produce output. The new holding company structures will be allowed to undertake investments that are much wider than those currently allowed. For example, activities can take place outside the bank: Consumer and corporate loans, investment counselling, real estate brokerage, and armoured car transportation are just some of the activities that will be permitted under the changes introduced in 2000.

holding company
a firm that does not produce any output but owns other firms that do produce goods and services

Other Canadian Dollar Assets

Apart from the major assets discussed so far, the banks' balance sheet contains a number of other assets listed in Table 13.3. Included is customer liability under acceptances, which is the counterpart of the acceptance listed as a liability. When a bank accepts a draft from a customer, the customer incurs a liability to the bank; this becomes an asset for the bank. Also included are Canadian dollar operating or other deposit balances with other banks (interbank loans), and bank premises.

Off-Balance Sheet Transactions

In recent years banks have increasingly provided services to their customers that are not recorded on their balance sheets except for the fees that they generate, which are included in their net income. While these off-balance-sheet activities have become an important source of revenue, they also have exposed the banks to additional risks in the form of contingent liabilities.

guarantees and letters of credit assurances given by a bank that it will make payments on behalf of customers to third parties in the event that the customers default

The banks give conditional commitments to provide funds to their customers for various lengths of time under specified conditions. Credit instruments used for this purpose are typically **guarantees and letters of credit** by a bank in favour of a third party. For example, a bank customer undertakes to provide funds to a third party; should the customer be unable to satisfy the obligation, the bank assumes it. Another indirect credit instrument offered is a conditional guarantee to extend credit under **revolving underwriting facilities** (RUF) or **note-issuance facilities** (NIF). Under these facilities a bank typically promises to extend credit to a customer should alternative sources of finance prove to be inadequate or too costly.

revolving underwriting facilities (RUF) or note-issuance facilities (NIF) undertakings by a bank when a customer issues short-term notes and, if unable to sell the notes at a prescribed price, the bank then buys them at that price

Other fee-generating off-balance-sheet transactions include interest rate and cross-currency swaps, financial futures, forward-rate agreements, foreign exchange–forward contracts, and foreign currency and interest rate options.

The banks enter these derivative contracts as part of the sales and trading activities to provide their clients with the ability to manage their risk exposure. As we saw in Chapter 10, the banks also use derivatives to manage their own asset–liability risk exposure.

Foreign Currency Operations of Banks in Canada

Canadian banks have been involved in accepting deposits and extending loans denominated in foreign currencies for more than 100 years. In the mid-nineteenth century, Canadian banks established their presence in the main international financial centres of London and New York to facilitate the foreign exchange requirements of their customers engaged in foreign trade, to arrange loans for Canadian governments, and to invest their liquid assets. In New York, agencies of Canadian banks accepted deposits and lent funds to U.S. residents, mainly in the broker call loan market, passing them through their books at their Canadian head offices. At about the same time, with the development of trade with the Caribbean and Central and South America, Canadian banks were the first to introduce banking to these areas. They established extensive branch networks to conduct domestic banking operations, most of which have since been nationalized by local governments. It was not until after the Second World War, and in particular during the past three decades, that the major Canadian banks expanded worldwide. In 1991, they had 300 foreign branches in addition to representative offices, agencies, subsidiaries, and associated companies in more than 55 countries.

The transformation of the major Canadian banks from primarily domestic to large and diversified transnational institutions is reflected in the growth of their foreign currency assets. By the mid-1980s, these assets accounted for some 45 percent of the total (domestic and foreign) assets of all Canadian banks and were important factors contributing to their earnings. Since then this percentage has declined. The decline resulted mainly from reduced lending as well as write-offs and sell-offs of existing loans following the debt crisis of the 1980s in the developing countries. However, the banks' foreign currency activities remain a significant contributor to their net income.

The composition of the banks' foreign currency assets and liabilities is shown in Table 13.4. Most of their foreign currency liabilities are "wholesale" deposits denominated in U.S. dollars. These large-denomination term deposits are accepted from other banks, multinational corporations, governments, and large institutional customers in Eurocurrency markets. These markets are described later in the book.

The 1980 *Bank Act* imposed for the first time a 3 percent reserve requirement against residents' foreign deposits booked in Canada.[4] Before the imposition of this requirement, the major proportion of the foreign currency deposits booked by Canadian residents was in the form of swapped deposits. A swapped deposit is a special Canadian dollar deposit that the bank converts into foreign currency, usually U.S. dollars for investment in the United States. The Canadian depositor assumes no foreign currency risk because the bank enters into a foreign exchange contract to convert the funds back into Canadian dollars at maturity of the foreign investment. The interest offered by the banks to their Canadian customers on swapped deposits combines the cost of forward cover with the yield on the foreign investment. Swapped deposits allow Canadians to take advantage of higher interest rates outside Canada without having to undertake any foreign exchange risk.

---

4. Of course today there are no reserve requirements against deposits in Canadian chartered banks.

TABLE 13.4	CHARTERED BANKS: TOTAL FOREIGN CURRENCY ASSETS AND LIABILITIES
	Millions of Canadian Dollars, January 2000

Assets

Call loans	11 918
Other loans	257 696
Securities	139 062
Deposits with banks	72 748
Other assets	77 521
	558 946

Liabilities

Deposits of banks	132 128
Other deposits	301 156
Other liabilities	151 500
	584 784
Net Foreign Assets	−25 838

Note: Errors due to rounding

SOURCE: *Statistics Canada,* CANSIM Database, Matrix 00920, April 2000.

More recently, the chartered banks, especially the foreign bank subsidiaries, have issued liabilities, in addition to accepting deposits, in Eurocurrency markets to fund their foreign currency lending operations. The foreign bank subsidiaries use guarantees from their parent bank to make their issues more attractive in international markets.

The foreign currency assets of the chartered banks include gold coin and bullion, foreign currency notes and coin, deposits denominated in foreign currencies, foreign-pay securities issued by Canadian borrowers, short-term loans such as day and call loans to investment dealers and stockbrokers, medium-term syndicated and other loans, and investments in foreign affiliates and subsidiaries. Foreign assets do not include bank premises abroad.

A major vehicle for lending by the banks in international markets has been syndicated credit, whereby a line of credit is extended by a group or a syndicate of banks rather than by a single bank. Participation in syndicated credits was viewed by banks in the early 1980s as a sign of prestige. The major Canadian banks, in addition to being members of syndicates, also initiate and manage them. The interest rate charged on these credits is usually based on the London Interbank Offered Rate (LIBOR). This rate is posted by the major banks in London and serves as an international "prime rate." The federal government has periodically arranged syndicated credits with the Canadian banks to replenish its foreign exchange reserves.

The chartered banks have also used their foreign currency deposits and borrowing to finance their domestic Canadian dollar loans. This is reflected in the banks' balance sheets when their total foreign currency liabilities exceed their total foreign currency assets (see Table 13.4). The foreign bank subsidiaries in particular have borrowed abroad to finance their Canadian dollar assets. The inspector general of banks had set a guideline limiting their foreign currency sources of funds to 50 percent of their Canadian dollar assets.

During the 1970s and early 1980s, a large proportion of the banks' international lending was to foreign governments and their agencies in the less-developed countries. By 1981 roughly 13 percent of the major assets of the domestically owned Canadian banks represented claims on developing countries. The banks' claims on 45 of the most heavily indebted countries rose from $15.6 billion at the end of 1980 to a peak of $27.5 billion at the end of 1985, before declining to $12.7 billion at the end of June 1991.[5] Most of the banks' exposure was concentrated in a relatively small group of middle-income countries, in particular Mexico, Brazil, Venezuela, Argentina, and Chile.

As we will learn later, with the world experiencing economic recession and a severe drop in oil prices during the early 1980s, many of the developing countries experienced difficulties servicing their loans from the banks (paying interest and repaying principal). This difficulty resulted in the international debt crisis. From the beginning of this crisis, the Canadian banks played a leading role in rescheduling the debts of the developing countries. They also reduced their exposure by selling their loans to developing countries on secondary markets, and by entering into debt-for-equity swaps. More recently they have also participated with other international banks in debt and debt-service reduction programs.

In 1984, the then-inspector general of banks asked the chartered banks to set up special reserves by October 1986 equal to 10 to 15 percent of their total loans to 34 designated indebted countries. This guideline was subsequently increased and for 1991 was set at 35 to 45 percent of the banks' exposure to 45 designated countries. The six major Canadian banks responded by actually setting aside $8.6 billion in reserves against their exposure of $12.4 billion to these countries. This amount exceeded by a wide margin the guidelines set by the Office of the Superintendent of Financial Institutions.

Because of their lending experiences with the less-developed countries, the banks have rationalized their overseas operations and withdrawn from certain countries or focused their activities more narrowly. Instead of granting general loans to governments (sovereign loans) they have focused on the more traditional types of international activities of trade financing and project lending. The major Canadian banks have also focused more of their international activities on the United States.

Banks Become Multiservice Institutions

Over the past few decades the Canadian chartered banks have evolved to become multiservice institutions offering a wide range of financial and related services to the public. This change can be attributed to financial deregulation, which has expanded their powers, and to increased domestic and foreign competition. In addition the banks have been able to take advantage of advances in

---

5. See James Powell. "The Evolution of Canadian Bank Claims on Heavily Indebted Developing Countries," *Bank of Canada Review* (November 1991), pp. 3–20.

computer and communications technology, and have seen greater financial sophistication on the part of corporations and individuals. Deregulation has allowed the banks to increase the variety of services they provide in-house through their branches and subsidiary institutions, as shown in Box 13–2.

BOX 13–2   CHARTERED BANK PERMISSIBLE SUBSIDIARIES

Subsidiaries	*Activities*
Securities dealers	• dealing in securities
Mortgage loan companies	• lending money on the security of real estate
Trust companies	• providing trust services
	• acting as receiver and liquidator
Insurance companies	• developing and marketing insurance products (including life annuities)
Mutual fund corporations	• investing of mutual funds
Mutual fund distribution corporations	• selling units, shares, or interests in mutual funds
Specialized financing corporations	• providing specialized management services
	• offering merchant banking
	• offering venture capital investment
	• providing financing and advisory services
Real property corporations	• holding, managing, and dealing in real property
Information services corporations	• providing information processing services
	• designing, developing, and marketing computer software
	• designing, developing, manufacturing, and selling ancillary hardware
Investment counselling and portfolio management corporations	• providing advice on investments
	• investing with discretion over money, property, deposits, and securities
Real property brokerage corporations	• acting as real estate agent
	• providing consulting and appraisal services
Financial leasing corporations	• leasing personal property other than automobiles and personal household property
Service corporations	• providing services to the bank and its financial subsidiaries
	• financing accounts receivable

As we have already seen, before the 1950s the chartered banks primarily offered the traditional banking services: deposit-taking and payment services and lending, mostly for commercial purposes. In the 1950s they started, somewhat reluctantly, to extend consumer credit and residential mortgage loans. It was only after the removal in 1967 of the ceiling on the interest rate they could charge on their loans, and after they received the authority to make conventional residential mortgage loans, that the banks moved aggressively into consumer credit and residential mortgage lending. Their provision of financial services to individuals in addition to their traditional corporate customers was enhanced with the introduction of credit cards in 1967.

Under the 1992 *Bank Act* revisions, the banks were allowed to offer their customers financial planning, investment counselling, and portfolio management services in-house. They were also authorized to promote merchandise and services to their payment, credit, and charge card holders.

The multiservice nature of Canadian banks has expanded as they have used their new powers granted in the 1992 *Bank Act* revisions to establish subsidiaries to provide financial and related services that were previously not permitted. A more detailed discussion of the services provided by some of these subsidiaries, shown in Box 13–2, is presented later in the book.

Aside from mortgage loan companies, factoring corporations, financial leasing corporations, venture capital corporations, real estate investment corporations, and investment dealers, all of which were added earlier to the list of permissible subsidiaries, the remaining subsidiaries were additions made to the list of permissible institutions resulting from the 1992 revisions to the *Bank Act*. Although restrictions remain, the banks have been able to retail the services of their affiliated institutions at their branches through networking arrangements. Restrictions still apply to the retailing of insurance products apart from those related to credit. Nor are the banks allowed to engage in any personal property leasing activity such as the leasing of automobiles.

The revisions introduced in June 2000 did not meet many of the banks' expectations regarding car leasing and insurance distribution. They had expected the government would allow them to compete with the financial subsidiaries of U.S. car manufacturers, but the legislation did not allow them "…the opportunity to give customers more competition and more choice in the insurance and car leasing area."[6]

In summary, the Canadian chartered banks, which historically were financial intermediaries, now also are capital market intermediaries. Not only are they personal and corporate bankers, but they have also become investment bankers and merchant bankers. In addition, they have become insurers and risk managers as well as administrators and managers of a wide variety of assets. In their transition, an increasing proportion of their revenue is in the form of income from fees and commissions rather than from the interest spread between their deposits and loans.

---

6. Macklem, K. "Bankers Agree Legislation Is Balanced and Step in Right Direction," *Financial Post,* Wednesday June 14, 2000, p. C9.

Electronic and Virtual Banking

The traditional delivery of routine commercial banking services at the hands of tellers standing behind counters at bank branches is rapidly disappearing. It was estimated that by 1997 the Canadian banks already were delivering some 85 percent of their banking products and services to their customers electronically.

electronic banking *banking done by telephone, direct deposit, debit cards, payment cards, ABM, or personal computer*

Electronic banking includes the use of automated banking machines, touch-tone telephone deposits, debit cards for point-of-sale payments, and personal computer banking employing private networks on the Internet. With recent advances in encryption technology that ensures confidentiality and security of information, it is expected that Internet and interactive television will become the predominant ways to deliver online financial services.

electronic data interchange (EDI) *a system that companies use to exchange business information electronically*

Canadian financial institutions have established a system that allows corporate clients to exchange payments and information electronically. This system is called **electronic data interchange** (EDI). The EDI reduces the cost of writing cheques and processing the related paperwork. It also speeds up payment flows.

virtual banking *where all banking services are delivered electronically*

Virtual banking is the delivery of banking services electronically, without the need of a branch bank. In August 1996, the Vancouver Savings Credit Union turned its Citizens Trust Company into a chartered bank to become Canada's first virtual, or branchless, bank. In October of the same year, the Bank of Montreal followed by setting up a separate division of the bank called m̲banx to provide virtual banking.

www.

Virtual banking gives individuals the convenience of 24-hour access, seven days a week, to banking services from any location served by touch-tone telephone or cable. From the banks' point of view, electronic banking has reduced transaction costs and provided a new source of income from fees charged. The banks also have been able to realize economies of scale and scope by applying their electronic technology to the delivery of services and products of their wholly owned subsidiaries, particularly the trading of securities, the sale of mutual funds, and the marketing of insurance products.

With the growth of electronic and virtual banking, the major Canadian banks have begun to reduce and transform their branches. In many cases, branches have been reconfigured to accommodate the delivery of the nontraditional banking services, especially those of their subsidiaries.

The Anatomy of Bank Failure

In September 1985 the Canadian Commercial Bank (CCB) was placed in liquidation, as was the Northland Bank in January of the following year. The CCB failure was the first for a Canadian bank in more than 60 years. The previous failure had been that of the Home Loan Bank of Canada in 1923. During 1985–86 three other banks—the Mercantile Bank of Canada, the Continental Bank of Canada, and the Bank of British Columbia experienced financial difficulties, and no doubt escaped ultimate liquidation by being taken over by other banks.

The failures of the two banks that were liquidated have similar characteristics. Both banks were formed in the 1970s in response to the demands from Western Canada for regional banks more attuned to their needs. As it turned out, the existing banks were already satisfying most of the legitimate lending requirements. The newer banks, in their desire to expand rapidly, extended loans with risks typically considered unacceptable by prudent bankers. Moreover, the newer banks undertook large loans concentrated in the cyclical, sensitive resource and real estate sectors in Western Canada, which were enjoying boom conditions at the time. When the Canadian economy experienced a sharp decline after 1981 and petroleum prices fell dramatically, many of the banks' borrowers were unable to meet their debt obligations. In their formative years, both banks committed a significant transgression of prudent banking: In their desire to grow quickly they accumulated loan portfolios that contained relatively large risky loans that were both sectorially and geographically undiversified. Furthermore, these loans were financed with fickle wholesale deposits. When a large proportion of these loans became nonperforming (that is, borrowers were unable to pay interest and meet scheduled principal repayments on time from their own funds), the banks introduced survival tactics that went well beyond the lines of proper and prudent banking practice. These survival tactics entailed "creative accounting" to give the appearance of the financial health necessary to hold depositors, who would be susceptible to flight at the first sign of trouble. Their survival tactics involved unorthodox banking practices with respect to interest capitalization and accrual, the setting of loan loss provisions, and the valuation of loans and the collateral securing them.

Capitalization of interest means adding unpaid interest to the principal value of a loan; the accrual of interest means adding interest to a bank's current income even though it has not been received by the bank. By capitalizing and accruing interest that was uncollected, the CCB and the Northland Bank added questionable value to the assets on their balance sheets and increased their stated income. While it is acceptable practice to provide loan agreements for interest capitalization during the initial years of some loans, both banks followed an unorthodox practice of capitalizing interest on loans after they were already in default and when the resulting accumulated amount of principal outstanding exceeded the value of the security collateralizing the outstanding amount.

It is also acceptable accounting practice for banks to count as income any interest that is due but not received, if it is less than 90 days overdue, or longer if there is little doubt of its eventual collectability. If subsequently its collection is considered improbable and it is classified as nonaccruing, interest previously accrued to income is reversed. Both banks followed the questionable practice of accruing interest long after 90 days, when there should have been little doubt that it could not be collected. Moreover, when they finally classified loans as nonaccruing, they did not immediately reverse interest on their income statements. By this deception they were able to show profitability when in reality this was far from a true picture.

It is also common practice for banks to classify loans as nonperforming (or simply bad) when the borrower's ability to pay becomes doubtful and when the value of the assets securing a loan falls substantially below the amount of its outstanding value. When loans are classified as nonperforming, prudent banking practice dictates that specific loss provisions be taken or that loans be written off the bank's balance sheets. The CCB and the Northland Bank at times used imaginative procedures to ascribe inflated and unrealistic values to bad loans or the assets securing them to avoid setting up specific loan loss provisions. In some instances no loss provision was taken even when the borrower was in receivership. The avoidance of the loan loss provision, as well as the reluctance to write off bad loans, also overstated the recorded value of their assets and their current income. The banks attempted to increase their income with fees earned from restructuring nonperforming loans and placing new loans. The Northland Bank hoped that by adding new loans it could dilute the nonperforming loans in its loan portfolio as a proportion of its total loans outstanding. However, when the banks' new loans rapidly became nonperforming as a result of the protracted economic recession, the additional fee income could not mask their underlying difficulties. Since the practices followed by the managers of the two banks were contrary to generally accepted accounting principles, you would have expected their board of directors and outside auditors and the inspector general of banks to impose corrective measures. But they either were not aware of what was going on until it was too late, or lacked the will to take appropriate action. On March 14, 1985, the general manager of the CCB reported to the governor of the Bank of Canada and the Office of the Inspector General of Banks that his bank could not survive unless "massive assistance was provided." Ten days later a $255 million support program for the bank was arranged without the participants being aware of the true state of the bank's affairs. If the magnitude of the bank's nonperforming loans had been known, the liquidity support probably would not have been undertaken.

Following the CCB bailout, professional money managers correctly assumed that the Northland Bank was in a similar situation and withdrew their deposits. During the summer months the Bank of Canada increasingly replaced the deposits of both banks with its advances. At the end of August, after more thorough inspections of both banks confirmed their "bizarre banking practices" and a last-minute attempt to find a merger partner for the Northland Bank proved unsuccessful, the Bank of Canada withdrew its liquidity support, and both banks were liquidated. The demise of the two banks resulted in a continual run on deposits of the Continental Bank of Canada and the Mercantile Bank of Canada. Although both these banks were soundly run, depositors associated their size and regional or sectorial concentrations with those of the two failures. When it was shown that regaining public confidence would be prolonged and difficult, mergers with other banks were successfully concluded.

In the aftermath of the failure of the CCB and the Northland Bank, the Bank of British Columbia also ran into difficulties that forced it to borrow some $97 million from the Bank of Canada. The public's growing loss of confidence in its operations was associated with its nonperforming loans related to the recession in Western Canada. In November 1986, after a merger partner could not be found, the bank's board of directors arranged to sell the bank's assets to the Hongkong Bank of Canada. The Canada Deposit Insurance Corporation advanced $200 million to cover potential future losses on the Bank of British Columbia's loan portfolio.

What lessons can be learned from this anatomy of bank failure? First, banks with poor quality and inadequately diversified asset portfolios financed by wholesale deposits are fragile financial institutions. Second, banks must be regulated and supervised to ensure that they are managed prudently. Third, liquidity support for banks that are no longer profitable, and indeed are insolvent, only postpones their eventual liquidation and thereby increases the social cost of bank failure. Finally, a bank can operate successfully only as long as the public has confidence in its soundness as well as in the soundness of the banking system.

KEY TERMS

BIS Capital Accord
brokered deposits
commercial loan theory
current accounts
disintermediation
double liability
electronic banking
electronic data interchange (EDI)

factoring
guarantees and letters of credit
holding company
impaired
line of credit
loan loss provision
master netting agreements
personal loan plan

pledge provisions
prime rate
revolving credit
revolving underwriting facilities or note-issuance facilities
virtual banking

REVIEW QUESTIONS

1. Distinguish between Schedule I banks and Schedule II banks.
2. What requirements must be met before a new foreign bank subsidiary is permitted to operate in Canada?
3. What was the function of the Office of the Inspector General of Banks (OIGB)? What was it replaced by, and how does the replacement differ from the OIGB?
4. What are the major sources of chartered bank funds?
5. What are the banks' capital funds? How do they protect the safety of the banks' deposits?
6. What are the "pledge provisions" of the *Bank Act*?
7. What are some of the major characteristics of chartered bank lending to business? to households?
8. Describe the foreign currency operations of Canadian banks.
9. Describe the banks' off-balance-sheet activities.

10. What were the major causes of bank failure in 1985–86?
11. How did the 1999 proposals for changes to the Canadian financial sector affect the chartered banks? Choose one proposal and write a two-page summary of how it is expected to change the way banks behave.
12. Explain what is meant by double liability. Would a restoration of this principle lead to a more stable banking system? Why or why not?
13. Can chartered banks sell insurance in their branches? Why or why not?
14. This question involves some research. Did chartered banks have the lion's share of the residential mortgage market in Canada in 2000? If not, why not? What changes led to an expansion of the banks' mortgage activities? Why were they introduced?

SELECTED READINGS

Armstrong, Jim. "The Changing Business Activities of Banks in Canada." *Bank of Canada Review* (Spring 1997), pp. 11–38.

Binhammer, H.H., and Jane Williams. *Deposit-Taking Institutions: Innovation and the Process of Change.* Ottawa: Economic Council of Canada, 1977.

Canadian Bankers' Association. *Bank Facts: The Chartered Banks of Canada.* Toronto, various years.

Department of Finance. *Reforming Canada's Financial Services Sector—A Framework for the Future.* Ottawa: Author, 1999.

Economic Council of Canada. *Efficiency and Regulations: A Study of Deposit Institutions.* Ottawa: Minister of Supply and Services Canada, 1976.

———. *Globalization and Canada's Financial Markets: A Research Report.* Ottawa: Minister of Supply and Services Canada, 1989.

Galbraith, J.A. *The Economics of Banking Operations: A Canadian Study.* Montreal: McGill University Press, 1963.

Macklem, K., "Bankers Agree Legislation Is Balanced and Step in Right Direction." *Financial Post,* Wednesday, June 14, 2000, p. C9.

Report of the Royal Commission on Banking and Finance. Ottawa: Queen's Printer and Controller of Stationery, 1964.

Rose, Peter S. *Commercial Bank Management: Producing and Selling Financial Services.* Homewood, Ill.: Richard D. Irwin, 1991.

Superintendent of Financial Institutions. *Annual Report.* Ottawa: Minister of Supply and Services Canada, various years.

Toulin, A. "Ottawa Resumes Control of Student Loan Program—Will Cost $155M More." *National Post,* March 10, 2000.

CHAPTER FOURTEEN

THE NEAR-BANKS

After reading this chapter you should be able to
1. *Outline the history and operations of credit unions and caisses populaires*
2. *Explain the history and functions of trust companies and mortgage loan companies*
3. *Explain why so many trust and mortgage loan companies have failed*
4. *Identify government savings institutions*

Near-banks are financial institutions that do most of the same financial intermediation as the banks, but by law are not allowed to call themselves banks. They are payments intermediaries that accept deposits from the public and make loans to businesses and especially, households. The near-banks include trust companies, mortgage loan companies, credit unions and caisses populaires, and government savings institutions.

The Montreal City and District Savings Bank (La banque d'épargne de la cité et du district de Montréal), before it became part of the Laurentian Bank of Canada in 1988, was the last institution to operate under the federal government's *Quebec Savings Banks Act*. Legislation to encourage the establishment of savings banks dates back to 1841. The early legislation restricted the operations of savings banks geographically; and to ensure the safety of individuals' savings accepted on deposit, savings banks were required to invest those deposits in government securities. Over the years the savings banks were absorbed by the chartered banks, whose activities evolved to encompass both businesses and households.

Credit Unions and Caisses Populaires

History and Structure

Caisses populaires and credit unions are financial cooperatives that trace their origins to the mutual savings bank movement in Europe during the eighteenth century and the people's bank movement during the nineteenth century. The first of these movements stressed the virtues of mutuality and thrift; the second, those of cooperation, self-help, and the democratic structure of management. In contrast to the savings banks, which were oriented toward encouraging the habit of saving, the people's banks emphasized the provision of credit facilities for the "little man." In Canada, the early formation of caisses populaires closely followed the concept of the European savings banks, while credit unions were modelled on the European people's banks.

The first Canadian financial cooperative was founded in Lévis, Quebec, by Alphonse Desjardins in 1900. Today two distinct cooperative credit movements exist: the caisses populaires centred in Quebec, and the credit unions in the rest of Canada. Sixty-five percent of the population of Quebec are members of caisses, and almost one-third of the population of the rest of Canada belongs to credit unions. Each movement has organized itself into a three-tier structure.

At the base of the caisse populaire structure in Quebec are some 1300 autonomous local caisses that provide financial services directly to their members, who must reside within the boundaries of a city or provincial electoral district. Membership also requires the purchase of at least one redeemable share of a local caisse. The original bond of association for all caisses was a parish. Membership in a caisse d'économie, of which there are only a few, is based on the bond of occupation or employer.

The local caisses are organized into 11 federations; 10 are regional Fédérations des caisses populaires Desjardins, and the other is la Fédération des caisses d'économie Desjardins. All federations have combined to form the Confédération des caisses populaires et d'économie Desjardins du Québec. The federations provide technical and financial services, and liquidity support in the form of loans and credit guarantees to their member caisses. Local caisses are required to hold deposits with their federations equal to a specified amount of their members' deposits and shares. The federations in turn must hold deposits with the La caisse centrale Desjardins du Québec, the central financial management facility of the caisse populaire movement in Quebec. In addition to providing liquidity support in the form of loans to the federations, the Caisse centrale Desjardins du Québec is for the caisses a direct clearer of the Canadian Payments Association.

The third or top tier of the caisse populaire movement in Quebec is the Desjardins Group. It consists of the Confédération des caisses populaires et caisses d'économie Desjardins du Québec together with affiliated financial and service organizations. These organizations include insurance companies, trust companies, and a securities firm whose financial services are offered by the local caisses to their members. Also included is the Corporation de fonds de sécurité de la confédération Desjardins, which, along with the federations, is responsible for stabilization services for the system. These services relate to loans and grants to local caisses experiencing solvency problems, and to the payment of insurance premiums to the Quebec Deposit Insurance Board, which guarantees members' deposits. On December 4, 1999, the member caisses of 10 federations approved a plan to amalgamate their federations and the confederation into a single new federation, effective July 1, 2001.[1]

---

1. The member caisses of the Fédération des caisses d'économie Desjardins du Québec did not approve the participation of their federation in the proposed amalgamation.

In English-speaking Canada, the credit union movement was initially conceived in the late 1920s at St. Francis Xavier University in Antigonish, Nova Scotia. Locals were organized in farming and fishing communities in much the same way as caisses populaires had been established in the rural parishes of Quebec. Unlike the caisses populaires, however, the Antigonish movement emphasized the provision of more adequate credit facilities for their members, rather than the virtues of thrift. Although still found mainly in the Maritime provinces, Antigonish-type credit unions have also been organized in the Prairies, particularly Saskatchewan.

In the 1940s the Credit Union National Association (now known as CUNA International) in the United States started to organize credit unions in Ontario. Locals were established on an industrial or occupational rather than a territorial basis, with many credit unions situated on employers' premises. They were formed essentially to provide a convenient source of low-cost credit to their members to finance consumer goods. More recently the traditional narrow bond of association has given way to a broader community membership.

The number of local credit unions and caisses grew rapidly during the 1940s and 1950s to a combined total of 5000 in 1965. Because of mergers and the formation of branch operations, however, their number declined. In the early 1990s there were some 1500 local credit unions. Although great diversity in their sizes exists, most hold assets of less than $100 000. The largest, Vancouver City Savings, had 39 branches, 260 000 members, and held $5 billion in assets in 1999. The three-tier structure of the credit union movement outside Quebec consists of local credit unions, provincial credit union centrals, and the Credit Union Central of Canada (Canadian Central). All provinces have credit union centrals with which local credit unions are affiliated. These centrals provide the same services to their local member credit unions that regional federations provide to caisses populaires.

The Canadian Central, chartered federally in 1953 under the *Cooperative Credit Associations Act*, is the national centre for credit cooperatives outside the Desjardins system. Its shareholder-members include provincial credit union centrals and other financial and nonfinancial cooperatives. The Canadian Central's main function is to provide financial services, particularly liquidity support, to the member credit union centrals. Both provincial and federal legislation specify statutory liquidity requirements. In addition, provincial centrals participate in a voluntary liquidity pool arrangement with their credit unions and the Canadian Central. The minimum level of operating liquidity has been set at 8 percent of the aggregate assets of local credit unions that are affiliated with centrals. Of this, 6 percent is maintained by centrals and 2 percent by the Canadian Central.

The Canadian Central receives deposits and shares from centrals and other member cooperatives and deposits from the federal government. It also borrows from other financial institutions and in domestic and foreign financial markets. It is a direct clearer and the credit union system's link to the Canadian Payments Association and the Bank of Canada.

A credit union or caisse populaire can be established by a handful of members (as few as 10), with a minimum share capital contribution from each member as low as $5. Membership is traditionally based on a shared "common bond of association," such as being in the same industry, trade union, club, or community. One of the most important aspects of the cooperative structure is the objective of providing services to members. Through providing loans and other services to its members, credit unions and caisses populaires assist in the economic development of many areas not served by the chartered banks.

Stabilization Corporations and Deposit Insurance

All credit unions and caisses populaires must be members of a stabilization corporation or a share and deposit insurance corporation. While the organization and powers of these institutions vary from province to province, their objectives are similar: They protect the safety of deposits and, usually, members' shares as well. They are typically empowered to monitor and supervise the management of credit cooperatives and to rehabilitate those with solvency problems. They are financed by annual fees assessed either on the value of member shares and deposits or on a credit cooperative's gross revenues. When such funds are insufficient, which was the case during the 1980s, additional funds are available from respective provincial governments and the Canada Deposit Insurance Corporation.

Financial Intermediation

Early in their history caisses populaires emphasized residential mortgage lending and deposit taking. The credit unions, meanwhile, concentrated more on providing their members with consumer loans, which were funded with members' shares rather than with deposits. Starting in the 1960s, however, the credit unions shifted their lending activities away from personal loans and toward market loans, and from share financing to deposits, particularly term deposits. The caisses populaires also started to emphasize term deposits. Because of these shifts, the asset and liability composition of the credit unions and caisses populaires became uniform.

Before the 1980s the credit unions and caisses populaires allowed their members to pre-encash their term deposits and to repay their residential mortgage loans with little or no penalty. When interest rates fell below contractual loan rates, borrowers refinanced their debt with lower-cost loans. When interest rates rose, borrowers held on to their lower-cost mortgage loans. At the same time, because interest rates increased, depositors pre-encashed existing term deposits and purchased new term deposits yielding higher interest rates. When interest rates decreased, depositors held their higher-yielding term deposits until maturity. This behaviour by borrowers and depositors created financial difficulties for the credit unions and caisses populaires when interest rates began to rise sharply through the 1970s.

Further financial difficulties were experienced, particularly during the 1980s, owing to losses on mortgage loans when, in many cases, the market value of mortgaged property dropped to less than the remaining value of the loan. These losses were particularly severe in Alberta, where the Law of Property prohibited lenders from recovering any loss due to the difference between property values and outstanding loan values. Losses on loans other than mortgage

TABLE 14.1	**LOCAL CREDIT UNIONS AND CAISSES POPULAIRES ESTIMATED ASSETS AND LIABILITIES** Millions of Dollars, December 1999		

Assets

Cash and deposits		17 549	
Government of Canada Treasury bills		81	
Other short-term paper and bankers' acceptances		391	
Bonds and debentures		1 215	
Personal loans		15 674	
Other loans		14 699	
Residential mortgages		56 861	
Nonresidential mortgages		8 230	
Other assets		3 279	**119 572**

Liabilities

Deposits:	chequable	23 903		
	nonchequable	9 719		
	term	69 042	102 664	
Loans payable			6 021	
Other liabilities			2 345	
Members' equity			8 542	**119 572**

Note: Errors due to rounding

SOURCE: Statistics Canada, CANSIM Database, Matrix 02564, April 2000.

loans also occurred because the caisses and credit unions had not been stringent enough in assessing borrowers' creditworthiness or in requiring sufficient collateral.

The caisses populaires and credit unions responded to the difficulties they experienced during the 1970s and early 1980s by closing weaker locals and caisses and merging smaller ones, by portfolio diversification, by asset and liability matching, and by introducing pre-encashment penalties on term deposits and prepayment penalties on fixed-term mortgages.

The financial intermediation activities of the local credit unions and caisses populaires are reflected in their assets and liabilities, as shown in Table 14.1. At the end of 1999 their total assets amounted to $119.6 billion. Most of these assets took the form of loans, especially mortgage and personal loans, indicating their orientation toward the household sector. This orientation is also indicated by their liabilities, which are predominantly members' deposits and equity contributions.

Trust and Mortgage Loan Companies

History and Structure

TRUST COMPANIES   Trust companies were originally organized because, under common law, corporations were not allowed to act as trustees. The administration of a trust was believed to require a conscience not possessed by corporations, which by their very nature are artificial beings. The concept of trust companies, first organized in the United States in the 1820s, probably came from the agency houses in India, which received money in trust for administering estates. In the United States, companies originally founded for trusteeship purposes were associated with life insurance companies; in the United Kingdom they were an adjunct to commercial banking. In the United States, most fiduciary or trust functions are now also performed by commercial banks. In Canada, trust companies were founded as separate institutions. They became closely associated with the chartered banks before the 1967 revisions of the *Bank Act*, which limited a bank's ownership to 10 percent of the voting shares of a trust company. The 1992 revisions to federal financial legislation again allowed banks to own trust companies but restricted them from offering most trust services through their branches.

Since the 1960s the structure of the trust industry has undergone almost constant change. Many trust companies failed and either exited the industry or were merged with healthier institutions. Others trust companies have merged to form larger firms or have been taken over by financial holding companies. These so-called financial service conglomerates include trust, mortgage, and insurance companies, as well as real estate brokerages, among other firms.

Following the 1992 legislative reforms that allowed regulated federal financial institutions to own one another, the domestic chartered banks and life insurance companies acquired many trust companies. In March 1996, for example, the Canada Deposit Insurance Corporation insured deposits of 11 wholly owned trust subsidiaries of the domestic banks and eight of the life insurance companies. In addition the CDIC insured the deposits of 20 companies not insured by the Quebec Deposit Insurance Board. Review question 10 requires you to find information on the number of trust subsidiaries of domestic banks and life insurance companies covered by deposit insurance in April 2000.

MORTGAGE LOAN COMPANIES   When first established in the 1850s, mortgage loan companies were patterned on the building societies that had developed in the United Kingdom during the early part of the nineteenth century. The purpose of these societies was to enable their members to acquire land, build homes, or develop farms. Over time, the building society phenomenon went through three phases of development. In the earliest phase, each member regularly contributed a certain amount of money to the society. When the accumulated funds reached a certain level, they were auctioned off to the highest bidder or made available to a member chosen by lot. The member receiving the funds assumed a mortgage that he repaid over a period of years while continuing his regular contributions to the society.

In the second phase of development, people could join building societies without the intention of eventually borrowing money from them. It was usual for these societies to sell two types of shares. People who did not want to avail themselves of the privilege of borrowing could purchase investment shares and participate in the profit of the society; for many, these shares were an attractive investment because they provided a way of escaping the early usury laws. People whose prime interest was to build a house, however, made regular contributions by purchasing advance shares, which did not allow them to participate directly in a society's profits.

The early building societies were "terminating"; that is, they were terminated when each member in turn had taken out and repaid his building loan. In the 1850s, in the third phase of development, "permanent" societies were established as companies. These companies accepted deposits from the public and later were allowed to issue debentures to fund mortgage loans.

Today's companies are known as the mortgage loan companies. Although their major activity remains that of granting residential mortgage loans, they also make nonresidential mortgage loans to finance commercial properties. They fund their mortgage loans with their deposit liabilities and by the issue of debentures. Most of the major companies are affiliated with other financial institutions, especially banks and trust companies.

Regulation and Supervision

Trust and mortgage loan companies may be incorporated under either federal or provincial legislation. Companies that are federally incorporated are licensed by each of the provinces in which they operate. Under section 29(13), the property and civil rights clause of the *Constitution Act*, 1967 (successor to the *British North America Act* of 1867), provincial governments have jurisdiction over trust and estate management and as such regulate these activities of all trust companies.

Provincially incorporated trust and mortgage loan companies are regulated and supervised by their respective provincial governments. In 1988 the Ontario government introduced the "equals approach" in the revisions to its *Loans and Trust Corporation Act*. Under this approach a trust company that operates in Ontario is subject to its regulation and supervision in all its activities, including those in other provinces, regardless of the jurisdiction of its incorporation.

Federally incorporated trust and loan companies come under the federal *Trust and Loan Companies Act*. These companies are regulated and supervised by the superintendent of financial institutions Canada. The ownership rules of these institutions changed under the 1992 federal financial institutions reform legislation. Today, no person, or entity controlled by a person, is allowed to own more than 10 percent of any class of shares of a company without government approval. Moreover, when a company's equity reaches $750 million, it is not allowed to increase its asset growth unless 35 percent of its voting shares are publicly held and traded. A nonresident, with the exception of a U.S. resident, cannot own more than 10 percent of the voting shares of a company, and total nonresident shareholding, also excluding U.S. citizens, is limited to 25 percent of a company's voting shares.

On June 25, 1999, the federal government announced plans to reform the financial services sector. Among the initiatives was a proposal to restructure the current three-tier system of local credit unions, provincial centrals, and the national central into a two-tier system. Another proposal involved the creation of a national cooperative bank. In addition, the proposals included the introduction of new rules regarding the activities of holding companies and changes in ownership rules that may strengthen the role played by credit unions in the marketplace.

In June 2000, the federal government introduced Bill C-38, which contained many of the proposals made the year before. Included among these changes is the potential for the creation of a single national services entity that would provide credit unions with a national structure and the ability to compete better with larger domestic and foreign-based institutions. Some of the services they might provide include discount brokerages, wealth management operations, and enhanced electronic banking systems. The national structure may allow credit unions to reduce their exposure to risk via risk-sharing ventures while retaining their local autonomy.

Trust Company Fiduciary Function

In their fiduciary function, trust companies administer estates, trusts, and agencies. Under the terms of deceased persons' wills, trust companies administer such estates as executors or trustees. As trustees, they also manage assets placed in trust for pension plans, charitable purposes, children's educations, and a wide variety of other purposes. In their role as administrators of agencies, they enter into agreements to manage real estate, mortgages, and the securities of others. As transfer agents, trust companies arrange for the transfer of ownership of a company's shares and the maintenance of shareholders' records. As administrators of estates, trusts, and agencies, trust companies do not have ownership of the assets under their administration. Funds and assets held in trust must be kept separate from a company's other assets. A company may invest trust funds in one or more common trust funds unless the instrument creating a trust provides otherwise.

Trust and Loan Company Financial Intermediation

The assets and liabilities of trust and mortgage loan companies, excluding those of the subsidiaries of the chartered banks, which are consolidated into their own balance sheets, are shown as at the end of 1999 in Table 14.2. The assets of this group of companies decreased from a peak of $135.5 billion in 1990 to $58 billion at the end of 1999. This decrease reflects the acquisition of existing trust and mortgage loan companies by the chartered banks.

TABLE 14.2	**TRUST AND MORTGAGE LOAN COMPANIES EXCLUDING BANK TRUST AND MORTGAGE SUBSIDIARIES: ESTIMATED ASSETS AND LIABILITIES** Millions of Dollars, December 1999

Assets

Liquid assets:

Cash and deposits	1 487	
Government of Canada Treasury bills	2 136	
Short-term paper	3 710	**7 333**

Loans:

Residential mortgages	19 223	
Nonresidential mortgages	1 394	
Personal loans	17 237	
Leasing contracts	344	
Other loans	538	**38 736**

Investments:

Canadian bonds	6 587	
Canadian preferred and common shares	1 195	7 782
Other assets, including items in transit		4 487
		58 338

Liabilities

Savings deposits:

chequable	8 134		
nonchequable	4 001	12 135	
Term deposits, guaranteed investment certificates and debentures		38 987	
Promissory notes and debentures		2 605	
Other liabilities		2 332	
Shareholders' equity		2 279	**58 338**

Note: Errors due to rounding

SOURCE: Statistics Canada, CANSIM Database, Matrix 00917, April 2000.

Trust and mortgage loan companies lend to households and businesses, but the provision of credit to households remains their major lending activity. One-third of their assets are residential mortgage loans. At the end of December 1999, 29 percent of their assets were personal loans, mainly credit card loans and variable-rate loans against personal lines of credit.

Their loans to businesses include nonresidential mortgages, privately placed corporate debentures, and leasing receivables. During the latter 1980s some companies increased their participation in commercial real estate markets, which created difficulties for them in the early 1990s when commercial real estate values dropped sharply. The federal *Trust and Loan Companies Act* forbids federally incorporated companies with less than $25 million in regulatory capital to make or acquire commercial loans. Moreover, companies with regulatory capital of $25 million or more require approval from the superintendent of financial institutions to hold commercial loans in excess of 5 percent of their assets. Portfolio limits also apply to the amount of real property and common shares that may be held. The amount of real property and equities (excluding those in prescribed subsidiaries) are each limited to 70 percent and together to 100 percent of regulatory capital, although proposed reforms to the financial sector may change these restrictions.

Trust and mortgage loan companies fund their assets primarily with chequable and nonchequable savings deposits, term deposits, guaranteed investment certificates (GICs), and debentures. Trust companies are allowed to accept deposits only as guaranteed trust money, which requires them to identify on their books assets equal to the aggregate amount of their deposits. Deposits are insured in Quebec by the Quebec Deposit Insurance Board and in the rest of Canada by the Canada Deposit Insurance Corporation. Both insurers also make loans to member institutions with liquidity difficulties. To protect the depositors and the deposit insurers, trust and loan companies are required to satisfy capital adequacy restrictions by having equity capital of at least 5 percent of total assets.

In the 1970s trust companies started to expand their retail savings deposits in competition with the other deposit-taking institutions by extending their branches into shopping centres, by maintaining convenient business hours, by adding to their number of automated banking machines, and by offering competitive interest rates and other inducements to attract new customers. With mergers and amalgamations among companies, some have extended their branch networks geographically. The few larger trust companies have national branch networks, but these are small in comparison to the chartered banks.

Trust and mortgage loan companies traditionally granted fixed-rate, long-term residential mortgages that were funded by their shorter-term guaranteed deposits. As long as the yield curve of the term structure of interest rates sloped upward, they enjoyed reasonably good spreads between their cost of funds and the return earned on mortgages. However, in the late 1970s and early 1980s, when the yield curve became negative and interest rates were volatile, many companies experienced difficulties. The trust companies responded by more closely matching the terms of maturity of their assets and liabilities and by matching variable-rate deposits with variable-rate assets. Because depositors' preferences, reflecting their inflationary expectations, shifted toward shorter-term deposits, the trust companies could achieve a closer match with their mortgage portfolios only by reducing the average term of their mortgage loans. Some of these were offered with terms as short as six months. As part of their longer-term portfolio strategy, the trust companies attempted to diversify their investment portfolios by expanding their commercial and personal lending. Regulatory restrictions on their lending activities caused them to demand regulatory reform. Provincial legislatures as well as the federal government subsequently expanded their lending powers.

Trust and mortgage loan companies hold liquid assets as a buffer to manage deviations between the growth in their loans and deposits. They tend to reduce their liquidity when the demand for loans exceeds funding available from deposits and increase it when the opposite occurs. Cash, deposits at the chartered banks, government of Canada securities, and money market instruments are their major sources of liquidity.

Trust and Mortgage Loan Company Failure

In the five years after 1979, 30 trust and mortgage loan companies experienced severe financial difficulties. Of these, 15 failed. In the aftermath of the Greymac affair of early 1983, the Ontario government passed special legislation to take control of three trust companies, and at the same time the federal government took over two related mortgage loan companies.

In the Greymac affair, 10 931 apartment units had been purchased by Greymac Credit Corporation for $270 million; it was the largest transaction of its kind ever made in Canada. These properties were "flipped" (immediately resold) for $312.5 million to another company, which in turn immediately resold them for $500 million to an unknown group of foreign investors. Greymac Trust Company, Crown Trust Company, and Seaway Trust Company facilitated the resale by advancing substantial amounts by way of third mortgages on the properties. Because these amounts not only were in excess of the trust companies' statutory lending limits, but also were based on questionable property values, the deals threatened the financial viability of the companies. The Morrison Report, commissioned by the Ontario Government, concluded that the objective for the transactions was to enable the principals who controlled the three trust companies to withdraw $152 million from these companies primarily for their own purposes. It was also revealed that they had used similar questionable methods before, but on a much smaller scale.

During the 1960s and 1970s, trust and mortgage loan companies expanded their operations as a result of a growing economy, residential construction, and real estate development. To allow these companies to satisfy the demand for funds, their regulators allowed them to make higher loan to value mortgage loans and to operate with higher debt to equity ratios. In the late 1970s, when interest rates moved sharply upward, many companies that had extended fixed-rate, long-term mortgage loans funded with shorter-term deposits and debentures faced financial difficulties. Most of them, unlike their counterparts in the United States, were able to overcome problems associated with mismatching the maturity of their assets and liabilities. Companies in Western Canada were not so fortunate, because of the depressed economic conditions and the sharp downturn in real estate values after 1982 in Alberta and British Columbia.

The failures of trust and mortgage loan companies over 1980–85 displayed many common characteristics. Some companies failed because they had been formed, or were taken over, by unscrupulous individuals who in some instances engaged in fraudulent practices. Many failed because of self-dealing transactions between major shareholders, directors, senior officers, and close associates. In some cases self-dealing abuses involved extremely complex and innovative arrangements that were difficult, if not impossible, for auditors and regulators to identify and monitor. Nearly all cases of failure involved inappropriate portfolio diversification, while companies assumed excessive risks that were made possible by deposit insurance protection and high leverage ratios. Part of the blame for failure must also be shared by the regulatory system and, in particular, lax enforcement of existing regulations.

In the decade after 1985 more than 15 trust and loan companies failed and were either liquidated, merged, or rehabilitated. Many of their failures occurred in the early 1990s when, with slower growth in the economy and a sharp drop in the price of commercial real estate, numerous companies experienced large losses on their assets.

Government Savings Institutions

The federal government established a Post Office Savings Bank in 1867 "to enlarge the facilities now available for the deposit of small savings…and to give the direct security of the nation to every depositor for repayment of all money deposited by him together with interest due thereon." Before it stopped accepting deposits at the end of 1969, the activities of the bank had been steadily declining. This decline was primarily the result of the growth of other deposit institutions, which tended to offer higher interest rates and a greater variety of services.

The Newfoundland Savings Bank was established in 1834, while the Province of Ontario Savings Office was opened in 1921. Similar institutions operated in Manitoba from 1924 to 1932, when they were taken over by the chartered banks. The Newfoundland Savings Bank ceased operations in 1962 when it was purchased by the Bank of Montreal.

www.

The Province of Ontario Savings Office is the only institution of its kind that has survived. Its original purpose was to gather funds from the public and to lend them to farmers through rural credit societies. Today the Savings Office offers savings accounts, term deposits, and guaranteed investment certificates to the public at 23 branches and 5 agencies in 22 communities across Ontario. In December 1999, funds on deposit amounted to $2.5 billion. All these funds are loaned directly to the treasurer of Ontario for general government purposes. The deposit liabilities of the Savings Office are in effect a debt of the province, and are guaranteed by it.

Treasury branches were established in 1938 by the government of Alberta in response to the belief that the chartered banks with head offices in Eastern Canada were not attuned to the financial requirements of Western Canada. As of April 2000, there are 144 branches and 130 agencies in more than 238 communities throughout Alberta. Total assets of Alberta Treasury Branches were $10.1 billion at the end of December 1999. These assets are held in residential mortgage loans and personal, commercial, and agricultural loans to Albertans. These loans are funded by demand, notice, and fixed-term deposits.

REVIEW QUESTIONS

1. Describe the structure of the credit union and caisse populaire movements.
2. Describe the fiduciary function of trust companies.
3. Why did the trust and loan companies run into financial problems in the 1970s and 1980s? How did they resolve these problems?
4. What have been the major causes of failure of trust and mortgage loan companies?
5. How do trust company deposit liabilities differ from those of the banks?
6. What is the essential difference between the banks and the near-banks?
7. What is the role of the two remaining government savings institutions?
8. Why would the government try to make it easier for near-banks to compete with banks?
9. How does the Quebec Deposit Insurance Board differ from the CDIC? Is there identical coverage?
10. In April 2000, how many trust subsidiaries of domestic banks and life insurance companies were covered by the CDIC? (Hint: You may find useful information at the CDIC Website!)

SELECTED READINGS

Department of Finance. *Canada's Credit Unions and Caisses Populaires—The Canadian Financial System.* Ottawa, February 2000.

———. *Reforming Canada's Financial Services Sector—A Framework for the Future.* Ottawa, 1999.

CHAPTER FIFTEEN

Nondepository Financial Institutions

After reading this chapter you should be able to
1. *Describe the functions of securities dealers and securities brokers*
2. *Discuss the economics of insurance*
3. *Define the various insurance and savings products offered by life insurance companies*
4. *Explain the nature of property and casualty insurance companies*
5. *Describe investment companies, particularly mutual funds*
6. *Explain Canada's retirement pension system*
7. *Identify financial leasing, venture capital, merchant banking, and financial holding companies*
8. *Provide a rationale for government participation in financial markets and identify major government insurance and lending institutions.*

Nondepository financial institutions supply specialized financial and related services to the public and to other financial institutions. As a group they tend to be much less homogeneous than depository institutions. For example, they may specialize in securities underwriting and brokerage, life insurance or general insurance underwriting and distribution, financial leasing, investment fund management, or the provision of other types of particular financial and related activities. However, as has been the case with the depository institutions, their individual distinctiveness has become blurred, since they too have diversified their product mix. Many of these institutions have become subsidiaries of depository institutions or are owned by other institutions, often within a holding company or financial conglomerate structure.

www.

Securities Dealers and Brokers

Securities dealers and brokers, also known as investment dealers, or investment bankers, primarily are market intermediaries. Unlike financial intermediaries, they do not transform the financial assets that they acquire into their own liabilities for distribution to the public. As market intermediaries, their major function is underwriting and trading securities. Underwriting, as we have previously described, is the acquisition of primary securities from ultimate borrowers for distribution to lenders. Securities dealers acquire securities issued by borrowers, either through competitive bidding or by negotiation. Traditionally, they promised borrowers to use their "best efforts" to sell the securities at the highest possible price. Today, dealers frequently purchase an entire issue directly from borrowers at a set price and assume the risk of reselling it at that price, or preferably a higher one, to the public. When dealers purchase large, new securities issues outright for distribution by their own sales force, the transaction is referred to as a bought deal.

bought deal the purchase by securities dealers of the entire issue of new securities for distribution

A **bought deal** usually involves a large stock or bond issue that is sold through a dealer syndicate. A so-called lead dealer negotiates a bought deal, forms the syndicate, manages the issue, and takes the largest share of the issue for resale. Other dealers in the syndicate take a proportionately smaller portion of the issue. The lead dealer earns both a management fee and a sales commission. Other dealers earn only a sales commission on the securities they take for resale to their clients.

brokers parties acting as agents who bring buyers and sellers together

Although many investment dealers are both brokers and dealers, a distinction exists between them. **Brokers** are agents who bring buyers and sellers together, either on listed securities markets such as the Toronto Stock Exchange or on over-the-counter markets. As middle parties, brokers earn a commission for buying and selling securities for their clients. In contrast, dealers underwrite new securities and assume part or all (as in the case of bought deals) of the risk in their distribution. Unlike brokers, **dealers** act as principals by holding inventories of securities they have purchased for subsequent resale. By holding inventories of securities, and standing ready to buy and sell at quoted prices, dealers also act as **market makers**, a role that is crucial for the efficient functioning of financial markets.

dealers parties acting as principals who underwrite and hold inventories of securities for resale

market makers those who hold inventories of securities and stand ready to buy and sell at quoted prices

A distinction is also made between full-service brokers and discount brokers. **Full-service brokers** engage in market research to provide investment advice and portfolio analysis to their clients. **Discount brokers** do not offer their clients these services, but, as a result, the commissions they charge for brokerage services are substantially less than those charged by full-service brokers and dealers. Discount brokers date from 1983, when the Toronto and Montreal stock exchanges allowed brokers to set their commissions competitively, and the Ontario and Quebec securities commissions allowed financial institutions to offer their customers discount brokerage service.

full-service brokers brokers offering a full range of brokerage services

discount brokers brokers offering low-cost execution of orders without investment advice

www.

Ownership and Regulation

Traditionally, Canadian investment dealers were organized as partnerships and the partners had to be securities brokers and dealers. This type of ownership was thought desirable because, by separating market intermediaries from financial intermediaries, abusive conflicts of interest could be avoided. So that the securities industry also remained in Canadian hands, in 1971 the Ontario government started to restrict ownership of securities firms to Canadian residents.

In the 1980s the major investment dealers, by acting more as principals than as agents, increased their exposure to risk and their need for capital resources. Some attempted to strengthen their capital base by reaching outside their fraternity and for the first time offering their stock to the public. Others merged with each other in the belief that size would enhance their access to more capital funds. However, without regulatory changes to allow wider ownership of investment dealers, the prospect for attracting more capital funds remained uncertain.

In December 1986, the Ontario Securities Commission announced that, beginning on June 30, 1987, Canadian financial institutions would be allowed 100 percent ownership of investment dealers and that foreign institutions would be allowed 50 percent, to be increased to 100 percent a year later.[1] The federal government shortly thereafter announced that it would amend its legislation to permit federally incorporated financial institutions to have wholly owned subsidiaries that would engage in all aspects of the securities business. These announcements marked the departure from traditional Canadian financial legislation that had attempted to separate market from financial intermediation.

The Canadian banks immediately took advantage of the announced legislative changes by arranging substantial ownership positions in existing securities dealers. Foreign banks as well as some Canadian trust companies also assumed ownership interests in investment dealers. Today, most of the major securities firms are owned by financial institutions; securities subsidiaries of the six major Canadian banks dominate the industry.

The regulation of securities brokers and dealers, as well as other aspects of the securities industry, falls under the jurisdiction of provincial governments. Some of the provinces have securities commissions or similar regulatory agencies to administer their securities regulation.

In 1965 the Royal Commission on Banking and Finance had recommended the establishment of a federal securities agency. More recently, it has been proposed that the federal government create a national securities commission similar to the Securities and Exchange Commission in the United States. It is argued that only a national authority can adequately deal with the already complex regulatory issues related to the internationalization of the securities market.

primary dealers
a subset of government securities dealers whose participation in the primary and secondary markets for government of Canada securities is above a threshold level

Market Intermediation

The major financial assets held by investment dealers are their inventories of securities awaiting sale in money and capital markets. Inventories of money market securities are funded primarily with day-to-day and call loans from the banks. A few investment dealers, known as **primary dealers**, who specialize in holding inventories of federal government securities, have short-term

1. This was a reversal of a new policy, announced earlier in the same year by the Ontario Securities Commission, that would have allowed Canadian financial institutions and nonfinancial firms as well as foreigners to own up to 30 percent of a securities firm. In addition, foreign securities firms doing business in Canada would have been required to become foreign dealer registrants subject individually and in aggregate to capital limitations.

borrowing privileges at the Bank of Canada. Inventories of securities that result from dealers' underwriting activities are funded with their own capital funds and collateral loans from financial institutions and large industrial corporations. Securities firms are not allowed to solicit deposits from the public; however, they hold clients' cash balances that accumulate from their trading activities. By allowing clients to write cheques against these balances, the accounts have become transactions accounts similar to the accounts where deposits are held with deposit-taking institutions. Investment dealers also make margin loans to their clients for the purchase of securities. These loans are secured by the securities being purchased.

book-based transactions
transactions made by electronic book entry

To improve efficiency, the securities industry has introduced **book-based transactions**, which means that transactions are made by electronic book entries between firms while the underlying securities remain on deposit with a securities depository such as the Canadian Depository for Securities. Because physical securities such as bond certificates do not change hands, it is generally not necessary to register securities in the owner's name. For the individual, ownership is recorded in the statements received from brokers and security dealers.

Consumer Protection

Canadian Investor Protection Fund
a fund that protects the interests of investors

www.

The Investment Dealers Association of Canada and the stock exchanges formed the national Contingency Fund in 1969. In 1992 the Fund was renamed the **Canadian Investor Protection Fund.** It protects the interests of individual investors as well as of corporations. Individual accounts are protected to a maximum of $1 000 000 which can be distributed between securities and cash holdings.

Insurance

The Economics of Insurance

Insurance companies are able to absorb their customers' risks by engaging in risk pooling and risk sharing which reduce the total amount of risk that has to be borne by them and their customers.

risk pooling
writing insurance policies with a probability that risks are independent of each other

RISK POOLING   A basic feature of insurance is the pooling of independent risks. For example, when an insurance company writes fire insurance covering a large number of houses located over a wide geographic area, it is **risk pooling**. The chance of fire burning down one house is independent of the chance of a fire burning down another. If an event causing fire, say a forest fire, were to engulf an extremely large area where an insurance company is providing most of the fire insurance coverage, the principle of reducing overall risk by pooling would be defeated.

BOX 15–1   BACKGROUNDER

Do You Have Protection?

Suppose your three friends present you with the following situation. Harry has $150 000 invested with his stockbroker, while Marv has $150 000 in his chartered bank account. Susan has $150 000 in cash available for withdrawal in a life insurance company. Now let's suppose each of the three firms goes bankrupt. Let's also suppose that during liquidation of each firm, the trustees are able to pay a dividend to creditors of 60 cents on every dollar, after expenses. Who has more protection? Marv, Harry, or Susan?

Three different compensation plans would affect each of your friends: the Canadian Investor Protection Fund (CIPF), the Canada Deposit Insurance Corporation (CDIC), and the Canadian Life and Health Insurance Compensation Corporation (COMPCORP). The following table illustrates that each investor has a find loss of $0, after the benefit of the consumer protection plan.

Customer	A	B		C	
Protected by	CIPF	CDIC		COMPCORP	
Cash insured for	$150 000	$60 000		$60 000	
Cash balance	$150 000	$150 000		$150 000	
		Insured	**Not Insured**	**Insured**	**Not Insured**
		$60 000	$90 000	$60 000	$90 000
Dividend from trustee at 60 cents per dollar equals	$90 000	$36 000	$54 000	$60 000	$30 000
Loss before coverage	$60 000	$24 000	$36 000	$0	$60 000
Paid by consumer protection plan	$60 000	$24 000	$0	$0	$0
Final loss	$0	$0	$36 000	$0	$60 000

In September 1999 the CIPF instituted several changes to its coverage, including the removal of a limit on cash coverage, which used to stand at $60 000. Today, investors are covered up to $1 million, independent of the combination of cash and securities in their accounts.

SOURCE: A. Moysey, "Deposit Insurance and Other Compensation Arrangements." Task Force on the Future of the Canadian Financial Sector. Department of Finance, Ottawa: 1998.

RISK SHARING   Suppose one of the rare paintings housed in the Hermitage Museum in St. Petersburg, Russia is to be shown at a special exhibition in Ottawa. Insurance is sought against the risk of loss while this painting is in transit and in Ottawa. No one insurance company will be prepared to underwrite by itself such a large risk of loss despite the very large premium to be earned. Under the circumstances, the market solution for providing insurance coverage is **risk sharing**. One or a group of insurance companies will write a

risk sharing when a very large insurance risk is shared by many insurers

master policy for the entire risk and then write a large number of sub-policies for sale to many other insurers. In this way, risk sharing makes it possible to provide insurance coverage for extremely large individual risks.

MORAL HAZARD AND ADVERSE SELECTION   Insurance creates incentive problems that reduce the ability of insurance companies to exploit fully the principles of risk pooling and risk sharing. Two such problems are moral hazard and adverse selection.

moral hazard *the tendency of insured parties to take more risk because they are insured*

Moral hazard is the tendency of those being insured to take a greater risk because they have insurance coverage. For example, a person whose auto is insured may not drive as carefully as someone without car insurance. Insurance companies have learned to cope with moral hazard problems by, among other things, requiring claimants to pay the first, say, $500 (the deductible) in the event of a claim and offering only partial coverage (coinsurance). They also undertake expensive monitoring of the risks that they insure. As we explained earlier, moral hazard is viewed as one of the major problems associated with government-sponsored deposit-insurance systems, where premiums paid by the insured institutions are not risk related.

adverse selection *tendency of worse risks to buy insurance, and of better risks not to buy it*

Adverse selection is the tendency of the most-likely claimants (the worst risks) to purchase insurance, and of the least-likely claimants (the best risks) not to purchase insurance. This is referred to as adverse selection because, from the insurer's point of view, the wrong people buy insurance.

When insurance companies cannot distinguish among different risks, they have to charge a high enough premium to all insured to allow for the increased risk for them due to adverse selection. These higher premiums can result in further adverse selection because those who know that they are high-risk individuals will purchase a policy because to them it will be relatively cheap. Adverse selection can create a situation in which insurance companies will not offer certain types of insurance because of their inability to price it appropriately. Although insurance companies have tried to deal with this problem by identifying human characteristics that are related to risk and by charging different premiums to individuals with different characteristics, governments now tend to make such discrimination illegal.

Life Insurance Companies

History and Structure

Life insurance companies offer insurance policies, annuity contracts, and investment funds to the public. Most life insurance companies also offer health and accident protection.

www.

The life insurance industry in Canada is made up of domestic and foreign-owned companies incorporated either federally or provincially, and Canadian branch operations of companies incorporated outside Canada. The industry dates from the middle of the 19th century; the oldest company still operating in Canada was founded in 1847. In addition to life insurance companies, there are fraternal benefit societies, such as the Knights of Columbus, that provide basic life insurance protection to members and their families.

Most of the life insurance sold in Canada is supplied by federally incorporated companies and by nonresident companies operating on a branch basis. These institutions are supervised by the Office of the Superintendent of Financial Institutions. Canadian life insurance companies and societies are required to maintain adequate capital. Foreign companies transacting business in Canada on a branch basis must maintain an adequate margin of assets in Canada to cover their Canadian liabilities. For these purposes, the superintendent has established minimum standards. All companies must be licensed in each province or territory where they conduct business.

Life insurance companies may be incorporated either as stock companies with common share capital or as mutual companies with no common shareholders. The management of a stock company consists of directors representing in part shareholders and in part participating policyholders. The latter share in a stock company's surplus earnings are distributed as "policy dividends." The directors of a mutual company represent the participating policyholders. More than 50 percent of all life insurance companies' coverage in Canada is provided by mutual companies. In the 1950s and 1960s, stock companies became mutual companies as a defence against hostile foreign takeovers. More recently, the move has been in the opposite direction, as mutual companies seek to expand their capital bases.

Changes in legislation in 1992 allowed federally incorporated life insurance companies to become subsidiaries of banks and near-banks. However, as we explained in the last chapter, these institutions are not allowed to offer their subsidiaries' insurance and annuity policies through their branches. Many life insurance companies are now subsidiaries of other financial institutions or financial holding companies. Federally incorporated life insurance companies are permitted to own other financial institutions in much the same way as are the banks and near-banks.

www.

demutualization
the conversion of a mutual company to a company owned by shareholders

In March 1999, Bill C-59 amended the *Insurance Companies Act* to allow federally incorporated mutual life insurance companies to convert to stock companies, a process called **demutualization**. It was argued that this process would allow the firms to raise additional capital, develop new technologies, and to clarify the ownership of the mutual companies. Policyholders will receive shares in the demutualized firm in proportion to the value they have placed with the mutual life insurance firm. The OSFI has been charged with overseeing the demutualization process.

Life Insurance Underwriting

term insurance
pure life insurance that pays a contractual amount in the event of death

Life insurance companies write two basic types of insurance contracts: term and whole life. **Term insurance** is pure life insurance that provides the policyholder with nothing more than death protection. The insurer contracts with the policyholder to make a cash payment to a beneficiary if the insured dies within the contract period. Under regular term policies, premia increase with each renewal, reflecting higher mortality rates at older ages. Under decreasing term policies, the premium rate is fixed over the contract period, but the

BOX 15–2   BACKGROUNDER

Demutualization

Canada's life insurance industry consists of both mutual and stock insurance companies. While the largest life insurance company is a stock company (Great West Life), the four next largest are mutual companies (Manulife, Sun Life, Mutual Life, and Canada Life).

Both mutual and stock insurance companies sell participating and nonparticipating policies. Participating policyholders have voting rights in the company and are entitled to receive profits of the company in the form of dividends and the remaining value of the company on dissolution. While nonparticipating policyholders do have voting rights in some mutual companies, they are not entitled to participate in profit distributions or to receive the remaining value of the company upon dissolution.

The objective of a mutual company is not to enhance shareholder value, but rather to use policy dividends to provide participating insurance "at cost," while ensuring the continued growth of the company. By their nature, mutual companies have no common shareholders. Instead, ownership of the companies resides with the voting policyholders, who are generally participating policyholders.

They elect the board of directors and approve all fundamental changes to the company. In comparison, participating policyholders of stock insurance companies elect at least one-third of the board of directors.

Policyholders will receive several benefits from demutualization. The regime being proposed will ensure that all of the company value will be allocated to current voting policyholders. Policyholders will also benefit from dealing with companies that have greater access to capital and a better understood system of ownership, and that are subject to greater scrutiny by the market. By taking advantage of their new corporate structure, demutualized companies may be able to provide more competitive insurance policy premiums and a wider array of new products.

By the end of 1999, Canada Life, Clarica (formerly known as Mutual Life of Canada), Manulife Financial and Sun Life had all demutualized. MetLife, operating in Canada as a branch of a New York firm, also became a publicly owned firm, as did Industrial-Alliance, a Quebec firm (subject to the Quebec National Assembly passing a bill to authorize its conversion).

Source: Department of Finance. *Demutualization Regime for Canadian Life Insurance Companies,* August 1998, p. 6.

---

whole-life insurance *a policy with level premiums that combines saving with term insurance*

cash surrender value *accumulated savings in a policy paid upon its termination*

amount of protection decreases from year to year, again reflecting higher mortality rates at older ages. Term policies are offered as group or individual contracts.

In contrast to term insurance, **whole-life insurance** (alternatively called straight life or permanent insurance) provides both protection and savings accumulation. Level premia are paid by the policyholder for a specified number of years or throughout his or her lifetime for a stated amount of protection. During the policy's earlier years the premium charged is higher than the actual cost of protection, and in later years it is substantially lower than the actual cost of protection. In the early years, the excess premium together with interest earned accumulate as savings of policy holders and provide insurance companies with a pool of funds for investment. These savings, known as the **cash surrender value** of a policy, are paid to the policyholder if the policy is terminated before the insured's death. The policyholder can borrow a portion of any accumulated savings in his or her policy.

Until the 1970s, life insurance companies sold mostly whole-life policies. However, when interest rates rose to reflect higher inflation rates, whole-life policies with fixed nominal returns lost their public appeal as a savings vehicle. Life insurance companies responded by offering new policies that were designed to give policy holders more control over their accumulated savings and to offer returns that reflected rising market rates. Three such policies are new money, universal life, and variable life. **New money policies** are life insurance policies for which the premia are revised periodically to take into account current and expected rates of interest. **Universal life policies** credit net premia to a policy account from which periodic charges for life insurance are deducted and to which interest is credited. The policyholder typically can vary the amount and timing of premium payments and change the amount of insurance coverage. In a **variable life policy**, benefits are not fixed, but vary with the market value of the assets in which the premia have been invested.

Annuities

A growing proportion of life insurance companies' operations is the sale of **annuity contracts** for pension plans. Under an annuity contract a life insurance company receives a lump sum or regular premium payments and agrees to pay the annuitant a stipulated sum of money (usually monthly) beginning at a specified time and extending for a designated period of years or for the remainder of the annuitant's life. Where an annuity is to be paid for life, a fixed number of years are usually guaranteed. For example, under an annuity payable for life with 10 years guaranteed, payment is made to the annuitant's estate for 10 years even if the annuitant dies the day payments are to start. While life insurance protects the beneficiary against financial difficulties resulting from the insured "dying too soon," an annuity contract protects the insured from financial difficulties resulting from "living too long."

More recently, insurance companies have offered variable annuities in addition to guaranteed annuities. In contrast to guaranteed annuities, where contracts call for the payment of a set amount, variable annuities pay a variable amount based on the performance of the underlying investments. However, most of these contracts guarantee to return at least 75 percent of premia on death or maturity of contracts. Insurance companies compete with depository institutions for personal savings by offering single-premium, short-term deferred annuities. Under these contracts the annuity payment is deferred for a short period, thereby making these contracts very similar to term deposits.

Individual annuity contracts also are classified as being either immediate or deferred. An **immediate annuity** involves a payment stream to the beneficiary beginning immediately after the contract has been purchased. With a **deferred annuity**, on the other hand, payments to the purchaser begin at a specified time in the future. The life insurance companies offer individual single-premium short-term deferred annuity contracts that resemble term deposits offered by the deposit-taking institutions. Life insurance companies are not legally permitted to receive deposits from their clients. The Bank of Canada

---

new money policy *a policy where the premiums are revised periodically to reflect current and expected interest rates*

universal life policy *a policy where the holder can vary the amount and timing of premium payments and change the amount of insurance*

variable life policy *a policy where benefits are not fixed, but vary with the market value of the assets in which the premiums have been invested*

annuity contract *a contract that provides income payments for a specified period*

immediate annuity *an annuity providing for income payments to begin immediately after the contract is purchased*

deferred annuity *an annuity providing for income payments to begin at some future date*

includes the individual deferred annuity contracts of the life insurance companies in its M2+ broad-based monetary aggregates.

Uses of Life Insurance Company Funds

Historically, life insurers have attempted to match the maturity or duration of their assets to the long-term nature of their liabilities. Their liabilities, as we have seen, represent the anticipated future payment of death benefits and retirement benefits. Hence, most of their assets (see Table 15.1) have been in the form of long-term securities.

At the end of 1998, the total assets held in Canada on behalf of Canadian life insurance policyholders amounted to $275 billion. Twenty-five percent of the assets of life insurance companies in Canada were invested in mortgage loans and real estate, 53 percent in bonds, and 5 percent in stocks. Investments in mortgages financed office buildings, shopping centres, manufacturing plants, and warehouses. Federally incorporated companies are allowed to hold real property and equities only up to 70 percent of their capital and 100 percent for both combined. Portfolio limits for total investments in real property and equities (shares in other companies) are also specified in terms of their liabilities in respect of life insurance policies.

Since 1991 all federally incorporated companies, except small ones with less than $25 million in capital, no longer have portfolio limits with respect to commercial and personal loans.

Fund Management

segregated funds
life insurance assets dedicated to specific liabilities

Since 1961, life insurance companies have been permitted to establish **segregated funds**. A life insurance company may manage more than one segregated fund. Assets held in these funds, while owned by the life insurance companies, have to be segregated from their other assets. Investors are able to participate in these funds by purchasing units at the net asset value of a fund at time of purchase. If investors wish to withdraw from a fund, the units are redeemed at the net asset value at the time of withdrawal.[2]

Segregated funds are used primarily for the investment of pension plan contributions. Some segregated funds are used to support variable rate annuity contracts. At the end of 1998, assets in segregated funds in Canada, as shown in Table 15.1, amounted to $153 billion.

Consumer Protection

In 1989, the life and health insurance industry created a consumer protection plan to safeguard life and health insurance policyholders. The plan is administered by the Canadian Life and Health Insurance Compensation Corporation

---

2. Although these funds resemble mutual funds in ease of trading, structure of portfolios, monthly valuation of assets, and sales charges, they differ in two important respects: They carry a specific term and they guarantee to return at least 75 percent of the original investment at the end of the term.

TABLE 15.1	**LIFE INSURANCE COMPANIES: ASSETS OF CANADIAN COMPANIES, 1998** Millions of Dollars	
		Total
Cash and short-term investments		11 240
Accrued investment income		3 300
Bonds		145 026
Policy loans		13 253
Mortgage loans		58 033
Shares		14 277
Real estate		9 767
Other loans and investment assets		2 491
Accounts receivable		4 459
Other assets		13 522
Total assets excluding segregated funds		275 369
Total assets in segregated funds		153 161

SOURCE: Office of the Superintendent of Financial Institutions, *Assets of Canadian Life Insurance Companies—Consolidated—1998.*

know as CompCorp. The federal government and most provinces require life and health insurers to be members of CompCorp and to pay assessments levied by it.

In the event that a member life insurance company becomes insolvent, CompCorp ensures that eligible policies will continue within limits, and generally according to the policies' terms. Individuals have up to $200 000 of life insurance protection and up to $60 000 in cash withdrawal guaranteed. Separate $60 000 limits apply to policies registered as Registered Retirement Savings Plans and Registered Retirement Income Funds.

The failure of Coopérants Mutual Life Insurance Society in 1992 was the first failure of a Canadian life insurer. The Sovereign Life Insurance Company failed in the same year. In 1994, the Confederation Life Insurance Company, Canada's fourth largest insurer at that time, was ordered into liquidation. These failures can be explained by insufficient provisioning for the decline in real estate investments following a sharp downturn in real estates markets and in some cases also by incompetent managers and their self-dealing.

When Coopérants Mutual Life Insurance Society failed, CompCorp paid claims of policyholders beyond its declared limits and sought reimbursement from its member insurance companies.

Accident and Health Insurance

Life insurers also provide accident and sickness insurance coverage in the form of extended health-care benefits, loss-of-income coverage for long-term dis-

BOX 15-3   COMPCORP PLAYS KEY ROLE IN ENSURING THAT CANADIAN POLICYHOLDERS OF CONFEDERATION LIFE RECEIVE FULL RECOVERY OF THEIR BENEFITS

Executive Summary

The liquidator of Confederation Life has announced that Canadian policyholders of the company will receive full recovery of their benefits. This news is very welcome to policyholders and to all those parties who have worked on the liquidation since August 11, 1994. One party that is particularly pleased with this announcement is CompCorp (Canadian Life and Health Insurance Compensation Corporation), the industry-funded consumer protection plan that worked with the liquidator to maximize value in the estate so that policyholders could be fully compensated.

As the shock wave of the demise of Confederation Life swept over the financial services sector in Canada and abroad, CompCorp moved quickly to alleviate Canadian policyholders' fears. CompCorp also reassured interested parties that the liquidation would be conducted in a prudent yet proactive manner, while at the same time keeping policyholders' rights and interests as its focus. CompCorp prepared its plan to help restore the value in the Confed estate, over time, towards full recovery for Canadian policyholders. It also began collaborating with the Superintendent of Financial Institutions, who was the liquidator in the early stages, to integrate its plan to support policyholders with his plan to liquidate the estate and untangle the international complexities.

CompCorp's plan was multi-dimensional. CompCorp provided immediate financial and guarantee support to all under-limit policyholders and also entered into loan agreements with the liquidator to ensure an uninterrupted flow of payments of claims up to the CompCorp limits. CompCorp ensured that a "hardship committee" was set up to deal with the cash needs and the cash surrender requests of policyholders in difficult financial circumstances. CompCorp also provided support to the liquidator so that he could conclude transactions to move complete blocks of business quickly to other insurers. Finally, CompCorp offered its in-house professional and insurance expertise to the liquidator, as well as cost-efficient actuarial support services. Through various mechanisms, the industry threw its support behind CompCorp's plan and contributed to the efficient resolution of this liquidation for Canadian policyholders.

In the case of all three life insurance insolvencies to date in Canada, but in particular with Confederation Life, CompCorp has been seen to be effective and efficient. It has found creative solutions to complex problems in an international context.

SOURCE: "CompCorp Plays Key Role in Ensuring that Canadian Policyholders of Confederation Life Receive Full Recovery of Their Benefits," Toronto: Canadian Life and Health Insurance Compensation Corporation, April 1999.

ability, dental coverage, and risk coverage against accidental death and dismemberment. In 1997 the federal government allowed life insurers (as well as property and casualty insurers) to write policies for loss of employment.

Since governments provide basic health care for all Canadians, private health insurance takes over where government coverage ends. Health insurance policies written by life insurance companies are mostly group policies sponsored by employers, unions, or professional groups. Under these policies,

www.

insured persons are typically responsible for a small dollar amount (the deductible) and a percentage of the cost (coinsurance). Disability income insurance usually supplements benefits available from the Canada/Quebec Pension Plans, Workers' Compensation, and Employment Insurance.

Property and Casualty Insurance Companies

In 1998 there were 87 federally regulated Canadian and 114 federally regulated foreign property and casualty insurance companies operating in Canada. Non-Canadian companies typically operate in Canada on a branch basis. The provinces of British Columbia, Saskatchewan, Manitoba, and Quebec operate government-owned companies that primarily provide automobile insurance. Property and casualty insurance policies protect individuals and organizations against loss due to theft, fire, and other physical damage, and against liability claims from injuries to others or the insured's property. There are many types of policies, each designed to cover specific classes of risk such as automobile, property, marine, aircraft, surety, and liability.

The main source of funds for property and casualty companies is premium income from insurance contracts. In contrast to life companies, these companies do not deliberately collect surplus premia, but they do accumulate pools of funds from premia and investment income. Since their liabilities are normally short-term in nature, and because claims against them are unpredictable, their assets are held in relatively liquid form. They invest very little in mortgages and concentrate their long-term investments in Government of Canada and provincial bond issues, which can be readily liquidated if the need arises. For immediate liquidity, they hold deposits with other financial intermediaries and invest in short-term market securities and paper. A small proportion of their assets is held in preferred and common stocks. At the end of 1998 their total assets amounted to $34 billion.

reinsurer an insurance company that insures risks assumed by other insurance companies

Property and casualty insurance companies, especially the smaller ones, as a rule do not assume all of the risks that they underwrite. They protect themselves against large and unexpected claims by passing some of their risks and ceding some of their premium income to **reinsurers**. Reinsurers are firms or exchanges that accept risks underwritten by other insurers. Lloyd's of London, which dates from the seventeenth century, is the largest and best-known insurance exchange in the world. It consists of groups or syndicates of investors who assume liability for any losses not covered by premium income from insurance contracts written directly on their behalf or from reinsuring risks initially underwritten by other insurance brokers.

In recent years, some of Lloyd's underwriting syndicates have experienced large losses due to catastrophes such as the Exxon Valdez oil spill off the coast of Alaska. In 1987, after the Ontario government passed enabling legislation and provided start-up funds, attempts to establish a Canadian insurance exchange in Toronto along the lines of Lloyd's of London were abandoned.

The property and casualty insurance industry has been subject to periods of intense price competition and falling profits, followed by periods of reduced availability of insurance coverage and premium-rate increases. For example, in the early 1980s Canadian general insurers competed aggressively for business by lowering their premium rates. Although the lower premia did not adequately reflect the larger and poorer risks underwritten, the insurers assumed that the increase in their investment income resulting from historically high interest rates would not only cover expected future insurance claims, but also produce healthy profits for them. At the same time, and for similar reasons, reinsurers actively competed for increased business by lowering their premium rates. When market interest rates fell at the very time that claims on liability policies rose in frequency and size, both direct insurers and reinsurers suffered losses. Within a relatively short period seven federally registered companies failed, while others escaped failure by merging with healthy institutions. To overcome their losses, insurers dramatically increased their premium rates after 1984 and refused to underwrite certain risks.

To reduce the tendency toward competitive cycles in the general insurance industry, which was resulting in institutional failure and wide fluctuations in premium rates, government regulators strengthened solvency requirements with respect to capital requirements and the amount of reserves insurers have to maintain at all times to meet their liabilities. Regulators also worked with the industry to design a plan to compensate policyholders for losses incurred when insurers fail. Subsequently, The Property and Casualty Insurance Compensation Corporation was established. In the event of the failure of a member company, this corporation will honour individual claims up to $200 000.

www.

Financial Corporations

There are two types of financial corporations: consumer loan companies, and sales finance or acceptance companies. These financial corporations primarily engage in providing credit to individuals and to commercial organizations for goods and services purchased at the retail, wholesale, and factory levels; and in making industrial loans and loans for the financing of inventories and capital expenditures.

Consumer Loan Companies

Consumer loan companies, which operated under the federal *Small Loans Act* before its repeal in 1981,[3] are commonly referred to as "small loan companies" when federally incorporated and as "money lenders" when provincially incorporated. Consumer loan companies specialize in direct cash lending to individuals. These loans are made for purposes of debt consolidation, for the purchase of consumer goods, and for financing vacations and other services.

---

3. The *Small Loans Act* was introduced in 1939 in an attempt to protect the public from usury. To do this, it set ceilings for interest rates charged on loans up to $1500. It was repealed after it was made obsolete by an anti-usury provision in the *Criminal Code*.

Traditionally, consumer loan companies made loans to lower-income groups who were unable to obtain credit elsewhere because of the perceived high risks involved. Since the mid-1960s, however, and in particular after the 1967 revisions to the *Bank Act,* which made it easier for the banks to make personal loans, both the banks and the near-banks have taken over much of the personal lending business formerly provided only by the consumer loan companies. Only four large companies with nationwide branches, together with a few smaller local companies, have survived the competition from the banks and the near-banks.[4]

Sales Finance Companies

Unlike consumer loan companies, sales or acceptance finance companies have little direct contact with the public. Almost all of their lending originates with other business firms, such as automobile and retail appliance dealers. For example, when a car is purchased but the customer does not pay cash, the automobile dealer writes a conditional sales contract whereby the customer does not assume full ownership until, through regular instalment payments, she or he has fully paid for it. The dealer in turn takes this contract to a sales finance company, which purchases or discounts the contract. The dealer receives the discounted amount of the contract from the sales finance company, which takes over the property rights to the car and collects the outstanding payments as they fall due. The sales finance company either assumes all of the risks or shares them with the dealer.

The major sales finance companies are affiliated with manufacturers and accept for discount the sales contracts of the manufacturers' dealers. For example, General Motors Acceptance Corporation discounts conditional sales contracts of General Motors' dealers. In addition it provides credit to dealers to finance their inventory of automobiles. In recent years, acceptance companies have diversified their lending activities by providing capital and term loans to companies and writing financial leases.

Before 1970, sales finance companies did not operate under specific legislation, chiefly because they did not deal directly with the public. Following the collapse of the Atlantic Acceptance Corporation and the Prudential Finance Corporation, the federal and provincial governments introduced legislation to regulate finance companies and protect consumers who buy on credit. A special feature of the federal *Investment Companies Act* is a provision to ensure that Canadian-controlled sales finance companies remain Canadian-controlled.

Financial Intermediation

Consumer loan and sales finance companies are consumer and business financing intermediaries. Most of their loans to households and businesses are

---

4. The four major consumer loan companies are Household Finance Corporation of Canada, Avco Financial Services Canada Limited, Beneficial Canada Holdings Inc., and Trans Canada Credit Corporation. In June 1979, IAC Limited, at that time Canada's leading sales finance and consumer loan company with some 140 offices, incorporated a wholly owned subsidiary, the Continental Bank of Canada, and was subsequently integrated into the bank.

secured by a chattel mortgage that enables them, in case of default, to repossess the chattel. These companies in turn borrow in the money market by issuing their own short-term paper secured by consumer durables or business inventories and equipment being financed. Their paper is referred to as finance company paper. To support their financing, the companies also issue long-term debt and obtain funding from parent and affiliated companies.

Under the federal Investment Companies Act, the Canada Deposit Insurance Corporation is authorized to be a lender of last resort to Canadian-controlled sales finance companies. A company may request a loan if it "has substantially exhausted the sources of funds reasonably available to it" and when such a loan is needed to "meet requirements for liquid funds needed to discharge its maturing debt obligations."

Investment Companies

There are two basic types of investment companies: closed-end companies and open-end companies. The latter are commonly referred to as mutual funds.

Closed-End Investment Companies

These companies trace their origin to the investment trusts developed in Europe during the 19th century. They first became popular in the United States and Canada in the 1920s, when they were established as a vehicle to gain control of other companies and to take advantage of leverage on a given amount of equity investment. For example, a typical company might be formed by the sale of shares for $100 000. After formation the company borrows $900 000 with an issue of bonds. The $1 million then available to the company is invested in the common shares of other companies. If in, say, a year's time the shares in these companies appreciate by 10 percent, the original investors in the investment company double their original investment of $100 000 less the costs incurred in borrowing. Most of the early companies were nothing more than highly speculative ventures.

Today's **closed-end investment companies**, unlike holding companies, do not invest in shares of other companies with the objective of ownership or control. They hold diversified portfolios of securities of other companies and are called closed-end because they issue only a limited number of shares of their common stock. These shares are traded in stock exchanges or over the counter by security dealers. These companies also issue marketable bonds and borrow from other financial institutions, depending on the extent to which they want to be leveraged.

Mutual Funds

Mutual funds are known as **open-end investment companies** because they constantly offer new shares, usually referred to as units, to the public. The first

closed-end investment companies investment companies that issue a fixed number of shares to invest in a portfolio of assets

open-end investment companies (mutual funds) investment companies that issue new shares and redeem old ones according to demand

Canadian mutual fund was Canadian Investment Fund Ltd., established by Calvin Bullock in 1931.[5] However, it is only within the last 25 years that mutual funds have become a popular investment vehicle, especially for registered retirement savings.

Mutual funds provide individuals with the opportunity to acquire shares in diversified, professionally managed asset portfolios. This allows them to improve their trade-off between risk and expected return. Fund managers reduce the overall credit risk by asset diversification and manage market risks with the use of financial derivatives.

ORGANIZATION AND MANAGEMENT   Mutual fund companies have been formed with the specific purpose of managing mutual fund portfolios. To avoid conflict of interest, the fund managers are usually excluded from owning the shares of the company that employs them. Since there are potentially large economies of scale in managing investment portfolios, mutual fund companies compete vigorously with each other, as is indicated by the proliferation and availability of different types of mutual funds.

Mutual funds are offered to the public by the deposit-taking institutions, insurance companies, securities dealers, and independent sponsors including affinity groups such as the Canadian Medical Association. Independent sponsors sell their funds through agents. These agents may be part of a mutual fund's direct sales force or insurance brokers, security dealers, or financial planners. Agents must be registered with provincial securities commissions.

Deposit-taking institutions promote their mutual funds through their branch networks. They must sell their proprietary mutual funds through subsidiaries that are registered under provincial securities acts. These acts also require that mutual fund units be sold by personnel registered to do so under their regulations.

TYPES OF FUNDS   Mutual funds vary according to the composition of their assets and, hence, according to the trade-off between risk and expected return. Funds can be broadly classified into three categories: money market funds, fixed income funds, and equity funds.

money market funds a mutual fund that invests in money market securities

Money market funds have their assets invested primarily in short-term commercial paper, bankers' acceptances, and treasury bills, all with very short maturities. The value of the units of these funds, especially those offered by the deposit-taking institutions, remains fixed, typically at $10. The interest earned is accrued daily and distributed monthly or quarterly in the form of additional units in such a way as to keep the value of each unit constant. Money market funds have become an alternative to direct holding of short-term securities and notice and term deposits of deposit-taking institutions. They were particularly popular during periods of declining interest rates in the mid-1990s because their yield adjusted, with a lag, to market rates.

---

5. For an interesting history of the development of mutual funds, see Hugh Bullock, *The Story of Investment Companies* (New York: Columbia University Press, 1959).

**fixed income
funds** *mutual
funds whose
assets are
invested primarily
in longer-term
fixed income obli-
gations such as
bonds*

Fixed income funds have their assets invested primarily in longer-term fixed income obligations. Income is distributed in cash or is reinvested in new units monthly or quarterly. The value of these units varies with the market value of the securities held in these funds, which in turn varies inversely with movements in interest rates. The most popular fixed income funds are bond funds and mortgage funds. The assets of mortgage funds are primarily residential mortgages insured under the *National Housing Act*.

Besides Canadian dollar funds, which hold fixed income securities denominated in Canadian dollars, there are funds that hold securities denominated only in foreign currencies.

equity funds
*mutual funds
whose assets are
invested primarily
in equities and/or
real estate*

Equity funds have their assets primarily invested in equities or real estate. Some of these so-called balanced funds contain both equities and fixed income securities. As with most other types of funds, earned income is distributed in cash or reinvested in new units monthly or quarterly. The value of the units varies from day to day according to market price changes in the underlying assets held.

A distinction is also made between equity funds that are invested in high-yielding common shares and fixed-income securities (so-called dividend funds), and those that invest only in common stock. The latter funds are referred to as growth funds since their managers attempt to pick the stock of companies that show a high potential for growth and in turn enhance the market value of their common shares.

Equity funds also differ in terms of the industry concentration of investment portfolios. For example, energy funds invest in the shares of companies operating in the energy sector, precious metals funds invest in shares of mining companies, and ethical funds invest only in shares of companies that meet certain criteria such as environmental standards.

Aside from Canadian equity funds, which hold Canadian common stocks, there are a variety of foreign equity funds such as "European" funds and "Asian" funds. There are many more types of mutual funds, each attempting to achieve a competitive advantage by holding a particular subset of assets that attract investors with different preferences.

PRICING OF MUTUAL FUND UNITS   As has already been observed, money market funds typically price their units at $10 and pass on the earnings and capital gains generated by the funds by way of additional units. Other types of mutual funds issue new units and redeem outstanding ones at the pro-rated net asset value of the portfolio. This is the market price of the portfolio less any fees.

LOAD AND NO-LOAD FUNDS   Some mutual funds charge their unit holders a fee at time of purchase (front-end), or at time of redemption. Such funds are referred to as load funds. Deposit-taking institutions as a rule do not charge such fees and, hence, their funds are no-load. All funds, however, both load and no-load, charge periodic management and administration fees.

MANAGED FUNDS AND INDEX FUNDS   Managed funds are actively managed and traded to achieve better risk-return trade-offs for their unit holders. Index funds, on the other hand, are passive investors and purchase securities

www.

that mimic a market portfolio in terms of the proportional holdings of a market index such as the TSE 300 stock composite index.

It is an open question whether, over the long run, managed funds outperform the market. If indeed they do not, one could conclude that the extra cost involved in managing these funds is a waste of valuable resources. Some evidence exists that, on average, actively managed equity funds tend to underperform when stock market behaviour is bullish, but do much better when a market behaviour is bearish.

Growth in Investment Funds

It is only within the past 25 years that investment funds have achieved much growth, most of which has taken place since the early 1990s. Because of the poor performance of the bond and equity markets during the 1970s, growth remained slow and by the end of that decade the market value of the assets held by these funds was only about $4 billion. It was not until the very strong securities markets following the 1981–82 recession that these funds achieved rapid growth and reached the $30 billion mark. About one-half of this growth was due to the increase in the purchase of shares and units, with the remainder due to the rise in stock prices. This growth ended with the stock market crash of October 1987. Following the crash, with the rising trend in interest rates until mid-1990, investment funds again lost some of their popularity. However, as interest rates began their decline in the early 1990s, and equity markets strengthened, growth of investment funds took off.

Other factors besides declining interest rates and buy-out stock markets explain this phenomenal growth. Two of these are the entrance of the banks into the mutual fund industry and the inclusion by individuals of mutual funds within their Registered Retirement Savings Plans.

Pension Plans

Old Age Security (OAS) a universal benefit that provides a flat-rate government pension to all Canadians aged 65 or over (though it is taxed back for high-income earners)

Pension plans are established to provide retirement incomes to individuals. At the beginning of 1994, Canada had 15 800 pension plans. Today there are well over 16 000 pension plans, affecting more than five million members. Canada's retirement income system consists of government-funded or sponsored pension plans, employers-sponsored registered pension plans, and personal pension plans.

Government-Funded or -Sponsored Pension Plans

The federal government funds two main programs. **Old Age Security (OAS)** and the **Guaranteed Income Supplement (GIS)**. The OAS is a universal benefit that provides a flat rate pension for persons aged 65 and over who meet

Canadian residency requirements. In recent years OAS benefits have been taxed (clawed) back for high-income earners. The GIS supplements the OAS for persons whose incomes are below a threshold level. Some provincial governments also have programs to supplement the federal OAS and GIS.

The Canada Pension Plan and in Quebec, the Quebec Pension Plan, are mandatory for all persons in the labour force. Contributions must be made by all employees and their employers based on earnings. Pension benefits of these plans are based on an individual's total lifetime contributions and pre-retirement income level. Surplus funds accumulated in the Canada Pension Plan are invested in nonmarketable provincial bonds. The Caisse de dépôt et placement du Québec administers surplus funds accumulated by the Quebec Pension Plan as well as by other public and private organizations in the province. In early 1997, the federal government announced that annual contributions paid by employees and employers into the Canada Pension Plan would increase from $969 to a maximum of $1635 by the year 2003. With this increase it was estimated that the plan's accumulated funds would rise from $35 billion to $100 billion by the year 2006 and to $300 billion by the year 2015. The Canada Pension Plan Investment Board will invest these funds in the market to earn a return that will make further increases in contributions unnecessary.

Employer-Sponsored Registered Pension Plans

registered pension plans *pension plans registered and supervised under government pension legislation*

Registered pension plans must be registered under the federal *Pension and Benefits Standards Act* or the appropriate provincial *Benefits Act*. These acts set out minimum standards to ensure protection of members' rights as well as a plan's viability. The federal Office of the Superintendent of Financial Institutions and respective provincial bodies ensure that all comply with these acts.

Registered plans must be funded; that is, sufficient assets have to be accumulated to pay pension commitments. The assets of pension plans must be administered according to the "prudent person rule." This defines the fiduciary responsibility of investment managers in terms of a guideline of prudence and a standard of care and professional competence.

To enjoy tax-shelter status, registered pension plans must also meet certain requirements under the federal *Income Tax Act*. For example, the maximum that pension funds could invest in foreign markets on a tax-sheltered basis was 20 percent of book value. In the 2000 federal budget, this was increased to 25 percent for 2000, and 30 percent in 2001.

defined benefit pension plan *a plan where benefits are predetermined by a formula and employer contributions depend on the cost of the benefit less the employee's contribution, if any*

TRUSTEED PENSION PLANS   These plans make up the largest proportion of registered pension plans. Trusteed pension plans are managed under a trust agreement. The trustee can be either a trust company or a private trustee consisting of at least three individuals, all residents of Canada and at least one independent of the sponsoring organization. Trusteed plans usually are sponsored by employers and funded through contributions by employers or by employers and employees.

Pension plans are either **defined benefit pension plans** or defined contributing plans (also called money purchase plans). In a defined benefit plan, benefits are determined by the employee's salary and length of employment, or are simply a flat amount for each year of employment. The sponsor of such a plan guarantees benefits regardless of the investment performances of accumulated benefits.

In a **defined contributing plan**, benefits are based on the accumulated contributions and their investment performance. The investment risk is assumed by members of the plan rather than by its sponsor.

defined contributing pension plan *a plan where contributions by employees and the employer are fixed and the benefits depend on the contributions and their earnings*

INSURANCE COMPANY CONTRACTS   While most large pension plans are funded through trusteed arrangements, most small-to medium-sized employer-sponsored plans are established under insurance company contracts. These include individual or group annuity contracts for employees; deposit-administered contracts, where employers contribute to interest-bearing deposit funds held with insurance companies; and segregated fund contracts. Under segregated fund contracts, the pension liability remains with the sponsoring employer, who also directs the asset-mix decisions with respect to fund investments.

OTHER TYPES OF EMPLOYER-SPONSORED ARRANGEMENTS   These include different types of profit-sharing plans and group Registered Retirement Savings Plans (group RRSPs). An employer-sponsored group RRSP is a collection of RRSPs for individual employees to which the employer contributes.

GOVERNMENT EMPLOYEE PLANS
Governments also have sponsored pension plans for their employees. These plans are registered, but not always funded. In the unfunded plans, employees' contributions are paid into a government's general revenue funds, and pension benefits are paid from these funds. Pension plans for federal public servants, the Canadian Forces, and the RCMP are examples of unfunded plans. More recently, the governments of Ontario and Alberta have changed the pension plans for their employees from unfunded to funded trusteed plans.

Personal Savings Plans

Registered Retirement Savings Plans (RRSPs) *tax-sheltered arrangements for investing savings for retirement*

Most individuals save for their own retirement and to supplement government and employer pension plans. Real assets as well as financial assets are accumulated by individuals to provide for their retirement income. Many individuals contribute earned income into **Registered Retirement Savings Plans (RRSPs).** Mutual funds have become a popular vehicle for these tax-sheltered plans. Life insurance with a savings component has long been a standard financial instrument used by Canadians to prepare for their retirement.

Other Financial Institutions

Financial Leasing Corporations

Financial leasing as an alternative to traditional modes of financing has grown rapidly in Canada since the mid-1960s. A lease is a method of financing the use of an asset as opposed to financing its purchase. It is important to distinguish between two basic types of leases: operating leases and financial leases (also called full payout leases). With operating leases, the lessee, or user, pays a rental fee for the possession and use of a specific asset for a fraction of the asset's useful life. Car rental or leasing is a common form of an operating lease.

With a financial lease, the contractual lease agreement usually extends over the full, expected useful life of the asset and is not cancellable. The contractual payments return the lessor's entire investment during the basic term of the lease, together with the desired yield on the asset. However, the lessee assumes most or all of the rights and obligations of ownership. The lessor pays for, and takes title to, the property selected and ordered by the lessee. The lessee, on the other hand, assumes all the costs associated with the use of the leased property.

In Canada leases are written by companies specifically incorporated for this purpose, and by finance companies, trust and mortgage loan companies, industrial corporations, and wholly owned leasing subsidiaries of banks. Financial leasing companies that are subsidiaries of the banks are not allowed to engage in leasing of automobiles and household property.

Financial leasing corporations finance their operations with loans from other financial institutions; the sale of short-term notes in domestic and foreign money markets; and the issue of long-term notes, bonds, and debentures. In addition, parent and affiliated companies provide loans and share capital.

Venture Capital Companies

venture capital company *a company that provides long-term capital and management assistance to new and expanding companies*

www.

Venture capital companies provide financing, and frequently managerial assistance, to firms in the early stages of their development or to small firms in the process of expansion. Most firms that receive financing from venture capital companies are unable to raise funds through bank loans, or are too small or too little-known to issue and distribute their own securities in the capital market. Investments by venture capital firms are as a rule in the form of common and preferred stock. Preferred stock is frequently taken up with either bonus common stock or conversion rights. You will recall we discussed the Canada Venture Exchange—whose aim is to provide venture companies with access to capital—in Chapter 6.

Some provincial governments have introduced development or venture corporation programs to encourage the private sector to set up venture corporations to invest in small businesses within their territorial jurisdictions. These programs encourage the establishment of small business venture capital corporations by offering investors loans, grants, or provincial income tax credits. The federal and some provincial governments have special programs that provide tax credits to labour-sponsored venture capital corporations to finance small and medium-sized enterprises. For example, in New Brunswick, an investor who put $5000 into a labour-sponsored venture capital corporation received a $1500 tax credit in 1999.

Merchant Banking

Although relatively new to Canada, merchant banking dates from the 18th century, when international trade was financed by bills of exchange drawn on big merchant houses, which also became known as acceptance houses. Over time, particularly in Britain, these houses developed into merchant banks, conducting a broad range of financial and nonfinancial activities. For example, they became engaged in foreign exchange and bullion trading, securities underwriting and trading, project financing, corporate restructuring, lending activities considered imprudent for commercial bankers, and the managing of funds for clients.

In Canada, companies engaged in merchant banking are not allowed to identify themselves as merchant banks. Hence, they refer to themselves as financial firms that provide merchant banking services. As agents, these firms are paid a fee to provide advice and a broad range of managerial services to corporations and institutions. For example, these services may be related to corporate mergers or acquisitions, debt financing and restructuring, and project financing. As principals they use their capital resources to make loans and acquire equity in companies that, because of the risks involved, are not able to obtain financing from other financial institutions. The banks and other financial institutions offer a variety of merchant banking services as agents. Some also own subsidiaries that act as both agents and principals.

Financial Holding Companies

financial holding company *a company that is the sole or major shareholder of a variety of different types of financial institutions*

In recent years **financial holding companies,** also referred to as financial conglomerates, have emerged. These holding companies have brought together under a single corporate umbrella one or more trust companies, life insurance companies, mutual funds, investment counsellors, general insurance companies, investment dealers, and banks. In addition to controlling financial institutions, many of these holding groups are also associated with major nonfinancial corporations. These holding companies may have become the harbingers of "financial supermarkets," providing access to "one-stop financing shopping."

In mid-1999 the federal government announced proposals for the reform of the financial sector, one of which was a new holding company structure that would allow widely held insurance companies and banks to organize within a widely held non-operating holding company. This change would allow for a broader range of investment activities, changes to capital requirements, and new ownership rules that would allow some firms to be closely held.

Government Insurance and Lending Institutions

The Role of Government

The role of government in financial markets is both large and diverse. As we have already seen, government is extensively involved in the financial intermediation process through its regulation of financial institutions. In addition, government is an important supplier of funds and, as such, is itself a financial intermediary. Government also participates in risk intermediation by guaranteeing repayment of loans from financial institutions and by insuring credits extended by them.

The rationale for direct government intervention in financial markets is market failure. Four potential sources of market failure have been identified: obstacles to the proper functioning of financial markets, externalities, public goods, and uninsurable risks.[6] Obstacles to the proper functioning of financial markets may take the form of regulatory restrictions imposed on the activities of financial institutions, the lack of competition, differences in taxation of various financial flows, self-imposed behaviour by financial institutions, and deficiencies in information gathering. These obstacles to the proper functioning of financial markets have been associated with "credit gaps" that are said to exist when potential borrowers facing similar risks and expected returns are treated differently with respect to the availability of funds.

Markets fail as a result of externalities because of a divergence between private and social costs and benefits. Public goods, whose consumption by one person does not rule out their consumption by others, cause market failure because their producers cannot receive adequate compensation. For example, insofar as information is a public good, financial institutions may be unwilling to lend to certain sectors because they cannot receive full compensation for gathering the necessary information with respect to risks and expected returns. The final potential source of financial market failure is the existence of uninsurable risks. These risks cannot be lowered by portfolio diversification and therefore cannot be insured. While government also cannot provide insurance against these risks, it can intervene and spread their burden over a greater number of participants. Such intervention is justified when high risks have the potential of generating significant social benefits.

Business Assistance

Financial and managerial assistance is offered to business enterprises by both the federal and provincial governments and their agencies.

In 1944 the Industrial Development Bank (IDB) was set up by the federal government as a subsidiary of the Bank of Canada to provide financial assistance to small businesses unable to obtain other financing on reasonable terms and conditions. The IDB was succeeded in 1975 by the Federal Business Development Bank (FBDB). Its objectives were to promote and assist in the

---

6. See Economic Council of Canada, *Intervention and Efficiency: A Study of Government Credit and Credit Guarantees to the Private Sector* (Ottawa, Minister of Supply and Services Canada, 1982).

establishment of business enterprises by providing not only financial assistance but also management, training, and planning services.

In 1995, the FBDB was succeeded by the **Business Development Bank of Canada** (BDC). Its mandate is to help create and develop small and medium-sized businesses. It is not a lender of last resort, as were its predecessors. Instead it complements private financial institutions and has entered into strategic alliances with them for joint lending and management support programs.

The BDC provides specialized financing for commercially viable business projects as well as a wide range of business counselling, training, and monitoring services. It makes term loans as well as venture loans, which combine characteristics of term loans with venture capital. It also does venture capital financing, often with other venture capital partners, by taking an equity position in small companies that demonstrate potential for growth.

The BDC funds its operations with capital and other appropriations from the federal government, and with the issue of its notes in domestic and foreign financial markets.

Farm Credit Assistance

The major government vehicle for providing credit assistance to farmers is the **Farm Credit Corporation (FCC)**. The FCC was set up as a Crown corporation in 1959 and as the successor to the Canadian Farm Loan Board, which dated from 1927. The FCC makes and administers loans under the *Farm Credit Act* and the *Farm Syndicates Credit Act*. In 1993 the FCC's mandate was broadened to include financing for rural diversification and farm-related business. The FCC also provides products and services to support the aquaculture industry.

The FCC can lend to new and established farmers for any size of operation. Loans are available for any agricultural or farm-related purpose, including the purchase of land, quotas, equipment, or livestock; construction of buildings including houses; debt consolidation; or any expenditure that will contribute to the development of a farm operation. In February 2000, the FCC offered capital leasing activities as an alternative to loans in an effort to help farmers secure greater access to capital equipment.

Farm-related business loans are available to anyone who is or will be engaged in farming or who is or will be a shareholder in a farm operation. The FCC can finance businesses on or off the farm that store, process, or transport farm inputs or farm produce to the farm of the business owner. Financial assistance for rural diversification allows the development of businesses on farm property even if the businesses are not directly farm related.

In addition to extending loans, the FCC offers extensive counselling and advisory services to borrowers. It also offers borrowers a group life insurance program to protect their estates in the event of premature death.

The FCC funds its operations with capital contributed by the federal government, through direct appropriations for specific government programs, and by the issue of its notes for sale to the federal government and in domestic and foreign capital markets.

Housing Assistance

The federal and provincial governments and their agencies provide a wide range of financial assistance to housing, including loans, loan guarantees, insurance, grants, and subsidies. The **Canada Mortgage and Housing Corporation (CMHC)** was established by the federal government in 1945 to administer its *National Housing Act*.[7] It is not only a financial institution, but also a quasi-department of government, administering all aspects of the federal government's housing policies and programs. Its mandate, as stated in the *Act*, is "to promote the construction of new housing, the repair and modernization of existing houses and the improvement of housing and living conditions."

In its role as a financial institution, CMHC makes direct loans and investments with funds borrowed from the federal government. Its original mandate was to be a direct residential mortgage lender of last resort. However, during the 1960s and 1970s it became the most important residential mortgage lender, financing nearly 20 percent of all new dwelling units being constructed. Its major involvement in housing finance at the time was the result of the government's policy to use government funds to counter the cyclical behaviour of residential construction. More recently, direct mortgage lending by CMHC has been used primarily for social housing; that is, to provide housing for low-income groups. It now funds its direct loans not only by borrowing from the government, but also by borrowing from the private sector with the issue of mortgage-backed securities. For its social housing program it also receives federal government appropriations to provide assistance in the form of grants, guarantees, and subsidies, frequently under cost-sharing agreements with the provinces and territories.

The CMHC is the primary supplier of residential mortgage loan insurance. It administers a Mortgage Insurance Fund that is the depository for insurance premiums and from which insurance claims are paid. For a time in the 1980s, the fund experienced deficits, the result of a large number of mortgage defaults. This liquidity problem was met by special advances from the federal government and an increase in the insurance premium rate.

To encourage the flow of funds into the housing sector, in 1985 CMHC introduced payment guarantees to holders of securities backed by NHA-insured mortgages. It also offers rental guarantees as well as grants and subsidies to organizations for housing projects where rents are related to low income. Financial assistance is also offered for home ownership by low-income groups.

---

7. The first federal housing legislation was the *Dominion Housing Act* of 1935, under which the government advanced funds at subsidized rates to approved lenders who in turn made 20-year mortgage loans with down payments of 20 percent rather than the traditional 40 percent or more of the value of the mortgaged property. In 1938 the *Act* was replaced by the *National Housing Act*, which provided for direct federal loans to borrowers in small and remote communities not served by private mortgage lenders. Amendments to the *Act* in 1944 resulted in the establishment of the Central Mortgage and Housing Corporation, later renamed the Canada Mortgage and Housing Corporation.

Export Insurance and Finance

**Export
Development
Corporation
(EDC)** *a federal
government insti-
tution that pro-
vides export credit
insurance and
export financing*

www.

The **Export Development Corporation (EDC)** is a federal government financial institution established in 1969 as the successor to the Export Credits
Insurance Corporation, which had been set up in 1944.

The primary function of EDC is to assist with financing Canadian export
sales through loans, loan guarantees, and credit insurance. Some provinces
also have special programs for financial assistance to exporters.

EDC export insurance protects exporters against 90 percent of their losses
due to nonpayment relating to commercial and political risks. Protected commercial risks include buyer insolvency, default on payments, repudiation of
goods, or termination of the contract. Political risk coverage protects exporters
against loss due to foreign exchange conversion or transfer payment difficulties; war, revolution, or insurrection preventing payment; or cancellation of
government import or export permits. Foreign investment insurance provides
coverage to Canadian investments in foreign countries, normally for periods
up to 15 years, against political risks.

EDC generally provides export financing for up to 85 percent of the contract value, at both fixed and floating rates of interest, to foreign buyers of
Canadian goods, equipment, and services. More recently, EDC has used lines
of credit and protocols to establish prearranged export financing facilities with
foreign banks and institutions. Lines of credit are used by EDC to lend money
to foreign banks, and to institutions that in turn re-lend it to foreign purchasers
of Canadian goods and services. Buyer credit protocols allow foreign institutions to guarantee EDC export loans to foreign buyers; and under supplier
credit protocols, foreign institutions guarantee promissory notes issued by foreign buyers to Canadian exporters. EDC, in turn, purchases these notes from
Canadian exporters.

The chartered banks have cooperated with EDC by purchasing participa-
tions in EDC loans and by co-lending or parallel lending with it. Parallel
lending refers to lending on the same project, but with separate loan agreements. EDC also provides guarantees to the banks with respect to some of their
export loans.

The interest rate charged by EDC on most of its loans is based on the cost
of funds to it. Concessional financing at less than commercial rates is available
under its *crédit mixte* program. This program allows for a lower interest rate by
mixing the standard commercial rate with a lower subsidized rate. The federal
government has established a special fund to meet the extra costs incurred as
a result of the subsidy portion of these loans.

The liability for outstanding loans and undisbursed commitments to foreign borrowers, as well as the liability on insurance and guarantees, is assumed
either directly by EDC or by the federal government. EDC finances its own
operations with capital contributions from the federal government and by borrowing in international capital markets.

The EDC was in the news in early 2000 when the chartered banks complained about its unfair advantage in providing loan guarantees. The EDC
wrote nearly $1.5 billion in loans during 1999, for which it could guarantee 85
percent of each loan using federal government assistance. The chartered banks
could guarantee only 64 percent of each loan. It was argued that levelling the

playing field would encourage competition and the provision of loans to small and medium-sized businesses. In addition, reports indicating that several EDC loans were overdue led to calls for changes to the manner in which the EDC provides export financing.

Government Trust Funds

Governments establish trust funds for a variety of purposes. Three of these, the Caisse de dépôt et placement du Québec, the Alberta Heritage Trust Fund, and the Saskatchewan Heritage Fund are of particular interest not only because of their size, but also because each one is considered by its respective government as a policy instrument for economic and social development.

The Caisse de dépôt et placement du Québec (the Caisse) was established in 1965 as the government's agency to administer contributions collected under the Quebec Pension Plan. Subsequently, it also received funds for investment from other public sector pension plans, the Quebec automobile insurance plan (Régle l'Assurance Automobile), the Workers' Compensation Board (Commission de la santé, et de la sécurité du travail), and the supplementary pension plan of the Quebec construction industry. By the end of 1996 the Caisse had accumulated a pool of investment funds of some $57 billion. By the end of 1999 this had risen to $105.5 billion.

The Caisse invests in equities, bonds, real estate, and money market securities. Over the years it has made significant investments in Canadian corporations, especially in corporations resident in Quebec. Its investments in the province have been associated with the government's industrial strategy aimed at strengthening and diversifying the Quebec economy. Instead of being a passive investor, the Caisse has frequently sought representation on the boards of directors of companies in which it holds substantial ownership shares. It has become the single largest investor in Canadian companies and the largest trader of securities on the Montreal Stock Exchange.

The Alberta Heritage Savings Trust Fund was created in 1976 by the government of Alberta to accumulate some of the royalty and other revenues collected by the government from nonrenewable oil and natural gas resources. At first, 30 percent of the government's nonrenewable resource revenue was transferred to the fund. In April 1983 this allocation was reduced to 15 percent, and no further transfers were made after January 1987. By 1987 the fund had accumulated some $15 billion. In 1982, because of the slowdown in the economy and the emergence of government budget deficits in Alberta, earnings on the fund's investments, formerly retained by it, began to be transferred to the government's general revenue.

In 1997, new legislation restructured the fund into two portfolios: a transitional portfolio with the objective of earning income to support the government's fiscal plan, and an endowment portfolio with the objective of maximizing long-term financial returns. The 1997 legislation also provides that, subject to certain conditions, sufficient investment income must be retained to protect the value of the fund from inflation.

At the end of 1996, the fund's assets amounted to $11.9 billion. By December 1999 this had risen to $12.3 billion. Much of this total was invested in highly liquid money market securities, marketable bonds, and Canadian equities.

The Saskatchewan Heritage Fund was set up in 1978 to collect and distribute all of the Province of Saskatchewan's nonrenewable resource revenue. The income earned on the fund is used for provincial development expenditures, for loans to and investments in Crown corporations, and to finance current government expenditures.

KEY TERMS

adverse selection
annuity contract
book-based transactions
bought deal
brokers
Business Development Bank of Canada (BDC)
Canada Mortgage and Housing Corporation (CMHC)
Canadian Investor Protection Fund
cash surrender value
closed-end investment companies
dealers
deferred annuity
defined benefit pension plan
defined contributing pension plan

demutualization
discount brokers
equity funds
Export Development Corporation (EDC)
Farm Credit Corporation (FCC)
financial holding company
fixed income funds
full-service brokers
Guaranteed Income Supplement (GIS)
immediate annuity
market makers
money market funds
moral hazard
new money policy

Old Age Security (OAS)
open-end investment companies
primary dealers
registered pension plans
Registered Retirement Savings Plans (RRSPs)
reinsurer
risk pooling
risk sharing
segregated funds
term insurance
universal life policy
variable life policy
venture capital company
whole-life insurance

REVIEW QUESTIONS

1. Distinguish between a securities broker and a securities dealer.
2. How do full-service brokers differ from discount brokers?
3. What is the difference between term insurance and whole-life insurance?
4. What are the life insurance companies' segregated funds?
5. How does a consumer loan company differ from a sales finance company, and a closed-end investment company from a mutual fund?
6. Illustrate how investment trusts, the forerunners of modern-day investment companies, used leverage to enhance the expected returns for investors.
7. What is the difference between a trusteed and an insured pension plan?

8. In what way are operating leases not the same as financial leases?
9. What reasons can be given to justify government participation in financial markets?
10. Describe the roles of the Farm Credit Corporation, the Canada Mortgage and Housing Corporation, and the Export Development Corporation.
11. Why would the chartered banks be critical of the EDC? What arguments did they make in early 2000?
12. Explain the difference between a defined benefit pension plan and a defined contributing plan.
13. Contact a local insurance company and ask them for literature on defined benefit and defined contributing pension plans. Provide suggestions on how they could improve their literature with respect to explaining the differences between the two plans.

14. What role does the CMHC play in the housing market today? Has it changed in the last 20 years?
15. What changes to the FCC have been introduced to provide greater assistance to farmers? Why were they introduced?
16. Are there both federal and provincial regulators of nondepository intermediaries? Why? Wouldn't it be more economical to consider a different regulatory structure?
17. If a no-load mutual fund has no sales commissions, how does a broker make money from offering these funds to her clients? Why offer a no-load fund? What are the benefits to holding one?

SELECTED READINGS

Brooks, S. "The State as Financier: A Comparison of the Caisse de dépôt et placement du Québec and the Alberta Heritage Savings Trust Fund." *Canadian Public Policy* (September 1987), pp. 304–29.

Canada. "Export Financing: Consultation Report." Ottawa: Government of Canada, January 1985.

——. "Trusteed Pension Funds: Financial Statistics." Ottawa: Statistics Canada, Catalogue 74–201 (Annual).

——. *Financial Institutions: Financial Statistics*. Ottawa: Statistics Canada, Catalogue 61–006 (Quarterly).

Canadian Co-operative Credit Society. *Annual Report*, various issues.

COMPCORP. *Annual Report*. 1998.

Department of Finance. *Demutualization Regime for Canadian Life Insurance Companies*. August 1998.

Economic Council of Canada. *Intervention and Efficiency: A Study of Government Credit and Credit Guarantees to the Private Sector*. Ottawa: Minister of Supply and Services Canada, 1982.

Fleming, James. *Merchants of Fear: An Investigation of Canada's Insurance Industry*. Toronto: Penguin, 1986.

Moysey, A. "Deposit Insurance and Other Compensation Arrangements." Task Force on the Future of the Canadian Financial Sector. Ottawa: Department of Finance, 1998.

O'Connor, Sean. "The Structure of the Co-operative Credit System in Canada." *Bank of Canada Review* (December 1988), pp. 3–19.

——. "The Evolution of the Co-operative Credit System in Canada." *Bank of Canada Review* (February 1989), pp. 3–17.

——. "New Directions for the Cooperative Credit System in Canada." *Bank of Canada Review* (March 1989), pp. 3–16.

Office of the Superintendent of Financial Institutions. *Assets of Canadian Life Insurance Companies—Consolidated—1998.*

Pesando, James E. *An Economic Analysis of Government Investment Corporations, with Attention to the Caisse de dépôt et placement du Québec and the Alberta Heritage Fund*. Discussion Paper No. 277. Ottawa: Economic Council of Canada, March 1985.

Smith, L.B., and James E. Pesando (eds.). *Government in Canadian Capital Markets*. Montreal: C.D. Howe Institute, 1978.

CHAPTER SIXTEEN

THE BANK OF CANADA AND THE OBJECTIVES OF MONETARY POLICY

> After reading this chapter you should be able to
> 1. Describe the founding of the Bank of Canada
> 2. Outline the functions and responsibilities of the Bank
> 3. Explain the management structure at the Bank and provide arguments for changing the mandate of the Bank
> 4. Examine the historical role of monetary policy
> 5. Present four national economic goals and explain why compromise and trade-offs have to be made to satisfy these national goals
> 6. Describe the objectives of monetary policy in Canada since 1991

Central banking is all about managing money. In 1873, Walter Bagehot, in the first and now famous account of a central bank, observed that "money will not manage itself...."[1] Bagehot was describing the role of the Bank of England, established in 1694. While not founded as a central bank, the development of central banking operations, associated with the issue of notes for circulation and the provision of cash at last resort to the banking system, is attributed to the Bank of England. Government institutions created specifically as central banks date only from the first part of the twentieth century. As we saw previously, Lord Sydenham, governor general of the Province of Canada, attempted unsuccessfully to establish a provincial bank of issue in 1841. In contrast, the *Finance Acts* of 1914 and 1923 allowed the Department of Finance to undertake the central bank function of providing cash at last resort to the chartered banks. It was not until 1934 that the Bank of Canada was established specifically as a central bank under the auspices of the federal government. The Federal Reserve System, made up of 12 regional central banks, had been established in the United States 20 years earlier.

www.

---

1. Walter Bagehot, *Lombard Street* (Homewood, Ill.: Richard D. Irwin), p. 10. Reprinted from Scribner, Armstrong edition, New York, 1873.

The Founding of the Bank of Canada

In 1933, in response to calls by the opposition parties in the House of Commons for the establishment of a central bank, the Conservative government appointed the Royal Commission on Banking and Currency. Under the chairmanship of Lord Macmillan, an eminent British jurist, the Commission began its work in August and, after 59 days, submitted a report to the government on September 28. The Macmillan Commission Report recommended the establishment of a central bank, against the wishes of the chartered banks. It cautioned, however, that such a bank "could not cure all of the economic ills of Canada." The chartered banks' opposition to a central bank was based on their reluctance to give up their own note-issuing power, which for them was a source of both profit and prestige.

In introducing the legislation to create a central bank, the government acted with the same unprecedented haste that the Macmillan Commission had shown in preparing its report. Parliament passed the *Bank of Canada Act* in 1934, and in March of the following year the newly founded central bank started operations.

It was the intention of the government to structure the new central bank in a way that would avoid excessive private interference and political pressure. Initially the central bank was privately owned, with all its stock sold to the public. Private interference was considered to have been minimized, since individual holdings of stock were limited and no one directly connected with a chartered bank was permitted to hold any shares. In addition, officers and employees of banks were not eligible for appointment as governor, deputy governor, or assistant governor of the Bank. Dividends paid to the stockholders were limited to 4.5 percent, with any excess profits accruing to the government. Although the government appointed all members of the Bank's first board of directors, provision was made for directors to be subsequently appointed by its shareholders. However, the deputy minister of finance was to remain a permanent member of both the Bank's board and executive committee. The government also appointed the Bank's first governor. Future appointments to the positions of governor and deputy governor could be made by the directors but would be subject to government approval.

In 1936, the Liberal government, which had assumed office in the fall of the previous year, fulfilled an election promise by bringing the Bank under closer government ownership. In an amendment to the *Bank of Canada Act*, the Bank issued additional shares that would be purchased by the government to give it 51 percent ownership. In 1938, the government acquired all of the Bank's remaining outstanding shares, thereby completing its nationalization.

www.

The Functions and Responsibilities of the Bank of Canada

The Bank's functions, as spelled out in the preamble to the *Bank of Canada Act*, are:

> *to regulate credit and currency in the best interests of the economic life of the nation, to control and protect the external value of the national monetary unit*

and to mitigate by its influence fluctuations in the general level of production, trade, prices and employment, so far as may be possible within the scope of monetary action, and generally to promote the economic and financial welfare of Canada.

Monetary Policy

A major reason for establishing a central bank in Canada was the need for an institution that would assume control over the rate of growth of the money supply. In Chapters 17 and 18 we will describe in detail how the Bank, by controlling the availability of ultimate cash to the banking system (the banks and the near-banks), also controls the growth of money. The Bank has primary responsibility for the conduct of monetary policy. However, as we describe below, that responsibility is shared with the federal government.

Lender of Last Resort

One of the primary functions of the Bank of Canada is to act as lender of last resort to the banking system. An important way in which the Bank is the ultimate source of cash to the banking system is by extending secured loans to the direct clearers of the Canadian Payments Association.

Issuance of Bank Notes

www.

The Bank of Canada is responsible for issuing the country's bank notes for circulation. The day it began operations, the Bank replaced the outstanding issue of Dominion notes, which had previously been issued by the federal government.[2] Provision was also made for the gradual removal of the note-issuing privilege of the chartered banks. However, it was not until 1945 that the banks completely stopped issuing their own notes for circulation and the Bank of Canada's notes became the only legal tender issue in the country.[3]

The *Bank of Canada Act* initially required the Bank to redeem its notes in gold "in the form of bars containing approximately four hundred ounces of gold." Although this provision remained in the Act until 1967, it was never used. Initially, the Bank was supposed to maintain a gold reserve of at least 25 percent against its outstanding notes and deposit liabilities. This requirement was suspended at the outbreak of the war in 1940, when the Bank's holdings of

---

2. When the Bank of Canada assumed responsibility for the redemption of Dominion notes, the government gave the Bank $69 million in gold, $1 million in silver, and $115 million in Dominion securities to offset this liability.

3. After 1934 the note issue of a chartered bank was limited to the amount of its paid-up capital. Beginning in 1936, however, this limit was reduced by 5 percent per annum, and beginning in 1940, by 10 percent per annum. By the end of 1945, the limit was 20 percent of a bank's paid-up capital. The 1944 revisions to the *Bank Act* prohibited any further issue or reissue of chartered bank notes. This restriction gave the Bank of Canada the sole privilege of issuing notes for circulation in Canada. In 1950, after the chartered banks made a cash payment to the Bank of Canada, the Bank assumed the liability for all chartered bank notes still outstanding.

gold and foreign exchange were transferred to the Foreign Exchange Control Board and later to the Foreign Exchange Fund Account. The Bank's gold reserve requirement against its note and deposit liability was repealed in 1967.[4]

Financial Advisor and Fiscal Agent to the Federal Government

The Bank of Canada's original legislation empowered it to act as financial advisor and fiscal agent for both the federal and provincial governments. The Bank never acted in this capacity for the provinces, and in 1967 the provision in the Act with respect to the provinces was repealed.

As the federal government's financial advisor and fiscal agent, the Bank assumes responsibility for debt management. It provides advice on matters relating to the public debt and is responsible for issuing debt, maintaining bondholder records, and making payments on behalf of the government for debt redemption and interest.

On behalf of the federal government, the Bank of Canada intervenes in the foreign exchange market and manages its foreign exchange reserves. The Bank also is the government's link with international organizations such as the International Monetary Fund.

Administration of Accounts and Cash Management

The Bank of Canada maintains deposit and safekeeping accounts for approximately 100 clients. These include the federal government, the directly clearing members of the Canadian Payments Association, international financial institutions, and other central banks.

As the federal government's banker, the Bank ensures that the government's operating accounts have enough cash to meet daily requirements while at the same time minimizing the cost to the government of holding these balances. As we will learn, this role involves the Bank raising funds to meet anticipated short-term needs and auctioning off excess funds as short-term deposits when balances are higher than required.

Other Functions of the Bank

Unlike central bank practice in many other countries, the Bank of Canada is not responsible for the prudential supervision of the chartered banks; this is the responsibility of the Office of the Superintendent of Financial Institutions. Nevertheless, the Bank plays an advisory role in the regulation and supervision of financial institutions.

---

4. When the Bank began operations, it actually held gold in excess of the 25 percent reserve requirement. In addition to the $69 million in gold received from the government for taking over the redemption of Dominion notes, the Bank also received $37 million in gold that the chartered banks had to surrender as part of their cash reserves. In 1935, when gold was revalued from U.S. $20.67 to U.S. $35.00 an ounce, the profit realized by the Bank was turned over to the chartered banks and to the Exchange Fund. The original legislation provided for profit distribution.

Payment Clearing and Settlement Act
the act that gives the Bank of Canada explicit responsibility for regulatory oversight of Canada's major payment and settlement systems

www.

The Bank also does not administer and operate the country's clearing system, as in some other countries; this is the responsibility of the Canadian Payments Association. However, the Bank is a member of the Association's governing body and is its most important participant since it provides settlement accounts for its directly clearing members.

The ***Payment Clearing and Settlement Act,*** enacted in 1996, gives the Bank of Canada explicit responsibility for the regulatory oversight of Canada's major payment clearing and settlement systems. The Bank examines all such systems to identify their potential to cause systemic risk, that is, the risk that problems affecting one participant in a clearing and settlement system will spread to other participants or throughout the financial system.

To date, the Bank's oversight has focused on three systems: the Large Value Transfer System (LVTS) that electronically clears and settles large-value payments; the Debt Clearing Service, operated by the Canadian Depository Securities Limited, an automated clearing and settlement system for bonds and money market securities; and the Multinet System for clearing and settling large-value foreign exchange transactions.

The *Payment Clearing and Settlement Act* gives the Bank authority to guarantee settlement of designated systems and to pay interest on special deposits from clearinghouses or participants.

The Management of the Bank of Canada

Overall corporate responsibility for the Bank's operations is assigned to a board of directors. The board comprises the governor, the senior deputy governor, and 12 outside directors who are appointed for a three-year term by the minister of finance, with cabinet approval. In addition, the deputy minister of finance is a nonvoting member of the board. A legal requirement exists that the outside directors of the board be drawn from various occupations, excluding banking. In practice, the overriding consideration for their appointment has been regional rather than occupational representation.

The board of directors appoints the Bank's governor and senior deputy governor, with cabinet approval, for seven-year terms. They serve during *good behaviour* and as such cannot be removed from office without a special Act of Parliament, or a joint address to both Houses of Parliament. This has happened only once: In June 1961, the government, to remove the Bank's governor, James Coyne, introduced a motion in the House of Commons declaring that the position of governor was vacant.

The Bank's board is required to meet at least four times a year, and in practice normally meets seven times. While the board of directors oversees the Bank's operations, the Bank is run day to day by its senior management. In 1994 the board established a new senior decision-making authority within the Bank, called the governing council. The council, chaired by the governor of the Bank, comprises the senior deputy governor and the four deputy governors.

BOX 16–1   BACKGROUNDER

Governors of the Bank of Canada

In May 2000, Gordon Thiessen, governor of the Bank of Canada, announced he would not seek a second term and that he would retire January 31, 2001. Many observers expect that the vacancy will be filled from within the ranks of senior Bank of Canada deputy governors rather than by someone from outside the Bank.

BANK GOVERNORS AND THEIR TERMS

Graham Towers, 1934–54
James Coyne, 1955–61
Louis Rasminsky, 1961–73
Gerald Bouey, 1973–87
John Crow, 1987–94
Gordon Thiessen, 1994–2001

SOURCE: Bank of Canada.

Responsibility for Monetary Policy

From its beginning, the Bank of Canada was assumed to be an independent body responsible for the conduct of monetary policy. While it was also assumed that monetary policy ultimately was the responsibility of the federal government, its day-to-day formulation and implementation remained the responsibility of the Bank. This was broadly the consensus as enunciated periodically before 1956 by both Graham Towers and James Coyne, the first and second governors of the Bank, respectively, as well as by all the ministers of finance up to that time. Moreover, it was understood that in the event of disagreement between the government and the Bank on an important question of monetary policy, the governor would resign.

In 1956, when the Bank was following a restrictive monetary policy despite high unemployment and slowed economic growth, Walter Harris, the Liberal minister of finance, stated that he would not accept responsibility for the monetary policy being conducted by the Bank. In 1959, the minister of finance, Donald Fleming, in the Conservative Diefenbaker government, reiterated his predecessor's position that the government of the day was not responsible for monetary policy.

In 1960, when the governor of the Bank of Canada publicly began to defend his tight monetary policy, the Bank increasingly became the target of public criticism, including condemnation by a group of prominent academic economists.[5] On May 30, 1961, the government requested the governor's resignation. When the governor refused to resign, the government introduced legislation declaring his position vacant. The so-called **Coyne Affair** was resolved during an acrimonious debate in the Senate, after which Governor Coyne tendered his resignation, thereby obviating passage of the legislation.

On July 24, 1961, Louis Rasminsky became the third governor of the Bank of Canada. On assuming office he issued a statement making public his views

Coyne Affair *the controversy between the government and the governor of the Bank of Canada that ended with the resignation of James Coyne, the governor of the Bank*

5. Scott Gordon, *The Economists versus the Bank of Canada* (Toronto: Ryerson Press, 1961).

on the relationship between the Bank and the government. It contained two main principles:

> ...*(1) in the ordinary course of events, the Bank has the responsibility for monetary policy, and (2) if the government disapproves of the monetary policy being carried out by the Bank, it has the right and the responsibility to direct the Bank as to the policy which the Bank is to carry out.*[6]

Rasminsky also added that "If this policy, as communicated to the Bank, was one which the governor felt he could not in good conscience carry out, his duty would be to resign and to make way for someone who took a different view." The government issued a concurrent statement to voice its approval.

The Porter Royal Commission, whose appointment was in part initiated by the Coyne Affair, accepted Governor Rasminsky's views and recommended "a dual system of responsibility under which the Bank formulates monetary policy and executes it from day-to-day but under which the government must accept full and continuous responsibility for the policy being followed, although not in the normal course for the details of its execution."[7] Furthermore, to avoid another bitter controversy between the governor of the Bank and the government, the Commission recommended that the *Bank of Canada Act* be amended to provide the minister of finance with the authority to issue a directive to the Bank if the government disapproved of its policy.

Amendments to the *Bank of Canada Act* confirmed the concept of dual responsibility for the conduct of monetary policy, specifying that there must be continual consultation between the government and the Bank. In the event of a disagreement over monetary policy, the minister of finance may, after consultation with the governor of the Bank and with the approval of the cabinet, issue a written directive to the Bank on the policy it is to follow. Such a directive, with which the Bank must comply, must be in specific terms and be applicable for a specific period. It also must be immediately published in the *Canada Gazette* and laid before Parliament within 15 days after it is issued, or, if Parliament is not sitting, during the first 15 days after it resumes sitting. The government has as yet not issued a directive to the Bank. A general reluctance to do so may exist because it would probably be followed by the governor's resignation, which could result in serious and adverse consequences in Canadian financial and foreign exchange markets.

www.

Reforming the Mandate and Governance of the Bank of Canada

In 1991, public controversy over the conduct of monetary policy arose again, centred on proposals for reform by David Laidler of the University of Western Ontario and by the federal government with respect to its recommendations

---

6. Bank of Canada, *Annual Report*, 1961, p. 3.

7. *Report of the Royal Commission on Banking and Finance* (Ottawa: Queen's Printer, 1964), p. 543.

for renewed federalism.[8] Both Professor Laidler and the government proposed that the mandate of the Bank of Canada be changed to make price stability the principal objective of monetary policy. Both also proposed changes to how the Bank is governed. Professor Laidler argued that the powers of the Bank were concentrated too narrowly in the hands of its governor and a small group of bureaucrats within the Bank. He suggested that this power be disseminated among a full-time rather than a part-time board of governors chosen in consultation with the provinces. The government proposed, as part of its plan for renewed federalism, consultation with the provinces in appointments to the Bank's board as well as the establishment of regional consultative panels to advise the board on regional economic conditions. The Constitutional Agreement reached in Charlottetown on August 28, 1992, included a consensus that the Senate have a role in ratifying the appointment of the governor of the Bank of Canada.

The House of Commons Finance Committee, after holding hearings, in February 1992 published its own report on the mandate and governance of the Bank of Canada.[9] In its report, the committee recommended that the mandate of the Bank not be changed to focus only on price stability, but should remain more broadly orientated, as set out in the preamble to the *Bank of Canada Act.* However, the committee recommended that the Act be amended to require the Bank to report to Parliament each year on current and anticipated economic conditions and on the intended course of monetary policy over the short and medium term, in light of those conditions. The committee also recommended that monetary policy continue to be formulated and conducted by the Bank of Canada, with ultimate responsibility resting with the federal government. With respect to the composition of the Bank's board of directors, the committee reaffirmed the existing practice of maintaining a regional balance in its representation.

One of the major reasons advanced for making price stability the principal objective of monetary policy is that it is the best contribution that monetary policy can make to the broader economic goals. We consider these goals later in this chapter. In the long run, as we will show, the rate of monetary expansion determines the rate of inflation, with no sustainable effects on output growth, employment, and other real variables. However, as pointed out by the Commons Finance Committee, to focus only on price stability would sell monetary policy short because in the short run, it can influence economic activity and the exchange rate. Monetary policy, therefore, should not be excluded from helping to cushion economic disturbances and shocks.[10]

Proposals to diffuse the powers of the Bank of Canada to make it more sensitive to regional concerns and more accountable to the government were based on the assumption that it would give monetary policy more legitimacy.

---

8. See David Laidler, *How Will We Govern the Governor? A Critique of the Bank of Canada* (Toronto: C.D. Howe Institute, 1991); Canada, *Canada, Canadian Federalism and Economic Union: Partnership for Prosperity* (Ottawa, 1991); Canada, *Shaping Canada's Future Together: Proposals* (Ottawa, September 1991).

9. Canada, House of Commons Finance Committee, *The Mandate and Governance of the Bank of Canada* (Ottawa, February 1992).

10. Ibid., Chapter 2.

This legitimacy in turn would make policy more effective. As we will argue, national money and capital markets preclude the implementation of regional monetary policies. Moreover, if the diffusion of the Bank's powers were to come at the expense of a loss in its independence, the goal of price stability could be put in jeopardy. History has shown that governments tend to minimize the long-run consequences of inflation as a result of excessive monetary growth. Researchers have shown that the rate of inflation has been lower in countries whose central banks enjoy a high degree of independence.[11]

Recently, the Bank has increased its professional staffs at its regional offices in Montreal, Toronto, and Vancouver to be better informed about regional developments when framing its policies. The Bank has also opened new offices in Calgary and Halifax.

Canadian Monetary Policy

While the term "monetary policy" is of comparatively recent origin, monetary policy has been pursued since time immemorial. In its broadest sense, monetary policy has been defined as "the attitude of the political authority towards the monetary system of the community under its control."[12] In ancient and early medieval times, the choice and maintenance of the monetary standard, the determination of the value of the monetary unit, and the enforcement of the state prerogative of coinage were all part of monetary policy. The attempts, at first of the medieval bullionists and later the mercantilists, to attract and maintain bullion and coin "within the realm" are further examples of early monetary policy.

Today, monetary policy is more narrowly defined and is commonly considered to be the *management of the monetary system toward the achievement of certain objectives.* These objectives should serve to enhance public welfare. Unfortunately, this has not always been the case, in either early or recent times. For example, Cleopatra debased Egypt's coinage to finance her life of luxury; Hitler pursued inflationary monetary policies in Germany after 1933 to prepare for and wage his imperialistic wars; and the communist-controlled regime in Hungary after the Second World War depreciated the currency to wipe out all "bourgeois" wealth and income.

Early Concepts of Monetary Policy

When banking institutions developed or were established to conduct central banking operations, their prime objectives were to finance the government, to

---

11. See Alberto Alesina, "Politics and Business Cycles in Industrial Countries," *Economic Policy* 8 (1989), pp. 55–98.

12. Paul Einzing, *Monetary Policy: Ends and Means* (Baltimore: Penguin, 1964), p. 48

establish and maintain a sound and stable currency system, to provide an elastic money supply, and to provide effective supervision of banking activities.

Both the United States and the United Kingdom provide excellent examples of the early intention to establish institutions to be used to finance government activity. During the First and Second World Wars the central banks in both these countries, and the Bank of Canada, played an important role in facilitating their respective governments' war expenditures.

www.

The early commercial banks were established to furnish an identifiable currency and a sound monetary system. A relatively long time passed before it was recognized that a commercial banking system's ability to supply money in the form of bank notes and deposits rested on a vulnerable foundation. The Bank of England, long before it was recognized as performing central banking operations, rescued the English banks and the English monetary system from disaster. It was able to play this role not because its notes were legal tender, but because they had general acceptability. When other countries developed or established their central banking institutions, they gave them the power to issue legal tender. The central banks thus became bankers' banks that could supply reserves to the banking system. A central bank that can supply reserves is a prerequisite of a sound monetary system.

At first, it was not intended for central banking institutions to use discretionary power to change the stock of money in circulation. It was thought that an automatic mechanism existed that would, over the long run, provide the proper amount of money. The commercial loan theory explained how the commercial banks supplied their liabilities (notes and deposits) to meet the needs of society. Central banking institutions existed to provide the commercial banks with adequate reserves to allow them to go about their business. The monetary system was regulated only by the fact that the amount of reserves central banking institutions could supply to commercial banks was limited by the gold reserves of the central banks. The amount of gold reserves at any one time depended on past accumulation, current production, and international flows. The discovery of gold in California and Australia toward the middle of the nineteenth century and in South Africa, the Klondike, and Alaska toward the end of that century resulted in rising trends in the volume of money and in prices. This trend was due not to discretionary monetary policy, but to the automatic working of the gold standard, whereby changes in the money supply were directly linked to changes in the country's gold reserves. However, the lack of discretionary monetary policy allowed deflationary conditions to occur between these two periods of gold rushes, when the world's monetary gold supply did not keep up with the growing demands of business.

After the First World War, the concept of a managed gold standard was introduced, aimed at maintaining stability by neutralizing the effects on the price level of unwanted increases or decreases in the gold reserves. During the early 1920s the return to the gold standard remained the major concern of monetary policy in many countries. There was, however, a growing tendency to focus more attention on internal economic conditions and the need for greater business and price stability. The newly created Federal Reserve System in the United States, for instance, considered that its main purpose was to meet the legitimate needs of business.

www.

In most countries during the 1920s, monetary stability was interpreted to mean monetary expansion, while price stability, a widely accepted objective of policy, was interpreted as the prevention of falling prices. Monetary expansion was hailed by many as the major reason for the prosperity of that time. Few realized that it was encouraging the speculative boom that was soon to end in collapse.

Economic collapse in the early 1930s ushered in a long period of stagnation and unemployment. Largely because of the new economic philosophy of John Maynard Keynes, monetary policy as a means to recovery was abandoned in favour of fiscal policy.

www.

During the Second World War monetary policy was directed toward facilitating government financial requirements, while direct controls were used to maintain price stability. Monetary policy was generally expansionary to make a sufficient amount of credit available and to hold interest rates at a level that would minimize the government's borrowing costs.

After the war, monetary expansion continued in the United Kingdom, the United States, and Canada. The primary reason was the fear of a postwar recession. Moreover, since all three governments had sold their debts during the war to a wide cross-section of their citizens, they considered it their moral obligation to allow the holders of this debt to cash it without loss. An expansionary monetary policy was one way of holding interest rates down and bond prices up. For some years after the war, monetary expansion and rising prices were a way of life. Indeed, many thought this situation was necessary to ensure an increase in output, and at the same time to secure a market for the larger output. Perhaps one reason why a policy of moderate inflation gained wide acceptance in the Anglo-Saxon countries was that none of these countries had experienced runaway inflation for more than a generation.

When monetary policy returned to its former respectability in the early 1950s, its attempts first to halt inflation and later to stop recurring conditions of deflation proved disappointing. Some thought that monetary policy had become an inadequate tool when used alone for short-run stabilization. Others felt that its failures were due not so much to its ineffectiveness as to its inappropriate use. Widespread criticism prompted a reassessment of monetary policy in the United Kingdom, the United States, and Canada. The reappraisal of the objectives that followed focused on defining broad national economic goals.

National Economic Goals

Today, the broad objectives of monetary policy are considered to be those of economic policy generally. Monetary policy must be conducted to assist a country in meeting its economic as well as its political and social goals. These goals include a high and stable level of employment, reasonable price stability, a high rate of economic growth, a sound external financial position, an equitable sharing of economic benefits and burdens, and an acceptable degree of economic freedom.

A High and Stable Level of Employment

When an economy fails to utilize its labour resources fully, as well as its other resources, it does not achieve its economic potential and produces at a level that creates economic and social hardships for a wide cross-section of the population. Unemployed labour services result in a loss of production that can never be recovered. National output does not realize its full potential, and certain sectors of the population are unable to share in what is being produced.

Full employment exists when all the owners of productive services, including labour services, are successful in voluntarily selling the desired amount of services at the prevailing market price. In a modern society where demands and technology are continually changing, 100 percent full employment is impossible, which is why we now speak of a high level of employment as distinct from full employment as an economic objective. Figure 16–1 plots the Canadian unemployment rate for the past 25 years. You can see that the rate cycles up and down over the business cycle.

In the case of labour, entry into the labour force and the shift out of one job into another take time because workers have to search for jobs. Individuals who are without jobs while undertaking job searches are referred to as the frictional unemployed. Unemployment may also be the result of a mismatch between the skill or location requirements of job vacancies and the present skills or location of unemployed individuals. This mismatch unemployment is frequently called structural unemployment. Taken together, frictional and structural unemployment make up what economists call the **natural rate of unemployment**. At the natural rate of unemployment, there is no tendency for

natural rate of unemployment
the rate of unemployment that results when expectations of inflation equal the actual inflation rate (implying all unemployment is structural and frictional); also referred to as NAIRU (nonaccelerating inflation rate of unemployment)

FIGURE 16–1   **CANADIAN UNEMPLOYMENT RATE, 1976 Q1 TO 2000 Q1**

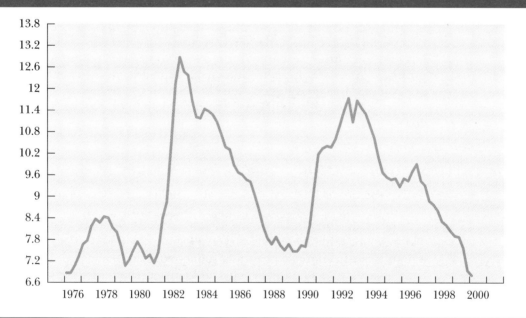

SOURCE: Statistics Canada, CANSIM Database, Series D980745, May 2000.

the rate of inflation to accelerate or decelerate. Actual unemployment in excess of the natural rate of unemployment is known as cyclical unemployment. It is the task of demand management (monetary and fiscal policy) to minimize cyclical unemployment. By contrast, reducing the natural rate of unemployment requires policies that reduce the time for job searches and that close skill and location mismatch gaps.

Not so long ago it was widely believed that the natural rate of unemployment was somewhere between 3 and 4.5 percent. Today, many economists set it between 6 and 7 percent, or even higher. Some economists argue that more generous social assistance and employment insurance benefits have significantly decreased the cost of leisure.[13] This decreased cost has discouraged workers from spending much more time in their search for jobs. Generous unemployment benefits may also encourage firms to lay off workers during periods of insufficient demand for their products rather than add to their inventories or reduce their prices.

Price Stability

price inflation *a sustained rising trend in the general price level*

Price inflation is broadly defined as a sustained rising trend in the general price level. It is usually measured as the year-over-year percentage change in the consumer price index (CPI). Figure 16–2 plots the Canadian inflation rate using the CPI. It is clear that the variability of inflation has fallen considerably since the late 1980s.

relative price *the price of one item relative to that of another*

While a strong case can be made for price level stability, an equally strong, if not stronger, case can be made for relative price flexibility.[14] The **relative price** of an item is its value in terms of another item; that is, the amount of one item that is exchanged for a unit of another item. Relative prices play an indispensable role as efficient allocators of resources. To play this role, relative prices must be allowed to change to signal the relative scarcity or abundance of goods and services. For example, when oil becomes scarce, its price should be allowed to increase relative to that of other goods to encourage further exploration, conservation in its use, and the search for alternative energy sources.

The costs to society of positive and variable rates of inflation, and hence the benefits from their avoidance, result from the often capricious redistribution of income and wealth, from resource misallocation, and from inefficiencies in the payment system. Income and wealth redistribution occur when contracts are written in nominal terms with expectations that real (inflation-adjusted) values will remain unchanged over the contract period. For instance, if inflation is not correctly anticipated, the young gain at the expense of the old, because the young can benefit from higher earnings while the old, on fixed-

---

13. The cost of leisure is measured as the difference between income when working and income when unemployed.

14. For relative prices to be efficient allocators of resources, the private marginal benefits and private marginal costs that they represent must be coincident with social marginal benefits and social marginal costs. When such coincidence is not present, market failures or externalities are said to be present.

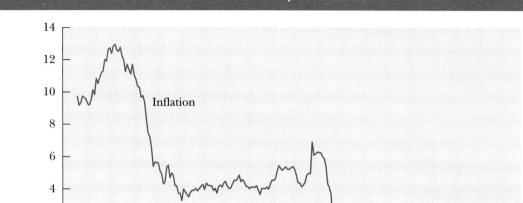

FIGURE 16–2   **CPI INFLATION IN CANADA, 1979–2000**

SOURCE: Statistics Canada. CANSIM Database, Series P119500, May 2000.

dollar incomes, experience a decline in their real income. Debtors gain at the expense of creditors because, when inflation is incorrectly anticipated, creditors do not recapture the real decline in the funds they lend, while debtors make repayments with dollars whose purchasing power has declined.

With inflation, homeowners gain at the expense of renters because they enjoy capital gains on their houses as well as lower real repayments on existing mortgage loans, while renters pay higher rents due to the higher cost of housing. However, inflation may also cause financial difficulties for homeowners who take new mortgages or renew existing mortgages at higher interest rates. Rising interest rates that capture higher rates of inflation cause borrowers to make higher real payments in the early life of a loan rather than making constant real payments over time. This so-called front-loading of real payments is known as the **mortgage-tilt problem**. Higher interest rates due to inflation also deny many people home ownership because the higher monthly payment relative to their income makes them ineligible for residential mortgage loans.

With inflation governments gain at the expense of taxpayers because, under a progressive income tax structure, inflation pushes taxpayers into income brackets subject to higher tax rates. Partial indexation in the income tax system has prevented some of this transfer of income from taxpayers.[15]

The federal government can also benefit from collecting an implicit inflation tax. The public may increase their nominal money holdings to offset the

mortgage-tilt problem *rising interest rates that capture higher rates of inflation cause borrowers to make higher real payments in the early life of a mortgage loan rather than making constant real payment over time*

15. For a discussion of indexation and safeguards against inflation, see Economic Council of Canada, *Eleventh Annual Review* (Ottawa, 1974), pp. 169–76. In its March 2000 budget, the federal government announced it would reintroduce full indexation to the tax system.

decline in the real value of their money balances due to inflation. By printing more money to accommodate the higher demand for it, the government raises revenue for itself. The revenue generated by this implicit inflation tax is called **seigniorage.**

seigniorage
profits from the issuing of money; the difference between the face value of money and its cost to produce

Undesirable income and wealth redistribution would be avoided if inflation could be completely anticipated and fully indexed. However, even if this were possible, the real costs to society of inflation would remain. Inflation decreases the purchasing power of money and increases the opportunity cost of holding money. For instance, at 5 percent inflation, the dollar loses half its purchasing power in only 14 years. Inflation can be viewed as an implicit tax on money. The public can reduce this tax burden by economizing on the use of cash, but this too has its costs in terms of the extra time and effort spent at automated banking machines to frequently replenish cash balances for transaction purposes. Economists refer to these costs as the "shoe leather" cost of inflation.

Serious inefficiencies in resource allocation occur because inflation distorts the price signals sent to the economy. Increases in the price of individual products often are mistakenly interpreted as relative price changes when in fact they are due to an increase in the inflation rate. Resources are also misallocated because resources that would otherwise be used for socially productive ends have to be devoted to coping with inflation. For example, employees have to be assigned to produce new catalogues announcing the higher prices. More time is taken up by more frequent renegotiation of labour contracts and is usually wasted in more frequent labour disputes and strikes.

Price inflation is of particular concern to Canadians, who depend on selling about 30 percent of what they produce to foreigners and on buying at least a similar proportion of what they consume from them. If we are reluctant to allow our dollar to depreciate in terms of the value of the currencies of our trading partners, then price inflation at home that is not matched abroad will shut our exporters out of foreign markets. However, if we allow our dollar to depreciate because of our relatively higher rate of inflation, the dollar price of our imports will increase. This situation can exacerbate existing inflationary conditions.

Finally, the danger is always present that by switching out of money into other assets whose prices are expected to increase along with inflation, the public will only push prices higher and higher. Inflation may become self-generating, ending in hyperinflation, where the value of money and its usefulness as a standard unit of account, a store of value, and a medium of exchange are destroyed. Hyperinflation usually leads to a general breakdown of a country's monetary system.

Economic Growth

For a long time it was thought by many that, in the long run, material progress, in the form of a rising standard of living and an increase of accumulated wealth, was a natural, automatic process. Whenever this secular process was interrupted by wars and crises, it resumed its course automatically. Before the Second World War totalitarian states introduced plans for stimulating secular

FIGURE 16–3   **ECONOMIC GROWTH IN CANADA, 1962–99**

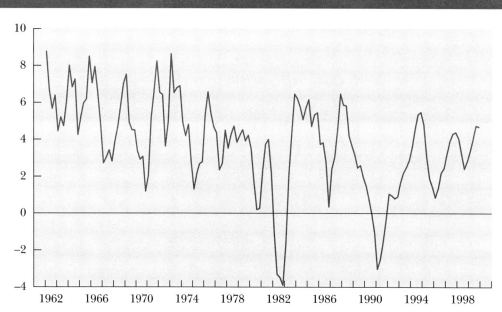

SOURCE: Statistics Canada, CANSIM Database, Series D14872, May 2000.

growth. Others relied on the maintenance of full employment as necessarily serving the cause of growth. It was not until after the mid-1950s that it became generally understood that policies aimed at full employment and those aimed at growth are not necessarily identical. Indeed, some people today would give policies directed toward long-term growth precedence over those directed at cyclical stabilization. They argue that far too often misdirected and ill-timed policies have accentuated rather than stabilized cyclical economic fluctuations. Figure 16–3 plots the growth rate of real GDP in Canada over almost the past 40 years, from which we can clearly see the recessions of the early 1980s and the early 1990s.

Long-run expansion of potential output or productive capacity depends on technological progress, the availability of productive resources that can be used, and the productivity of these resources. Productivity is a measure of how efficiently resources are used; it calculates output per factor, such as a worker or a machine, used in the productive process. Labour productivity is measured in terms of either output per employee or output per work-hour. Increases in factor productivity are generally considered the main long-term source of improvement in living standards.

The annual growth rate of output (real GDP) increased from 3.6 percent over the 1929–53 period to 4.9 percent over the 1975–83 period. Labour productivity—that is, output per employed worker—grew at an annual rate of around 2.2 percent from 1929 to 1974, after which time its growth declined on average to less than 1 percent per year. Other industrial countries experienced similar deceleration in the growth rates of their output and labour productivity.

Economists have suggested a wide range of explanations for the productivity slowdown, including some decline of the rate of growth of capital-to-labour ratios, a reduction in the quality of the labour force due to the entry of inexperienced and less skilled workers, more government regulations, major changes in the economic environment such as the large increases in the relative price of energy, and uncertainty created by higher underlying rates of inflation.[16]

Economic growth requires not only the availability of an appropriate amount of resources and an increase in their productivity, but also a high level of employment of resources on a sustained basis. Hence, economic policy must be oriented at not only maintaining the supply capabilities of the economy, but also at maintaining stable and sustained expansion of final demand for goods and services. Canada's success in pursuing appropriate policies to facilitate steady and balanced economic growth also depends on the rate of growth being maintained in the world economy.

Most economists now agree that the long-run rate of real economic growth is determined by nonmonetary factors such as increases in the availability of resources, in productivity, and in technology. At the same time, monetary policy can contribute to long-term economic growth by fostering price stability, so that economic decisions can be made based on reliable information on changing relative prices. Price stability, without the uncertainties associated with inflation, is also accompanied by a higher rate of saving and of investment expenditures.

A Sound External Position

Under the international gold standard, the maintenance of the standard itself became the overriding objective of most countries, even if it meant an increase in unemployment or price fluctuations. Canada played an important role in the negotiations that led to the establishment of the International Monetary Fund and the Bretton Woods system of fixed exchange rates after 1944. This system, described later in the book, was intended to retain the apparent advantages of a fixed exchange rate regime, but without subjecting the economies of member nations to the adverse effects of the earlier gold standard. When Canada assumed its full membership obligations in the International Monetary Fund and maintained a fixed foreign exchange rate for the Canadian dollar until September 1950 and again from 1962 to 1970, its external policy goal was to hold adequate foreign exchange reserves to defend the fixed external value of its monetary unit. As such, the soundness of our external position was reflected by the degree to which our balance of payments was in equilibrium.

When a country has a floating or flexible exchange rate, the soundness of its external position is reflected by the size of the movements of the exchange rate. Excessive appreciation or depreciation of the Canadian dollar in terms of the currencies of our major trading partners could adversely affect the international flow of goods and services. This is important for a country such as Canada, whose exports and imports each account for over 30 percent of its

---

16. See the entire issue of the *Canadian Journal of Economics* (April 1999), for more on the productivity paradox.

gross domestic product. Overvaluation of the dollar could close foreign markets to Canadian exporters; undervaluation of the dollar could raise the cost of imports, promote inflation, and impair growth.

Other Objectives

Economic objectives are not ends in themselves; they cannot be defined in a vacuum. Attention must be focused on the ultimate ends of the socioeconomic activity of the nation; that is, on the combined social, political, economic, environmental, and technological aspects of society. For instance, we expect the attainment of our economic goals to be accompanied by enhancement of the quality of life, as reflected in improvements in housing, health, and the natural environment. Furthermore, economic growth is undesirable if, as a result, the poor become poorer while the rich grow richer, which is why we include as an objective the equitable sharing of economic benefits and burdens in a country. Moreover, economic benefits are undesirable, and probably not attainable, if a society's economic freedoms are taken away. The definition of "equitable" and the degree of economic and social freedom considered desirable vary from country to country. Once these decisions are made, however, it becomes the objective of the society to see that they are preserved in the attainment of its other goals.

Compromise and Tradeoffs

Ideally, we would like to achieve all economic and social goals simultaneously. In practice, this has not been possible. Economists have shown that inconsistencies or conflicts may exist since the greater achievement of one goal may be accomplished only at the expense of a shortfall in meeting another goal. For example, a country may simultaneously experience a high level of unemployment (internal disequilibrium) and an undesirable balance of payments deficit (external disequilibrium). If policies are introduced to expand aggregate demand to correct unemployment, the resulting increase in demand may spill over into foreign markets and aggravate the country's balance of payments deficit.

The economic objectives we have outlined cannot be achieved simultaneously by using only one policy instrument such as monetary policy. While monetary policy may be used to achieve a particular objective, its use may at the same time create a divergence from the achievement of another objective. For example, let us assume that the monetary authorities put upward pressure on interest rates to induce an inflow of foreign capital to meet a balance of payments objective. While higher interest rates may achieve the policy objective of maintaining the country's foreign exchange reserves, they may at the same time lead to a reduction in domestic investment and thereby deflect the economy from the goal of full employment.

Jan Tinbergen of the Netherlands School of Economics has shown that a solution exists, at least theoretically, for achieving multiple divergent goals simultaneously.[17] Two conditions are necessary. One is that there must be at least as many instruments or strategies of policy as there are economic objectives or constraints. The other condition is that policy instruments must be paired with the policy objectives over which they have the greatest influence. For example, assume that the two immediate economic objectives are to reduce unemployment and to prevent a further decline in the country's foreign exchange reserves under a system of fixed foreign exchange rates. As has been shown by Nobel Laureate Robert Mundell, under a system of fixed exchange rates, and with international capital flows sensitive to interest-rate differentials between countries, monetary policy has a comparative advantage for achieving external equilibrium.[18]

In our example, to stop the loss of foreign exchange reserves, monetary policy may be used to put upward pressure on interest rates to halt or reverse the outflow of capital and therefore the loss of foreign exchange reserves. As we have already noted, however, higher interest rates may reduce domestic aggregate demand and thereby add to an already high rate of unemployment. To meet its employment objective—that is, internal equilibrium—the authorities can use fiscal policy (reduction in taxes and an increase in government expenditures) to stimulate and add to aggregate demand.

Even if the minimum conditions for simultaneously achieving multiple goals are met, available policy instruments must be mixed and blended properly. Canadian experience has proven that an overconcentration in the use of one instrument to meet a particular objective can lead to an undesirable shortfall in achieving other objectives.

Monetary Policy and Ultimate Goals

A central bank's ultimate policy goals emanate from the government's macroeconomic objectives. The two major ultimate policy goals usually focus on the level or rate of growth of real national income and the price level. Economists have shown that in the short run, monetary policy can influence both real output and the price level, but it cannot independently affect one or the other. Since it cannot determine the division between real output and the price level, nominal income, which combines both these economic variables, is frequently taken to be the appropriate short-run policy goal. In the long run, monetary policy affects only the price level; therefore, stabilizing the price level is the only credible long-term policy goal for a central bank to achieve.

Before the 1970s, central banks focused their attention on achieving short-run real output and employment goals. They used NAIRU (the nonaccelerating inflation rate of unemployment) as the measure of the goal to be achieved. Since this rate tended to increase over time as a result of changes in

17. Jan Tinbergen, *On the Theory of Economic Policy* (Amsterdam: North-Holland, 1952).

18. Robert A. Mundell, "The Appropriate Use of Monetary and Fiscal Policy for Internal and External Stability," *International Monetary Fund Staff Paper 9* (March 1962), pp. 70–79. Reprinted in Robert Mundell, *International Economics* (New York: Macmillan, 1968).

minimum wage laws, employment insurance benefits, and demographic shifts, the unemployment goals turned out to be set too low and at inflationary rates. It is now widely held that policy initiatives in the 1960s and early 1970s that were meant to achieve real output and employment goals sacrificed long-run price level goals.

In the January 1988 Hanson Memorial Lecture at the University of Alberta, Bank of Canada Governor John Crow explicitly announced that price stability was the Bank's long-term objective for monetary policy. He said that "monetary policy should be conducted so as to achieve a pace of monetary expansion that promotes stability in the value of money. This means pursuing a policy aimed at achieving and maintaining stable prices."[19] The governor's statement was interpreted to imply a goal of zero inflation, which opened the debate about whether the goal of price stability should be zero inflation or a positive but low and stable inflation rate.[20]

In February 1991, the Bank of Canada and the federal government made a formal commitment to price stability as the objective of monetary policy.[21] Moreover, to make the commitment clear and credible, specific targets were announced to which monetary policy would be directed over the medium term.

The objective of monetary policy was reaffirmed in a joint statement by the government and the Bank at the time of Gordon Thiessen's appointment as governor of the Bank in December 1993.[22] At that time, a target range for inflation control of 1 to 3 percent was specified for the 1995–98 period.

In 1996 Governor Thiessen made the following observation concerning the ultimate goals of Canadian monetary policy:

> *The focus of Canadian monetary policy is on price stability. However, the Bank of Canada does not pursue stability for its own sake but rather as a means of contributing to a well-functioning, productive economy, capable of providing Canadians with a rising standard of living.*[23]

Canadian monetary policy remains focused on price stability at the start of the twenty-first century, but debate continues about whether monetary policy should be targeted in this fashion. We'll return to a full analysis of the subject after we look at some of the tools in the Bank of Canada's arsenal. Knowing how these tools work (and sometimes don't work) will help us interpret the policy debate.

---

19. John W. Crow, "The Work of Canadian Monetary Policy," Eric J. Hanson Memorial Lecture, University of Alberta, Edmonton, Alberta, January 18, 1988. Reprinted in *Bank of Canada Review*, February 1988, pp. 4–17.

20. See Robert C. York, ed., *Taking Aim: The Debate on Zero Inflation*; and Richard G. Lipsey, ed., *Zero Inflation: The Goal of Price Stability* (Toronto: C.D. Howe Institute), Policy Studies 10 and 8 respectively, 1990.

21. Bank of Canada, "Targets for Reducing Inflation: Announcements and Background Material," *Bank of Canada Review*, March 1991, pp. 3–21.

22. Bank of Canada, "Statement of the Government of Canada and the Bank of Canada on Monetary Policy Objectives," *Bank of Canada Review*, Winter of 1993–94, pp. 85–86.

23. Notes for remarks by Gordon G. Thiessen, governor of the Bank of Canada, to the World in 1996 Conference, Toronto, January 19, 1996. Reprinted in *Bank of Canada Review*, Spring 1996, pp. 67–72.

KEY TERMS

Coyne Affair
mortgage-tilt problem
natural rate of unemployment

Payment Clearing and Settlement
    Act
price inflation

relative price
seigniorage

REVIEW QUESTIONS

1. How is the Bank of Canada managed?
2. Outline the major functions of the Bank of Canada.
3. How is the responsibility for monetary policy shared in Canada?
4. What was the Coyne Affair?
5. Why, and in what ways, might the mandate and governance of the Bank of Canada be reformed?
6. Define monetary policy. What are the goals or objectives of economic policy? Why does monetary policy

have to concern itself with intermediate as well as ultimate economic objectives?

7. What is the difference between frictional, structural, and cyclical unemployment?
8. Why should price stability be a major policy goal of monetary policy?
9. Define labour productivity. How can you account for its slowdown?
10. What is Jan Tinbergen's solution for simultaneously achieving multiple divergent goals?

SELECTED READINGS

Bagehot, Walter. *Lombard Street.* Homewood, Ill.: Richard D. Irwin, 1962. Reprinted from Scribner, Armstrong edition, New York, 1873.

Bank of Canada. *Evidence of the Governor before the Royal Commission on Banking and Finance.* Ottawa, May 1964, pp. 113–5.

Canada. House of Commons Finance Committee. *The Mandate and Governance of the Bank of Canada.* Ottawa, February 1992.

Canada. Senate. *Report of the Senate Standing Finance Committee on National Finance on Growth, Employment and Price Stability.* Ottawa: Information Canada, 1971.

Economic Council of Canada. *Annual Review* (various issues).

Fullerton, Douglas H. *Graham Towers and His Times.* Toronto: McClelland and Stewart, 1986.

Gordon, Scott H. "The Bank of Canada in a System of Responsible Government." *Canadian Journal of Political Science* 27 (February 1961), pp. 13–22.

Howitt, Peter. "Constitutional Reform and the Bank of Canada," in Robin Boadway et al., *Economic Dimensions of Constitutional Change.* Kingston: Queen's University, 1991, Vol. 2, pp. 383–408.

Laidler, David E.W. *How Will We Govern the Governor? A Critique of the Governance of the Bank of Canada.* Toronto: C.D. Howe Institute, 1991.

Lipsey, Richard G., ed. *Zero Inflation: The Goal of Price Stability.* Toronto: C.D. Howe Institute, 1990.

Muller, P., and M. Zelmer. "Greater Transparency in Monetary Policy: Impact on Financial Markets," *Bank of Canada Technical Report* 86, 1999.

O'Reilly, B. "The Benefits of Low Inflation: Taking Stock." *Bank of Canada Technical Report* 83, 1998.

Parkin, M. "Unemployment, Inflation, and Monetary Policy." *Canadian Journal of Economics* 31 (November 1998), pp. 1003–32.

Paulin, Graydon. "The Changing Face of Central Banking in the 1990s." *Bank of Canada Review,* Summer 2000, pp. 3–13.

Rasminsky, Louis. "The Role of the Central Banker Today." Per Jacobson Memorial Lecture, Rome, November 9, 1966. Reprinted in *Canadian Banker* 74 (Spring 1967), pp. 25–44.

Riddell, C. *Dealing With Inflation and Unemployment in Canada*. The Collected Research Studies, Vol. 25. Royal Commission on the Economic Union and Development Prospects for Canada. Toronto: University of Toronto Press, 1986.

Sargent, J., Research Coordinator. *Macroeconomics*. The Collected Research Studies, Vols. 19 to 24, inclusive. Royal Commission on the Economic Union and Development Prospects for Canada. Toronto: University of Toronto Press, 1986.

Scarfe, Brian L. "Economic Fluctuations and Stabilization Policy in Canada: The State of the Art." *Canadian Public Policy—Analyse de Politiques*, March 1987, pp. 75–85.

Srour, G. "Inflation Targeting under Uncertainty." *Bank of Canada Technical Report* 85, 1999.

Tinbergen, Jan. *Economic Policy: Principles and Design*. Amsterdam: North-Holland Publishing Co., 1956.

Watts, George. "The Origins and Background of Central Banking in Canada." *Bank of Canada Review*, May 1972, pp. 15–27.

———. "The Legislative Birth of the Bank of Canada." *Bank of Canada Review*, August 1972, pp. 13–26.

York, Robert C., ed. *Taking Aim: The Debate on Zero Inflation*. Ottawa, C.D. Howe Institute, 1990.

CHAPTER SEVENTEEN

MONETARY CONTROL: CENTRAL BANK INSTRUMENTS

After reading this chapter you should be able to
1. *Define the monetary base*
2. *Describe the payments clearing and settlement systems*
3. *Show how the central bank's open market operations affect the availability of cash in the financial system*
4. *Describe lending by the central bank and the role of its Bank Rate*
5. *Discuss the use of moral suasion and selective credit controls*
6. *Describe the nature of government financial transactions*
7. *Explain how government cash balances are managed*
8. *Show how the Bank of Canada uses Exchange Fund Account swaps*
9. *Show how government borrowing can affect the money supply*
10. *Describe the dimensions and management of the federal government's debt*

The Monetary Base

A country's monetary base consists of those financial assets that by custom, or more usually by law, serve as ultimate means of payment. Under a commodity monetary standard, a particular commodity, or set of commodities, is the country's monetary base. For example, under the gold standard, gold was the ultimate means of payment and all other monetary instruments were convertible by law into a specified amount of gold. Under a pure paper standard, the ultimate means of payment are certain liabilities of the government or of its central bank, together with subsidiary coin.

monetary base
the total amount of currency (Bank of Canada notes and coin) plus direct clearer's settlement balances at the Bank of Canada

In Canada today, where we have a pure paper standard, the **monetary base** consists of liabilities of the Bank of Canada in the form of Bank of Canada notes, deposits held at the Bank by directly clearing members of the Canadian Payments Association (described in the following section), and coin with a face value of $2 or less.

The monetary base should not be confused with the money supply. Although the two are closely related and their composition includes some of the same financial instruments, the two are not identical. The major difference is that only money supply measures include deposits held with depository financial institutions other than the central bank. While in practice these deposits are used to make final payments, they serve this purpose only because the public has full confidence in the depository institutions' ability to convert them into currency—that is, cash, the ultimate means of payment.

www.

To satisfy the obligation to convert their deposit liabilities into cash, deposit-taking institutions require ready access to currency to meet cash withdrawals by their depositors and to provide cash settlement for deposit transfers between depository institutions by cheque, electronically, or via other payment orders. The total amount of cash in the monetary system is the monetary base. In addition to currency—Bank of Canada notes and coin, which the public identifies as cash—the monetary base includes the deposits held at the Bank by directly clearing members of the Canadian Payments Association. These deposits are similar to cash since their holders can in effect withdraw them in Bank of Canada notes. The Bank of Canada's prerogative to print its notes for circulation makes it the ultimate source of cash in the monetary system. At any given time, the total amount of cash is held by the public to satisfy its hand-to-hand daily payments transactions, and by the depository institutions as primary reserves to satisfy the public's demand for cash withdrawals and to settle claims that arise in the daily clearing of cheques and other payments orders.

The Clearing and Settlement System

clearing system
the system for collecting and processing cheques and other payment items

settlement system the process whereby cash payment is made for net claims following clearing

www.

Central to the payments system (and especially to the Bank of Canada's management of the availability of cash to depository institutions) are the institutional arrangements for clearing and settling payments. The concept of clearing was introduced in an earlier chapter with a simple example of clearinghouse operations. As explained there, in the course of any business day, a bank or other deposit-taking institution receives on deposit cheques and other payments items drawn on deposit accounts in other institutions. To arrive at a cash settlement between institutions, their claims against each other are netted so that instead of paying each claim separately, only one cash transfer need be made. The process of settling claims against each other by netting, and the exchange of cheques or other payments items that document these claims, is called the **clearing system**. The process whereby cash is transferred to pay net claims is the **settlement system**. Since the founding of the Bank of Canada, settlement has been made by the transfer of deposits held with the Bank by participants or their representatives in the clearing system.

In 1980, federal legislation established the Canadian Payments Association (CPA) with the mandate "to establish and operate a national clearings and settlements system and to plan the evolution of a national payments system." In 1983 the CPA assumed full responsibility for the clearing and settlement system previously operated by the Canadian Bankers' Association. In the following year it introduced the Automated Clearing Settlement System (ACSS), which replaced a largely paper-based, manually operated system.

www.

Membership in the CPA is mandatory for all banks, including the Bank of Canada, and voluntary for other federally and provincially regulated and supervised deposit-taking institutions. In May 2000 the CPA had 143 members. The CPA's board of directors is made up of a designated number of representatives from five specified membership classes: (1) the Bank of Canada, (2) chartered banks, (3) centrals of credit unions and caisses populaires, (4) trust and loan companies, and (5) other financial institutions such as provincial savings institutions and credit unions not affiliated with a central. The representative from the Bank of Canada serves as chairperson of the CPA's board of directors, and the superintendent of financial institutions supervises its affairs.

Members of the CPA may be either direct clearers or indirect clearers. **Direct clearers** participate directly in the clearings and maintain settlement accounts at the Bank of Canada. To be a direct clearer, an institution must also be responsible for at least 2 percent of the number of payment items passing through the clearings and participate daily in at least one of the seven regional settlement points operated by the CPA across the country. In May 2000, 12 members were direct clearers, in addition to the Bank of Canada.[1] **Indirect clearers** do not maintain settlement balances at the Bank of Canada and retain another member of the CPA to represent them in the clearing and settlement process.

A single day's clearings and settlement is referred to as a clearing round or cycle. The cycle begins when a depository institution receives cheques and other payment items to be deposited to a customer's account. Payment items, mostly cheques, are magnetically encoded for computer processing and sorted according to the institutions on which they are drawn. Financial institutions with many branches operate regional data centres where most of these functions are performed.

Starting late afternoon or early evening on each business day, the physical exchange of cheques and other payment items, including electronic transfers on magnetic tape, begins at the CPA's regional settlement points. This exchange is usually completed around midnight local time; next, all paper items go back to the branches where the accounts against which they are drawn are held. As exchanges are concluded, the dollar amounts of the associated claims are entered by the CPA into its ACSS. Early the next morning each direct clearer is informed of the outcome of the previous day's clearings. Around four o'clock in the afternoon, Ottawa time, the previous day's clearing cycle officially ends and final settlement is made retroactively by debiting or crediting each direct clearer's demand deposit account at the Bank of Canada.[2] With retroactive (back-dated) settlement, introduced in 1986, clearing results on the books of the Bank are dated on the same day as the

direct clearers *members of the CPA who participate directly in the clearings and maintain settlement balances with the Bank of Canada*

indirect clearers *members of the CPA who do not maintain settlement balances with the Bank of Canada and are represented by direct clearers in clearing and settlement processes*

---

1. The 12 direct clearers are Alberta Treasury Branches, Bank of Montreal, the Bank of Nova Scotia, La Caisse centrale Desjardins du Québec, Canada Trustco Mortgage Company, Canadian Imperial Bank of Commerce, Credit Union Central of Canada, HSBC Bank Canada, Laurentian Bank of Canada, National Bank of Canada, Royal Bank of Canada, and Toronto-Dominion Bank.

2. As explained later, the books of the Bank of Canada are held open until the late afternoon to allow the direct clearers to replenish their settlement balances by borrowing from the Bank, and to allow the Bank to manage the availability of cash to meet its monetary policy objectives.

Large Value Transfer System (LVTS) *an electronic funds transfer system that provides final settlement on a same-day basis*

www.

dating of the associated deposit or transactions between financial institutions and their clients.[3]

In 1997 the Canadian Payments Association introduced its **Large Value Transfer System (LVTS)**. It came into effect in February 1999. While the system clears and settles payments of any size, it was designed primarily to handle large value payments. Although payments of more than $50 000 represented only one-third of 1 percent of the total number exchanged among the banks and other financial institutions in the mid-1990s, they accounted for more than 94 percent of their value, or some $80 billion per day. The LVTS supplements rather than replaces the CPA's ACSS, which is essentially paper-based and clears cheques. In its first year of operation, the LVTS processed an average of 13 000 transactions daily. Its peak value for one day was more than 21 000 transactions (July 2, 1999). More than $100 billion in payments pass through LVTS every day. Nearly half the payments are for values less than $50 000.

The LVTS is an electronic transfer system that provides certainty of settlement on an item-by-item basis as payment messages are accepted in real time. Users of the LVTS are assured of receiving funds that are not subject to reversal if either the payer or its financial institution cannot meet its obligations. In the CPA's ACSS, when a deposit-taking institution accepts for credit to a customer's account a cheque drawn on another institution, the credit does not represent final payment until the next day, when final settlement is transacted in the books of the Bank of Canada. All of us have experienced a returned cheque with "NSF" notification. This is not the case with LVTS even though each day's net clearings are not settled until the end of the day with settlement balances held by the Bank of Canada.

multilateral netting *where each clearer's net credit or debit position vis-à-vis all other clearers is calculated for settlement*

The CPA's LVTS, as with its ACSS, employs **multilateral netting** in which the net amount of any one clearer vis-à-vis the other clearers as a whole is calculated. Netting significantly reduces the need for settlement funds because clearers need only have a sufficient amount of settlement balances to cover net amounts at the end of each clearing cycle.

Because financial institutions make payments during a clearing period in anticipation of sufficient incoming payments, the failure of a major institution to settle its net obligation at the end of the clearing cycle could have a domino effect: Other institutions that are counting on the institution's payments might be unable to meet their own obligations.

The LVTS was designed to avoid such systemic risks associated with the transfer of huge amounts of funds. The size of each participant's net debit position is limited—a so-called debit cap. In addition, each member sets a net credit limit on other participants in the LVTS to establish a maximum intraday credit that it is willing to grant to each counter-party. Moreover, each participant provides collateral in an amount of 30 percent of the largest net bilateral credit limit that it has extended to a counter-party. In the event of a default, the defaulting institution's collateral is used first to cover its settlement obligation. If this amount is insufficient, the collateral of the surviving LVTS participants

---

3. Before 1986 the Bank of Canada did not hold its books open into the next day for settlement of daily clearings, and as a result there was a one-day lag between the time when institutions' customers received credit for cheques deposited to their accounts and when the associated gains were registered in institutions' own settlement accounts at the Bank of Canada.

will be used to cover the shortfall. In the unlikely event that this second amount is insufficient, the Bank of Canada in its role of lender of last resort guarantees to provide the residual amount.

Central Bank Open Market Operations

Open market operations by the Bank of Canada involve it in the purchase and sale of securities. As a rule, the Bank buys and sells securities in market transactions with the chartered banks and other directly clearing members of the Canadian Payments Association and with the primary dealers. The Bank is allowed to use a wide variety of securities to facilitate its open market operations, including Government of Canada Treasury bills, bonds, and securities issued by municipal, provincial, and specified foreign governments. The Bank is also allowed to buy a broad range of chartered bank or bank-guaranteed short-term paper and commercial paper maturing in 180 days or less, issued by private firms. In practice, the Bank conducts most of its open market operations in Government of Canada securities, which have several advantages. These securities are available in a broad range of maturities. Furthermore, they are traded by all financial institutions, investment dealers, and the general public. As a result, the Bank can usually conduct its open market operations by simply responding to market bids and offers.

A distinction is usually made between the Bank's purchase of securities in the open market and its purchase of securities directly from the government of Canada at the time of issue. The Bank regularly takes some of each new issue of Government of Canada bonds to facilitate growth of the monetary base and to assist the government's debt management operations.

As shown in Table 17.1, the purchase of securities by the central bank increases the amount of cash in the financial system, while the sale of securities reduces the available amount of cash in the system. Unlike the practice in most other countries, the Bank of Canada no longer uses open market operations as a primary technique for day-to-day management of the cash reserves of the chartered banks and the other direct clearers of the Canadian Payments Association. Instead, as we will learn later in this chapter, the Bank targets the overnight interest rate and uses special purchase and resale agreements and sale and repurchase agreements to bring the overnight interest rate back on track. The Bank could use open market operations to intervene directly in the money market to achieve short-term rates consistent with its monetary policy objectives. Open market operations by the Bank directly affect interest rates by changing the demand and supply of securities in secondary markets, as well as by changing market expectations of future interest rates.

Open Market Operations and Cash Availability

When the Bank of Canada purchases securities in the open market it increases the availability of cash to the direct clearers, and when it sells securities in the open market it decreases the availability of cash to them. An open market pur-

www.

TABLE 17.1   **OPEN MARKET PURCHASE FROM PRIMARY DEALERS**
Millions of Dollars

BANK OF CANADA

Assets		Liabilities	
Treasury bills	+ 10	Direct clearer deposits	+ 10

DIRECT CLEARERS

Assets		Liabilities	
Deposits at Bank of Canada	+ 10	Deposits	+ 10

chase of $10 million in Treasury bills from the primary dealers is illustrated in Table 17.1.

When the Bank of Canada buys Treasury bills from primary dealers, it writes payment cheques on itself. The dealers, in turn, deposit these cheques in a deposit-taking institution. In the daily clearing and settlement process, the deposits of the direct clearers at the Bank of Canada, and hence their cash balances, are increased by the value of the Treasury bills purchased by the Bank.

If the Bank of Canada purchases $10 million in Treasury bills from the direct clearers rather than from the primary dealers, the changes in the books of the Bank and the direct clearers would be recorded as shown in Table 17.2.

The increase in the availability of cash to direct clearers is the same whether the Bank of Canada buys securities from them or from the primary dealers. However, when the chartered banks want to hold minimum reserves against their deposits, an open market purchase from them will increase their excess reserves more than an open market purchase from the primary dealers will. In the case shown in Table 17.2, the deposit liabilities of the chartered banks do not change, and therefore no additional reserves are necessary. The entire $10 million increase in direct clearers' deposits at the Bank of Canada represents an increase in the chartered banks' cash reserves.

TABLE 17.2   **OPEN MARKET PURCHASE FROM DIRECT CLEARERS**
Millions of Dollars

BANK OF CANADA

Assets		Liabilities	
Treasury bills	+ 10	Direct clearer deposits	+ 10

DIRECT CLEARERS

Assets		Liabilities	
Deposits at Bank of Canada	+ 10		
Treasury bills	− 10	Deposits	+ 0

Discounts, Advances, and the Bank Rate

A central bank is the ultimate source of cash for a country's payments system. When deposit-taking institutions are unable to encash their deposit liabilities, the public quickly loses confidence in their solvency and financial crisis can follow. To ensure the stability of the payments system, central banks act as **lender of last resort** to commercial banks and in some cases to other financial institutions as well. The central bank is a unique lender of last resort since it is the only institution that is the ultimate supplier of cash.

lender of last resort *the central bank, as the ultimate supplier of cash, can come to the assistance of financial institutions in times of financial crisis*

The concept of central banking was developed by the Bank of England when the commercial banks issued their own notes, which were redeemable into cash in the form of gold and Bank of England notes. The commercial banks put their own notes into circulation by discounting good-quality commercial bills for their customers. When they required additional cash, especially during periods of economic expansion, the commercial banks sold the bills they had previously discounted to the Bank of England, which paid for them by crediting deposit accounts held with it. These accounts could be drawn down in gold and Bank of England notes that were redeemable into gold on demand. The Bank of England was guided in the amount of bills it was willing to purchase (rediscount) by the adequacy of its gold reserves. It attempted to control the volume of its rediscounting, and hence its lending, by the quality of the bills it would accept and the rediscount rate it charged. This rate became known as the Bank Rate.

A rise in the Bank Rate usually served as a signal for other lending rates to follow, while the opposite was the case when the Bank Rate was lowered. By changing the Bank Rate, the Bank of England controlled the availability of cash to the financial system, and thereby the growth of the money supply, and the inward and outward flow of gold from its vaults.

Early in the development of central banking in the United Kingdom, the Bank of England began the practice of rediscounting bills for the London discount houses rather than for the banks. This change was made because it was thought that the public might lose confidence in a bank seen to be in need of cash by having the Bank of England rediscount bills of exchange for it. Alternatively, the banks could obtain cash indirectly from the Bank of England by calling their loans to the discount houses, which in turn replenished their cash by rediscounting their bills at the Bank of England. To discourage the discount houses from abusing their privilege of obtaining cash from the Bank, the Bank Rate (the rediscount rate) was ordinarily set above money market rates. In this way the Bank of England was a lender of last resort.

In 1913, when the Federal Reserve System was established in the United States, its role as lender of last resort was considered one of its principal functions. During its early years of operation, its member banks regularly took commercial paper they had discounted to the Federal Reserve for further discount. Rediscounting of commercial paper by the Federal Reserve was thought to ensure that growth in the money supply would always accommodate itself to the needs of business. This perception was rooted in the commercial loans theory. According to this theory, during periods of economic upswing, the banks, and in turn the Federal Reserve, would generate appropriate growth in the money supply by discounting commercial paper. During periods of eco-

discount window *refers to borrowing from the U.S. Federal Reserve Bank*

discount rate *the term used in the United States that is equivalent to the Bank Rate in Canada*

nomic downturn, growth in the money supply would appropriately decline as businesses repaid their loans to the banks and the banks in turn reduced their indebtedness to the Federal Reserve.

From its early practice of discounting commercial paper, the Federal Reserve's lending role became known as the **discount window** and the interest charged as the **discount rate**. Both these terms are still used today, even though discounting by the Federal Reserve has been replaced by direct advances by it to its member banks.

Bank of Canada Overdraft Loans and Advances

Unlike the early practice of central bank discounting in the United Kingdom and the United States, the Bank of Canada, from the time of its establishment, offered loans to the chartered banks in the form of direct advances secured by government bonds and other eligible financial assets. Before the founding of the Bank, the federal Department of Finance offered a lender of last resort facility to the chartered banks. To encourage the banks to finance the grain crop during the financial crisis of 1907, the government provided for cash advances to them in the form of Dominion notes. This facility was extended to the banks in the spirit of the real bills doctrine. The *Finance Acts* of 1914 and 1923 allowed the banks to obtain Dominion notes by depositing government bonds with the Department of Finance.

Since the establishment of the Canadian Payments Association in 1980, the chartered banks and nonbank members who are direct clearers have had access to advances from the Bank of Canada. These advances were ordinarily given to meet temporary day-to-day shortfalls in a direct clearer's settlement balances with the Bank, and to meet cumulative cash deficits of a direct clearer at the end of a cash-averaging period. As explained earlier, with the phasing out of primary reserve requirements for the banks, the Bank of Canada introduced lending procedures whereby all direct clearers were forced to take overnight overdraft loans from the Bank whenever they held insufficient daily settlement balances, and advances from the Bank at the end of each averaging period when this was necessary to maintain their cumulative settlement balance at the end of each monthly averaging period at zero or above.

Before the phasing in of zero primary reserve requirements for the banks, the Bank of Canada charged Bank Rate (one-quarter of 1 percent above the average weekly auction rate of 91-day federal Treasury bills) for advances within a line of credit preauthorized for each direct clearer, up to once per averaging period for banks and twice per month for nonbanks. Successive advances within an averaging period were charged successively higher margins over Bank Rate. In some cases these charges doubled the Bank Rate. After the move to zero primary reserves for the banks, both overdraft loans and advances became available at the Bank Rate.

With the introduction of the LVTS, the Bank of Canada eliminated the averaging period for settlement balances, because the direct clearers prefer a system in which negative settlements balances require overdraft loans financed at the overnight interest rate, while positive settlement balances are paid interest. Direct clearers who find themselves in a net deficit position may borrow from the Bank of Canada at the Bank Rate, while direct clearers in a net surplus settlement position are paid interest on their positive settlement balances by the Bank of Canada. The interest rate is 50 basis points below the Bank Rate, that is, the lower bound of the operating band for overnight interest rates (to which we will turn shortly).

A deficit clearer faces the Bank Rate if it borrows from the Bank of Canada and a surplus clearer earns 50 basis points below Bank Rate on its positive balances, so the overnight financing rate should lie somewhere within the target range specified by the central bank. Deficit clearers have an incentive to borrow from surplus clearers, since they will pay a lower rate of interest (lower than the Bank Rate), while surplus clearers want to lend out their surplus funds and receive more than the Bank Rate less 50 basis points. Hence, the overnight financing rate usually falls within the target range.

Historically, Canadian chartered banks have been infrequent borrowers from the Bank of Canada. Their reluctance to take advances from the Bank has been explained by their fear that such borrowing might be interpreted by the market as a sign of liquidity problems. From the Bank's point of view, it has always considered its lending as a last resort facility and has charged a penalty cost with rates above alternative money market borrowing. For example, its rules in 1991 governing advances to financial institutions stated:

> *While the Bank of Canada is conscious of its responsibility as the lender of last resort, it expects potential borrowers to make every effort to adjust their cash positions through the money market and to use their lines of credit at the central bank sparingly.*

Bank of Canada advances have normally been made for only a few days and usually just overnight to cover shortfalls in the direct clearers' settlement balances that result from unexpected payment flows in the daily clearing cycle. However, in 1985 when it appeared that the stability of the financial system could be threatened by the failure of the Canadian Commercial Bank and the Northland Bank, extraordinary advances, both in terms of their length and their amount, were granted. Total advances outstanding to these two institutions amounted to $1.8 billion. Extraordinary advances also were granted to the Bank of British Columbia and the Continental Bank of Canada when they experienced large withdrawals of deposits due to a loss of public confidence in the viability of their regional operations.[4] The governor of the Bank of Canada explained that the role of the Bank's advance facility

> *...is one of providing liquidity support to solvent banks that are encountering withdrawals of funds they cannot readily meet out of their own resources. It would be foolish to force a bank to call its loans and sell off its assets at fire-sale prices because of a temporary withdrawal of funds. The duty of the Bank of Canada is to advance funds to banks needing help on these occasions in order*

---

4. The only other time that the Bank of Canada had made an extraordinary advance was in 1977 to the Unity Bank, which experienced financial difficulties due to problem loans. These difficulties resulted in a loss of confidence that led to a run on the bank by wholesale depositors.

to prevent a loss of confidence from spreading and to give a sound institution time to demonstrate that a loss of confidence by its depositors was unjustified.[5]

Overdraft Loans, Advances, and Cash Availability

Overdraft loans and advances by the Bank of Canada to the direct clearers immediately increase their demand deposits at the Bank of Canada and, hence, the availability of cash to them. The changes in the balance sheets of the Bank and the direct clearers following a $10 million advance or loan are shown in Table 17.3.

TABLE 17.3 **OVERDRAFT LOAN OR ADVANCE** Millions of Dollars			
BANK OF CANADA			
Assets		**Liabilities**	
Overdraft Loans	+ 10	Direct clearer deposits	+ 10
DIRECT CLEARERS			
Assets		**Liabilities**	
Deposits at Bank of Canada	+ 10	Overdraft loans and advances	+ 10

The Bank Rate

As we have already observed, the Bank Rate is the minimum rate at which the Bank of Canada makes loans to members of the Canadian Payments Association. It has been the tradition in Canada, following that in Britain, to make the Bank Rate a penalty rate, but at the same time to keep it low enough so as not to jeopardize the central bank's role as lender of last resort. In the United States, the Federal Reserve Bank's discount rate is usually kept below market interest rates. The Federal Reserve Bank, however, uses "administrative counselling" for those borrowers that are judged to be using the discount window privilege inappropriately.

Changes in the Bank Rate can assist the central bank in achieving its monetary policy objectives because of their possible announcement effect and cost effect. The announcement effect refers to the use of Bank Rate changes by the central bank to signal desired changes in monetary policy.[6] The cost effect refers to the behaviour of the direct clearers in response to a change in the cost

---

5. *Bank of Canada Review*, October 1985, p. 23.

6. M.L. Kilman has investigated to what extent changes in the Bank Rate have had a predictable announcement effect. See M.L. Kilman, "The Administered Bank Rate and Its Announcement Effect," *Canadian Journal Economics* 7 (November 1974), pp. 625–41; and Anselm London, "Bank Rate Changes and the Exchange Rate: A Test for Anticipation and Announcement Effects," *Canadian Journal of Economics* 14 (February 1981), pp. 115–9.

fixed Bank Rate regime *when the central bank uses its discretion to change its Bank Rate*

floating Bank Rate regime *when the Bank Rate is tied to and varies with a specified market rate*

operating band for overnight rates *when Bank of Canada monetary policy action keeps overnight interest rates within a band of 50 basis points*

of borrowing cash from the central bank. The degree to which these two effects may assist monetary policy depends on the method the central bank employs for setting its Rate.

In Canada, two methods have been used for setting the Bank Rate. One is called a **fixed Bank Rate** regime and the other a floating Bank Rate regime. Under a fixed Rate regime the central bank uses its discretion to change the rate. With a **floating Bank Rate regime,** the rate is tied to a specific market rate. In Canada we had a floating Bank Rate from November 1, 1956, to June 1962, and again from March 13, 1980, to February 13, 1994. At that point it was automatically set each week equal to the average interest rate established at the auction of three-month Government of Canada Treasury bills, plus one-quarter of a percentage point. Figure 17–1 shows the Bank Rate in Canada since 1998.

Since mid-1994, the operational objective of the Bank of Canada's monetary policy action has focused on the **operating band for overnight rates—** where overnight interest rates are kept within a band of fifty basis points. On February 22, 1996, the Bank adopted an approach in which the Bank Rate is set at the upper limit of the operating band for the overnight financing rate— the Rate at which major participants in the money market borrow and lend one-day funds. The Bank of Canada adopted this new method in anticipation of the introduction of the Large Value Transfer System, which provides overnight financing at a cost equal to the upper limit of its operating band.

FIGURE 17–1   THE BANK RATE IN CANADA

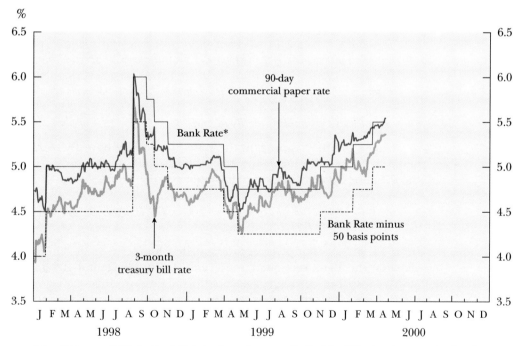

* As of February 1996, the Bank Rate has been the upper limit of the 50-basis-point operating band for the overnight rate.

SOURCE: Bank of Canada, *Monetary Policy Report,* May 2000.

A major advantage claimed for a fixed Bank Rate regime is its use by the central bank to announce its intentions about the direction or stance of monetary policy. Critics point out that the announcement effect of a Bank Rate change can be perverse, because a change in the Rate by itself does not always contain sufficient information to allow markets to interpret the central bank's intention accurately. Changes in the Bank Rate are particularly subject to misinterpretation when they are announced frequently to keep the Rate at a penalty level. Critics suggest that a simple statement by the central bank when making a change in its rate is a more efficient method for making known its monetary policy intentions.

The major advantage of a floating Bank Rate regime is that it automatically guarantees that the rate is continually a penalty rate. It avoids the dangers of misinterpretation of changes that have to be made under a fixed rate regime to keep it at a penalty level. Critics point out that under a floating Bank Rate, the central bank gives up an important discretionary power to influence (or control) money market interest rates directly. This need not be the case, however, because with the Bank Rate tied to the Treasury bill rate, the Bank of Canada can influence its level by the amount of its own purchases and sales of Treasury bills. On various occasions since 1980, the Bank has aggressively intervened in the Treasury bill market to influence the floating Bank Rate directly and thereby the movement of money market rates.

In September 2000 the Bank of Canada announced it would adopt eight pre-specified dates each year for announcing changes to the bank rate, effective November 2000. The Bank reported that

> "…*fixed dates will reduce uncertainty in financial markets associated with not knowing exactly when the Bank might announce an interest rate change. They should also focus greater attention on the economic and monetary situation in Canada; put greater emphasis on the medium-term perspective that underlies monetary policy; and increase the Bank's transparency, accountability, and ongoing dialogue with the public. Together, these improvements should contribute to better public understanding of the factors influencing monetary policy and increase the public's ability to anticipate the direction of policy.*[7]

Under the new approach, the Bank would still have the option of acting between fixed announcement dates, but it would exercise this option only in the event of extraordinary circumstances.

Buy-Back Techniques

In 1954, in its attempt to encourage development of the money market in Canada, the Bank of Canada entered into Purchase and Resale Agreements (PRAs) with the money market jobbers. These were a small group of investment firms that made markets for money market instruments by holding trading inventories of short-term securities, and by posting bid and ask quotes at which they were prepared to trade in these securities. They have since been replaced by primary dealers.

---

7. Bank of Canada, Press Release, September 19, 2000.

A PRA involved the Bank of Canada buying Treasury bills and other short-term assets from the primary dealers, who in turn agreed to buy them back at a prearranged price within 15 days, but in practice usually the next day. Each dealer could initiate PRA transactions up to an assigned limit at the Bank Rate when other financing was unavailable or unduly expensive. In effect, with PRA transactions, the Bank of Canada extends lender of last resort privileges to the primary dealers, just as it did to the direct clearers with overdraft loans and advances.

In 1985 the Bank of Canada introduced the Special Purchase and Resale Agreements (SPRAs). They are similar to the PRAs, but are initiated by the Bank rather than the primary dealers. Moreover, the Bank sets the rates and the amounts at which it offers SPRAs to the primary dealers and occasionally also to the chartered banks. In 1986 the Bank added Sale and Repurchase Agreements (SRAs). These transactions are essentially the opposite of SPRAs in that they involve the Bank selling short-term government of Canada securities with an agreement to repurchase them on the next business day.

SPRAs and SRAs are money market intervention techniques employed by the Bank of Canada to directly influence short-term, and in particular overnight, interest rates. The Bank uses SPRAs to offset what it considers undesirable upward pressure on overnight rates or to place pressure on the rates to move down. Alternatively, it uses SRAs to counteract undesirable downward pressure on the overnight rate or to encourage an upward movement in the rate.

SPRAs are open market transactions that increase the direct clearers' settlement balances at the Bank of Canada. So that the impact of SPRAs is on interest rates alone, the Bank usually neutralizes their effect on settlement balances via its cash-setting technique, as we will quickly learn.

SPRAs and SRAs assist the Bank in three ways in the implementation of its monetary policy objectives. First, they are usually used to provide immediate support to the level and direction of short-term interest rates sought by the Bank's daily cash setting. Second, they have been used as a safety valve to offset unexpected sharp changes in overnight interest rates in response to the Bank's cash setting. Third, the use of these buy-back techniques has also served as a signal to financial markets of the direction of short-term interest rates sought by the Bank.

With the introduction of the LVTS, the Bank of Canada eliminated the PRA so that only the Bank can initiate a Purchase and Resale Agreement (SPRA). As we will learn later in this chapter, this allows the central bank to effectively control the overnight financing rate.

Moral Suasion

The central bank is said to use moral suasion when it attempts to persuade financial institutions to pursue some objective of financial policy voluntarily. Moral suasion can take the form of informal or formal agreements, or simply a statement by the central bank or the minister of finance, expressing their views regarding the desirable or undesirable behaviour of financial institutions.

The cooperation that the central bank as persuader can expect to receive from the financial community critically depends on the success or failure of its leadership in the past. The prestige gained from a history of success undoubtedly makes it easier for the central bank to solicit cooperation. Under most circumstances it is probably also true that the smaller the number of institutions whose support is being sought, the easier it is to gain support. When a large group is being persuaded to follow a certain course of action, the possibility of sidestepping is increased because individual institutions may believe that their deviations influence the outcome insignificantly. The relatively small number of banks in Canada before the 1980 *Bank Act* revisions probably encouraged the Bank of Canada to use moral suasion as a policy tool.[8] The support that the central bank can expect from financial institutions also depends on the nature, frequency, and duration of its requests. For instance, it may request that the chartered banks reduce a certain type of profitable lending. If the banks are persuaded that this is in the national interest and that it is for a relatively short period, they will probably comply. However, even if the requests call for only temporary compliance, their increased frequency may meet a cool reception.

The chartered banks may generally also be inclined to respond to moral suasion by the central bank because they know that it can manage the cash reserves available to them so as to affect their ability to expand, and thereby their ability to enhance their profits.

In recent years the Bank of Canada has not used moral suasion as a tool of monetary policy.

Selective Credit Controls

Selective credit controls are directed to types of lending rather than to the lending of particular institutions. Because they involve direct interference with the free play of market forces, they have been used reluctantly and only during times of war and periods of postwar readjustment. The authority to impose such controls was granted to the Bank of Canada during the Second World War by an order-in-council under the *War Measures Act*. The more common type of selective credit controls that have been employed includes those on margin requirements, consumer credit, real estate credit, and new capital issues.

margin requirements the proportion of the price of a security that must be paid at time of purchase

Margin requirements are the part of the purchase price of securities listed on stock exchanges that must be paid directly by the purchaser. When the margin requirement is 60 percent, a buyer of a listed stock with a current value of $1000 has to put up at least $600 of his or her own funds and may borrow no more than $400 using the stock as collateral. By increasing margin requirements, the authorities make it more difficult for those who must borrow funds to speculate on the stock market. The authority to set margin requirements was given to the board of governors of the Federal Reserve System in the United States in the *Securities Exchange Act* of 1934, and has been used continually since then. The Bank of Canada has no such authority but, instead, has used moral suasion to this end.

---

8. For a somewhat different point of view on why the Bank of Canada may have preferred the use of moral suasion, see John F. Chant, and Keith Acheson, "The Choice of Monetary Instruments and the Theory of Bureaucracy," in *Canadian Banking and Monetary Policy*, ed. James P. Cairns, H.H. Binhammer, and Robin Boadway (Toronto: McGraw-Hill Ryerson, 1972).

Government Financial Transactions

The financial transactions of the central government influence the monetary system and credit conditions to almost as great a degree as do the activities of the central bank. Management of the government's cash deposits brings indirect influence to bear on credit conditions by affecting the cash positions of the directly clearing members of the Canadian Payments Association. Direct influence on credit conditions may be exerted by the management of government assets (other than cash deposits) and of government debt.

The Nature of Government Financial Transactions

During any given period the federal government requires cash to meet its budgetary and nonbudgetary obligations. These cash requirements can be met by increasing debt (borrowing), by running down cash balances, or by liquidating assets held in the investment account and sinking funds. When, however, the federal government's overall transactions result in cash surpluses rather than deficits, it is able to reduce its overall debt or increase its cash balances, or add to the security holdings of the investment account and sinking funds.

The federal government's financial operations are reflected in its fiscal position, as shown for its fiscal year ended March 31, 2000, in Table 17.4.[9] The government's financial budget, together with nonbudgetary receipts and expenditures, indicates its overall cash surplus or cash requirements.

www.

Budgetary revenue is derived from personal and corporate income taxes, various excise taxes and duties, the goods and services tax (GST), employment insurance contributions, returns on investments, and net earnings of Crown

TABLE 17.4	**GOVERNMENT OF CANADA, FISCAL POSITION, 1999–2000** Billions of Dollars, Fiscal Year Ended March 31		
Budgetary Transactions			
Revenue		119.8	
Expenditures		−108.8	
Budgetary surplus (+) or deficit (–)			+11.0
Nonbudgetary Transactions			**−5.4**
Requirement for Foreign Exchange Transactions			−0.3
Total Cash Requirements			+5.3
Financed by			
Increase in cash balances		+4.7	
Increase in debt outstanding		−0.6	−5.3

SOURCE: Statistics Canada, CANSIM Database, Series D94080, D94092, D94122, D94123, D94132, D94146, and D94133, August 2000.

---

9. The federal government's financial transactions can be presented either on a public accounts basis (actual payments), as is done in this chapter, or on a national accounts basis (accrual).

corporations including the Bank of Canada and the Royal Canadian Mint. Budgetary expenditures consist of charges on the government for work performed, goods received, and services rendered. Interest paid on the public debt, and government subsidies, grants, and other transfers also are part of the government's budgetary expenditures.

Nonbudgetary expenditures comprise transactions that involve the acquisition or disposal of assets or the creation or discharge of liabilities. For example, loans and advances to, and investments in, Crown corporations such as the Canada Deposit Insurance Corporation and the Export Development Corporation are nonbudgetary transactions, as are loans to provincial and territorial governments, international organizations, and developing countries. Other nonbudgetary transactions are the maintenance of specified-purpose accounts such as the Canada Pension Plan, and government superannuation and annuities accounts. Nonbudgetary foreign exchange transactions are financial claims and obligations of the government involving changes in its foreign assets and liabilities. The most important type of transaction resulting in an increase or decrease in the government's Canadian dollar financing requirements is an advance to the Exchange Fund Account or the repayment of such an advance. We will learn later that such advances and repayments can affect the availability of cash to the financial system.

As shown in Table 17.4, in its 1999–2000 fiscal year, the federal government had a cash surplus of $5.3 billion. This figure was the result of a $11 billion budgetary surplus, a $5.4 billion deficit due to nonbudgetary transactions, and a requirement of $0.3 billion to finance foreign exchange transactions. The federal government's total cash surplus allowed it to increase its cash balances by $4.7 billion, and reduce its debt outstanding by $0.6 billion.

Management of Government Deposits

The government of Canada maintains cash balances in the form of current and special accounts in the name of the receiver general for Canada with the Bank of Canada, the chartered banks, nonbank members of the Canadian Payments Association, and banks in some foreign countries. By statutory definition, the total of these deposits constitutes the Consolidated Revenue Fund of the Government of Canada.

The Bank of Canada, as the government's fiscal agent, is its main banker and as such holds its operating account. Day-to-day receipts and disbursements of the federal government are handled through its account with the Bank. Daily Canadian dollar receipts, whether in the form of cash, cheques, or electronic transfers, are received by the Bank of Canada's agencies throughout the country and credited to the receiver general's account. When a cheque received by the government is cleared by the Canadian Payments Association, the government's deposit account with the Bank is credited, and simultaneously a direct clearer's account with the Bank is debited. Similarly, when the government writes a cheque received by the public, this cheque is taken to a financial institution for deposit or to be cashed. The institution in turn has the government's cheque cleared through the Canadian Payments Association. In

TABLE 17.5	CASH EFFECT OF A NET INCREASE IN FEDERAL EXPENDITURES
	Millions of Dollars

BANK OF CANADA

Assets	Liabilities	
	Deposits:	
	Government of Canada	−$25
	Direct clearers	+$25

DIRECT CLEARERS

Assets		Liabilities	
		Deposits:	
Deposits at central bank	+$25	Government of Canada	0
		Public	+$25

the clearing process, the government's deposit account with the Bank of Canada is debited and that of the direct clearer is credited.

If the government were to maintain a deposit account with the central bank alone, the cash position of the chartered banks and other deposit-taking institutions would fluctuate with the daily ebb and flow of the government's financial transactions. If on balance the government's receipts from the public were to exceed its payments to the public, the direct clearers' deposits with the central bank, and therefore their cash holdings, would decrease. Conversely, if on balance the government's payments to the public were to exceed its receipts from the public, the direct clearers' deposits with the central bank would increase, as would their cash holdings. This is illustrated in Table 17.5, where it is assumed that the government has undertaken an expansionary fiscal policy. As a result it has incurred a budgetary deficit of $25 million, which it finances by writing cheques on its deposit balances with the central bank. When these cheques are cleared and settled, the direct clearers' cash in the form of deposits with the Bank of Canada have increased by $25 million, the same amount by which the government's balance at the Bank has declined.

The public's deposits have increased by the same amount as a result of crediting the government's cheques to their accounts at depository institutions. The increase in cash available to the depository institutions can lead to a multiple expansion of their loans, investments, and deposits and can result in undesirable money market conditions and changes in interest rates. To avoid such undesirable changes stemming from federal government funds flowing in and out of its account at the central bank, the federal government also maintains deposit accounts at private financial institutions.

As part of its function of fiscal agent for the government of Canada, the Bank of Canada in consultation with the Department of Finance manages the federal government's cash balances. These balances are held as demand and term deposits with the Bank and the directly clearing members of the Canadian Payments Association.

Before 1986, the government held only demand deposits with the direct clearers, and each clearer's share of total government deposits was equal to its share of Canadian dollar deposit liabilities as of December 31 of the previous year. Balances in excess of $100 million earned interest based on the rate for new 91-day Treasury bills. In 1986 the method of calculating the interest rate paid on demand deposits held by the government with the direct clearers was changed to the chartered banks' prime rate minus 250 basis points (2.5 percentage points). For the government to earn higher market-related interest rates on its cash balances in excess of the daily requirements to fund its transactions and for monetary policy operations, the Bank also started in 1986 to auction excess government balances for fixed terms to the direct clearers. From September 1989 until early 1999, in addition to auctioning government balances in excess of daily requirements, the Bank also auctioned the government's demand deposit balances. These auctions were held each week and allowed the direct clearers to determine, within limits, their share of total government demand deposits over a cash-averaging period. To ensure a reasonably wide distribution of government demand deposits among the direct clearers, the auction procedure limited the total amount of each clearer's bid at the auctions. Bids for a share of these deposits were accepted in terms of basis point spreads against the average of the "big six" banks' prime lending rates, with a minimum permissible bid of prime minus 350 basis points.[10]

With the introduction of the LVTS in 1999, the Bank of Canada changed how it used government deposits to manage the settlement process. Until 1999, the Bank used drawdowns and redeposits (described in Appendix 17.B) to both neutralize the effects of government disbursements and to affect the level of settlement balances. Since then, the Bank has primarily used the transfer of government deposits to neutralize the impact of government flows between the central bank and the direct clearers. Initially, the Bank did not attempt to achieve a particular level for settlement balances, which had been targeted around a net settlement flow of zero. However, in the latter half of 1999, the overnight financing rate approached or exceeded the upper band of the target range, partly due to month-end "technical tightness" during which a great degree of uncertainty regarding net flows and payment volumes existed. Rather than change the level at which the operating band had been set, the Bank of Canada decided to introduce a target level for settlement balances of $200 million, with a higher target value possible on "technically tight" days.

How does this relate to the overnight financing rate? We know that the upper band of the target range is the Bank Rate, and we know that direct clearers with positive settlement balances receive the lower bound of the target range from the central bank as interest. Surplus and deficit clearers have an incentive to trade since deficit clearers face the Bank Rate on loans from the Bank of Canada, while surplus clearers earn 50 basis points below the Bank Rate on their balances. The overnight financing rate will lie somewhere within this band. As the government's banker, the Bank of Canada knows, with cer-

10. For a description of auction procedures and characteristics, see "Receiver General Deposit Auctions: A Technical Note," *Bank of Canada Review*, August 1991, pp. 21–34. In July 2000 the Bank of Canada released a discussion paper containing proposed revisions to the auctioning process. See *Proposed Revisions to the Rule Pertaining to Auctions of Receiver General Term Deposits*, Bank of Canada, July 18, 2000.

tainty, the size of the transfers from government deposits into the direct clearers (resulting from federal disbursements). By mid-afternoon the Bank will be informed of the direct clearers' claims on government deposits. The neutralization component of government deposit flows is based on the difference between these two amounts. Neutralization occurs through the twice-daily auction of government deposits.

To achieve the $200 million target for settlements balances, the Bank may use a SPRA or an SRA. These actions will not only affect the net amount of total settlements, but they will ensure that the overnight financing rate remains within the target band. To see why, suppose the overnight rate rises to the Bank Rate. The Bank can undertake a special PRA to increase liquidity in the financial system, with the overnight rate falling back toward the mid-point of the range. In the event the overnight financing rate were to approach the lower bound of the target range, the Bank would undertake a SRA, thereby reducing liquidity, which tends to bring the overnight rate back up to the mid-point of the target.

Asset Management

The federal government maintains nondeposit accounts in which it holds domestic and foreign financial assets. The Bank of Canada, in its role as government fiscal agent and debt manager, helps to manage the assets held in those accounts. The Bank has fairly wide powers to manage some of these accounts, especially the Securities Investment Account, the Purchase Fund Account, and the Exchange Fund Account, for either debt management policy or cash reserve management. However, in the case of Special Investment Accounts such as the Employment Insurance Account, the Canada Pension Plan Account, and Superannuation Accounts, the Bank plays a small role in their management because these accounts can be used only to serve the special purposes for which they have been set up.

The Securities Investment Account was originally established to facilitate investment of the government's temporary excess cash balances in its own securities at a time when the chartered banks did not pay any interest on government deposits held with them. During and for some time after the Second World War, the account was used to purchase and sell Government of Canada bonds to stabilize their prices. Since then the Bank has occasionally also used this account for its cash reserve management policy. For example, in 1963, the Bank sold $50 million in Treasury bills to the account on February 1 and repurchased the bills on March 1 to offset a seasonal change in the chartered banks' till money.

The Purchase Fund Account was established in 1961 to provide for the orderly retirement of government debt, and at the same time to contribute to the stability of the long-term government bond market. Since 1974 all long-term bond issues of the federal government provide for the Bank, in its role as agent, to buy for the Purchase Fund each quarter a prorated amount of the principal amount of each issue outstanding. These purchases are usually timed to complement the Bank's monetary policy. For example, to keep interest rates from rising in the first quarter of 1983, the Bank bought bonds for the Purchase Fund relatively early in the quarter rather than at the end, as is usually the case. When the Bank buys bonds for the Purchase Fund, the government's deposit balances with the Bank are decreased by an equivalent amount, as is the cash available to members of the Canadian Payments Association. Any undesirable increase in the chartered banks' cash reserve can be offset by the Bank of Canada with open market sales and drawdowns.

Exchange Fund Account *the fund managed by the Bank of Canada, on behalf of the government of Canada, that holds the country's official foreign exchange assets*

The **Exchange Fund Account** is the major vehicle used by the Bank of Canada on behalf of the government to manage the country's foreign exchange reserves. The foreign currency assets held by the Exchange Fund (primarily foreign-currency-denominated government Treasury bills, bonds, and bank deposits) may be used to maintain a particular level for, or to prevent undesirable fluctuations in, the value of the Canadian dollar. For example, if the value of our dollar is falling, the Bank may attempt to prevent or moderate such a fall by purchasing Canadian dollars in the foreign exchange market with the foreign currency assets held by the Exchange Fund. The Canadian dollars purchased are deposited in the government's account with the Bank. Alternatively, if the external value of the Canadian dollar is rising, the Bank may attempt to prevent or moderate the increase by purchasing foreign currency assets with Canadian dollars. The Canadian dollars used in this way reduce the government's deposit account held with the Bank.

Exchange Fund Account Transactions

Direct intervention by the Exchange Fund Account in the foreign exchange market, by purchasing or selling foreign exchange to moderate downward or upward movements in the value of the Canadian dollar, affects the availability of cash to the direct clearers. This effect is illustrated in Table 17.6, where it is assumed that the Exchange Fund sells the equivalent of $50 million in foreign exchange to moderate downward market pressures on the Canadian dollar's value.

TABLE 17.6   INTERVENTION USING GOVERNMENT DEPOSITS
Millions of Dollars

BANK OF CANADA

Assets			Liabilities		
EFA transaction			Government deposits:		+50
			Direct clearer deposits		−50
Sterilization (redeposit)			Government deposits		−50
			Direct clearer deposits		+50

DIRECT CLEARERS

Assets			Liabilities		
EFA transaction	Deposits at Bank of Canada	−50	Public deposits:		−50
Sterilization	Deposits at Bank of Canada	+50	Government deposits		+50

When the Exchange Fund sells from its foreign exchange holdings, the Canadian dollar receipts from this sale are credited to the federal government's deposit account at the Bank of Canada. Purchasers pay the Exchange Fund by writing cheques against their Canadian dollar deposit accounts at Canadian financial institutions. As is shown in the table, after the daily clearing and settlement of these cheques, the direct clearers' demand deposits at the Bank are reduced by $50 million, as are their deposit liabilities.

As a rule the Bank of Canada offsets the cash effects of Exchange Fund transactions in a process known as **sterilization**. In the example in the table, the Bank sterilizes the fund's sale of foreign exchange with a $50 million redeposit of government deposits. In the past, the Bank has used transfers of government deposit balances to sterilize the cash effects of Exchange Fund intervention in the foreign exchange market.

sterilization
exchange market intervention that leaves the monetary base unchanged

Exchange Fund Account Swaps and Bank of Canada Cash Setting

The Bank of Canada regularly uses Exchange Fund Account swaps to increase federal government demand deposit balances to facilitate the Bank's daily cash-setting exercise. Since 1986, when the government started to place its money for fixed terms with the direct clearers, the amount of its demand deposits has typically been insufficient to allow the Bank to achieve its desired cash setting objectives.

Foreign exchange swap transactions involve the matching of a spot purchase (or sale) with a forward sale (or purchase) of foreign exchange assets. Typically, the Bank temporarily purchases foreign exchange assets from the government's Exchange Fund, and at the same time agrees to resell these assets to the fund at a set price and at a future date. As shown in Table 17.7, the initial effect on the Bank's books of the swap purchase of $100 million of foreign exchange from the Exchange Fund is to increase the Bank's assets of foreign exchange and, at the same time, its holdings of government demand deposits. This increase now allows the Bank to engage in a transfer of government deposits to the direct clearers of $100 million, recorded in Table 17.7 by a $100 million decrease in government demand deposits at the Bank and a corresponding increase in government deposits at the direct clearers. At the same time the direct clearers' availability of cash has increased with a $100 million increase in their demand deposits at the Bank of Canada. In their books, the redeposit is recorded as an increase in cash held on deposit with the Bank of Canada and a corresponding increase in government deposit liabilities.

The Bank of Canada normally resells the foreign exchange assets it has temporarily purchased from the Exchange Fund (known as unwinding or reversing the swap) when it reduces the quantity of cash available to the direct clearers. As we have explained, swap foreign exchange transactions are made directly between the Exchange Fund Account and the Bank of Canada to facilitate the management of cash available to the banking system. In February 1991, the minister of finance announced that swap transactions between the Exchange Fund Account and major financial institutions would be used to help the government manage its domestic cash balances in a cost-effective manner.

TABLE 17.7	**FOREIGN CURRENCY SWAP AND A REDEPOSIT**
	Millions of Dollars

BANK OF CANADA

Assets			Liabilities	
EFA swap	Foreign exchange	+ 100	Government deposits	+100
Redeposit			Government deposits	−100
			Direct clearer deposits	+100

DIRECT CLEARERS

Assets			Liabilities	
Redeposit	Deposits at Bank	+100	Government deposits	+100

These swaps are now used regularly as a cost-effective alternative to borrowing by issuing cash management Treasury bills for temporarily replenishing the government's balances.[11]

Debt Management and the Money Supply

The federal government borrows to finance its budget deficits most often by issuing securities. We will now show the effects of government borrowing on the money supply when newly issued securities are purchased by the Bank of Canada, depository institutions, and the public.

Borrowing from the Bank of Canada

Federal government borrowing by the sale of its securities to the central bank is referred to as debt monetization or money financing because the monetary base is increased. This is illustrated in Table 17.8 where we assume that the federal government, in anticipation of a cash deficit, sells a new issue of securities directly to the Bank of Canada.

When the Bank buys securities directly from the federal government, cash settlement, as shown in Stage 1 in Table 17.8, takes place by crediting the government's deposit account at the Bank.[12] The cheques written against this account to pay the government's additional expenditures end up in the public's deposits with the direct clearers. Following clearing and settlement (Stage 2), the direct clearers' deposits with the Bank and, hence, the monetary

---

11. See George Norlan, "Exchange Fund Account Cash management Swaps: A Technical Note," *Bank of Canada Review*, May 1992, pp. 3–10.

12. This table and the following tables have been divided into "stages" to simplify our exposition. The stages do not necessarily identify the actual timing of transactions.

TABLE 17.8	**FINANCING DEFICIT BY BORROWING FROM THE CENTRAL BANK**
	Millions of Dollars

BANK OF CANADA

Stage 1	Assets		Liabilities	
Securities purchase	Government bonds	+	Government deposits	+
Stage 2			Government deposits	–
			Direct clearer deposits	+

DIRECT CLEARERS

Stage 1	Assets		Liabilities	
Stage 2				
Government deficit	Deposits at Bank of Canada	+	Government deposits	0
expenditures			Public deposits	+
Net effect	Cash:		Government deposits	0
	Deposits at Bank of Canada	+	Public deposits	+

base are increased. The net effect of a government deficit financed by borrowing from the Bank of Canada is an expansion of the money supply.

Borrowing from Depository Institutions

When depository institutions such as the banks and trust companies buy securities newly issued by the federal government to finance its budget deficit, their assets increase as shown in Stage 1 in Table 17.9. Settlement for these securities in the books of the Bank of Canada (Stage 2) takes place by crediting the government's deposits account and debiting the direct clearers' accounts by an equivalent amount. As the government writes cheques to pay for the expenditures that cause its deficit (Stage 3), its deposits at the Bank decline while the direct clearers' deposits at the Bank increase by the same amount as do the public's deposits at depository institutions. (We assume that the public's deposits are held with the direct clearers.)

The net effect of an increase in government purchases of goods and services from the public matched by a corresponding increase in government borrowing from depository institutions is to leave the cash held by the direct clearers unchanged. However, their demand deposits, and therefore the money supply, have increased. These increases can only be sustained if the direct clearers are prepared to hold a lower cash-to-total-deposits ratio, if the Bank provides them with additional cash, or if they can induce the public to deposit more cash with them. The last of these options could be accomplished by offering higher deposit interest rates.

TABLE 17.9	**FINANCING DEFICIT BY BORROWING FROM DEPOSITORY INSTITUTIONS**

BANK OF CANADA

Stage 1	Assets		Liabilities	
Stage 2			Government deposits	+
			Direct clearer deposits	–
Stage 3			Government deposits	–
			Direct clearer deposits	+

DIRECT CLEARERS

Stage 1	Assets		Liabilities	
Securities purchase	Government bonds	+		
Stage 2				
Clearing and settlement	Deposits at Bank of Canada	+		
Stage 3				
Government spends funds	Deposits at Bank of Canada	+	Public deposits	+
			Government deposits	0
Net Effect	Deposits at Bank of Canada	0	Government deposits	0
	Securities	+	Public deposits	+

Borrowing from the Public

We now assume that the government sells a new issue of its securities directly to the public. The public pays for these securities with cheques drawn against deposits held at depository institutions (see Stage 1 in Table 17.10). After these cheques are cleared and settlement is made, the government's deposit balances at the Bank of Canada are increased and those of the direct clearers are decreased by the same amount (see Stage 2). When the government writes cheques drawn on its increased deposits, the public's deposits and the depository institutions' cash at the Bank are built back up (see Stage 3).

The net effect of these transactions, as summarized in Table 17.10, is to leave the money supply unchanged. However, because these transactions may not occur simultaneously, both the monetary base and the money supply can experience temporary changes.

Ricardian Equivalence Theorem

Whether the public views its holdings of government securities as an asset, and hence net wealth to society, is a question first raised by David Ricardo, a famous classical economist of the early nineteenth century. Robert Barro of Harvard University posed the question again more recently.

TABLE 17.10 FINANCING DEFICIT BY BORROWING FROM THE PUBLIC

BANK OF CANADA

Stage 1	Assets	Liabilities	
Stage 2		Government deposits	+
		Direct clearer deposits	−
Stage 3		Government deposits	−
		Direct clearer deposits	+

DIRECT CLEARERS

	Assets		Liabilities	
Stage 1				
Securities purchase			Public deposits	−
Stage 2				
Clearing and settlement	Deposits at Bank of Canada	−		
Stage 3				
Government spends funds	Deposits at Bank of Canada	+	Public deposits	+
Net effect	Deposits at Bank of Canada	0	Public deposits	+

According to the Ricardian equivalence theorem, government debt is not part of society's net wealth. This idea is based on the assumption that individuals believe that they will have to pay additional taxes to service and retire increases in the debt. Because they perceive an increase in the present value of their taxes as just offsetting deficit-financed expenditures, the government debt is not part of society's net wealth. Moreover, it has been argued that the public will increase its saving to meet its future tax liability. With an increase in loanable funds because of higher saving, government debt financing is not accompanied by higher interest rates.

The opposite point of view is that when the government issues debt, the debt holders see it as an asset, but taxpayers do not view it as a liability. That is, they do not perceive that they will have to pay additional taxes to service or retire the debt. Consequently, their saving behaviour is unaffected by government debt issues. As a result, the supply of loanable funds may remain unchanged while the demand increases with additional government borrowing. The excess demand puts upward pressure on market interest rates. Higher interest rates can crowd out consumer and investment expenditures sensitive to higher interest costs. A debt-financed increase in government expenditures intended to expand aggregate expenditures may be frustrated by the crowding-out effect of higher interest rates.

Dimensions of the Federal Government's Debt

At the beginning of 1992, the outstanding direct and guaranteed debt of the government of Canada was $348 billion. By 2000, this figure had risen to more than $580 billion. This debt represents the net accumulation of the government's total cash deficits and cash surpluses since Confederation in 1867. During the Second World War it rose to some 150 percent of national income. Because of large deficits, the debt increased almost threefold in the 1970s, from $26 billion to $71 billion, and almost fivefold in the 1980s. After the Second World War, the debt–income ratio declined almost steadily until 1974 when the debt was some 5 percent of GDP. However, after the mid-1970s, because of the government's large deficits, it increased to more than 60 percent of GDP before it started to decline again in the second half of the 1990s.

At the end of 1999, the Bank of Canada held only 7.7 percent of the $458 billion in total outstanding Government of Canada direct securities and loans, which indicates that a relatively small amount was monetized. Financial institutions held about 50 percent, and nonresidents 22 percent of the federal government's outstanding securities and loans. Much of the federal government's debt consists of marketable securities, and the remainder of nonmarketable securities. The latter include Canada Savings Bonds and bonds issued to the Canada Pension Plan Investment Fund.

The average term to maturity of the federal government's unmatured direct and guaranteed securities was seven years and two months in 1979. The average term to maturity steadily decreased during the inflationary 1980s, and was down to four years in the early 1990s. During 1996, however, it increased, reaching five years and six months. By May 2000, the average term had risen to six years, four months. This higher average maturity reflected the lower and stable inflation rates of the mid- to late 1990s. A similar story can be told regarding the proportion of the government's outstanding debt held in Treasury bills. During the years of high inflation, this proportion rose to more than 42 percent in the early 1990s. Thereafter, the proportion declined and stood at 30.2 percent in 1996. By early 2000 it had declined further to just over 20 percent.

Debt Management

The primary objectives of the government of Canada's debt management operation are to meet the government's financing requirements in an efficient and cost-effective manner. The government also has an interest in promoting efficient, competitive, and liquid markets to facilitate domestic market activity and to minimize its own debt costs. Because of the "risk-free" nature of the federal government's securities, they provide an important benchmark against which domestic securities are issued. Government bonds have been the basis for the creation of stripped zero-coupon bonds. The government Treasury bills as well as repose have played an important role in the execution of monetary policy. Moreover, as we have shown, our money is nothing more than monetized federal government debt.

primary dealers
the federal government distributes its securities through a syndicate of investment dealers and banks; members of the syndicate are called primary dealers

The federal government's marketable securities are distributed through a syndicate of investment dealers and banks. The members of this syndicate are called **primary dealers**. Investment dealers, banks, and any nonbank members of the Canadian Payments Association that hold a settlement account with the Bank of Canada are eligible for primary dealer status. To be conferred such status, eligible distributors must maintain a certain threshold level of activity in the market for Government of Canada securities. Primary dealer status may be in either Treasury bills or marketable bonds, or both.

The Bank of Canada as fiscal agent for the federal government is responsible for the administration and business arrangements of the auctions for the distribution of all new issues of the government's marketable debt. The primary dealers are eligible to bid at all Government of Canada Treasury bill and bond auctions, and they can act as Canada Savings Bond sales agents.

Before 1983 government bonds were issued exclusively through an allotment system. Under this system investment dealers were allotted a proportion of each new issue of bonds to be sold to the public at a price set by the government. In return, the dealers received a sales commission.

To satisfy the primary objective of meeting its financial requirements, the government's debt management operations must be tailored to investors' preferences. In the past this tailoring has involved adding features such as extendible options to enhance the appeal to investors. During periods of high and rising market interest rates, the government mainly issued Treasury bills rather than long-term fixed-interest bonds. In 1991 Government of Canada Real Return Bonds were introduced. By fixing the real rate of return, these bonds minimize investors' risk associated with inflation. By late 1999, real return bonds represented only 0.4 percent of the total stock of domestic Government of Canada bonds and 3 percent of bonds with maturities over 10 years.

www.

Canada Investment and Saving *federal government agency responsible for all of the government's retail debt operations*

In 1995, to place more of the government's debt with individuals, the federal government established a special agency, known as **Canada Investment and Saving**, responsible for all of the government's retail debt operations. The retail debt is that part of the debt held by individuals rather then institutions. This agency also handles Canada Savings Bond campaigns and is responsible for the development of new retail products and market initiatives. In January 2000 the agency introduced Canada Premium bonds that guarantee annual interest rates that rise from 5.25 percent in the first year to 6.25 percent in the third year.

In an attempt to reduce the cost of the debt, the Bank of Canada initiated interest-rates swap transactions in 1988. Now, at the beginning of each fiscal year, the Bank and the Department of Finance establish a swap strategy for the coming year. Swaps typically have been used to convert fixed-rate payments on part of the longer-term government debt into floating-rate payments. In effect, interest-rate swaps have been used to artificially create three-month debt with a lower rate than the government would have to pay by issuing a three-month Treasury bill. The savings in interest cost derives from the fact that the federal government enjoys a comparative advantage on the market for longer-term, fixed debt securities.[13]

---

13. For a detailed discussion on these swap transactions, see Francois Thibault, "The Role of Interest Rate Swaps in Managing Canada's Debt," *Bank of Canada Review*, Autumn 1993, pp. 21–31.

The Integrity of Government Debt Markets

market squeeze
when market participants gain control of a particular securities issue and withhold its supply to manipulate its price

For government securities markets to operate efficiently, auctions of these securities must be free. They must also be perceived as being free of manipulation, so that purchasers receive a fair value. Large investors and brokers have been increasingly able to manipulate interest rates in Canada's debt markets, a practice that can undermine the integrity of the market and investor confidence in it.

When one or a small group of market participants monopolizes a particular government bond or Treasury bill issue, the potential exists to use this control to squeeze the market. A **market squeeze** occurs in the primary market when the participants who gain control of a particular security at the auction withhold its immediate distribution and then make it available at exorbitant prices. As a result, other market participants who have entered contracts to deliver the particular security at some future date find themselves unable to purchase or borrow it for delivery on the specified date at a price close to that anticipated in the contract.

A squeeze, for example, occurred on July 2, 1996, when an investor reportedly established a large position in the six-month Treasury bill auction through purchase from a number of dealers in the when-issued market. The investor gained such tight control over the issue that it often could not be obtained at any price in secondary markets. In another case, several market participants were able to squeeze the Government of Canada bond maturing in March 1998. Its shortage was so acute that between late August and late September, its yield plummeted to nine basis points below the one-year Treasury bill rate from forty basis points above.

The fear of being caught in a squeeze may discourage trading in when-issued contracts, which have come to serve the important role of price discovery for to-be-issued securities. In when-issued markets, participants contract with each other to buy or sell securities to be distributed at a forthcoming auction that has been announced.

The general public can also suffer from a squeeze because the market for government securities is likely to become less liquid and efficient, which means the cost of borrowing will be higher.

www.

The Bank of Canada has introduced changes in the rules of the auctions for federal government securities and in its surveillance of the auction process. One change puts further bidding limits on primary dealers. Another change increases the Bank's auction-related monitoring activities to reduce the potential for manipulative behaviour before and during auctions.[14]

---

14. See Bank of Canada, *Revised Rules Pertaining to Auctions of Government of Canada Securities and the Bank of Canada's Surveillance of the Auction Process.* August 1998.

$\mathscr{A}$PPENDIX 17A

Some History on the Tools of Canadian Monetary Policy

Reserve Requirements at Chartered Banks

Legal, minimum cash (primary) reserve requirements were originally imposed on the chartered banks in the belief that they were necessary to protect depositors and the stability of the banking system. It was thought that in their pursuit of profits, the banks were inclined to hold an insufficient amount of noninterest-earning cash at all times to satisfy their obligations to encash their deposit liabilities on demand or on short notice. With the founding of central banks, the primary purpose for imposing legal, minimum primary reserve requirements was to give central banks effective control over the money supply. For purposes of monetary control, commercial banks were usually required to hold more cash than they would ordinarily hold in the absence of the specified legal amount. This requirement assured the central banks that the commercial banks would at all times work close to the legal minimum amount and quickly change their loans and deposits in response to any increases or decreases in the availability of cash to them by the central bank.

From the commercial banks' point of view, the requirement to hold noninterest-earning cash in excess of the amount they considered necessary to satisfy the timely conversion of their deposit liabilities into cash was an unfair implicit tax on them. Moreover, since other deposit-taking institutions were not subject to legal, minimum primary reserve requirements, the banks argued that they were placed in a disadvantageous competitive position. For this reason, and because the Bank of Canada no longer considered legal minimum reserve requirements a necessary condition for its conduct of monetary control, the federal government made provision in the 1991 revisions to the *Bank Act* to phase them out.

When the Bank of Canada commenced operations in 1935, each chartered bank was required to maintain a daily cash reserve in the form of Bank of Canada notes and deposits equal to 5 percent of its Canadian dollar deposit liabilities. Because of the difficulty in satisfying the 5 percent reserve ratio every business day, the banks, in practice, kept their cash reserves equal to 10 percent of their deposit liabilities to avoid falling short of the legal requirement because of unexpected daily fluctuations.

In 1954, the minimum required reserve ratio was increased to 8 percent, and the basis of its calculation was changed from a daily to an average monthly requirement. This change allowed the banks to offset a deficiency in required reserves on any one day with excess reserves on other days over the monthly averaging period. At the same time the Bank of Canada was empowered to vary the cash ratio between 8 percent and 12 percent. However, it was not allowed to increase the ratio at any one time by more than one percentage point, and then only after one month's notice. The Bank never used its discretionary power to vary the banks' cash reserve ratio before the power was withdrawn in 1967.

Variable Cash Reserve Requirements

A central bank's discretionary power to set cash reserve ratios is one of the most powerful tools it can have for controlling the commercial banks' ability to expand their deposit liabilities. Changes in the reserve ratio affect not only the total amount of cash reserves the banks are required to hold, but also the deposit-creation multiplier. A simple example illustrates this point.

Suppose the banking system has $50 billion in deposit liabilities and holds $5 billion in cash reserves. The legal minimum reserve ratio is 8 percent. Given their deposit liabilities, the banking system is required to hold cash reserves amounting to $4 billion; since it holds $5 billion, it has $1 billion in excess cash reserves. This $1 billion can support $12.5 billion in additional deposits, using a simple money supply multiplier (1/0.08). Now assume that the legal reserve ratio is increased from 8 percent to 12 percent. The legal required reserves become $6 billion and the banks are now left with a $1 billion deficiency in their required reserves. To bring their reserve requirement in line again, they will have to decrease their deposit liabilities by $8.3 billion, a 17 percent decline from their initial $50 billion level (the deposit expansion multiplier falls from 12.5 percent to 8.33 percent).

Such a large required decline would undoubtedly create undesirable monetary conditions, a situation the Canadian government attempted to avoid by restricting the Bank's discretionary use of the variable reserve requirement. Because of this limit, any potential decline in the banks' deposit liabilities would have been relatively small since the Bank could only vary the ratio by one percentage point at any one time instead of the four percentage points shown above. Moreover, since the Bank had to give a month's notice before increasing the ratio, the banks would have had ample time to adjust their cash positions to avoid a sudden decline in their deposit liabilities.

In 1992 the federal government passed legislation providing for the complete phasing out of the legal cash reserve requirements over a two-year period. However, the direct clearers of the CPA are required to hold cash balances, referred to as settlement balances, with the Bank of Canada.

Split Reserve Requirements

Split reserve requirements, whereby different cash reserve ratios apply to different types of deposits, were first introduced in the *Bank Act* revisions of 1967. Starting in February 1968, the chartered banks were required to hold minimum cash reserves equal to 12 percent of their Canadian-dollar demand deposits and 4 percent of their Canadian-dollar notice deposits. In 1980 these ratios were changed to 10 percent on reservable demand deposits, 2 percent on reservable notice deposits up to $500 million, and 3 percent on notice deposits in excess of this amount. In addition, a 3 percent reserve ratio was introduced on foreign-currency deposits held by Canadian residents. Deposits held under Registered Retirement Savings Plans and Registered Retirement Income Funds, and deposits of one bank held at another bank (interbank deposits), as well as certain other deposits, were excluded from any reserve requirements.

With split reserve requirements, the banks can decrease their overall total required cash reserves by persuading the public to shift from reservable deposits with high reserve ratios to reservable deposits with lower reserve ratios. This shift can be prevented with the imposition of interest rate ceilings on types of deposits with lower reserve requirements. In the United States, the so-called Regulation Q, before it was phased out after 1980, regulated the interest rates U.S. banks were allowed to pay on notice deposits. In Canada, under the so-called Winnipeg Agreements in effect from June 1972 to January 1975, the Canadian chartered banks voluntarily observed interest rate ceilings on large Canadian dollar short-term deposits.

Lagged Reserve Accounting

Central banks can use either a contemporaneous or a lagged accounting method to calculate legally required reserve ratios. With contemporaneous accounting, actual reserves and deposits during the averaging period over which the ratios are calculated are used in the calculation. With lagged reserve accounting, the value of some or all the items entering into the calculation are based on a previous period. The Bank of Canada started to employ the following lagged reserve accounting methodology after 1980:

$$
\begin{array}{l}
\text{Average cash} \\
\text{reserve ratio} \\
\text{during half-} \\
\text{monthly} \\
\text{averaging} \\
\text{period}
\end{array}
=
\dfrac{
\begin{array}{l}
\text{Average holdings of coin} \\
\text{and Bank of Canada notes} \\
\text{on four Wednesdays} \\
\text{ending with the second} \\
\text{Wednesday of the pre-} \\
\text{vious month}
\end{array}
+
\begin{array}{l}
\text{Average daily deposits} \\
\text{with the Bank of Canada} \\
\text{during the current aver-} \\
\text{aging period}
\end{array}
}{
\begin{array}{l}
\text{Statutory deposits: average of deposit liabilities to which} \\
\text{reserve apply held on four consecutive Wednesdays} \\
\text{ending with the second Wednesday of the previous month}
\end{array}
}
$$

The reserve calculation was based on a two-week averaging period. The Bank of Canada had changed from a monthly to a half-monthly averaging period in January 1969. The two-week averaging period gave the Bank closer control over the banks' cash reserves since it left them with fewer days to make up any one day's cash reserve deficiency.

With the lagged cash reserve calculation shown above, at the beginning of each month the Bank of Canada and the chartered banks knew the exact amount of their required legal reserves over the two bimonthly averaging periods, because the amount of reservable (statutory) deposits was already known. The amount of reservable deposits was the amount of statutory deposits the chartered banks held on the four consecutive Wednesdays ending with the second Wednesday of the previous month. Moreover, since the dollar amount of coin and Bank of Canada notes, which were part of their required reserves, was counted in the same lagged manner as their statutory deposits, the only variable that could be adjusted during any averaging period to satisfy the minimum ratio was the daily average amount of the chartered banks' deposits at the Bank of Canada.

Weighted Daily Average Reserve Requirement

As we have seen, with the lagged reserve accounting used by the Bank of Canada after 1980, chartered bank deposits at the Bank of Canada were the only element in the reserve calculation that was not predetermined at the beginning of each month. Until September 1983, the required amount of reserves was a simple average of reserves held for each business day of each two-week averaging period. Since weekends and holidays were nonreservable days, it was profitable for the banks to invest some of their cash over these days in interest-bearing money market instruments. Banks started the practice of investing their cash on regular weekends for three days (Friday, Saturday, and Sunday). Since settlement for each day's clearings was recorded in the books of the Bank of Canada on the following business day, the investment of cash on Fridays did not show up in the calculation of a bank's average of daily reserves until the next business day, which was a Monday. Large shifts of cash into the monetary market to start earning interest on Fridays, and then out again on Mondays, or Tuesdays when Monday was a nonreservable holiday as well, produced undesirable large fluctuations in short-term money market rates.

To discourage the banks' weekend cash management practice and thereby avoid the large weekend fluctuations in short-term money market rates, the Bank introduced a weighting system based on "one plus the number of immediately preceding nonreservable days." For example, for regular weekends, Monday was given a weight of three; for holiday weekends, Tuesday was given a weight of four. In June 1986, the Bank revised its weighting procedure, following the introduction of retroactive settlement of daily clearings (each day's clearing, although settled on the next business day, is retroactively recorded as a change in a bank's cash position on the day the clearing actually takes place). It started to base its weighting system on "one plus the number of immediately succeeding nonreservable days." Fridays were now given a weight of three for regular weekends and a weight of four when Monday was a holiday. Similar adjustments were made to take account of midweek holidays and longer holidays at Christmas and New Year.

Zero Reserve Requirements

In the revision to the *Bank Act* passed by Parliament in 1992, provision was made to phase out over a two-year period the statutory requirement on the banks to hold primary reserves against their deposit liabilities. In November of the same year, the Bank of Canada introduced new procedures for the implementation of monetary policy in a system with zero reserve requirements. These procedures were as follows:

overdraft loans
overnight loans to direct clearers experiencing temporary shortfalls in balances because of daily clearings

cumulative computed settlement balance *the cumulative weighted sum of the daily settlement balances*

1. Direct clearers of the Canadian Payments Association have to maintain a zero or positive settlement balance each day in their accounts at the Bank of Canada. On days in which a direct clearer has a negative position at the Bank as a result of the day's clearings, it has to take from the Bank an overnight overdraft loan of sufficient size to offset the negative position. Such **overdraft loans** are at the Bank Rate.

2. In addition, each direct clearer is required to maintain its **cumulative computed settlement balance** equal to or in excess of zero over an averaging period of four or five weeks ending on the third Wednesday of each calendar month. The cumulative computed settlement balance is defined as the weighted sum of daily positive settlement balances less the sum of all daily overdraft loans taken to offset a negative daily position. Balances are weighted by a factor related to the day of the week. A balance on Friday or the day before a holiday is assigned a weight of one plus the number of nonbusiness days that follow.

3. If a direct clearer has a negative cumulative computed settlement balance on the last day of an averaging period, it has to take an advance from the Bank of Canada equal to its cumulative deficiency. The advance is at the Bank Rate. In lieu of taking an advance, a direct clearer can pay a fee to the Bank of Canada equal to the Bank Rate (expressed as a daily rate) times the cumulative deficiency. While the fee option is financially equivalent to an advance, unlike an advance it does not require direct clearers to post collateral.

4. All borrowing from the Bank of Canada, whether overdraft loans or advances, has to be collateralized. No collateral is required in the case of a fee paid in lieu of an advance.

5. No restrictions are placed on the frequency of overdraft loans or advances.

Although the chartered banks have not been required to hold a minimum amount of primary reserves since 1994, directly clearing members of the Canadian Payments Association hold settlement balances with the Bank of Canada. The Bank's procedures for these balances, as outlined above, substantially increase the cost to the banks of unexpected clearing gains and losses. Two costs are associated with large cash losses that result in negative settlement balances at the Bank. The first cost is the interest rate that has to be paid on a Bank overdraft to make up the day's clearing deficiency. The second cost can take one of two forms. It can be the opportunity cost of holding noninterest-bearing excess balances on other clearing days to satisfy the cumulative computed settlement balances requirement, or it can be the penalty cost of not meeting this requirement.

To minimize additional costs due to clearing gains and losses, the direct clearers have instituted new procedures to manage their daily cash flows. For example, customers who make large cash deposits late in the day may not be paid interest immediately, unless the direct clearer has received sufficient notice or it has the opportunity to invest the cash in the overnight market. Alternatively, customers who make large unannounced cash withdrawals that result in overdraft loans from the Bank of Canada may be asked by direct clearers to pay some or all of the additional costs undertaken to satisfy a client's demand for cash.

Chartered Bank Secondary Reserve Requirements

Commercial banks hold a proportion of their assets in relatively liquid form for a variety of reasons. Liquid assets can be readily turned into cash to satisfy large, unexpected cash withdrawals. By holding a cushion of liquid assets, the banks also have greater flexibility to take advantage of attractive lending opportunities that may arise. In addition, when yield curves are negatively sloped, liquid assets, which typically have short maturities, become an attractive investment for the banks for no other reason than the relatively high return and income they generate.

Large holdings of liquid assets by the banks can present difficulties for central banks in their conduct of monetary policy. This is particularly the case when central banks are committed to maintaining a certain level and pattern of interest rates that allow the banks to sell their liquid assets with little or no loss to obtain cash to expand their loans. This situation can frustrate a monetary policy that attempts to restrict the availability of cash reserves to the banks to constrain their ability to expand their loans and deposits.

During postwar expansionary periods, the chartered banks frequently responded slowly to restrictive monetary policy actions by the Bank of Canada. When the Bank reduced the amount of cash it made available to them, the banks sold liquid assets to replenish their cash to expand their loans and deposits. In 1956, on the urging of the Bank of Canada, the chartered banks agreed to hold a combination of Treasury bills, day-to-day loans, and cash in excess of their primary reserve requirements equal to 7 percent of their deposits.

In the 1967 revisions to the *Bank Act*, the Bank was empowered to impose on the banks a minimum secondary reserve requirement within the range of 0 to 12 percent. However, any increase in an existing requirement could not be more than one percentage point per month (and then only with effect one month after the announced increase). The secondary reserve ratio was calculated as follows:

$$\text{Average during any month} = \frac{\begin{array}{l}\text{Coin + Notes of any deposits with the Bank of Canada not}\\\text{required for primary reserves + Treasury bills with terms}\\\text{of one year or less + Loans to investment dealers}\end{array}}{\begin{array}{l}\text{Canadian currency deposit liabilities + Foreign currency}\\\text{deposits of residents of Canada with branches of the bank}\\\text{in Canada, or with offices in Canada of subsidiaries of the}\\\text{bank, held on the four consecutive Wednesdays ending}\\\text{with the second Wednesday of the previous month}\end{array}}$$

The history of changes in the legal secondary reserve ratio before its abandonment in June 1992 is shown in Table 17A.1. The changes in the ratio have served two purposes: to assist the Bank in its conduct of monetary policy, and to act as a technical complement to the federal government's debt management policy. The Bank first used its new authority to vary the minimum liquid asset ratio of the chartered banks in January 1968, when it announced that the ratio would be 6 percent in March and would rise to 7 percent in April. This increase, together with the further increase to 8 percent in June 1969, was for monetary policy objectives. At the time, the Bank wanted more restrictive credit conditions, and the higher liquidity requirements prevented the banks from reducing their liquid assets to expand their loan portfolios.

The increase in the secondary reserve ratio in 1970 was the first time a change in the ratio was used to assist debt management policy. At that time, to replenish its cash balances, which had been depleted as a result of intervention in the foreign exchange market, the government offered a special $250 million issue of Treasury bills. By requiring the banks to increase their liquid asset ratio, they took up a large proportion of this issue and thereby reduced the possibility of a large rise in short-term money market rates.

TABLE 17.A1	HISTORY OF THE SECONDARY RESERVE RATIO	
1968	March	6.0
	April	7.0
1969	June	8.0
1970	July	9.0
1971	December	8.5
1972	January	8.0
1974	December	7.0
1975	January	6.0
	March	5.5
1977	February	5.0
1981	December	4.0

Except for the reductions in the ratio in March 1975 and February 1977, which were associated with an easing in the Bank's monetary policy, the reductions in the Bank Rate after 1970 complemented domestic debt management policy. Large sales of Canada Savings Bonds reduced the government's need to increase its Treasury bill issues. Since expansion in bank deposits required the banks to add to their Treasury bill holdings, a decline in the availability of bills would have reduced their yields. As the Bank of Canada did not want to see lower money market yields, it reduced the banks' demand for bills by reducing their required secondary reserve ratio. By reducing the captive demand for bills, the Bank also hoped to develop a bigger nonbank demand that would add breadth, depth, and resiliency to the short-term money market.

Unlike an increase in the cash reserve ratio, which reduces the banks' ability to increase the overall volume of credit and deposits, an increase in the liquid asset ratio only affects the composition of credit flows. An increase in the liquid asset ratio directs credit to day loans and Treasury bills and away from other assets usually acquired by the banks. The immediate impact of an increase in the secondary reserve ratio is usually on the availability of credit rather than on the general level of interest rates. The Bank of Canada has defended the use of a variable liquid asset ratio rather than a cash reserve ratio on the basis that its effects are not as blunt, and therefore do not lead as readily to undesirable money market disturbances.

Both primary and secondary reserve requirements inhibit the earning ability of the banks if as a result they must hold more reserves than they would ordinarily consider prudent. A secondary reserve is the lesser of the two evils from the banks' point of view because they can earn at least some interest on liquid assets. Where the money market is not well developed, secondary reserves have served to provide governments with a captive market for their Treasury bills. A minimum cash reserve requirement, conversely, determines the profit (seigniorage) split between the central bank and the private banking system that is obtained from creating money.

The Bank of Canada's authority to impose a secondary reserve requirement was removed at the same time that the government phased out the primary reserve requirement.

History of the Use of Open Market Operations by the Bank of Canada

The Bank of Canada has traded in government securities from the time of its establishment in 1935. Its early open market operations were concerned less with managing the cash reserves of the banks than with the development of a market for government bonds. After 1938, for instance, the Bank attempted to make a market for these securities by adopting the practice of submitting to the market a daily list of bids it would accept and the offers it was prepared to make.

During and after the Second World War, the Bank of Canada considered it government policy to peg the yield structure of government securities. This pegging was done so that the public, who had purchased large quantities of government bonds during the war, could cash them without loss and so that interest rates would be held at a level that would make the peacetime transition easier.

Once relieved of its assumed obligation to support the price of government bonds on a continuing basis, and particularly after 1953 with the development of a money market in Canada, the Bank was able to use open market operations actively to manage the cash reserves of the chartered banks and to indirectly influence short-term interest rates. It accomplished this goal by confining its open market operations to the short end of the market. The shorter the term of a security, the closer it is to the cash for which it is being exchanged, and the smaller the impact will be on its price and yield when traded.

Since the early 1970s the Bank has tended to depend less on its use of open market operations for day-to-day management of the cash reserves of the chartered banks, and more on the use of shifting government deposits between it and the banks. The Bank now uses open market operations essentially to affect short-term interest rates directly via changes in the demand and supply in securities markets.

The Bank's open market operations have come to play a particularly important role for managing the value of the dollar, by directly affecting short-term Canadian interest rates to maintain a desired differential with interest rates in the United States. For example, during the first week of February 1986 speculators were responsible for forcing the exchange value of the Canadian dollar to a low of U.S. 69.13¢. To punish them and to prevent further speculation, the Bank undertook unprecedented aggressive actions to raise Canadian interest rates and thereby also the exchange value of the Canadian dollar. Included in these actions was the sale of $545 million of Treasury bills at progressively lower prices. Again in August 1998, when the Canadian dollar was falling to a low of U.S. 63¢, the Bank came to its rescue by increasing the Bank Rate and by intervening in the foreign exchange market with the purchase of Canadian dollars.

The Bank has also employed open market operations to avert disorderly conditions in security markets. Disorderly market conditions can arise from unexpected shocks such as substantial shifts of assets caused by large-scale private or public debt operations, or sudden changes in the public's expectations of future market yields. For example, during the Cuban missile crisis in October 1962 there was a sudden shift in investment out of Government of Canada bonds. As a result their prices began to fall sharply. The Bank of Canada intervened to steady the market by purchasing $111 million of these bonds over three days, $73 million of them in a single day.

Finally, the Bank, in its role as the federal government's debt manager, at times intervenes in the securities markets with open market operations. These steps are undertaken to prepare the financial market for large government debt operations and to prevent disorderly market conditions when such operations are being undertaken.

Canada's Bank Rate

When the Bank of Canada began operations in 1935, the Bank Rate was set at 2.5 percent, where it remained until 1944 when it was decreased to 1.5 percent. The decrease was announced to indicate the Bank's desire to maintain a low level of interest rates during the postwar reconstruction period. In 1950, with the threat of inflation because of the Korean War, the Rate was raised to announce that the Bank desired market interest rates at higher levels.

Early in 1955 the Bank Rate was again reduced to 1.5 percent. The Bank made this reduction not to signal a shift in the direction of monetary policy, but to bring the Bank Rate into closer relation with rates in the developing money market in order to facilitate its more flexible use in the future. Subsequently, from August 1955 to November 1956, the Bank Rate was increased on six separate occasions. Although most of these increases were of a technical nature to keep the Rate at a penalty level, their upward movement came at a time when the Bank wanted to impose monetary restraint. During this period the Bank Rate, for the first time, had important cost effects. The chartered banks not only had to make frequent use of central bank advances, but also adjusted their own rates with reference to changes in the Bank Rate. Although the Bank Rate had become an important factor influencing market rates, the frequent changes required to keep it at a penalty level increased the possibility not only of misinterpretation of the Bank's intentions, but also of the creation of disorderly money market conditions. The Bank therefore abandoned the fixed Rate regime for a floating Rate regime in November 1956.

The Bank reintroduced a fixed Rate regime in June 1962, as part of a program for dealing with a decline in the foreign exchange value of the Canadian dollar. At the time the Bank Rate was increased from 3.5 percent to 6 percent to signal to the rest of the world Canada's determination to defend the external value of its dollar. During most of the 1960s and the first half of the 1970s, the Bank of Canada announced frequent changes in the Bank Rate for similar reasons.

The use of the Bank Rate to protect the external value of a nation's currency, while new to Canada at the time, had a long history in Britain. As explained earlier, changes in the Bank of England's rate were first introduced primarily to protect its gold reserves, which at the time constituted most of the country's foreign exchange reserves. In the heyday of the gold standard, it was commonly believed that by setting the Bank Rate at 7 percent, the Bank of England could produce an inflow of foreign capital sufficient "to bring gold from the moon." Under a system of fixed foreign exchange rates, as was the case in Canada from June 1962 to May 1970, administered changes in the Bank Rate were a useful tool to assist in maintaining the external value of the currency.

After November 1975, when the Bank of Canada started to set targets for the growth rate of the M1 monetary aggregate, the Bank Rate assumed yet another new role. In the years following, the Bank frequently changed its Rate to obtain market rates that would result in a demand for money consistent with its target rates of growth. For example, when the growth rate of M1 exceeded its upper target rate, the Bank usually set the Bank Rate higher and managed the excess cash reserves of the banks to move market rates to the higher Bank Rate level. Conversely, when the Bank wanted to raise the trend rate of M1 growth, it reduced the Bank Rate and provided more cash reserves to the banks.

During the 1970s the Bank of Canada announced 34 changes in its Rate, usually to move market rates to protect the external value of the currency or to meet its money growth targets. However, to again avoid misunderstanding, and to ensure that the Bank Rate would consistently remain at a penalty rate, the Bank reintroduced a floating Bank Rate regime beginning on March 13, 1980. The Bank continued, however, to directly effect changes in the Bank Rate by its intervention in the secondary market for Treasury bills and by its bids for bills at the weekly auction.

The Use of Moral Suasion and Selective Credit Controls in Canada

When the Bank of Canada opened its doors in 1935, there were only 10 chartered banks. The small number of chartered banks before the recent entrance of foreign bank subsidiaries made possible an intimate relationship between them and the Bank of Canada. Although the chartered banks accepted the establishment of the Bank of Canada in 1934 with much suspicion, Graham

Towers, the first governor of the Bank, quickly gained the respect of his fellow bankers, and the Bank soon established a favourable reputation.

The Bank of Canada first used moral suasion in 1936. In that year the governor of the Bank held meetings with committees of the stock exchanges and the banks to request them to raise margin requirements for loans intended for speculation. Ten years later the Bank of Canada requested that the banks restrict their holdings of Government of Canada bonds to an amount not exceeding 90 percent of their Canadian personal savings deposits and that they restrict their net earnings on such securities to a specified maximum.

In February 1948 the banks agreed to a request by the Bank of Canada to refrain from making term loans to or directly purchasing bonds and debentures from corporate customers in amounts exceeding a certain limit. This request was withdrawn a year later.

A more detailed and extensive agreement by the banks was reached following the Bank of Canada's request in 1951 to limit credit expansion. The banks agreed to not allow further expansion in their loans under existing inflationary conditions, to stop making term loans or purchase corporate securities in amounts in excess of a certain sum, to request at least a 50 percent margin in the case of loans to carry corporate stock, and to allow no further increases in total loans to finance companies. This agreement was extended in January 1952 and was suspended later in the year.

Although the Bank of Canada has used moral suasion primarily to influence the lending policies of the banks, it has been used for other purposes. In 1956, as in 1936, the Bank had discussions with members of the governing bodies of the stock exchanges to request them to limit any further increases in the volume of credit used in stock market trading. During the same year the Bank also met with representatives of the major instalment finance companies and the major department and chain stores to seek voluntary agreement to prevent significant increases in the volume of consumer credit extended by them. On this occasion no general agreement was reached. The Bank was not entirely unsuccessful, however; the banks were persuaded to curtail the credit extended to finance companies and retail stores providing instalment finance facilities. However, companies that were subsidiaries of large foreign corporations had access to funds through them and could still escape monetary restraint.

Until the end of 1956 the use of moral suasion in Canada was concerned primarily with the restriction of credit. The only exception to this was the persuasion, more in the form of advice than request, used by the Bank after 1953 to encourage the development of a money market in Canada.

In 1957 moral suasion by the Bank of Canada was used for the first time as a qualitative control to encourage the flow of credit to a certain sector of the economy. In March of that year the Bank of Canada requested that the banks resume their residential mortgage lending activity under the *National Housing Act* on the same scale as in 1956. In the early months of 1957 the chartered banks had virtually withdrawn from the insured residential mortgage market as other market yields became more attractive. The Bank of Canada indicated that if the banks increased their *NHA* lending to the 1956 scale, it would provide extra reserves to the banking system. The banks would then be able to maintain a flow of funds for insured mortgages without having to dispose of other assets.

The minister of finance, rather than the governor of the Bank, applied moral suasion to the banks and other financial institutions in 1981 to get them to expand their lending to small businesses under the federal government's Small Business Development Bond Programs.

In 1965, after the failure of Atlantic Acceptance Corporation, the governor of the Bank of Canada consulted with the chartered banks. He indicated that the Bank was prepared to provide the necessary reserves so that the banking system could accommodate any creditworthy finance company that might find itself in a difficult liquidity position. The banks responded by making additional credit available, and at least some of the uneasiness in the market was relieved. In this case, the Bank used moral suasion in an attempt to maintain confidence in the financial system.

The Bank of Canada has also used moral suasion on the chartered banks and other institutions to influence their behaviour and reduce the impact of foreign policy measures and foreign market conditions on Canada. In an attempt to solve its continuing balance of payments problem, the U.S. government introduced a guideline program in 1965 to stem the flow of capital from the United States and to encourage the repatriation of funds in foreign countries. The Bank foresaw that subsidiaries of U.S. companies might seek to raise substantially larger amounts of capital from the banks and securities markets in Canada. It therefore asked the banks to meet in full the normal demands for business loans from their creditworthy customers and to give priority to customers who had relied on them in the past for credit needs.

In 1968, a new balance of payments program in the United States could have led to an outflow of capital from Canada. However, the Bank received agreement from the chartered banks to discourage Canadian subsidiaries of U.S. corporations from using bank credit to facilitate an abnormal transfer of funds abroad or to replace funds normally obtained in the past from parent firms. In a further attempt to control the outflow of capital during 1968, the Bank asked the chartered banks and other financial intermediaries to refrain from extending "swapped" deposit facilities to new customers and to disallow renewals on existing contracts. Under different circumstances in 1970, to discourage the inflow of foreign capital, the minister of finance and the Bank suggested to borrowers that they carefully explore the domestic market before placing issues abroad.

Following the devaluation of the pound sterling by the United Kingdom in November 1967, speculation developed in other countries. This speculation was reflected in large-scale purchases of gold. In a spirit of international cooperation, the Bank of Canada requested that Canadian chartered banks and other financial intermediaries refrain from extending credit for the purchase of gold or to facilitate the forward purchase of gold. In addition, in a spirit of international cooperation, the Bank requested in 1968 that the financial institutions conduct their foreign currency business in a way that would prevent them from being used as a "pass-through" by U.S. institutions to escape their country's balance of payments guideline program. Similarly, in April 1980, following a request made by the Federal Reserve Board in the United States, the governor of the Bank asked all Canadian financial institutions not to lend to U.S. borrowers either directly or indirectly where such demands would allow borrowers to circumvent restrictive monetary and credit controls in the United States.

In 1981, in response to the government's National Energy Program introduced in October of the previous year, there was a sharp increase in takeovers by Canadians of foreign-controlled businesses in the petroleum industry. The banks financed many of these takeovers by converting Canadian dollars into foreign currencies. This conversion put undesirable downward pressure on the external value of the Canadian dollar, and in late July the minister of finance requested the banks limit such financing, especially for takeovers not directly related to the National Energy Program.

The Canadian banks have traditionally financed their foreign currency loans to customers outside Canada with funds borrowed abroad. As a result, their external business has operated virtually separately from their domestic business. In 1984, when called on to reschedule the debts of debtor countries that found themselves in increasing difficulties, the banks also switched the currency denomination of some of the rescheduled debt repayments from foreign to Canadian dollars. The Bank of Canada "expressed the view" that such switching on a large scale was undesirable because it had a potentially disruptive effect on Canadian interest rates and the foreign exchange rate.

With the additional competitive freedom allowed to the chartered banks by the revisions to the *Bank Act* in 1967, the banks competed vigorously for large blocks of short-term corporate funds. The Bank felt that the disproportionate share of funds that flowed into the banks and the sharp increase in term deposit rates would introduce instability and distortions into the financial system. The Bank, therefore, requested that the banks moderate their activities in competing for term deposits. This occasion was the first one in which the Bank used moral suasion to influence the rate of interest paid by the banks. In another attempt to influence interest rates, the Bank requested in 1969 that the banks accept a temporary ceiling on "swapped" deposits. The banks' "swapped" deposit business had expanded rapidly in response to the higher interest rates paid in the Eurodollar market. The Bank of Canada did not want these higher rates to be transmitted to the Canadian financial markets. In January of the following year, investment dealers and trust companies were asked not to arrange similar transactions.

The use of moral suasion to influence interest rates has occurred on at least two occasions. In the Winnipeg Agreement, in effect from June 12, 1972 to January 5, 1975, the Bank of Canada proposed ceilings on the interest rates the chartered banks offered on their large-denomination wholesale deposits with terms of one year or less. At times during the agreement, the banks circumvented its spirit by offering these deposits at higher rates, but with terms of one year plus one day.

In March 1987, the federal government's Standing Committee on Finance, Trade, and Economic Affairs recommended that there be "a substantial downward movement in credit-card interest charges and other related charges." The minister of state for finance supported the recommendations and urged the card issuers to reduce their rates, which they subsequently did.

In 1969 the Bank of Canada used moral suasion in an attempt to soften the impact of its restrictive monetary policy on certain sectors of the economy. It asked the banks to meet the demands of borrowers in the less prosperous areas of the country and to pay particular attention to requests by small businesses, which, unlike large corporations, normally do not have ready access to alternative sources of bank credit. The chartered banks were also asked to maintain seasonal continuity in their lending on housing mortgages and to give priority to Canadian borrowers over U.S. corporations that might seek accommodation from Canadian banks because of the lower rate prevailing in Canada. A somewhat similar request was made in 1973, when the Bank asked the chartered banks to moderate their lending policies, but in ways that would minimize the impact on small business borrowers, on borrowers in the less buoyant regions of the country, and on mortgage flows.

As is evident from the above survey, the Bank of Canada has used moral suasion to influence bank lending policy, and in some cases that of other institutions, in a wide variety of ways and for a wide variety of objectives. It may be argued that at times the Bank relied too much on moral suasion when more forceful techniques would have been appropriate.

More recently, the use of moral suasion by the Bank of Canada as a technique of monetary policy has fallen into disuse. However, standing committees of Parliament have been using moral suasion on financial institutions to change certain aspects of their behaviour. Two such examples involve banks' interest-rate charges on credit-card balances and banks' lending practices to small businesses.

Selective Credit Controls

Consumer credit controls were employed in Canada during the Second World War and the Korean War. The Bank of Canada issued regulations that set minimum required down payments for the purchase of consumer goods and the maximum number of months allowed to pay the balance. Consumer credit controls have been used to decrease the demand for consumer goods, to restrain inflationary pressures during periods of scarcity, and to make resources available for such purposes as essential war industries. Because they postpone the demand for consumer durables during war periods, they also help to prevent the recessionary tendencies that usually follow the sudden decline of government demand for war materials when war is over.

Real estate credit controls are similar to the controls on consumer credit discussed above. They are intended to restrict the purchase of real estate, and thereby restrict construction and speculation, by prescribing minimum down payments for the purchase of real estate and maximum maturity dates for loans.

The *National Housing Act* has had effects similar to those resulting from selective credit controls. Under the Act, the government guarantees loans made by the Canada Mortgage and Housing Corporation and approves institutional lenders for the construction of new houses. By setting down payment requirements, the minimum maturity of the loans, and the maximum interest chargeable, the government has influenced the demand for funds for residential construction.

In the United Kingdom direct control was exercised over new capital issues in the 1950s to limit overseas borrowing in that country and to allocate domestic funds for capital investment purposes. Because direct controls that attempt to affect the allocation of credit are usually difficult to administer, they are used only in emergencies.

APPENDIX 17B

Government Deposit Management before the LVTS

As we explained earlier, the directly clearing members of the Canadian Payments Association hold cash balances in the form of demand deposits at the Bank of Canada to settle their daily clearings of cheques and other money transfers. This Appendix describes how the Bank of Canada used government deposits to manage settlements balances before the Large Value Transfer System came into effect in 1999.

The Bank implemented monetary policy on a day-to-day basis by controlling the supply of these cash balances, which constituted the ultimate settlement of the direct clearer's payment obligations. The Bank controlled the supply of these cash balances by transferring government deposits between it and the direct clearers.

drawdown *the transfer of government of Canada deposits with the direct clearers to the governments' deposit account with the Bank of Canada*

A transfer of government demand deposit balances from the direct clearers to the Bank of Canada was called a **drawdown**, and a transfer from the Bank to the direct clearers was a **redeposit.** A drawdown reduced the supply of cash available to the direct clearers, while a redeposit increased it.

The increase in the cash balances available to the direct clearers as a result of a $100 million redeposit is illustrated in Table 17B.1. Government deposits are reduced by $100 million at the Bank and at the same time increased by $100 million at the direct clearers. This transfer was settled with an increase by $100 million in the direct clearers' deposits at the Bank, which represented the increase in the supply of cash available to them to settle their daily clearings.

redeposit *the transfer of government of Canada deposits from the Bank of Canada to the direct clearers*

The decrease in the quantity of cash balances to direct clearers as a result of a drawdown of $100 million in government deposits is illustrated in Table 17B.2. Government deposits were increased at the Bank of Canada and simultaneously reduced by $100 million at the direct clearers. This transfer of government deposit balances was settled with a $100 million reduction in the direct clearers' deposits at the Bank, which represents the decrease in the supply of cash available to them to settle their daily clearings.

cash setting *the Bank of Canada's use of drawdowns and redeposits to adjust the settlement balances of the direct clearers following daily clearings*

The Bank of Canada's control of the supply of settlement balances through drawdowns and redeposits of federal government deposits with direct clearers was referred to as cash management or **cash setting**. The Bank made its drawdown or redeposit decision shortly after 5 p.m. each business day, and informed each direct clearer early the next morning (typically by 8:30 a.m.) of its new settlement balance at the Bank as a result of the transfer from or to the clearer's government demand deposit account. Under the system of retroactive settlement accounting, although actual settlement usually took place on the day following the evening's cash-setting decisions, it was dated to the previous day.

TABLE 17B.1 REDEPOSIT OF GOVERNMENT DEPOSITS
Millions of Dollars

BANK OF CANADA

Assets		Liabilities	
		Government deposits	−$100
		Direct clearer deposits	+$100

DIRECT CLEARERS

Assets		Liabilities	
Deposits at Bank of Canada	+$100	Government deposits	+$100

TABLE 17B.2 DRAWDOWN OF GOVERNMENT DEPOSITS
Millions of Dollars

BANK OF CANADA

Assets		Liabilities	
		Government deposits	+$100
		Direct clearer deposits	−$100

DIRECT CLEARERS

Assets		Liabilities	
Deposits at Bank of Canada	−$100	Government deposits	−$100

The Bank's daily cash setting had two components: a neutralization component and a monetary policy component. In late afternoon each day when the Bank made its cash-setting decision, it had a good estimate of the potential change in the total supply of the direct clearers' cash balances as a result of the amount of government receipts and payments, official foreign exchange transactions, its own money market intervention, and other transactions. The neutralization component offset the effects of these items on the direct clearers' cash balances at the Bank. The monetary policy component, on the other hand, constituted the additional drawdowns or redeposits made by the Bank to change the direct clearers' availability of cash in order to achieve overnight interest rates, and in turn money market rates, consistent with the Bank's monetary policy objectives.

KEY TERMS

Canada Investment and Saving
cash setting
clearing system
cumulative computed settlement
  balance
direct clearers
discount rate
discount window
drawdown

Exchange Fund Account
fixed Bank Rate regime
floating Bank Rate regime
indirect clearers
Large Value Transfer System (LVTS)
lender of last resort
margin requirements
market squeeze
monetary base

multilateral netting
operating band for overnight rates
overdraft loans
primary dealers
redeposit
settlement system
sterilization

REVIEW QUESTIONS

1. What is the monetary base? How does it differ from the money supply?
2. What are the characteristics of the Canadian clearing settlement system?
3. Describe the procedures the Bank of Canada introduced in 1991 for implementing a regime of zero reserve requirements.
4. Are direct clearers required to hold positive clearing balances under the LVTS? Why?
5. Show on the balance sheets of the Bank of Canada and the direct clearers how the availability of cash to the financial system is affected with an open market sale of $25 million in Treasury bills by the Bank of Canada to the direct clearers.
6. Under what conditions might the Bank of Canada employ SPRAs and SRAs?
7. Show on the balance sheets of the Bank of Canada and the direct clearers the effect on the availability of cash to the direct clearers of a $25 million advance to them by the Bank.
8. Why might a floating Bank Rate regime be preferred to a fixed Bank Rate regime?
9. What is "moral suasion"? Give examples of its use in Canada.
10. Explain how and why selective credit controls have been used.
11. Why is it necessary for the government of Canada to hold its cash deposits with both the central bank and the depository institutions?
12. How does the Bank of Canada keep the overnight financing rate within the target range? Did the introduction of the LVTS change their operating procedure?
13. Use the balance sheets of the Bank of Canada and the direct clearers to show the effects on cash in the system of a sale of the equivalent of $100 by the Foreign Exchange Fund Account in the foreign exchange market.
14. What is an Exchange Fund swap, and why are these swaps used by the Bank of Canada?
15. Why would the public not consider an increase in its holdings of federal government bonds to be an increase in its net worth?
16. What considerations may guide the government's debt manager when undertaking an additional bond issue?

SELECTED READINGS

Bank of Canada. "The Role of the Bank of Canada in Debt Management." Submission by the Bank of Canada to the Royal Commission on Banking and Finance, May 31, 1962.

———. "Cash Reserve Management." *Bank of Canada Review*, June 1975, pp. 3–12.

———. *Implementation of Monetary Policy in the Absence of Reserve Requirements.* Discussion Paper No. 1, September 30, 1987.

———. *Implementation of Monetary Policy in a System with Zero Reserve Requirements.* Discussion Paper No. 2, February 2, 1989.

———. "The Implementation of Monetary Policy in a System with Zero Reserve Requirements." *Bank of Canada Review*, May 1991, pp. 23–34.

———. "Amendments to the Administrative Arrangements Regarding the Auction of Government of Canada Securities." *Bank of Canada Review*, Summer 1996, pp. 55–60

———. *The Framework for the Implementation of Monetary Policy in the Large Value Transfer System Environment.* Discussion Paper, January 1999, pp. 1–16.

———. *Proposed Revisions to the Rule Pertaining to the Actions of Receiver General Term Deposits.* Discussion Paper, July 18, 2000, pp. 1–11.

Bouey, Gerald K. "Monetary Policy—Finding a Place to Stand." The 1982 Per Jacobsson Lecture. *Bank of Canada Review*, September 1982, pp. 3–17.

Branion, Andrew. "The Government of Canada Bond Market since 1980." *Bank of Canada Review*, Autumn 1995, pp. 3–21.

Clinton, Kevin. "Bank of Canada Cash Management: The Main Technique for Implementing Monetary Policy." *Bank of Canada Review*, January 1991, pp. 3–25.

Clinton, Kevin, and Kevin Fetting. "Buy-Back Techniques in the Conduct of Monetary Policy." *Bank of Canada Review*, July 1989, pp. 4–17.

Courchene, Thomas J. *Monetarism and Controls: The Inflation Fighters.* Montreal: C.D. Howe Institute, 1976.

———. *Money, Inflation and the Bank of Canada: An Analysis of Canadian Monetary Policy from 1970 to Early 1975.* Montreal: C.D. Howe Institute, 1976.

Crow, John. "The Work of Canadian Monetary Policy." Eric J. Hanson Memorial Lecture, University of Alberta, January 12, 1988, reprinted in *Bank of Canada Review*, February 1988.

———. "Clearing and Settlement of Financial Transactions: A Perspective from the Bank of Canada." *Bank of Canada Review*, November 1990, pp. 11–9.

Dingle, James F. "Technical Note: Introduction of Retroactive Settlement for Daily Clearing of Cheques and Other Payment Items." *Bank of Canada Review*, August 1986, pp. 3–7.

———. "The LVTS—Canada's Large Value Transfer System." *Bank of Canada Review*, Autumn 1998, pp. 39–55.

Faure, Frank. "Technical Note on Temporary Bank of Canada Exchange Swaps." *Bank of Canada Review*, July 1977, pp. 15–20.

Fettig, Kevin. "The Government of Canada Treasury bill Market and Its Roles in Monetary Policy." *Bank of Canada Review*, Spring 1994, pp. 35–53.

Howard, D. "A Primer on the Implementation of Monetary Policy in the LVTS Environment." *Bank of Canada Review*, August 1998, pp. 57–66.

Martin, Peter. *Inside the Bank of Canada's Weekly Financial Statistics: A Technical Guide*, 2nd ed. Vancouver: Fraser Institute, 1989.

"Memorandum on Monetary Policy." *Bank of Canada Review*, June 1981, pp. 19–23.

Rasminsky, Louis. "Central Banking in the Canadian Financial System." In *Challenges and Trends in Modern Banking.* Toronto: Canadian Bankers' Association, 1967.

Report of the Royal Commission on Banking and Finance. Ottawa: Queen's Printer, 1964, Ch. 22. Reprinted in part in *Canadian Banking and Monetary Policy*, ed. James P. Cairns and H.H. Binhammer. Toronto: McGraw-Hill, 1965.

CHAPTER EIGHTEEN

THE IMPLEMENTATION OF MONETARY POLICY

After reading this chapter you should be able to

1. *Differentiate between instruments, operational targets, intermediate targets, indicators, and ultimate targets in the design and implementation of monetary policy*
2. *Describe the Bank of Canada's concept of monetary conditions and its use as an operational target*
3. *Describe the Bank of Canada's operating range for the overnight interest rate*
4. *Explain why the Bank of Canada cannot simultaneously set both quantity of money and interest rate targets*
5. *Describe base control and interest rate control of the money supply*
6. *Outline the Bank of Canada's monetary targeting experience*
7. *Describe the government's and the Bank of Canada's inflation control targets*
8. *Discuss the day-to-day implementation of monetary policy in Canada*

Instruments, Indicators, and Targets

In their design and implementation of monetary policy, central banks employ a series of variables ranging from instruments of policy at one end, to the ultimate goal or target of policy at the other. In between, as illustrated in Figure 18–1, there are operational targets, intermediate targets, and indicators or information variables. As we have already explained, in Canada price stability is the declared goal of monetary policy, with specified inflation targets.

policy instruments the techniques that allow the central bank to control base money

base money the monetary base, comprising Bank of Canada notes and settlement balances held by the direct clearers with the Bank

The **policy instruments** available to a central bank are the techniques that allow it to control the means of ultimate settlement, which is base money. In Canada, **base money** (that is, the monetary base) comprises Bank of Canada notes and settlement balances held by the direct clearers with the Bank. In its monetary policy actions, the Bank affects the level of base money by changing the amount of the direct clearers' balances held with it. The Bank of Canada is able to control these balances because final settlement of all transactions occurs in the direct clearers' accounts on the books of the Bank. As we saw in the last chapter, the Bank can change the level of these balances.

FIGURE 18–1   FRAMEWORK FOR THE CONDUCT OF MONETARY POLICY

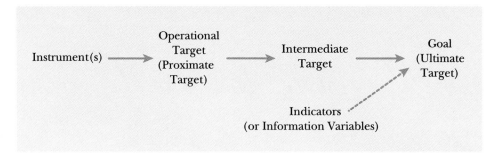

SOURCE: Charles Freedman, "The Use of Indicators and of the Monetary Conditions Index in Canada," in *The Transmission of Monetary Policy in Canada*, Ottawa, Bank of Canada, 1996. Reproduced with permission.

intermediate target *a variable that can be directly influenced by central bank policy instruments*

www.

Since monetary policy actions usually do not affect ultimate goals or targets directly—and only with long and variable lags—central banks have preferred to set intermediate targets for themselves. An **intermediate target** can be viewed as a surrogate for the ultimate target; the intermediate target can be directly influenced by the central bank's policy instruments. Various variables have been proposed and used as intermediate targets.

It is generally agreed that the variables selected as intermediate targets should satisfy three criteria. First, information about them must be readily available on a timely basis. Second, they must be predictably related to ultimate policy goals. This implies that their movements are closely related to those of the policy goals. Third, the central bank must be able to exercise a high degree of control over the chosen intermediate targets.

Monetary aggregates or nominal interest rates typically have been used as intermediate targets; to a lesser extent, other credit aggregates have been used, as have nominal spending and the nominal exchange rate. As explained below, the central bank cannot attempt to control a monetary aggregate and the interest rate simultaneously; it must choose one. Before the 1970s the Bank of Canada usually used its influence on nominal interest rates to affect the growth of total spending and to smooth cyclical fluctuations in economic activity. With rising rates of inflation and the development of inflationary expectations, the effect that a change in nominal interest rates had on total spending became uncertain. Although nominal interest rates rose, real interest rates declined because of the increase in the rate of inflation. Since real rather than nominal interest rates influence total spending, a tight monetary policy as indicated by high nominal interest rates turned out to be an easy monetary policy because real interest rates declined.

When nominal interest rates became an unreliable intermediate policy target, central banks in the industrial world chose to formally target a monetary aggregate,[1] but this approach also turned out to have its problems.

---

1. See Dallas S. Batten et al., *The Conduct of Monetary Policy in the Major Industry Countries: Instruments and Operating Procedures*, Occasional Paper 70, International Monetary Fund, Washington, July 1990.

From 1975 to 1982, as will be explained later, the Bank of Canada used the rate of growth of the narrow money aggregate, M1, as its intermediate target variable to bring about a gradual decline in the rate of inflation. As it turned out, this target variable, although useful initially, did not enable the Bank to hold down the rate of inflation when demand pressures built up in the late 1970s.[2]

An **operational target** is a variable that the central bank can influence fairly directly when it changes the setting of its policy instrument variable. It is frequently called the *proximate target* by central bankers. For many years the Bank of Canada used short-term interest rates as its operational target. In the early 1990s it started to use the concept of **monetary conditions**, which focuses on the movements of both the short-term interest rate and the exchange rate.

Two major reasons were given by the Bank for the change in its operational target. First, under a flexible exchange rate regime, monetary policy actions have their effect on the economy through both interest rates and the exchange rate. Hence, when the Bank takes action to tighten or ease its policy stance, it must take account of both channels through which its actions influence aggregate demand. Second, when there is an exogenous shift in the exchange rate, such as a depreciation of the Canadian dollar due to political or other concerns, the monetary conditions concept indicates the expansionary nature of the shock and the need to tighten interest rates to offset it.

The Bank constructs a **monetary conditions index (MCI)**. The index is a weighted sum of the changes in the short-term interest rate (the 90-day commercial paper rate) and the C6 exchange rate, from a given base period.[3] The weighting for the interest rate versus the exchange rate is three to one, which is based on empirical studies that estimate that a three percentage point change in the interest rate has about the same effect on aggregate demand as a one percentage change in the exchange rate. In the past, the Bank has focused on a nominal MCI over short horizons.

Figure 18–2 plots the MCI from 1980 until mid-2000. It is constructed as:

$$MCI = (CP90 - 7.9) + (100/3) \times [\ln(C6) - \ln(91.33)]$$

operational target *a variable that the central bank can influence fairly directly by changing the setting of its policy instruments*

monetary conditions *an operational target that focuses on the movements of both short-term interest and exchange rates*

www.

monetary conditions index (MCI) *the Bank of Canada's index of monetary conditions, which is a weighted sum of changes in the short-term rate of interest and the effective multilateral exchange rate from a given base period*

---

2. See G .G. Thiessen, "The Canadian Experience with Monetary Targeting," in *Central Bank Reviews on Monetary Targeting*, P. Meek, ed. (New York: Federal Reserve Bank of New York, 1982), pp. 100–4; and C. Freedman, "Financial Innovation in Canada: Causes and Consequences," *American Economic Review* 73, 2 (1983), pp. 101–6. It has been suggested that the failure of the Bank's policy due to its difficulty in predicting the demand for M1 was an example of the so-called Lucas critique. This critique asserts that econometric relationships estimated from past data trends tend to change when policy implementation takes advantage of them. Professor Courchene has advanced the hypothesis that the Bank's monetary graduation policy encouraged the chartered banks to use computer technology to introduce daily interest savings accounts so that their customers would switch out of M1 accounts and thereby allow the financial institutions to beat the Bank's M1 growth targets. See Robert E. Lucas, Jr., "Econometric Policy Evaluation: A Critique," in Karl Brunner and Allan H. Metzler, ed., *The Phillips Curve and Labour Markets*, Carnegie-Rochester Series on Public Policy 1 (Amsterdam: North Holland, 1976), pp. 19–46; and Thomas J. Courchene, *Money, Inflation and the Bank of Canada, Volume II: An Analysis of Monetary Graduation 1975–80* (Montreal: C.D. Howe Institute, 1981).

3. The C6 exchange rate is a trade-weighted Canadian dollar exchange rate index. The six currencies in the index are the U.S. dollar, the Euro, the yen, the U.K. pound, the Swedish krona, and the Swiss franc.

FIGURE 18–2   THE CANADIAN MONETARY CONDITIONS INDEX

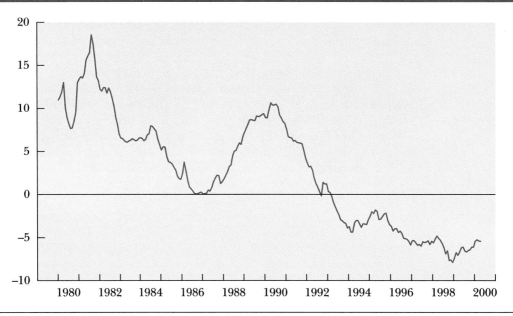

SOURCE: Bank of Canada, May 2000.

where CP90 denotes the 90-day commercial paper rate, C6 is the C6 exchange rate, and the average 90-day commercial paper rate (exchange rate) for January 1987 was 7.9 (91.33). The MCI is an index with a value equal to 0 in January 1987, so we interpret the index relative to that date to determine whether monetary conditions are more expansionary or more contractionary relative to that date. An increase in the index indicates tighter monetary conditions, while a reduction in the index represents an easing of monetary conditions.

A change in the MCI provides a measure of the overall degree of tightening or easing in monetary conditions. However, the Bank has noted that the MCI should not be taken as a very precise measure; therefore, its information content is supplemented by other indicators, which are considered separately below. This view is consistent with results reported by Eika, Ericsson, and Nymoen (1996), who argue that the MCI is, at best, an imperfect gauge of monetary conditions.

The Bank of Canada sets a desired target path for monetary conditions that is judged to result in a rate of inflation within its inflation target band six to eight quarters ahead. The forward-looking approach is necessary because of the relatively long lags between monetary policy action and its effects on the rate of inflation. In arriving at its desired path of monetary conditions, the Bank also uses information provided by indicator variables.

The Bank constantly assesses that level of monetary conditions necessary to achieve its inflationary control target. If on balance the analysis indicates a lessening of inflationary pressures in the economy relative to what had been expected, the desired path of monetary conditions is revised downward. If inflationary pressures have increased relative to earlier expectations, the desired monetary conditions are adjusted upward.

Since 1997, the Bank has relied on changes in the target for overnight interest rates to achieve a desired level of monetary conditions. The MCI serves as an intermediate target along with other indicators such as the yield curve and rates of growth of certain monetary aggregates.

indicators variables that provide the central bank with information for its conduct of monetary policy

Indicators are variables that provide information to central banks for their conduct of monetary policy. Historical data show that accelerated growth in the real value of the M1 monetary aggregate is typically followed by an increase in the rate of growth of real GDP. Growth of broad definitions of money, such as M2, M2+, and, more recently, M2++ have been good leading indicators of inflation.

Empirical work has also shown that the slope of the term structure of interest rates is a good predictor of near-term changes in the inflation rate in Canada. Sharp increases in the slope of the yield curve have been followed by a rapid expansion of economic activity during the next year. Changes in the spread between the yield on conventional long-term federal government bonds and that on its Real Return Bonds capture changes in inflation expectations. When this spread declines, expectations in the financial markets tend to be for low inflation. These indicators or information variables are only a few of the many that have been used by the Bank of Canada.

Money Supply or Interest Rate Targets

The Bank of Canada cannot simultaneously set both the quantity of money and the interest rate at any given levels that it desires. If the Bank wants to achieve a given interest rate target, say 8 percent, it then has to supply the amount of money that is demanded at that interest rate. Alternatively, if the Bank wants to achieve a given money supply target, say $60 billion for the M1 monetary aggregate, it then has to allow the interest rate to adjust to the level that will equate the demand for money to its money supply target.

Figure 18–3 illustrates these alternatives available to the central bank. The M_d curve in the figure shows the public's demand for money balances as a function of short-term interest rates, assuming a given level of real income. (In Chapter 19 we describe in some detail the determinants of the demand for money.) If the Bank of Canada decides that it wants to set the interest rate level at i^*—a policy known as pegging the interest rate—it then has to supply the amount of money demanded at this interest rate. By pegging the interest rate, the Bank also gives up its control over the money supply. As shown in the figure, when pegging the interest rate at i^* it has to supply an amount of money equal to M, which is equal to the demand for money at that interest rate.

If, instead, the Bank wants to retain control over the money supply, and desires it to be at M^*, it must allow the interest rate to be at i, which equates the demand for money to the Bank's target amount of M^*. The various combinations of interest rate and money supply at which the supply of money is equal to the demand for money lie along the demand curve. As we will learn

FIGURE 18-3   TARGETING MONEY SUPPLY OR INTEREST RATES

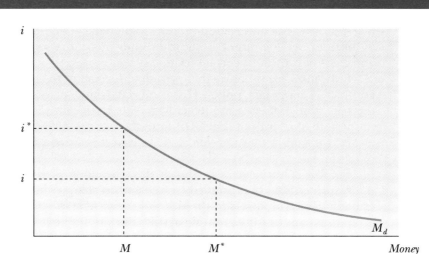

The demand for money curve is drawn assuming a given level of income. If the central bank targets the money supply at M^* it must accept the interest rate level i. Conversely, if the central bank sets a target for the interest rate of i^*, it has no choice but to supply a quantity of money equal to M.

later, these equilibrium combinations can change because of shifts in the demand for money curve or changes in the shape of the curve, which reflect the sensitivity of the demand for money to various levels of the rate of interest.

Policy Instruments for Money Supply Control

Can the Bank of Canada control the level or the rate of growth of the money supply, and if so, how should it go about it? If the Bank has the ability to control the money supply and uses this ability, we say that the money supply is exogenously determined. Conversely if the Bank is deprived of control, or has it but does not use it, the money supply is said to be endogenously determined.

The Bank can use one of two operational procedures to control the money supply. It can use either so-called base control or interest rate control. Base control involves estimating the size of the appropriate base multiplier and controlling the monetary base to achieve the targeted amount of money supply. Interest rate control involves estimating the demand for money and controlling the level of short-term interest rates so that the demand for money is equal to the targeted amount of money supply.

Base Control of Money Supply

Base control requires the Bank of Canada to correctly estimate the value of the appropriate base (money) multiplier and then to set the quantity of the monetary base at a level consistent with its money supply target. For example, suppose the Bank wants to hit an M1* target of $60 billion and that its estimate of the M1 base multiplier is $m = 1.5$. Since M1* $= mB^*$, where B^* is the required amount of the monetary base

$$B^* = \text{M1}^*/m$$

From this equation it follows that the monetary base must be controlled at $40 billion:

$$B^* = \$60 \text{ billion}/1.5 = \$40 \text{ billion}$$

The monetary base consists of the total amount of currency (coin and Bank of Canada notes in public circulation and held by the chartered banks) plus deposits and settlement balances held by direct clearers at the Bank of Canada. Except for coin, all the components of the monetary base are liabilities of the Bank of Canada. It should therefore follow that the Bank should be able to control the size of the monetary base with the changes it can make on its balance sheet. Table 18.1 shows the Bank's balance sheet as at December 31, 1999.

The determinants of the monetary base are readily identifiable from the Bank's balance sheet by keeping in mind that its total assets must always equal its total liabilities. Hence, any change in its total assets not accompanied by a change in its nonmonetary liabilities must be associated with an equivalent change in its monetary liabilities (that is, the monetary base). Alternatively, any change in its nonmonetary liabilities not accompanied by a change in its total assets must also be associated with an equivalent change in the monetary base. In other words, the amount of the monetary base is determined by changes in the central bank's assets and nonmonetary liabilities. While coin in public circulation is part of the monetary base, it is not part of the Bank of Canada's balance sheet. However, since coin is a relatively small proportion of the monetary base, changes in the public's preference to hold coin do not seriously affect the Bank's ability to control the overall size of the monetary base.

As shown in Table 18.1, most of the assets held by the Bank of Canada are Government of Canada securities. The Bank depends on the direct purchase of these securities at the time of their issue for the long-term growth of its assets and the monetary base. On a day-to-day basis it manages its holdings of these securities to offset short-term interest rates, either directly with open market operations, or indirectly by changing the availability of cash to direct clearers.

Overdraft loans and advances by the Bank of Canada to the direct clearers do not serve to provide long-term growth of the Bank's assets and the monetary base. As we learned earlier, advances from the Bank are initiated by the direct clearers to manage their day-to-day cash needs. Except in 1985 and 1986, the Bank's advances have been an insignificant proportion of its total assets. In those two years, the Bank made advances in unprecedented amounts in response to the banking system's liquidity needs due to the failure of two banks and the shifts in deposits this caused at other banks. In order to prevent those large demands for advances from creating an undesirable increase in the monetary base, the Bank reduced its holdings of government securities.

TABLE 18.1   BANK OF CANADA BALANCE SHEET
December 31, 1999, Millions of Dollars

Assets

Foreign currency deposits	610.0
Advances to members of the Canadian Payments Association	560.7
Investments	
Treasury bills of Canada	12 020.6
Other securities issued or guaranteed by Canada maturing within three years	7 515.1
Other securities issued or guaranteed by Canada not maturing within three years	12 975.7
Other Investments	5 130.9
Total Investments	37 642.3
Bank premises	175.2
Other assets	
Securities purchased under resale agreements	3 669.6
All other assets	405.5
TOTAL ASSETS	43 063.3

Liabilities

Non-monetary liabilities

Government of Canada deposits	11.8
Deposits other than by members of the Canadian Payments Association	428.5
Foreign currency liabilities of government of Canada	454.5
Other nonmonetary liabilities	78.6
Total nonmonetary liabilities	973.4

Monetary liabilities

Bank of Canada notes in circulation	40 142.6
Deposits by members of the Canadian Payments Association	1 947.3
Total monetary liabilities	42 089.9
TOTAL LIABILITIES	43 063.3

SOURCE: Bank of Canada, *Annual Report* 1999.

www.

In addition to Canadian dollar assets, the Bank holds assets denominated in foreign currencies. These assets include foreign currency deposits that the Bank holds as working balances with Canadian and foreign banks and with foreign central banks. The Bank also holds foreign currency securities, identified as other investments on its balance sheet. Some of these securities are held temporarily under swap agreements with the government's Exchange Fund Account. As we learned earlier, these transactions are undertaken periodically to replenish temporarily the government's cash balances to facilitate cash management.

All other assets of the Bank consist mainly of accrued interest on investments and the cost of the Bank's premises and equipment.

In Table 18.1, the total liabilities of the Bank of Canada are divided into nonmonetary and monetary liabilities. The nonmonetary liabilities are primarily Canadian-dollar deposits, other than those by the directly clearing members of the Canadian Payments Association, held at the Bank. These liabilities include deposits by the Government of Canada, foreign central banks, and official institutions such as the International Monetary Fund and the World Bank. Other Canadian-dollar deposits at the Bank are privately owned balances that have to be transferred to it by the chartered banks after they have remained unclaimed for ten years. Foreign currency liabilities are deposits denominated in foreign currencies, primarily U.S. dollars, held at the Bank by the federal government and foreign central banks.

Other nonmonetary liabilities of the Bank are its net revenue (profits) payable to the receiver general of Canada, its paid-up capital, its rest fund, and cheques that remain outstanding. The Bank's paid-up capital is $5 million and its rest fund is $25 million. In December 1955 the rest fund reached the maximum permitted under the *Bank of Canada Act* of five times the paid-up capital; thereafter, all of the Bank's net revenue was remitted to the federal government. These remittances are now timed to replenish the government's deposit account at the Bank to facilitate cash management.

The monetary liabilities of the Bank of Canada are its notes issued and settlement deposits held with it by the direct clearers, which are the most important components of the monetary base. Coin, the other component of the monetary base, is not a monetary liability of the Bank. Coin is provided by the Royal Canadian Mint, a Crown corporation since 1969. The production of coin and its distribution for circulation are determined primarily by the demands of the public. Unlike the other components of the monetary base, which are the result of debt monetization, the production of coin involves monetization of the metals of which they are made.

Control of the monetary base by the Bank of Canada implies control of its monetary liabilities. Since the Bank exercises close control over the amount of its assets with its purchase and sale of securities, and since it can fairly accurately predict changes in most of its nonmonetary liabilities and it initiates changes in some, such as federal government deposits, it follows that it can exercise close control over its monetary liabilities and therefore over the monetary base.

As we already observed, to exercise base control effectively over a monetary aggregate, the Bank of Canada must be able not only to control the monetary base, but also to predict correctly the size of a base multiplier. While the Bank's control over the monetary base is certain, its ability to correctly forecast the size of base multipliers is somewhat uncertain.

In Chapter 9 we derived base multipliers for M3 and M1. The multiplier expressions shown there are composed of ratios that express the demand for cash by the public and the depository institutions relative to these institutions' deposit liabilities. The currency ratio expresses the public's demand for cash as a proportion of the depository institutions' total demand liabilities. The depository institutions' cash reserve ratio shows their demand for cash relative to their respective deposit liabilities. When no minimum legal cash reserve requirements exist, these reserve ratios reflect the institutions' perceived need for cash to satisfy their obligations to encash cheques and other payment orders drawn against their deposit liabilities. Since the chartered banks and the near-banks may have different reserve ratios, our multiplier expressions also contain a ratio that specifies the relative size of their deposit liabilities. Finally,

FIGURE 18–4   **MONEY MULTIPLIERS**

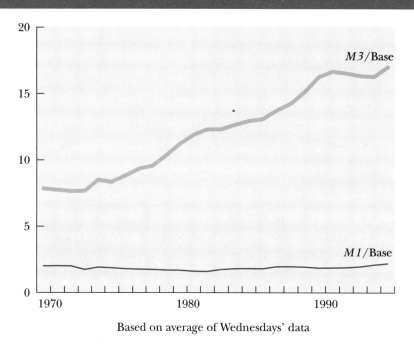

Based on average of Wednesdays' data

SOURCE: Canada, Department of Finance, *Economic Reference Tables*, Table 7–4, August 1996, p. 125. Reproduced with the permission of the Minister of Public Works and Government Services Canada, 1997.

the M1 base multiplier also contains a ratio that takes into account the proportion that the chartered banks' demand deposits is of their total deposits. The size of all these ratios and, hence, the size of the base multipliers are determined in one way or another by the various participants' preferences, and the institutional arrangements that affect the demand for cash. All these determinants are subject to changes that are difficult to predict, particularly in the short run.

Figure 18–4 shows the variability in the size of base multipliers over the years. Most critics of the use of base control underscore its shortcomings in terms of the instability and unpredictability of base multipliers. However, those who do not view this problem as a serious one suggest that its use may result in undesirably sharp, possibly explosive, oscillations of short-term interest rates. With international capital flows extremely sensitive to interest rate differentials between countries, sharp changes in Canadian short-term interest rates also can be accompanied by undesirable exchange rate volatility.

Interest Rate Control of Money Supply

Interest rate control of the money supply, also illustrated in Figure 18–3, involves the central bank estimating the demand for the monetary aggregate it has targeted, and keeping the interest rate at the level that equates demand with targeted supply. The central bank's success when using this procedure to meet its money supply target depends on its ability to estimate accurately the demand for money. As we will learn below, the Bank of Canada abandoned its attempt to target the growth rate of M1 after 1981, when it could no longer adequately estimate the demand for it.

The choice between base control and interest rate control of a monetary aggregate depends on the relative stability of base multipliers and the demand for money. The choice may also depend upon whether the growth of a broad or narrow monetary aggregate is to be targeted. Insofar as the demand for broad monetary aggregates is not very sensitive to interest rate changes, interest rate control may require unacceptably large changes in rates.[4]

The Bank's Monetary Targeting Experience

In 1975 the Bank of Canada started to announce interim targets for money growth defined in terms of M1. The Bank chose to target M1 rather than other monetary measures because M1 satisfied two principal requirements. First, the Bank's econometric analysis had shown a stable relationship between the real demand for M1 and variations in real income and short-term interest rates. Second, since the assets included in M1 are mostly noninterest bearing, the demand for it is highly sensitive to interest rate changes. This sensitivity, the Bank hoped, would allow it to control the annual growth rate of M1 without generating large movements in short-term interest rates, and, at worst, prevent instability and uncertainty in financial and foreign exchange markets. With an assumed stable demand function for M1, the Bank attempted to achieve its target levels by using its daily cash setting and, when necessary, direct intervention in the money market as policy instruments to achieve a level of short-term interest rates that would produce a demand for M1 consistent with its targeted growth rates.

Beginning in 1975, on six separate occasions the Bank preannounced target growth ranges for M1: 10 to 15 percent (November 1975), 8 to 12 percent (August 1976), 7 to 11 percent (October 1977), 6 to 10 percent (September 1978), 5 to 9 percent (December 1979), and 4 to 8 percent (February 1981). By setting successively lower target ranges, as shown in Figure 18–5, the Bank hoped to reduce the rate of inflation gradually without impairing the real economy unnecessarily.

The dark line in Figure 18–5 traces the actual growth rate of M1 during the years of growth targets. Except for disruptions caused by three postal strikes, during which times the demand and hence the supply of M1 temporarily shot up, the Bank generally kept monetary growth within its target ranges until the second half of 1981.

However, with innovations in banking practices and the instability these created for the demand for M1, the Bank found it increasingly difficult, and

---

4. See Thomas Courchene, "On Defining and Controlling Money," *Canadian Journal of Economics* (November 1979), pp. 604–15.

FIGURE 18–5   **TARGET GROWTH RANGES FOR M1**
Billions of Dollars, Seasonally Adjusted; Ratio Scale

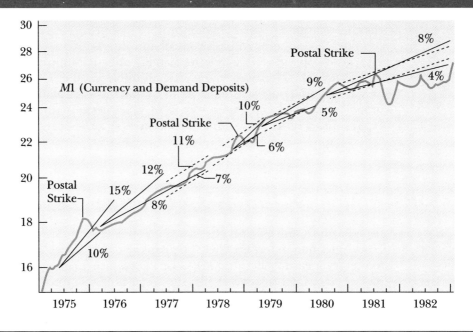

SOURCE: Bank of Canada, *Annual Report,* 1982. Reproduced with permission

after 1981 all but impossible, to hold M1 within its target ranges. Major financial innovations included the introduction of daily interest chequing and savings accounts, and the development of cash management techniques for corporate accounts. Daily interest chequing accounts, facilitated by the use of new computer technology, induced the public to shift out of noninterest-bearing deposit accounts in the M1 money measure. At the same time, businesses increasingly economized on their M1 balances by taking advantage of the cash management packages offered by the banks. These packages made it possible to consolidate funds from geographically dispersed sources into a single account, thereby allowing businesses to reduce the level of their M1 working balances. Payroll service plans and arrangements for shifting surplus funds overnight to interest-bearing accounts not part of M1 further reduced the demand for M1. These financial innovations made it increasingly difficult for the Bank to determine the appropriate level of short-term interest rates that would hold M1 growth within its targeted range. The Bank chose to resolve its difficulties by abandoning the setting of M1 targets.[5]

The Bank's announcement in November 1982 that it was no longer using a target range for M1 growth came as no surprise because, as shown in Figure

5. For an evaluation of Canada's experience with MI targeting, see T. J. Courchene, *Money Inflation and the Bank of Canada,* Vol. 2, (Montreal: C.D. Howe Institute, 1992); G.K. Bouey, "Monetary Policy— Finding a Place to Stand," Per Jacobsson Lecture (1982); G. Thiessen, "The Canadian Experience with Monetary Targeting," in *Central Bank Views of Monetary Targeting,* Paul Meek, ed. (New York: Federal Reserve Bank of New York, 1983).

18–5, the Bank had allowed M1 to consistently remain below its target range after mid-1981. Beginning in late 1979, when a sharp increase and greater volatility in interest rates occurred in the United States, the Bank had to choose between allowing Canadian rates to follow U.S. rates or allowing the Canadian dollar to depreciate to accommodate the differential in interest rates between the two countries. The Bank chose to resist depreciation of the exchange rate because it was afraid that this would worsen inflation. Hence, in addition to the difficulties associated with estimating the demand of M1, the Bank also stopped targeting money growth and concentrated instead on stabilizing the external value of the Canadian dollar. The control of interest rates became a major instrument for meeting this policy objective. When exchange rate stabilization and interest rates, rather than the level and growth of a monetary aggregate, are major monetary policy targets, the Bank leaves the money supply to be endogenously determined.

Targets for Reducing Inflation

On February 26, 1991, the governor of the Bank of Canada and the minister of finance announced the setting of targets for reducing inflation and reaching price stability.[6] These targets provided for a year-over-year rate of increase in the consumer price index of 3 percent by the end of 1992, 2.5 percent by the middle of 1994, and 2 percent by the end of 1995. Thereafter, further reductions in the inflation rate were to be achieved until price stability was secured. No explicit target was set for 1991, but 5 percent was considered an interim guidepost. As shown in Figure 18–6, the targets are regarded as the mid-point of a target range of plus or minus one percentage point. Since 1993 the core CPI inflation rate (excluding food and energy prices and the effects of indirect taxes) has been within the Bank's target band.

In December of 1993, the government and the Bank agreed to extend the targets to the end of 1998. On February 24, 1998, the Bank of Canada and the federal government agreed to extend the targets until the end of 2001. The inflation target range stood between 1 percent and 3 percent in May 2000.

With the setting of inflation targets, the consumer price index (CPI) assumed the role of information variable for the framing of monetary policy over the intermediate and long run. Over the short run, the Bank of Canada has used the CPI, excluding its food and energy prices components, as its operational target. Changes in prices of these components reflect temporary demand and supply conditions that do not necessarily affect the trend rate of inflationary conditions. The same is true for changes in indirect taxes; as a result, the Bank makes temporary adjustments to its inflation targets to account for them.

www.

---

6. See "Press Release: Targets for Reducing Inflation," and "Background Note on the Targets," reproduced in *Bank of Canada Review*, March 1991, pp. 5–15; "Targets for Reducing Inflation: Further Operational and Measurement Considerations," *Bank of Canada Review*, September 1991, pp. 5–6.

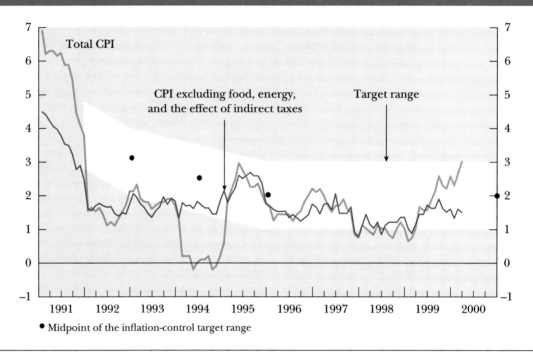

FIGURE 18–6 **INFLATION TARGETS**

● Midpoint of the inflation-control target range

SOURCE: Bank of Canada, *Monetary Policy Report,* May 2000.

The formal setting of inflation targets that indicated both the path and the timing for lowering the rate of inflation served two important purposes for the achievement of price stability. It provided the public with a clear indication of the Bank's intermediate and longer-term policy action on which to base their inflationary expectations and economic decision making. (As we will learn in later chapters, the transitional costs for achieving price stability in terms of higher rates of unemployment are closely related to the lowering of inflationary expectations.) The other purpose served by the announcement of formal targets was that it provided a better basis than before for judging the performance of monetary policy and for holding the Bank accountable for its actions.

Essential to the success of setting inflation targets is the public's expectations that they can and will be achieved, which is particularly critical during the transition toward price stability, when misunderstanding of the need to increase monetary growth temporarily can call into question the credibility of the central bank. As the inflation rate and interest rates begin to fall, the M1 narrow interest-sensitive money aggregate can be expected to increase rather than decline. This increase in M1 may last up to one year or longer before the public fully adjusts its desired M1 balances to the lower interest rates. It may take up to two years or longer before a decline in interest rates is fully reflected in a decline in the less interest-sensitive, broader money aggregates. Interest rates affect the demand for these aggregates only indirectly via their induced effects on changes in prices and output.

The Bank's Operating Range for the Overnight Interest Rate

Since mid-1994, the operational objective of the Bank of Canada's monetary policy has been to keep the overnight rate within a band of 50 basis points (× of 1 percent). The overnight rate is the average rate at which investment dealers are able to arrange their overnight financing of their inventories of money market securities.[7]

The Bank changes its operating range when it wants to effect an increase or decrease in the level of monetary conditions or to rebalance monetary conditions (for example, lower interest rates as a result of an appreciation of the Canadian dollar). On occasion, the Bank has increased its operating range for overnight rates to stabilize financial markets. The Bank typically changes overnight rates to ratify movements that have already taken place in the market.

The Bank can influence the overnight rate through changes in its supply of settlement balances to the direct clearers of the Canadian Payments Association. The Bank offers Special Purchase and Resale Agreements (SPRAs) to signal a change in its operating range for the overnight rate. To indicate the top end of the band, the Bank offers SPRAs to the primary dealers at a rate equal to the desired top end of the band. More recently, an announced change in the Bank Rate has served the same purpose. SPRAs are also offered to relieve market pressure that threatens to move the overnight financing rate above the current operating band.

Alternatively, the Bank may use Sale and Repurchase Agreements (SRAs) to indicate a new lower end of the band. More often, however, SRAs are offered to the major banks to offset undesired downward pressure on overnight financing costs to levels below the current operating band. In addition to using SRAs the Bank may undertake a reverse-repo-type operation whereby it offers to sell Treasury bills to the primary dealers under an agreement to repurchase them the next day.

Outright purchases or sales of Treasury bills are used by the Bank to indicate its desire to moderate the pace of movements in the interest rate. On occasion the Bank may engage in switches (purchasing longer-term maturities and selling shorter-term maturities) to help relieve market pressures.

Changes in the Range of Overnight Rates

Following the introduction of the operating band for overnight rates in mid-1994, the Bank moved the band down on several occasions. These shifts reflected the decline in the Bank's monetary conditions index during the first half of the year. In the latter part of 1994 and the early part of 1995, however, depreciation of the Canadian dollar and higher commodity prices pushed the inflation rate toward the upper part of the inflation target range. The Bank

---

7. There are other "overnight" or one-day interest rates, including interbank rates, wholesale deposit rates, swap rates, and "repo" rates.

FIGURE 18–7 **THE BANK OF CANADA'S OPERATING BAND FOR OVERNIGHT RATES, 1996–2000**

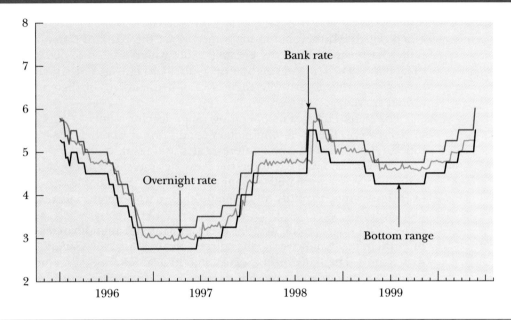

SOURCE: Statistics Canada, CANSIM database, Series B114038 and B113862, May 2000.

responded by increasing its operating band of overnight rates twice in the latter part of 1994, and five more times in January and February alone in 1995.

In the second quarter of 1995, after the Canadian dollar strengthened, and with expectations of a drop in interest rates in the United States, the Bank took the opportunity to rebalance the mix of monetary conditions by offsetting the effects of stronger exchange rates through a reduction in its operational range of the overnight interest rate. Eight further reductions in the operational range were made by the end of 1995. In response to the firming of the Canadian dollar and the lacklustre performance of the economy, a significant easing of monetary conditions had become desirable.

In February 1996, the Bank of Canada adopted a new method of setting the Bank Rate, tying it to the top of its band for the overnight rate. During that year the Bank reduced the Bank Rate and its operating band for overnight interest rates eight times. As is shown in Figure 18–7, reductions in the operating range were typically 25 basis points. Two reductions in the operating range in 1996 were again made to rebalance the mix of monetary conditions. However, all of the reductions during the year were consistent with the Bank's desire for a distinct easing of monetary conditions. The inflation rate had moved firmly into its lower range, and aggregate demand remained sluggish. At the same time, short-term interest rates were declining not only in the United States but also globally. There was also a marked improvement in Canada's balance of payments and the Canadian dollar traded in a narrow range.

In 1997 the Bank raised the Bank Rate and hence its operating band four times and twice more in 1998, often to match increases announced by the Federal Reserve Bank in the United States, as well as to counter the undesirable easing of monetary conditions and to forestall the potential loss of confidence in the Canadian dollar resulting from turbulence in global financial markets following the Asian crisis and the Russian debt moratorium. The last increase in August 1998 of a full percentage point, as well as each of the two preceding increases of one-half of 1 percent were made primarily to arrest the decline of the dollar against its American counterpart. In the latter part of 1998 and the first part of the following year, the Bank Rate and the operating band were lowered by one-quarter of 1 percent on five occasions, thereby reversing most of the previous increase.

Into 2000, the Federal Reserve began to aggressively raise interest rates, with a 50 basis point increase in May 2000. The Bank of Canada followed suit the next day with a similar 50 basis point increase in the Bank Rate. Fed-watchers expected further increases in American interest rates during the summer, and much of the financial community wondered whether the Bank of Canada would be able to match expected changes in U.S. rates. The market, at least initially, did not believe the Bank would follow the Fed, and the Canadian dollar lost value immediately after Canadian interest rates rose. Rather than raise the value of the dollar, higher Canadian interest rates led to a depreciation. Why? As we learned in Chapter 7, expectations play a critical role in determining the behaviour of exchange rates in the short term.

The Bank of Canada's Day-to-Day Implementation of Monetary Policy under the Large Value Transfer System (LVTS)

The method used by the Bank of Canada to implement monetary policy is closely linked to the characteristics of the system whereby payments are cleared and settled daily. As we have described, before the introduction of the LVTS, payments were cleared overnight and settled the next day on a retroactive (backdated) basis. As a result, direct clearers did not know the outcome of the daily clearings, or of the end-of-the-day level of their settlement balances at the Bank of Canada, until the following morning. This uncertainty had been central to the way in which the Bank had acted to influence the overnight interest rate. This uncertainty was removed when the Large Value Transfer System (LVTS) became operational in 1999. Participants in the LVTS are able to track their receipts and payments in real-time and know the net outcomes of these flows by the end of the day, when settlement is made in the books of the Bank of Canada. Hence, the Bank had to accommodate its day-to-day implementation of monetary policy to the LVTS.

The key features of the framework in place today are as follows:[8]

www.

1. The Bank continues to use an operating band of 50 basis points for the overnight interest rate.

2. The upper limit of the band is the Bank Rate, which is also the rate charged participants (institutions with settlement balances at the Bank) requiring an overdraft loan to cover a clearing deficit following end-of-day settlement. The lower limit of the band (Bank Rate less 50 basis points) is the rate paid participants with surplus settlement balances at the end of the LVTS clearing day.

3. Changes in the operating band, and hence the Bank Rate, are announced at 9 a.m. on the effective date. If there happens to be a shock that requires an immediate response, the Bank announces a change in the Bank Rate effective the following day. The announcement ordinarily has an immediate impact on monetary conditions.

4. Within the operating band for the overnight rate, the Bank has specified a policy target rate, which is the midpoint of the band. The Bank is prepared to enter into open market operations at this target rate. At 11:45 in the morning, if overnight funds are generally trading above the target level, the Bank enters into SPRA transactions with primary dealers. Conversely, if overnight funds are generally trading below the Bank's target level, it enters into SRA transactions with the primary dealers. When the overnight rate is at the target level, the Bank does not intervene. By not intervening in the market before 11:45 a.m., the Bank encourages participants in the LVTS to adjust their cash positions by trading with each other at the target level that is known to them early in the day, rather than with the Bank.

5. By 3 p.m. each day, the Bank has full information on the payment flow throughout the LVTS resulting from public sector transactions. With this information in hand, the Bank can neutralize the potential impact of public sector transactions on the supply of settlement balances by auctioning Government of Canada deposits for same-day settlement through the LVTS. An initial auction takes places at 9:15 a.m., with a second auction held after the government's receipts and payments are known.

6. The LVTS has a presettlement trading period of about half an hour, after the close of client business (6 p.m.). Participants with surplus settlement balances as a result of client transactions can lend to other participants with a deficit balance. This lending allows each participant to achieve a zero balance, regardless of the distribution of client payments.

7. The paper-based payment items continue to be cleared through the Canadian Payments Association's Automated Clearing and Settlement System (ACSS), with the retroactive settlement of cheques. Direct clearers, however, are remunerated for positive settlement balances as well as charged for overdrafts when they experience deficit balances. Since April 1, 1999, the charge for daily overdrafts is Bank Rate plus one and one-half percentage points, and the rate received on positive balances is equal to

---

8. Bank of Canada, *The Framework for the Implementation of Monetary Policy in the Large Value Transfer System Environment,* January 28, 1999.

TABLE 18.2	**THE MARKET TIMETABLE**
9 a.m.	Announcement of change in operating band (if any; a change implies change in target, i.e., intervention rate)
9:15 a.m.	Cutoff time for bids on receiver general (RG) term deposit auction
9:30 a.m.	Release of RG term deposit auction results
11:45 a.m.	SPRAs or SRAs offered and transacted (if any)
2:15 p.m.	Second round of SPRAs possible if overnight rate above target
3 p.m.	Cutoff time for presentation of government items to Bank of Canada
4 p.m.	Payment exchange for Debt Clearing Service
4:15 p.m.	Cutoff time for bids for RG deposit auction
4:30 p.m.	Release of RG auction results
4:45 p.m.	Announcement of the previous day's target settlement balance
6 p.m.	Close of LVTS client (third-party) transactions
6–6:30 p.m.	Presettlement trading
8 p.m. or earlier	Settlement of LVTS balances at the Bank of Canada

SOURCE: Bank of Canada, *The Framework for the Implementation of Monetary Policy in the Large Value Transfer System Environment*, January 28, 1999; and Bank of Canada, *The Framework for the Implementation of Monetary Policy in the Large Value Transfer System Environment:* Addendum II, November 1999.

the LVTS positive balance interest rate less one and one-half percentage points.

Table 18.2 shows the timelines involved in the LVTS process. While the Bank initially targeted a settlements balance of zero, in late 1999 it adopted a positive balance of $200 million for the system. The Bank also introduced a second round of SPRAs, which takes place early in the afternoon. The Bank had found that on "technically tight" days, the overnight rate tended to rise above the target. These month-end effects were usually due to payment volumes and net flows that exhibited greater than average uncertainty. The Bank introduced these changes to shelter the overnight rate from this volatility and increase its ability to achieve its target for the overnight interest rate.

Rules versus Discretion in Monetary Policy

"100-percent money" a system of banking proposed by Irving Fisher in which a bank's deposit liabilities would be matched by an equal amount of cash reserves

Should the monetary authorities be allowed to conduct monetary policy at their own discretion, or should they be subject to legislated or otherwise mandated rules? This question has a long history and concerns both how money growth should be controlled and who should exercise such control.

In the 1920s, Irving Fisher saw the mismanagement by the commercial banks of their deposit-creating powers as the major cause of cyclical disturbances in the U.S. economy. He blamed the banks for expanding the money supply too quickly during periods of economic expansion and contracting it during economic recessions. He proposed **"100-percent money"** to resolve this problem. Under such a system each dollar of the bank's deposit liabilities would have to be matched by a dollar of cash reserves.[9] The central bank would have complete control of the money supply since it controls the amount of cash available to the commercial banks to expand their deposit liabilities.

Those who mistrusted the commercial banks' use of their deposit-creating powers usually also mistrusted the central bank's use of its discretionary power in providing cash reserves to the commercial banks. Some proposed circumscribing the central bank's ability to supply cash to the banking system by returning to the pure gold standard. Under a gold standard the central bank's ability to provide the banking system with cash reserves in the form of the central bank's own liabilities depends on the availability of gold reserves to the central bank. Gold standard rules require the central bank to convert its monetary liabilities into a specified amount of gold. The gold standard had already been tried but was abandoned because it tied money supply growth to the availability of gold reserves, which did not necessarily reflect the economy's monetary growth requirements.

Realizing the shortcomings of a gold standard rule for providing the banking system with an adequate amount of cash to allow them to expand their deposits and hence, the money supply, Benjamin Graham proposed a **commodity reserve dollar**.[10] Under such a system the value of the dollar would be defined in terms of a specified bundle of representative basic commodities rather than gold. The monetary authorities would be required to buy and sell a composite group of commodities at a stated price. Since the price of the chosen commodities was representative of prices in general, the monetary authorities' commitment to buy and sell them would serve to stabilize the price level, since the right combination of money to goods would be automatically maintained. While at first sight Graham's proposal appeared attractive, it too had its shortcomings. Two of these problems were the difficulty of storing perishable goods, which certainly would have to be included in the representative bundle of commodities, and the depletion of commodity reserves during lengthy periods of economic expansion when the monetary authorities would be forced to sell them at their fixed price.

During the 1930s attention turned away from the use of the banking system's, and in particular the monetary authorities', discretionary power to expand the money supply too rapidly. The slowness with which the money supply increased was held by many as the root cause of the economic depression being experienced. In Alberta, C.H. Douglas proposed that the government mandate the central bank to allow an increase in the money supply to provide it with funds to be distributed as a "**National Dividend**" to increase spending and thereby end the depression.[11] Similar proposals were put forward in the United States by Upton Sinclair and the Townsend Clubs.[12]

As alternatives to the schemes for expanding the money supply, proposals were made to increase spending by forcing an increase in the velocity of circu-

commodity reserve dollar *proposed by Benjamin Graham whereby the value of the dollar would be defined in terms of a specified bundle of commodities*

"National Dividend" *C.H. Douglas proposed that the central bank be mandated to increase the money supply, which would be distributed as a national dividend*

---

9. Irving Fisher, *100-Percent Money,* rev. ed. (New York: Adelphi Company, 1963).

10. Benjamin Graham, *Storage and Stability* (New York, McGraw-Hill, 1937).

11. C.H. Douglas, *Credit Power and Democracy* (London: Cecil Palmer, 1920).

12. See, for example, *Economic Meaning of the Townsend Plan,* Public Policy Pamphlet 20 (Chicago University of Chicago Press, 1936).

lation of money. One such proposal had already been made around the turn of the century by a German economist named Silvio Gesell.[13] He suggested issuing paper money, or **script money** as it became known, that would remain legal tender only as long as a required monthly stamp was affixed to it. Holders of script money would be inclined to spend it quickly to avoid the cost of the stamps.

In 1935, shortly after the Social Credit Party formed the government of Alberta, it began to issue "Prosperity Certificates." These were similar to bank notes, but on the back of each note were 104 little squares for each week over two years. A one-cent stamp had to be pasted each week into one of these squares to keep the certificate valid. Alberta's enabling legislation for the issue of this script was disallowed by the federal government. The disallowance ruling was later sustained by the Supreme Court of Canada. In practice, the script circulated for a very short time since the public quickly became suspicious of the value of what they perceived to be "funny money."

In the 1950s and 1960s, central banks increasingly used their discretionary powers to manage monetary expansion for short-term stabilization of the economy. Milton Friedman and Edward Shaw, in the United States, were among the first to point out that such behaviour was more likely to destabilize than stabilize the economy.[14] Moreover, long-run price stability was inevitably being sacrificed to achieve short-run income stabilization. Friedman proposed replacing central bank discretion with a constant money growth rule designed to provide price stability. Other economists have subsequently joined Friedman in advocating fixed rules for monetary growth. They have pointed out that rules would limit the damage that can be done by central bankers with an unjustifiable confidence in their ability to control the economy. Finn Kydland and Edward Prescott have shown that discretionary monetary policy that attempts to avoid both inflation and unemployment tends to produce more inflation than would result with a monetary rule, with no additional employment obtained in compensation.[15]

In 1991, Professor Thomas Courchene at Queen's University in Kingston suggested that Canada should fix the value of its dollar to that of the U.S. dollar. If this were the case, the Bank of Canada would have to follow a monetary growth rule that maintains the fixed value between the two currencies. Courchene argued that since the United States had a better record than Canada in controlling its inflation, Canada's own record would improve.

More recently, economists have proposed nondiscretionary feedback rules as an alternative to a constant money growth rule. Feedback rules would specify how the monetary authorities would have to change money growth in

13. The work of Gesell was not noticed or was completely forgotten until it was mentioned by Keynes. See *The General Theory of Employment, Interest, and Money* (London: Macmillan, 1951), Ch. 23.

14. See Edward S. Shaw, "Money Supply and Stable Economic Growth," in American Assembly, *United States Monetary Policy* (New York: Columbia University Press, 1958); and Milton Friedman's testimony before the Joint Economic Committee, *Employment, Growth and Price Levels*, Hearings (1959–60), Part 4, pp. 605–37. Friedman elaborates his proposals in *A Program for Money Stability* (New York: Fordham University Press, 1960).

15. Finn E. Kydland, and Edward C. Prescott, "Rules Rather Than Discretion: The Inconsistency of Optimal Plans," *Journal of Political Economy* 85 (June 1977), pp. 473–91.

script money *the issue of paper money that would remain legal tender as long as a required monthly stamp was affixed to it*

response to changes in certain economic variables.[16] For example, a simple nondiscretionary feedback rule might take the following form:

$$\Delta M = 1.0 + 0.5(U_{t-1} - 6.0)$$

where ΔM is the quarterly rate of growth of M1, and U_{t-1} is the unemployment rate, in percentage terms, in the previous quarter. According to this rule, the monetary authorities would be obliged to control M1 to grow at a rate of 1 percent per quarter, if during the previous quarter the unemployment rate was 6 percent. If in the last quarter the unemployment rate was higher, say 8 percent, the money supply in this quarter would have to be made to grow at $1.0 + 0.5(8.0 - 6.0) = 2$ percent. Similarly, if in the previous quarter the unemployment was less than 6 percent, money supply growth during the current quarter would have to be less than 1 percent.

Designing an appropriate feedback formula is not an easy matter. Armour and Coté (2000) provide an accessible review of the literature as it applies to inflation control. We can specify formulae that include a variety of variables. For example, we can include variables that capture temporary departures of the velocity of money from its average level and deviations of nominal income and the price level from their targeted paths. The variables chosen must have a stable relationship with money growth. The possibility exists that once the rules are made known these relationships may change—the so-called Lucas critique. The feedback formula must also contain a rule specifying how fast the monetary authorities must adjust money growth when the included economic variables diverge from their targeted amounts. A wrong choice in setting target levels or rates, as well as the time allowed to adjust the money supply to maintain these targets, can result in the time inconsistency problems referred to earlier.

John Taylor (1993) proposed that the central bank follow a feedback rule in which nominal interest rates are set on the basis of the difference between output (Y) and its target (Y^*) and the inflation rate (π) and its target (π^e):

$$i = i^* + 1.5(\pi - \pi^e) + 0.5(Y - Y^*)$$

where the coefficients on the inflation error and the output gap were determined by examining the U.S. evidence on interest rates, inflation, and the

---

16. See Bennett T. McCallum, "The Case for Rules in the Conduct of Monetary Policy: a Concrete Example," *Federal Reserve Bank of Richmond Economic Review* 73 (September–October 1987), pp. 10–18; Bennett T. McCallum, "Robustness Properties only a Rule for Monetary Policy," *Carnegie-Rochester Conference Series on Public Policy 29* (Autumn 1988), pp. 173–203; Robert E. Hull, "Monetary Strategy with an Elastic Price Standard," *Price Stability and Public Policy,* a symposium sponsored by the Federal Reserve Bank of Kansas City, August 1984, pp. 137–59; A. Steven Englander, "Optimal Monetary Policy Design: Rules versus Discretion," *Federal Reserve Bank of New York Quarterly Review* 15 (Winter 1991), pp. 65–79; John P. Judd, and Brian Motley, "Nominal Feedback Rules for Monetary Policy," *Federal Reserve Bank of San Francisco Economic Review* (Summer 1991), pp. 3–17; and John B. Carlson, "Rules versus Discretion: Making a Monetary Rule Operational," *Federal Reserve Bank of Cleveland Economic Review* 3 (1988), pp. 2–12.

output gap.[17] Taylor's "rule" appeared to do very well at explaining the behaviour of the Federal Reserve Board, until Orphanides (1998) examined whether using historically revised data made a difference in the fit of the rule, relative to using the data that policymakers had at their disposal when decisions had been made.[18] The Taylor rule lost some of its lustre, but it remains a useful example of the fragility of activist feedback rules.

Unfortunately, money will not manage itself, nor is monetary policy a precise science that allows it to be conducted according to a rule set in stone. Gerald Bouey, a former governor of the Bank of Canada, noted that a central bank

> *...must operate to a considerable extent by the method of successive approximation, constantly adjusting its operations in the light of all evidence it can get, as it becomes available, about changing economic and financial conditions.*[19]

This implies that discretion has a role in the conduct of monetary policy. As Paul Samuelson has put it:

> *In principle, the choice has never been between discretionary and nondiscretionary action; for when men set up a definitive mechanism which is to run forever afterward by itself, that involves a single act of discretion which transcends, in both its arrogance and its capacity for potential harm, any repeated acts of foolish discretion that can be imagined.*[20]

KEY TERMS

"100-percent money"
base money
commodity reserve dollar
indicators

intermediate target
monetary conditions
monetary conditions index
"National Dividend"

operational target
policy instruments
script money

17. Taylor, John B., "Discretion versus Policy Rules in Practice," Carnegie-Rochester Conference Series on Public Policy, 39, December 1993, pp. 195–214.

18. A. Orphanides, *Monetary Policy Evaluation with Noisy Information*, Finance and Economics Discussion Paper Series, No 1998-50, Federal Reserve Board, 1998.

19. Bank of Canada, Evidence of the Governor before the Royal Commission on Banking and Finance (Ottawa, May 1964), p. 127.

20. Paul A. Samuelson, "Reflections on Central Banking," *National Banking Review*, September 1963, p. 16.

REVIEW QUESTIONS

1. Explain the determination of the monetary base in terms of balance sheet changes of the Bank of Canada.
2. How have an increasing currency ratio and increasing time deposit ratio affected the M1 and M3 multipliers? Why has the time deposit ratio increased?
3. Why did the Bank of Canada decide to target a positive settlements balance in 1999?
4. Explain how the central bank can try to control the money supply. Why did the Bank of Canada stop setting money growth targets in the early 1980s?
5. Why can the Bank not simultaneously control both the money supply and the rate of interest?
6. Is a monetary conditions index an infallible indicator of the stance of monetary policy? Explain.
7. The Taylor rule was initially framed in terms of real interest rates. What form did his initial rule take, and how it is possible to express this in terms of nominal interest rates as in the text?
8. How does the Bank of Canada use the LVTS in its implementation of monetary policy? Over the past year or so, what has been the daily volume and value of transactions in the LVTS ?
9. This question involves doing some research. Courchene argued that the United States had a better record at controlling inflation than Canada did. Obtain annual data on the U.S. inflation rate and the Canadian inflation rate from 1990 until 2000, and plot the figures on the same graph. In which country has inflation been the lowest over this period, on average? Does it make sense to fix the value of the Canadian dollar? Why or why not?
10. This question involves research. Obtain monthly data on M1, M2+, and M2++ in Canada from 1990 until December 2000. Calculate growth rates on a year-to-year basis (i.e., December 2000 relative to December 1999). Plot the growth rates on the same graph. Using information in Atta-Mensah (2000), does any one of these plots appear to be more consistent with the Bank of Canada's operating band for the overnight interest rate? Explain.

SELECTED READINGS

Armour, J., and A. Coté. "Feedback Rules for Inflation Control: An Overview of Recent Literature." *Bank of Canada Review*, Winter 1999–2000, pp. 43–54.

Atta-Mensah, J. "Recent Developments in the Monetary Aggregates and Their Implications." *Bank of Canada Review*, Spring 2000.

Bank of Canada. *Money Markets and Central Bank Operations*. Proceedings of a Conference Held by the Bank of Canada (November 1995). Ottawa, 1996.

———. *The Framework for the Implementation of Monetary Policy in the Large Value Transfer System Environment*, January 28, 1999 (revised March 31, 1999).

———. *The Framework for the Implementation of Monetary Policy in the Large Value Transfer System Environment: Addendum II*, November 1999.

———. *Monetary Policy Reports*. Semi-annual reports, starting May 1995.

———. *The Transmission of Monetary Policy in Canada*. Ottawa, 1996

Barro, Robert J. "Recent Developments in the Theory of Rules versus Discretion." *Economic Journal* 95 (Supplement, 1985), pp. 23–37.

Barro, Robert J., and David B. Gordon. "A Positive Theory of Monetary Policy in a Natural-Rate Model." *Journal of Political Economy*, August 1983, pp. 589–610.

Clinton, Kevin. "Implementation of Monetary Policy in a Regime with Zero Reserve Requirements." Bank of Canada Working Paper, 97–8. Ottawa: Bank of Canada, April 1997.

Clinton, Kevin, and K. Lynch. "Monetary Base and Money Stock in Canada." Bank of Canada Technical Report, No. 16. Ottawa: Bank of Canada, 1979.

Courchene, Thomas J. "In Defining and Controlling Money." *Canadian Journal of Economics* 12 (November 1979), pp. 604–15.

———. *Money, Inflation and the Bank of Canada, Volume II: An Analysis of Monetary Gradualism, 1975–80*. Montreal: C.D. Howe Institute, 1981.

———. *No Place to Stand? Abandoning Monetary Targets: An Evaluation.* Montreal: C.D. Howe Institute, 1983.

Dittmar, R., W. Gavin, and F. Kydland. "Price-Level Uncertainty and Inflation Targeting," *Federal Reserve Bank of St. Louis Economic Review* (July/August 1999), pp. 23–34.

Dufour, Jean-Marie, and Daniel Racette. "Monetary Control in Canada." In *Fiscal and Monetary Policy*, research coordinator John Sargent. Toronto: University of Toronto Press (for the Royal Commission on the Economic Union and Development Prospects for Canada), 1986, pp. 199–256.

Eika, D., N. Ericsson, and R. Nymoen. "Hazards in Implementing a Monetary Conditions Index." Board of Governors of the Federal Reserve System International Finance Discussion Paper No 568, October 1996.

Fortin, Pierre. "Monetary Targets and Monetary Policy in Canada: A Critical Assessment." *Canadian Journal of Economics* 12 (November 1979), pp. 625–46.

Howitt, Peter. *Monetary Policy in Transition: A Study of Bank of Canada Policy, 1982–83.* Montreal: C.D. Howe Institute, 1986.

Johannes, J.M., and R.H. Rasche. "Predicting the Money Multiplier." *Journal of Monetary Economics* 5 (1979), pp. 301–25.

"Memorandum of Monetary Policy Prepared for the Treasury and Civil Service Committee of the U.K. House of Commons." *Bank of Canada Review*, January 1981, pp. 18–23.

Orphanides, A. "Monetary Policy Evaluation with Noisy Information." Finance and Economics Discussion Paper Series, No 1998-50, Federal Reserve Board, 1998.

Sparks, Gordon R. "The Theory and Practice of Monetary Policy in Canada." In *Fiscal and Monetary Policy*, research coordinator John Sargent. Toronto: University of Toronto Press (for the Royal Commission on the Economic Union and Development Prospects for Canada), 1986, pp. 54–83.

Taylor, John B. "Discretion versus Policy Rules in Practice," Carnegie-Rochester Conference Series on Public Policy, 39, December 1993, pp. 195–214.

———. "The Robustness and Efficiency of Monetary Policy Rules as Guidelines for Interest Rate Setting by the European Central Bank." *Journal of Monetary Economics* 43 (1999), pp. 655–79.

Taylor, John B., ed. *Monetary Policy Rules.* Chicago: University of Chicago, 1999.

Thiessen, Gordon. "The Canadian Experience with Monetary Targeting." In *Central Bank Views on Monetary Targeting*, ed. P. Meek. New York: Federal Reserve Bank of New York, 1982.

White, W.R. "Alternative Monetary Targets and Control Instruments in Canada: Criteria for Choice." *Canadian Journal of Economics* 12 (November 1979), pp. 590–604.

CHAPTER NINETEEN

THE DEMAND FOR MONEY

After reading this chapter you should be able to
1. Provide a basis for the transactions and speculative demands for money
2. Explain the inventory–theoretic approach to modelling the demand for money
3. Demonstrate how the portfolio approach can be used to determine the demand for money
4. Summarize some of the empirical evidence on the demand for money
5. Differentiate between two forms of the quantity theory of money and describe how they are related
6. Demonstrate how the quantity theory can be used to predict the inflation rate

Previously, we examined the determination of the money supply and the role of the Bank of Canada and the chartered banks in the money creation process. With this chapter, we begin to examine the relationship between the money supply and aggregate economic activity. In particular, we want to analyze the channels through which changes in the quantity of money impinge on the aggregate demand for goods and services.

The nature and form of the demand for money are at the heart of a great deal of controversy over the role of money in determining economic activity and the ability of the monetary authorities to pursue their monetary policy objectives. The theory of the demand for money traces its lineage to classical and neoclassical economics, where it was assumed that money has no utility per se other than facilitating transactions. In other words, its only useful purpose was assumed to be as a medium of exchange. This purpose explained why individuals would want to hold a certain quantity of money at any given time. This concept was an integral part of the early quantity theory of money, which is explained later in this chapter.

Keynes identified three motives for holding money: the transactions motive, the precautionary motive, and the speculative motive. His transactions motive corresponds to the classical explanation of why people hold money: to use to make payments. Keynes's precautionary motive is the desire to hold money to meet unforeseen contingencies or opportunities. This motive, too, is closely related to the classical explanation. It is with his third reason for holding money, the speculative motive, that Keynes makes an important depar-

459

ture from his predecessors. The speculative motive is the desire to hold money as an asset or store of value.

In this chapter we will first consider the demand for money within the framework of the three Keynesian motives for holding it. This discussion will give us the necessary background to formulate the theory of the demand for money, and then we will see whether our theories are supported by the available empirical evidence. Then we will move on to the roles that money and monetary policy can play in the economy.

The Transactions Demand

transactions balances money held for transactions purposes

transactions demand the demand for money for transactions purposes

We all hold money balances to carry on ordinary day-to-day exchanges. Money held temporarily in the form of cash to meet day-to-day expenditures for goods and services between the intervals when money income is received has already been referred to as **transactions balances**. But what determines how much money the community will want to hold to satisfy what we call its **transactions demand**? As a first approximation, we can define five determinants of the transactions demand for money:

1.   the community's payment habits
2.   the degree of vertical integration of production
3.   the development of the financial system
4.   the level of income
5.   the rate of interest

PAYMENT HABITS   By the community's payment habits we mean the time pattern of its expenditures and the payment interval—that is, the frequency with which income payments are made. An individual who regularly receives income on the first day of each week has a payment interval of one week, or seven days. If, for example, an individual receives $140 per week on the beginning of the first day of each week and spends $20 on each of the seven days during the week, she holds from the beginning of the first day to the end of the last day of the week an average balance of $70. This pattern is illustrated by the solid lines in Figure 19–1.

Our assumption of a time pattern of expenditures where the individual spends her weekly money income at a constant rate ending with a zero money balance at the end of the last day of the week is an oversimplification. (The assumption of a fixed weekly income is also an oversimplification.) Under normal circumstances, rents and utilities are paid at the beginning of each payment interval, with the result that money balances decrease rapidly immediately after receipt of income and more slowly thereafter until they are exhausted just before the next receipt of income. Under these circumstances our straight-line curve in Figure 19–1 showing the time pattern of expenditures would be curvilinear.

Now let us assume that with no change in her income, the individual is paid on the first day of each month rather than each week. What effect will this have

FIGURE 19–1   **TRANSACTIONS DEMAND AND PAYMENT INTERVALS**

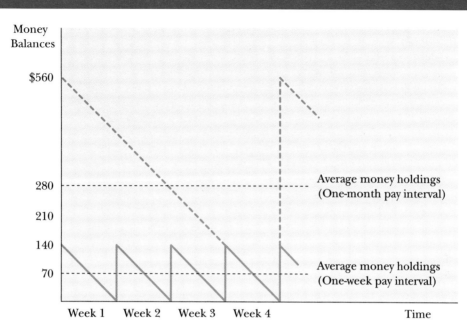

An individual has a monthly income of $560 and spends her money evenly over the payment interval ($20 per day) so as to have nothing left at the end. If she is paid $140 at the beginning of each week (a one-week pay interval, shown by the solid line) her average money balance is $70. If she instead is paid the full $560 at the beginning of each month (a one-month pay interval, shown by the dotted line) her average money balance increases to $280.

on her average money holdings if she spends her income at a constant rate throughout the month? This spending pattern is represented in Figure 19–1 by the broken straight-line curve. We have divided the month into four weeks for the sake of simplicity. With a constant expenditure pattern but a monthly instead of a weekly payment interval, her average money holdings increase from $70 to $280. Thus, all other things remaining the same, a simple lengthening of an individual's payment interval will result in larger average money holdings. The opposite, of course, is true for a shortening of the pay interval.

The individual's average money balances are also affected by changes in her expenditure pattern, as we have already noted. In Figure 19–2 we assume that the pay interval remains at one month (four weeks), but the time pattern of expenditures changes. The solid line shows income being spent at a constant rate over a four-week period, and the broken line shows the same income being spent over only a two-week period. In the first case the individual's average money holdings over the month are $280. In the second they are only $140, since during each day of the last two weeks in the month her actual money holdings are zero. Thus, if the individual spends her income so as to run out of money before the next payment receipt, her average money holdings during the month are smaller than they would be if they were equally distributed throughout the month.

FIGURE 19–2 TRANSACTIONS DEMAND AND EXPENDITURE PATTERNS

An individual has a monthly income of $560 paid in full at the beginning of each month. If she spends it evenly over the month so as to have no money left at the end (expenditures of $20 per day shown by the solid line), her average money holdings would be $280. If, however, she spends all her money evenly over the first two weeks (expenditures of $40 a day for the first two weeks shown by the dotted line) and spends nothing in the last two weeks, her average money balance would be only $140.

VERTICAL INTEGRATION   So far we have considered only the average money holdings of an individual. Let us now go back to Figure 19–1 and assume that it represents the total cash holdings of all individual income recipients in an economy. Let us go one step further and assume that all businesses are organized into one giant firm (they are vertically integrated) and that there is no government. In other words, on the first of each week, our giant business firm pays out wages, salaries, interest, and profits that are received by individuals during the same day. During the week, as individuals spend their income, this money flows back to the giant firm. Thus, while individuals run down their cash balances, those of the business are increased by exactly the same amount. The pattern of business cash balance, shown in Figure 19–3, is shown as the mirror image of cash balances held by all individuals.

Of course, it would have been more realistic to assume that the productive process is carried out by many firms, all of which hold transactions cash balances, rather than by one huge firm. It is reasonable to assume that the smaller the degree of vertical integration of production, the larger the total transactions balance held at any given time.

DEVELOPMENT OF THE FINANCIAL SYSTEM   The amount of transactions cash balances that individuals and firms are required to hold to meet their day-to-day exchanges will depend on the development of the financial system. Where this system is highly developed and borrowing to finance needed pur-

FIGURE 19–3   TRANSACTIONS AND VERTICAL INTEGRATIONS OF PRODUCTION

(a) INDIVIDUALS

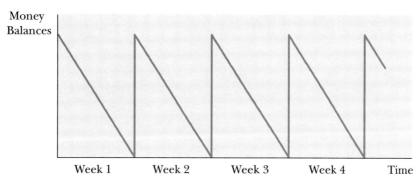

(b) BUSINESS

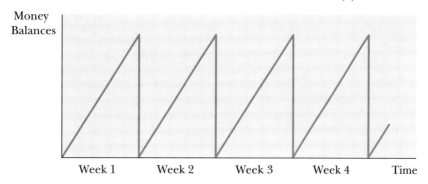

(a) The expenditure pattern for all the individuals in an economy as a whole is assumed to be the same as that in Figure 19–1. They receive their payments at the beginning of each week and spend them evenly so as to have no money left at the end of the week. (b) Business, assumed in this case to be one giant firm, has the opposite pattern. It makes all its payments (wages, etc.) at the beginning of the week and receives the money back evenly during the course of the week as the individuals spend their money balances.

chases is both easy and economical, businesses and individuals will be able to facilitate their purchases by holding smaller transactions balances. They will also hold smaller balances if nonmonetary interest-bearing assets exist that can readily, and at small cost, be transformed into a medium of exchange. We can say that, other things being equal, the more highly developed the financial system, the lower the transactions demand for money.

INCOME LEVEL   The determinants of the amount of transactions cash balances that we have discussed so far—the community's payments habits, the degree of vertical integration of production, and the development of the financial system—can be considered to change only slowly over time. Therefore, we must look elsewhere to explain variations in the level of transactions balances

FIGURE 19–4   TRANSACTIONS DEMAND AND INCOME

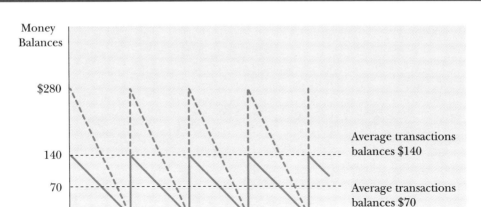

An individual is paid at the first of the week and spends her pay evenly so as to have no money left at the end of the week. If she has an income of $280 per week (the dotted lines) she would have an average transactions balance of $140; with an income of $140 per week (the solid lines), her average transactions balance would be only $70.

in the short run. Two determinants listed earlier remain to be considered: the level of income and the rate of interest. Let us assume for the moment that interest rates, along with all the other determinants of the transactions demand for money, except income, remain constant.

In Figure 19–4 the solid lines show an individual receiving $140 at the beginning of each week and spending this income evenly over the week. The broken lines show the same individual after weekly income has increased to $280 per week. The figure shows that an increase in income is accompanied by an increase in the individual's average money balances (the transactions demand for money). With income of $140 paid on the first day of the week, the average transactions balance is $70, while with an increase to $280 also paid at the beginning of the week, the average balance for the week rises to $140. If we add to these money balances those of business, then the total average transactions demand for money is $140 in the first case and $280 in the second.

An alternative and more usual way to show the relationship between the total transactions demand for money in a community and changes in the level of income is depicted in Figure 19–5.

Economists assume that the demand for nominal money balances varies proportionately with the price level, since what matters to individuals and firms is the purchasing power of their nominal money balances (the money in their pockets). For example, if the price of all goods and services were to double, all other things remaining unchanged, the amount of money needed to purchase a given quantity of goods and services would also double, and so would the nominal quantity of money demanded. Individuals who concern themselves with the nominal or dollar amount of their money balances, rather than with the purchasing power it represents, are said to suffer from **money illusion.** We

money illusion
when individuals mistakenly care about nominal variables rather than about real variables

FIGURE 19–5 TRANSACTIONS DEMAND FOR MONEY

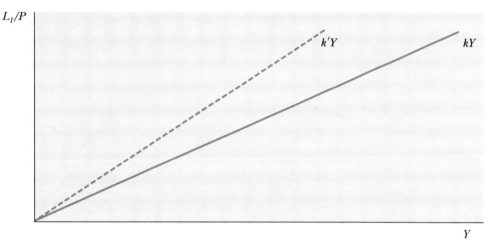

The positive slope of the transactions demand curve (the solid line) shows that as real output (Y) increases, the money demanded for transactions purposes (L_1/P) also increases. k is that proportion of real output that people want to hold for transactions purposes. If k increases (to k') then the transactions demand by the community increases for each level of income (as shown by the dotted line).

www.

real balances *the purchasing power of money balances; nominal balances divided by the price level*

nominal balances *the nominal amount of money held by individuals*

velocity of circulation *the number of times money is turned over for transactions purposes in any given period*

assume that individuals' demand for money is a demand for real balances and that they are therefore free of money illusion.

Since real money and real income are nothing more than their nominal values divided by an appropriate price index (P), we can readily specify the demand for money in either real terms (the demand for **real balances**) or in nominal terms (the demand for **nominal balances**). In Figure 19–5 we demonstrate the demand for real balances. Real output, Y, is shown on the horizontal axis, and the amount of real transactions balances demanded, L_1/P, is shown on the vertical axis. The transactions demand curve for money, kY, is linear and slopes up from left to right. By drawing a straight-line curve through the origin, we assume that the amount of transactions balances demanded is the same proportion of real income no matter what the level of income. What this proportion (expressed by the slope of the line) will be depends on all the determinants, other than income, of the transactions demand for money. The upward slope of the line indicates the community will want to hold larger balances as real income increases. The equation of the demand curve for transactions balances is

(19.1)
$$\frac{L_1}{P} = kY$$

where L_1 is the nominal money supply available for transactions balances (so L_1/P are real transactions balances), Y represents real output, and k is the proportion of real output that the country wants (or needs) to hold as transactions balances; k is also the slope of the curve, and $k = L_1/PY$. Later we will show that k is the reciprocal of the **velocity of circulation**, which is the number of times money is turned over for transactions purposes in any given period. A linear demand curve, which assumes k remains constant, also assumes a constant velocity of circulation. An increase in velocity as a result of, for instance, a change in payment habits, the vertical integration of business, or a change in the financial system will cause the demand curve to become flatter—for example, if the broken demand curve $(k'Y)$ changes to the solid demand curve (kY) in Figure 19–5.

INTEREST RATES   We now turn to the last item on our list of the determinants of the demand for transactions balances—the rate of interest. Economists are still uncertain as to the effect of the rate of interest on the demand for transactions balances. We could make a theoretical case to show why changes in the rate of interest may affect the demand for transactions balances. For example, assume that an individual is paid $1000 (in real terms) on the first day of each month and spends his income evenly throughout the month so that his saving per month is zero. This pattern is shown in Figure 19–6(a). For convenience, we again assume that the month consists of four weeks. In the middle of the first week, the individual will have spent $125 and will be holding $875 to meet his purchases during the three and a half weeks left in the month. In the middle of the last week, he will have spent $875 and will be holding $125 to meet his needs during the remaining half-week in the month. The average transactions demand for the individual is $500 for the month as a whole.

If the individual requires $250 in each of the four weeks during the month to meet his purchases of goods and services, he holds $750 that he does not require during the first week, $500 during the second, and $250 during the third. On the first day of the month, therefore, he can use the $750 he does not require to purchase an interest-bearing asset. On the first day of each subsequent week he can redeem $250 of his earning assets to meet his weekly requirement. His average cash transactions balances will then be reduced from $500 to $125 for the month, as shown in Figure 19–6(b). Part (c) of the figure shows his earning asset holdings during the month, the average of which is $375 for the month.

Whether or not an individual behaves in the manner we have outlined depends on several factors. The financial system must be sufficiently developed to allow him or her to buy and sell interest-earning assets in the very short run. The individual must weigh the cost of buying and selling and the inconvenience of frequent entry to and exit from the securities market against the net interest he or she can earn from holding interest-bearing securities. The same is true for firms. However, large corporations with millions of dollars not immediately needed for transactions purposes will be more inclined to put money into interest-earning assets if a profit can be realized than will be an individual who has only a few hundred dollars. Moreover, the costs involved are lower, and entry to and exit from the securities market is much easier, when the amounts involved are substantial. With a given cost of participating in the money and capital markets, switches by the community from idle transactions balances into interest-bearing securities are probably influenced by the rate of interest, particularly at the higher levels.

FIGURE 19–6   **TRANSACTIONS DEMAND AND THE RATE OF INTEREST**

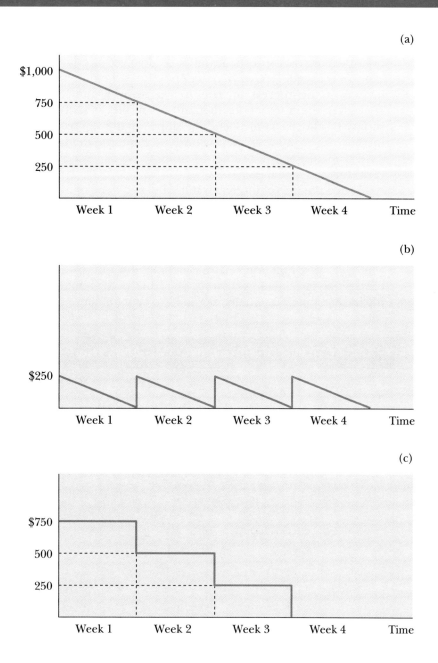

(a) If an individual were to receive $1000 at the beginning of each month and spend it evenly ($250 per week), holding it all for transactions purposes, his transactions balance would be a straight line, as shown. (b) When the month is broken down into four weeks, however, it can be seen that he only needs to hold $250 at the beginning of each week to satisfy his transactions demand. (c) If he puts the excess money holdings (above $250 per week) into assets to earn interest, his asset holdings will have this step-like pattern as he invests $750 at the beginning of the month and draws out $250 at the start of each week for transactions purposes.

The relationships among the level of income, the rate of interest, and the transactions demand for money for the economy as a whole are shown in Figure 19–7. Here, two transactions demand curves for money are shown at two different levels of income. When, for example, the rate of interest is below 5 percent, the community will not switch from cash to interest-bearing securities because the costs and inconvenience involved are larger than the gains that can be realized. Above 5 percent some switching will take place and will increase as the interest rate rises to progressively higher levels. Above the 5 percent level, the transactions demand for money is said to be interest elastic, as shown by the backward-bending slope of the curve. Thus, given a level of income, Y_1, at interest rates below 5 percent, the demand for transactions balances remains at OA; at interest rates above 5 percent, it declines. At 10 percent, for instance, it is OA'.

When the rate of interest is included as a determinant, the equation for the transactions demand for money previously shown is modified and becomes

(19.1a) $$\frac{L_1}{P} = f(Y, i)$$

where $f(\cdot)$ is a function relating income and interest rates to the demand for transactions balances. As before, the other determinants are not shown explicitly in the equation and are assumed to remain constant.

FIGURE 19–7   TRANSACTIONS DEMAND, INCOME AND THE RATE OF INTEREST

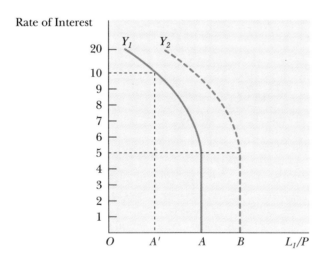

Shown are two transactions demand for money curves for two different levels of income (the solid line and the dotted line, with $Y_1 < Y_2$), where L_1/P is the amount of money demanded for transactions purposes. When the interest rate is below 5 percent, no one will switch cash into interest-bearing assets because the costs exceed the benefits. Above 5 percent, as the interest rate goes up, the transactions demand goes down because increasing gains can be made from assets. At the 10 percent rate of interest, for instance, the transactions demand for the level of income Y_1 has shrunk to OA'.

The Transactions Demand for Cash: The Inventory–Theoretic Approach

It is possible to view the decision to hold money for transactions purposes in terms of an inventory control problem—that is, the inventory is the medium of exchange.[1] In this case, the principles determining the optimum amount of inventory of a commodity should apply to determining the optimum amount of money held for transactions purposes. This leads to the **inventory–theoretic approach** to money demand.

inventory–theoretic approach *the idea that the demand for money is based on individuals desire to hold an inventory of money for transaction purposes*

Let us assume that at the beginning of each period, say a month, an individual receives his or her income in the form of a nonchequable savings deposit with a nonbank financial intermediary, which in our example is assumed not to be part of the money supply and demand. The amount of the deposit is T, and interest received on the deposit is equal to i per period. The individual's total expenditures during the month are also equal to T. These expenditures are perfectly foreseen and occur at a steady rate over the month. The individual makes evenly spaced visits to the nonbank intermediary during the month, withdrawing the same amount of cash, W, each visit. The total number of visits, and therefore withdrawals, are equal to T/W.

opportunity cost *the revenue or benefit forgone by using a resource in one way rather than in its best alternative use*

The individual bears certain costs by holding cash (that is, money) rather than interest-bearing deposits with a nonbank financial intermediary. An optimizing individual will attempt to minimize these costs. What are these costs? It is evident that by holding cash we forgo the interest that would be received by holding deposits. This forgone interest is an **opportunity cost** for the individual. The average cash holdings during the month are equal to $W/2$, and assuming that withdrawals are equally spaced, leaving a zero balance at the end of the period, the loss of interest as a result of holding this amount of cash, rather than interest-bearing deposits with a nonbank intermediary, is given by:

$$i \frac{W}{2}$$

brokerage fees *charges made by intermediaries for cash withdrawal, transportation costs to and from the intermediary, and the subjective cost of having to make regular trips to get cash*

In addition to the interest cost of holding cash rather than deposits, there are noninterest costs (called **brokerage fees**). These include the charge made by the intermediary for each withdrawal, the cost of transportation to and from the intermediary, and the subjective cost in the form of the inconvenience of having to make regular trips to get cash. We assume that the brokerage fee for each withdrawal is the same and equal to b. Since the number of withdrawals during the month is T/W, the total noninterest cost to the individual is given by:

$$b \frac{T}{W}$$

---

1. See William J. Baumol, "The Transactions Demand for Cash: An Inventory Theoretic Approach," *Quarterly Journal of Economics* 66 (November 192), pp. 545–56. See also James Tobin, "The Interest-Elasticity of the Transactions Demand for Cash," *Review of Economics and Statistic 38* (August 1956), pp. 241–47; and Robert W. Clower and Peter W. Howitt, "The Transactions Theory of the Demand for Money: A Reconsideration," *Journal of Political Economy* 86 (June 1978), pp. 449–66.

The total cost, TC, to the individual for holding an inventory of cash to meet transactions needs may be written as:

$$(19.2) \qquad TC = i(W/2) + b(T/W)$$

As the number of withdrawals increases, the brokerage cost increases while the interest cost decreases. The optimal number of withdrawals that minimizes the total cost of holding cash occurs when the increase in brokerage fees, as the result of an additional withdrawal, is just offset by the reduction in the interest cost as a result of this withdrawal. To find the optimal value of W that minimizes the total cost of holding cash, we differentiate TC with respect to W, set the derivative equal to zero, and solve for W:

$$(19.3) \qquad \delta TC/\delta W = (i/2) - b(T/W^2) = 0, \text{ or}$$

$$i/2 = b(T/W^2)$$

so that

$$(19.4) \qquad W = \sqrt{\frac{2bT}{i}}$$

The amount of the individual's average cash holdings over the month is $W/2$, which we can express as

$$(19.5) \qquad \frac{W}{2} = \frac{1}{2}\sqrt{\frac{2bT}{i}} = \sqrt{\frac{bT/2}{i}}$$

This equation tells us that given the price level and fixed brokerage fees, the individual will minimize his or her cost by holding average cash balances in proportion to the square root of the average transaction value and in inverse proportion to the square root of the rate of interest. This means that the higher the rate of interest paid on financial assets other than money (i.e., the greater the opportunity or interest cost of holding money), the greater will be the number of withdrawals and, hence, the lower the average cash balances held. In other words, the transactions demand for money is inversely related to the rate of interest.[2]

The brokerage fee (the noninterest cost) also plays an important role in determining average cash balances held. From equation 19.5 you can see that if there was no brokerage fee (if $b = 0$), then no cash would be held. Since there would be no cost for changing deposits into cash, the individual would synchronize cash withdrawals with the purchase of goods and services. The individual would make a withdrawal every time he or she wished to make a purchase, so cash would be held only in the brief interval between withdrawal and purchase. Although in the absence of a brokerage fee the individual would hold no cash, in reality there is always some cost to converting deposits into

---

2. From equation 19.5 it follows that the interest rate elasticity of demand is –0.5. For example, a quadrupling of i leads to a halving of $W/2$. Conversely, because the price level and real income vary directly with T and the implied elasticity of T is +0.5, a quadrupling of either prices or real income leads to a quadrupling of T, which in turn leads to a doubling of $W/2$.

cash, and therefore *b* takes a value greater than zero. The higher *b* is, the fewer withdrawals will be made by the optimizing individual. Given the same size of initial deposit, *T*, the fewer the withdrawals, *T/W*, the larger will be the cash balances, *W/2*, held by the individual. Intuitively, what we are saying is that if the cost of making a withdrawal is high, the individual will want to hold more cash and make fewer withdrawals rather than hold less cash and make more withdrawals.

economies of scale when output increases proportionately more than inputs increase; if inputs double and output more than doubles

The square root rule outlined above suggests that there are **economies of scale** in the use of cash, or more generally the use of money. Equation 19.5 states that the demand for money, *W/2*, rises at a less than proportional rate to the volume of transactions, *T*. Since a close relationship exists between an individual's level of income and the volume of his or her transactions, the equation also shows that the individual's transactions demand for money increases at a less than proportional rate to an increase in income.

Two important implications arise from these economies of scale. The first is that the more that total transactions—and therefore income—are concentrated in a few hands, the smaller the total transactions demand for money. This means that not only the level of income, but also the distribution of income, should be considered a determinant of the transactions demand for money.

The second implication of economies of scale in holding money has to do with the effectiveness of monetary policy. Let us assume that the square root rule applies and that the monetary authorities double the amount of money. Some resources are unemployed, and all the additional money is used to purchase goods and services. Then, with the price level and the interest rate held constant, for the doubled money supply to be absorbed, real transactions will have to quadruple. These results can be shown as

(19.6)
$$T = \frac{2i}{b}\left(\frac{W}{2}\right)^2$$

Without economies of scale in holding money and under similar circumstances, the doubled money supply would be absorbed by real transactions increasing only in the same proportion. Thus, the larger the economies of scale in holding money, the more effective is monetary policy in periods of unemployment, because real transactions have to increase more to absorb any increase in the money supply. If, however, increases in the money supply are accompanied by higher prices, interest costs, and brokerage fees, the change in real transactions will be more in proportion to the change in the money supply.

The Precautionary Demand

precautionary balances money held to meet unpredictable increases in expenditures and unpredictable delays in receipts

Persons and businesses hold money in the form of cash as a precaution essentially because of the uncertainty of their future receipts and expenditures. In other words, **precautionary balances** are held to meet unpredictable increases in expenditures and unpredictable delays in receipts. For example, a business may be confronted with having to pay a higher price for a material necessary

BOX 19–1   THE CUBE ROOT RULE

We've seen how the demand for money can be viewed in terms of an inventory model. If we extend this analysis to other models of inventory behaviour, we can arrive at another specification determining the demand for real balances. For example, Miller and Orr (1966) and Milbourne (1987) demonstrate that money holdings will fluctuate according to a cube root rule, which sets upper and lower bounds. In these models, money is seen as a "buffer stock." Individuals will replenish their money holdings to bring them back to their average value if they hit the lower bound; and

they will invest in interest-earning assets, thereby reducing their money holdings if they hit the upper bound. The following figure demonstrates the path of money holdings.

Average money holdings are denoted by the dashed line. If actual money holdings fall to the lower bound, individuals go to the bank and withdraw additional funds to take them back to the average. If actual money holdings rise to the upper bound, individuals revisit the bank and reduce their money holdings. The actual path of an individual's money balances will fluctuate within these bounds.

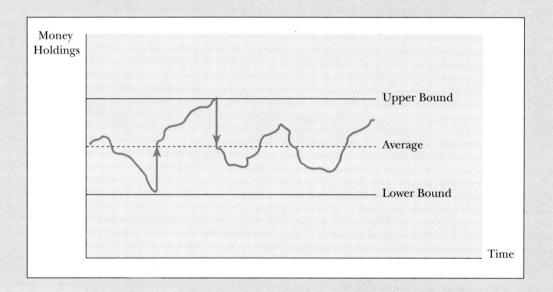

to its productive process, or it may find that an important customer to whom it has extended credit has gone bankrupt. To protect itself from such unforeseeable increases in its expenditures or losses in its receipts, it will hold cash as a margin of safety. At the same time a business may hold cash to allow it to take advantage of unexpected future bargains that will reduce its costs and increase its profits.

Money in the form of cash may also be held as a margin of safety to reduce what has been described as "the linkage of risks." For example, a man with very little cash takes a car trip from Ontario to British Columbia. In Alberta he is arrested for speeding and, since he does not have enough cash to pay his fine, is thrown into jail. But his troubles are only beginning. After the humiliating experience of telephoning a friend to send him money, he finds that he must remain in Alberta for several days to appear in court. As a result he arrives back at his job several days late, and his employer fires him. Not only has he lost a few days' pay, but also his job—one misfortune leads to another. A business can have the same kind of experience. By holding cash as a margin of safety, individuals and businesses are able to weaken the linkage of risks so that one misfortune need not be followed by a host of others. Alternatives to holding cash are the ability to obtain credit or the holding of "near-moneys," which can be readily converted into cash. While credit and "near-moneys" may be substituted for precautionary cash holdings, in the final analysis cash becomes a prerequisite.

Most individuals and firms hold money as a margin of safety to maintain a certain financial respectability. In our earlier example, for instance, the individual who had insufficient cash to pay his speeding fine suffered the ignominy of asking a friend to send money to him. Since the stigma attached to borrowing money has now generally disappeared, individuals and businesses today rely more on their overall wealth holdings rather than on their money holdings to give them desired financial respectability.

Changes in the amount of money held for precautionary purposes are usually considered to depend on changes in income. We can assume that as individuals' incomes rise, their "obligations" also increase, and consequently their need for larger precautionary money balances. Against this assumption is the possibility that at higher income levels, it becomes easier to borrow money, thus obviating the necessity of holding large money balances. The usual assumption, however, is that changes in precautionary balances are a positive function of the level of income.

The precautionary demand for money may also be expected to vary inversely with the rate of interest. At high rates of interest individuals and businesses may be willing to assume the greater risk of holding a smaller precautionary balance in exchange for the higher interest rate that can be earned by holding interest-bearing assets.

Although the precautionary demand can be formally distinguished from the transactions demand, as we have done above, for analytical purposes the two now are usually considered together. This merging involves describing only one function called the transactions demand for money, which includes the precautionary demand, and relating this function positively to the level of income and to some extent inversely to the rate of interest.

The Speculative or Asset Demand for Money

We have already noted that classical economists assumed that individuals would not hold more money than they needed to meet their transactions (including precautionary) requirements. It was considered irrational to hold idle money that could be invested to earn interest. But Keynes argued that if individuals expect the rate of interest to rise in the near future, holding idle money balances in excess of those required for transactions (and precautionary) purposes is eminently rational. When individuals hold money rather than bonds, they are "speculating" that the rate of interest will rise in the near future and that the price of bonds will fall.

We have already seen that the prices of marketable bonds rise when interest rates fall, and vice versa. Hence, the possibility exists of making a capital gain or incurring a capital loss by holding bonds. Keynes assumed that the choice between holding money and holding bonds is determined by individuals' expectations about future changes in the rate of interest, and that individuals hold money because they speculate that interest rates will rise in the future (future bond prices will be lower).

According to Keynes, individuals view the current rate of interest as high or low because they have a normal range of interest rates in mind to which they can compare the current rate. An individual's conception of the normal range of interest rates is based on recent experience. If rates have fluctuated from, say, 5 percent to 8 percent, an increase to 10 percent may be regarded as a temporary aberration and a return to the normal range will be expected. Alternatively, a drop in the rate to, say, 2 percent may be regarded as abnormally low and an increase to the normal range will be expected in the near future. Keynes assumed that when current rates diverge from what is assumed to be the normal range, individuals always expect that the rates will tend to return to the normal range in the near future. Individuals who see current rates rise (or fall) but expect future rates to be lower (or higher) are said to have inelastic interest rate expectations.

When the current rate of interest rises above the normal range of rates and an individual expects it to decline in the future, that person will shift from money to bonds to realize expected capital gains. Alternatively, when the current rate of interest falls below the normal range of rates, the individual—to avoid expected capital losses and to be in a "cash position" to purchase bonds when they are expected to be "cheap"—will shift from bonds to money. Keynes assumed that each individual, according to his or her expectations, will make a complete shift and hold either bonds or money. At any given time, however, different individuals will have a different view of what is the normal range of interest rates, and therefore, a different expectation about the future direction of rates. The higher the current rate of interest, the larger the number of individuals who will expect interest rates to fall (bond prices to rise) and who will switch out of money into bonds. Alternatively, the lower the current rate of interest, the larger the number of individuals who will expect interest rates to rise (bond prices to fall) and who will hold only money. It follows that, taking all individuals together, the community's total demand for speculative balances is inversely related to the rate of interest.

speculative balances money held to finance a speculative opportunity in securities markets

The relationship between the demand for **speculative balances** and the rate of interest, which Keynes called liquidity preference, is shown by the speculative demand or liquidity preference curve (see Figure 19–8). The equation expressing this relationship is

(19.7)
$$\frac{L_2}{P} = l(i)$$

The community's speculative demand for money in Figure 19–8 is drawn assuming that individuals have, on the average, a fixed concept of the normal range of interest rates. A change in their concept of the normal range of rates

FIGURE 19–8 SPECULATIVE DEMAND FOR MONEY

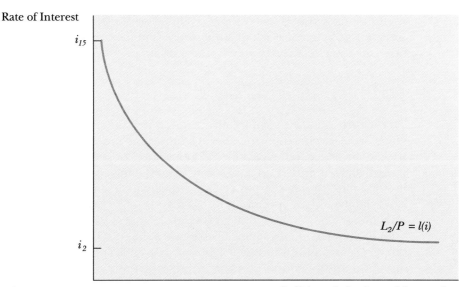

L₂/P (speculative demand for money)

This curve shows the speculative demand for money (L_2/P) at each rate of interest (i). As i goes up, L_2/P falls until i_{15}, where there is no speculative demand for money because everyone feels i is above its normal range and will fall (thereby giving capital gains to assets other than money). When i gets very low, everyone expects i to rise, giving capital losses on assets (therefore people switch all their wealth into money). This situation is the liquidity trap.

liquidity trap *a situation in which interest rates (bond prices) get so low (high) that everyone expects them to rise (fall); hence, no one will want to hold bonds (because of capital losses) and the speculative demand for money will become infinitely sensitive*

would be reflected by a shift in the curve. The curve is drawn to show that when the rate of interest reaches 15 percent, all individual expectations will converge; all individuals assume the rate of interest to be above its normal range and expect that it can only fall. The community will therefore hold no speculative balances. In reality, the curve will probably always lie a little to the right of the vertical axis because individuals distributing their wealth between cash and bonds probably prefer to hold a fixed minimum in the form of speculative balances rather than invest it all in bonds, even at extremely high rates of interest.

While the demand for speculative balances curve in its extreme left portion is perfectly interest inelastic at rates above 15 percent, as shown in Figure 19–8, in its extreme right portion it is perfectly elastic at an interest rate of 2 percent. The horizontal portion of the curve is what Keynes described as the **liquidity trap**. It implies that some low rate of interest exists, in our example 2 percent, below which no additional money will be lent. Any amount of money that might be created by the banking system, as well as any amount that individuals can save after meeting their current demands for consumption, is added to their speculative balances. At a very low rate of interest, individuals will feel that holding bonds will mean almost certain capital loss as interest rates return to their normal range. The assumption is that interest rates are so low that the consensus of expectations is that they cannot fall any lower; there is a floor to the rate of interest. Although the existence of a liquidity trap is doubtful, except perhaps during extended periods of deep economic depression, as we shall see in later chapters, the liquidity trap has important implications for the effectiveness of monetary policy.

Risk and Portfolio Choice

Viewing the choice to hold money from a portfolio perspective has led to an alternative explanation of the demand for money independent of the Keynesian one-sided expectational behaviour. As we have seen, Keynes maintained that, although an individual is uncertain about the future course of interest rates, he or she has certain expectations about its direction and acts accordingly. If the expectation is that the rate will rise, the individual will hold only money; however, if, the expectation is that it will fall, only bonds will be held in the individual's financial asset portfolio. But because Keynes also maintained that, at any given time, different individuals hold different expectations about the future course of interest rates, the entire community of individuals will, at any given time, hold both bonds and money. In other words, given this Keynesian assumption, it is possible to draw a total speculative demand for money curve such as in Figure 19–8, even though it is not possible for any one individual.

James Tobin has shown that portfolio choice need not be an "either/or" decision for an individual; he or she can at any given time hold both bonds and money.[3] Tobin's theory is based on an individual's behaviour toward risk, while Keynes's is based on uncertainty and expectations.

The total return, R, that an individual receives from holding bonds and money depends on the proportion, λ, of his or her portfolio held in bonds; the rate of interest, i, paid on bonds; and the capital gain or loss, s, he or she may receive when selling bonds. In addition, the individual's total return will depend on the gain or loss, m, from holding money (in proportion $(1 - \lambda)$, resulting from a change in the price level, which affects the purchasing power of money. We may show the individual's total return as

(19.8) $$R = \lambda(i + s) + (1 - \lambda)m$$

The individual's expected return is

(19.9) $$E(R) = \mu = \lambda E(i) + [\lambda E(s) + (1 - \lambda)E(m)]$$

where $E(i)$, $E(s)$, and $E(m)$ denote the expected or mean values of the rate of interest, the capital gain on bonds, and the capital gain on money, respectively. If we assume that the expected capital gain on bonds is zero and that the

---

3. See James Tobin, "Liquidity Preference as Behavior Towards Risk," *Review of Economic Studies*, February 8, pp. 65–86.

expected return on money is known with certainty to be m, then the expected total return is

(19.10) $$\mu = \lambda E(i) + (1 - \lambda)\, m$$

The individual's total expected return, μ, depends on the rate of return on money, the proportion of his or her asset portfolio held in bonds, and the expected rate of interest received from holding these bonds.

The individual's risk in holding bonds and money may be measured by the standard deviation or variability of the return from holding bonds, σ_B, and the standard deviation of the gain from holding money, σ_M, respectively. Since we assume the return to money is known to be m with certainty (which implies the price level remains constant), there is no risk to holding money, so $\sigma_M = 0$. The total risk assumed by holding a portfolio of bonds and money is therefore

(19.11) $$\sigma = \lambda \sigma_B$$

Let us assume that our individual is risk averse. She considers risk to be a disutility, but the expected return from her portfolio to be a utility. With given wealth holdings, by switching from money into bonds she will increase both her risk and her expected return. If her utility from an increment of return exceeds her disutility from an increment of risk, she will be induced to switch from money to bonds. She will be induced to increase the proportion of bonds in her portfolio only as long as by so doing her marginal utility of expected return exceeds her marginal disutility of risk.

The behaviour of a risk averter is shown by a set of indifference curves, I_1, I_2, and I_3 in Figure 19–9. Each curve shows the various combinations of expected return and risk that give the individual a given level of utility. Successively higher curves (moving to the left) represent successively higher levels of utility. This relationship is easy to see if you hold portfolio risk constant and consider utility for different levels of expected portfolio returns. Higher expected returns lead to higher satisfaction; hence, utility rises as one moves to indifference curves to the left. Each indifference curve is upward sloping, indicating that the individual requires a higher expected return to compensate for an increase in risk. Each indifference curve is drawn convex downward because we assume that the individual is subject to diminishing marginal utility of expected return and increasing marginal disutility of risk.

Now we turn to Figure 19–10. Consider the upper quadrant, where we begin to look at the ability of the investor to trade risk for expected return. Starting at the origin, where no bonds and only money are held, a movement to the right along the horizontal axis represents a switch from money into bonds—the proportion of bonds in the portfolio rises. As the investor holds more and more bonds, portfolio risk rises. If all wealth is held in the form of bonds, then portfolio risk is equal to the risk on bonds, $\sigma = \sigma_B$ (since $\lambda = 1$). The expected return on the portfolio at this level of risk is $\mu = E(i)$ (again, since $\lambda = 1$). Point A presents the combination of risk and expected return when only bonds are held in the portfolio (assuming $E(i) > m$).

Now consider what would happen if all wealth were held as money. The expected return on the portfolio would be $\mu = m$, known with certainty, and the

FIGURE 19–9   TASTES FOR EXPECTED RETURN AND RISK

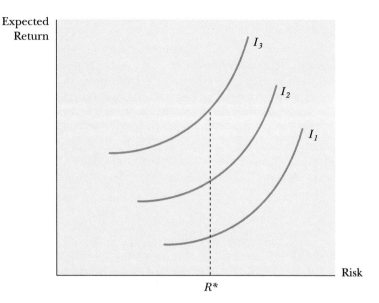

For a given level of risk R^*, higher levels of expected return provide greater satisfaction. Indifference curves increase in utility as one moves from the right to the left (from I_1 to I_2 to I_3).

risk to the portfolio would be zero. Point *B* plots this combination of risk and expected return. Now join points *A* and *B*. This line demonstrates the rate at which the investor can trade risk for expected return. To enhance portfolio return above the known rate related to holding only money, the investor will have to hold more bonds—thereby raising portfolio risk.

Figure 19–10 also provides a way for us to determine the demand for money (which is, after all, what we're after). Given a fixed level of wealth, we can plot a line in the lower quadrant of Figure 19–10 to determine the composition of the portfolio—the proportion of wealth held in bonds and the proportion held in money. If all wealth is held in the form of bonds, portfolio risk is equal to bond risk. Move along the horizontal axis to the level of risk associated with point *A*. Now measure down in the lower quadrant, stopping at the fixed level of wealth. Point *C* labels this point; only bonds are held in the portfolio, so all wealth is held in the form of bonds. This suggests that if we begin at the origin and measure down, we are measuring bond holdings in the portfolio.

Continue to consider Figure 19–10 and ask, what would portfolio risk be if only money were held? You should have no difficulty seeing that portfolio risk is zero at this point. (The return to holding money was assumed to be known, so there is no risk). If we begin at the fixed level of wealth, W_0, and measure up until we hit the origin, *O*, we measure money holdings in the portfolio. Now join points *O* and *C*. This line provides information on the composition of the portfolio. Measuring down from the origin measures bond holdings, while

FIGURE 19–10 RISK, EXPECTED RETURN, AND PORTFOLIO BALANCE

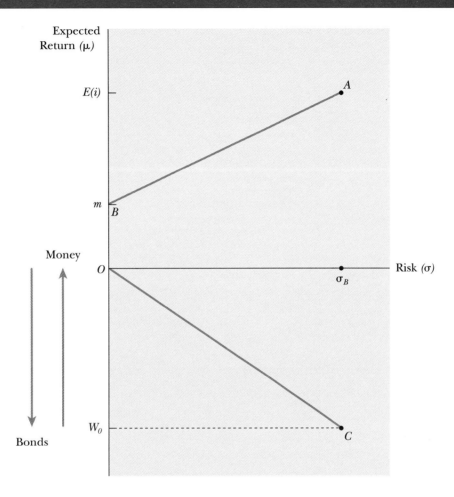

If no bonds are held in the portfolio, the expected return to the portfolio is known with certainty to be μ. In this case portfolio risk is zero and all wealth is held as money. If only bonds are held in the portfolio the expected return would be $E(i)$ and risk would equal σ_B.

The lower quadrant allows us to measure the composition of our portfolio. Given fixed wealth of W_0, if all wealth is held in bonds, we measure down from the origin to W_0. If all wealth is held as money, we measure up from W_0 to measure our money holdings. Points along OC provide information on the demand for money and bonds.

measuring up from the fixed level of wealth measures money holdings. (Alternatively, we could simply subtract bond holdings from the fixed level of wealth to determine money holdings.)

All that is left is to determine the individual's optimal portfolio. Figure 19–11 presents this information, blending the indifference curves of Figure 19–9 with the framework of Figure 19–10. The investor optimizes when the rate at which he is willing to trade expected return for risk (the slope of his indifference curves) is equal to the rate at which he is able to trade expected return

FIGURE 19-11   **OPTIMIZATION**

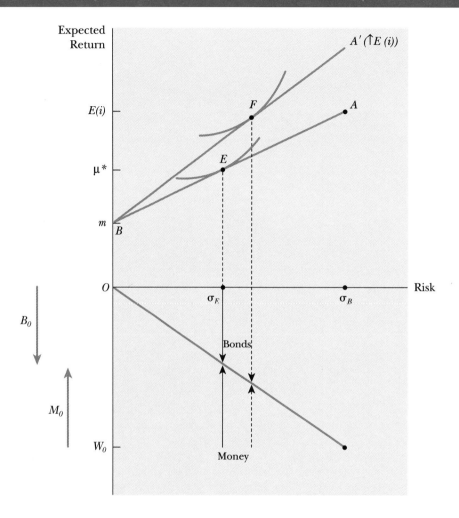

An investor maximizes his utility at point *E*. The expected return on the portfolio is μ* while the risk of the port-folio is σ_E. At point *E* this investor holds both money and bonds. Total wealth, W_0, is equal to money holdings, M_0, plus bond holdings B_0.

An increase in the expected return on bonds rotates *AB* to *A'B* and the new optimum is at point *F* (if tastes do not change), leading the investor to hold a greater proportion of his wealth as bonds, and the demand for money falls from M_0. This is how we derive the demand for money in the portfolio balance model.

for risk (the slope of line *AB*). When the investor has maximized his utility at point *E*, portfolio risk is denoted by σ_E with the expected return on the port-folio given by μ. Total wealth, W_0, is distributed between money and bonds, with M_0 money and B_0 bonds in the portfolio.

If the expected rate of interest on bonds increases and if tastes remain unchanged (so the slopes of the indifference curves don't change), curve *AB* rotates upward to *A'B*. The individual's equilibrium point now shifts to *F*, which is to the right of E and therefore represents a higher proportion of bonds in his portfolio. In other words, at higher interest rates our individual switches out of money and, conversely, at lower interest rates he switches into money. You can see this in the lower quadrant, where proportionately more bonds are held after the investor has reoptimized. Hence, Tobin arrives at the same conclusion as Keynes. Tobin, however, shows that the individual need not make an either/or decision, but may at any time hold a portfolio consisting of both bonds and money.

It must, however, be pointed out that Tobin's conclusions depend on the assumptions we make about the individual's preference map. For example, at higher interest rates, the individual's behaviour toward risk may change. As the expected return increases, the individual may feel wealthier and may be willing to assume proportionately more risk. This behaviour would be represented by steeper indifference curves. As a result, the new equilibrium position may lie to the left of E and the individual may hold a smaller (rather than a larger) proportion of bonds in his portfolio. In this case the relationship between the rate of interest and the demand for money is opposite to that postulated by Keynes.

Tobin's analysis of behaviour toward risk is easily extended to include not only bonds and money, but also other assets. It can also be used to show that under certain conditions the individual can reduce his risk for any given expected return by portfolio diversification.

The Total Demand for Money

We have defined three separate demands for money—the transactions demand, the precautionary demand, and the speculative or asset demand. The transactions and precautionary demands have been combined and expressed by the equation $L_1/P = kY$. The speculative demand has been expressed by the equation $L_2/P = f(Y, i)$. Combining these two equations, we have an equation describing the total demand for money

(19.13)
$$\frac{M_d}{P} = kY + f(Y, i)$$

If we recognize that the rate of interest also determines the transactions demand [in the form $g(Y, i)$], equation 19.13 can be written:

(19.13a)
$$\frac{M_d}{P} = g(Y, i) + f(Y, i)$$

or more generally

(19.13b)
$$\frac{M_d}{P} = l(Y, i)$$

Equation 19.13b can be amended to explicitly include total wealth, W, as a variable, and by adding a variable, say X, to represent all the other factors that may influence the demand for money. Our equation for the total demand for money now becomes

(19.13c) $$\frac{M_d}{P} = L(Y, i, W, X)$$

Represented by X are such diverse factors as the distribution of income, price expectations, the degree of uncertainty about business forecasts, the community's payment habits (which change when there are postal strikes), the degree of vertical integration of production, the development of the financial system, and the desired distribution of the various wealth forms. Traditionally, most of these factors have been considered to change only slowly over time, or wealth holders' reactions to changes in them have been considered as being very slow. As a result they have been regarded as playing an insignificant role in determining the demand for money. More recently, with the increased attention being given to the portfolio approach, many of these factors are now being considered as having more than just a long-term effect on the demand for money. For example, since changes in the expected rate of inflation are incorporated in nominal interest rates, they affect the demand for money. If the rate of inflation is expected to rise, corresponding higher nominal interest rates increase the opportunity cost of holding money. As a result, individuals will want to reduce their money balances and hold alternative interest-earning assets.

The Demand for Money Schedule

Since there is no way to show variations of the five variables included in our demand for money in a two-dimensional diagram, explicit reference to three variables must be eliminated. Our choice, as indicated in Figure 19–12, is to retain M_d/P, the total demand for money, and i, the nominal rate of interest. In the figure, we have drawn a family of demand for money curves. Each curve shows the amount of money demanded at a particular level of real income and various rates of interest, assuming that other factors that affect demand remain constant. Each curve slopes downward from left to right, indicating an inverse relationship between the demand for money and the rate of interest. If we follow the Keynesian assumption that at very high rates of interest no money is held for speculative purposes, the upper left portion of the demand for money curve is perfectly vertical (perfectly interest inelastic). If we allow for the Keynesian hypothesis that at some low rate of interest the community will hold all additions to its money idle, the curve becomes perfectly horizontal (infinitely elastic) in its extreme right portion. In drawing the total demand for money curve, we have omitted these two assumptions because we consider them to be very special cases.

If the level of income increases we can expect to find a new demand curve appropriate to this level of income. Thus, in Figure 19–12 we have drawn separate demand for money curves labelled $L(Y)$ where the curves reflect successive higher levels of income from Y_1 to Y_4. But what about the position of these $L(Y)$ curves with changes in the other determinants we have included in our X variable? If, for example, people expect their future incomes to change from expected levels, they may change their expenditures in the present by holding

FIGURE 19–12   INCOME AND THE TOTAL DEMAND FOR MONEY

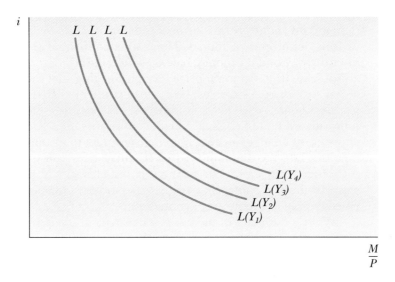

As the level of income increases from Y_1 to Y_2 the demand for money curve shifts up from $LL(Y_1)$ to $LL(Y_2)$, indicating that at each rate of interest more money is demanded as income increases. Four demand for money curves are shown with $Y_1 < Y_2 < Y_3 < Y_4$.

less money. Such a change would move the position of the total demand for money curve to the left, just as would a decrease in the level of income.

With the development of financial markets and the introduction of what the community considers to be better alternatives for holding its wealth, the desired composition of wealth has changed. The community holds these new forms of wealth in preference to money. As a result, other things remaining the same, the demand for money curve has shifted to the left. Various other examples can be given to explain the position and shifts of the demand for money curve. As we shall see, economists have been concerned with the stability of the demand for money curve because, aside from its slope, shifts in the curve have important implications for monetary policy.

Empirical Evidence

In the mid-1970s many economists were confident that reasonably stable demand functions could be estimated for narrow definitions of money. Indeed, a consensus had emerged among monetarists that the evidence confirmed that money demand was one of the more stable relationships in economics and sufficiently reliable as the basis for formulating monetary policy. Unfortunately, by the time central bankers had formulated their monetary policy on the estimated relationships, their estimates for narrow money were already starting to break down owing to financial innovations.

Representative of the various empirical studies of the demand for money in Canada undertaken in the 1970s is that by William White. White estimated demand for money functions over the period 1959–74 using monthly data and various definitions of money. His results confirmed the proposition that the quantity of nominal money balances demanded increased proportionately to an increase in the general price level, indicating that the demand for money is a demand for real balances. White also confirmed Baumol's theory that there are economies of scale in holding money balances. White's estimates of the long-run or equilibrium elasticities, after the demand for money has fully adjusted to changes in real income, were less than one, implying that as real income rises, the demand for real balances rises, but by a smaller proportion. Although White's estimate of the income elasticity of narrow money falls just short of unity, it shows that an increase in real income raises money demand considerably less than proportionately.

White's estimates of the interest elasticity of the demand for narrow money support the theoretical conclusion that it should be negative. White found the interest elasticity of narrow money to be –0.142: A 1 percent decrease in interest rates (the opportunity cost of holding money) should lead to a 0.142 percent increase in the demand for real money balances.

For the conduct of monetary policy, the monetary authorities will want to know not only the size and sign (positive or negative) of income and interest rate elasticities, but also the stability; that is, the reliability of their estimates for predicting the demand for money. White, as well as others who did earlier studies for other countries, found that prediction errors were relatively small, and therefore concluded that the estimated demand for narrow money functions could be considered to be quite stable. This conclusion provided the foundation for the Bank of Canada's experiment with money growth targeting in 1975.

In the mid-1970s, however, S.M. Goldfeld discovered that previously estimated demand for narrow money functions in the United States overpredicted money demand. The sudden downward shift in the demand for narrow money in the United States was characterized by Goldfeld as "the case of missing money." Subsequently, a similar downward shift in the narrow money function, which led to the abandonment of money growth targeting by the Bank of Canada, was observed in Canada. These shifts in the demand for narrow money have been attributed to innovations in the banking system that have made it attractive for individuals and businesses to economize on their holdings of M1 balances. In 1982, the governor of the Bank of Canada observed that

> *as a result of these innovations, a substantial reduction has taken place in the growth of M1 relative to that which one would have expected, given movements in total expenditures in the economy and interest rates.*[4]

Since the breakdown in stability of the demand for narrow money functions, more attention has been focused on the demand for broad money, such

4. *Annual Report of the Governor of the Bank of Canada* (Ottawa, 1982), p. 27.

as M2 and M2+. Kim McPhail and Francesco Caramazza, for example, estimated demand functions for these broad money aggregates between 1970 and 1987. They reported the following results:

- *Prices.* A given percentage change in prices is reflected in an equal percentage change in M2 and M2+ after 12 months. Approximately 80 percent of the adjustment of money demand to price changes occurs within six months.

- *Real Income.* The estimated income elasticities are 0.50 and 0.67 for M2 and M2+, respectively. A 1 percent increase in real GDP, all other variables remaining unchanged, is estimated to raise the demand for M2 by 0.50 percent and that of M2+ by 0.67 percent. It is estimated that the adjustment of money demand to a change in real GDP is quite fast; more than 50 percent after three months, over 75 percent after six months, and complete adjustment after one year.

- *Interest Rates.* The estimated net effect of raising the 90-day interest rates on commercial paper and bank and trust company deposits by 100 basis points (or about 1 percent at the average level of interest rates over the 1970–87 period) is to lower the demand for M2 by 0.16 percent and for M2+ by 0.27 percent after nine months. The implied interest rate elasticities of –0.15 and –0.26 for M2 and M2+, respectively, are extremely low. These elasticities indicate that broad money demand is insensitive to changes in the general level of interest rates that are not accompanied by changes in relative yields.

- *Other Factors.* Canada Savings Bonds (CSBs) and personal deposits are close substitutes. It is estimated that a 1 percent increase in the constant-dollar stock of CSBs reduces M2 by 0.12 percent and M2+ by 0.09 percent. CSB sales are concentrated in November of each year; depending on the size of each year's offering of these bonds, the broad money aggregates can fluctuate widely over this month.

www.

Scott Hendry examined the demand for M1 from 1961 to 1993, taking into account structural changes in the financial system that would affect M1 demand. He found evidence that supported the view that the demand for money is a demand for real balances, since the estimated coefficient on the price level was insignificantly different from unity. He also found that the income elasticity of demand for M1 was between 0.43 and 0.6 (depending on how the price level was measured), and that interest rates had negative effects on M1 demand that were similar to previous results published by the Bank of Canada.

More recently, Aubry and Nott demonstrated that financial innovation has had a major impact on the demand for narrowly defined money. The advent of virtual banking, new types of accounts at financial intermediaries, and easier access to the payments system have led to money demand functions that are not well suited to linking monetary policy to the transactions demand for money. These changes make the design and implementation of monetary policy subject to a great degree of uncertainty, as was argued by David Laidler:

> ...*the interaction of the supply and demand for money is crucial, not only to the impact of monetary policy, but also to the way in which a number of other shocks impinge upon the economy. Instability in the demand-for-money function does*

not alter the importance of this interaction. It simply makes it more difficult to apply our understanding of it to the design of monetary policy...when it comes to monetary policy designed to achieve an inflation goal, it would be appropriate and helpful to move towards using one or more transactions-money aggregates as the basis of an intermediate target variable.[5]

Kim McPhail recently provided evidence of stable long-run money demand functions using a variety of measures of "broadly defined money." Income elasticities of demand ranged between 1.4 and 1.8, and increases in the opportunity cost of holding money tended to reduce money holdings, as expected. McPhail also reported that measures of wealth did not seem to affect the demand for money, and that the estimated equations appeared to capture the financial innovations of the past 30 years, since the demand for money equations appeared to be structurally stable. This result is one we might expect, given that broadly defined money captures more of the savings role played by money than its transactions role; and should therefore be subject to fewer structural shifts.

Summary

Both theory and empirical evidence allow us to make the following five observations with respect to the properties of the demand for money function:

1. The demand for nominal balances is proportional to the price level; therefore, the demand for money is a demand for real balances.
2. The demand for real money balances increases with the level of real income. The demand for real money balances increases less than proportionally to an increase in real income (income elasticity of less than one), which implies that there are economies of scale in holding money.
3. The demand for real money balances increases with a decrease in the rate of interest and vice versa (interest elasticity is negative). However, the direct effect of changes in the overall level of interest rates on money demand is very small.
4. The long-run stability of demand for money functions is open to question. In the short-run, shifts have been the result of postal strikes, Canada Savings Bond sales, the introduction of the GST, and financial innovation. On broadly defined measures of money, McPhail reported evidence of a set of stable long-run money demand functions.
5. Finally, the search for a policy-relevant money demand function is not as simple a task as it may appear, as succinctly stated by Aubry and Nott:

   ... the basket of financial instruments that are available and desired by economic agents for the purpose of transactions evolves over time, and thus the set of instruments that most adequately captures transaction money today is not the

---

5. See David Laidler, "Passive Money, Active Money and Monetary Policy," *Bank of Canada Review*, Summer 1999, pp. 15–25.

same as it was yesterday, nor will it be the same tomorrow. Technology reduces operating costs and thus ensures ongoing financial innovation in the future, and the continuous evolution of the financial instruments used for the purpose of settling transactions.[6]

The Quantity Theory

quantity theory of money
changes in the price level are determined primarily by changes in the quantity of money in circulation

One of the oldest surviving economic doctrines is the **quantity theory of money**, which in its simplest and crudest form states that changes in the general price level are determined primarily by changes in the quantity of money in circulation. The quantity theory of money existed as long ago as the Greek and Roman periods. In the sixteenth century, Jean Bodin explained the price inflation in Spain and elsewhere in Europe following the inflow of gold from the New World in terms of the quantity theory.[7] In the seventeenth and eighteenth centuries, Richard Cantillon and David Hume attributed the general rise in prices to increases in the quantity of money.[8] In the nineteenth and early twentieth centuries, the quantity theory of money was the centrepiece of what we now refer to as classical and neoclassical macroeconomics.

The theory fell into disrepute during the 1930s, when it failed to explain the Great Depression. Moreover, the income–expenditure theory then being developed came to be considered a better explanation of economic activity. It was not until the 1950s, when Keynesian theory failed to explain re-emerging inflationary conditions, that the quantity theory of money again started to assume a life of its own. Its resurgence was assisted by its restatement by Don Patinkin of Hebrew University and by Milton Friedman and his students at the University of Chicago.[9] Their reformulation of the theory led to the "monetarist revolution," or simply **monetarism**. Unlike the earlier quantity theory, which concerned itself with the causal relationship between changes in the stock of money and the price level, the monetarists' concern is with showing that while changes in the quantity of money in the long run are primarily reflected in changes in the price level, in the short run they can also cause a change in real income.

monetarism *a school of thought in which changes in the money supply are the primary cause of economic fluctuations, implying that a stable money supply would lead to a stable economy*

---

6. See Aubrey and Nott, "Measuring Transaction Money in a World of Financial Innovation." Prepared for the Annual Bank of Canada Conference, Bank of Canada, November 1999.

7. Jean Bodin, "La Réponse de Jean Bodin aux paradoxes de Malestroit touchant l'enchérissement de toutes choses et le moyen d'y remédier," reprinted in *Early Economic Thought*, ed. Aruther E. Monroe (Cambridge, Mass.: Harvard University Press, 1924).

8. "Richard Cantillon and the Nationality of Political Economy," reprinted from *Contemporary Review*, 1881, in Richard Cantillon, *Essai sur la nature du commerce en général*, trans. H. Higgs (London: Macmillan, for the Royal Economic Society, 1931), p. 342, reprinted by Augustus M. Kelley (New York, 1964); and David Hume, *Essays and Treatises on Several Subjects* 2 vols. (London, 1772), available in *Essays: Moral, Political and Literary* (Oxford: Oxford University Press, 1963).

9. Don Patinkin, *Money, Interest and Prices* (Evanston, Ill.: Row, Peterson and Company, 1956); and Milton Friedman, ed., *Studies in Quantity Theory of Money* (Chicago: University of Chicago Press, 1956).

We begin this section with a discussion of the approaches to the quantity theory of money in classical and neoclassical macroeconomics, followed by a review of Milton Friedman's restatement of the theory and a description of its monetarist conclusions. We then show how the quantity theory can be used to predict the rate of inflation in the economy, and touch briefly on the reasons why the monetary authorities might be concerned about the level of inflation in the economy.

Velocity Approaches to the Quantity Theory of Money

The Transactions-Velocity Approach

transactions-velocity approach *a relationship between money and prices based in part on the number of transactions that occur in the economy in a year*

The **transactions-velocity approach** to the quantity theory of money, as formulated by Irving Fisher at the turn of the century, is considered to be the definitive analysis of the quantity theory in classical economics.[10] To show the relationship between money and prices, Fisher started with a simple identity known as the **equation of exchange,** which can be written as

$$(19.14) \qquad\qquad MV \equiv PT$$

where M is the quantity of money; V is the transactions **velocity of money,** or the number of times it turns over; P is the price level; and T is the volume of transactions. This **identity** (note the use of an identity sign rather than an equality sign) tells us nothing more than that the dollar value of everything bought equals the dollar value of everything sold. Each side of the identity is merely a different way of expressing the same phenomenon—expenditures. The left side of the identity tells us that the value of money spent on purchases, MV, is equal to the quantity of money in circulation multiplied by the number of times it is used, or turned over, to complete the total value of transactions, PT, specified on the right side of the identity. Hence, we can learn little from the equation that is not self-evident.

equation of exchange *an identity that relates the value of nominal transactions or income to the nominal money supply and the velocity of circulation*

However, once we make certain assumptions about the behaviour of the four variables that make up the equation, we can say something about the relationship between the quantity of money and the price level. In other words, we can turn the definitional identity into a monetary theory by the assumptions we make about the behaviour of the variables—M, V, P, and T—in the equation of exchange. Traditionally, the quantity of money theorists made the following four assumptions:

velocity of money *the average number of times per year each dollar is spent, either on final goods and services (income velocity) or on everything (transactions velocity)*

1. The quantity of money, M, is independent of the other variables—P, T, and V—and is determined solely by the monetary authorities.
2. The velocity of money, V, is also independent of the other variables in the equation of exchange. Its determinants were thought to be basically institutional (such as the community's system of payments and the habits of individuals). Because its determinants change only gradually and smoothly

identity *a relationship that always holds by definition, independent of any theory*

---

10. Irving Fisher, *The Purchasing Power of Money* (New York: Macmillan, 1911, 1922).

in the long run, velocity had generally been taken to be constant in the short run. Today, economists believe the velocity of circulation is primarily a function of the opportunity cost of holding money. That is, the higher the opportunity cost of holding money, the less money will be held, consequently, the greater the velocity of circulation as agents reduce their money holdings in favour of interest-bearing assets. Orphanides and Porter demonstrate that this is the case for U.S. data.[11] An end-of-chapter Review Question asks you to look at the Canadian evidence.

3. The volume of transactions, T, is constant. This conclusion was based on the assumption that transactions are a fixed ratio of output (since the number of transactions depends on the extent and variety of human wants, the facilities of transport, and other factors affecting trade, all of which change only slowly over time) and that the level of output remains constant at full employment.

4. The price level, P, is a passive variable in the equation of exchange. While it exerts no influence over the other variables, it may be influenced by them. But because both V and T are assumed to remain constant, only changes in M can produce changes in P.

If all these assumptions can be shown to be valid, it follows that changes in the money supply lead to proportional changes in the price level. This can be expressed in the following way (note that we have used the equality sign now since we have introduced some assumptions that may or not be true, and hence the relationship need not hold as an identity):

(19.15) $$\Delta M = (\frac{\overline{T}}{\overline{V}})\Delta P$$

with the bars on T and V, $\overline{T}$ and $\overline{V}$ signifying that they are constants. Remember the Greek letter delta (Δ) represents "the change in."

The Income-Velocity Approach

In the 1930s, following the work of the Swedish economists and that of John Maynard Keynes, attention shifted away from the concept of total expenditures to that of expenditures on only final goods currently produced, which we know today as Gross Domestic Expenditures. This change was reflected in what has become known as the **income-velocity equation of exchange**, expressed as

income-velocity equation of exchange a relationship between money and prices based in part on nominal income

(19.16) $$MV_{\text{Y}} \equiv PT_{y} \equiv PY$$

In the income-velocity equation, T_Y is the physical volume of final goods currently produced and P is the average price of this output. The total value of final output currently produced during a given period is shown as PT_y, or the more commonly used symbol of nominal income, PY (where Y is real income). As in the earlier transactions-velocity equation, M is the quantity of money, but now V_y is its income velocity. Since the physical volume of final goods currently

---

11. A. Orphanides, and R. Porter, "P* REVISITED: Money-Based Inflation Forecasts with a Changing Equilibrium Velocity," *Journal of Economics and Business* (2000) Vol. 52, 1–2, pp. 87–100.

produced is smaller than the physical volume of all transactions taking place in an economy over a given period, it follows that for a given quantity of money the income velocity, V_y, is smaller than the transactions velocity, V.

If we now assume that the economy operates at full employment, and therefore T_y remains constant, and V_y is also constant, we can repeat the conclusions of the transactions-velocity approach: The price level is determined by the money supply, and changes in the money supply lead to equiproportionate changes in the price level in the same direction. We can also state, if V_y, but not T_y, remains constant, a change in the money supply is reflected in a proportionate change in the level of nominal income (PY).

The Cash-Balance Approach to the Quantity Theory of Money

cash-balance approach *a theory of the demand for money based on the transactions demand for money*

While Irving Fisher was formulating the velocity approach to the quantity theory of money in the United States, Alfred Marshall, A.C. Pigou, J.M. Keynes, and D.H. Robertson at Cambridge University in England were developing the cash-balance approach.[12]

Unlike the transactions approach, which asks how much money individuals have to hold to carry out a given volume of transactions, the **cash-balance approach** asks how much money individuals want to hold to facilitate their transactions. It is assumed that individuals want to hold money primarily for transactions purposes. Although the Cambridge economists usually expressed individuals' desired nominal cash balances in terms of their total wealth, it is now generally shown as a fraction of their money income. The demand for money equation is

$$(19.17) \qquad M^d = kPY$$

where M^d is the transactions demand for money; Y is real income or physical output; P is the price level; and k is the proportion of their money income, PY, that individuals desire to hold in cash or money form. In equilibrium, the supply of money, M^s (determined by the monetary authorities exogenously at M_0), is equal to the demand for money ($M^s = M^d$).

$$(19.18) \qquad M^s = M_0$$

and by substitution from equation 19.17

$$(19.19) \qquad M_0 = kPY$$

12. Alfred Marshall, *Money, Credit and Commerce* (London: Macmillan, 1924); A.C. Pigou, "The Value of Money," *Quarterly Journal of Economics* (November, 1917), pp. 38–65; J.M. Keynes, *A Treatise on Money* (London: Macmillan, 1930); D.H. Roberson, *Money* (Cambridge: The University Press, 1922).

cash-balance equation *a relationship between the demand for money and nominal income*

which is referred to as the **cash-balance equation**. If we now assume that Y (real income) is constant and that k remains fixed and independent of the money supply, then changes in the money supply cause proportionate changes in the price level, as shown by

$$(19.20) \qquad \Delta M_0 = (k^* Y^*)\Delta P$$

neutral *when only nominal variables change (as opposed to real variables)*

where the asterisks denote that variables are assumed to remain constant. Except for the variables between the brackets, equations 19.15 and 19.20 are similar in that both provide identical conclusions. When changes in the money supply lead only to changes in the price level with no changes in real variables (output, employment, and interest rates), money is said to be **neutral**.

The Relationship between the Two Approaches

stock concept *a variable that doesn't have an associated time dimension*

flow concept *a variable that does have an associated time dimension*

While the velocity and cash-balance approaches to the quantity theory produce the same conclusions, there are significant differences between them. The first and most basic distinction between the two approaches has to do with stocks and flows. In the cash-balance equation, as in the equation of exchange, M is the total amount of money in circulation at a moment in time. Economists refer to this as a **stock concept**—a variable that doesn't have an associated time dimension. Money remains a stock concept whether we define it as the absolute amount in existence in any one day, or the average amount in any one month or year. In both equations, conversely, $P_Y T_Y$ (or PT) and PY are **flow concepts** in that they express the value of final output produced (or in the case of PT, total transactions) over a period. The basic difference between the equation of exchange and the cash-balance equation is that the former is transformed entirely into a flow concept—a variable that does have an associated time dimension—and the latter is transformed entirely into a stock concept. These two transformations are accomplished by including VY (or V) on the left side of the equation of exchange, and k on the right side of the cash-balance equation.

In the equation of exchange, multiplying the money stock M by its income velocity V_Y produces MV_Y, the total money expenditures on final output over a period. The inclusion of V_Y transforms the left side of the equation into a flow concept and equates it to the right side of the equation, $P_Y T_Y$, also a flow concept.

In the cash-balance equation, the left side of the equation, the money stock, remains a stock concept, while the right side of the equation undergoes a transformation from a flow to a stock concept when PY is multiplied by k. The product, kPY, tells us that the total amount of money held by the community is equal to the fraction k of the value of nominal output. The total amount of money held by the community at any moment in time must be equal to the total money stock in existence at the same moment in time because, by definition, the money supply is the total amount of money in public circulation. The cash-balance equation, therefore, like the equation of exchange, is nothing more than a truism where kPY is a different way of expressing M, just as MV_Y is a different way of expressing $P_Y T_Y$ (or MV is a different way of expressing PT). In the equation of exchange we note that over any period of time money expenditures are equal to the value of goods and services sold (or purchased). In the cash-balance equation we note that at any moment of time the total amount of money in existence is equal to the total amount of money held by the community.

While the two versions of the quantity theory differ in their approach because one uses V while the other uses k, a close relationship exists between V and k, shown as follows:

$$(19.21) \qquad\qquad MV_Y = P_Y T_Y, \text{ or}$$

$$(19.22) \qquad\qquad V_Y = \frac{P_Y T_Y}{M}$$

$$(19.23) \qquad\qquad M = kPY$$

In equation 19.21, by substituting the value for M from equation 19.23, we derive

$$(19.24) \qquad\qquad V_Y = \frac{P_Y T_Y}{kYP}$$

and since $P_Y T_Y \equiv PY$

$$(19.25) \qquad\qquad V_Y = \frac{1}{k}$$

Algebraically, therefore, V_Y and k are simply the reciprocal of each other. If, for example, a unit of money passes from hand to hand four times a year, each unit of money must remain in someone's hands for an average time of three months, or one-quarter of the year.

Thus, we can clearly see a close relationship between the two approaches to the quantity theory of money and why they are said to be two sides of the same coin. D.H. Robertson identified the cash-balance approach as "money sitting" and the velocity approach as "money on the wing."[13]

For analytical purposes, the cash-balance approach is more useful than the velocity approach because it can lead to a direct examination of individuals' motives for holding money. While the Cambridge economists recognized this, they generally assume that k, like V or V_Y, remained constant in the short run and changed only slowly but smoothly over the long run, because it was essentially determined by institutional factors that display these patterns of change. As we have already observed, by assuming that k and V (or V_Y) together with real income remain constant, both approaches to the quantity theory could show that changes in the quantity of money produce proportional changes in the price level.

---

13. D.H. Robertson, *Money* (Chicago: University of Chicago Press, 1959), Ch. 2.

This proportionality conclusion came to be seriously questioned once Keynes observed that we cannot assume that the economy will continually operate near or at the full employment level, and that individuals desire to hold money for other reasons in addition to the transactions motive. With the inclusion of the precautionary motive and particularly the speculative motive for holding money, one could no longer assume that V and k would remain constant. In fact, Keynesian economists have questioned not only the constancy of V and k, but also their predictability with respect to the factors that are assumed to determine them.

www.

The P-Star Model of Inflation

Operationally, the quantity theory can be used to help predict the rate of inflation. If the central bank sees inflation jump above its target level (which changes over time according to Bank policy), then it can introduce policies to restrain the rate of monetary growth. These policies, according to quantity theory, should restrain inflationary pressures. One method the Bank uses to determine whether inflationary pressures are building is the **P-Star Model**. It was originally proposed by Hallman, Porter, and Small.[14]

P-Star Model an indicator model of inflation using the quantity theory

Suppose the long-run equilibrium price level, P^*, long-run velocity, V_Y^*, and long-run real output, Y^*, are related to the current level of the money stock, M, according to equation 19.26:

(19.26)
$$P^* = \frac{MV_Y^*}{Y^*}$$

Now, suppose the current price level, P, current velocity, V, current real output, Y, and the current money stock, M are related by

(19.27)
$$P = \frac{MV_Y}{Y}$$

Now take the natural logarithms of both sides of equations 19.26 and 19.27, and denote the logarithms as lower-case letters to obtain equations 19.26a and 19.27a:

(19.26a)
$$p^* = m + v_Y^* - y^*$$

(19.27a)
$$p = m + v_Y - y$$

Now subtract equation 19.27a from equation 19.26a to obtain

(19.28)
$$p^* - p = (v_{Y^*} - v_Y) + (y - y^*)$$

14. See Atta-Mensah for recent evidence on Canadian data, and Humphrey for a historical view of P-Star.

output gap the difference between the current value of real output and its long-run value

The P-Star model of inflation suggests that the difference between the long-run equilibrium price level and the current price level (in logarithms) is equal to the difference between the long-run value of velocity relative to its current value and the output gap. The **output gap** is the difference between the current value of real output and its long-run value. If we rewrite equation 19.8 using $\pi = p^* - p$ as the actual inflation rate (there is positive inflation if the current price level is below its long-run value; the price level is rising toward its long-run value), we obtain

(19.28a) $$\pi = (v_{Y^*} - v_Y) + (y - y^*)$$

From equation 19.28a you can see that when velocity is fixed at its long-run value, inflation is purely the result of the output gap. Indeed, when output exceeds its long-run value, inflation is positive. If velocity and output are at their long-run values, inflation is zero.

If we allow for short-run dynamics in the inflationary process (because of the effects of lags in the adjustment of wages over time, as an example), we arrive at:

(19.29) $$\pi = (v_{Y^*} - v_Y) + (y - y^*) + \text{lagged inflation}$$

The Bank of Canada and other central banks use equations like 19.29 to predict the inflation rate. The P-Star model provides early warning of the future path of inflation, and accommodates several views of the inflationary process.

This subject leads us to the next chapter, where we begin to examine the role and efficacy of Canadian monetary policy.

KEY TERMS

brokerage fees	liquidity trap	real balances
cash-balance approach	monetarism	speculative balances
cash-balance equation	money illusion	stock concept
economies of scale	neutral	transactions balances
equation of exchange	nominal balances	transactions demand
flow concept	opportunity cost	transactions-velocity approach
identity	output gap	velocity of circulation
income-velocity equation of	precautionary balances	velocity of money
exchange	P-Star Model	
inventory–theoretic approach	quantity theory of money	

REVIEW QUESTIONS

1. What are the three Keynesian motives for holding money?
2. An individual spends his salary cheque at a constant rate, leaving him with no money when the next cheque is received. His monthly salary is $2240. What is his average daily money balance if his monthly salary is paid at the beginning of each week? What is his average daily monthly balance if all of his monthly salary is paid at the beginning of the month?
3. What is the square root rule for holding money?
4. Assume that the square root rule for holding money is correct so that the income elasticity is 1/2. What is the increase in the real demand for money if nominal GDP rises from $100 billion to $240 billion while the price level doubles?
5. Demonstrate how Tobin explains that the speculative demand for money is inversely related to the rate of interest.
6. What determines the slope of the demand for money schedule?
7. How does the demand for money curve shift with an increase in income?
8. Summarize the major characteristics of demand for money suggested by empirical estimates of demand for money functions.
9. What do we mean by money illusion?
10. How did Keynes explain that the speculative demand for money is inversely related to the rate of interest?
11. Show what happens to the demand for money when wealth rises, all other factors remaining the same. Does portfolio risk rise? Why, or why not? What happens to the proportion of money held in the portfolio?
12. Show what happens to the demand for money when the expected return on money falls, all other factors remaining the same. What happens to portfolio risk? Why?
13. In our analysis of the portfolio approach to money demand, we assumed $E(i) > m$. Now assume that $E(i) < m$ and derive the demand for money following the approach we presented in the text. Do changes in the interest rate affect the demand for money when the expected return on the risky asset is less than the return to holding money? Why?
14. Why are V and T assumed to be constant in the transactions-velocity approach? To what conclusion do these assumptions lead?
15. What is the difference between the transactions-velocity approach and the income-velocity approach? Does it affect the conclusion?
16. How is the emphasis changed between the velocity approaches and the cash-balance approach? Explain the concepts of stock and flow variables, and how they relate to the velocity approaches and the cash-balance approach. What is the relationship between V and k?
17. Using the portfolio approach to money demand, explain the conditions under which an investor would hold only money.
18. What does the liquidity trap imply about the ability of a central bank to reduce interest rates through an expansion of monetary policy?
19. Did Atta-Mensah find evidence that interest rates helped predict inflation? He found two other variables to be significant predictors of inflationary pressures. What are they?
20. Suppose the equilibrium price level is rising at a fixed rate. On two separate graphs, plot the path of the equilibrium price level and the associated inflation rate for five periods. Now suppose the equilibrium rate of growth of the price level rose because of an increase in the rate of growth of the money supply. If actual prices adjust with a lag, demonstrate graphically and verbally explain the relationship between the actual rate of inflation and the new equilibrium rate of inflation. Does the price gap indicate a rise in the inflation rate?
21. Using data on M2+ (CANSIM series B1633), the opportunity cost of holding M2+, calculated as the difference between the three-year Government of Canada bond yield and the 91 day Treasury bill rate (CANSIM series B14068 and B14007, respectively), and Real GDP (CANSIM series D14872), calculate an estimate of M2+ velocity in Canada from 1965: Q1 to 2000: Q4. Plot velocity against the opportunity cost of holding M2+. Is there a positive relationship? Explain.

SELECTED READINGS

Atta-Mensah, J. "A Modified P* Model of Inflation Based on M1." Bank of Canada Working Paper 96–15, 1996: Ottawa.

Aubry, J., and L. Nott. "Measuring Transaction Money in a World of Financial Innovation." Prepared for the Annual Bank of Canada Conference Bank of Canada, November 1999.

Dean, Edwin, ed. *The Controversy Over the Quantity Theory of Money.* Boston: D.C. Heath, 1963.

Fisher, Irving. *The Purchasing Power of Money.* New York: Augustus M. Kelley, 1963.

Friedman, Milton, ed. "Money: Quantity Theory," in *International Encyclopedia of the Social Sciences.* New York: Macmillan and Free Press, 1968.

———. *Studies in the Quantity Theory of Money.* Chicago: University of Chicago Press, 1956.

———. "A Theoretical Framework for Monetary Analysis." *Journal of Political Economy* 78 (March/April 1970), pp. 193–235.

———. *The Optimum Quantity of Money and Other Essays.* Chicago: Aldine, 1970.

Gilbert, J.C. "The Demand for Money: The Development of an Economic Concept." *Journal of Political Economy* 61 (April 1953), pp. 144–59.

Gordon, Robert J., ed. *Milton Friedman's Monetary Framework.* Chicago: Aldine, 1974.

Hallman, J., R. Porter, and D. Small. "Is the Price Level Tied to the M2 Monetary Aggregate in the Long-Run?" *American Economic Review* 81 (1991), pp. 841–58.

Hendry, S. "Long-Run Demand for M1." Bank of Canada Working Paper 95–11: Ottawa

Humphrey, T. "Precursors of the P-Star Model." *Federal Reserve Bank of Richmond Review* 4 (1989), pp. 3–9.

Laidler, David E.W. *The Demand for Money: Theories, Evidence and Problems*, 3rd ed. New York: Harper & Row, 1985.

Laidler, David. *Monetarist Perspectives.* Oxford: Philip Allan Publishers, 1982.

———. *The Golden Age of the Quantity Theory.* Princeton, N.J.: Princeton University Press, 1991.

———. "Passive Money, Active Money, and Monetary Policy." *Bank of Canada Review*, Summer 1999, pp. 15–25.

Keynes, J.M. *The General Theory of Employment, Interest and Money.* London: Macmillan, 1936.

McPhail, K. "Broad Money: A Guide for Monetary Policy." Paper prepared for the Annual Bank of Canada Conference, November 1999.

McPhail, K., and F. Caramazza. "La demande de M2 et M2+ au Canada; quelques resultats recents," Bank of Canada Working Paper 90–3.

Milbourne, R. "Re-examining the Buffer-Stock Model of Money." *Economic Journal* 97 (1987), pp. 130–42.

Miller, M., and D. Orr. "A Model of the Demand for Money by Firms." *Quarterly Journal of Economics* (1966), pp. 413–35.

Rousseau, Stephen. *Monetary Theory.* New York: Knopf, 1972.

CHAPTER TWENTY

THE ROLE AND EFFECTIVENESS OF MONETARY POLICY

After reading this chapter you should be able to

1. *Explain the orthodox Keynesian approach to monetary policy*
2. *Show how the credit approach and the neo-Keynesian approaches to monetary policy differ*
3. *Demonstrate the salient features of monetarism as they relate to monetary policy*
4. *Show how New Classicals and neo-Keynesians approach the conduct of monetary policy*
5. *Identify the lags in the monetary policy process*
6. *Argue against a regional monetary policy*
7. *Use Phillips curves to demonstrate gradualism versus cold turkey approaches to eliminating inflation*
8. *Identify the appropriate choice of monetary policy instrument*

The raison d'être of monetary policy is to influence the demand for goods and services so as to achieve the objectives of overall economic policy—price stability, a high and stable level of employment, external balance, and economic growth. In this chapter we shall specifically consider the interrelationships between theory and policy. The various theoretical explanations of the monetary mechanism will be reviewed, and the policy implications will be shown.

The Orthodox Keynesian Approach

In the orthodox Keynesian model of the economy, monetary policy affects economic activity indirectly through its prior effect on interest rates. An increase in the money supply results in a fall in interest rates, which, in turn, leads to an increase in investment expenditure and, via the income multiplier, to an increase in aggregate demand and income. The relationship between changes in the quantity of money and interest rates is explained by the Keynesian

**liquidity prefer-
ence function** *the
relationship
between changes
in the quantity of
money and
interest rates*

liquidity preference function. Except for the possibility of a liquidity trap, Keynes assumed that this function was downward sloping, so that an increase in money could generally be assumed to be accompanied by a decline in interest rates. The relationship between changing interest rates and investment expenditures is explained by the Keynesians' belief that this function is relatively interest inelastic. As a result, an increase in the money supply, which causes a fall in interest rates, has little or no effect on investment and, therefore, on aggregate demand and income.

Studies undertaken at Oxford University in the late 1930s showed that business operators in Britain were affected to a very limited extent by changes in interest rates. These studies, which received wide attention, contributed to the early skepticism concerning the effectiveness of monetary policy. Further studies in 1956 and 1957 confirmed the earlier observations that businesses in Britain reacted only marginally to changing credit conditions. The Committee on the Working of the Monetary System (the Radcliffe Committee, appointed in 1957 to investigate the British monetary system) noted that "when we confined our questions strictly to the direct effects of interest rate changes in making businessmen alter their decisions to buy and sell goods and services, we were met by general scepticism." Studies in the United States, both before and after the Second World War, discovered a similar insensitivity of business decisions to changes in credit conditions. Robert Eisner, for example, after making a survey of business decisions during 1951–52 and 1954–55, concluded that "Questions directed at the role of interest rate received almost uniform negative response."

Because of the studies, which all showed that changes in interest rates had little if any effect on investment and, therefore, on income, many economists came to consider monetary policy an ineffective instrument for use in stabilizing economic activity.

**debt manage-
ment** *the manage-
ment of the
federal debt and
its composition*

In Canada, the Porter Commission conducted a mail survey of businesses with follow-up interviews to ascertain the correlation between credit conditions and business investment during three periods of monetary restraint, 1956–57, 1959–60, and mid-1962. The Commission's studies explicitly interpreted credit conditions to include both the cost of money (the rate of interest) and the availability of money. Moreover, they explicitly assumed that credit conditions were influenced by both monetary and **debt management** policies. The Commission found that credit restraint during the years under review did not affect a significant proportion of businesses, because they were able to respond to credit conditions in ways that left their financial arrangements unaffected. The significance of this point had been largely overlooked in the earlier studies of restrictive credit conditions in Britain and the United States.

The Availability of Credit Approach

www.

In the early 1950s, central bankers, particularly those associated with the Federal Reserve System in the United States, advocated the return to a more flexible use of monetary policy. They accepted the popularly held view of the time that saving, investment, and spending generally were insensitive to

availability doctrine the idea that monetary policy works through restricting the availability of credit, and its effects on lenders

changes in interest rates, but they did not believe that this necessarily made monetary policy ineffective. Their defence of a more flexible use of monetary policy was embodied in what is variously known as the "**availability doctrine**," the "new theory of credit control," the "credit rationing doctrine," and the "Roosa effect."

The basic proposition of the availability doctrine is that monetary policy works much more through restricting the availability of credit than through increasing its costs, and much more through its effects on lenders than its effects on borrowers. According to the theory, in the postwar financial environment, government debt had become an important part of the asset holdings of most financial institutions, and small changes in the yields of government securities induced substantial changes in the lending patterns of these institutions. With only a small increase in the yield of government securities, say, because of open market sales by the central bank, institutions were assumed to increase their holdings of such securities at the expense of extending private loans.

The 1959 Radcliffe Report in Britain and the 1961 Report of the Commission on Money and Credit in the United States attached considerable importance to availability effects in the explanation of the transmission mechanism of monetary policy. In Canada, the Bank of Canada, in its testimony in 1964 before the Porter Commission, included availability effects in its perception of how monetary policy is transmitted to the real sector of the economy. In its assessment of postwar Canadian monetary policy, the Porter Commission explicitly included the availability concept in its definition of credit conditions. (The Radcliffe Committee included the same concept implicitly when it considered the whole liquidity of the British economy.) In its assessment of postwar Canadian monetary policy, the Porter Commission found that alterations in the availability of funds for residential construction played an important role in determining the activity in this important sector of the economy.

A significant part of postwar residential construction was financed under the *National Housing Act* (NHA). Under the Act, approved lenders made residential mortgage loans guaranteed by the government, which also specified the maximum interest lenders could charge. The interest rate allowed on NHA mortgages also did not fluctuate with market rates. Whenever alternative lending offered attractively higher rates, lenders turned away from NHA loans. As market rates rose, fewer funds were available for residential construction, and this sector was forced to contract. While the total funds in the economy did not decline, the flow of new loanable funds was redirected into different types of assets. This redirection, in turn, influenced the spending pattern of the economy in a way that assisted monetary policy.

The Neo-Keynesian Portfolio Balance Approach

Earlier in the textbook we introduced the theory of portfolio selection to demonstrate how financial intermediaries choose an optimum portfolio of financial assets. We later used this theory to explain the demand for money

portfolio balance approach a theory attempting to determine the demand for money within a general portfolio approach to the selection of assets

and, in particular, to show why individuals hold money in a diversified portfolio of money and bonds. The **portfolio balance approach**, describing how monetary policy is transmitted to the real sector of the economy, is a further application of the theory of portfolio selection. Instead of holding only money and bonds in their portfolios, the public is assumed to hold a variety of both financial and real assets that are less than perfect substitutes for each other. The total of all assets held by the public represents its wealth. The proportionate amount of any asset that the public wants to hold in its portfolios depends on its total wealth (wealth effects), and the relative yields (substitution effects) that it perceives on all the various assets.

According to James Tobin, a leading neo-Keynesian, because of the relatively higher degree of substitution between money and financial assets, the public will initially attempt to rid itself of any excess of money by purchasing financial assets. As a result, the yield on financial assets will fall and be less than the yield on real assets. This yield decline will induce the public to acquire real assets. The availability of real assets cannot, however, be increased quickly, and a gap develops between the desired and existing amount of real assets. The excess demand for real assets drives up their price relative to their cost of new production, stimulating investment expenditures until the gap between actual and desired holdings of real assets is closed. Tobin notes that because the higher price of existing real assets is reflected in the price of equities, the latter may be a good indicator of the thrust of monetary policy.

In the portfolio balance approach, the public's desired portfolio may be disturbed not only by a change in the stock of money, but also by a change in the stock of any asset included in the public's desired portfolio. Moreover, it is possible that a change in the relative supplies of assets results in a change in their relative prices and yields that produces a change in nominal income in the opposite direction from the change in the money supply. The implication for monetary policy is that it should be gauged in terms of the supplies of all assets held by the public, not just by the supply of money. Hence, neo-Keynesians argue that while money matters, it is not the only asset that matters when explaining the direction of economic activity. Furthermore, debt management operations may be every bit as effective as monetary policy in attempting to change the course of economic activity by disturbing the composition of the public's asset portfolio.

The public's portfolio balance may be disturbed not only by a change in the composition of its assets, but also by a change in the size of its assets, or wealth, of which money is a part. There are two types of wealth effects: direct wealth effects, which result from additions to wealth owned by the private sector; and indirect wealth effects, which result from an increase in the value of existing assets owned by the private sector.

With an expansionary monetary policy and the substitution effects explained earlier, yields on existing assets may decline and their market price increase. If as a result the public feels wealthier, it may increase both its investment and its consumer expenditures. But since real expenditures depend on real wealth, if monetary expansion is accompanied by an increase in the price level, wealth effects from a change in asset yields may be negated.

While substitution effects are typically assumed to have a direct and prior effect on investment expenditures, the wealth effects are assumed to have a more direct effect on consumer expenditures. However, the strength of the wealth effect remains an unsettled issue.

The Modern Quantity Theory (Monetarism)

Today's approach to the quantity theory, while following the general framework of the cash-balance approach of the Cambridge economists, differs from it in three important ways. First, instead of regarding real income as fixed, the modern quantity theory assumes that in the short run real income can depart from its long-term, full-employment and, hence, fixed level. Second, instead of assuming that the only motive for holding money is for transactions purposes, the theory recognizes that individuals also hold money for precautionary and speculative motives, as described in the previous chapter. Third, instead of regarding k (or V) as constant, the theory assumes the demand for money is a stable function of a small number of variables, particularly income and interest rates.

monetarist approach the view that the quantity theory can be used to model the economy

While there are various versions of the modern quantity theory that are frequently referred to as the **monetarist approach**, all of them stem from Milton Friedman's restatement of the theory.[1] Friedman states that the quantity theory must be viewed as a theory of the demand for money. He analyzes the demand for money within the same general framework that economists use to study the demand for other goods and services by utility-maximizing economic agents. Hence, in Friedman's restatement, the demand for money is related to an individual's wealth (the budget constraint), the expected relative rates of return from holding various assets (the relative price effect), and the utility or satisfaction associated with the services rendered by holding money as determined by individual tastes and preferences.

Individuals may hold their wealth in five different forms: money; bonds and other interest-bearing financial assets; equities; physical capital such as houses, automobiles, and furniture; and human capital. The part of their wealth that they choose to hold in the form of money—that is, their demand for money—can be expressed by the following equation:

$$(20.1) \qquad \frac{M_d}{P} = f(Y_p, \; r_M, \; r_B, \; r_E, \; \pi^E, \; h, \; u)$$

where M_d/P is the real demand for money; Y_p is "permanent" real income; r_M is money's own rate of return; r_B is the rate of return from bonds and other fixed-interest financial assets; r_E is the return from equities such as common stock, including both dividends and capital gains; π^E is the expected rate of inflation; h is the ratio of human wealth to total wealth; and u represents tastes or preferences.

Friedman assumed that nominal money balances change in exact proportion to the level of prices, and therefore the demand for money is a demand

---

1. Milton Friedman, "The Quantity Theory of Money: A Restatement," in *Studies in the Quantity Theory of Money*, ed. M. Friedman (Chicago: University of Chicago Press, 1956), pp. 3–21.

*permanent real
income* the
average level of
income expected
to prevail over a
long period

for real balances. Although wealth is the appropriate constraint on asset holding, and therefore on money, in the absence of direct estimates of wealth, Friedman uses **permanent real income** as a proxy. Permanent income refers to the average level of income expected to prevail over a long period.[2] A distinction is also made between human and nonhuman wealth. To a limited extent individuals can substitute between human wealth and other forms of wealth. For example, other assets may be sold to pay for education and training to enhance one's future earning capital. This investment in "human capital" represents a substitution of human wealth for nonhuman wealth. For any given level of wealth, the larger the proportion invested in human capital, the less liquid the individual's wealth holdings. To compensate for this reduction in liquidity, individuals may increase their demand for real money balances as the ratio of human wealth to total wealth increases.

The rates of return from holding assets other than money represent the opportunity cost of holding money. At the margin, each individual adjusts his or her money holdings to the point at which the extra utility or satisfaction from the last dollar held just compensates for the opportunity cost of holding wealth in the form of money. If these opportunity costs of holding money increase, the portion of wealth held in money will decline. Some forms of money itself, such as bank deposits, may earn interest. If money's own rate of return increases relative to the rates of return on other assets, individuals will be induced to substitute money for these other forms of wealth holdings.

The expected inflation rate in Friedman's demand for money equation can be viewed as a tax on money as well as a nominal rate of return on real capital such as durable goods. The higher this expected "tax rate," the greater the cost of holding money and, hence, the smaller the amount of money that will be demanded.

Finally, given wealth and the expected rates of return on assets that compose it, individuals' preferences for money will be conditioned by the subjective utility they derive from holding it. Money provides a service to individuals in that it represents immediate purchasing power. It may also give them a "sense of security" since it provides what we described in the last chapter as "a margin of safety."

In his studies of U.S. monetary history, Friedman found that the nominal demand for money varies directly with and in proportion to the level of prices. In addition, real income exerts an overriding influence on the demand for real balances. But while an inverse and systematic relationship exists between the demand for money and interest rates, this relationship is generally quite weak. The stable relationship between nominal money and prices (the real demand for money) and real income, and the stable but weak and inverse relationship between the real demand for money and interest rates, provided the cornerstones for Friedman's restatement of the quantity theory of money. He summarized the modern quantity theory propositions in the following way: "There is a consistent though not precise relation between the rate of growth of the quantity of money and the rate of growth of nominal income." He qualified that statement, however, by saying

---

2. Most researchers use a weighted average of current and past measured income, with the weights declining exponentially, as a proxy of permanent income.

it takes time for changes in monetary growth to affect income and how long it takes is itself variable.... The changed rate of growth of nominal income typically shows up first in output and hardly at all in prices....In the short run, which may be as much as five to ten years, monetary changes affect primarily output. Over decades, on the other hand, the rate of monetary growth affects primarily prices.[3]

Using the Quantity Theory in the Design of Monetary Policy

The quantity theory provides us with the answers to several questions about the role of monetary policy, particularly with respect to the Canadian economic environment. First, reconsider the income–velocity approach to the quantity theory:

(20.2) $$MV_Y = PY$$

We know that if velocity and real output are fixed, any change in the money supply leads to an equiproportionate change in the price level, suggesting that as long as velocity and real output are fixed, monetary policy will have no impact on real economic variables. The implication is that monetary policy cannot be used to change physical production in the economy (which, after all, is what real output measures). If we extend this reasoning, then monetary policy will not be able to affect the inputs used to produce that physical output (as long as velocity and real output are fixed). The direct implication is that monetary policy cannot be used to change or influence the level of employment (and thereby unemployment) in the economy.

This belief was at the heart of Bank of Canada policy in the 1990s. The central bank took the long run view that monetary policy had no real lasting effects, and hence it should be focused on achieving price stability—typically defined to be a low and stable rate of inflation. Proponents of Bank policy argue that this was the only responsible action the central bank should consider. Their arguments were based on an elementary macroeconomic principle: Inflation is undesirable because it imposes costs on the economy. What are some of these costs? Just to name four, inflation

1. erodes the purchasing power of money and leads to a breakdown in what is used as the medium of exchange (and economic activity falls since there is little confidence in the medium of exchange).

2. makes it difficult for firms to distinguish between changes in the absolute price level (which should not affect production decisions) and changes in relative prices (on which production decisions should be based).

---

3. Milton Friedman, *The Counter Revolution in Monetary Theory* (London: the Institute of Economic Affairs, 1970) pp. 22–3.

Phillips curves
the inverse relationship between inflation and unemployment in the short run; the lack of a link between inflation and unemployment in the long run

3. creates "menu costs" associated with reticketing and repricing items because of frequent changes in prices.

4. leads to higher nominal interest rates, which restrains aggregate demand and raises the costs of servicing both private and publicly issued debt.

We can understand this view if we consider the **Phillips curves** in Figure 20–1. The long-run Phillips curve is based on the assumption that a natural rate of unemployment exists to which the economy would gravitate if all markets cleared (that is, if all resources were used at their normal levels of intensity, and expectations were fully realized). This idea isn't difficult to accept, at least in theory, since when everyone is able to do what they had planned to do, real output should be independent of the inflation rate (and hence, by implication, the rate of unemployment). For example, suppose you signed a contract with your employer that gave you a 5 percent wage increase over the year because you expected inflation to be 5 percent ($\pi^e = 5\%$). If inflation turns out to be what you had expected, you'll be happy with the decisions you made based on your expectations. If that's true across the economy, then it doesn't matter whether the inflation rate is 3 percent or 6 percent, as long as it turns out to be what everyone expected.

Indeed, the long-run Phillips curve demonstrates the long-run view of the quantity theory: Any change in the money supply will cause a change in the price level (an inflation). Real variables won't change.

Figure 20–1 also plots a series of short-run Phillips curves, each drawn for a specific level of expected inflation. If you look at the plot carefully you'll see that the long-run Phillips curve intersects each short-run Phillips curve at the

FIGURE 20–1 THE PHILLIPS CURVES

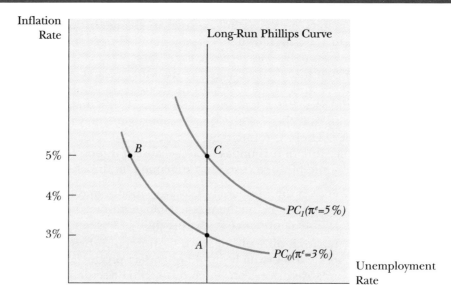

In the long run, there is no tradeoff between inflation and unemployment. In the short run, the central bank may be able to reduce unemployment by creating more inflation than had been expected.

point where expected inflation equals actual inflation. So, when expectations are fully realized, there's no tradeoff between inflation and unemployment.

Critics of Bank of Canada policy suggest that monetary actions could have real effects in the short run and that these would change the rate of unemployment. They base their arguments on several factors, the first of which is that expectations are not always fully realized. People do make expectations errors; they may sign contracts that give them a 3 percent increase in their nominal wages, but if inflation turns out to be higher than expected, say 5 percent, their real wages (the nominal wage adjusted for the effects of inflation) will fall, making it cheaper for firms to hire workers, since in real terms, the cost of labour has fallen. Firms hire more workers and produce more output. This may, for example, take us from point *A* in Figure 20–1 to point *B*.

Next-period workers will revise their expectations of inflation up, in response to their errors of the last period—and the short-run Phillips curve will shift to PC_1. Next period, if expected inflation turns out to be equal to the actual rate, real output (and, hence, unemployment) returns to its original level (point *C*). But the central bank could frustrate the market by allowing more monetary growth than it had announced—creating expectations errors and reducing the unemployment rate again, but at the cost of a steadily increasing inflation rate.

Figure 20–1 provides us with two views of monetary policy. The first is the long-run view that suggests the authorities should focus on the long run. The second is that by creating expectations errors, the central bank may be able to "fool people" into taking sub-optimal positions that would have real effects. (Of course, there are dynamic consistency problems here; if central bank policy statements always turn out to be falsehoods, soon no one will believe them.) Critics of Bank of Canada policy suggest that the social costs of unemployment are much larger than the costs of inflation, and that the central bank should accept—and in fact create—greater inflation. They argue that the benefits outweigh the costs. Early in 1997 the Bank of Canada revisited the arguments in favour of price stability to set the course of future monetary policy. They decided to maintain the inflation target of 1 percent to 3 percent, with a plan to review the target early in the new millennium.

Monetarism—A Summary

The monetarist approach is associated with Professor Milton Friedman who, during the 1960s while at the University of Chicago, formulated its major tenets. The antecedents of monetarism are found in the quantity theory of money. Monetarism may be summarized in terms of six basic propositions.

First, money supply growth is exogenously determined by the monetary authorities, and changes in the money supply are the primary determinants of changes in total spending and nominal income.

Second, monetary changes are transmitted directly into spending and do not have to await prior changes in interest rates. Monetarists have argued that history has shown a stable demand function for real money balances, which has a strong positive relationship with real income but only a weak negative relationship with interest rates. Thus, when the nominal money supply is increased, individuals rid themselves of undesired excess real balances by spending them first on goods and services, and only subsequently by purchasing financial assets. As individuals rid themselves of their excess money balances, nominal income increases. As this happens, the public will want to absorb its excess balances into its desired money holdings. In this way excess money balances are transformed into desired balances.

Third, unanticipated increases in the money supply only temporarily affect real output; in the long run, increases in the growth rate of money translate themselves into price inflation. According to Friedman, "Inflation is always and everywhere a monetary phenomenon."

Fourth, the monetary authorities should not attempt to control nominal interest rates or use these rates as indicators of monetary policy. Investment spending is affected by real interest rates, over which the monetary authorities exercise little or no control because they cannot directly control changes in the public's inflationary expenditures.

Fifth, changes in private sector spending subsequent to variations in the growth rate of the money supply occur with long and variable lags. As a result, a monetary stimulus may come too late, when the economy is already recovering, fuelling excess expansion. Because of the unpredictability of these lags, monetarists argue that monetary policy should not be used to "fine-tune" the economy. Instead, monetary growth should follow a specified monetary rule and not be left to the discretion of central bankers.

natural rate of unemployment
the rate of unemployment that results when expectations of inflation equal the actual inflation rate (implying all unemployment is structural and frictional); also referred to as NAIRU (nonaccelerating inflation rate of unemployment)

Sixth, long-run real economic growth is independent of money growth and is determined by real growth factors such as the amount of capital stock, the size and structure of the labour force, and the rate of technological growth. There is no long-term tradeoff between the rate of unemployment and the rate of inflation. When the public's inflationary expectations become fully incorporated into its economic behaviour, any level of inflation is consistent with the **natural rate of unemployment**. Therefore, the long-run Phillips curve is a vertical line, positioned at the natural rate of unemployment. Hence, monetarists have recommended that the rate of growth of money should approximate the long-run rate of growth of real productive capacity if undesirable price inflation is to be avoided. Monetarists hold that the private sector is inherently stable and, if left to its own devices, tends to stabilize over time at the full-employment level of income.

The New Classical Approach

New Classical *a school of thought emphasizing rationality, wage and price flexibility, and efficient information processing*

The enunciation of this approach in the early 1970s is associated with Robert Lucas and Thomas Sargent and is based on two propositions: (1) that people form their expectations rationally; and (2) that money wages and prices are flexible; that is, they adjust quickly to bring supply and demand into equilibrium to clear factor, commodity, and asset markets. Insofar as the market-clearing assumption is in a sense borrowed from the classical economists, this approach is referred to as **New Classical.**

adaptive expectations *expectations formed by looking backward; an average of past changes*

rational expectations *expectations formed by looking forward and using all available information*

Two explanations exist for how people may form their expectations: one is called **adaptive expectations**, the other **rational expectations**. Adaptive expectations are formed by looking backward. Anticipated expectations essentially are an average of past changes, and expectations change slowly because the weight of past changes overshadows more recent changes. In contrast, rational expectations are formed by looking forward. More specifically, the following three assumptions underlie the concept of rational expectations:

1. Individuals form their expectations by using all available information efficiently. This means that they not only consider what happened in the past, but also what available evidence indicates may happen in the future. Robert Lucas has made the point, now referred to as the Lucas critique, that government policy changes influence the way expectations are formed.

2. In forming their expectations, individuals are knowledgeable about how the economy functions and therefore make informed predictions similar to those derived from economic theory.

3. Individuals' predictions may turn out to be wrong. But since errors can be costly, people learn quickly from their mistakes, so that on average their forecasts turn out to be correct. It is said that individuals do not make systematic errors in their expectations.

New Classical economists sharply distinguish between the effects of anticipated and unanticipated changes in the money supply. With rational expectations, complete information, and flexible wages and prices, anticipated expansionary monetary policy affects only the price level, leaving the real economy undisturbed. This idea is known as the **policy ineffectiveness proposition**, first suggested by Thomas Sargent and Neil Wallace. The proposition is illustrated in Figure 20–2. As shown in the figure, the economy initially is in equilibrium E_0, with the inflation rate constant at zero (by assumption, it is expected to be zero before the policy is announced) and output at its long-run full-employment level, Y^*.

policy ineffectiveness proposition *the idea that systematic monetary policy is known to all agents; hence, it will have no effect on the real side of the economy because it will have been planned for*

A permanent increase in the money supply raises expectations of inflation. Workers and firms, fully informed and behaving rationally, will immediately realize that the increase in money supply will raise the price level (and thereby the inflation rate). Workers will demand higher money wages to compensate for the expected higher prices, and firms will incorporate this increase into their costs and prices. As a result, the short-run Phillips curve immediately shifts upward from $SRPC_0$, to $SRPC_1$, and a new equilibrium position is established at E_2. Hence, it can be seen that all that anticipated monetary expansion has accomplished is to raise the price level, leaving real output undisturbed.

If, however, changes in the money supply come as a surprise, workers and firms won't have planned for the higher price level. The unanticipated expansion will reduce real wages, and employment and output will rise (and unemployment will fall). The economy will move to E_1 in the short run. As inflationary expectations adjust, the short-run Phillips curve will shift to $SRPC_1$; the new equilibrium could be at E_2 if workers and firms expect the central bank to increase the money supply again (thereby maintaining the higher inflation rate). However, as soon as expected price changes catch up to actual price

FIGURE 20–2   **THE POLICY EFFECTIVENESS PROPOSITION**

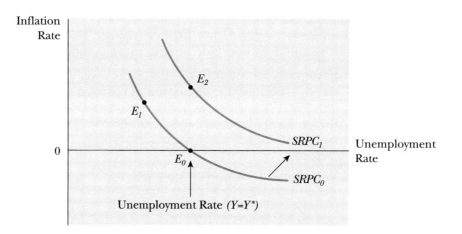

If everyone is rational and wages and prices are perfectly flexible, the economy will move from E_0 to E_2 when the central bank increases the money supply. Only nominal variables will change since unemployment (and, hence, real output) won't change.
If the increase in the money supply is unanticipated, monetary policy can have short-run real effects. In the long run, depending on what people expect the central bank to do next period, the economy may adjust from E_0 to E_1 to E_2.

changes, the economy will return to its long-term, full-employment equilibrium position.

The policy ineffectiveness proposition critically depends on the assumptions on which it is based. Critics have pointed out that, in the short run, monetary policy can be effective because the public's expectations become rational only over time, and because since the monetary authorities have better information than the public, they can engineer surprises. But fooling the public has its limitations. Since the public learns quickly from deceptions, systematic fooling does not work. Moreover, central bankers are reluctant to use deception, which can erode their cherished **credibility**.

credibility *the extent to which the market believes what policymakers have to say*

New Keynesian Approach

New Keynesian *a school of thought that blends traditional Keynesian models with market imperfections*

The **New Keynesian** theory of the effectiveness of monetary policy is based on a monetary adjustment mechanism in an economy with sticky wages and prices. We can interpret New Keynesian policies to be those that create a "wedge" between the actual inflation rate and the expected rate of inflation. For example, suppose you signed a two-period wage contract that set out the wage increases you were to receive over the two periods. You signed this contract based on your expectations of what the central bank would do over the contract period. This situation leads to "sticky" wages and prices, since your wage can't change from the value you signed in the contract, even in the face of new information. If you were wrong about the central bank policy (or if the policy changes because of some unforeseen event), we can get the same process as that described in Figure 20–2. In the short run, an unanticipated (as of the time you signed your multi-period contract) expansionary monetary policy can lead to an increase in real output via a reduction in the unemployment rate. In Figure 20–2, that's a movement from E_0 to E_1 in the short run.

In contrast to the New Classicals, the New Keynesians do not believe that markets are sufficiently flexible to produce continuous market-clearing conditions. The major reason usually cited for sticky wages is that money wages are set for a fixed contract period, frequently as long as three years. In addition, overall wages only adjust slowly because all labour contracts are not subject to renegotiation at the same time. If firms set their prices in terms of a constant percentage over cost, and wages are the main component of cost, then sticky wages also imply sticky prices. Another explanation of sticky prices has been so-called **menu costs**. In certain circumstances prices may not be regularly adjusted to reflect higher costs precisely because of the adjustment costs involved. For example, it is costly for restaurants to reprint their menus and for firms to print and distribute new catalogues.

menu costs *the costs of frequent price changes*

When wages and prices are sticky, then, as shown in Figure 20–2, expansionary monetary policy is effective in increasing real output in the short run (but not the long run).

A review of the salient features of arguments in favour of an inflationary bias, and their pitfalls, was recently provided by William Poole. Poole, the president of the Federal Reserve Bank of St. Louis, provides a central banker's perspective, which can be applied to both the Canadian and American economies. His analysis suggests that the Bank of Canada should continue to follow a policy of price stability, as the empirical evidence in support of the neo-Keynesian view is weak and ill-founded.

www.

Lags in the Effect of Monetary Policy

Monetary policy influences the economy only after long and variable lags (delays). Economists have distinguished between two lags in the conduct of stabilization policy: the **inside lag** and the **outside lag**. The inside lag is the time between an economic disturbance and the policy response to correct it. The outside lag is the time between a policy response and its influence on the economy. As shown in Figure 20–3, the inside lag consists of a recognition lag and an implementation lag. The recognition lag is the time it takes for the monetary authorities to recognize that a problem exists that requires their attention. This lag arises because it takes time to collect, tabulate, and analyze statistical data. Once the need for policy action has been recognized, it takes time to decide what policy action, and how much of it, is necessary; this is the implementation lag.

inside lag *the time between an economic disturbance and the policy response to correct it*

outside lag *the time between a policy response and its influence on the economy*

FIGURE 20–3   LAGS IN MONETARY POLICY

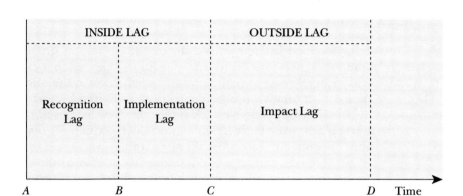

At time *A*, a disturbance arises in the economy that can be solved with monetary policy. At time *B*, the monetary authorities recognize that a problem exists, and by time *C* they are ready to implement appropriate policy. However, it takes from time *C* to time *D* before the implementation of a policy change has a significant effect on the economy.

In Canada, monetary policy probably has a relatively short inside lag, since the day-to-day conduct of policy is in the hands of the governor of the Bank of Canada and a small group of the governor's senior advisors. In contrast, the inside lags in the implementation of fiscal policy, which often requires legislative approval, can be both long and variable.

The outside lag, the time it takes for monetary policy to have an impact on the economy, can also be quite long and variable. Suppose the Bank of Canada has decided to implement a more expansionary monetary policy. It increases the monetary base, which through its liquidity effect reduces short-term interest rates, which in turn may result in a depreciation of the Canadian dollar. It takes time for businesses to change their business plans to take advantage of lower interest rates and a depreciated dollar. Moreover, it may take a while before business believes that the Bank's policy stance is sufficiently permanent for it to change its expectations accordingly.

The available evidence suggests that on average it may take at least one year before a change in monetary policy has its peak effect on real output. However, this lag can be as short as six months and as long as a year and a half. On average the peak effect of a change in monetary policy on the price level appears to be about two years, but it can be as short as one year.

The Differential Impact of Monetary Policy

The Bank of Canada's monetary policy has frequently been criticized because of its differential impact on businesses, sectors, and regions. As we have learned, the immediate impact of a restrictive monetary policy is on the cost and availability of funds provided by the banking system. Hence, those businesses that have to depend on bank loans as their major source of financing are more severely affected by a restrictive monetary policy than are those with alternative sources of financing. Smaller firms usually have to depend on the banks as their major source of funds. Larger firms can turn to the capital market as well as to foreign financial markets.

The housing construction sector usually has been more severely affected than others by the Bank's monetary policy. Before 1966, for instance, the maximum rate of interest on *National Housing Act* mortgage loans was administratively set. Because the maximum rate the banks were allowed to charge on NHA mortgages did not always reflect the higher market rates, the institutional lenders turned away from making NHA mortgage loans. Since these loans were the major source of residential mortgage financing, residential construction suffered. At times, the Canada Mortgage and Housing Corporation (formerly the Central Mortgage and Housing Corporation) came to the rescue with direct loans funded by the federal government.

The Bank of Canada conducts national monetary policy based on national levels of economic activity and inflation. Since economic conditions can differ from region to region, a national policy has frequently been viewed as discriminating between regions. In the late 1980s, for example, Canada's inflation rate was fuelled by an increase in spending in Ontario. When the Bank of Canada introduced a deflationary policy, the politicians in other regions (especially Atlantic Canada, where the economy remained relatively depressed) criticized the Bank's monetary stance. The Bank responded by noting: "A country with a common currency and well developed financial markets cannot have in any way levels of interest rates, or rates of monetary expansion, that would be systematically different in different regions or provinces." In a banking system with national branch networks, the banks employ their cash reserves according to their portfolio preferences and to maximize their profits. Assuming the Bank of Canada could make more cash available to the branches of the chartered banks in Atlantic Canada, there is no assurance that this cash would be used to expand loans in the region. Monetary policy cannot be used effectively to offset regional disparities.

At times during periods of tight credit conditions, the Bank has used **moral suasion** on the chartered banks to induce them not to restrict their lending in less prosperous regions. *The Small Business Loans Act*, the *Fisheries Loans Act*, and the *Farm Improvement Loans Act* were designed to assist certain sectors and regions that can be adversely affected by national monetary and financial policies.

A more radical proposal for dealing with perceived regional monetary and financial discrimination has been the creation of regional (or optimal) currency areas, each with its own central bank. Such a proposal involves complex economic and political issues. In an attempt to assuage critics of "made in Ontario" monetary policy, the Bank of Canada increased its staff in its regional offices (and even opened several new offices). Senior bank economists spend up to two years in these regional offices to try to help explain Bank policy to local business and consumer groups, and at the same time get a better feel for the impact of Canadian monetary policy on the cost and availability of credit at the regional level.

moral suasion
used by the central bank when persuading financial institutions to voluntarily pursue some objective of financial policy

Monetary Policy for Controlling Inflation

money growth targeting *the idea that monetary policy should be based on setting growth objectives for monetary aggregates*

As we learned, **money growth targeting** was introduced by the Bank of Canada in 1975 as part of the government's attempt to control inflation. Two alternative monetary policy strategies were available to the Bank. It could lower money supply growth *gradually* (the strategy it chose to follow), or it could lower it all at once (called a *cold turkey* strategy). As we shall see, the degree of success of either strategy in reducing the rate of inflation depends on the credibility of the Bank's policy (whether the public believes its objectives will be met), the structure of contracts in the economy, and the manner in which expectations are formed.

Under gradualism, the money supply is reduced slowly but steadily. In Figure 20–4, for example, the economy is initially in full-employment equilibrium, with the inflation rate at π_0. With slower money growth, the short-run Phillips curves will shift down. To the degree that there are minor rigidities in the system, the unemployment rate will rise slightly during the process of adjustment to a new lower rate of inflation, shown by the arrows along the path labelled 1. The short-run Phillips curve shifts downward as people change their price expectations and firms' input costs fall. Because of the steady shifts of the short-run curve, the inflation rate continually declines, while the rate of unemployment increases for a time (output decreases) but gradually returns to the full-employment level. With a gradual downward drift of the short-run curve as expectations adjust, the rate of inflation falls over time to the desired lower level, while in the process the rate of unemployment is kept relatively low.

The cold turkey approach claims to be able to reduce inflation rapidly, but this may be at the cost of a very high rate of unemployment for a short period. In Figure 20–4, when the monetary authorities induce a sharp decrease in money supply growth, expectations may not have taken the severity of the monetary contraction fully into account. The economy rapidly moves along the initial short-run Phillips curve to point *C*, where the rate of inflation is lower but unemployment is high. With lower inflation and a high rate of unemployment, people will change their inflation expectations, which, together with lower costs of production than expected, are reflected by a downward shift of the short-run Phillips curve to $SRPC_1$. Equilibrium is again achieved at full employment, but at a lower rate of inflation. In the cold turkey approach, the economy follows path 2 shown in Figure 20–4. It is assumed that the economy quickly proceeds along this path toward the desired lower rate of inflation, but with a short period of relatively high unemployment before full employment is regained.

According to the New Classical economists, who assume that expectations are formed rationally and that goods and money markets are in continuous equilibrium, a credible cold turkey policy will automatically reduce the inflation rate without causing any unemployment. Once a credible anti-inflationary policy is announced, people are assumed to change their inflationary expectations immediately, workers to lower their wage demands quickly, and firms to lower their prices. In terms of Figure 20–4, the reduction in the rate of monetary growth is simultaneously accompanied by a downward shift of the short-run Phillips curve. The policy announcement by itself may cause the Phillips

FIGURE 20–4   **GRADUALISM VERSUS COLD TURKEY**

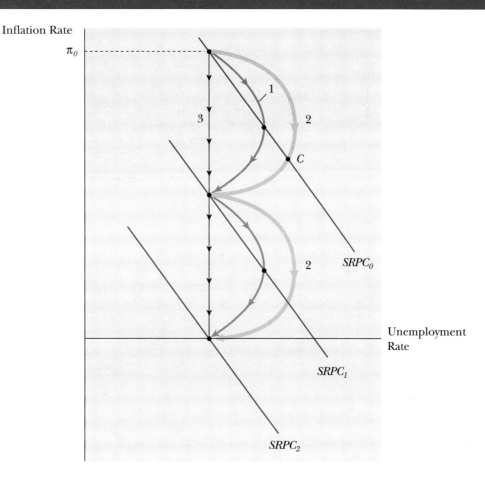

Under gradualism, the economy follows arrow 1 and eventually attains a low inflation environment. A cold turkey approach induces greater unemployment effects, with the economy following arrow 2. New Classical economists believe the economy moves along path 3 so that there are little or no unemployment effects of contradictory monetary policy.

curve to shift even before a reduction in money growth occurs. As shown by the adjustment path 3, the desired lower rate of inflation is quickly attained without the economy having to suffer any increased unemployment.

Although rational expectations have been acknowledged as playing an important role in economic agents' decision processes, the New Classical theorists' continual market-clearing assumption is generally viewed as being unrealistic because of institutional arrangements in the labour market. Workers are hired under implicit or explicit contracts that are usually for long periods. Money wages are set when contracts are negotiated and, unless indexed, remain fixed during the contract period. Contracts overlap in that they do not end at the same time. As a result, average money wages cannot continually adjust to incorporate all changes in inflationary expectations, and labour market equilibrium is not continuously maintained. This is true even if rational expectations play an important role at the time each contract is negotiated. Because of overlapping labour contracts, the short-run Phillips curve does not immediately shift down following an announcement of lower money growth and a consequent lowering of labour's price expectations.

Even with rational expectations the short-run Phillips curve can only shift downward over time as old contracts are renegotiated to reflect the change in expectations. Hence, we cannot expect that a credible cold turkey anti-inflationary policy will bring about a lower rate of inflation without causing some unemployment. During extended periods of high inflation, however, labour contracts are usually written for much shorter periods, and therefore more frequent renegotiation allows average money wages to be more immediately related to changing inflationary expectations. As a result, shifts in the Phillips curve take place much more rapidly, and unemployment caused by an anti-inflationary policy is less severe.

The short-run Phillips curve may also only shift down slowly following the announcement of an anti-inflation policy, when expectations are assumed to be formed adaptively rather than rationally. As explained earlier, with adaptive expectations people are assumed to base their expectations on what happened in the immediate past without taking into consideration how present events may determine the future. Hence, expectations are updated only gradually, and as a result the Phillips curve only shifts downward slowly over time.

Both strategies, as explained, reduce the level of inflation and return the economy to full employment, but at different rates and levels of unemployment, as shown by the three possible paths of adjustment traced out in Figure 20–4. The equilibrium of a gradualist strategy may suffer from an additional difficulty not yet mentioned. A gradualist strategy may lack credibility in the eyes of the public, which may not feel that it represents a definite move toward reducing inflation. The public may be skeptical that it will be kept up, because political changes, which can lead to policy changes, can happen over the long period that the strategy needs to be in place. These changes can come about because of a change in government, or a change in policy by the existing government, if it either views its gradualism strategy as unfavourable to itself or develops new goals. The cold turkey strategy, on the other hand, is more likely to have credibility, because people can see that the government is determined to reduce inflation and is prepared to take drastic steps to do so.

The disinflation policy introduced in Canada in the early 1990s attempted to address the credibility problem in two ways. First, the announcement of the policy was made jointly by the governor of the Bank of Canada and the minister of finance, signalling that the Bank had the full support of the federal government. Second, specific targets for reductions in the rate of inflation by the end of 1995 were announced (we'll return to this issue at the end of the textbook). These defined targets made it much easier for the public to monitor the Bank's progress in achieving its goals and in holding it accountable for any shortfalls. This, in turn, may have put additional pressures on the Bank to ensure its credibility. The strategy appears to have worked, at least in its early stages, since the adjustments in wages and prices that followed indicate that the public expects the Bank and the government to be committed to reducing the inflation rate and achieving price stability.

Sources of Instability and Choice of Policy Target

We noted earlier that monetarists contend that the quantity of money impinges directly on spending decisions of all types. If this is indeed the case, the appropriate variable for the monetary authorities to control is the quantity of money. However, Keynesians contend that monetary policy influences the economy indirectly through credit conditions. Therefore, from the Keynesian point of view, the appropriate variables to be controlled are interest rates and the availability of credit. The existence of two schools means a dilemma exists: The monetary authorities cannot control both the quantity of money and the interest rates at the same time. They must do one or the other. If they choose to control the quantity of money, interest rates (the price of money) will move passively to whatever level clears the money market. Alternatively, if they decide to determine interest rates, they have to passively furnish whatever quantity of money clears the market.[4]

Both interest rates and the money supply are affected by forces other than those resulting from policy changes. Moreover, quite frequently the authorities are unable to ascertain whether a shift in the proximate target variable is the result of their own actions or of forces outside their immediate control. William Poole and others have pointed out that the choice between money supply targets and interest rate targets depends on the relative importance of the various sources of instability in the economy.[5] This fact can be illustrated using a model of money demand and money supply as well as the rudimentary savings equals investment equilibrium condition you might recall from your introductory economics course.[6]

Let's refresh your memory. Panel (a) of Figure 20–5 plots the demand and supply of money as a function of the interest rate. The money supply is initially assumed to be fixed by the central bank, while the demand for money is a negative function of the interest rate (since the higher the opportunity cost of holding money, the lower is the demand for money). Panel (b) of Figure 20–5

---

4. You may see this more clearly if you think about the market for a commodity, like wheat. If the government were to control price, the quantity supplied would be market determined. If the authorities controlled quantity supplied, the market would determine the price of wheat. Hence, if the central bank controls interest rates, it loses control of the money supply. If it controls the money supply, the interest rate will be market determined.

5. This reasoning has been extended to the open economy. See Peter Sephton, "The Choice of Monetary Policy Instruments in Canada: An Extension," *Canadian Journal of Economics* 20 (February 1987), pp. 55–60.

6. One way to think about this is to consider a closed economy without government. If all income is either consumed or saved, and all production is for consumption and investment purposes, then when income equals production, consumption plus savings must equal consumption plus investment. The consumption terms cancel out, leaving "savings equals investment" for equilibrium.

FIGURE 20–5   EQUILIBRIUM IN MONEY AND OUTPUT MARKETS

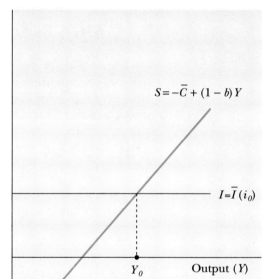

(a) MONEY DEMAND AND SUPPLY

(b) SAVINGS AND INVESTMENT

Money demand and money supply determine the equilibrium interest rate in panel (a). In panel (b) we describe equilibrium income Y_0 as the point at which savings equals investment. Note that investment is independent of income but is a function of the interest rate (i_0).

plots the familiar savings equals investment equilibrium condition, where production equals income in the economy. Investment and savings are on the vertical axis, with the level of income on the horizontal axis. The savings function is a positive function of income; the investment function is independent of income but is a negative function of the interest rate. Every time the interest rate changes, the investment function shifts, leading to a new level of equilibrium income.

REAL SHOCKS   Now suppose the economy begins at point A in each panel of Figure 20–6 and autonomous consumption rises exogenously. (Recall that the vertical intercept of the savings function is the negative of the level of autonomous consumption.) This rise shifts the savings function to the right in panel (b) and raises equilibrium income. An increase in income stimulates money demand (for transactions purposes), and the money demand curve shifts right in panel (a). If the central bank were to use the interest rate as its policy instrument, the money supply would rise so that the new equilibrium at

FIGURE 20–6 POLICY INSTRUMENTS WHEN THERE ARE REAL SHOCKS

(a) MONEY DEMAND AND SUPPLY

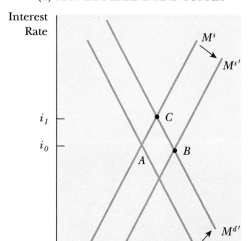

(b) SAVINGS AND INVESTMENT

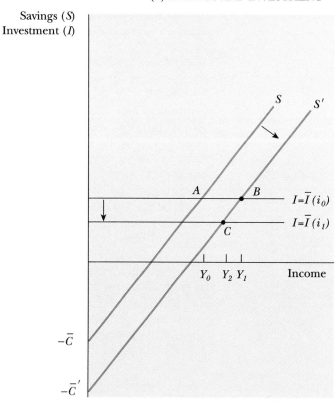

A positive real shock shifts the savings right to S'. If the central bank fixes the interest rates, the higher level of money demand (resulting from an increase in income) must be met with an increase in the money supply, taking us from point A to point B in panel (a). Since interest rates don't change, investment remains fixed and output rises from Y_0 to Y_1.

If the central bank controls the money supply, the nominal interest rate rises, thereby reducing investment and, hence, output rises, but by less than under interest rate control.

If the object is to keep output as close to its original value as possible, the central bank should control the money supply when there are real shocks.

point B was at the controlled interest rate i_0. In panel (b), this implies that the investment function would not shift (since interest rates remained fixed), and output would rise to Y_1 from Y_0.

If the central bank were to control the money supply rather than the interest rate, the increase in money demand would lead to an increase in interest rates to i_1, taking the equilibrium in panel (a) to point C from point A. As interest rates rise, investment falls, and the investment function shifts down in panel (b). This shift reduces the expansionary effect of the real shock so that output rises from Y_0 to Y_2 rather than Y_1.

These figures make it clear that if the central bank believes the economy is subject to shocks that are primarily real in origin (that is, they affect the real side of the economy rather than being monetary in nature), the optimal choice of policy instrument is controlling the money supply. This policy is *optimal* in the sense that it minimizes fluctuations in real output from its original value (admittedly penalizing positive shocks in the same manner as negative shocks).

MONETARY SHOCKS   Now consider the potential for shocks to the demand for money within the same framework as Figure 20–6. If the demand for money were to fall exogenously, the money demand curve would shift to the left in panel (a) of Figure 20–7. If the central bank were to control the money supply (and let interest rates be market determined), the interest rate would fall, and the economy would move to points *B* from points *A* in both panels. Notice that the lower interest rate stimulates investment, thereby raising equilibrium income.

If the central bank were to control the interest rate (and let the money supply be market determined), the reduction in money demand would be met with a reduction in the money supply, leaving the interest rate unchanged. If the rate of interest remains constant, so too does the level of investment, and equilibrium output does not change.

These arguments indicate that if there are disturbances to money demand, the policy instrument that leads to the least fluctuation in equilibrium income from its initial value is the interest rate. This leads to the famous "Poole policy prescription": If there are real shocks, the central bank should use the money supply as its policy instrument, while if there are money demand shocks, the central bank should use the interest rate as its instrument of monetary policy.

During most of the postwar period up to 1975, the Bank of Canada used credit conditions (reflected by market interest rates and the availability of credit) as both the indicator and the target of its policy actions. In part, this followed from its adherence to the Keynesian view of the transmission mechanism of monetary policy and in part from its underlying desire to develop the Canadian money and capital markets as well as to minimize the cost of debt management. To a large degree, it was also the result of the government's policy of either maintaining a fixed exchange rate or managing the exchange rate to confine the value of the Canadian dollar within a very narrow range.

In an open economy with a fixed exchange rate, the appropriate indicator of monetary policy is the domestic rate of interest and the proximate target developments in the country's balance of payments. The Bank of Canada has not always followed this prescription, especially during 1958–60. Moreover, as Thomas Courchene has pointed out, especially after Canada again adopted a flexible exchange rate system in 1970, the Bank's use of credit conditions, as reflected by the nominal rate of interest and the chartered banks' liquid asset ratio, produced an expansionary policy in terms of the growth rate of the money supply. This led inevitably to an increase in the rate of inflation. Courchene argued that nominal interest rates can be a misleading indicator, in that during inflationary periods a rise in nominal interest rates reflects the rate of expected inflation and not a tight monetary policy. Moreover, the Bank was also misled when using the chartered banks' liquid asset ratio as an indicator of the availability of credit, because a fall in this ratio did not signal a decrease

FIGURE 20–7   POLICY INSTRUMENTS WHEN THERE ARE MONEY DEMAND SHOCKS

(a) MONEY DEMAND AND SUPPLY

(b) SAVINGS AND INVESTMENT

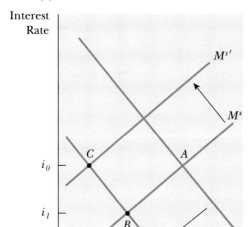

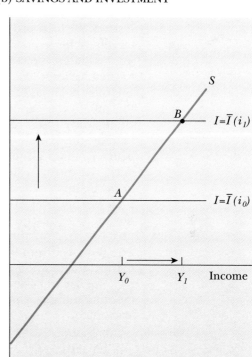

When the demand for money falls in panel (a), the central bank can choose to fix the interest rate or the money supply. When it chooses to control the money supply, the interest rate falls to clear the money market. This stimulates investment leading to an increase in output from Y_0 to Y_1.

If the central bank chooses to fix the interest rate, the money supply would have to fall in response to a lower level of money demand. Investment would remain unchanged, and real output would not change.

This situation suggests that the interest rate is the optimal policy instrument in the wake of shocks to money demand.

in the future availability of credit. Instead, it reflected a change in the chartered banks' behaviour with respect to what they considered the threshold level of this ratio. A change in their behaviour followed the introduction of liability management and financial innovations.

In 1975 the Bank of Canada switched from credit conditions to the growth rate of the money supply as the appropriate indicator and target of its policy. It chose M1 as the appropriate monetary aggregate to monitor and control because of the belief that it could control M1 in a reasonably prompt and predictable way, and because M1 appeared to be related in a predictable and systematic manner to GDP and short-term interest rates. Not everyone agreed with the Bank's contentions at the time. Courchene, in particular, argued that the Bank could control a broader aggregate of money supply better than it could the M1 measure, and that a broader aggregate, which was more inclusive of the public's transactions balances, was more closely related to economic activity.

Courchene also questioned the manner in which the Bank attempted to control M1. As we have previously argued, the Bank used interest rates as its instrument to control M1 and keep its growth within announced growth-rate targets. Whenever M1 growth approached the upper target limit, the Bank nudged interest rates up indirectly by rationing the availability of cash reserves to the chartered banks, and, at times, directly by intervening forcefully in the Treasury bill market. With the higher opportunity cost of holding M1 balances, the public was expected to reduce its demand for M1. Alternatively, by providing cash reserves to the banks and by intervening in the Treasury bill market, the Bank attempted to keep the rate of money growth from falling below its lower target limit. As shown in Figure 20–8, until 1981 the Bank was fairly successful in holding M1 growth within its set target levels. After 1981, however, this was no longer the case, owing to innovations in banking practices such as daily interest savings accounts and cash management accounts for businesses. As a consequence of these innovations, the demand for money became unstable. In 1982 the Bank abandoned money targeting. This move is what we would expect from our earlier analysis, which showed that money targeting is inappropriate when a major source of disturbance is the money market.

The Bank of Canada walks a fine line when it comes to adopting and implementing monetary policy, as we shall see when we review the history of mone-

FIGURE 20–8   TARGET GROWTH RANGES FOR M1
Billions of Dollars, Seasonally Adjusted; Ratio Scale

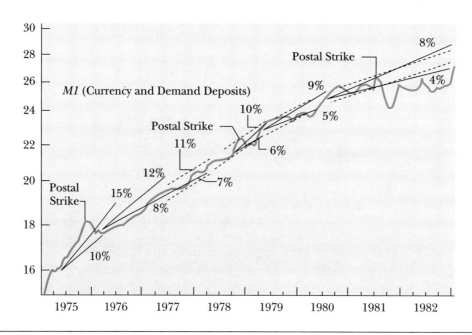

tary policy in Canada. The problem with ensuring the efficacy of any monetary policy is that the goals of policy need to be clearly defined, and the state of the economy has to be gauged with precision. The wrong interpretation of events can lead to deleterious policies that only further exacerbate the disturbances impinging on the economy. Economic policymaking is an art that takes experience and talent to finely hone. Remember that the next time the central bank's policies are subjected to ridicule. Does the group criticizing current policy have a firmer grip on economic conditions than the Bank? Does it have a credible alternative that will address the problems it has identified? Perhaps so, but remember it's much easier to ride the bus than to drive the bus.

KEY TERMS

adaptive expectations
availability doctrine
credibility
debt management
inside lag
liquidity preference function
menu costs

monetarist approach
money growth targeting
moral suasion
natural rate of unemployment
New Classical
New Keynesian
outside lag

permanent real income
Phillips curves
policy ineffectiveness proposition
portfolio balance approach
rational expectations

REVIEW QUESTIONS

1. How did the orthodox Keynesians explain the transmission of monetary policy?
2. Explain the availability of credit approach and contrast it with the neo-Keynesian approach to explain the effectiveness of monetary policy.
3. Outline the major tenets of monetarism.
4. What are the assumptions underlying the concept of rational expectations?
5. Explain the policy ineffectiveness proposition of the new-classical economists.
6. How do the neo-Keynesians explain the effectiveness of monetary policy in the short run?
7. Outline the various lags in the effect of monetary policy.
8. Could we implement regional monetary policies in Canada?
9. Compare a gradualist with a cold turkey disinflationary monetary policy.

10. How does central bank credibility reduce the short-run costs of a disinflationary monetary policy?
11. How does the relative importance of the sources of economic instability affect the choice of monetary targets?
12. Suppose the demand for money falls. Which policy instrument should the central bank adopt if it wants to encourage fluctuations in output from its current value? Make sure to use graphs in your answer.
13. Suppose autonomous consumption falls. Which policy instrument will minimize fluctuations in equilibrium income? Which instrument will maximize fluctuations in equilibrium income? Make sure to use graphs in your answer.

SELECTED READINGS

Bosworth, Barry. "Institutional Change and the Efficacy of Monetary Policy." *Brookings Papers on Economic Activity* 1 (1989), pp. 77–124.

Brunner, Karl. "The Role of Money and Monetary Policy." *Federal Reserve Bank of St. Louis Review*, July 1968, pp. 9–24. Reprinted in *Federal Reserve Bank of St. Louis Review*, September/October 1989, pp. 4–22.

Friedman, Milton. "The Role of Monetary Policy." *American Economic Review* 58 (March 1968), pp. 1–17. Reprinted in Milton Friedman, *The Optimum Quantity of Money and Other Essays*. Chicago, Ill.: Aldine Publishing Co., 1969, pp. 95–100.

Gordon, Robert. "What Is New Keynesian Economics?" *Journal of Economic Literature* (September 1990), pp. 1115–71.

Holland, Steven. "Rational Expectations and the Effects of Monetary Policy: A Guide for the Uninitiated." *Federal Reserve Bank of St. Louis Review*, 67 (May 1985), pp. 5–11.

Laidler, David. "The Legacy of the Monetarist Controversy." *Federal Reserve Bank of St. Louis Review*, March/April 1980, pp. 49–64.

———. "Taking Money Seriously." *Canadian Journal of Economics* (November 1988), pp. 687–713.

———. *Monetarist Perspectives*. Cambridge, Mass.: Harvard University Press, 1982.

Maddock, R., and M. Carter. "A Child's Guide to Rational Expectations." *Journal of Economic Literature* 20 (March 1982), pp. 39–51.

Mankiw, N. Gregory. "Recent Developments in Macroeconomics: A Very Quick Refresher Course." *Journal of Money, Credit and Banking* (August 1988), Part 2, pp. 436–49.

Mankiw, N. Gregory, and David Romer, eds. *New Keynesian Economics*. Cambridge, Mass.: MIT Press, 1991.

Poole, William. "Great Monetary Myths." Great Issues Series, St. Louis University (February 24, 2000).

Purvis, Douglas D. "Monetarism: A Review." *Canadian Journal of Economics* 13 (February 1980), pp. 96–122.

Sephton, Peter S. "The Choice of Monetary Policy Instruments in Canada: An Extension." *Canadian Journal of Economics* 20 (February 1987), pp. 55–60.

Tobin, James. "The Monetarist Counterrevolution Today— An Appraisal." *Economic Journal* 91 (1981), pp. 29–42.

CHAPTER TWENTY-ONE

FOREIGN EXCHANGE REGIMES

After reading this chapter you should be able to
1. Explain how exchange rates are determined in the short run using interest rate parity
2. Describe absolute and relative purchasing power parity and relate these theories to exchange rates in the long run
3. Provide the mechanics underlying fixed exchange rates
4. Show how a central bank could operate a managed exchange rate
5. Argue why developing nations frequently introduce exchange controls
6. Discuss Bank of Canada foreign exchange market intervention policy
7. Differentiate between sterilized and unsterilized intervention
8. Explain exchange rate volatility in terms of exchange rate overshooting
9. Argue the pros and cons of both fixed and flexible exchange rate regimes
10. Enter the debate on the choice of the exchange rate regime for Canada

A foreign exchange regime refers to the institutional arrangements countries establish for determining the foreign exchange value of their currencies. Four types of foreign exchange regimes exist: (1) a floating exchange rate, (2) a fixed exchange rate, (3) a managed floating exchange rate, and (4) an exchange control regime. In this chapter we describe how foreign exchange rates are determined under each of these regimes.

Floating Exchange Rate Regime

flexible exchange regime nominal exchange rates are determined in competitive markets, without government intervention

Under a floating or **flexible exchange regime**, nominal exchange rates are determined in competitive markets by the forces of demand and supply, without government intervention. The net demand for a country's currency on the foreign exchange market arises from the net international demand for its goods, services, and assets. Until recently, the net demand for most countries' currencies was essentially for the payment of goods and services. Hence, it was generally assumed that foreign exchange rates were primarily determined by net demands for settlement of current account imbalances in international payments. Moreover, exchange rates were seen as adjusting to make the flow supply of a country's currency equal to its flow demand. The flow supply and demand were directly related to current imbalances and international borrowing or lending to settle these imbalances.

More recently, following the closer integration of international capital markets, which has been accompanied by almost perfect international capital mobility and a very high degree of asset substitutability, the net demands for the currencies of the major industrial countries have come to be dominated by transactions in financial assets. Hence, it is now widely held that, at least in the short run, exchange rates adjust to make the demanded stock of financial assets denominated in a country's currency equal to the supplied stock. This adjustment is explained by the **portfolio balance theory of the exchange rate** and the **monetary theory of the exchange rate**. While both of these theories focus on the role of financial assets as the major short-term determinants of exchange rates, the portfolio theory includes all financial assets denominated in a country's currency, whereas the monetary theory considers the country's quantity of money to be the only relevant asset.

What follows are short-run and long-run theories of exchange rate determination. The short-run theory is based on a portfolio balance model that assumes that exchange rates are essentially determined in asset markets, as explained by financial arbitrage and interest rate parity. The long-run theory is based on the proposition that, in long run, equilibrium nominal exchange rates are determined by purchasing power parity, international competitiveness, and international commodity arbitrage.

portfolio balance theory of the exchange rate all financial assets denominated in a country's currency help determine its exchange rate

monetary theory of the exchange rate only a country's quantity of money determines its exchange rate

Short-Run Determinants of Exchange Rates

Let us consider the short-run determinants of the value of the Canadian dollar in terms of its U.S. counterpart. We assume that in the short run the value of the Canadian dollar is primarily determined in asset markets, as explained by uncovered interest rate parity, introduced in Chapter 7. This illustration of interest rate parity is similar to the one found there.

Suppose one U.S. dollar is invested for a year in the United States. By the end of the year $(1 + i^{US})$ will be accumulated, where i^{US} is the U.S. interest rate. Alternatively, the U.S. dollar can be converted at the current exchange rate into Canadian currency and invested in Canada, earning the Canadian interest rate $i^{CAN.}$ By the end of the year this investment will accumulate to $(E_t)(1 + i^{CAN})$ Canadian dollars, where, recall, we have defined E_t (the exchange rate at time t) to be the Canadian dollar price of a U.S. dollar.

If the U.S. dollar exchange rate is expected to be E^e_{t+1} at the end of the year, one can expect to retrieve $(E_t/E^e_{t+1})(1 + i^{CAN})$ U.S. dollars at that time. The investment strategy chosen—Canadian or U.S. dollar-denominated assets—depends on the interest rate parity (*IRP*) ratio:

(21.1)
$$IRP = \frac{1 + i^{US}}{(1 + i^{CAN})(E_t / E^e_{t+1})} = \left(\frac{1 + i^{US}}{1 + i^{CAN}}\right)\left(\frac{E^e_{t+1}}{E_t}\right)$$

When $IRP > 1$, investors buy U.S. dollar-denominated assets; and when $IRP < 1$, they buy Canadian-dollar-denominated assets. When $IRP = 1$, they are indifferent about the currency denomination of their financial assets. Profit-seeking interest rate arbitragers drive the ratio to unity so that, given the existing interest rates in Canada and the United States as well as the expectations of the future value of the U.S. dollar against the Canadian dollar, the short-run equilibrium U.S. dollar rate in terms of the Canadian dollar is given by

(21.2)
$$E_t = \left(\frac{1 + i^{US}}{1 + i^{CAN}}\right)(E^e_{t+1})$$

Alternatively, we can write the equilibrium condition for the Canadian dollar in terms of its American counterpart. We define the Canadian dollar's spot rate as S_t. (This is equal to $1/E_t$ where E_t is the U.S. dollar's spot price in terms of the Canadian dollar.) The short-run equilibrium condition of the Canadian dollar is given by

(21.2a)
$$S_t = \left(1 + \frac{i^{CAN}}{1 + i^{US}}\right)(S^e_{t+1})$$

In Figure 21–1 we have drawn supply and demand curves for financial assets denominated in Canadian dollars. Under a floating exchange rate regime, in the short run the supply curve of Canadian-dollar assets is upward sloping. These assets include Canadian dollar currency, deposits, bonds, and money market securities. The supply of Canadian-dollar assets changes over time, and therefore the supply curve shifts. Such shifts can occur because of federal government budget changes and the Bank of Canada's monetary policy. For example, the supply curve shifts to the right if the government increases its budget deficit, financing it with a new issue of Canadian dollar bonds purchased by the Bank of Canada. Canadian-dollar-denominated assets also increase when the Bank of Canada buys foreign-currency-denominated assets with an expansion of the Canadian money supply.

The quantity of Canadian-dollar assets demanded is shown by the downward-sloping D_0 curve. The curve is drawn for given Canadian and U.S. interest rates and expectations of the Canadian dollar's future value. It slopes downward because as the Canadian dollar loses value, interest rate arbitragers respond to this profit opportunity by increasing the quantity of Canadian-dollar assets they desire to hold. A decline in the Canadian dollar's value will also increase the quantity of Canadian-dollar assets demanded to finance any increase in the net demand for Canadian exports of goods and services.

The market establishes the short-run equilibrium value of the Canadian dollar at S_0, the intersection of the demand and supply curves for Canadian-dollar assets where the interest parity condition is satisfied.

The value of the Canadian dollar changes when the demand curve shifts owing to a violation of the interest parity condition. For example, an upward shift in the D_0 curve to D_1 increases the value of the Canadian dollar from S_0 to S_1. Such a shift can be caused by an increase in Canadian interest rates, a

FIGURE 21–1   FLEXIBLE EXCHANGE RATES

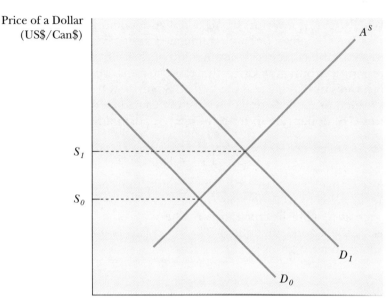

A perfectly flexible exchange rate regime allows the value of the dollar to be market determined. An increase in the demand for dollar-denominated assets leads to an appreciation of the dollar under flexible exchange rates.

decline in U.S. interest rates, or an expected increase in the future value of the Canadian dollar.

Long-Run Determinants of Exchange Rates

purchasing power parity (PPP) under ideal conditions, the exchange rate should reflect relative prices across countries

absolute PPP the exchange rate should be the ratio of the domestic price of a commodity relative to its foreign price

We assume that the profit-seeking activities of commodity arbitrageurs tend to establish long-run equilibrium exchange rates based on the **purchasing power parity** (**PPP**) theory of exchange rates. There are two versions of this theory: the absolute version, and the comparative or relative version. **Absolute PPP** is an extension of the law of one price. It states that if international commodity arbitrage is possible and if arbitrageurs exploit price disparities for profit by simultaneously buying a commodity where it is cheap and selling it where it is expensive, then its price will be the same in every market. Any price discrepancies that may remain are attributed to transportation and transactions costs. Hence, if Can.$400 buys an ounce of gold in Toronto, it should also, after conversion into U.S. dollars at the existing spot exchange rate, buy an ounce of gold in New York. While it may be advantageous in the short run for Canadians to cross-border shop, in the long run the exchange rate should adjust to remove most price advantages.

According to PPP, the law of one price as it relates to a single commodity also applies to the prices of all traded goods, as reflected in a country's general price level.[1] As a result, the long-run equilibrium value of the nominal exchange rate of the currencies of any two countries should equal the ratio of their price levels. For example, suppose that P_t and P_t^* are the price levels in Canada and the United States, respectively, and E_t is the Canadian dollar price of one U.S. dollar at time t. If absolute purchasing power parity holds, then

(21.3)
$$P_t = E_t P_t^*$$

or

(21.4)
$$E_t = \frac{P_t}{P_t^*}$$

Purchasing power parity as implied in equations 21.3 and 21.4 does not hold exactly, because the calculation of general price levels includes nontraded goods not subject to international commodity arbitrage. Moreover, countries' price indices are not strictly comparable because they include different goods and services as reflected by their individual production and consumption preferences.

relative PPP
exchange rates should change over time according to the relative changes in domestic and foreign prices

The comparative or **relative PPP** theory attempts to avoid the price level pitfalls inherent in the absolute version. It asserts that with freely fluctuating exchange rates, the percentage change in exchange rates from a given base period is equal to the difference between the percentage changes from the same base period between two countries' price levels (so we work in rates of change rather than in levels). This relationship is shown by

(21.5)
$$\Delta E_t = \Delta P_t - \Delta P_t^*$$

where Δ denotes "percentage changes" from the same base period.

Despite the statistical problems inherent in calculating purchasing power parity, empirical evidence confirms the long-run tendency toward the price relationships predicted by the PPP theory.

K. Rogoff, summarizing the relevance of PPP to the behaviour of exchange rate notes that "real exchange rates...tend to converge towards purchasing power parity in the very long run....The speed of convergence...is extremely slow; deviations appear to damp out at a rate of roughly 15 percent a year."[2] D.R. Johnson, using Canadian data, reports results similar to Rogoff, with more than a decade having to pass after any disturbance for PPP to reassert itself. However, he also finds that "shorter samples show little support for purchasing

1. As we will see shortly, this assumes all goods in the price index are traded goods. When some goods in the price index are not subject to international trade, absolute PPP does not hold. Empirical evidence suggests PPP works well in the long run, but that it is incapable of explaining the evolution of exchange rates in the short run. See Yangru Wu (1996) for some recent evidence.

2. K. Rogoff. "The Purchasing Power Parity Puzzle." *Journal of Economic Literature* 34 (June 1996), pp. 647–68.

power parity, particularly after 1970."[3] A similar study by Murray van Norden and Vigfussen for the period 1959: Q1 to 1995: Q1 also firmly rejects the relevance of the PPP.[4]

Some economists have combined the quantity theory of money with the purchasing power theory to derive a theory of exchange rate determination. Largely, this so-called monetary model of exchange rate determination has been rejected owing to the instability of the demand for money and its failure to adequately account for real shocks to the economy.[5]

Fixed Exchange Rate Regime

fixed exchange rate regime *the central bank sets the exchange rate and intervenes to ensure the rate does not deviate substantially from its fixed level*

par value *the value at which a monetary authority fixes its exchange rate*

gold standard *when each country defines the value of its monetary unit in terms of a given amount of gold*

gold (mint) par of exchange *the rate at which a country defines its monetary unit in terms of gold*

Under a **fixed exchange rate regime**, a country declares a central or **par value** for the value of its currency. The country's monetary authorities, usually its central bank, assume the responsibility to maintain the exchange rate within prescribed limits, or a "band," of the declared par value. This requires the central bank to stand ready to buy and sell its currency on the foreign exchange market for a price dictated by these prescribed limits. Under the gold standard, a country's monetary authorities were obliged to buy and sell domestic financial assets for a stated amount of gold. Under the Bretton Woods system, between 1945 and 1971, member countries were required to buy and sell financial assets denominated in their national currencies for a prescribed amount of assets denominated in foreign currencies, typically U.S. dollars.

Under the international **gold standard** (which we will describe in a later chapter), each country defined the value of its monetary unit in terms of a given amount of gold. Since gold was the common denominator of the value of each country's currency, a definite pattern of currency values existed among countries. For example, with the re-establishment of the gold standard in the 1920s, the Canadian dollar was valued at 23.22 grains and the British pound at 113.0016 grains of fine gold. The exchange value of the pound in terms of Canadian dollars was therefore

$$\frac{113.0016}{23.22} = \$4.8665$$

This ratio is known as the **gold** or **mint par of exchange**. The market rate of exchange could fluctuate freely around this mint par of exchange within a narrow band determined by what were known as the gold export and gold

3. D.R. Johnson "Co-integration Error Correction, and Purchasing Power Parity between Canada and the United States." *Canadian Journal of Economics* 23 (November 1990), pp. 839–955; and by the same author, "Unit Roots, Cointegration and Purchasing Power Parity" in *Exchange Rate and the Economy*. Proceedings of a conference held at the Bank of Canada, June 22–23, 1993. Ottawa, Bank of Canada.

4. S. Murray, van Norden and R. Vigfussen. "Excess Volatility and Speculative Bubbles in the Canadian Dollar: Real or Imagined?" *Technical Report 76* (1996), Ottawa, Bank of Canada.

5. See H.G. Johnson, "The Monetary Approach to the Balance of Payments: A Nontechnical Guide," *Journal of International Economics* (1977), pp. 252–68; and J.T. Bilson, "Recent Developments in Monetary Models of Exchange Rate Determination," *IMF* Staff papers (1979), pp. 201–23.

import points. These gold points were given by the cost of shipping gold between Canada and the United Kingdom. The exchange rate remained within the gold points because of **gold arbitrage**.

For instance, suppose that because of an increase in net exports from Britain to Canada, the accompanying increase in the demand for pound-denominated financial assets forced the pound's value to rise to $4.895. Gold arbitragers could now profit by simultaneously buying gold in Canada and selling it to the British government. The purchase of $4.867 worth of gold in Canada could be shipped at a cost of approximately 2.5 cents to Britain, where it was purchased by the government for £1 sterling, and in turn could be sold in the market for $4.895. With the cost of the pound to the arbitrager of $4.892 ($4.867 plus 2.5 cents) and the $4.895 realized from its sale, a profit of 0.3 cents was realized from each pound sterling traded. With continuous gold arbitrage and the consequent increase in the supply of pounds on the foreign exchange market, the price of the pound would remain only briefly above its export point (the mint par plus the cost of acquiring and shipping gold from Canada to Britain).

In similar fashion, the activities of gold arbitrageurs established a floor value of the pound in terms of the Canadian dollar at the gold import point (the mint par value of $4.867 less the cost of acquiring and shipping gold from Britain to Canada).

Under the Bretton Woods system, member countries declared a par value (or peg) for their currencies in terms of the U.S. dollar. Insofar as until 1971 the United States was prepared to convert its dollar into a specified amount of gold for foreign monetary authorities, the par value of other member countries' currencies also was indirectly pegged to gold. Between 1946 and 1950, the Canadian dollar's value was pegged at one U.S. dollar.

Under a pure fixed exchange rate regime, it is assumed that the regime will be maintained indefinitely, and that the country devotes all the tools of macroeconomic policy to maintaining the exchange rate in place. With a pegged rate system, where a country pegs the value of its currency to that of another country or a group of countries, the authorities usually reserve the right to shift the peg from time to time and hence lack a commitment to a fixed value for their currency.

The operation of a fixed exchange rate regime is illustrated in Figure 21–2. We assume that the Canadian dollar is pegged at U.S.$1.00; in this case, the Bank of Canada stands ready to supply the quantity of Canadian-dollar assets required to maintain the pegged value of the exchange rate. The demand for Canadian-dollar assets, shown by the D_0 curve, initially intersects the supply curve at A, the pegged value of the Canadian dollar.

Now suppose that the demand for Canadian-dollar assets increases and the demand curve shifts from D_0 to D_2. If the exchange rate were perfectly flexible, the value of the Canadian dollar would rise to S_2. However, under fixed exchange rates, the central bank must stand ready to supply all of the dollars the market wants at the fixed rate. Hence, the Bank of Canada intervenes directly in the foreign exchange market by increasing the supply of Canadian dollars until the market clears at the fixed exchange rate. It does this by purchasing an equivalent amount of U.S.-dollar-denominated assets, thereby adding to its foreign currency reserves.

gold arbitrage
the process of simultaneous buying and selling of gold and currencies under the gold standard

www.

FIGURE 21–2   **FIXED EXCHANGE RATES**

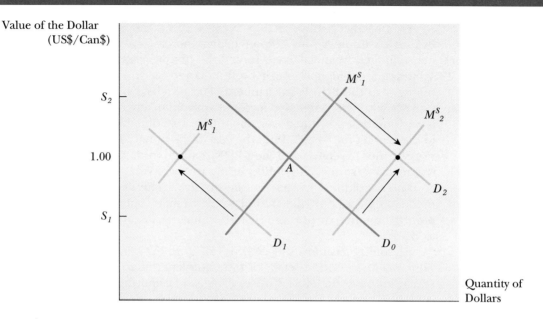

Under a fixed exchange rate, the central bank stands ready to supply all the domestic currency the market wants. If the demand curve shifts to D_2 the Bank of Canada must increase the supply of dollars to keep their value fixed. If the demand for dollars falls, the money supply must fall to keep the exchange rate fixed.

revaluation when a central bank increases the value at which it will support its currency under fixed exchange rates

devaluation when a central bank reduces the value at which it will support its currency under fixed exchange rates

When the Bank of Canada purchases foreign currency assets on the foreign exchange market, the Canadian money supply is increased. We know from the quantity theory of money that this could be inflationary (unless real output and velocity are changing). To avoid the inflationary consequences of increasing the money supply in response to an increase in its demand, the Canadian government could instead change the par value of its currency—the value at which it will support the dollar. This process is known as **revaluation**. Revaluing the Canadian dollar to S_2 would require no market intervention by the Bank of Canada.

Now suppose that the demand for Canadian-dollar assets declines and, as shown in Figure 21–2, the demand curve shifts leftward from D_0 to D_1. Without intervention by the Bank of Canada in the foreign exchange market, the value of the Canadian dollar would fall below its par value to S_1. To prevent this from happening, the Bank intervenes in the foreign exchange market by selling U.S.-dollar-denominated assets. This process is equivalent to buying Canadian-dollar-denominated assets. The quantity of Canadian-dollar assets on the foreign exchange market is reduced in response to the decline in demand for dollars, and the value of the dollar is restored to its par value.

Instead of intervening in the foreign exchange market to prevent the Canadian dollar from falling below its par value, the Canadian government could decrease the par value, which is known as **devaluation**.

For purposes of intervening in foreign exchange markets, countries hold international reserve assets in exchange stabilization or exchange equalization accounts. Canada established such an account, known as the Exchange Fund Account, in 1935 with part of the profits from the revaluation of its gold reserves. Today, direct intervention in the foreign exchange market with the use of this account is carried out by the Bank of Canada as fiscal agent for the minister of finance. The bulk of Canada's official international reserve assets are held in the Exchange Fund Account, which is funded by advances from the federal government's Consolidated Revenue Fund. The Bank of Canada and various government departments and agencies hold small working balances of foreign-currency-denominated assets, but these are not used to intervene in the foreign exchange market.

The success of an international fixed exchange rate regime critically depends on the adequacy of international reserve assets that allow national monetary authorities to defend the values set for their currencies. The relative shortage of gold and its uneven distribution among nations were important reasons for abandoning the gold standard in 1931.

The Bretton Woods system of pegged exchange rates, introduced after the Second World War, depended on U.S.-dollar-denominated financial assets and credit facilities provided by the newly created International Monetary Fund (IMF) as the major sources of international reserve assets. When these sources were considered insufficient for the efficient functioning of the international monetary system, the IMF created a new international reserve asset called a Special Drawing Right (SDR). The Bretton Woods system worked reasonably well as long as countries were willing to hold U.S.-dollar-denominated financial assets to intervene in foreign exchange markets, and the United States supplied these assets by running balance of payments deficits. When this could no longer be relied upon after 1970, the Bretton Woods system broke down.

Managed Exchange Rate Regime

Today, the monetary authorities of most countries intervene directly in the foreign exchange market because the exchange rate is considered too important to be left to the mercy of capricious market forces. The degree to which exchange rates are managed varies among countries. Where monetary authorities intervene only occasionally to preserve orderly market conditions, they are said to be following a **clean float policy.** Where they regularly intervene, they follow a dirty float policy. In the extreme, where a **dirty float policy** attempts to hold the exchange rate within an announced range, it is akin to a fixed exchange rate regime. This policy was the one followed by the countries of the European Monetary Union before the introduction of the Euro.

In some countries the monetary authorities influence the movements of the exchange rate through active intervention in the foreign exchange market without specifying or precommitting to a preannounced path for the exchange rate. Many countries manage their currencies within **target zones** in which a country pegs its currency (formally or defacto) at a fixed rate to a major currency such as the American dollar, or to a basket of currencies. The pegged rate is managed to float within a declared target zone, say plus or minus 1 percent, around the central rate. Target zones can have narrow or wide bands of permissible exchange rate variation.

clean float policy a policy of infrequent intervention in exchange markets

dirty float policy a policy of regular intervention in exchange markets

target zone specifies the zone within which a currency is managed to fluctuate

crawling peg *the currency is adjusted periodically at a fixed pre-announced rate*

In a **crawling peg** arrangement, the value of the currency is adjusted periodically in small amounts at a fixed preannounced rate, or in response to changes in selective quantitative indicators. The rate of crawl, for example, can be set to generate inflation-adjusted changes in the currency's value.

Exchange Control Regime

Exchange control regimes take different forms, depending on the objectives to be satisfied. In their extreme form, they are used to control all of a country's economic transactions with the rest of the world; this form is what is generally implied by an **exchange control regime**. Nazi Germany and the former Soviet Union had such regimes. Exchange restrictions, however, when their imposition is only temporary or when they affect only a limited number of selected international transactions, need not be incorporated into a comprehensive exchange control system.

exchange control regime *regulations used to control all of a country's economic transactions with the rest of the world*

www.

In an exchange control regime the government monopolizes the country's foreign exchange transactions. All foreign-currency-denominated assets acquired by the country's residents must be turned over to the government, which in turn dictates their reallocation. The authorities set the rates at which foreign currency assets are turned over to it and at which it will make them available for use. Where governments use a variety of different buying and selling rates, the control regime is known as a **multiple exchange rate system**.

multiple exchange rate system *a system of multiple exchange rates based on sources and uses of funds*

Exchange regimes in which the government rations the availability of foreign exchange invariably give rise to **black markets**,[6] also called **parallel markets** in that they are illegal free markets that exist alongside the official government markets for foreign exchange. By overinvoicing imports (that is, overstating the value of an approved import), importers can obtain additional foreign exchange at the official rates, which can be resold at a profit in the black markets. Similarly, exporters, by underinvoicing (understating) the value of exports, can sell the unreported foreign exchange from their exports on the black market. Tourism is also a typical source of foreign exchange in black markets.

black (parallel) markets *illegal markets in controlled currencies*

While most of the Western industrial countries abandoned quantitative foreign exchange restrictions and multiple exchange rates in the early 1990s, they still remain a common feature of the exchange rate systems of some developing countries.[7] These countries typically set low prices for foreign exchange used to pay for imports required for their development; and, to discourage the import of luxuries, set high prices for imported goods for sale on the domestic market. Furthermore, foreign exchange is priced to attract foreign investment and to discourage the external flight of capital.

---

6. See Michael Novak, "Black Markets in Foreign Exchange: Their Causes, Nature and Consequences," *Finance and Development*, March 1985, pp. 20–23.

7. See International Monetary Fund, *Exchange Arrangements and Exchange Restrictions: Annual Report 1990.*

Managing the Canadian Dollar

In the early 1980s the Canadian government's policy for managing the exchange rate was aimed at dampening fluctuations in the value of the Canadian dollar against the U.S. dollar, described as follows:

Following the adoption of a floating exchange rate on June 1, 1970, official operations in the foreign exchange market by the Canadian authorities have been directed towards smoothing out erratic movements in the Canadian dollar–U.S. dollar rate of exchange and avoiding disorderly market conditions.

There has been no attempt, through intervention, to achieve or maintain a particular value of the rate over time, although there have been short periods when movements in the rate have been more firmly resisted than others.[8]

With a managed floating exchange rate regime, the Bank of Canada adjusts the quantity of Canadian-dollar-denominated assets outstanding to smooth fluctuations in the value of the Canadian dollar, shown by shifts in the supply curve of Canadian-dollar assets in Figure 21–3. To dampen sharp upward movements in the value of the dollar, the Bank supplies additional Canadian-dollar assets to the foreign exchange market by purchasing foreign currency assets. Alternatively, to dampen downward movements in the value of the dollar, the Bank reduces the availability of Canadian-dollar assets by selling foreign currency assets on the market.

In Figure 21–3, given the D_0 demand curve for Canadian-dollar assets, the Canadian dollar's value against the U.S. dollar is initially at S_0. Suppose that the demand curve shifts up to D_1 in response to expectations by investors that falling short-term U.S. interest rates will be accompanied by a rise in the Canadian dollar's value. Under a perfectly flexible exchange rate regime, the Canadian dollar's value will rise until it achieves a new equilibrium at S_2. Under a managed exchange regime, intervention in the market by the Bank of Canada will hold the rise to S_1. However, under a fixed exchange rate regime, the Bank's intervention in the market would hold the dollar's value at its fixed level, which in our example is the initial equilibrium rate of S_0.

Murray, Zelmer, and McManus have described the Bank's intervention policy and how it changed in the mid-1990s. Before April 12, 1995, the official policy of the Bank of Canada was to resist changes in the exchange rate that fell outside a narrow nonintervention band. This band was initially set as 25/100ths of a Canadian cent, but was raised to a full cent in the late 1980s. When the value of the Canadian dollar fell below the lower bound, the central bank would sell U.S. dollars in return for Canadian dollars—at a rate of about $4 million U.S. dollars for every 1/100 of a cent that the market value of the dollar differed from the lower bound. This process would continue (in most cases) until the value of the Canadian dollar stabilized. In the event that the dollar did not stabilize when markets closed, the next day the lower bound

---

8. Department of Finance, "Foreign Exchange Market Intervention in Canada: A Report Submitted to the Working Group on Exchange Market Intervention of the Economic Summit," Ottawa, September 1982 (Mimeo).

FIGURE 21–3   MANAGED EXCHANGE RATES

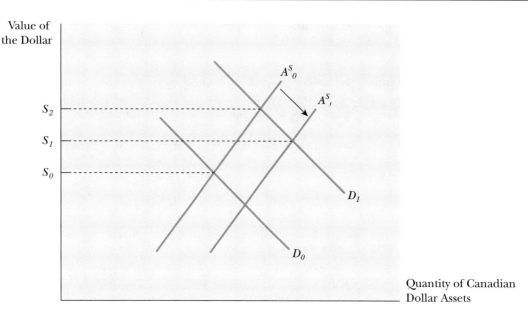

Under a managed exchange rate the central bank resists market forces. If the demand for dollars rises, the value of the dollar would rise to S_2 under a perfectly flexible exchange rate system. The central bank can resist this appreciation by increasing the money supply as shown by a shift in the Canadian dollar asset curve from A^S_0 to A^S_1, leading to an increase in the value of the dollar to S_1, rather than to S_2.

would be reset at the previous market closing value of the dollar. If the dollar had stabilized and regained some of its value before closing, the lower bound would be set at the previous day's market low. Figure 21–4 shows the extent of Canadian foreign exchange intervention over the early 1990s.

In April 1995 the Bank of Canada changed its official intervention policy to reflect changes in the market for Canadian dollars (the market had matured and was now well developed). The new policy was

> *designed to (1) reduce the frequency of intervention and give the market more play; (2) raise the average intensity of intervention when authorities did enter the market; (3) make intervention practices more consistent with the objectives of maintaining orderly markets; and (4) allow scope for greater variability and discretion in the application of intervention guidelines when conditions warranted.*[9]

Increasing the nonintervention band and resetting it each day by putting the middle of the band at the previous market close satisfied objectives 1 and 3. This resetting had the effect of reducing the likelihood of intervention, since the exchange rate could now fluctuate more before attracting central bank

---

9. Murray, Zelmer, and McManus, "The Effects of Intervention on Canadian Dollar Volatility," Mimeo. (Bank of Canada: Ottawa, October 1996), p. 9.

FIGURE 21–4   **INTERVENTION AND THE DOLLAR**

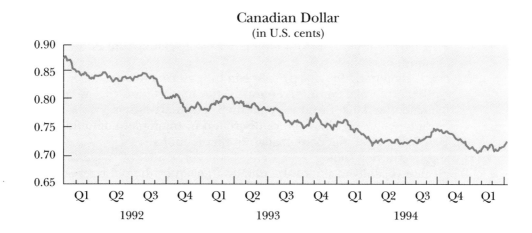

Canadian Dollar
(in U.S. cents)

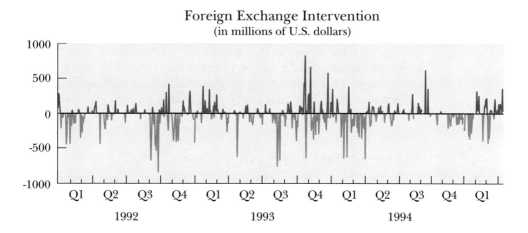

Foreign Exchange Intervention
(in millions of U.S. dollars)

As you can see, the Bank of Canada actively supported the value of the dollar over the 1992–95 period.

SOURCE: Murray, Zelmer, and McManus (1996).

attention than it could under the previous policy. The second objective changed the degree to which the Bank of Canada intervened when intervention was warranted (presumably at more than U.S.$4 million per 1/100 of a Canadian cent). Finally, the fourth objective allowed the Bank of Canada the discretion to act in advance of what it perceived to be speculative activities that would create destabilizing movement in the value of the dollar. Additionally, this change in intervention policy made it somewhat more difficult to predict how the Bank of Canada would react in certain situations, thereby making it riskier for the private sector to engage in speculative trades against the Canadian dollar.

During the first two years of the Bank's new intervention policy, it intervened only on 56 days or on 9 percent of all business days compared with almost 50 percent under the pre–April 1995 intervention regime. Moreover, the Bank used discretionary intervention on only nine occasions. This low rate changed in 1997 following the beginning of the Asian financial crisis, and in 1998 because of global exchange market volatility caused by the Russian debt moratorium.

Following the sharp decline in the external value of the Canadian dollar in 1998, the massive intervention in the market, and the increase in the Bank Rate, the Bank introduced another new intervention policy. This policy is less automatic and allows more discretion in timing and amount of intervention. During 1999, the Bank made no interventions.

Murray, Zelmer, and McManus report evidence suggesting that exchange rate volatility was not substantially affected by the old intervention policy and that only unexpected and substantial intervention by the central bank under the new policy has had an effect on the value of the Canadian dollar against the U.S. dollar.

In a more recent study, Neil Beattie and Jean-Francois Fillion investigated whether Canada's intervention policy in the two and a half years after 1995 affected currency volatility within each trading day.[10] They found that expected rule-based intervention had no direct impact on the reduction of foreign exchange volatility, but that the nonintervention band provided a small stabilizing influence. At the same time, unexpected discretionary intervention appeared to be somewhat more effective in moderating the volatility of the Canadian dollar than had previously been reported by Murray, Zelmer, and McManus.

Sterilized and Unsterilized Intervention

unsterilized intervention *exchange market intervention that leads to a change in a country's money supply*

sterilized intervention *exchange market intervention that does not lead to a change in a country's money supply*

Official intervention in the foreign exchange market by a country's monetary authorities may be either unsterilized or sterilized. With **unsterilized intervention** a country's monetary supply changes. The effect is similar to central bank open market operations in the domestic money market. The only difference is that in exchange intervention, the central bank buys or sells foreign currency rather than domestic-currency-denominated assets. Our earlier analysis of a managed exchange rate assumed unsterilized intervention.

Sterilized intervention leaves the domestic money supply unchanged. It involves offsetting cash management operations by the central bank that prevent any change in the monetary base resulting from exchange intervention. For example, suppose, to avoid a sharp upward movement of the value of the Canadian dollar, the Bank of Canada intervenes directly in the foreign exchange market by purchasing foreign-currency-denominated assets. This purchase, taken by itself, increases the monetary base and, via the money multiplier, the money supply. The Bank can negate—that is, *sterilize*—the expansion of the monetary base with open market sales of Government of Canada

10. Neil Beattie and Francois Fillion, An Intraday Analysis of the Effectiveness of Foreign Exchange Intervention, Bank of Canada Working Paper 99-4, Ottawa, February 1999.

securities. The net effect is to leave the monetary base and the money supply unchanged. The monetary base remains unchanged because all the Bank has done is to replace Canadian with foreign-currency-denominated assets on its balance sheet.

Instantaneous sterilization of exchange market intervention that leaves the money supply constant should have little immediate effect on the exchange rates, and requires that domestic and foreign-currency-denominated securities be imperfect substitutes in investors' portfolios (otherwise one cannot "separate" the market for Canadian dollars from the market for Canadian dollar–denominated securities). Instantaneous intervention may also affect the exchange rate if it signals central bank intentions on future monetary policy and, thereby, expected future spot rates. In practice, central bank sterilization lags behind intervention so that temporary changes in the money supply and the interest rate have an immediate impact on exchange rate movements.[11]

BOX 21–1   HOW SUCCESSFUL IS INTERVENTION?

How effective has official intervention been in reducing exchange rate volatility? Two tests have been applied to answer this question. One, first suggested by Milton Friedman, estimates whether intervention has made money for the authorities.[12] According to Friedman, only profitable speculation in foreign exchange markets is stabilizing, because to make a profit speculators have to buy low and sell high. Since intervention by monetary authorities is nothing more than "official speculation," it follows that if intervention is profitable it, too, must be stabilizing.

The other test of the effectiveness of official intervention has been proposed by Paul Wonnacott.[13] This test estimates "success ratios," which measure the percentage of times intervention by monetary authorities has managed to push exchange rates toward rather than away from their long-run trend.

Applying both these tests, John Murray and his colleagues at the Bank of Canada found that the Bank's intervention policy to stabilize the Canadian–U.S. dollar rate between 1975 and 1988 was quite successful.[14] Indeed, they estimated that the Bank realized some Can.$1.65 billion in profit.

---

11. For a timely discussion of sterilized intervention, see Jang-Yung Lee, "Sterilizing Capital Inflows," *Economic Issues* 7 (Washington, D.C.: IMF, 1997).

12. See Milton Friedman, "The Case for Flexible Exchange Rates," in *Essays in Positive Economics* (Chicago, University of Chicago Press, 1953), pp. 157–203.

13. See P. Wonnacott, *U.S. Foreign Exchange Market for DM, 1977–80,* Princeton Studies International Finance, No. 51 (Princeton, N.J.: Princeton University Press, 1982).

14. See John Murray, Mark Zelmer, and Shane Williamson, *Measuring the Profitability and Effectiveness of Foreign Exchange Intervention: Some Canadian Evidence,* Ottawa, Bank of Canada Technical Report No. 53 (March 1990).

Exchange Rate Overshooting

exchange rate overshooting *the tendency of exchange rates to overreact in the short run because of rigidities of one kind or another*

The volatility observed since the introduction of more managed, flexible rates in the early 1970s has been associated with **exchange rate overshooting**.[15] Overshooting occurs when, in response to an economic disturbance, in the short run (daily/weekly) the exchange rate moves more than is required for it to attain its long-run equilibrium level. Exchange rates overshoot their long-run equilibrium values because they adjust much more quickly to a disturbance than do commodity prices.

Suppose, for example, a disturbance in the form of an unanticipated permanent increase in the money supply takes place. If foreign prices remain constant, and purchasing power parity holds over the long run, then when the exchange rate attains its new long-run equilibrium value, the domestic price level will have increased and the value of the domestic currency will have fallen by the same rate at which the money supply was permanently increased. In the shorter run, however, before the domestic price level begins its sluggish rise, real money balances increase and the domestic interest rate rapidly falls below foreign interest rates. If we further assume that the interest parity condition holds, domestic interest rates can remain below foreign interest rates only if the value of the domestic currency is expected to rise. But how can the domestic currency be expected to appreciate if, as already noted, it will depreciate over the long run at the rate at which the money supply has increased? Clearly, such appreciation is only possible if initial depreciation exceeds (overshoots) its long-run depreciation. This allows the exchange rate to appreciate in the intermediate period to achieve the long-run rate of depreciation consistent with the rate of increase of the money supply, as demonstrated in Figure 21–5. Hence, exchange rate volatility can be explained by instantaneous adjustments to maintain continuous interest rate parity and, subsequently, long-run adjustments to maintain purchasing power parity.

misalignment *when changes in the exchange rate are not related to changes in the fundamentals that determine it*

Changes in the exchange rate for extended periods not related to changes in the fundamentals that determine it are called **misalignment**. When such disparity is protracted, it can be costly to an economy because of its adverse affects on resource allocations.

Murray, Zelmer, and Antia examined the behaviour of the Canadian dollar from 1997 to 1999 to look for evidence of excess volatility or significant overshooting.[16] They found that over this period, overshooting was not a major problem. Furthermore, periods of extreme exchange rate volatility, such as during the 1997–98 Asian and Russian financial crises, are typically explained by changes in economic fundamentals rather than by destabilizing speculation.

---

15. See Rudiger Dornbush, "Expectations and Exchange Rate Dynamics," *Journal of Political Economy* 84, pp. 1161–76.

16. John Murray, Mark Zelmer, and Zahir Antia, *International Financial Crises and Flexible Exchange Rates: Some Lessons from Canada*, Bank of Canada Technical Report No. 88, Ottawa, April 2000.

FIGURE 21–5 **OVERSHOOTING**

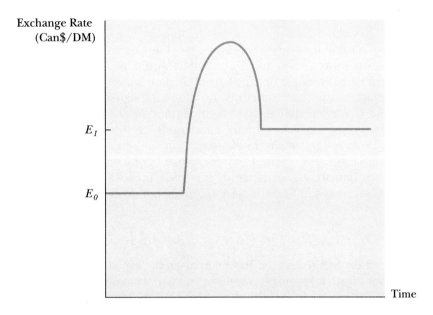

In the long run, an increase in the money supply leads to an equiproportionate increase in the exchange rate. Because prices are sluggish, interest rates adjust to clear the money market in the short run, leading to a greater than proportionate short-run reduction in the value of the domestic currency. As prices adjust, the pressure on interest rates to clear the money market is reduced and the exchange rate is allowed to return to its new long-run value.

Freely Floating versus Fixed Exchange Rates: Some of the Arguments

"Fixed Rates Promote International Trade and Investment"

Fixed exchange rates are said to promote international trade because they reduce both transactions costs (the cost of exchanging different currencies) and exchange rate risk (due to exchange rate volatility and misalignment). Some research has shown that the welfare loss due to exchange rate volatility can be substantial at close to a full percentage point of GDP.

It has been argued that the certainty of fixed rates promotes international trade and investment, while the uncertainty of flexible rates does the opposite. Experience with floating exchange rates since the early 1970s does not indicate that they have had much of an adverse effect on international trade and investment.[17] There may be two explanations for this. One is that real world output

17. See A Coté, "Effets de la variabilité des taux de change sur le commerce international: Une analyse pour le Canada," *L'Actualité Économique* 62 (1986), pp. 501–20.

is a much more important determining factor of the volume of world trade than is exchange rate variability and uncertainty. The other is that financial markets have been extremely innovative in introducing new instruments and techniques to hedge exchange risks.

Nevertheless, opponents of flexible exchange rates maintain that flexible rates have had adverse consequences. They claim that exchange rates have frequently moved away from levels that would be justified by economic fundamentals, and in particular, by purchasing power parity. They also claim that exchange rates have remained misaligned for prolonged periods. For example, large U.S. trade deficits have been blamed on the overvalued U.S. dollar in the early 1980s. The overvalued Canadian dollar in the early 1990s was blamed for jeopardizing successful implementation of the Free Trade Agreement between Canada and the United States. Alleged long-run misalignment of currency values has increased demands for trade protection laws in the United States and proposals in Canada for a fixed exchange rate against the U.S. dollar.[18]

"Fixed Exchange Rates Impose Monetary Discipline"

Fixed exchange rates, it has been argued, provide necessary discipline against otherwise irresponsible monetary expansion and inflation. Reference is frequently made to the gold standard's "golden anchor" or "golden brake." Expansionary monetary policies and the consequent inflation under fixed exchange rates cause external deficits and losses in international monetary reserves. The loss of reserves plus the loss of national prestige in the event of devaluation are said to deter governments from pursuing inflationary policies.

While fixed rates may provide better discipline against inflation, they can also have an undesirable deflationary bias. The limited availability of gold, as well as its uneven distribution among countries, is claimed to have prevented more rapid growth in many countries during the gold standard era.

Supporters of fixed exchange rates point to the undisciplined monetary expansion and consequent inflation following the move to more flexible rates in the early 1970s. However, it should be noted that the restoration of anti-inflationary policies in the mid-1970s, in the face of both high unemployment and political pressures for monetary expansion, shows that discipline need not be absent in a flexible exchange rate regime.

In recent years international capital markets have assumed an important role in disciplining domestic monetary and fiscal policy in flexible and fixed exchange rate regimes. In the summer of 1998, for example, in the wake of the Russian debt default, a worldwide capital "flight to quality," specifically to U.S. dollar securities, drove the Canadian dollar down to U.S.63¢. The Bank of Canada initially intervened heavily in the foreign exchange market and subsequently raised the Bank Rate by a full 100 basis points to stabilize financial markets. This incident was interpreted as a wakeup call from capital markets to the federal government to reduce its appetite for fiscal deficits and to decrease the debt to GDP ratio.

---

18. See Thomas J. Courchene, "Zero Means Almost Nothing: Towards a Preferable Inflation and Macro Stance." Background paper prepared for the House of Commons Standing Committee on Finance, Ottawa, June 7, 1990; and Robert Mundell, "The Overvalued Canadian Dollar." Paper prepared for the Canadian Monetary Policy Review Board, Montreal, April 4–5, 1990.

"Fixed Rates Sacrifice Independent Monetary Policy"

It can be shown that in a fixed exchange rate regime, discretionary monetary policy for domestic stabilization is sacrificed because it has to be used to defend the fixed value of the exchange rate. (If you fix your currency's value, you have to allow your money supply to fluctuate with the demand for your currency.) During the 1962–70 period of fixed parity between the U.S. and Canadian dollars, it was asserted by some that Canada had lost its monetary independence and had become the 13th Federal Reserve District of the U.S. central banking system. A simple illustration can be used to show that monetary independence can be sacrificed under a fixed exchange rate regime.

Suppose the Canadian economy is experiencing less-than-full employment, a situation that calls for an expansionary monetary policy. The Bank of Canada undertakes open market purchases of government securities, which expand the availability of cash and, via the money multiplier, the money supply. As a result, Canadian interest rates fall below world interest rates, and currency arbitragers and speculators switch from Canadian- to U.S.-currency-denominated assets. The value of the Canadian dollar will fall. However, if Canada has a fixed exchange rate regime, the Bank is committed to prevent the depreciation by directly intervening in the foreign exchange market. This prevention involves selling foreign-currency-denominated assets for Canadian dollars. As the Bank absorbs these Canadian dollars, the availability of cash is reduced and now, via the money multiplier, the Canadian money supply declines. This decline offsets the increase in the money supply initiated by the expansionary monetary policy to stabilize the economy. Hence, it can be seen that the Bank's obligation to preserve a fixed exchange value for the Canadian dollar limits the Bank's use of monetary policy for domestic stabilization.

Alternatively, it is argued that a flexible exchange rate allows a country to use discretionary monetary policy for stabilization. However, now that international capital has become extremely mobile, much of the monetary independence claimed for flexible exchange rate systems has eroded.

"Fixed Rates Facilitate the International Transmission of the Business Cycle"

It has been claimed that with fixed exchange rates the business cycle is readily transmitted from one country to another. The transmission mechanism may be explained in the following way. Suppose that Americans tolerate higher inflation rates than Canadians. With relatively lower prices in Canada, Canadian exports to the United States are encouraged, while Canadians are inclined to do their shopping at home rather than across the border. The increased demand for Canadian goods at home and from south of the border will tend to force up Canadian prices. Hence, Canada is made to follow the higher inflation rate in the United States.

Purchasing power parity suggests that international commodity arbitrage will tend to bring inflation rates into equality across countries with fixed exchange rates over time. Earlier we showed that when PPP holds between two trading nations

(21.3) $P_t = E_t P_t^*$

where P and P^* are the domestic and foreign price levels, respectively, and E_t is the exchange rate (units of domestic currency per unit of foreign currency). If we now denote change by Δ (the Greek letter delta), equation 21.3 can be rewritten as

(21.4) $\Delta P_t = (E_t \, \Delta P_t^*) + P_t^* \Delta E_t$

Dividing equation 21.3 by equation 21.4 and cancelling the common terms, we obtain

(21.5) $\Delta P_t / P_t = \Delta P_t^* / P_t^* + \Delta E_t / E_t$

or

$$\pi = \pi^* + \zeta$$

where π and π^* are the domestic and foreign inflation rates, respectively, and ζ (pronounced zeta) is the rate of depreciation of the domestic currency. With a fixed exchange rate, $\zeta = 0$ and, therefore, $\pi = \pi^*$.

Under a flexible exchange rate and PPP, a country is insulated from inflation in the rest of the world. This is because the difference between the domestic inflation rate and the higher foreign inflation rate is offset by the rate of depreciation of the domestic currency:

(21.6) $\zeta = \pi - \pi^*$

If, for example, the U.S. inflation rate is 10 percent while that in Canada is only 5 percent, the higher rate in the United States will not be transmitted to Canada if PPP holds and the Canadian dollar in terms of the U.S. dollar appreciates by 5 percent.

A major cause of the breakdown of the Bretton Woods system of pegged exchange rates was the unwillingness of other countries, particularly West Germany and Japan, to continue to allow higher inflation rates in the United States to be transmitted to their economies. After the introduction of more exchange rate flexibility in the early 1970s, it became possible for countries to choose their own inflation rates if they were also willing to accept consequent movements in exchange rates. However, as international inflation rates increasingly diverged during the 1980s, concern mounted over the volatility of exchange rates. In the Plaza Accord in 1985 among the G-5 countries (the United States, West Germany, Japan, the United Kingdom, and France), and again in the **Louvre Accord** among the G-7 countries (the G-5 countries plus Canada and Italy), members agreed to reduce the degree of exchange rate volatility. This was to be achieved both by greater coordination of their economic policies and by joint intervention by members in foreign exchange markets.

Louvre Accord *an international agreement (1987) aimed at reducing exchange rate volatility and coordinating monetary policies across countries*

"Flexible Exchange Rates Act as Insulators against Foreign Shocks"

An alleged advantage of flexible exchange rates is that they insulate the domestic economy from economic disturbances beyond its borders. The Bank of Canada, in its defence of the flexible Canadian dollar regime, employs this so-called buffer argument. The Bank points to the sharp drop in world prices of primary commodities, which are major Canadian exports. The associated depreciation of the Canadian dollar has allowed Canadian exporters to remain competitive. Without exchange rate flexibility, adjustments to this external shock would have had to come about through wage and price reductions, or failing this, through a fall in output, resulting in unemployment. It should be noted, however, that even under the best of circumstances, flexible exchange rates can deliver only partial insulation from adverse real external shocks.

"Floating Exchange Rates Promote Payments Adjustments"

A major advantage attributed to a floating exchange rate regime is that it facilitates continuous, if not automatic, payments adjustments. It is also claimed that the burden of adjustment is more equitably shared between deficit and surplus countries.

Relative price changes resulting from flexible exchange rate adjustment are believed to effectively maintain a country's international competitiveness and prevent large and persistent trade imbalances. According to the **Marshall–Lerner Condition**, the more price elastic the demand for a country's exports and imports, the more stable its exchange rate and the more likely that a depreciation or devaluation of its currency will improve its trade balance.[19] However, even if this condition is satisfied, the beneficial effects on the trade balance of depreciation or devaluation may be frustrated if labour unions are successful in maintaining their real wages by forcing the same percentage increase in their money wage as the percentage decline in the value of the domestic currency.

Economists have also shown that soon after a devaluation or depreciation of its currency, a country's trade balance is likely to worsen before it improves. This short-run phenomenon is known as the **J-curve** effect because when a country's trade balance is plotted on the vertical axis and time is plotted on the horizontal axis, as in Figure 21–6, the response of the trade balance to devaluation or depreciation traces out the letter J. The J-curve effect is explained by

Marshall–Lerner Condition *a condition required for a domestic depreciation to raise the trade balance*

J-curve *the relationship between the exchange rate and the trade balance; a depreciation may temporarily reduce the trade balance, but eventually it should rise*

---

19. According to the Marshall–Lerner condition, when the supply elasticities of a country's exports and imports are infinite, and the sum of the absolute values of the price elasticities of demand for its exports and imports is greater than 1, a devaluation or depreciation of its currency will improve its trade balance.

the slow adjustment in the quantities of imports and exports to a change in relative prices.[20]

Relative price changes resulting from movements in exchange rates are no guarantee that persistent external trade imbalances can be avoided. In fact, large and persistent external trade imbalances have been the rule rather than the exception since the introduction of more exchange rate flexibility in the early 1970s.

The Debate about Canada's Exchange Rate Regime

Thomas Courchene and Richard Harris have argued that Canada's floating exchange rate is not serving the country's economic interests well.[21] They propose that Canada work toward establishing a North American Currency Union. Since it would take a decade or two, if not more, to accomplish, they suggest that in the interim, Canada should fix its currency to the American dollar (see Box 21–2 for an explanation of alternative fixed rate arrangements).

They argue that the Canadian economy has been damaged by a quarter century of secular currency depreciation, as well as by bouts of serious "excess volatility" and "serious misalignment" of our dollar during this period.

Courchene and Harris note that our living standard has not increased relative to that of the United States because our manufacturing productivity has lagged. This lag is blamed on the behaviour of the exchange rate. The secular decline in the value of the Canadian dollar in terms of the American dollar is alleged to have sheltered Canadian firms from foreign competition, thereby reducing their incentive to make productivity-enhancing investments. Any significant relationship between the exchange rate and productivity growth is questionable. It has been shown that much of the relative decline in our standard of living is explained by lower participation and employment rates in Canada then in the United States.[22]

---

20. The trade balance is given by $(P \bullet Q_X) - (E \bullet P^*)\ Q_M$ in terms of the domestic currency, where P and P^* are the price levels of the domestic and foreign countries respectively; Q_X and Q_M are the domestic country's export and import quantities, respectively; and E is the domestic currency price of foreign exchange. When E increases in response to a devaluation or depreciation of the domestic country's currency, the total value of its imports increases while that of its exports, also valued in terms of the domestic currency, remains unchanged. Hence in terms of the domestic currency, the trade balance immediately worsens since P, Q_X, and Q_M are assumed to remain unchanged.

21. See Thomas Courchene, "Towards a North American Common Currency: An Optimal Currency Area Analysis," in T.J. Courchene, ed., *Room to Manoeuvre? Globalization and Policy Convergence.* Bell Canada Papers on Economic and Public Policy. McGill-Queens University Press, Kingston, Montreal 1999; Thomas J. Courchene and Richard Harris, "From Fixing to Monetary Union: Options for North American Currency Union," Commentary 127, C.D. Howe Institute, Toronto, June 1999; A Freeman, "Nobel Economist Urges Tying Loonie to U.S. Greenback," *The Globe and Mail,* Toronto, October 14, 1999, p. A11.

22. See Robert Lafrance, and Lawrence L. Schembrie, "The Exchange Rate, Productivity, and the Standard of Living," *Bank of Canada Review,* Winter 1999–2000, pp. 17–21. See also, "The Canadian Economy, Productivity, and Our Standard of Living." Remarks by Gordon Thiessen, governor of the Bank of Canada to the Fraser Institute. *Bank of Canada Review,* Winter 1999–2000, pp. 59–63.

FIGURE 21–6 **THE J-CURVE**

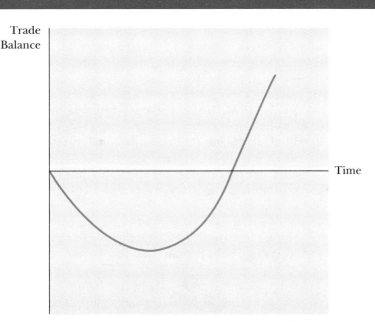

A reduction in the value of the dollar initially reduces the trade balance. As exports and imports respond to changes in prices, the trade balance improves.

BOX 21–2 **FIXING THE CANADIAN DOLLAR TO ITS AMERICAN COUNTERPART**

1. **Fixed Exchange Rate**. The Exchange Fund Account intervenes in the foreign exchange market and macroeconomic policies are used to hold the value of the Canadian dollar at a fixed value in terms of the U.S. dollar.
2. **Pegged Exchange Rate**. The Canadian dollar is pegged to the American dollar at a specified rate of exchange. It is managed to remain within a target zone around the specified rate. The degree to which the Canadian dollar is fixed depends on the adjustability of the peg and the width of the target zone.
3. **Currency Board**. The Canadian government sets up a currency board responsible for the issue of Canadian currency. The currency board must exchange Canadian dollars at a fixed rate for American dollars on demand. To satisfy the obligation it must at all times hold a sufficient amount of liquid U.S. dollar assets. The board cannot undertake independent monetary policy since its operations are circumscribed by the availability of U.S. dollar assets to it. It has been said that a currency board arrangement would represent an "unabrogatable" commitment to the U.S. dollar.

Exchange rate volatility can be costly to exporters and imports with respect to both uncertainty and hedging currency risk. However, it is hard to believe that the cost of undertaking a currency hedge has been sufficiently high to cause much damage to the growth of international trade and investment.

Currency misalignment can cause damage to an economy in that it sends false price signals that result in a misallocation of resources. Courchene and Harris contend that the Canadian dollar was overvalued in the late 1980s when it reached U.S.89 cents and undervalued when it dropped to U.S.63 cents in August 1998. If the currency remains overvalued for an extended period, firms have the incentive to leave the country, and if it remains undervalued, skilled labour has the incentive to migrate (the so-called brain drain). Alternatively, some have argued that the U.S. dollar's appreciation in the 1980s created the foundation for the subsequent noninflationary growth of the U.S. economy because the overvalued currency forced corporations to face global competition.

David Laidler has seriously questioned the contentions of Courchene and Harris.[23] Laidler has argued that the flexible exchange rate has served us very well and certainly better than the fixed rate would have done. Gordon Thiessen, the governor of the Bank of Canada, has taken a similar point of view. Laidler notes that most of the exchange rate fluctuations have been related to variations in its fundamental determinants. Accordingly, the major causes of real exchange rate variations after 1970 have been the sharp decline in the world prices of primary products and the differences in the Canadian and U.S. short-term interest rates.[24]

The flexible exchange rate is said to have served Canada well because it has helped us to cope with the decline in world primary product prices. Primary products represent 35 percent of Canada's exports, 80 percent of which go to the United States. If we had had a fixed exchange rate, adjustments to the external shock of world commodity prices would have had to come about through lower domestic wages and prices or, failing this, through lower output and depressed economic conditions.

---

23. See David Laidler, "What Do the Fixers Want to Fix? The Debate about Canada's Exchange Rate Regime," Commentary 131, C.D. Howe Institute, Toronto, December 1999; David Laidler, "The Exchange Rate and Canada's Monetary Order." Working Paper 99-7, Bank of Canada, Ottawa 1999; J. Murray, "Why Canada Needs a Flexible Exchange Rate." Working Paper 99-12, Bank of Canada, Ottawa 1999; J. Crow, "The Floating Canadian Dollar in our Future," in J.C. Courchene, ed. *Policy Frameworks for a Knowledge Economy*. Bell Canada Papers on Economic and Public Policy, John Deutsch Institute, Queens University, Kingston 1996, pp. 11–36; J. McCallum, "Seven Issues in The Choice of Exchange Rate Regime for Canada," *Current Analysis*, Royal Bank of Canada, February 1999.

24. This is verified by the so-called "Bank of Canada equation," which indicates that the world price of primary products and the Canada–U.S. short-term interest rate differential best explain the movements of the Canadian dollar exchange rate since 1970.

Abandoning the "Loonie"

www.

dollarization *refers to the growing use of the American dollar around the world*

market dollarization *the informal use of the American dollar alongside the local currency*

policy dollarization *the official adoption by a country of the U.S. dollar as its legal tender*

seigniorage *the profits earned from issuing currency*

amero *the name suggested for the currency in a North American Currency Union*

An old joke says the exam questions in economics remain the same every year—only the answers change. The debate about the best exchange rate has been with us forever, but new answers keep appearing. The newest answer to what is the best exchange rate for Canada is "none." That is, we should forgo using our own currency entirely and adopt as our legal tender that of another country, or that of a yet-to-be-established North American Monetary Union.

Dollarization is a term of recent vintage referring to the growing use of the American dollar around the world as a unit of account and a medium of exchange. Countries hold around 60 percent of their foreign exchange in U.S. dollars. It is estimated that as much as two-thirds of the American dollars in circulation are held by people outside the United States.

A distinction can be made between market dollarization and policy dollarization. **Market dollarization** refers to the informal use of the American dollar alongside the local currency. For example, if you have travelled in many parts of the world, you probably have taken American dollars with you for everyday cash transactions. Or, you may have read about professional hockey and baseball players in Canada being paid in American dollars.

Policy dollarization is the official adoption by a country of the American dollar as its legal tender. Policy dollarization in Canada would mean abandoning the Canadian dollar and much more. The Bank of Canada would close its doors and Canada would lose some $1.5 billion each year in **seigniorage,** the profits the Bank earns each year from issuing its own currency; the Americans may not want to share some of the additional seigniorage they would earn if a country officially adopted its dollar. By giving up our dollar, we would also relinquish an important national symbol. Since we could no longer conduct an independent monetary policy, we would give up some economic sovereignty as well since it is unlikely that the United States would allow us little more than observer status on the Federal Reserve board's policy committees.

We would also have to abandon the *loonie* were Canada to become a member of a North American Monetary Union (NAMU). A newly created central bank of the NAMU would issue a common currency. Herbert Grubel has suggested this be called an **amero.**[25] The bank also would set a common monetary policy for all Union members. While its board of governors would include Canadians, given the size of the American economy relative to other members of the Union, Canada's voice would hardly be audible; again, we would give up our conduct of an independent monetary policy.

The economic viability of a NAMU, even a narrow one that includes only Canada, the United States, and Mexico, is in doubt. It would not satisfy many of the critical determinants of an optimum currency area. We have summarized these determinants in Box 21–3. The creation of a NAMU also poses serious political difficulties because countries jealously guard their economic and political sovereignty.

---

25. Herbert Grubel, "The U.S. Dollar Makes Sense for Us," *National Post,* January 28, 2000, A15; Herbert Grubel, *The Case of the Amero: The Merit of Creating a North American Monetary Union.* Fraser Institute, Vancouver 1999.

The Choice of an Exchange Rate for Canada

A country's choice of an exchange rate regime depends, among other things, on the type of shocks its economy is prone to, on the flexibility of its wages and prices, on the credibility of its monetary and fiscal authorities, and on its openness vis-à-vis the rest of the world. Even when all these factors are taken into account, the choice remains a difficult one and the right one today could turn out to be the wrong one tomorrow. No exchange rate regime is perfect or without costs and risks, nor will it work on every occasion.

BOX 21–3   DETERMINATES OF AN OPTIMUM CURRENCY AREA

What is the optimum currency area, that is, the area best suited for a common currency? Robert Mundell, a Canadian and 1999 Nobel Laureate, was the first to pose the question.[1] He answered that it is a region within which factors of production are sufficiently mobile to bring about adjustments to economic shocks. An optimum currency area could be a country or smaller, such as the Atlantic provinces in Canada, or it could encompass several countries.

Ronald McKinnon has argued that the major determinant of an optimum currency area is openness to interregional trade.[2] Based on the pioneering work of Mundell and McKinnon, it is now generally taken that the following four criteria must be met for the region to be an optimal currency area:

1. Countries should be exposed to similar sources of disturbances (common shocks).

2. The relative importance of these shocks should be similar (symmetric shocks).
3. Countries should have similar responses to common shocks (symmetric responses).
4. If countries are affected by country-specific sources of disturbance (idiosyncratic shocks) they must be able to adjust quickly.

If countries satisfy these four criteria, they would have similar business cycles so that a common monetary response would be an option.

Where regions within a common currency area are not highly symmetric and do not face common sources of disturbance to which they respond in a similar way, the viability of the common currency area can be sustained by a system of fiscal transfers. To the degree that Canada does not strictly satisfy the four criteria, a well-developed fiscal transfer system brings about compensatory adjustments.

1. Robert A. Mundell. "A Theory of Optimum Currency Areas." *American Economic Review* 51 (1961), pp. 657–65.

2. Ronald I. McKinnon. "Optimum Currency Areas." *American Economic Review* 53 (September 1963), pp. 717–25. See also Peter B. Kenen. "The Theory of Optimum Currency Areas: An Eclectic View," in Robert Mundell and Alexander Swoboda, eds. *Monetary Problems of the International Economy*. Chicago: University of Chicago Press, 1969, pp. 41–60; T. Bayoumi. "A Formal Model of Optimum Currency Areas." Centre for Economic Policy. Research Discussion Paper 968; Robert Lafrance and Pierre St.-Amant. "Optimal Currency Areas: A Review of the Literature." Bank of Canada Working Paper 99-16. Ottawa: October 1999 (also <www.bank-banque-canada.ca>).

KEY TERMS

absolute PPP
amero
black (parallel) markets
clean float policy
crawling peg
devaluation
dirty float policy
dollarization
exchange control regime
exchange rate overshooting
fixed exchange rate regime
flexible exchange regime

gold arbitrage
gold (mint) par of exchange
gold standard
J-curve
Louvre Accord
market dollarization
Marshall–Lerner Condition
misalignment
monetary theory of the exchange
   rate
multiple exchange rate system
par value

policy dollarization
portfolio balance theory of the
   exchange rate
purchasing power parity (PPP)
relative PPP
revaluation
seigniorage
sterilized intervention
target zone
unsterilized intervention

REVIEW QUESTIONS

1. What is purchasing power parity? What are the implications of purchasing power parity for the exchange rate and for the domestic price level under a fixed rate regime and a flexible rate regime?
2. How can the interest rate parity ratio explain an increase in the short-term spot exchange rate of the Canadian dollar?
3. How did gold arbitrage hold foreign exchange rates within the gold points under the gold standard?
4. What is the role of the Exchange Fund Account?
5. What is sterilized intervention in the foreign exchange market? What tests have been used to measure the effectiveness of official intervention?
6. How can one explain short-run overshooting of the exchange rate?

7. Show why inflation is transmitted between countries under a fixed exchange rate regime, but not necessarily under a floating exchange rate regime.
8. "Economists believe that central bank intervention has its greatest impact on market expectations. Direct intervention by central banks is small in quantitative terms relative to total market volume trading, so it is not expected to have substantial direct effects on exchange rates." Do you agree with this statement? Why?
9. From the arguments presented, what do you think is the best exchange rate regime for Canada?
10. What is "dollarization"? What would be the advantages and disadvantages to Canada of officially adopting it?

SELECTED READINGS

Argy, V. *Exchange Rate Management in Theory and Practice*. Princeton Studies in International Finance, No. 50. Princeton, N.J.: Princeton University Press, 1982.

Bergstrand, Jeffrey. "Selected Views of Exchange Rate Determination After a Decade of Floating." Federal

Reserve Bank of Boston, *New England Economic Review*, May/June 1983, pp. 14–29.

Bigman, David, and Taya Teizo, eds. *The Functioning of Floating Exchange Rates: Theory, Evidence and Policy Implications*. Cambridge, Mass.: Ballinger Publishing Co., 1980.

Black, Stanley W. "International Money and International Monetary Arrangements," in Ronald W. Jones and Peter B. Kenen, eds. *Handbook of International Economics,* Vol. II. Amsterdam: North-Holland, 1984, pp. 1153–94.

Chipman, John S., and Charles Kindleberger, eds. *Flexible Exchange Rates and the Balance of Payments.* Amsterdam: North-Holland, 1980.

Coeuré, Benoit, and Jean Pisani-Ferry. "The Case Against Benign Neglect of Exchange Rate Stability." *Finance and Development,* September 1999, pp 5–8.

De Grauve, P. *The Economics of Monetary Integrations,* 2d ed., Oxford University Press, New York, 1994.

Frankel, Jeffrey. *No Single Currency Regime is Right for All Countries or at All Times.* Essays in International Finance, no. 215. Princeton University, Princeton, August 1999.

Laidler, David E.W., and William B.P. Robson. "The Fix Is out: A Defence of the Floating Canadian Dollar." C.D. Howe, Commentary, 18, July 1990.

Lee, Jang-Yung. "Sterilizing Capital Inflows." *Economic Issues* (7). International Monetary Fund, February 1997.

Longworth, D., P. Boothe, and K. Clinton. *A Study of the Efficiency of Foreign Exchange Markets.* Ottawa: Bank of Canada, 1983.

Murray, John, and Ritha Khemani. *International Interest Rate Linkages and Monetary Policy: A Canadian Perspective.* Technical Report No. 52. Bank of Canada, December 1989.

Murray, John, Mark Zelmer, and Des McManus. "The Effect of Intervention on Canadian Dollar Volatility." Mimeo. Bank of Canada, October 1996.

Murray, John, Mark Zelmer, and Zahir Antia. *International Financial Crises and Flexible Exchange Rates: Some Policy Lessons from Canada.* Technical Report no. 88, Ottawa, Bank of Canada, April 2000.

Yangru Wu, "Are Real Exchange Rates Stationary? Evidence from a Panel-Data Test." *Journal of Money, Credit and Banking* 28 (February 1996).

CHAPTER TWENTY-TWO

INTERNATIONAL FINANCIAL MARKETS

After reading this chapter you should be able to
1. *Describe the Eurocurrency and international banking markets*
2. *Explain international bond, equity, and derivative markets*
3. *Outline some of the implications of the globalization of financial markets*
4. *Explain some of the steps already taken to make international money markets safer*
5. *Describe the international debt crisis, the Mexican peso crisis, the Asian crisis, the Russian debt default, and the implications of these crises for international financial markets*

The ongoing integration of financial markets around the world has produced today's global financial environment. This topic is large enough for a separate book; hence, this chapter can do little more than provide an introduction to the nature of international financial markets, point out some difficulties experienced with these markets, and review the solutions sought.

Eurocurrency and International Banking Markets

Eurocurrency *a bank deposit held in one country that is denominated in another country's currency*

Eurodollar *a U.S.-dollar-denominated deposit held with banks or bank branches outside the United States*

Eurocurrencies are defined as bank deposits held in one country that are denominated in another country's currency. A deposit denominated in Canadian dollars held in a bank in France is a Eurocurrency, or it may be referred to as a Euro-Canadian dollar. The U.S. dollar dominates Eurocurrencies in terms of volume and market trading, and is known as the **Eurodollar**. Over time, external markets have developed for other major international currencies (Euro-DM, Euro-yen, Euro-Swiss francs, among others). To London and other European financial centres, where Eurocurrency markets first developed, have been added markets in the Caribbean, the Middle East, Singapore, Hong Kong, and Tokyo. Since intermediation services for borrowing and lending are now offered by banks in a variety of currencies other than that of the country where they are located, and since these banks are spread around the world, the prefix Euro has become somewhat misleading.

www.

Eurocurrency markets are found in international banking centres, where there is a concentration of banks (Eurobanks) that negotiate, book (record), and administer Eurocurrency business, free of most domestic financial regulations and taxes. Some of these centres, such as the Cayman Islands, are primarily used to book business because of the tax concessions they offer. In 1981 the United States allowed U.S. banks to participate in the Eurodollar market from within the country by establishing International banking facilities (IBFs).[1] These IBFs are a set of books, kept at U.S. banks or at branches and agencies of foreign banks in the United States, that record deposits and loans with nonresidents and are not subject to most domestic regulatory requirements. Various state governments have encouraged banking institutions to establish IBFs by granting favourable tax treatment under state and local laws.

In December 1987, following much controversy, the Canadian government passed legislation that designated Montreal and Vancouver as international banking centres (IBCs).[2] In these centres, the banks are allowed to set up separate facilities, free of certain taxes and regulatory requirements, to transact business with nonresident customers. It was the government's hope, in setting up these centres, to repatriate offshore Eurocurrency business conducted by Canadian banks in tax havens such as the Cayman Islands, the Channel Islands, and Panama.

Long before the term *Eurodollar* came into general use, Canadian banks regularly booked U.S. dollar deposits with their head offices in Canada and relent them in the New York "call" and "street loan" markets. Because the Canadian banks were not required to hold cash reserves against these deposits, they had a competitive advantage in relending them in the United States. At one time Canadian banks provided over 50 percent of all call loan money on Wall Street.

Large-scale arrangements that permit not only banks but also other financial intermediaries to draw on and lend funds denominated in currencies other than that of the country in which they are domiciled are of quite recent development. The Eurodollar market as we know it today began in the 1950s. Its origin has been attributed to the Soviet-controlled Banque Commercial pour l'Europe du Nord, whose cable address was EUROBANK. Eastern-bloc countries are said to have withdrawn their deposits from banks in the United States and redeposited them with this bank in Paris to conceal from the American authorities the size of their dollar holdings and to avoid the possibility of the U.S. government "freezing" or expropriating deposits held with banks in the United States.[3]

---

1. See Alec Chrystal, "International Banking Facilities," *Federal Reserve Bank of St. Louis Review*, April 1984, pp. 5–11.

2. See *Canada as an International Banking Centre*, A Report to the Department of Finance, by L. Rasminsky and R.W. Lawson (Ottawa: Minister of Supply and Services Canada, 1986). For a discussion of the controversy related to the establishment of these centres, see Robert MacIntosh, *Different Drummer: Banking and Politics in Canada* (Toronto: Macmillan, 1991), Ch. 14.

3. In 1979 the U.S. government froze Iranian government bank deposits held in the United States, and in 1982 during the Falkland Island War the British government froze Argentinean deposits in London banks.

Aside from political considerations, the impetus for the development of Eurocurrency markets was the avoidance of domestic regulatory requirements. In 1957, for example, when a run on sterling occurred, the government of the United Kingdom imposed controls to prevent sterling credits being used to finance non-British foreign trade. Restricted in the amount of sterling trade credit that they could grant, the British banks resorted to lending U.S. dollars to traders who would otherwise have purchased pounds sterling. The resultant demand by the British banks for U.S. dollar deposits and the placing of these dollars outside the United States on a large scale are viewed as having sparked the development of an active Eurodollar market in London.

Further impetus for the development of the Eurodollar market came in 1963, when the United States introduced the *Interest Equalization Act*, which made foreign borrowing in the U.S. more costly and the Eurodollar market an attractive source for funds. Other measures introduced by the U.S. authorities to deal with their overall balance of payments problems also encouraged the use of the Eurodollar market. Moreover, since Regulation Q restricted U.S. banks in the amount of interest they could pay on deposits, depositors were attracted by the higher rates offered in the unregulated Eurodollar markets. At times the large U.S. banks also borrowed heavily in Eurodollar markets through their overseas branches, as did the Canadian chartered banks, in an attempt to escape tighter monetary policies in their domestic markets.

Eurobank *a bank that regularly accepts deposits denominated in foreign currency and makes foreign currency loans*

When a Eurocurrency deposit is made in a **Eurobank**, the depositor ultimately writes a cheque on a deposit account in a bank situated in the country in whose currency the deposit is denominated. This usually involves a covered interest arbitrage transaction. The Eurobank ends up with a claim on a bank in another country, while the Eurocurrency depositor has a claim on a time deposit in a Eurobank.[4] The Eurobank may use these funds to make loans to ultimate borrowers or relend them to other banks. In the 1960s and 1970s a large proportion of Eurodollar deposits were the result of interbank deposits.

The Eurocurrency deposit market is primarily a brokered market where fixed-term deposits at Eurobanks are actively traded. Maturities typically range from thirty days to one year, but can be longer or as short as overnight. Interest rates paid on deposits as well as those charged on loans funded with these deposits are based on Interbank Offered Rates, of which the **London Interbank Offered Rate** (**LIBOR**) is most commonly used. The purchase and sale of Eurodollars are usually cleared through the Clearing House Interbank Payment System (chips), operated by New York banks. Other currencies are cleared through domestic payments mechanisms in their respective countries. The Society of Worldwide Interbank Financial Telecommunications (SWIFT), headquartered in Belgium, typically handles international financial telecommunications.

London Interbank Offered Rate (LIBOR) *the interest rate at which banks in London, England, will lend Eurocurrencies in the interbank market*

With the introduction of the Euro in January 1999, the LIBOR, which had been denominated in the national currencies of member European countries

---

4. Eurobank acquires a Eurodollar deposit by accepting a dollar deposit and entering it in its books in favour of the depositor. This liability is in turn offset by a "due from Bank's asset," which is the dollar deposit standing to the Eurobank's credit in a U.S. bank. While Eurodollar deposit transactions cause a change of ownership of Eurodollar deposits on the books of Eurobanks, the claim of Eurobanks on U.S. banks does not change. Such transactions involve no loss of deposits for U.S. banks as a whole.

as well as the European Currency Unit, was replaced by Euro-denominated benchmark interest rates. For example, the ECU LIBOR has become the **EURO LIBOR,** measured daily from a panel of London banks, while the **EURIBOR (Euro Interbank Offered Rate)** is based on European domestic rates.

EURO LIBOR and the EURIBOR (Euro Interbank Offered Rate) are Euro-denominated benchmark interest rates

Euroloans funded by Eurocurrency deposits usually have been made by syndicates of banks formed on a loan-by-loan basis. A lead manager, consisting of one or more banks, is responsible for negotiating the conditions of the loan with the borrower in return for a management fee. The lead manager, in turn, offers other banks the possibility to join the syndicate and to participate in the loan. Euroloans usually have a floating interest rate with relation to LIBOR and a fixed maturity ranging from 1 to 12 years; on average, maturity is about five to seven years.

The zenith of the Eurocurrency market was in the 1970s, when the large surpluses realized by the members of the Organization of Petroleum Exporting Countries (OPEC), following increases in world oil prices, were deposited with Eurobanks. These deposits, by and large, were used for loans to developing countries and, as explained later, became an important cause of the world debt crisis.

More recently, repurchase agreements (or repos), which involve the sale of securities against cash with a future buy-back agreement, have become a substitute for traditional international interbank credit. According to international accounting practices, funds advanced by purchases under these agreements are generally treated as collateralized loans, and the underlying security is maintained on the balance sheet of the seller. Such collateralized loans are generally extended between financial institutions for very short periods (a few days) and as such are part of the global interbank market.

Changes have also taken place in the international syndicated loan market. Before the international debt crisis in the early 1980s, described later, most of these loans were for general-purpose use by the governments of developing countries. Now, most syndicated bank loans are extended to private sector enterprises. Many of these have been arranged to facilitate transactions related to mergers and acquisitions, and for project-related financing worldwide.

International Bond and Equity Markets

International Bond Markets

The international bond markets may be divided into three broad groups: foreign bonds, Eurobonds, and global bonds.

foreign bonds bonds issued by nonresidents in a country's domestic capital market

Foreign bonds are bonds issued by foreign borrowers in a country's domestic market and are denominated in the domestic currency. What makes foreign bonds different from ordinary domestic bonds is that they are typically subject to different tax laws and regulatory requirements with respect to disclosure and registration. Foreign bonds issued in the United States are referred to as Yankee bonds; those issued in Japan are called samurai; those issued in the Netherlands and the United Kingdom are called Rembrandt bonds and bulldog bonds respectively. Before a domestic bond market developed in Canada, foreign bonds denominated in sterling were frequently issued on behalf of Canadian firms and governments in London, England.

Eurobonds are denominated in a currency other than that of the country in which they are issued. For example, a Canadian dollar bond issued in London, New York, or Tokyo is a Eurobond (referred to as a Euro-Canadian bond). As with the Eurocurrency market, a major reason for the emergence of the Eurobond market was its relative freedom from taxation and regulation.

Eurobonds **bonds that are denominated in a currency other than that of the country in which they are issued**

Multinational bank syndicates usually manage Eurobond issues. The managing banks negotiate the acquisition of bonds from borrowers and in turn sell them to other banks, which as underwriters and sellers place them with investors. Bonds are issued as straight bonds, which pay fixed interest; as equity-related bonds; or as floating rate bonds or floating rate notes (FRNs). Equity-related bonds are convertible or they have equity warrants. An FRN is a security with a floating-rate interest payment where the rate is reset at regular intervals, typically quarterly or half-yearly, in relation to a reference rate such as LIBOR.

Unlike regular bonds, which are issued through public offerings, FRNs are issued through security dealers. As such, the amount of their issue is not limited to a minimum amount, as is typically the case with public offerings. Borrowers are also given flexibility with respect to the size and currency denomination of drawdowns (calling on funds as needed).

Banks and other financial institutions have used FRNs to increase their subordinated capital and to remove assets from their balance sheets by securitizing loans. Bank loans may be put in a trust and used as collateral against FRNs. During the 1980s, the composition of new international credit shifted away from syndicated bank loans to securitized assets. While bonds and FRNs became an important form of long-term credits, Note Issuance Facilities (NIFs) and Euro-commercial paper became the main forms of short-term credit.

An NIF is an arrangement whereby borrowers issue short-term notes (Euronotes) supported by an undertaking by the banks that if the borrowers are unable to issue their notes at predetermined prices, the banks will buy them at these prices or extend credit. Since these notes may be underwritten, and usually are issued at periodic intervals, the facility may be called a revolving underwriting facility (RUF). Euronotes that are not underwritten are known as Euro-commercial paper.

A major trend in international financial markets has been the shift away from syndicated bank loans to marketable debt instruments. The maturing of the Eurobond markets, which have become broader and more homogeneous and which have developed standardized trading practices, has fostered this securitization. Moreover, a secondary market for Eurobonds has developed. This market is relatively free of official regulations and is self-regulated by the Association of International Bond Dealers. Eurobonds are cleared through one of two major clearing systems: Euroclear, founded in Brussels in 1968, and Cedel, founded in 1970 in Luxembourg by a group of European banks. Each of these systems has a group of depository or custodian banks to which bond certificates are delivered in bulk. When bonds are purchased or sold, book entry settlements are made transferring ownership while the bonds themselves remain in the custody of the depository banks.

The distinctive feature of the Euro market (which used to refer to offshore issues) has been progressively eroded by the liberalization of underwriting and trading practices. The creation of the single currency (the Euro) by the European Monetary Union has further compounded the difficulty of distinguishing between domestic and offshore issues in these countries. While the American dollar continues to be the main currency of issuance, it is losing ground to Euro-denominated securities.

global bonds
bonds issued simultaneously in more than one country

Global bonds are bonds issued simultaneously in more than one country. The World Bank undertook the first issue of global bonds in 1989. In May 1992, the Province of Ontario offered a U.S. $2 billion bond issue simultaneously in North America, Europe, Asia, and the Middle East. Global bonds backed predominately by U.S. credit card and automobile lease receivables have also been issued.

International Equity Markets

The markets for international equities encompass the underwriting and distribution of stocks by international syndicates of security firms or banks to investors in markets outside the issuers' domestic market. The three types of placements are (1) offerings of common or preferred equity in the Euromarket, (2) issues targeted at particular foreign markets, and (3) registered stocks traded on foreign markets as domestic instruments, such as American Depository Receipts (ADRs).[5] The listing and secondary market trading of international equities takes place on the domestic market of the issuer as well as on the foreign market where a listing has been secured.

The settlement of transactions takes place either in the issuers' country of residence or through domestic depositories that maintain a pool of foreign stocks and settle according to local procedures or, increasingly, through international depositories such as **Cedel and Euroclear**.

Cedel and Euroclear depositories for the settlement and clearing of foreign stock issues

The expansion of international trading in equities has been associated with the development in telecommunication systems, which have made market information more readily available to increasingly more sophisticated potential investors. The introduction of electronic trading and clearing systems also provided easier access to these markets. Investors, particularly fund managers, use these markets to diversify and maximize their wealth portfolios. Firms have used these markets to widen their shareholder base and to make offerings of their shares in amounts that could not be accommodated in their own domestic markets. For similar reasons, governments have used these markets for privatization issues.

It is not uncommon today for large firms to have their stock interlisted and simultaneously traded on several markets. Most of the major exchanges have electronic trading systems and are in the process of introducing remote access links. For example, the European Eurex exchange has been allowed to place trading terminals in the United States. These innovations and others are transforming domestic exchanges into international marketplaces that can be

---

5. ADRs are receipts issued by U.S. banks certifying that they hold a foreign security on behalf of the owner. European and Global Depository Receipts are the European and international equivalents of ADRs.

BOX 22–1   BOWRSE, BOERSE, TORIHIKI-JO, EXCHANGE

The beginning of the millennium saw a flurry of activity as stock exchanges around the globe were in the midst of merging or forming alliances. In Europe several smaller exchanges had already come together. Markets in Paris, Amsterdam, and Brussels were forming Euronext, while a group of Scandinavian markets agreed to form Norex. These deals prompted the London Stock Exchange and Frankfurt's Deutsche Boerse, which had been discussing merger for some time, to announce plans to merge into a new European market called iX.

In North America, NASDAQ joined ventures and alliances in Japan, Hong Kong, Australia, and Quebec. It has also arranged a joint venture focusing on growth stocks with iX when it gets going.

In June 2000, 10 stock exchanges from around the globe (New York Stock Exchange, Toronto Stock Exchange, exchanges in Australia, Tokyo, Hong Kong, Amsterdam, Brussels, Mexico, and Brazil, and the bourses in Paris) announced their alliance to create a new global exchange to be called Global Equity Market (GEM). GEM would replace their respective electronic systems and provide a 24-hour trading market worldwide for companies with the biggest capitalization on each of the participating exchanges. The GEM group represents some 60 percent of the market capitalization of worldwide trading, with a value of about U.S.$20 trillion.

accessed directly via the Internet. At the same time, stock exchanges around the globe have been in the process of merging or forming alliances and joint ventures (see Box 22–1).

It is estimated that the value of international equities issues was U.S.$1 trillion in 1997 and U.S.$900 billion in 1998.[6]

Global Derivative Markets

Among the fastest-growing financial markets have been those for interest rate and currency futures, options, and swaps. Since 1982 options and futures exchanges have been opened outside North America. Growth in these markets has been in response to the need for hedging instruments to manage the high variability of interest rates, exchange rates, and stock prices.

Despite the establishment of more exchanges around the world for the trading of financial derivatives, over-the-counter (OTC) derivatives predominate exchange trading by a wide margin. In its first triannual central bank survey of OTC derivatives in April 1995, the Bank for International Settlements found that the national value of outstanding foreign exchange, interest rate, equity, and commodity derivatives was an estimated U.S.$47.5 trillion (after adjusting for double counting). In addition to OTC derivatives, the intermedi-

---

6. See Bank for International Settlements, *International Banking and Financial Market Developments*, Basel, Quarterly.

aries that were involved in the survey reported that they held a further U.S.$16.6 trillion in notional value of exchange-traded derivatives. In the tri-annual survey at the end of June 1998, the aggregate national value of OTC derivatives outstanding had grown to U.S.$72 trillion.

It was found in the 1995 survey that 55 percent of all outstanding OTC interest rate and currency derivatives involved counter-parties in different countries. This reflected the global nature of derivative contracts. Globalization of derivative markets is also observed in the growth of interconnections among derivative markets worldwide. For example, derivative contracts are being cross-listed by exchanges throughout the world. This, together with the proliferation of after-hour trading, is moving us closer to a 24-hour global derivative market.

Globalization of Financial Markets

Globalization refers to the growing interdependence among world financial markets that has resulted in unprecedented financial integration, international capital mobility, and competition. Advances in information processing and telecommunications, the liberalization of restrictions on cross-border capital flows, and the deregulation of domestic financial markets have driven these developments. Profit-maximizing financial intermediaries have taken advantage of these changes by expanding their operations worldwide, and by introducing new, sophisticated financial instruments that allow investors to diversify their portfolios internationally and to hedge risks associated with volatile exchange rates, interest rates, and equity prices.

Many observers see the globalization of financial markets as bringing about more efficient markets. This should be reflected in lower costs of intermediation, a narrowing of the differences in the cost of funds between markets, the pooling of risks across countries, and the more equitable distribution of world savings. Globalization should also make available a wider range of financial services; access formerly depended on a customer's geographic location.

Despite the actual and potential benefits, certain aspects of financial globalization may give cause for concern for public policy. One such concern is global systemic failure as a result of a financial crisis in one country quickly spreading to other countries. The October 1987 crash of the New York stock market and its almost simultaneous effect on other major world stock exchanges, and more recently the Mexican peso crisis in 1994–95 and the Asian crisis in 1997–98, which spilled over into neighbouring countries and beyond, focused attention on potential systemic risks in global financial markets.

A related concern has been the anticipated concentration of the worldwide financial service industry in relatively few institutions. If this should happen, the failure of any one institution could threaten the viability of the world financial system, resulting in panic and crisis.

Yet another concern for public policy has been the adequacy of domestic institutional regulatory and supervisory systems and the need internationally to harmonize at least minimum standards of conduct. As explained below, the

www.

money laundering *the conversion or disposal of funds derived from illegal activity to conceal their illicit origin*

Basel Committees and others have addressed some of these policy issues. As also explained below, steps have been taken to deal with settlement risk in the global foreign exchange market.

International coordination efforts have been initiated to make money laundering a criminal offence. **Money laundering** is the attempt to convert or dispose of funds derived from illegal activities to conceal their illicit origin. Discussions have also been initiated to design safer systems for the clearing and settlement of international financial transactions.

Surveillance over Global Financial Markets

Various international organizations share responsibility for arrangements concerning the supervision and surveillance of the international financial system.

The International Monetary Fund (IMF) has responsibility under its Articles for surveillance of all member countries. It monitors developments in the global economy and financial markets. Each year it reviews economic developments and policies of member countries and holds consultations with them. It also regularly publishes world economic and financial surveys and, once a year, the *World Economic Outlook.*[7]

The IMF has promulgated the Special Data Dissemination Standard, a standard of good practices in the dissemination of economic and financial data provided by countries engaged in international capital markets.[8]

The World Bank, under its mandate, uses its expertise to assist countries in the design and implementation of reforms to strengthen financial systems, including banking, capital markets and market infrastructure.[9]

The Bank for International Settlement (BIS) and its affiliated Basel Committees, described in Box 22–2, have played a particularly influential role in forming the institutional infrastructure of the international financial system.

Basel Concordat *an agreement among the Group of Ten countries establishing the principle that the home country is responsible for supervising the global operations of international banks in its jurisdiction*

The Basel Committee for Banking Supervision has reached two important agreements related to the successful supervision of global financial markets. The first, the so-called **Basel Concordat**, in 1975 established the principle that the home country is responsible for supervising the global operations of international banks in its jurisdiction based on a consolidated balance sheet. In 1992 the Concordat was supplemented with agreement on a set of minimum standards for the supervision of international banks and their cross-border establishments. Agreement has also been reached on the imposition of restrictive measures if these standards are not met. For example, the host country supervisor can deny access to banking institutions from countries whose oversight over the consolidated activities of institutions is not in keeping with the

---

7. See for example, *International Capital Markets, Development Prospects and Key Issues* (September 1999), and *World Economic Outlook: International Financial Integration* (October 1999). In addition the IMF publishes working and policy papers. More recent issues are accessible from its Website, <www.imf.org>.

8. The database is accessible on the IMF Website, <www.imf.org>.

9. The World Bank is officially known as the International Bank for Reconstruction and Development.

BOX 22–2   BANK FOR INTERNATIONAL SETTLEMENTS (BIS)

The BIS is a bank for central banking based in Basel, Switzerland. It provides a broad range of financial services to central banks for managing their external reserves. It was originally created to coordinate German reparation payments after the First World War. It serves as an agent or trustee for facilitating the implementation of various international financial agreements.

The BIS does not accept deposits from or ordinarily provide financial services to private individual firms.

The BIS functions as a forum for international monetary and financial cooperation.

The BIS also serves as the secretariat of the so-called **Basel Committees,** which were estab-

lished by the governors of the Group of Ten countries in the 1970s.

- **Basel Committee on Banking Supervision.** It is an important rule-setting body in the field of banking standards and supervision.

- **Basel Committee on Payments and Settlement Systems.** It analyzes payment systems and makes recommendations with the aim of reducing risks in these systems.

- **Basel Committee on Global Financial Systems.** It analyzes global financial system conditions and makes recommendations for improving the functioning of markets.

Basel Accord an agreement among the Group of Ten countries covering regulatory risk-weighted capital requirements for internationally active banks

agreed minimum standards. More recently, discussions have been held on the supervision of international financial conglomerates.

The second major set of agreements negotiated by the Basel Committee for the G-10 countries concerns regulatory capital requirements. In 1988, the so-called **Basel Accord** established minimum risk-weighted regulatory capital ratios for banks in the G-10 countries. This accord was amended in 1997 to encompass the management of market risks in banks' trading activities. However, in formulating this extension, the committee realized that the traditional supervisory approach based on compliance with a prescribed set of balance-sheet ratios was no longer a necessary—or sufficient—condition for risk management by international financial intermediaries. Instead, the committee proposed that internationally active banks should use their own risk management models to estimate and control the net loss that they could sustain during a specified number of trading days (the value-at-risk methodology we discussed in earlier chapters), with the regulatory minimum capital requirement determined as a multiple of the banks' value-at-risk estimate.

In 1999, the Basel Committee proposed a new capital adequacy framework to replace the Accord.[10] The new framework is designed to better align regulatory capital requirements with underlying risks, and to recognize the improvements made in recent years in risk measurement and control. It consists of three pillars: minimum capital requirements based on a more comprehensive approach to addressing risks, supervisory review of an institution's capital adequacy and internal assessment process, and the effective use of

---

10. *Basel Committee on Bank Supervision, A New Capital Adequacy Framework.* BIS, Basel, June 1999. See also *The Core Principles of Methodology,* Basel, 1999. This committee has issued a large number of policy papers covering a wide range of topics. More recent papers can be downloaded from the Website <www.bis.org>.

market discipline as a lever to strengthen disclosure and encourage safe and sound banking practices.

In September 1997 the Committee on Banking Supervision issued a comprehensive set of core principles representing a global standard for prudential regulation and supervision. The vast majority of countries have endorsed the core principles and have declared their intention to implement them.

The Basel Committee on Global Financial Systems also has been working on the desirability of developing international norms or standards in a wide variety of areas. The IMF also has been fostering the development, dissemination, and implementation of internationally acceptable standards or codes of practice for economic, financial, and business activities.

In April 1999 the IMF approved the creation of Contingent Credit Lines (CCLs) for its member countries as a readily available precautionary defence against balance of payments problems arising from international financial contagion.

The ministers and governors of the G-7 countries initiated the Financial Stability Forum in February 1999, which then set up three study groups, each with its own goal: (1) establishing the potential of highly leveraged institutions to do harm to the international financial system, (2) avoiding excess reliance on volatile short-term capital flows, (3) assessing progress made by financial offshore centres in enforcing international prudential standards and exchange of information.

The June 1999 G-8 Summit of Leaders made proposals aimed at the better management of global capital flows and financial crises. These proposals focused on a framework for involving the private sector in preventing and resolving international financial crises.

Banking, securities, and insurance supervisors in the G-10 countries have also undertaken cooperative initiatives in financial surveillance. The Basel Committee and the International Organization of Securities Commissions have issued guidelines for derivatives. These guidelines are based on three basic principles: appropriate oversight by boards of directors and senior managements, adequate risk management, and comprehensive internal controls and audit procedures.

Settlement Risk in the Global Foreign Exchange Market

The global foreign exchange market is at the centre of the international financial system. It is the largest market in the world. In April 1995, when the Bank for International Settlements completed its fifth triennial survey of foreign exchange markets, the total estimated average daily net turnover in these markets was U.S.$1.2 trillion. There were an estimated 125 000 to 150 000 transactions every day, necessitating 250 000 to 300 000 exchanges of currency.[11]

11. See also Bank for International Settlements, *Central Bank Survey of Foreign Exchange and Derivative Market Activity* (Basel, October 1999).

Because the foreign exchange market is at the core of the international financial system and the global network of interbank payments, a major disruption in this market could have disastrous consequences for the global economy. The risk of such a disruption arises from the cross-currency nature of international currency settlement. Because settlements must occur through the payment systems of two countries that are not always open at the same time, final payment in each currency cannot take place simultaneously. The inability to finalize payments simultaneously gives rise to the risk that after the first counter-party has already delivered one side of the transaction, the other counter-party may go bankrupt and fail to deliver the offsetting currency. This risk is called **Herstatt risk**, named for the failure of the German bank Bankhaus Herstatt, in 1974. Since it is not uncommon for a major international bank to have a U.S.$2 billion unsecured foreign exchange exposure with just one other bank as a result of one day's transactions, Herstatt risk has received attention. The Bank for International Settlements has documented four recent potentially threatening events involving foreign exchange settlement failures, or the possibility of one: the failure of Bankhaus Herstatt in 1974; the collapse of Drexel Burnham Lambert in 1990; the collapse of the Bank of Credit and Commerce International (BCCI) in 1991, the attempted Soviet coup d'état in 1991; and the Barings Bank crisis in 1995.[12] Fortunately, in each case timely intervention by major central banks avoided what could have resulted in serious systemic consequences for the international financial system.

Herstatt risk the risk that after one counter-party delivers on one side of a foreign exchange transaction the other counter-party will fail to deliver on the other side

Foreign exchange settlement risk could be substantially reduced and even eliminated if the two payments of a foreign exchange transaction were to be finalized simultaneously. Two changes in international payments arrangements could bring this about: the elimination of existing gaps in the operating hours of the major national payments clearing and settlement systems, and the linking of these payments systems in real time to achieve intraday payments finality.

The CLS Bank International has been set up with headquarters in New York. Its ownership is open to qualified financial institutions worldwide, and its shareholders include Canadian banks. When fully in operation, it will provide an electronic currency clearing and settlement system, reducing and controlling the risks associated with settlement of foreign exchange transactions. The Bank of Canada has indicated that it will provide a settlement account and act as an agent for the CLS Bank.

Some progress has already been made in reducing the gaps in operating hours of the U.S. and Japanese and the U.S. and German payments systems. The major industrial countries have introduced, or are in the process of introducing, real time gross settlement systems (RTGS) for large value (wholesale) payments. However, linking these domestic payments systems involves large issues of public policy. A major concern of establishing payment systems link-

12. See Bank for International Settlements, *Settlements Risk in Foreign Exchange Transactions* (Basel, March 1996). See also *Report of the Committee on Interbank Netting Schemes of the Central Banks of the Group of Ten Countries* (Basel, November 1990). This report, called "The Lamfalussy Report," sets out minimum standards for the design and operation of cross-border and multicurrency netting and settlement schemes; *Reducing Foreign Exchange Risk: A Progress Report*, Committee on Payments and Settlement Systems of the Central Banks of the Group of Ten Countries, Basel, July 1998.

TARGET *an EU-wide system for settling Euro payments*

bilateral netting system *a netting arrangement that periodically aggregates payments between counter-parties and calculates one payment per currency for each pair of counter-parties*

multilateral netting system *a netting system that nets the amounts among a group of counter-parties through a clearing-house arrangement, resulting in one payment each day in a given currency to or from the clearing house by each counter-party*

ages is the increased exposure of domestic payment systems to cross-border spillovers from disturbances in other countries. Members of the European Union have developed the so-called **TARGET** system to link together their national RTGs systems.[13]

Alternatives for reducing Herstatt-type risk are netting arrangements, which private initiatives have introduced. Netting arrangements allow counter-parties to reduce the number of financial payments and the amounts involved. **Bilateral netting systems** periodically aggregate the amounts owed between counter-parties and calculate one payment per currency for each pair of counter-parties. Bilateral netting can reduce amounts at risk by an estimated 50 percent on average. Two widely used netting systems are FXNET and the swift Accord system.

Multilateral netting systems net the amounts among a group of counter-parties through a clearing-house arrangement resulting in one payment each day in a given currency to or from the clearing house by each counter-party. Two such systems are ECHO, based in the United Kingdom and MULINET a system that is being developed under the sponsorship of a group of Canadian and U.S. banks.

The International Debt Crisis

The international debt crisis refers to the difficulties many of the developing countries experienced in the early 1980s in servicing (paying interest and repaying principal) their external debt. This debt had grown from under U.S.$100 billion to some U.S.$572 trillion during the 1970s. Attention was first drawn to the debt problem of the developing countries in August 1982 when Mexico announced a moratorium on servicing its external debt.

During the early 1970s, commercial banks in the industrial countries increased their lending to the developing countries whose economies were growing rapidly in response to rising world prices of their export commodities. Bank lending to these countries reached flood proportions in 1973–74 as a result of the first sharp increase in world oil prices by members of OPEC. The major oil-exporting countries deposited most of the massive surplus revenue from the higher oil prices with banks in the Eurodollar market. The banks in turn recycled these so-called petrodollars to the oil-importing countries faced with higher oil costs. As the volume of petrodollars increased, especially after another sharp price hike by OPEC in 1979, competition intensified between the banks placing loans. Borrowing by developing countries was not limited to oil-importing countries; oil-exporting countries such as Mexico and Venezuela borrowed heavily to finance expansion of their own oil production.

Bank lending took the form of syndicated loans at floating interest rates, typically six months LIBOR. Most of these loans were sovereign loans; that is, loans to governments that borrowed to finance their countries' balance of payments deficits. Some critics of the banks' lending behaviour claim that they misjudged the risks associated with sovereign loans and that with loan syndication, many banks did not make their own independent risk assessments.

---

13. TARGET is the acronym for Trans-European Automated Real Time Gross Settlement Express Transfer System.

debt rescheduling *a postponement of principal repayments but not interest payments*

www.

Paris Club *an arrangement whereby the government of France hosts and chairs rescheduling negotiations between creditor and debtor countries*

In response to the inflationary pressures that followed the second oil price increase in 1979, the major industrial countries introduced restrictive monetary policies. This resulted not only in a sharp increase in interest rates but also in a global recession in 1980–82. As prices and demand for their export commodities declined and their interest costs increased, the developing countries experienced difficulties servicing their external debts. These difficulties were exacerbated in many of the developing countries by inappropriate domestic policies, including overvalued exchange rates that encouraged imports and discouraged exports, and huge flights of capital in search of safe refuge.

At first it was generally held that the debt problem of the developing countries was merely one of liquidity, which would be resolved as their terms of trade and the world economy improved. The immediate response by creditors was country-by-country debt rescheduling agreements. **Debt rescheduling** involves a postponement of principal repayments, but not of interest payments. However, agreements usually provide for new credits to help debtors to meet their interest obligations.

Between 1983 and 1985, rescheduling agreements were arranged between commercial banks and some 30 developing countries. During the same period, the **Paris Club** assisted in restructuring loans that governments had made directly to many developing countries. The Paris Club is an arrangement whereby the government of France hosts and chairs rescheduling negotiations between creditor and debtor countries.

In October 1985, U.S. Secretary of the Treasury James Baker proposed new initiatives for resolving the international debt crisis. He emphasized the need for the principal debtor countries to adopt comprehensive macroeconomic and structural policies assisted by increased lending by the international banks. He suggested that the banks commit U.S.$20 billion in new lending over a three-year period. The additional financing from the banks, together with additional funds from official sources (government, the World Bank, and the IMF) was to be made conditional on debtor nations following growth-oriented macroeconomic and structural reforms.

The commercial banks were reluctant to increase their lending to the developing countries and took steps to decrease their external risk exposure. In 1987, following the lead taken by Citicorp of New York, other major banks started to set aside unprecedented amounts of reserves against the possibility of not recovering their loans to developing countries. By the end of 1989, the Canadian banks' loan loss provisioning was on average equal to 75 percent of their outstanding loans to low-income countries. The amount of this provisioning eroded the banks' net income and their capital base. The most severely affected banks had to raise additional capital in financial markets.

The creditor banks used a wide range of techniques to reduce their risk exposure on outstanding claims to problem countries. These included a variety of debt conversion schemes such as buy-backs, swaps, and exchanges. Most of these schemes were made possible by the development of a secondary market after 1985 in the debt of developing countries.

With buy-back agreements, indebted countries or private firms agree to repurchase their own debt, usually at a deeply discounted price. These agreements are usually viewed as a final alternative for countries that appear to have virtually no hope of repaying their debt. Under debt-for-equity swaps, banks sell their loan claims at a discount to investors who in turn swap them for equity investments in debtor countries. Loan claims have also been swapped for a debtor country's anticipated exports (debt for export swaps), and for commitments to undertake specified environmental policies (debt for nature swaps). Debt exchanges have involved creditors exchanging existing debt claims for a new debt instrument with a lower principal value and backed by government securities or other acceptable collateral. When an exchange is made for so-called exit bonds, typically in association with a debt-restructuring agreement, a creditor is freed of existing commitments to make any further contribution to a debtor country's financial needs.

The countries of sub–Saharan Africa, encumbered with high rates of population growth and disastrous climatic changes, have struggled in particular with their external debts, which are largely owed to official creditors. Following a commitment at the 1988 Toronto G-7 Summit meetings, the governments of the major industrial countries forgave nearly U.S.$5 billion in official development assistance loans to these countries.

In 1996 the World Bank and the International Monetary Fund undertook a joint initiative to ensure that the most heavily indebted countries with a sound track record of economic adjustment attain a sustainable debt burden over the medium term. Sustainability implies sufficient export earnings to service external debt. Under the initiative, debt relief is available from the World Bank and the IMF, but only after these countries have pursued convincing economic policies over several years. Despite the progress already made, the initiative was enhanced in late 1999.

Debt-rescheduling and conversion agreements, together with economic restructuring programs, did not significantly reduce the external debt of the developing countries. As a result, these countries were unable to obtain new financing from private sector sources to develop their economies. To deal with this problem, early in 1989, U.S. Treasury Secretary Brady proposed new private sector initiatives to help countries undertake growth-oriented adjustment while reducing their debt burden. The Brady Plan called for debt relief or debt reduction rather than rescheduling for countries that implement comprehensive economic reform programs. A number of debtor countries, including Mexico, the Philippines, Costa Rica, Venezuela, and Uruguay, worked out debt-restructuring agreements in 1990 with their bank creditors within the framework of the Brady Plan. These agreements typically involved a combination of outright debt reduction, debt service relief, and the provision of new money by creditor banks. The banks were induced to enter these agreements by enhancements provided by the World Bank, the IMF, and governments of the major industrial countries, in the form of collateralization of principal and interest guarantees on restructured debts. Bonds issued under the Brady Plan are known as **brady bonds** and are actively traded in secondary markets.[14]

Between 1990 and 1993, countries participating in the Brady Plan were able to reduce their debt loads by as much as 20 percent by discounting original loans and by exchanging their bank debt for bonds that bore below-market

brady bonds
bonds issued under the Brady Plan for debt reduction and rescheduling

---

14. The BIS together with the IMF, OED, and the World Bank now publish statistics on external debt. See *Statistics on External Indebtedness,* Quarterly. Data are accessible on the sponsors' respective Websites.

interest rates. Stabilization and reform programs by debtor countries also resulted in their stronger external positions that allowed them to accumulate reserves for debt reduction.

In the early 1990s, attention became focused on the chronic debt problems of countries in Eastern Europe as they began their transition from centrally planned to market-oriented economies.

The Paris Club came to their assistance by negotiating debt reduction and debt-restructuring agreements. For example, in March 1991, the Paris Club agreed in principle that Poland's bilateral debt to official creditors be reduced by one-half in net present-value terms. The Paris Club also agreed, following Bulgaria's moratorium on servicing its bank debts, to reschedule that country's debts to foreign official creditors.

Private Capital Flows to Developing Countries

In the first half of the 1990s, private capital flowed to the developing countries in unprecedented amounts. During the debt crisis of the 1980s, these flows had all but dried up and had to be replaced with funds from government and multilateral institutions.

The emerging markets in Latin America and East Asia explain much of the increase in private capital flows to the developing countries. The composition of these flows is changing accordingly. Most funds are now going to private rather than to government borrowers and have come from nonbank rather than bank lenders. Moreover, private bank lending is being supplemented and in some cases replaced by the sale of bonds and equities and by direct private investments.

Part of the shift in the composition of funds reflects international asset diversification that has taken place in the industrial countries. Institutional investors in these countries, particularly pension funds and mutual funds, are investing in private enterprises in emerging markets displaying political and macroeconomic stability. At times, as was the case in the early 1990s, the decline in interest rates in the major industrial countries has also provided an incentive to investors to place some of their funds into higher-yielding assets in the developing countries.

For their part, many of the developing countries have attracted foreign capital with the privatization of many of their state enterprises, the liberalization of their markets, and deregulation of their financial systems. However, above all, they have been able to attract more foreign private capital as a result of restructuring their economies and providing political and macroeconomic stability.

The Mexican Peso Crisis

On December 20, 1994, the government of Mexico's announced devaluation took financial markets by surprise and precipitated the so-called Mexican peso crisis. During the previous three years, Mexico had been following an exchange-rate policy of maintaining the peso within a well-defined band against the U.S. dollar. However, during 1994, this policy came under pressure as Mexico's current account deficits rose and its international reserves declined. The Mexican authorities tried unsuccessfully to support the peso by drawing down their reserves and by financing the large and increasing current account deficit with the sale of short-term debt to foreigners. The devaluation of December 20 failed to stabilize the peso in currency markets, and two days later the authorities were forced to allow the peso to float freely. Its value immediately plummeted. The Mexican authorities had been unwilling to defend the peso by tightening monetary policy because higher interest rates would have strained an already vulnerable banking system and conflicted with their attempts to promote economic activity in an election year.

In the years immediately before the crisis, Mexico was the recipient of large capital inflows since it had established a good reputation among international investors as a result of its ongoing fundamental improvements in its economic and financial structure. It had restructured its foreign debt under the Brady Plan. Budget deficits and inflation rates were sharply reduced. Various government-owned enterprises had been privatized and trade barriers removed. The negotiation of the North American Free Trade Agreement (NAFTA) also led investors to believe that Mexico was a very promising place to invest.

In 1994, however, investors increasingly became less confident about the Mexican economy, owing to uncertainties caused by rebellion in the southern province of Chiapas, political assassinations, and the August election. With this rather sudden loss of confidence, foreign money not only stopped flowing into Mexico, but also rapidly moved out and made it impossible for the authorities to finance the current account deficit and, hence, to hold the peso within its band against the U.S. dollar. A major concern for the government was its ability to roll over its large short-term debt that had been built up to finance the growing current account deficit.

Since the Mexican situation was seen as having the potential for systemic harm to the global financial system, an unprecedented international support package amounting to some U.S. $50 billion was negotiated under American leadership. These funds were made available to Mexico to undertake stabilization programs and to restore a climate of confidence in international financial markets.

Investors that had been taken by surprise when the Mexican peso was devalued immediately looked around to see if other Latin American countries were in a similar situation. As a result, Argentina and Brazil also experienced a sudden withdrawal of foreign funds.

The major lessons that were to be learned by the Mexican crisis were that a country experiencing large capital inflows could suddenly experience an equally large outflow when investors revise their views about the country's prospects. Moreover, with the international integration of financial markets, crises are contagious; they can spill over into other countries and have the potential to put the entire international financial system at risk. Crisis prevention calls for countries involved in global financial markets to manage their economies prudently and to respond promptly to changes in economic and financial conditions.

These lessons were taken up by the leaders of the major industrial countries at their Halifax Summit meetings in June 1995. As a result of the summit proposals to strengthen the international financial system, the International Monetary Fund intensified its surveillance of national policies. It also has set out new standards for the timely publication of financial statistics for countries involved in international financial markets. Furthermore, the IMF subsequently negotiated an arrangement that allows it to borrow some U.S.$47 billion to be used to deal with exceptional situations that could threaten the stability of the international monetary system.

Massive foreign official assistance to Mexico had allowed holders of short-term dollar-linked Mexican government paper to escape without loss. Some observers have suggested that this may have weakened investors' sense of responsibility for their own actions (moral hazard). Furthermore, because holders of other forms of Mexican debt (equities, long-term bonds, or peso-denominated debt) did not suffer losses, this may have changed the future pattern of capital flows to emerging market countries from equity to debt, from long- to short-term debt and from local to foreign currency denomination. In fact, this may have been a major factor in the Asian Crisis, to which we now turn.

The Asian Financial Crisis

The Asian financial crisis during 1997–98 had far-reaching consequences and is a classic example of contagion (spillover) at work in global capital markets. The crisis started in Thailand, engulfed Malaysia, Indonesia, South Korea, the Philippines, and eventually proceeded to affect Russia, Brazil, and Argentina.

In the decade preceding the crisis, the economic performance of the emerging market countries of East Asia had been impressive. Average annual growth rates in the region had been 7.5 percent with modest inflation. Much of the growth came from increasing openness in most of the economies in the region, which attracted massive flows of foreign capital. In retrospect, however, the strong macroeconomic features masked difficulties these countries were experiencing in their financial sectors and elsewhere. The underlying causes of the crisis are summarized in Box 22–3

Strong speculative pressure began to mount against the Thai baht in early 1997 as investor confidence in Thailand began to wane with the revelation of deep-seated financial and economic vulnerabilities. Intervention could not stem large capital outflows, and in July the Thai baht was cut from its dollar anchor and quickly depreciated.

Indonesia was the next victim. It had been enjoying strong economic growth, moderate inflation, and a modest current account deficit. Nevertheless, international investors focused on the country's financial weakness, in particular a fragile and poorly supervised financial sector and a highly indebted corporate sector. When investor confidence failed and former capital inflows reversed, the rupiah also had to be freed from its dollar anchor and suffered dramatic devaluation.

BOX 22–3   UNDERLYING CAUSES OF THE ASIAN FINANCIAL CRISIS

Foreign investors and lenders overlooked the underlying fragility of East Asian countries' financial systems because of apparent exchange rate stability and high levels of economic growth accompanied by modest inflation. Six important factors contributed to the crisis:

1. Longstanding policies of fixed or quasi-fixed exchange rates nurtured a misconception of exchange rate stability by both Asian borrowers and international lenders.
2. Weak supervision and prudential regulations of financial institutions invited reckless risk taking.
3. Creditors (both foreign financial institutions and domestic lenders) perceived their funds to be protected by implicit or explicit government guarantees, providing the incentive for excessive risk taking.
4. Excessive expansion of bank credit fuelled overinvestment, leading to creation of unprofitable industrial capacity, especially in the electronics industry, and asset price boom–bust cycles.
5. Heavy dependence on short-term foreign loans denominated in foreign currencies made these countries vulnerable to capital flow reversals.
6. Herd behaviour by international investors who rushed to East Asia at the beginning of the decade with scant regard for risk, and later bolted with scant regard for the consequences to the economies of the affected countries.

Malaysia was next to suffer from reversal in investor confidence and a large capital outflow, particularly in equity capital. The authorities depreciated the ringgit and imposed administrative measures to control capital outflows.

South Korea was placed on international lenders' watch lists in early 1997 following the bankruptcies of large industrial conglomerates and evidence of loan performance problems in the financial sector. The pressure on the Korean won could not be successfully stemmed by intervention, and by the end of the year the country appeared to be on the brink of defaulting on its short-term external debt. This default was prevented by a large international bailout.

To quell the Asian crisis and restore international confidence in financial and exchange markets, the International Monetary Fund together with bilateral and multilateral assistance provided international liquidity support to the affected countries. A total of U.S.$117 billion was offered to Thailand, Indonesia, and Korea, with the size of commitments growing with each successive assistance package. The reason for this escalation was to ensure that the announced size of the package would have a psychological impact on markets and halt the erosion of foreign confidence.

In the countries most severely affected by the crisis—Thailand, Korea, Malaysia, and Indonesia—high interest rates and the reversal of foreign capital inflows reduced capital investment. Together with some tightening of macro policies and widespread failures in financial sectors, the economies collapsed. Economic depression with high levels of unemployment led to wide social distress in the region.

The Russian Debt Moratorium

The official announcement of the floating of the rouble and the unilateral moratorium on Russia's debt in mid–August 1998 sent further shock waves through global financial markets. These markets were still recovering from the Asian crisis. The unexpected Russian announcement re-ignited global market turbulence. The Russian default was a catalytic event in that the international community did not come to its immediate assistance, and thereby changed the rules of the game for investors who had counted on some form of bailout.

The Russian default left Long-Term Capital Management (LTCM) extremely vulnerable as deteriorating positions in international markets brought it to near insolvency. LTCM, a large American-based hedge fund, had U.S.$120 billion of balance sheet exposure and U.S.$1.3 trillion of notional derivatives exposure. It is said that LTCM lost almost U.S.$2 billion in a single month as a result of the collapse of markets in Russia. Hedge funds are described in Box 22–4.

BOX 22–4   HEDGE FUNDS

Hedge funds comprise a heterogeneous group of investment partnerships that have operated in a regulatory and supervisory "no man's land." For tax advantages, many are located in offshore centres.

Contrary to what their name implies, hedge funds deliberately assume risk in pursuit of their performance targets. Hedge fund managers are given wide freedom of action to enable them to respond quickly whenever new market opportunities arise. Managers' remuneration can include between 15 and 20 percent of the gain realized. To avoid moral hazard problems, managers themselves are required to hold a fairly high participation in the fund. Since partnership shares can be acquired for thousands of dollars, their owners are high net worth individuals (the very rich) and institutional investors.

Hedge funds frequently are highly leveraged by borrowing from banks and other financial institutions to supplement their owners' contribution. Moreover, with the aid of derivatives they can build up market positions that vastly exceed their asset base.

The following are four of the more common types of hedge funds.

Macro: These funds speculate worldwide on price changes of shares, bonds currencies, or exchange-traded commodities in connection with presumed changes in economic or economic policy conditions.

Market-neutral: These funds take up long-term and short-term positions that are wholly or partly hedged in terms of value in more or less closely related securities to minimize market risk. They buy undervalued assets and simultaneously sell overvalued ones.

Short selling: These funds borrow shares from brokers that they regard as overvalued and immediately sell them in the market in the hope that they will be able to repurchase them later at a lower price to return them to the broker and realize a profit.

Value: These funds buy or sell securities of firms that they regard as overvalued relative to their estimated fundamental value.

Other types of hedge funds are emerging markets, aggressive growth, sectoral, and market timing.

SOURCE: See International Monetary Fund, *Hedge Funds and Financial Market Dynamics*, Occasional Paper No 166, 1998; Basel Committee on Banking Supervision, *Sound Practices for Banks' Interactions with Highly Leveraged Institutions* (Bank of International Settlements). Basel, January 1999.

Failure of such a large hedge fund could have had serious consequences for the American and global financial systems. Hence, the Federal Reserve Bank of New York arranged a meeting of 17 large financial institutions to recapitalize the ailing LTCM hedge fund. A U.S.$3.6 billion bailout package was required. Since no public funds were offered to guarantee the bailout, it can be viewed as a private sector solution to a private sector problem threatening systematic failure of the financial system.

KEY TERMS

Basel Accord	Eurobank	London Interbank Offered Rate
Basel Concordat	Eurobonds	(LIBOR)
bilateral netting systems	Eurocurrency	money laundering
brady bonds	Eurodollar	multilateral netting systems
Cedel and Euroclear	foreign bonds	Paris Club
debt rescheduling	global bonds	TARGET
EURO LIBOR AND EURIBOR	Herstatt risk	

REVIEW QUESTIONS

1. What are Eurocurrencies? Where does one find Eurocurrency markets? How can one explain their emergence? What are Eurocurrency syndicated bank loans?
2. What is the difference between foreign bonds and domestic bonds?
3. What is an FRN, a RUF, and a NIF? What is LIBOR?
4. What explains the rapid growth of international equity markets?
5. What are the potential benefits and what are some of the concerns of public policy with respect to financial globalization?
6. What are some of the factors attributed to causing the international debt crisis?
7. What explains the large increase in the external debt of the developing countries during the 1970s? Why did this develop into the debt crisis of the 1980s?
8. What is debt rescheduling? Describe some of the debt conversion schemes that have been employed.
9. What are the Basel Concordat and the Basel Accord?
10. Define "Herstatt risk."
11. What is the difference between a bilateral netting system and a multilateral netting system?
12. What are the lessons to be learned from the Mexican and Asian crises?
13. What are hedge funds? How do they differ from mutual funds?
14. What changes have already been made to reform the financial infrastructure? List some further reforms that have been suggested.

SELECTED READINGS

Abken, Peter A. "Globalization of Stock, Futures and Options Markets." Federal Reserve Bank of Atlanta, *Economic Review*, July/August 1991, pp. 1–21.

Andrews, David, Anthony Boote, et al. (eds.). *Debt Relief for Low Income Countries: The Enhanced HIPC Initiative.* Pamphlet Series 51, World Bank, Washington, D.C., March 2000.

Bank for International Settlements. *Recent Innovations in International Banking.* Basel, Switzerland, April 1986.

Brau, E., et al. *Recent Multilateral Debt Restructuring with Official and Bank Creditors.* International Monetary Fund, Occasional Paper 25. Washington: IMF, December 1985.

Bryant, Ralph C. *International Financial Intermediation.* Washington, D.C.: The Brookings Institution, 1987.

Canada. Department of Finance. *Canada as an International Banking Centre.* A Report to the Department of Finance by L. Rasminsky and R.W. Lawson. Ottawa: Minister of Supply and Services Canada, 1986.

———. The Senate Standing Committee on Foreign Affairs. C*anada, the International Financial Institutions and the Debt Problems of Developing Countries.* Ottawa: Minister of Supply and Services Canada, April 1987.

Clendenning, F. Wayne. *Euro-Currency Markets and the International Activities of Canadian Banks.* Ottawa: Economic Council of Canada, 1976.

Cline, William R. "International Debt and the Stability of the World Economy." *Policy Analysis in International Economics* 4. Washington, D.C.: Institute for International Economics, September 1983.

Harvavini, Gabriel, and Eric Rajendra. *The Transformation of the European Financial Services Industry: From Fragmentation to Integration.* Monograph Series in Finance and Economics 1989–4. New York University Salomon Center.

Huang, Roger D., and Hans R. Stoll. *Major World Equity Markets: Current Structure and Prospects for Change.* Monograph Series in Finance and Economics 1991–3. New York University Salomon Center.

International Development Research Center. *The Global Cash Crunch: An Examination of Debt and Development.* Ottawa, 1992.

International Monetary Fund. *International Capital Markets: Development and Prospects.* Washington, D.C.: IMF, various years.

Kapstein, Ethan B. *Supervising International Banks: Origins and Implications of The Basel Accord.* Essays in International Finance No. 185. Princeton, N.J.: Princeton University Press, 1991.

Leipold, Alessandro, et al. *Private Market Financing for Developing Countries.* Washington, D.C.: International Monetary Fund, December 1991.

McKenzie, George W. *The Economics of the Euro-Currency System.* London: Macmillan, 1976.

McKinnon, Ronald I. *The Euro-currency Market.* Essays in International Finance. Princeton, N.J.: Princeton University Press, 1977.

McLeod, Ross H. and Ross Garnant. *East Asia in Crisis: From Beginning a Miracle to Needing One?* London, Rout Redge, 1998.

Melnik, Arie, and Steven E. Plant. The Short-Term Eurocredit Market. Monograph Series in Finance and Economics 1991–1. New York University Salomon Center.

Powell, James. "The Evolving International Debt Strategy." *Bank of Canada Review*, December 1990, pp. 3–25.

———. "The Evolution of Canadian Bank Claims on Heavily Indebted Developing Countries." *Bank of Canada Review*, November 1991, pp. 3–20.

Report of the Working Group on International Financial Crisis (Willard Group), October 1998.

Roll, Richard. "Price Volatility, International Market Links and Their Implications for Regulatory Policies." *Journal of Financial Services Research*, 1989, pp. 211–46.

Watson, Maxwell, et al. *International Capital Markets: Developments and Prospects.* Occasional Papers No. 43. Washington, D.C.: International Monetary Fund, February 1986.

White, William. *Some Implications of International Financial Integration for Canadian Public Policy.* Technical Report No. 57. Ottawa: Bank of Canada, December 1991.

World Bank. *East Asia: The Road to Recovery.* Washington, D.C., 1998.

CHAPTER TWENTY-THREE

HISTORY OF INTERNATIONAL MONETARY RELATIONS BEFORE 1939

After reading this chapter you should be able to
1. *Describe the institutional arrangements that contributed to the functioning of the international gold standard between 1870 and 1914*
2. *Outline the factors that contributed to the eventual failure of the international gold standard*

The Golden Era

In 1821 Great Britain became the first country in modern history to base its monetary unit on only one metal. The Province of Canada adopted gold monometallism in 1853. It was not until the 1870s, however, that the major countries of the world abandoned silver and bimetallism for gold. Germany and Sweden turned to gold in 1871; Norway, Denmark, and Belgium in 1873; Switzerland, Italy, Greece, and France a year later; Holland in 1875; and Uruguay in 1876.

Although the United States went on a defacto gold standard in 1879 when specie payment resumed, it did not formally adopt the gold standard until 1900. By 1914, after some forty countries had accepted the gold standard, it had become a truly international standard. In most countries acceptance of the gold standard had come to be considered part of the natural order of things and an indication of political and economic maturity.

During most of the 35 years from the late 1870s to 1914, the international payments mechanism operated fairly smoothly. Exchange-rate fluctuations were relatively small, international movements of capital and trade expanded, and chronic balance of payments disequilibria were avoided. The existence of an international gold standard no doubt played an important role in this stability. However, it was only allowed to play this role because of the particular political and economic conditions and institutional arrangements of the time, and because countries were willing to play according to the rules of the gold standard game.

Except for minor wars, peace was maintained during the period, essentially because of the military and economic supremacy of Great Britain. Britain was the leading industrial nation and the world's chief trader and financier. It supplied the other countries with the fruits of its industrial expansion in return for food and raw materials. Surpluses and deficits in Britain's balance of payments were absorbed by the free movement of gold and capital, which induced balance of payments adjustments. Money supply changes were sensitive to gold and capital movements; changes in incomes and prices were sensitive to variations in the money supply; and international trade in goods and services was sensitive to changes in incomes and prices. All this was the result of institutional arrangements and behaviour for which Great Britain assumed the major responsibility.

Most of the world trade, even when it did not originate in or was not destined for Great Britain, was financed through Britain. Sterling bills and deposits served as the principal medium of international payments. Trade credit to finance imports or exports was generally obtained in London. The most important institutional arrangement for the smooth functioning of the gold standard was probably the London money market. It was the financial nerve centre of the world. If at any given time an excess supply of bills was drawn on London, their discount rate would tend to rise. When crisis threatened, other interest rates in the London money market usually moved in the same direction as the discount rate on bills, assisted by the Bank of England. With higher interest rates in London, foreign exporters were inclined to hold sterling bills to maturity, and short-term capital would tend to flow to London. Hence, countries with balance of payments surpluses financed such surpluses with relatively small gold imports and large short-term capital exports. Conversely, deficit countries escaped exhaustion of their gold stock with an inflow of short-term capital. An outflow of capital from a surplus country had the same result as an inflow of gold: the money supply would increase, as would prices and money income. The country's exports declined, while its imports increased and its balance of payments equilibrium was restored. At the same time that these adjustments were taking place in the surplus country, opposite adjustments were taking place in the deficit country. With an outflow of gold and an inflow of capital, its money supply declined, as did prices and money income. This stimulated an increase in exports and a decrease in imports, leading to balance of payments equilibrium.

Three important institutional arrangements are implied in the above adjustment process: a financial nerve centre; flexible prices, wages, and money income; and unrestricted trade. Furthermore, during this era the authorities in the respective countries played by the rules of the gold standard game. The most important of these rules was that balance of payments or external equilibrium had to receive preference over domestic or internal equilibrium. This implied that the monetary authorities would allow or even assist the required monetary changes to take place following gold and short-term capital flows. Moreover, if price inflation or unemployment resulted, these sacrifices had to be made.

www.

The assumed automatic self-correcting adjustments to guarantee balance-of-payments equilibrium were explained by David Hume's **price–specie flow**

***price–specie flow
mechanism*** *if a
country experi-
enced balance of
payments surplus,
it gained gold
(specie), this
added to its
money supply, its
prices rose, and
its balance of pay-
ments was
restored to
equilibrium*

mechanism.[1] For instance, the loss of gold by a deficit country would reduce its money supply and the reciprocal gain of gold by a surplus country would increase its money supply. With both economies already at full employment, then, according to the quantity theory of money, prices would rise in the surplus country and fall in the deficit country. These price level changes would lead to expansion of the deficit country's exports and a reduction in its imports from the surplus country; equilibrium in both countries' balance of payments would be restored and specie (gold) flows would halt.

During the 1920s economists questioned whether price elasticities of demand for imports were sufficiently large for one to assume that trade imbalances would quickly respond to relative price changes. In the 1930s, with less than full employment, the assumed relationship between changes in money supplies and price levels was also questioned. Attention was turned to the role of changes in national income in the adjustment process under an international gold standard.

The End of an Era

The outbreak of war in 1914 marked the beginning of the piecemeal dismantling of the international gold standard. At first, most countries made a valiant attempt to hang on to at least the outward symbols of the gold standard. For example, in Britain no restrictions were placed on gold export until 1919, and the Bank of England's legal obligation to buy and sell all gold offered to it at the official price remained in effect until much later. After 1914, however, redemption of bank notes in gold and the export of gold were virtually prevented by appeals to patriotism. Moreover, by pegging the dollar–sterling rate (at about U.S.$4.77) and by making illegal the purchase and sale of gold at a premium, gold export was made unprofitable. Furthermore, wartime shipping risks discouraged gold movements. On the continent there was a general tendency to suspend redemption in gold coin and to place embargoes on gold exports. However, gold importing and official obligations to buy gold at fixed prices remained legal. The exceptions to this general rule were the Scandinavian countries, particularly Sweden, which restricted the flow of gold into their monetary systems as an anti-inflationary measure. On the North American continent, Canada suspended gold convertibility of Dominion notes and bank notes in 1914; in the United States gold exports became subject to official licence in 1917. During the war, the restrictions on free convertibility of currencies and on gold movements broke the former link among national price systems. Prices in the different countries were free to move independently. Varying degrees of inflation ensued, as most countries depended on monetary expansion to finance their war requirements.

---

1. David Hume, "Of the Balance of Trade," in *Gold Standard in Theory and History,* Barry Eichengreen (London: Methuen, 1985), pp. 38–48.

The Return to Gold

After the war, almost everyone considered a return to the international gold standard as the natural course of events; any other course would have been sacrilege. The United States, with comparatively little wartime inflation, discontinued controls over gold exports and returned to the full gold standard in June 1919. However, its relatively high tariff barriers and its insistence on debt repayment by wartime allies and on reparations by Germany made it difficult for other countries to follow the American lead immediately. In 1918 the Cunliffe Committee in Britain recommended the removal of all restrictions "without delay" to allow the traditional gold standard adjustment mechanism to function again. By 1920 Britain had relaxed most of its controls on the import and export of capital, and the pound fluctuated freely without government intervention. Finally, in 1925, after Britain had received an American loan of $300 million, the Chancellor of the Exchequer, Winston Churchill, announced that gold export would again be allowed. But in order to economize on gold and yet have the benefits of the gold standard, the Bank of England was permitted to purchase gold only in bars, valued at around U.S. $8300. Hence, a return to gold by Britain meant a gold bullion standard. The pound was convertible at its prewar parity of U.S.$4.867, making it overvalued by about 10 percent. This made Britain's period of readjustment rather painful. High interest rates became the chief weapon against gold outflows, but high interest rates and trade depression led to business stagnation and chronic unemployment. At times the pound received some support from inflows of capital seeking refuge from still weaker continental currencies, and from central bank deposits as other countries adopted gold exchange standards.

In France, with government deficits, inflationary finance, and recurrent political crises, the franc was not stabilized until mid-1926. Two years later the gold content of the franc was redefined at the prevailing exchange rate and the gold bullion standard was adopted. The new par value for the franc left it undervalued.

By 1929 most countries were back on the gold standard. Some countries, like France, chose new parities that undervalued their currencies. Others, like Britain, returned to prewar parities that overvalued their currencies and necessitated painful adjustments. Still other countries, such as Austria, Hungary, Poland, Germany, and the U.S.S.R., adopted new currency units after hyperinflation had destroyed their old currencies. Most of the parities chosen did not adequately reflect the different degrees of inflation in the various countries, a fact that led to the disintegration of the international monetary system.

The Fall from Gold

We noted earlier that the apparent success of the prewar gold standard depended on existing institutional arrangements and behaviour. Of prime importance was the London money market. London set the pattern of interest rates, which with relative political and economic stability induced appropriate stabilizing capital movements. After the war London was no longer the financial nerve centre of the world; it had to compete now with New York and Paris. With more than one major financial centre, international clearing became more complex and less efficient. Moreover, because of the recommendations of the Genoa conference in 1922, many countries linked their currencies not directly with gold but rather with gold-standard currencies. Thus, they held a large proportion of their reserves in the form of bank accounts and liquid securities in the main financial centres of gold-standard countries. This practice created a large amount of "ballast capital," which tended to shift with each change of wind. Such shifts took place in response to erratic changes in interest rates and to a loss of confidence in currencies resulting from economic and political instability; at times, they were a result of irrational behaviour by central bankers. Attempts to liquidate foreign exchange holdings played an important role in the collapse of 1931. The uneven distribution of gold among the nations of the world and the pyramiding of claims on a relatively narrow gold base produced an international monetary system unable to cope with sudden and large shifts from one currency to another and from currencies to gold.

rules of the game refer to the practices governments of gold standard countries were supposed to follow to facilitate the operations of the gold standard adjustment mechanism

Another reason why the traditional gold standard balance of payments adjustments no longer operated was the reluctance by most countries to follow the **rules of the game**. One of the prime defectors was the United States. During most of the 1920s the United States sterilized gold flows, preventing them from producing appropriate changes in its domestic money supply. In the early 1920s it made loans for relief, for rehabilitation, and for stabilizing European currencies. While these charitable acts compensated for America's inappropriate gold sterilization activities, much of their usefulness in stabilizing currencies and adjusting the balance of payments was negated by U.S. insistence on repayment of war loans and payment of reparations. After mid-1920, when official loans and credits ended, private lending took their place. Unfortunately, a large proportion of the loans made in the U.S. capital markets were for unproductive commercial purposes, and this ultimately aggravated rather than assisted the balance of payments difficulties of recipient countries.

France was another major defector from the rules of the gold game. The Bank of France, because it was not allowed to conduct open market operations, was unable to reinforce gold movements. Britain, on the other hand, was one of the few countries that almost consistently responded to gold flows with appropriate domestic money and credit changes.

Even if all countries had desisted from gold sterilization and allowed appropriate domestic money and credit changes to take place, there remained other obstacles to smooth adjustment. The concentration of business enterprise and government support programs prevented downward price flexibility. Governments also introduced social legislation to prevent excessive declines in money incomes. At the same time, when changes in prices and money incomes did occur, international trade could not fully respond because of trade restrictions. In 1921, for example, Britain inaugurated the Key Industries Duties. The United States replaced its low Underwood Tariff of 1913 with the high Fordney–McCumber Tariff in 1922.

Inappropriate parities that left currencies either undervalued or overvalued, large international balances that moved erratically in response to economic and political instability, the insensitivity of monetary systems to changes in reserves, the unsympathetic movement of prices and incomes to the balance of international payments, and restrictions on the free movement of international trade all resulted in a very fragile international monetary system. This system was unable to withstand the disturbances created by economic depression and financial panic.

Symptoms of economic decline first appeared in the primary producing countries. These countries had expanded their production to meet the demands created by wartime dislocations. After the war various support programs encouraged them to maintain and expand production once producers, cut off by war, had been rehabilitated. The result was overproduction and a downward drift in primary goods prices. Aside from the deflationary pressures of overproduction, an inherent deflationary bias existed in the international monetary system itself. This bias was the result of the uneven distribution of the world gold stock. The United States in the early 1920s and France in the late 1920s had a disproportionately large share of the world's gold stock. As a result, other countries had only small gold holdings and were reluctant to expand their money supplies as fast as they otherwise might have. Conversely, countries with ample gold stocks were reluctant to pursue inflationary policies that would have relieved the strains on other nations.

After 1927, Australia, the Dutch East Indies, Germany, Finland, Brazil, Poland, Argentina, and Canada experienced economic recession. But worldwide depressionary forces did not become serious until after the downturn of industrial activity in the United States in July 1929 and the stock market crash in October of that year. American lending abroad virtually ceased, and the repatriation of funds from abroad began. During the following year the U.S. government introduced the Smoot–Hawley Tariff, which increased tariff rates on both agricultural and industrial goods. Other countries responded by imposing tariff barriers or increasing the height of existing barriers. Some went a step further and imposed trade embargoes. By 1931 hope still existed that the Depression had run its course and recovery was on its way. However, the events following a financial crisis in Austria shattered any such hopes.

In May 1931 it became known that the Credit–Anstalt, one of the most influential and largest banks in Austria, was insolvent. This led to the withdrawal of foreign short-term credits, which did not subside even after foreign loans were made to Austria. Subsequently, a standstill agreement was made by the Credit–Anstalt's chief creditors, and President Hoover of the United States proposed a one-year moratorium on all government war debts and reparations. The plight of Austria raised doubts about the solvency of banks in Hungary, Romania, and Germany. Foreign central banks came to Germany's assistance by discounting the equivalent of $100 million in Reichsbank bills. This proved inadequate, and a further flight from marks to foreign exchange ensued, particularly after the failure of the Darmstadter und National Bank. To preserve its gold and foreign exchange, a temporary stock exchange and bank holiday was declared, and exchange controls were introduced. A standstill agreement reached in August immobilized for six months funds owned by Germans in foreign banks. About U.S.$70 million in British short-term assets were frozen, and the liquidity panic spread to England. An outflow of capital from London had been under way since midyear. Indeed, in its report the Committee on Finance and Industry (the Macmillan Committee) had already warned of the vulnerability of sterling. Advances of U.S.$650 million by American and French banks in August were quickly exhausted and the reserves of the Bank of England continued to decline.

When no more foreign assistance was forthcoming and devaluation seemed inevitable, the Bank of France gave orders to sell £6 million. This final blow pushed Britain off the gold standard. On September 21, 1931, Parliament passed legislation suspending the Bank of England's obligation to sell gold. During the first week the pound, with a previous mint par of U.S.$4.87, fluctuated between about U.S.$4.30 and $3.40. The depreciation cost the Bank of France an amount equal to seven times its capital. The Netherlands Bank also lost heavily. The decline in the external value of sterling was soon moderated by domestic credit restraints, temporary exchange controls, and the adoption in November 1931 of a general tariff. In 1932 the Exchange Equalization Fund was established to smooth out excessive short-run rate fluctuations, and the pound became in effect pegged. In the same year, at a conference in Ottawa, final arrangements were made to promote greater economic unity within the British Empire through a system of trade preferences—the Imperial Preferences. To stop further trade discrimination, the League of Nations was requested, at a conference in Lausanne in the summer of 1932, to call another conference and prepare studies on the problems of trade discrimination and exchange instability.

In 1929 Uruguay, Argentina, and Brazil left the gold standard. In the following year they were joined by Australia, New Zealand, and Venezuela. The move from gold was accelerated after Britain's departure; Canada was among the first to follow, in September 1931. Many countries with strong trade and financial ties with Great Britain pegged their currencies to the pound sterling to retain their traditional trading markets. This change marked the beginning of the sterling area. These countries held the major part of their international reserves in the form of sterling deposits and other liquid assets in London, which served as their clearing centre.

After the formation of the sterling area, only five countries still remained on the gold standard: the United States, France, Switzerland, Belgium, and the Netherlands. Germany, the Balkan countries, and the Latin American countries adopted exchange control systems.

After Britain left the gold standard, attention was focused on the United States, where deflation was growing worse. To stop the exodus of gold the Federal Reserve increased its rediscount rate, which, in turn, increased the deflationary tendencies and encouraged the further hoarding of gold. The Federal Reserve was unable to offset the deflationary forces by open market purchases. It was required to back its notes dollar for dollar with gold and commercial paper discounted by borrowing member banks. Under conditions of economic depression, member bank borrowing declined and Federal Reserve holdings of commercial paper decreased. Therefore, more gold had to be used as collateral, but the amount available was dwindling because of external and internal drains. In February 1932, the *Glass–Steagall Act* permitted the Federal Reserve to use government securities as collateral for its notes, and it immediately began to purchase such securities. By this time, however, many banks were in no position to increase the availability of credit. Loans from the Reconstruction Finance Corporation, established by Congress early in the year, kept many banks and other businesses from failing.

By midyear there were signs of a business revival. Unfortunately, the Central Republic Trust Company of Chicago became vulnerable to runs, and in the following year, when the Union Guardian Trust Company of Detroit failed, financial panic broke out. On February 14, 1933, the governor of Michigan declared an eight-day statewide bank holiday. By March every state in the country had declared banking holidays, and bank deposits were generally no longer redeemable. Soon after Franklin D. Roosevelt became president, he declared a four-day nationwide bank holiday. On March 9, 1933, Congress passed the *Emergency Banking Act*, which affirmed the president's power to regulate or prohibit transactions in gold or foreign exchange as well as the hoarding of gold. This was followed on April 18 by an announcement that the government would issue no further gold export licences. With the embargo on gold exports, the United States left the gold standard. The U.S. dollar, free to fluctuate, immediately depreciated. However, since the embargo on gold was considered temporary and because the U.S. balance of payments position was relatively strong, the initial depreciation of the dollar on the foreign market was relatively small.

In June 1933 representatives of 64 countries met in London, ostensibly to find a way back to gold. The conference floundered because agreement could not be reached on which should come first, a reconstituted gold standard or the lowering of trade barriers. Moreover, as one observer put it: "Delegates wandered around in a fog trying to learn by remote control what Mr. Roosevelt was currently thinking. The whole conference fell to pieces."[2]

Unlike Great Britain, the United States had not been forced off the gold standard. In large part it had deliberately gone off because of the mistaken belief by many that an increase in the price of gold would cause domestic prices to rise—a principle of the commodity theory of money. Toward this end the government adopted a gold-buying program under the authority given to the president in the Thomas Amendment to the *Agricultural Adjustment Act* passed in May 1933. The price of gold was gradually bid up, and at the end of January 1934 the *Gold Reserve Act* fixed it at U.S.$35 an ounce. Before the departure from the gold standard, it had been fixed at U.S.$20.67 an ounce. The Gold Reserve Act also transferred the gold stock of the Federal Reserve System to the Treasury in exchange for gold certificates. Furthermore, with the profits from gold revaluation, the Exchange Stabilization Fund was established. In effect, the United States adopted a limited gold bullion standard. The government would buy all gold offered to it at U.S.$35 an ounce, but would redeem dollars in gold only for foreign central banks and governments.

With the United States' gold price settled and the U.S. dollar devalued and stabilized, American capital that had fled abroad during the protracted depreciation of the dollar in 1933–34 was gradually repatriated. Moreover, gold flowed into the United States because of its export surplus and the attraction of high gold prices for foreign gold producers. Thus began the "golden avalanche,"[3] which continued until checked by foreign restrictions during the Second World War. During the latter part of the 1930s much of the gold

---

2. Quoted in B.M. Anderson, *Economics and Public Welfare* (New York: Van Nostrand, 1949), p. 331.

3. Frank D. Graham and C.R. Whittlesey, *Golden Avalanche* (Princeton, N.J.: Princeton University Press, 1939).

coming into the United States was seeking refuge from impending war conditions.

After the U.S. dollar was devalued, the British Equalization Account kept the pound–dollar rate in the neighbourhood of U.S.$5, and most of the sterling area countries followed Britain's move. Canada, whose dollar had fallen relative to the U.S. dollar in 1931–32, came back to a dollar-for-dollar exchange rate. The gold bloc countries, finding it increasingly difficult to defend the gold parities of their currencies, one by one devalued and aligned their currencies with the U.S. dollar. Among the last to sever itself from gold was France, which did so in September 1936.

The announcement of the devaluation of the franc was accompanied by the announcement of the Tripartite Monetary Agreement. France, Britain, and the United States, later joined by Belgium, Holland, and Switzerland, agreed to maintain convertibility of their currencies at their pegged rates. All countries were urged to do the same to avoid further competitive exchange depreciation, and were exhorted to start relaxing trade restrictions and exchange controls. The initial devaluation of the franc was not enough, and further devaluation took place in May 1938. In effect, France became a member of the sterling bloc, because it then stabilized the franc in terms of the pound sterling at a rate of 179 francs to the pound.

Thus in 1938 tranquility was almost restored to the foreign exchange markets. Sterling was pegged to the U.S. dollar, and the currencies of most other countries, directly or indirectly, were pegged to either sterling or the dollar. The exceptions to this arrangement were those countries, notably Germany and the Balkan countries, which had exchange control systems.

KEY TERMS

price–specie flow mechanism
rules of the game

REVIEW QUESTIONS

1. What did the apparent success of the gold standard depend on between 1870 and 1914? What factors contributed to its failure after its restoration in the 1920s?
2. It is usually assumed that for the gold standard to have provided an efficient payments mechanism, countries had to follow the "rules of the game." What were these rules, and why would countries be reluctant to follow them?
3. What was the sterling area? What brought about its introduction?

SELECTED READINGS

Bloomfield, Arthur. *Monetary Policy under the International Gold Standard, 1880–1910*. New York: Federal Reserve Bank of New York, 1959.

Cassel, Gustav. *Money and Foreign Exchange after 1910*. London: Constable, 1922.

———. *The Downfall of the Gold Standard*. Oxford: Clarendon Press, 1936.

Condliffe, J.B. *The Commerce of Nations*. New York: W.W. Norton, 1950.

Dick, Trevor J.O., and John E. Floyd. *Canada and the Gold Standard: Balance of Payments Adjustments under Fixed Exchange Rates*. New York: Cambridge University Press, 1992.

Ellsworth, P.T. *The International Economy*. New York: Macmillan, 1950, Ch. 16, 17, and 18.

Graham, Frank D., and C.R. Whittlesey. *Golden Avalanche*. Princeton, N.J.: Princeton University Press, 1939.

Hawtrey, Ralph G. *The Gold Standard in Theory and Practice*, 5th ed. New York: Longmans, Green, 1947.

Keynes, John Maynard. *The Economic Consequences of the Peace*. New York: Harcourt Brace and World, 1920.

League of Nations. *Commercial Policy in the Interwar Period—International Proposals and National Policies*. Geneva: League of Nations, 1942.

———. *International Currency Experiences—Lessons of the Interwar Period*. Geneva: League of Nations, 1944.

Rich, George. *The Cross of Gold, Money and the Canadian Business Cycle, 1913–1967*. Ottawa: Carleton University Press, 1988.

Ropke, Wilhelm. *International Economic Disintegration*. London: William Hodge, 1942.

Yeager, Leland B. *International Monetary Relations*, 2nd ed. New York: Harper & Row, 1976, Part II.

Young, John Parke. *Interwar Currency Lessons*. New York: Monetary Standard Inquiry, 1944.

CHAPTER TWENTY-FOUR

RECENT INTERNATIONAL MONETARY RELATIONS

After reading this chapter you should be able to

1. Describe the history, structure, and operations of the International Monetary System
2. Describe the role of the World Bank and its affiliates
3. Explain the transition in the international monetary system from dollar shortage to dollar glut and the steps taken to defend the U.S. dollar
4. Discuss the problems with the gold–dollar exchange standard
5. Describe the Smithsonian Agreement and events that precipitated it
6. Show how the reformed international monetary system after the early 1970s differs from what it had been
7. Argue for and against the merits of managed exchange rate flexibility
8. Outline the transition toward a European Monetary Union
9. Explain the Euro, the European System of Central Banks, and monetary policy in the EMU
10. Outline some of the key issues in the debate to strengthen the international financial architecture

The Second World War shattered any hopes there might have been after the Tripartite Monetary Agreement of 1936 for consolidating the international monetary system and for a return to multilateral trade. Most countries pegged their currencies to either sterling or the American dollar, while the pound was rigidly pegged to the American dollar at $4.03. The sterling area, which before the war had consisted of a rather loose arrangement, became a cohesive monetary union held together by an elaborate system of controls. Canada was one of the countries that pegged its currency to the American dollar.

During the years preceding the war, Canada had a net current account deficit with the United States. As long as sterling was convertible, this deficit could be financed with Canada's net current account surplus with the sterling area. With the advent of war, however, sterling was no longer convertible. To protect Canadian foreign exchange reserves, especially the reserves of American dollars, the Canadian government introduced foreign exchange controls, administered by the newly established Foreign Exchange Control Board. At the same time the Canadian dollar was depreciated by about 10 percent vis-à-vis the American dollar and pegged at this level. Because Canada was one of Britain's chief suppliers of essential goods and services, Canadian sterling surpluses expanded. As a temporary measure the Canadian government provided dollars to Britain by repatriating direct debt held there. (Later, a large part of the accumulated sterling balances in London was converted into interest-free loans and gifts.) Although Canada's sterling balances grew, the shortage of American dollars became acute with the import of essential materials from the United States. The Hyde Park Agreement in April 1941 provided for some integration of war production between Canada and the United States in an attempt to increase Canada's net earnings of American dollars.

Departing from the practice they had followed during the First World War, most countries introduced price controls and rationing during the Second World War to prevent excessive inflation. Moreover, taxation rather than inflationary finance was the more common source of war finance. As a result, compared to the situation after the earlier war, price distortions among the major nations were relatively small at the end of the Second World War.[1] An effort was also made to avoid creating a morass of interallied war debt like that which had plagued many countries during the interwar period. Starting in 1941, under its Lend–Lease program, the United States supplied war materials with settlement to be worked out after the war. Eventually, 38 countries were included under this program. By the end of 1946, the United States had supplied goods and services amounting to almost $50 billion and had, in turn, received about $8 billion in reverse lend–lease.

www.

Reconstruction and Development

Committee of European Economic Cooperation *committee formed in Europe to deal with post–Second World War recovery and aid programs*

Economic Cooperative Administration (ECA) *organization set up in the United States to administer Marshall aid funds for European recovery*

Before the end of the war, plans were made to meet the immediate postwar problems of European reconstruction. The long-range problem of providing institutional arrangements for an efficient and stable mechanism of international payments and for the development of world trade and production were also pressing matters.

Physical destruction was far greater during the Second World War than during the First. An enormous reconstruction program was called for. Even before hostilities ended, large grants for relief had been made either directly by Canada and the United States or indirectly through the United Nations Relief and Rehabilitation Administration. By 1947, realizing that Europe needed a much larger and more coordinated program of assistance, the U.S. Secretary of State, George Marshall, called for massive American assistance, with European cooperation. European countries immediately responded by forming the **Committee of European Economic Cooperation**, which formulated a program of recovery that extended from 1948 to 1951. In 1948 the United States established the **Economic Cooperation Administration (ECA)**

---

1. Four countries experienced hyperinflation either during or immediately after the Second World War: Hungary, China, Romania, and Greece.

Organization for European Economic Cooperation (OEEC) *an organization set up for promoting postwar recovery of Europe with American aid*

Marshall Plan *program proposed by American secretary of state, George Marshall, for postwar recovery of Europe with massive financial assistance*

with an initial appropriation of $4 billion. At the same time seventeen European countries formed the **Organization for European Economic Cooperation** (**OEEC**) to establish priorities and administer the American aid program, which became known as the **Marshall Plan**. By the end of 1951 nearly $13 billion had been spent under the plan. Aid was given in the form of goods and services, which were sold by recipient countries to their residents for local currencies known as "counterpart funds." Five percent of these funds were allocated to the use of the United States, essentially to meet administrative costs, and the remaining 95 percent was spent mostly on public investment projects. Insofar as counterpart funds were held idle from time to time, they served to check inflation.

Institutional arrangements to provide for the mechanism of international payments and the development of world trade and production took form at the Bretton Woods Conference, held in New Hampshire in July 1944. The centre-piece of the postwar international monetary system was to be the new International Monetary Fund (IMF). Its sister institution, the International Bank for Reconstruction and Development (known as the World Bank), was to concentrate on the tasks implied by its name. However, the role envisaged for it in promoting the flow of long-term development capital soon fell far short of the needs. As a result two affiliated institutions were established, the International Finance Corporation and the International Development Association. Regional development banks later joined these institutions.[2]

The Bretton Woods System and the International Monetary Fund and the World Bank

bancor *the name for an international reserve asset proposed by John Maynard Keynes*

At the Bretton Woods Conference two proposals were considered for the creation of an international monetary institution—the British Keynes Plan and the American White Plan.[3] The Keynes Plan proposed the establishment of an international body to be known as the Clearing Union, which would create an international means of payment called bancor. Both the gold value of **bancor** as well as the bancor value of national currencies would be fixed. Each member country's central bank would accept payment from other central banks by the transfer of bancor to its credit in the books of the Clearing Union. Countries with balance of payments deficits could obtain bancor by using automatic overdraft facilities with the Union. The total amount of each central bank's overdrafts would be limited in advance to a specified amount of its country's average trade turnover (exports plus imports). To further discourage the irresponsible use of overdrafts, taxes would be levied on both debtor and creditor

---

2. The Website of the IMF is <www.imf.org> and that of the World Bank and its affiliates <www.world-bank.org>.

3. See S.E. Harris, *The New Economics: Keynes' Influence on Theory and Public Policy* (London: Dennis Dobson, 1947); and Robert W. Oliver, *Early Plans for a World Bank*, Princeton Studies in International Finance, No. 29 (Princeton University, 1971).

BOX 24–1   **PURPOSE OF THE IMF**

Article I of Agreement of the International Monetary Fund set forth the Fund's purposes.

Article I: Purposes

(i) To promote international monetary cooperation through a permanent institution which provides the machinery for consultation and collaboration on international monetary problems;

(ii) To facilitate the expansion and balanced growth of international trade, and to contribute thereby to the promotion and maintenance of high levels of employment and real income and to the development of the productive resources of all members as primary objectives of economic policy;

(iii) To promote exchange stability, to maintain orderly exchange arrangements among members, and to avoid competitive exchange depreciation;

(iv) To assist in the establishment of a multilateral system of payments in respect of current transactions between members, and in the elimination of foreign exchange restrictions, which hamper the growth of world trade;

(v) To give confidence to members by making the Fund's resources available to them under adequate safeguards, thus providing them with the opportunity to correct maladjustments in their balance of payments without resorting to measures destructive of national and international prosperity;

(vi) In accordance with the above, to shorten the duration and lessen the degree of disequilibrium in the international balance of payments of members.

The Fund shall be guided in all polices by the purposes set forth in this Article.

accounts in excess of specified amounts. Creditor accounts were also to be taxed so that creditors would assume at least some of the responsibility for overall balance of payments adjustments.

The Keynes Plan was abandoned largely for the American White Plan, which proposed an International Stabilization Fund very similar to the International Monetary Fund agreed on at the Bretton Woods Conference.

The International Monetary Fund

Purpose of the IMF

The Bretton Woods conference led to the Articles of Agreement that established the International Monetary Fund (IMF). Article I of the Agreement, reproduced in Box 24–1, describes the original purposes of the IMF. A world currency system based on adjustable pegged exchange rates was inaugurated and the IMF was given administrative oversight responsibilities to preserve the stability of this currency system. It did this, in part, by making short-term emergency loans to member countries experiencing balance of payments problems.

In the early 1970s when exchange rates between major currencies became flexible, part of the Fund's original mission was lost and it began to reinvent itself in other ways. In the 1980s the IMF concerned itself with the debt crisis—the difficulties experienced by countries in Latin America in servicing and repaying their debts. In the early 1990s the Fund turned its attention to providing assistance to countries in Eastern Europe and the former Soviet Union to help their transition to market economies. More recently, it has made poverty reduction, debt relief, and sustained economic growth in its poorest member countries an explicit objective of its programs. These initiatives by the Fund since the early 1970s have tended to shift much of its lending to providing long-term rather than temporary financing for strictly short-term balance of payments problems. However, with the introduction of Contingent Lines of Credit within the framework of the Fund's Supplementary Reserve Facility, the "balance of payments needs" as a condition of lending, a principle enshrined in its Articles of Agreement, has again taken on more importance.

Structure and Organization

MEMBERSHIP   The International Monetary Fund is an autonomous organization affiliated with the United Nations. At the outset 35 national governments became members; by 1991 this number had grown to 155 countries. The Union of Soviet Socialist Republics (U.S.S.R.) was not a member; it signed the Bretton Woods Agreement but did not ratify it. In 1992, 14 states of the former U.S.S.R. became members. Switzerland did not become a member until 1992, although it had associated itself with some of the Fund's programs. Czechoslovakia was expelled in 1950 (but later readmitted) for failure to provide information. Cuba withdrew in 1964. The Polish People's Republic withdrew in 1950 but was readmitted in 1986. The People's Republic of China represented China in the Fund starting in April 1980. Romania became a member in 1972; the Hungarian People's Republic joined in 1982. With the addition of Albania, the Marshall Islands, and San Marino in 1992, membership stood at 173. Subsequently, with the addition of many states of the former Soviet Union, membership increased further and by 1999 reached 182 and was almost universal.

GOVERNING BODY   The highest authority of the International Monetary Fund is its board of governors, in which a governor and an alternate governor represent each country. In most cases, the governors are ministers of finance or central bank governors in their countries or hold comparable rank. The board has delegated many of its powers to an executive board, which in 1999 was composed of 24 executive directors: five appointed (by the United States, the United Kingdom, the Federal Republic of Germany, France, and Japan); and 19, with the exception of Saudi Arabia and Russia, elected by groups of the remaining members. A 24-member International Monetary and Financial Committee, formerly the Interim Committee, advises the board of governors on broad policy issues. A Development Committee advises and reports to the board of governors of both the IMF and the World Bank on all aspects of the transfer of real resources to the developing countries. The voting power of each member country is determined by 250 "basic votes" plus one vote for each

100 000 of SDR (see below) quota. As at April 30, 1999, Canada had 63 942 votes representing some 3 percent of the total.

PAR VALUES: ADJUSTABLE PEG   One of the main objectives in establishing the International Monetary Fund was to provide for foreign exchange stability. Toward this end, each member country, in consultation with the Fund, was supposed to declare a par value of its currency in relation to the gold content of the U.S. dollar in 1944. (Few member countries failed to declare par values, but even those that did not maintained de facto parities.) The par values chosen by the original members in 1946 were the exchange rates then in effect. Realizing that many countries probably would have difficulty in maintaining their parities, the IMF condoned the use of exchange controls during a transition period.

The framers of the agreement to establish the IMF also recognized that structural changes in the world economy during postwar reconstruction would make it difficult for countries to defend their chosen par values. Hence, member countries were allowed to propose a change in the par values of their currencies to correct *fundamental disequilibrium* in their balance of payments. The IMF could not object if a proposed change was less than 10 percent away from an initial parity. However, a country making a change of more than 10 percent without prior approval faced the possibility of having its privileges withdrawn or even being expelled from the organization. The Fund's Articles of Agreement did not define fundamental disequilibrium; in practice, during the period in which the par value requirement existed, it was interpreted to mean chronic balance of payments difficulties that could not be corrected without excessive deflation or inflation, or resorting to restrictive import barriers.

Until 1971 each member country was required to prevent the external value of its currency from fluctuating more than 1 percent above or below its declared value. Following the Smithsonian Agreement in December 1971, the IMF authorized its members to widen this range to 2.25 percent above or below their parities or "central rates." Starting in 1973, most of the major countries no longer abided by the par value requirement, and with the Second Amendment to the Fund's Articles of Agreement, provision was made for its discontinuance.

The negotiators of the Bretton Woods system sought an exchange rate system that would combine the advantages of both the fixed and the flexible exchange rate systems. In the short run, exchange rate stability was to be ensured by the observance of a fixed system in terms of par values or pegged rates. Longer-term stability would result from countries making appropriate adjustments to their par values to reflect the fundamental disequilibrium in their balance of payments. As we shall see, although the system allowed for exchange rate stability in terms of an adjustable peg, before 1973 countries were reluctant to adjust their par values.

www.

Special Drawing Rights (SDRs)

In 1967, at the International Monetary Fund's annual meeting, held in Rio de Janeiro, the board of governors approved a plan to establish a new facility "to

Special Drawing Right (SDR) book-keeping account created by IMF to serve as an international reserve asset

meet the need, as and when it arises, for a supplement to existing reserve assets." This supplement to international reserve assets, the **Special Drawing Right** (**SDR**), was introduced in 1970 as the major feature of the First Amendment to the Articles of Agreement in 1969.

An SDR is a simple bookkeeping entry in the Special Drawing Account established for each member country. Insofar as the member receives a gratuitous credit entry in the books, it can be said that the Fund creates international reserve assets. A total of 21.4 billion SDRs have been created in six allocations since 1970. Members have received SDRs in proportion to their fund quotas (described below) at the time of each allocation. Canada has received an accumulated amount of 779 million SDRs (some Can.$1.6 billion).

More than one-fifth of the IMF's member countries have never received an SDR allocation because they joined the IMF after 1981. In addition, other members have not participated in every allocation. To ensure that all participants in the SDR Department receive an equitable share of cumulative SDR allocations, in 1997 the Fourth Amendment was proposed to the IMF's Articles of Agreement. When approved, the Amendment will authorize a special one-time allocation of SDR 21.4 billion, which would raise all participants' ratios of cumulative SDR allocations to quotas to a common benchmark ratio.

When the SDR was first introduced in 1970, its value was set at 0.888671 grams of gold, which at the time was the gold equivalent of U.S.$1. In July 1974, however, following the U.S. decision to no longer convert its dollar into a specified amount of gold and to allow the market to determine its value in terms of gold and other currencies, the value of the SDR became a weighted average of the exchange rates of the currencies of 16 member countries. A further change was made in 1981, when the SDR's valuation became determined based on a basket of the currencies of the five countries with the largest exports of goods and services over a previous five-year period. The five currencies included in the SDR valuation in 1981, and retained following the reviews in 1990 and 1996, are the U.S. dollar, the deutschemark, the Japanese yen, the French franc, and the British pound sterling.

With the introduction of the Euro in January 1999, the currency amounts of the deutschemark and the French franc in the SDR basket were replaced with equivalent amounts of the Euro, based on the fixed conversion rates between the Euro and the deutschemark and the French franc.

The U.S. dollar value of SDR is calculated daily by the Fund as illustrated in Table 24.1

The value of the SDR in terms of currencies other than the U.S. dollar is determined by applying the representative exchange rate for that currency in terms of the U.S. dollar to the SDR value of the dollar. For example, in August 1999 the monthly Canadian dollar price of the U.S. dollar was Can.$1.4923. Hence, the Canadian dollar value of one SDR was 1.36986 × 1.4923 = Can.$2.0549.

Since August 1, 1983, the interest rate on the SDR has been determined weekly as the weighted average of the interest rate on specified short-term domestic obligations in the money markets of the same five countries whose currencies are included in the SDR valuation basket. A member with holdings of SDRs in excess of its allocations earns net interest on those excess holdings, and a member with holdings below its total allocations pays interest on its net use of SDRs.

TABLE 24.1	**SDR VALUATION ON AUGUST 31, 1999**		
	1 **Currency** **Amount**	**2** **Exchange Rate**	**3** **U.S. Dollar Equivalent** **on August 31**
Euro (Germany)	0.2280	1.05450	0.240426
Euro (France)	0.1239	1.05450	0.130653
Japanese yen	27.2000	109.550	0.248288
Pound sterling	0.1050	1.60370	0.168389
U.S. dollar	0.5821	1.00000	0.582100
		TOTAL	1.369856

SDR 1 = U.S.$1.36986

U.S. $1 = SDR 0.73004[1]

Column 1: The currency components of the SDR basket.

Column 2: Exchange rates in terms of currency units per U.S. dollar, except for the Euro and pound sterling, which are expressed in U.S. dollars per currency unit.

Column 3: The U.S. dollar equivalents of the currency amounts in Column 1 at the exchange rates in Column 2.

1. The official SDR value of the U.S. dollar, which is reciprocal of the total of Column 3; that is, 1 ÷ 1.369856, rounded to six significant digits.

Source: *IMF Survey*, supplement, Vol. 28, September 1999, p. 27. Reproduced with permission of the International Monetary Fund.

Members use SDRs in discharging their financial obligations to the IMF. Their obligations mainly take the form of charges levied on members' use of IMF resources, repurchases (repayments) and quota subscriptions. The IMF transfers SDRs to members primarily for purchases (drawings), interest paid on member's creditor positions, and repayments of and interest payments on IMF borrowing.

To meet their balance of payments needs, member countries may also use SDRs. Transactions in SDRs are facilitated by arrangements between the IMF and 12 members that are prepared to buy or sell SDRs for one or more usable currencies as long as their SDR holdings remain within certain limits. These "two-way" arrangements have helped ensure the liquidity of the SDR system. The IMF can also designate members with strong balance of payments and gross reserve positions to provide freely usable currencies to members with a balance of payments need in exchange for SDRs.

The International Monetary Fund's Financial Resources

The IMF is a quota-based institution, that is, it is financed primarily from its members' quota subscriptions. It is authorized to borrow, if necessary to supplement its resources. To date, it has borrowed only from official sources (such as governments and central banks), but it may also borrow from private sources.

Quotas

Each member country is assigned a quota. Quotas determine members' financial subscription to the Fund, their relative voting power, and their maximum access to financing from the Fund. The size of a country's quota is related to economic factors such as national income and the values of external trade and payments. Up to 25 percent of a quota subscription has to be paid in reserve assets specified by the Fund, and the remainder in the member's own currency. Before 1980, each member had to pay 25 percent of its subscription in gold and the balance in its own currency.

Total quotas initially assigned in 1947 were equal to U.S.$7.7 billion. The Fund's Articles of Agreement require its board of governors to conduct a general review of quotas at intervals of no more than five years. After all but three of the 11 reviews up to 1999, quotas were increased and adjusted. As a result of general quota increases, adjustments to quotas of individual members, and the addition of new members, total quotas had risen to SDR 208 billion (some Can.$426 billion) by April 1999. Canada's quota, the eighth largest, was SDR 6.4 billion, the equivalent of Can.$13 billion.

The General Agreements to Borrow (GAB)

General Arrangements to Borrow (GAB)
lines of credit from 11 industrial countries that are available for use by the IMF under specified circumstances

In 1962, 10 of the IMF's main industrial members (who subsequently became known as the Group of Ten)[4] concluded a four-year agreement to lend the Fund up to the equivalent of SDR 6.4 billion if this should be needed to "forestall or cope with an impairment of the international monetary system." **The General Arrangements to Borrow (GAB)** was renewed for a further four years in 1966 and subsequently at five-year intervals. In 1983, when disagreement arose over the amount of a proposed increase in quotas and the Fund's resources appeared inadequate because of difficulties experienced by some of its members in meeting their international debt obligations, the GAB was revised and enlarged. The maximum amount available was increased to SDR 17 billion for a five-year period. An additional SDR 1.5 billion is available to the IMF under an associated arrangement with Saudi Arabia. Canada has agreed to provide SDR 892.5 million (Can.$1.8 billion).

The Fund has borrowed under the GAB to help finance large drawings by the United Kingdom, France, Italy, and the United States. Borrowed funds, which until 1983 could be used only to provide assistance to the GAB participants, can now also be used for the benefit of nonparticipants. In 1998 Russia became the first nonparticipant to borrow. Loans under GAB are made at market rates of interest.

In June 1995, in the aftermath of the Mexican financial crisis and with the growing realization that substantially more resources might be needed for possible future financial crises, the Group of Seven industrial countries, at their Halifax Summit, called for the development of a new financing arrangement that would double as soon as possible the funds available under the GAB to

---

4. United States, United Kingdom, Deutsche Bundesbank, France, Italy, Canada, Netherlands, Belgium, Japan, the Sveriges Riksbank, and the Swiss National Bank. Switzerland, while not a member of the Fund at the time, joined as an associate in 1964 and as a full participant in 1984.

respond to financial emergencies. Subsequently, the G-10 countries reached agreement in principle on the features of a new borrowing arrangement.

New Arrangements to Borrow (NAB)

New Arrangements to Borrow (NAB)
additional lines of credit from other financially strong countries that can be activated by the IMF in the event of systemic financial crisis

In January of 1998 the IMF approved a new borrowing arrangement to enhance its ability to safeguard the international monetary system. Under the **New Arrangements to Borrow** (**NAB**), 25 member countries and institutions stand ready to lend the IMF up to SDR 34 billion (about Can.$69 billion) to supplement its regular quota resources. Canada's share is SDR 1.4 billion, or some U.S.$2.9 billion. These additional funds are to be made available when needed to forestall or cope with an impairment of the international monetary system or to deal with an exceptional situation that threatens the stability of the system.

The NAB does not replace the GAB, which remains in force. However, the NAB will be the facility of first recourse. NAB credit lines may be drawn for the benefit of all NAB participant countries, or for nonparticipants under circumstances similar to those under the GAB. The NAB were activated for the first time in December 1998 when the IMF borrowed SDR 9.1 billion (U.S.$12.5) to help finance drawings under a standby arrangement for Brazil.

Other Borrowing Arrangements

Borrowing has come to provide an important temporary supplement to the Fund's ordinary resources. Under guidelines adopted in 1983, its outstanding borrowing plus unused lines of credit cannot exceed the range of 50 percent to 60 percent of the total quotas. Aside from the General Arrangements to Borrow, the Fund has entered into arrangements to borrow from its members, Switzerland, and central banks and other official institutions in these countries. Most of its borrowed funds have been used for the various financial facilities discussed below, which have been introduced to meet specific needs of its members.

Uses of the Fund's Resources

Members may draw on the Fund's resources to meet their balance of payments needs as reflected by their balance of payments position, their foreign reserve position, and developments in their reserve position. When a member draws on the Fund's resources, it actually uses its own currency to purchase the currencies of other member countries or SDRs held by the Fund. Thus, a purchase (drawing) results in an increase in the Fund's holdings of the borrowing member's currency, and a corresponding decrease in the Fund's holdings of other currencies or SDRs equal to the amount sold to the borrowing country. The purchaser must reverse the transaction, within a prescribed time, by repurchasing—that is, buying back—its own currency with SDRs or specified currencies. Repurchases must ordinarily be made within three to five years after the date of purchase, except for purchases under some of the special facilities described below. A member is also normally expected to repurchase earlier if its balance of payments and reserve positions improve sufficiently.

Reserve Tranches

tranches specifies the amount of other countries' currency that a member may draw (borrow) from IMF's ordinary resources

The amount of other countries' currency that a member may draw from the Fund's ordinary financial resources is defined in terms of **tranches**. When the Fund's holding of a member's currency is less than that country's quota, the difference is called a reserve tranche. Although a member must show balance of payments needs, drawings within the reserve tranche are virtually automatic, free of specified repurchase requirements, and not subject to any charges. As such, countries consider their reserve tranche as part of their own foreign exchange reserve assets.

Credit Tranches

The credit tranche policy is the Fund's regular or basic lending policy. A member can make purchases in four credit tranches (segments), each equivalent to 25 percent of its quota. Use of Fund resources in the first credit tranche (which raises the Fund's holdings of the member's currency to 125 percent of the member's quota)[5] requires only that the member demonstrate reasonable efforts to overcome its difficulties. Use of Fund resources in the other three credit tranches, known as the upper credit tranches, requires a member to adopt policies that provide substantial assurance that its payments difficulties will be resolved within a reasonable time. A member may request use of the first credit tranche either in the form of a direct purchase or under a Standby Arrangement. In the upper credit tranches the Fund's resources are usually made available through Standby Arrangements that stipulate that access to successive instalments of drawings depends on preconditions and on performance criteria. Repurchases of drawings in the credit tranches have to be made by a member within three to five years.

Conditionality

conditionality a term employed by the IMF that refers to restrictions it imposes on borrowing countries

Except for drawings in the reserve tranche, a country making use of the Fund's resources is generally required to carry out an economic policy program aimed at achieving a viable balance of payments position over an appropriate period of time. This requirement is known as **conditionality**. It has become an essential element of the Fund's role in helping to alleviate the balance of payments problems of member countries and facilitating the international adjustment process. The conditionality requirement has been severely criticized by some countries that considered the conditions imposed for their drawings on the Fund to be too severe and interfering unduly in their own domestic affairs.

---

5. Utilization of the reserve tranche raises the Fund's holdings of a member's currency from 75 percent to 100 percent of its quota and the four credit tranches raise holdings to 200 percent of its quota.

Standby Arrangements

Standby Arrangements give members the right to draw up to a specified amount of IMF finance during a prescribed period. Funds are released only if members meet the conditionality requirements under which the standby arrangement was approved.

In 1995 the IMF approved a standby arrangement of SDR 12.1 billion for Mexico. This financial commitment was the largest in IMF history.

Extended Fund Facility

Under the Extended Fund Facility, introduced in 1974, the Fund may provide assistance to members to meet their balance of payments deficits for longer periods, and in larger amounts in relation to quotas, than under the credit tranche policies. The facility is available to members who have serious payments imbalances relating to structural maladjustments in production, trade, and prices and who intend to implement a comprehensive set of corrective policies over two or three years. The facility may also be used by a developing country dependent on a few export goods whose markets have deteriorated, leaving it unable to carry out development programs. Drawings outstanding under the facility may not exceed 140 percent of quota, and repayment must be made in twelve equal instalments within four and one-half to 10 years after each drawing.

Access Limits

Access to the use of IMF resources by its members is determined primarily by a member's balance of payments needs, the strength of its adjustment policies, and its ability to repay the IMF. With the exception of access under the Supplemental Reserve Facility and Contingent Credit Lines, annual and cumulative access limits under other facilities and policies are set in proportion to members' quotas. For example, an annual limit of 100 percent of a member's quota, and a cumulative limit of 300 percent of its quota, apply to the credit tranches and the Extended Fund Facility. With the Enhanced Structural Adjustment Facility, a member country may borrow up to 190 percent of its quota under a three-year arrangement, and in exceptional circumstances up to a maximum of 255 percent of quota.

Concessional Facilities

In May 1976 a special Trust Fund was created to provide additional balance of payments assistance on concessionary terms to low-income developing countries. A total of SDR 3 billion was disbursed over four years to 55 members. These resources came from the profits realized by the market sale of one-sixth (25 million ounces) of the Fund's gold holdings. In 1987, the Structural Adjustment Facility (SAF) was set up to employ the repayments from the Trust Fund loans for further assistance on a concessionary basis to low-income developing countries in need of structural adjustments to solve their balance of payments problems. Subsequently, the Successor Facilities to the SAF, described below, have been financed through the Trust Fund. In turn, the Trust Fund is now financed primarily with special grants and loans from member countries and multilateral organizations.

Poverty Reduction and Growth Facility (PRGF) *the principal means by which the IMF provides concessional financial support to low-income member countries*

The Poverty Reduction and Growth Facility (PRGF) became the successor in 1999 to the Enhanced Structure Adjustment Facility (ESAF). This in turn, had been an extension and enlargement in 1994 of the Structural Adjustment Facility (SAF) first set up in 1987. Like its predecessors, the PRGF has become the principal means by which the IMF provides concessional financial support to low-income member countries, and as its name implies, has placed poverty reductions at the centre of IMF support programs among its poorest nations.

Eligible member countries seeking assistance must develop a Poverty Reduction Strategy Paper (PRSA) in consultation with the IMF and the World Bank. This PRSA is the basis for receiving concessional loans under the Facility. The interest rate on loans is 0.5 percent a year, and loans are to be repaid over a 10-year period. The IMF closely monitors progress made by countries in meeting their objectives of poverty reduction and durable growth.

HIPC Initiative *joint World Bank–IMF initiative to provide debt relief to heavily indebted poor countries*

In 1996 the IMF and the World Bank jointly launched the Heavily Indebted Poor Countries Initiative (**HIPC Initiative**) to provide debt relief for the poorest of countries to escape the vicious circle in which debt-servicing costs wipe out any gains these countries achieve from economic growth. The HIPC Initiative has become closely associated with the Fund's PRGF Facility. A joint World Bank and IMF Committee has been set up to oversee the implementation of the HIPC and the poverty-reduction strategies of the poorest countries. The HIPC also is financed through a Trust Fund that depends on bilateral contributions from donor countries, the World Bank, and other multilateral institutions.

Buffer Stock Financing Facility

This borrowing facility was introduced in 1969 to help finance members' contributions to approved international commodity buffer stock schemes. Drawings may be made for buffer stock financing up to the equivalent of 45 percent of quota. To date, the Fund has authorized the use of this facility for tin, cocoa, rubber, and sugar buffer stocks, but drawings have been made only with respect to tin, rubber, and sugar. The facility has not been used since 1984.

Oil Facility

In 1974 the Fund established a temporary oil facility, with funds borrowed from seventeen countries, to assist members in financing payments deficits related to the increase in the cost of petroleum. By March 1976, when the facility was terminated, 55 countries had used SDR 6.9 billion. In 1975 the Fund also set up an oil facility subsidy account with contributions from 25 countries to provide subsidies to countries to reduce their interest costs related to drawings under the oil facility.

Systemic Transformation Facility

This temporary facility was created in April 1993 to respond to the needs of economies in transition. It provided financial assistance to members with balance of payments difficulties resulting from shifting their trade at nonmarket prices to multilateral market-based trade. No new approvals under the facility were made after May 1, 1995. Most of the funds advanced were to countries of the former Soviet Union and central and Eastern European countries.

Compensatory and Contingent Financing Facility

In 1988, this facility superseded the Compensatory Financing Facility, which was introduced in 1963 to help members with balance of payments difficulties caused by temporary shortfalls in their export receipts due to circumstances beyond their control. In 1981 the facility was extended to provide compensation for countries faced with an excessive rise in the cost of imports of cereal products. More recently other goods, as well as services, have become eligible for compensatory financing by the Fund. The contingency element of the Facility helps members to keep their adjustment programs under IMF arrangements on track when faced with unexpected adverse external shocks.

Supplemental Reserve Facility (SRF)

In the wake of the financial crisis in Asia, in December 1997 the IMF established this borrowing facility. The SRF provides financing to members experiencing exceptional balance of payments difficulties owing to a large short-term outflow of capital due to a disruptive loss of market confidence. Access under the SRF is not subject to the usual access limits but is based on the financing needs of the member, its capacity to repay, and the commitment to measures undertaken for early correction of its difficulties. Financing is subject to a surcharge in addition to the usual rate of charge for other IMF loans.

Contingent Credit Lines (CCL)

In April 1999 CCL were introduced for a two-year period and are intended to serve as a new instrument of crisis prevention. Contingent credit lines are available to member countries with strong economic policies as a precautionary line of defence against future balance of payments problems that might arise from international financial contagion—that is, circumstances largely beyond the member's control stemming primarily from adverse developments in international capital markets and in other countries. Unlike the SRF, which is for members already in the midst of a crisis, the CCL is a preventative measure solely for members concerned with their potential vulnerability to contagion.

Emergency Financing Mechanism

The Emergency Financing Mechanism consists of procedures that allow immediate IMF financial support while ensuring the conditionality necessary to warrant such support. It is to be used in rare circumstances representing or threatening a crisis in a member's external accounts requiring immediate attention. It was established in 1995 and was used in 1997 for the Philippines, Thailand, Indonesia, and Korea, and in 1998 for Russia.

Emergency Assistance

The IMF also provides emergency financial assistance to members facing balance of payments difficulties caused by natural disasters. In 1998, for example, the Dominican Republic, Haiti, St. Kitts, and Nevis received emergency assistance to recover from Hurricane Georges.

In 1995 the policy on emergency assistance was expanded to cover countries emerging from political turmoil, civil unrest, or armed international conflict that are unable to implement regular IMF support programs because of damage to their institutional and administrative capacity. In 1998, for example, the Republic of the Congo and Sierra Leone received such support.

Surveillance

Central to the IMFs purposes of operations is its oversight of the operations of the international monetary system. Its Articles of Agreement direct it to exercise firm surveillance over the exchange rate policies of its members. Surveillance is intended to identify issues and problems in a timely manner so that member countries can implement suitable corrective measures more quickly.

Traditionally, IMF surveillance has focused on encouraging countries to correct macroeconomic imbalances. More recently surveillance has also included structural and institutional reforms.

The IMF carries out its surveillance responsibilities primarily through regular consultations with individual member countries and through multilateral discussions.

The World Bank

International Bank for Reconstruction and Development (IBRD) *known as the World Bank; makes long-term loans in the developing countries*

The International Bank for Reconstruction and Development (IBRD) is commonly known as the World Bank. It was set up in 1944 as a sister institution of the IMF to provide long-term loans for rebuilding Europe after the Second World War. When the rebuilding was finished, particularly with the help of the Marshall Plan, the World Bank started to make long-term loans for projects and programs in the developing countries. Today, through its loans, policy advice, and technical assistance, the IBRD supports a broad range of programs aimed at reducing poverty and improving the living standards in developing countries.

The World Bank has become the world's largest source of development assistance, providing some U.S.$30 billion in loans each year. Its operations are financed by member country subscriptions and the sale of its bonds in global markets.

The **International Development Association (IDA)** is an affiliate of the IBRD. The IDA makes concessional loans to the poorest of the IBRD member countries—those with per capita income in 1998 of less than U.S.$895—that lack the ability to borrow from the IBRD. The IDA loans, known as credits, have maturities of 35 or 40 years with a grace period of 10 years on repayment of principal. No interest is charged, but credits do carry a small service charge. The IDA is funded largely by contributions from the governments of the richer member countries.

The **International Finance Corporation (IFC)** is another affiliate of the World Bank. It is the largest multilateral loan and equity-financing establishment for private sector projects in the developing countries. Its focus is promoting growth of productive private enterprise in developing countries, as well as efficient capital markets in the emerging countries. The IFC's 174 member countries provide its share capital and determine its policies. Most of its funds are raised by the sale of its bonds and by arranging syndication and underwriting for the companies that it assists in international markets.

International Development Association (IDA)
an affiliate of the Word Bank that offers concessional loans to the poorest developing countries

International Finance Corporation (IFC)
an affiliate of the Word Bank that provides loans and equity financing for private sector projects in developing countries

The Dollar Shortage in the 1950s

Despite the aid received after the war from the United States and, to a lesser extent, from Canada, European countries' needs for goods and services from North America, first for reconstruction and then for military purposes to thwart the spread of communism, left them with a chronic dollar shortage. Added to their overall requirement for dollars was their inability to earn them. In part this was due to the overvalued currency parities that European countries had established with the International Monetary Fund. Once established, the Fund was reluctant to approve currency depreciation and was unwilling to lend its resources. Since the Fund could not begin to cope with the foreign exchange problems associated with European reconstruction, it retired into relative obscurity until the early 1950s. European countries drifted toward tighter exchange controls and bilateral payment agreements to protect their dollar reserves.

Under the Anglo-American Financial Agreement in 1946, the United States came to the assistance of Britain by giving it credits of $3.7 billion. Canada added another $1.2 billion. The agreement was of benefit to Canada, which was also caught in a dollar shortage. Some of the American dollars supplied to Britain were to settle British import surpluses with Canada, thus providing Canada with U.S. dollars to meet its import surplus with the United States. Unfortunately, the Americans insisted that their advances to Britain be conditional on the pound becoming convertible during 1947. Britain met its commitment in July, but immediately lost $1 billion worth of gold as foreigners took the opportunity to rid themselves of pounds accumulated as a result of credit extended during the war. Convertibility had to be abandoned in August.

France devalued the franc before registering its official parity with the International Monetary Fund in 1946. Two years later the franc was devalued further when France adopted a complex system of multiple exchange rates. A general round of devaluation came in 1949 when Britain, with little or no consultation with the International Monetary Fund, announced a 30 percent devaluation of the pound from U.S.$4.03 to U.S.$2.80. Twenty-three countries followed the British move within one week; seven more followed later.

Canada was among the countries to follow Britain's move. In 1946 Canada had declared a par value with the Fund at parity with the American dollar. The Canadian dollar was appreciated at the time from its wartime level in order to reduce the inflationary price movements resulting from the early abandonment of price controls in the United States. In 1947, however, with continuing inflation and with the large drawing down of loans extended to foreigners, Canada's foreign exchange reserves declined precariously. The Canadian government responded by borrowing $300 million from the Export–Import Bank of Washington and by imposing temporary exchange controls and restrictions. After the 1949 devaluation of sterling, Canada was again forced to protect its dollar. The dollar was depreciated in terms of the U.S. dollar by about 9.1 percent. During the following year, with rumours of revaluation and a large inflow of speculative capital, Canada too flouted the intent of the Fund by abandoning a par value for its currency and thereby allowing its dollar to float.

The European Payment Union

One way to alleviate the dollar shortage was to revive trade within Europe and thereby make European countries less dependent on supplies from North America. Intra-European trade was hampered by the inconvertibility of currencies. Any one country with a balance of payments surplus with another country could not use that country's currency to purchase goods and services from a third European country. Large surpluses in some currencies and large deficits in others could not be offset against each other. This encouraged bilateral payments agreements, which were usually accompanied by bilateral trade agreements discriminating in favour of certain imports from bilateral partners and against similar goods obtainable more cheaply elsewhere.

European Payments Union (EPU) a clearing arrangement from 1951 to 1958 for the major European currencies

A major step toward currency convertibility and multilateral trade was taken in 1951 with the establishment of the **European Payments Union** (**EPU**).[6] The EPU comprised seventeen European countries and, with British membership, overlapped with the sterling area. It functioned as a European clearinghouse very similar to the Clearing Union proposal of Keynes. At the end of every month, each member country reported its net debit or credit position vis-à-vis the other member countries to the Bank for International Settlements in Switzerland, which acted as the clearing agent for the EPU. The Bank consolidated each member's debts and claims into an overall net debt or claim on the EPU. Each member was allotted a quota that served as the basis for settlement

---

6. The EPU was preceded by a more modest move to convertibility with the First Agreement on Multilateral Monetary Compensation, signed in 1947, and by the Agreements for Intra-European Payments and Compensations, signed in 1948 and 1949.

with the EPU. Countries in surplus agreed to accumulate credits with the EPU up to a certain proportion of their quotas, after which they could demand gold or U.S. dollars from it. These credits could be used to make purchases from any member country and thereby removed much of the former trade discrimination. Deficit countries were allowed to accumulate debt with the EPU up to a certain proportion of their quotas, beyond which complete settlement in gold or U.S. dollars was required. Under the original arrangements, the EPU could be called on to pay out more gold and dollars to creditors than it received from debtors. To meet this possibility the United States provided it with a $350 million fund of working capital. The EPU paid interest to creditors and collected interest from debtors, which increased with the duration of their debt.

As both intracontinental and intercontinental trade in Europe expanded, member countries were able to settle a larger proportion of their debts with the EPU in gold and American dollars. The EPU gradually reduced debtor countries' access to credit with it and required them to pay a larger fraction of their debts to it in gold or U.S. dollars.

In December 1958, the EPU was terminated when most of its members made their currencies externally convertible. It was replaced by the European Monetary Agreement, which, through a European Fund of $600 million, provided short-term loans of up to two years to aid members in balance of payments difficulties. The EPU has been described as a miniature International Monetary Fund, and its success suggested that regional clearing unions might be an excellent supplement to the operations of the Fund.

From Dollar Shortage to Dollar Glut

During the 1950s world trade gradually began to flourish again. A high rate of domestic saving and foreign aid allowed a high rate of productive investment in Europe. As Europe rebuilt its productive capacity, new technology and more efficient production methods were introduced. This, together with only a moderate increase in prices, made it a keen competitor in world markets. What was considered a chronic dollar shortage soon became a dollar glut. U.S. aid for economic development and U.S. military commitments throughout the world, combined with the accessibility of the U.S. capital market, created a pervasive flow of dollars into every nook and cranny of world commerce. Not only did the American dollar become the chief trading currency, a position long held by the pound sterling, but it also became an important foreign reserve asset. Foreigners were induced to hold their accumulation of foreign exchange in dollar assets because New York provided a much greater variety of savings outlets than any other financial centre. Moreover, there was always the inducement for foreign governments and central banks to hold dollars because the U.S. Treasury was willing to convert them into gold at a fixed price.

Next to the American dollar, sterling remained the most important trading currency. However, its role as an international reserve asset was confined to the sterling-area countries. These countries still kept close trading ties with the United Kingdom and held substantial reserve balances in London. But these balances tended to decline rather than increase.

In the prewar period, when sterling reigned, the international monetary system was a gold–sterling exchange standard. With the eclipse of sterling it became a gold–dollar exchange standard. Finally, when the U.S. dollar was no longer convertible into gold, it became the dollar exchange standard or a key currency system.

Problems with the Gold–Dollar Exchange Standard

By the early 1960s general concern focused on the weakness of the gold–dollar exchange system that had evolved. Concern centred on three major areas: the confidence problem, the liquidity problem, and the adjustment problem.

The Confidence Problem

The confidence problem arose from the increasing amount of U.S. dollar liabilities being accumulated by other countries as their major international reserve asset. The demand for American dollars as reserve assets was, in large part, conditional on the U.S. government's willingness and ability to convert other countries' official dollar holdings into gold. As the amount of dollars held as reserve assets increased, confidence in the U.S. government's willingness and ability to satisfy any large-scale attempt to convert dollars into gold began to be questioned.

The Liquidity Problem

The liquidity problem, closely associated with the confidence problem, related to the composition and adequacy of international reserves. The two major components of a country's international reserves were its owned reserves and its unconditional drawing rights with the International Monetary Fund. Owned reserves consisted principally of gold, U.S. dollars, and sterling. But with small annual additions to the gold stock, and a general turning away from sterling, the major increase in owned reserves depended on an increase in the foreign liabilities of the United States. As already observed, however, any increase in international liquidity in the form of American dollars threatened the confidence of foreigners to hold them. The United States also became concerned with the vulnerability of its gold stock, because by law a 25 percent gold cover was required for Federal Reserve Credit (notes and deposits of its central bank).[7] When the United States responded by introducing measures to correct its overall balance of payments deficits, the adequacy of international reserves was threatened and in turn so was the ability of other countries to stabilize the value of their currencies relative to their par values.

The International Monetary Fund addressed the liquidity problem with an increase in drawing rights to its members, financed by a 50 percent general

---

7. Following a request by the president, the Congress of the United States provided for ending this requirement in 1968.

increase in quotas in 1958–59, and further increases of 25 percent in both 1965 and 1970. The General Arrangements to Borrow in 1962 also allowed the Fund to temporarily increase its loans to (drawings by) members in crisis situations.

The Adjustment Problem

The adjustment problem arose because of the reluctance of countries to change the par values of their currencies to reflect fundamental changes in their trade and payments, or their reluctance to adopt appropriate domestic stabilization policies consistent with a fixed exchange rate regime. Since the par values of exchange rates were expressed in terms of the U.S. dollar, and most countries used the dollar in their intervention in foreign exchange markets, the United States itself could not change the value of its currency relative to that of any other country. Under these circumstances it followed a policy of "benign neglect," expecting other countries to revalue their currencies in terms of the dollar. Failing this, it expected other countries to introduce appropriate domestic policies. All too often, however, when flights of capital out of dollars and into other currencies occurred, the recipient countries not only hung on to the parities of their currencies but also sterilized the monetary effects of exchange intervention on their domestic economies. This exacerbated the adjustment problem and thereby added to the liquidity and confidence problems.

Defending the Dollar

During the 1960s various arrangements and measures were introduced to maintain confidence in the American dollar for its use as the major international reserve asset.

The Gold Pool

Loss of confidence in the American dollar was usually reflected by a flight out of dollars and into gold. The major gold market was London, which had reopened in 1954. It is here that speculation against the dollar was reflected in a rise in the market price of gold. The official price of gold was U.S.$35 an ounce, meaning that the United States Treasury converted American dollars for central banks into gold at this price.

In October 1961 speculation on the possible devaluation of the American dollar caused the price of gold in the London money market to shoot up briefly from $35 to over $40 an ounce. To catch gold speculators at their game, the Federal Reserve System in the United States began feeding gold to the London market through the intermediation of the Bank of England. Later, European central banks joined the Bank of England in an arrangement, known as the **gold pool,** to stabilize the price of gold. Until March 1968 the central banks participating in the pool provided gold for sale when necessary

gold pool *an arrangement between 1961 and 1968 to stabilize the price of gold*

to prevent speculators from driving the price abnormally high. They also coordinated their own gold purchases to stabilize price fluctuations of gold.

Until early 1968 the transactions by the pool members in the London gold market were fairly successful in stabilizing the price of gold and in reducing speculation against the future gold price of the U.S. dollar. The operations of the pool prevented an extreme rise in the price of gold during the Cuban missile crisis in October 1962, and during the sterling crisis at the end of 1964, which followed the French government's announced intention to convert part of its dollar reserves into gold. But when further speculative attacks on the pound in 1967 resulted from the United Kingdom's difficulties in resolving its chronic balance of payments problems, the gold pool found it increasingly difficult to stabilize the price of gold. Although the pool succeeded in maintaining the established price of gold following the devaluation of the pound in November 1967, gold speculation continued and reached unprecedented postwar proportions early in March 1968.

With heavy foreign expenditures by the United States to carry on the war in Vietnam and with the reluctance of Congress to adopt the restrictive fiscal measures recommended by the president, fear spread that the United States would soon be unable to continue to convert dollars into gold for foreign governments at $35 an ounce. On March 15, 1968, when the stampede for gold reached crisis proportions, the United Kingdom, in response to a request from the United States, closed the London gold market. Following a meeting in Washington of the governors of the central banks participating in the gold pool and the managing director of the International Monetary Fund, a new policy on gold was announced. In order to conserve the stock of monetary gold, the governors agreed to stop supplying gold from monetary reserves to the London gold market or any other gold market. They also agreed to continue to sell gold at $35 an ounce to monetary authorities so long as this gold would not be used to replace gold stocks sold in private markets.

The immediate effect of the new two-price gold system was that the price on the Paris market rose from the official price of $35 an ounce to about $45. The price quickly fell back when speculators realized that the gold pool's decision also implied that the support floor for gold in the free markets had been removed. The price of gold fell again to about $38 an ounce when the London gold market reopened in April.

The two-price gold system was considered an interim measure that, with the announcement of appropriate fiscal measures by the leading countries of the world, would restore confidence in the international monetary system and allow time for major reforms to the system to be instituted. In November 1973, when the 1968 agreement by the central banks not to sell gold to private markets terminated, the two-tier price system ended.

Reciprocal Currency Arrangements

Central banks came to recognize the need for joint action among themselves to neutralize the disruptive effects of flights of "hot money" in and out of dollars and other currencies. The Basel Agreements established the pattern for central bank cooperation. In 1961, after the German mark and the Netherlands guilder were revalued, a large movement of capital took place from London to Frankfurt and Amsterdam in anticipation of further revaluations. The continental central banks bought and held sterling under an arrangement worked out in Basel, Switzerland, at the Bank for International Settlements. With central banks buying sterling as fast as speculators sold it, fear of further revaluation soon subsided.

reciprocal currency arrangements temporary currency swaps between central banks

Swap or **reciprocal currency arrangements,** whereby central banks temporarily hold another country's currency, had become common. One such arrangement in the 1960s was between the Bank of Canada and the Federal Reserve in the United States. In 1962, when Canada experienced a large capital outflow, the Bank of Canada arranged to buy spot U.S. dollars from the Federal Reserve. At the same time it sold U.S. dollars forward to the Federal Reserve. The consequent spot purchase of Canadian dollars in the market signalled Canada's determination not to devalue its dollar at the time. Speculation against the Canadian dollar subsided, and as American dollars flowed back, the forward commitment to the Federal Reserve was met.

Central Bank Transactions in Forward Markets

One way to try to control undesirable international capital movements is with central bank transactions in forward exchange markets. This method was recommended by Keynes in the 1920s, but was not generally employed until the Federal Reserve in the United States started to use it in 1962 to defend its dollar. When speculators sell dollars for foreign exchange, the Federal Reserve sells forward foreign currencies (buys forward U.S. dollars). With a fall in the forward price of foreign currencies (a rise in the forward price of the dollar), speculators may become convinced that they will be unable to sell foreign currencies spot at a profit in the future and so will stop using their dollar holdings to buy it spot now. If a capital outflow is the result of interest arbitrage, Federal Reserve purchases of American dollars forward by increasing the forward rate will tend to offset any gains from interest rate differentials and to stop capital outflows on this account.

Further Control of U.S. Dollar Speculation

To protect itself from a sudden sale of dollars for gold, the U.S. government started in 1962 to sell special medium-term bonds to foreign central banks. These were known as Roosa bonds (named after Under Secretary of the Treasury Robert Roosa, who was instrumental in their introduction). Purchasers of these bonds gave up their immediate dollar claim to gold.

To further eliminate doubts as to the potential strength of the American dollar, steps were taken to correct the large overall balance of payments deficit of the United States. The U.S. government requested that other countries assume a larger share of foreign aid to the developing countries and a larger proportion of mutual defence expenditures. To encourage foreigners to invest their dollar balances in the United States, in 1962 Congress suspended interest ceilings on time deposits held by foreign and international monetary authorities with banks in the United States. On the other hand, to reduce the outflow of U.S. dollars as a result of foreign borrowing, in mid-1963 the United States imposed an interest equalization tax on the value of foreign securities purchased by U.S. residents. Except for the various exempted securities (those of Canada, developing countries, and international financial institutions), the tax had the effect of sharply curtailing the U.S. market for new foreign bonds. The exclusion of Canada was made conditional on its not allowing its official foreign exchange reserve holdings to amount to more than approximately $2700 million. This proved to be an expensive price for Canada to pay, because the use of monetary policy to control subsequent inflationary tendencies was restricted by the fear that higher interest rates in Canada would attract an inflow of foreign capital and expand Canadian reserves beyond the agreed level.

interest equalization tax *a tax imposed in 1963 on foreign bonds issued in the United States and extended in 1964 to foreign loans by U.S. financial institutions; it was repealed in 1974*

The **interest equalization tax**, which remained in effect until January 1974, added about one percentage point to the effective interest rate on foreign bonds sold in the United States. As a result of the higher bond financing costs, foreigners turned to the U.S. banks for direct loans. Guidelines were introduced setting out a voluntary program for banks and other financial institutions to limit their credit and loans to foreigners, and to repatriate some of their liquid holdings abroad. Guidelines were also issued suggesting how business firms could assist in reversing the country's payments deficits, and in particular how they might control their direct foreign investment.

Proposals for More Flexibility in Exchange Rates

During the 1960s it became increasingly apparent that excessive reluctance by countries to change parity levels not only encouraged exchange speculation, but also eliminated an effective means of achieving international adjustment. While most economists considered the extremes of fixed and floating rates unacceptable, some felt that a solution could be found somewhere in between. George Halm proposed the retention of the par value system, but with a wider band for currency fluctuation.[8] A step in this direction was taken with the Smithsonian Agreement in 1971, when the band was widened from 1 percent to 2.25 percent on either side of parity. Another proposal, falling between the extremes of purely fixed and floating rates, was the **crawling peg**, also referred to as the gliding peg, or sliding parity.[9] For instance, countries might allow their exchange rates to drift slowly and steadily within a given maximum annual rate of change. Changes within the year could be either automatic or guided deliberately. Countries might be required, under a par value system, to change their parities according to an appropriate indicator. There was wide disagreement, however, as to possible objective indicators, as well as to the use of sanctions should countries not move their parities when called to do so by the chosen indicator.[10]

crawling peg *the exchange rate is held fixed in the short run but is adjusted at regular intervals to reflect supply and demand conditions*

---

8. George Halm, *The "Band" Proposal: The Limits of Permissible Exchange Rate Variations* (Princeton, N.J.: Princeton University, International Finance Section, Department of Economics, 1965).

9. See J.H. Williamson, *The Crawling Peg*, Essays in International Finance, No. 50 (Princeton, N.J.: Princeton University, International Finance Section, Department of Economics, 1965).

10. See "Report of Technical Group on Indicators," in *International Reform: Document of the Committee of Twenty* (Washington: IMF, 1974), pp. 51–75.

Perpetual Foreign Exchange Crises in the 1960s

Throughout the 1960s Britain had continual balance of payments problems. Despite internal policies to correct excess demand and inadequate growth and productivity, confidence in sterling weakened. Finally, on November 18, 1967, the British government announced a devaluation of 14.3 percent of the pound sterling. With the United States's balance of payments in substantial deficit, speculative pressure next turned against the dollar, primarily in the form of a huge rise in gold purchases in the London market. Speculation against the dollar was moderated only after coordinated central bank action. Reciprocal currency arrangements between central banks were extended and strengthened. Some European central banks purchased American dollars forward at rates designed to provide an incentive for funds to move into the Eurodollar market. The German Federal Bank agreed to invest in medium-term mark-denominated securities issued by the United States. For its part, Canada sold U.S.$150 million in gold to the United States during 1967 and purchased U.S.$200 million in medium-term nonmarketable bonds from the U.S. Treasury.

Following the devaluation of the pound, a number of sterling area countries, having suffered an exchange loss as a result of the devaluation of the pound, switched relatively large amounts of officially owned sterling into dollars and other currencies. These withdrawals, together with the British government's delay in introducing comprehensive measures to correct balance of payments deficits, led to further speculative pressures against the pound in early 1968. At the same time, with widespread rumours of a change in the U.S. gold policy, there were again heavy speculative demands in the London gold market. On March 17, the central bank governors of the gold pool announced that they would no longer support private gold markets. The absence of an assured floor on its market price introduced an element of risk into gold speculation, and private speculative gold purchases subsided.

In May and June 1968, following widespread civil disorders in France and the government's promise of substantial wage and benefits increases to all segments of the French labour force, the French franc came under severe speculative pressure. The government responded by tightening exchange controls and imposing monetary restraints. In August, however, with rumours of revaluation of the German mark, the French franc moved into Germany and the reserve assets of France continued to decline. Rather than revalue the mark, the Germans introduced fiscal restraints. To support the existing parities of the French franc and the pound sterling, the central banks and the IMF extended unprecedented amounts of credit to France and Britain.

Speculation in foreign exchange markets continued throughout most of 1969. In February the central banks introduced an innovation to bolster their defensive arrangements. They agreed on a joint central banking facility for the recycling of short-term capital flows back to central banks suffering large reserve losses as a result of speculation. But with political uncertainty in both France and Germany and with further rumours of German revaluation, massive flows of funds into Germany resumed in April. Finally, on August 8, the French franc was devalued by 11.1 percent, and on October 24, after having floated since September, the German mark was revalued by 9.3 percent from its former parity.

Compared to the previous few years and the following year, exchange markets during 1970 were relatively free of extreme speculative pressures. The Canadian dollar had risen to its ceiling in December 1969, and except for a brief easing in February 1970, remained at or near its ceiling level through May. The strength of the Canadian dollar reflected a widened trade surplus and an inflow of capital. Relatively high interest rates resulting from vigorous anti-inflationary policies attracted short-term capital inflows, including some repatriation of funds previously placed in the Eurodollar market. In its defence of the dollar's upper ceiling, the Exchange Fund Account ran down government cash balances. In mid-May the government replenished its cash balances by the sale of a special issue of $250 million in Treasury bills. The Bank of Canada offset the effect of this on the available liquidity of the chartered banks by raising the chartered banks' minimum secondary reserve ratio from 8 percent to 9 percent of their deposit liabilities. At the same time, in an attempt to reduce the capital inflow, it decreased the Bank Rate from 8 percent to 7 percent. The dollar fell below its ceiling only temporarily, and on May 31 the minister of finance announced that its upper level would no longer be defended. He noted, however, that the Exchange Fund would be used to prevent excessive appreciation and to maintain orderly conditions in the exchange market. He also announced that the International Monetary Fund had been informed of the Canadian government's intention and that Canada would resume its Fund obligation as soon as circumstances permitted.

Although the world's foreign exchange markets remained relatively calm during 1970, this can be characterized as the calm before the storm. During 1970, international interest rate differentials widened in response to monetary and fiscal restraint in Europe and monetary ease in the United States. A massive flow of short-term funds from the United States to Europe developed in early 1971. On May 5, Germany countered the capital inflow by adopting a floating rate for the mark. This was followed by a 7.07 percent revaluation of the Swiss franc (the first parity change of the Swiss franc since 1936 when it was fixed in terms of gold), a 5.05 percent revaluation of the Austrian schilling, and the suspension of the par value obligation by the Netherlands. France and Belgium introduced various controls to cope with capital inflows. By early August neither European currency nor the Japanese yen was immune to disruptive capital flows. The basic cause of these disruptive capital flows was a loss of confidence in the American dollar, particularly after the announcement that the United States was experiencing the first deficit in decades in its merchandise trade balance.

On August 15, 1971, the president of the United States announced the introduction of measures to "protect the dollar from the attacks of international monetary speculation," to improve employment, and to resist inflation. These measures included the "temporary" suspension of the convertibility of the dollar into gold or other reserve assets, a 10 percent reduction in foreign economic aid, and a 10 percent surcharge on dutiable imports into the United States. This surcharge was to be removed when a realistic realignment of foreign exchange rates was completed.

Most foreign exchange markets were closed following the U.S. announcement, and when they reopened, a week later, nearly all the major currencies were in effect floating for the first time since the 1930s. Some exchange controls were introduced to discourage the inflow of capital, and some moves were made, as was the case in Canada, to maintain international trade patterns. The entire international monetary system was immobilized and in danger of complete collapse.

The Smithsonian Agreement

During the summer of 1971 the international monetary crises remained unresolved. The Americans held to their position that currency realignment should come about through having other countries, particularly Germany and Japan, revalue their currencies in terms of gold. While these countries agreed to increase the gold parities of their currencies, they insisted that the United States should also reduce the gold parity of the dollar. Finally, the Group of Ten countries meeting at the Smithsonian Institute in Washington on December 17–18, 1971, reached a tentative agreement. The Fund immediately concurred. The United States agreed to raise the official price of gold from $35 to $38 per ounce—an effective devaluation of the American dollar of 8.57 percent against gold. The agreement set new "central rates," with an allowable fluctuation of 2.25 percent above or below these new rates. This wider range of allowable fluctuations constituted a major departure from the 1 percent fluctuation on either side of the parity under the Bretton Woods Agreement.

The newly adopted "central rates" constituted an upward revaluation against the American dollar of 16.88 percent for the Japanese yen, 13.58 percent for the German mark, 11.57 percent each for the Dutch guilder and the Belgian franc, 8.57 percent for the pound sterling and the French franc, and 6.36 percent for the Swiss franc over its parity established in May 1971. The Italian and Swedish governments revalued their currencies in terms of dollars by about 7.5 percent. Among the Group of Ten countries, only Canada continued to maintain a floating exchange rate, and it had appreciated by about 8 percent since it was floated in May 1970. Once the Smithsonian Agreement on Exchange Rates was reached, the United States withdrew the 10 percent import surcharge, and the discriminatory "Buy American" provision of the investment tax credit was rescinded.

www.

Smithsonian Agreement an agreement among G-10 governments in December 1971 that provided for realignment of participating countries' exchange rates and the maintenance of their currency values within 2.25 percent on either side of their official par values

Although the **Smithsonian Agreement** provided a much overdue realignment of exchange rates, it left unresolved the question of major reform of the international monetary system. Such reform was necessary to deal with destabilizing capital flows resulting from the integration of international capital markets. The development of Eurocurrency markets had provided a mechanism for the movement of liquid funds in response to interest rate differentials and changes in confidence of one kind or another. Moreover, the growth and proliferation of multinational corporations, which used the financial facilities in several countries, had further intensified the sensitivity of short-term capital movements to interest rate differentials and to expectations of changes in exchange rates.

snake in the tunnel *an arrangement among European governments dating from early 1972 to keep the market value of their currencies within 2.25 percent on each side of their official par values*

In April 1972 the members of the European Economic Community (EEC) introduced the **snake in the tunnel** to narrow the fluctuations among their currencies. The member countries agreed to hold the margins of fluctuations between their currencies within 2.25 percent (the snake) and to allow fluctuations against the dollar of up to 4.5 percent (the tunnel).[11] Soon thereafter, however, the United Kingdom ran large deficits with its EEC partners and, in June, left the snake and allowed sterling to float. Iceland and Denmark soon followed the United Kingdom, and special arrangements had to be made to hold the Italian lira within the snake. Sterling's float set off further speculation against the dollar, and West Germany, Japan, the Netherlands, and Switzerland introduced new exchange controls to counter inflows of unwanted dollars. In July the United States intervened in the foreign exchange market, for the first time since August 1971, and this proved to be sufficient to ease speculation against the dollar.

Bretton Woods System *the international monetary system in existence from 1947 to August 1971 that was based on the concept of the adjustable peg for exchange rates*

The watershed in the **Bretton Woods System** came in 1973. Early in the year, cracks in the Smithsonian Agreement widened as speculation against the lira spread to other currencies. On February 12 the United States announced a second devaluation of the dollar—by 10 percent, equivalent to an increase in the price of gold from $38.00 to $42.22 per ounce. By year-end, most of the major industrial countries had allowed their currencies to float, temporarily and "dirtily," while eight European countries were operating a joint float against the American dollar. It had become evident that the original Bretton Woods arrangement had passed de facto into history.

The Reformed International Monetary System

In the early 1960s, Robert Triffin of Yale University, as well as other economists, was already proposing reforms to the Bretton Woods system.[12] In the First Amendment to its Articles of Agreement in 1969, the International Monetary Fund addressed the question of the adequacy of international reserves by introducing the SDR. In 1971 a resolution by the Fund's board of governors called for an immediate study of measures to improve or reform the international monetary system. In the following year, the Fund established the Committee of Twenty on the Reform of the International Monetary System and Related Issues. This committee of its board of governors was set up specifically to negotiate a reformed international monetary system. The Interim Committee succeeded it in 1974, until provision was to be made for a permanent Council of Governors with decision-making powers. When agreement for setting up the council failed, the Interim Committee continued its advisory role and has

11. See G. Wittich and M. Shiratori, "The Snake in the Tunnel," *Finance and Development* 10 (June 1973), pp. 9–13.

12. See Robert Triffin, *Gold and the Dollar Crisis* (New Haven, Conn.: Yale University Press, 1960); Roy Harrod, *Reforming the World's Money* (New York: St. Martin's, 1965); and Albert G. Hart, Nicholas Kaldor, and Jan Tinbergen, *The Case for an International Commodity Reserve Currency*, a memorandum submitted to the United Nations Conference on Trade and Development, Geneva, March 28 to June 15, 1964.

become a vital part of the Fund's policymaking process in that it has provided political leadership to the Fund. Most of the recommendations of these committees were implemented before they received legal status in the form of acceptance by the members of the Second Amendment to the Fund's Articles of Agreement on April 1, 1978.

The Second Amendment, in effect, legalized the system of managed floating exchange rates adopted by the major countries in 1973. Fund members were now free to choose their own exchange arrangements, except for a prohibition against maintenance of the value of a currency in terms of gold. At the same time each country was to undertake "to collaborate with the Fund and other members to assure orderly exchange arrangements and to promote a stable system of exchange rates." The Fund was required to engage in firm surveillance over members' exchange rate policies to ensure that they are consistent with this broad objective. To perform this function, the Fund adopted the following three principles for the guidance of exchange rate policies.

(a) A member shall avoid manipulating exchange rates or the international monetary system in order to prevent effective balance of payments adjustment or to gain an unfair competitive advantage over other members.

(b) A member should intervene in the exchange market if necessary to counter disorderly conditions that may be characterized inter alia by disruptive short-term movements in the exchange value of its currency.

(c) Members should take into account in their intervention policies the interests of other members, including those of the countries in whose currencies they intervene.[13]

The Fund's procedures for surveillance oblige each member to notify it promptly of any change in exchange arrangements and to hold regular consultations with the Fund. In addition to annual consultations with each member, the Fund initiates informal and confidential discussions with members whose behaviour it considers as not conforming to their obligations.

Although no definite return to fixed par values is envisaged, the Fund can, by a decision taken by at least 85 percent of its total voting power, recommend exchange arrangements that are in accord with the development of the international monetary system, or determine conditions that will permit an international system based on stable but adjustable par values. However, any member may freely choose whether or not to enter such a system, and, having entered it, may freely leave unless the Fund objects by an 85 percent majority vote.

Gold has been removed from the central position it occupied in the Bretton Woods par value system. The use of gold as a peg for a currency under any future exchange rate system, including a par value system, is prohibited. The once official price of gold maintained by central banks no longer exists, and the Fund is required to avoid actions that would manage the price of gold in the market or establish a fixed price.

---

13. Executive Board Decision No. 5392 (77/63), adopted April 19, 1977. See *Annual Report*, 1977, pp. 107–09.

As part of the program for gradually reducing the role of gold in the international monetary system, in May 1980 the Fund completed the sale of 50 million ounces of gold, or about one-third of its gold holdings as at August 3, 1975. One-half of the amount, 25 million ounces, was sold to member countries at the former official price of U.S.$35 an ounce. The other 25 million ounces were sold in public auctions over a period of four years, and profits from these sales (the sales proceeds in excess of U.S.$35 an ounce) were transferred to the Trust Fund for the benefit of developing countries. The Second Amendment of the Articles of Agreement gave the Fund a wide range of powers to dispose of its remaining gold holdings of about 104 million ounces. However, an 85 percent majority of the voting power is required before the Fund can exercise any of these powers.

The descent of gold in the international monetary system was to be accompanied by the ascent of the SDR. Members were called on to collaborate with the Fund in the pursuit of making the SDR the principal international reserve asset. The Fund has taken steps to make the SDR a more useful unit of account and thereby facilitate its wider use. As we have already observed, the valuation of the SDR has been simplified in terms of a basket of only five currencies. The reconstitution requirement, whereby participants had to maintain over time a minimum amount of SDRs in relation to their net cumulative allocations, has been abrogated. The range of official holders of SDRs has been extended beyond the Fund and its member countries. Finally, the interest rate paid by the Fund to members on SDRs in excess of their allocations has been set to reflect more closely market-related rates.

With the increase in the market value of gold from around SDR 95 in 1973 to around SDR 435 in 1980, the proportion of the value of countries' total official holdings of reserve assets represented by gold increased. Over the same period the amount of foreign exchange assets almost quadrupled from SDR 101 billion. Hence, the role of the SDR as an international reserve asset has tended to decrease rather than increase. Its role as a unit of account, however, has expanded as, increasingly, private and public transactions are denominated in SDRs.

Further proposals for reform still remain outstanding. For example, it has been proposed that a Substitution Account be established within the Fund to strengthen the basis for centralized world monetary reserves in an international institution. It has also been suggested that central banks be allowed to deposit their foreign exchange assets, particularly U.S. dollars, in excess of their anticipated needs for working balances with the Fund in exchange for SDRs.[14] This would involve a move away from the use of national currencies as reserves and to their simultaneous replacement by SDRs.

---

14. See Dorothy Meadow Sobol, "A Substitution Account: Precedent and Issues," Federal Reserve Bank of New York, *Quarterly Review*, Summer 1979, pp. 40–48.

The Present System of Managed Exchange Rate Flexibility

The post–Bretton Woods international monetary system has been character-ized by large volatility and overshooting of the exchange rates of the major industrial countries. Moreover, substantial exchange rate disequilibria have persisted for several years at a time. For example, the U.S. dollar was subject to large depreciation from 1978 to 1980 and again after 1985, and to excessive appreciation between 1980 and 1985. Because the variability of nominal exchange rates has not always reflected international inflation rate differen-tials, real exchange rates have also been volatile, which has had real economic effects. This has resulted in calls for trade protection, as was the case in the United States in the early 1980s.

Two major policy approaches exist for dealing with exchange rate volatility. One approach is to view exchange rate variation as the product of national eco-nomic policies, and therefore to stabilize exchange rates with the "conver-gence" of these policies. The other approach is to consider exchange rates as a requisite of a healthy world economy and therefore manage them correctly. In practice, both approaches have been used. In September 1985, meeting at New York's Plaza Hotel, the Group of Five (G-5) industrial countries—the United States, the United Kingdom, West Germany, France, and Japan negotiated the so-called **Plaza Accord**. They agreed to coordinated intervention in the foreign exchange market to lower the value of the American dollar. During the seven weeks following the Accord, the monetary authorities of the G-5 countries sold nearly U.S.$9 billion, which resulted in a sharp drop of the American dollar; by year-end it had fallen 17 percent against the yen and 14 percent against the Deutschemark compared to its levels just before the Accord.

Plaza Accord an agreement reached in 1985 by the G-5 nations to coordinate their efforts to lower the exchange value of the U.S. dollar

At the Tokyo Economic Summit in May 1986, the leaders of the G-7 (G-5 plus Canada and Italy) countries agreed to the use of economic indicators to improve policy coordination and to strengthen multilateral surveillance. In the **Louvre Accord** in 1987 and at subsequent Economic Summit meetings, they reconfirmed their commitment to exchange rate stability by coordinated inter-vention in the foreign exchange market and with greater coordination and convergence of their economic policies.

Louvre Accord an Agreement by the G-7 countries to stabilize their cur-rencies at the exchange rates prevailing at the time

Despite the volatility of exchange rates in the two decades following the collapse of Bretton Woods, the international monetary system can be consid-ered a success. It is doubtful whether the Bretton Woods system would have suc-ceeded as well, given the many shocks to the system over these two decades: the dramatic change in the world price of oil in the 1970s; the world debt crisis starting in the early 1980s; the failure of major financial institutions; major stock market crashes in New York in 1987 and Tokyo in 1991; the Gulf War in the same year, 1991; the political and economic transformation of the U.S.S.R. and the countries in eastern Europe; and the Mexican peso crisis in 1994–95.

The European Monetary System

In July 1978, the European Council, composed of the heads of state and gov-ernment of the then-member countries of the **European Economic Community**

European Economic Community (EEC) an organization dedicated to the economic integration of Europe

European Monetary System (EMS) an exchange rate system formed in the EEC from 1979 to the end of 1989 that fixed the exchange rates of participating countries within a defined band

www.

European Currency Unit (ECU) the currency unit used in the European Monetary System before the Euro was introduced

Exchange Rate Mechanism (ERM) an exchange rate mechanism that provided for fixed but adjustable exchange rates for participating countries of the EMS

EMR II an exchange rate mechanism that links all EU members outside the Euro area to the Euro

(**EEC**), agreed that closer monetary cooperation between their countries should be promoted through the creation of the **European Monetary System** (**EMS**). The EMS formally came into being on March 13, 1979, and was heralded as representing a major new commitment toward harmonization and integration within the EEC.[15]

The EMS had three main features: the **European Currency Unit** (**ECU**), the Exchange Rate Mechanism (ERM), and a credit mechanism. As initially envisaged, the ECU was to become the centre of the system. It replaced the European unit of account in the former "snake" arrangement. The European Monetary Cooperation Fund (EMCF) created ECUs in exchange for three-month swaps by member countries' central banks of 20 percent of their gold and U.S. dollar reserves. The amount of these swaps, and therefore the amount of ECUs, changed every three months in line with changes in the quantity and value of the central banks' gold and dollar reserves.

The ECU was a composite currency defined as a basket (or "cocktail") containing a fixed amount of each member's currency. The value of one ECU in terms of any currency was equal to the sum of these amounts expressed in that currency. The value of the ECU was thus a weighted average of its component currencies. The weight of each currency, reviewed every five years, was based on its country's gross domestic product and importance in intra-EEC trade. The ECU's main functions were as a numeraire for setting central rates in the exchange rate mechanism; as a unit of account for intervention and for the credit mechanism; and as a reserve instrument and means of settlement among EMS central banks. On December 31, 1998 the ECU was replaced by the Euro.

The **Exchange Rate Mechanism** (**ERM**) provided for fixed but adjustable exchange rates for participating countries. Among the original nine countries in the EMS, the United Kingdom did not participate in the ERM until October 1990, Spain joined in 1989, while Greece and Portugal had not joined by 1991, instead preferring for their currencies to float. A central exchange rate was set for each currency in the ERM in terms of the ECU. These central rates established a parity grid of bilateral exchange rates among the currencies. Hence, with 10 participating countries there existed a grid of 100 bilateral exchange rates. These bilateral rates were adjusted periodically following a multilateral consultation and decision process, to reflect changes in a member country's relative economic position. During the 1979 to 1990 period, twelve such realignments took place. The ERM limited each member currency to fluctuations of 2.25 percent on either side of these bilateral exchange rates. An exception was made in the case of the Italian lira, which was allowed a 6 percent fluctuating band until 1990. The Spanish peseta and the pound sterling were granted a similar exception when they joined the ERM.

In 1998 when the Euro was introduced, both the EMS and the EMR, which played a key role in the progress toward European Monetary Union, were replaced by a new exchange mechanism, **EMR II**. This exchange mechanism provides the framework for exchange rate policy cooperation between the

15. See Horst Ungerer, "Main Developments in the European Monetary Fund," *Finance and Development* 20, 2 (June 1983), pp. 16–9; and Horst Ungerer et al., *The European Monetary System: The Experience, 1979–82*, International Monetary Fund, Occasional Paper 19 (Washington: IMF, May 1983).

Euro area and EC members not participating in the Euro. Membership in the mechanism is voluntary.

When a currency's market exchange rate diverged sufficiently from its central rate, a divergent indicator provided an early warning signal that some corrective action was necessary. As a result, central bank intervention followed to ensure that fluctuations remained within the specified limits.

A further realignment followed the currency crisis in Europe in September 1992. Higher fiscal expenditures to achieve reunification with East Germany had led to relatively higher inflation and interest rates in Germany than in its neighbours. Higher interest rates attracted capital to Germany, causing the mark to appreciate within the ERM. On September 8, Finland, which was not an ERM member but which was shadowing the ERM, allowed its currency to float. This triggered a speculative attack against the Swedish krona (also not an ERM currency), the British pound, and the Italian lira. To defend its currency, the central bank of Sweden increased its marginal lending rate by an unprecedented 500 percent. The pound and the lira as well as the Spanish peseta were subsequently devalued. The United Kingdom and Italy suspended their participation in the ERM while Spain, Ireland, and Portugal reimposed capital controls. In another relatively minor realignment in 1995, the Spanish peseta and the Portuguese escudo were devalued. In 1996 Finland joined the ERM. Italy rejoined after having allowed the lira to float for four years.

Three credit mechanisms were available to finance intervention in EMS currencies to support the exchange rate arrangement. A very-short term financing facility consisting of lines of credit by participating central banks provided unlimited amounts to finance intervention at the limits. A system of short-term monetary support provided financial assistance to member countries with temporary balance of payments deficits. Medium-term financial assistance was available in the form of loans to member countries that were experiencing, or were seriously threatened by, difficulties in their balance of payments. Such assistance was, however, subject to the recipient undertaking economic policies as could be specified by the Community's Council of Ministers.

European Monetary Union (EMU)

In 1969 the EEC decided to pursue complete monetary union. The Werner Plan, adopted in 1971, called for fixed exchange rates and a common monetary policy within ten years. As an initial step, member countries were to keep exchange rate fluctuations within designated ranges called margins. The plan was abandoned, but the concept of monetary coordination re-emerged in 1978 with the development of the European Monetary System.

The *Single European Act* adopted in 1986 and known as "Europe 1992" called for the elimination of all barriers to the movement of persons, goods, services, and capital between member countries of the community by the end of 1992. The Second Banking Directive, adopted in December 1989, proposed an increase in the range of activities that banks be allowed to engage in and that banks be permitted to operate in any member state on a single banking licence. With these initiatives the creation of a single financial area was envisaged.

In June 1988 the European Council established a committee of central bank governors and other experts to develop concrete stages toward complete economic and monetary union in Europe. The committee's report (The Delors Report) was presented to the Council in April of the following year. The Delors Report defined monetary union as total and irreversible convertibility of currencies, full liberalization and integration of capital markets, and irrevocable fixed exchange rates with no fluctuation margins between member currencies.

Three stages toward the realization of complete unification were outlined. In the first stage, member countries would achieve greater economic convergence through closer economic policy coordination. This stage was officially launched on July 1, 1990. In the second stage, a European System of Central Banks (ESCB) would be established. It would include the 12 national central banks and a European central bank. Its initial task would be to start the transition from the coordination of independent monetary policies to the implementation of a common monetary policy. In the third and final stage, the introduction of a single common currency would take place, and monetary together with external exchange rate policies would come under a single monetary authority.

Maastricht Treaty

Maastricht Treaty
the treaty sets out the framework for achieving monetary union in the European Economic Community

In December 1991, in the Dutch city of Maastricht, 15 member states of the newly founded European Union (EU) agreed to a treaty, to be ratified by each member state, that provides a framework for the transition to a common monetary policy and a single currency managed by an independent central bank.[16] Under the **Maastricht Treaty**, European monetary union is to be reached in three stages. During the first two stages member governments are to achieve greater "convergence" of their economies as measured by four criteria: price stability, interest rates, exchange rate stability, and the sustainability of the fiscal position. In the third stage, which according to the treaty could begin as early as 1997 but no later than 1999, member states who meet the convergence criteria are to irrevocably fix their exchange rates, and a single European currency will be issued by a newly established European Central Bank (ECB).

In 1994, the European Monetary Institute (EMI) another requirement of the treaty, was set up. The EMI now administers the EMS and is preparing the groundwork for the ECB, which will replace it.

---

16. The 15 member states of the European Union are: Austria, Belgium, Denmark, Finland, France, Germany, Greece, Ireland, Italy, Luxembourg, the Netherlands, Portugal, Spain, Sweden, and the United Kingdom.

The Madrid Summit

In December 1995, at the European Council meeting in Madrid, it was decided that the third and final stage of the European Monetary Union would begin on January 1, 1999. It was further decided that a country's eligibility according to the Maastricht convergence criteria for admission to the EMU would be resolved in the spring of 1998. It was also agreed to adopt the name **Euro** for the new European currency. By July 1, 2002, the national currencies of the member countries are to be withdrawn from circulation and to be replaced by the Euro.

According to the Maastricht Treaty, eligibility for EMU membership was to be assessed on the convergence criteria shown in Box 24–2.

BOX 24–2   EMU CONVERGENCE REQUIREMENTS FOR MEMBERSHIP

Price stability: A country's annual rate of inflation must not exceed that of the three best-performing countries by more than 1.5 percentage points.

Interest rates: A country's long-term interest rates must not be more than 2 percentage points above the average long-term interest rates of the three member countries with the lowest inflation rates.

Fiscal and debt position: The government's budget deficit must not exceed 3 percent of a country's GDP and the government's outstanding debt must not exceed 60 percent of GDP.

Exchange rate stability: A country must have participated in the Exchange Rate Mechanism (ERM) of the EMS for the two years prior to the convergence examination date (set for early 1998) and have respected the normal fluctuation margins without severe tensions. Furthermore, a candidate for the EMU must not have devalued its currency during this period.

The precise definition of what constitutes the normal fluctuation margin needs clarification. When the treaty was drafted, the ERM fluctuation limits were narrowly defined at 2.25 percent on each side of the central rate with the exception of 6 percent for newer members. In 1992 the margins were "temporarily" increased to 15 percent on either side, where they still remain. The question now is whether the narrower or wider margins should be the criterion.

The Council of Ministers of the European Union, meeting in Brussels on May 1, 1998, declared that 11 of its members had sufficiently satisfied the criteria: Austria, Belgium, Finland, France, Germany, Ireland, Italy, Luxembourg, the Netherlands, Portugal, and Spain. Greece and Sweden failed to fulfil the conditions for the introduction of the Euro, while the United Kingdom and Denmark chose not to introduce the Euro.

The Euro

On January 1, 1999, the Euro was launched as the common currency in the 11 member states of the European Community.[17] The values of their national cur-

---

17. In June 2000, it was announced that Greece had gained membership.

BOX 24–3   DETERMINATION OF THE EURO CONVERSION RATES

Conversion rates between the national currencies of the 11 member countries and the new Euro were irrevocably fixed at midnight, local time, on December 31, 1998. Between January 1, 1999, and June 30, 2002, one Euro will be equivalent to the following amounts of each of the 11 currencies:

Austrian shilling	13.7603	Irish punt	0.787564
Belgian franc	40.3399	Italian lira	1936.27
Dutch guilder	2.20371	Luxembourg franc	40.3399
Finnish markka	5.94573	Portuguese escudo	200.482
French franc	6.55957	Spanish peseta	166.386
German mark	1.95583		

Thus, a German mark is a bit over half a Euro, and a French franc is a bit more than 15 Euro cents.

SOURCE: European Central Bank.

---

rencies were irrevocably fixed to the Euro at exchange rates shown in Box 24–3. The conversion rates were based on the market value of the ECU on December 31, 1998. The ECU was replaced 1:1 by the Euro. The national currencies in essence became nondecimal subunits of the Euro.

The Euro, however, is available only in the form of deposit money for a transitional period of three years. Beginning January 1, 2002, Euro banknotes and coins will be issued. In the interim, therefore, existing national currencies will remain legal tender. However, in cashless payments, everyone can choose whether to issue payment orders in a national currency unit or in Euros. The amount of the payment is debited or credited to the respective account of the payer and payee, in the desired currency unit in accordance with conversion rates and the rounding rules. Prices are already frequently quoted in both Euros and national currencies.

European System of Central Banks

The European System of Central Banks consists of the European Central Bank (ECB); the 11 national central banks of the EMU member countries; and the four national central banks of the European Union countries that did not initially join the 11-country "Euro zone."

The most important decision-making body within the ECB is the Governing Council. It consists of an executive board (six members, including the president and vice president of the ECB, appointed by common accord of the governments of the 11 EMU countries) and the central bank governors of the 11 EMU countries (appointed by their respective governments). Each member of the council has one vote in the decision-making process.

There is also a general council. It gives some representation to the four EU countries that did not initially join the EMU. The council is made up of the president and vice president of the ECB and the governors of all 15 European national central banks. Among other things, the council provides input concerning monetary and exchange rate policies for European countries both inside and outside the EMU.

Monetary Policy in the EMU

The Governing Council of the ECB is responsible for formulating and implementing a single monetary policy for the Euro area. The national central banks, being an integral part of the ESCB, execute the monetary policy for the ECB in their respective member states. In the formulation of monetary policy, the members of the governing council are independent. They act as "guardians of the Euro" and not as defenders of national interests. Every member of the council only has one vote on monetary policy issues, and monetary policy decisions are made by a simple majority of votes.

The primary objective of monetary policy is to maintain price stability in the monetary union. Price stability is defined in terms of the Harmonized Index of Consumer Prices (HICP) of less than 2 percent. To achieve this objective, monetary policy strategy is based on two pillars. The first consists of a prominent role for money. A quantitative reference value of 4.5 percent for the growth rate of the broad monetary aggregate M3 is regarded as being compatible with price stability. The second comprises a broadly based assessment of the outlook for price developments and the risks to price stability using financial and other economic indicators.

The ECB has three tools for conducting monetary policy: reserve requirements called "minimum reserves," open market operations, and the provision of standing facilities. Reserve requirements are applied to a wide range of financial intermediaries in the Euro area.[18] Interest is paid on minimum reserve holdings. Open market operations consist of the purchase and sale of securities initiated by the ECB and executed by the 11 EMU national central banks. Standing facilities allow eligible banks to borrow from or lend to the national banks overnight. They provide reserves (when banks borrow) or absorb reserves (when banks lend). The ECB uses standing facilities to signal the general stance of monetary policy and to provide upper and lower bounds for overnight market interest rates.

Strengthening the International Financial Architecture

Globalization, the growth and volatility of international capital flows, and the international financial crises of the 1980s and 1990s have spawned widespread

---

18. A list of monetary financial institutions subject to reserve requirements is available at the ECB Website at <www.ecb.int>.

calls for strengthening the "international financial architecture"—the current buzzword for reform of the system. Much of the debate has centred on the prevention, management, and resolution of international currency and financial crises. We survey here some of the issues in the ongoing debate.

Increased Transparency and Information

International financial markets would work more efficiently if there were greater transparency of national government policies, of private sector reporting, and of international financial institutions. The IMF has developed a Code of Good Practices on Fiscal Transparency to guide member countries in enhancing the accountability and credibility of fiscal policy. Member countries are encouraged to adopt the Code voluntarily. Agreement also has been achieved on a code on the transparency of monetary and financial policies.

A need exists to improve both the quality and amount of information to financial market participants to prevent investor herd behaviour, which can cause major disruptions in capital markets. When an investor is perceived to have inside knowledge, others frequently blindly follow regardless of whether the so-called informed investor is following fundamentals or responding to unrelated signals. Improvements in the general availability of good information require efforts in the private sector to adopt sound accounting practices and appropriate standards of disclosure to investors, financial institutions, and official agencies. Better information on government policies, the state of countries' economics, and on individual firms would make financial markets more efficient and less prone to disruptive capital flows.

The IMF has been at the forefront of the movement to improve the provision of economic and financial data by emerging countries to the public. By the end of 1999, 47 of these countries had subscribed to its Special Data Dissemination Standards (SDDS).

Developing International Standards and Principles

The need to develop, adopt, implement, and monitor international codes of good practices is considered essential for the smooth functioning of international capital markets. These practices include standards for accounting, auditing, banking supervision, bankruptcy laws, corporate governance, insurance and securities market regulations, payment systems, and so on. Much has already been achieved in this regard. A Basel Committee has developed the Core Principles for Effective Banking Supervision, which will serve as the basic reference and minimum standard for supervisory authorities. The International Organization of Securities Commissions (IOSCO) has been working to establish universal principles for securities market regulation and to improve disclosure standards. The International Accounting Standards Commission has published international standards aimed at achieving uniformity in international accounting practices. The International Federation of Accounting has established auditing standards.

Although good progress has already been made in developing international standards of best practices, it still remains for most countries to adopt and implement them. It has been suggested that as an incentive, the IMF should base access to its lending facilities on the degree to which a country implements some or all of these standards, which would also require appropriate monitoring.

Increased Private Sector Involvement

Various proposals have been made to involve the private sector more effectively in efforts to forestall financial crises, and if they do occur, to resolve them. To help protect countries from contagion, the private sector might follow the lead of the IMF and also offer contingent lines of credit to protect countries with sound fundamentals that are attempting to meet relevant international standards. Private sector "bailins" also have been suggested; that is, under certain conditions specified in advance, private creditors would be obliged to retain or expand their exposure to a country. This obligation would probably raise the cost of borrowing for many emerging market countries, which would not be a bad thing if the increased cost reflects the higher risk of international borrowing.

Shifting more of the burden of dealing with international financial crises to market and private participants may be necessary because of the difficulty the public sector may encounter in obtaining funds for ever larger international bailouts. Moreover, with more private sector participation, some of the moral hazard problems associated with such bailouts may be mitigated.

Private sector participation also has been sought in changing provisions in loan contracts to facilitate the more orderly restructuring of a country's external debts. It is generally agreed that protracted and often costly debt restructuring could be reduced if majority rather than unanimous consent were required by creditors to the terms of any restructuring.

Occasions arise in which firms and even countries cannot pay their external debts and consequently have to declare bankruptcy. The absence of international bankruptcy procedure creates the possibility of creditor panics. The establishment of an international bankruptcy court has been proposed to oversee orderly debt workouts and to arrange an equitable reduction of payment to foreigners. To date legal obstacles have prevented the establishment of such a court.

Capital Controls

While the further liberalization of capital flows has wide support, it has been suggested that emerging nations might use capital controls, either of outflows or of inflows, to avoid and to manage financial crisis. The use of controls to limit capital outflows generally has not been effective because controls are easily circumvented and encourage corruption. Controls on the inflow of capital to encourage long-term rather then short-term flows and to redirect flows into emerging countries toward equity and direct investment might prove helpful. In any case, if controls are used to deal with financial crises, the controls should be temporary at best.

Since exchange rate instability often results from short-term speculative international capital flows, it has been suggested that restrictions be placed on these flows. However, such restrictions should not be in the form of direct capital controls, but rather in the form of a transactions tax on capital flows. James Tobin, for example, has proposed the imposition of a worldwide 1 percent tax (the **Tobin tax**) on all spot conversions of one currency into another.[19] Admittedly, this tax would impose an added burden on international trade, but in Tobin's view its negative impact on short-term capital flows would more than compensate for this defect. Because the tax would be a function of transaction size, it would be more discouraging for short-term flows than for long-term ones. Hence, it would promote exchange rate stability, but at the same time have little or no consequence for longer-term investments.

Tobin tax pro-posal for a universal tax on all spot conversions of one currency into another

Critics of the Tobin tax contend that a universal and uniform tax on all spot currency conversions would be difficult, if not impossible, to administer and to enforce. It would also have to be applied to forwards, futures, and swap transactions, since a spot transaction can be replicated easily by a combination of debt and forwards, futures, and swaps. Such a tax would generate large economic distortions unrelated to capital flows. There also is the troublesome issue of the distribution of potentially large revenues among countries.

Exchange Rates

No clear answer exists to the question of which exchange rate system or monetary regime is the best. In the final analysis, if domestic policies are right, how much does it matter which exchange rate regime is adopted? The new conventional wisdom is that in view of the high degree of capital mobility, countries will move increasingly toward the ends of the regime spectrum that ranges from pure floating to fixed rates exemplified in currency boards and dollarization. If the Euro is to serve as an example (if it is successful), we also may be moving toward a world of fewer currencies and more currency unions. But such a movement will be measured in decades rather than months and years.

International Financial Assistance

It is generally agreed that financial assistance remains an important aspect of the resolution of international financial crisis. However a prominent concern is that expectations of such assistance create moral hazard. That is, the possibility of assistance is the incentive for reckless behaviour by both lenders and investors. Domestic firms and governments may also be inclined to borrow more in anticipation of international bailouts. The conditionality requirements that are a prerequisite for loans by the IMF, greater participation by private sector lenders, and the implementation of codes of best practices will serve to mitigate moral hazard problems.

---

19. James Tobin, "A Proposal for International Monetary Reform," *Eastern Economic Journal*, July/October 1978, pp. 153–9; and *International Currency Regimes, Capital Mobility and Macroeconomic Policy*, Cowles Foundation Discussion Paper, No. 993, New Haven, Yale University, 1991. See also Paul Bernd Spahn, "The Tobin Tax and Exchange Rate Stability," *Finance and Development*, Vol. 33, No. 2 (June 1996), pp. 24–6.

Regional agreements, such as the one by the financial ministers of the 13 largest Asian economies in May 2000 to protect each others' currencies from adverse capital flows, can be an important addition to the international arsenal of crisis prevention and resolution.

KEY TERMS

bancor
Bretton Woods System
Committee of European Economic Cooperation
conditionality
crawling peg
Economic Cooperative Administration (ECA)
ERM II
Euro
European Currency Unit (ECU)
European Economic Community (EEC)
European Monetary System (EMS)
European Payments Union (EPU)

Exchange Rate Mechanism (ERM)
General Arrangements to Borrow (GAB)
gold pool
HIPC Initiative
interest equalization tax
International Bank for Reconstruction and Development
International Development Association
International Finance Corporation
Louvre Accord
Maastricht Treaty
Marshall Plan

New Arrangements to Borrow (NAB)
Organization for European Economic Cooperation (OEEC)
Plaza Accord
Poverty Reduction and Growth Facility
reciprocal currency arrangements
Smithsonian Agreement
snake in the tunnel
Special Drawing Right (SDR)
standby arrangements
Tobin tax
tranches

REVIEW QUESTIONS

1. What are the major differences between the Keynes Plan and the White Plan for the creation of an international monetary institution?
2. What was the original purpose of the IMF and how has this changed?
3. What was the Bretton Woods adjustable peg system?
4. How is the IMF financed?
5. What is the SDR? Why was it developed, and how is its value determined?
6. Describe the IMF's tranche facilities for lending to its members. What are some of its other lending facilities, and what purpose do they serve?
7. What role does conditionality play for borrowing from the IMF?
8. How do the IMFs Supplementary Reserve Facility, Emergency Financing Mechanism, and Contingent Credit Lines attempt to deal with international financial crisis?

9. Outline the three major problems that the gold–dollar exchange standard is said to have experienced.
10. How did the European Payments Union help to relieve the so-called dollar shortage?
11. What were some of the early proposals for more flexible exchange rates?
12. What was the Smithsonian Agreement?
13. What is a member's responsibility for its exchange rate under the reformed international monetary system? What is the role of IMF surveillance?
14. What was the ECU, and how was its value determined?
15. How did the Maastricht Treaty set the stage for the introduction of the Euro?
16. How is monetary policy conducted in the EMU?
17. How can the international financial architecture be strengthened?

SELECTED READINGS

Aliber, Robert Z. *The International Money Game*, 3rd ed. New York: Basic Books, 1979.

Chandavarkar, Anand G. *The International Monetary Fund: Its Financial Organization and Activities*. Pamphlet Series No. 46. Washington, D.C.: IMF, 1984.

de Vries, Margaret G. *The International Monetary Fund, 1966–1971*. 2 vols. Washington, D.C.: IMF, 1976.

———. *The IMF in a Changing World, 1945–85*. Washington, D.C.: IMF, 1986.

Eichengreen, Barry. *Toward a New International Financial Architecture: A Practical Post-Asia Agenda*. Institute of International Economics, Washington D.C., 1999.

Fellner, William, et al. *Maintaining and Restoring Balance in International Payments*. Princeton, N.J.: Princeton University Press, 1966.

Goldstein, Morris, *Safeguarding Prosperity in a Global Financial System: The Future International Financial Architecture*. Herndon, Virginia: Institute for International Economics, 1999.

Grubel, Herbert G., ed. *World Monetary Reform: Plans and Issues*. Palo Alto, Calif.: Stanford University Press, 1963.

Halm, George N., ed. *Approaches to Greater Flexibility of Exchange Rates: "The Burgenstock Papers."* Princeton, N.J.: Princeton University Press, 1970.

Hansen, Alvin H. *The Dollar and the International Monetary System*. New York: McGraw–Hill, 1965.

Harris, Seymour, ed. *The Dollar in Crisis*. New York: Harcourt, Brace & World, 1961.

Harrod, Roy. *Reforming the World's Money*. New York: St. Martin's, 1965.

Horsefield, J.K., ed. *The International Monetary Fund, 1945–1965: Twenty Years of International Monetary Co-operation*. 3 vols. Washington, D.C.: IMF, 1970.

International Monetary Fund. *The Exchange Rate System: Lessons of the Past and Options for the Future, A Study by the Research Dept*. Occasional Paper No. 30. Washington: IMF, July 1984.

———. *A Guide to Progress in Strengthening the Architecture of the International Financial System*. <www.imf.org/external/np/cxr/facts/arch.htm>.

———. *Financial Organization and Operations of the IMF*. Pamphlet Series No. 45, 2nd ed. Washington, D.C.: IMF, 1991.

———. *The Role of the SDR in the International Monetary System*. Occasional Paper No. 51. Washington: IMF, 1987.

Kenen, Peter B. (Col.). *Making EMU Happen, Problems and Proposals: A Symposium, Essays in International Finances*. No. 199, Princeton, N.J.: Princeton University Press, August 1996.

La france, Robert, and James Powell. "Canada and International Financial Institutions." *Bank of Canada Review*, Autumn 1996, pp. 37–61.

MacDougall, Donald. *The World Dollar Problem*. New York: St. Martin's, 1958.

Machlup, Fritz. *Plans for Reform of the International Monetary System*, rev. ed. Princeton, N.J.: Princeton University Press, International Finance Section, 1964. Reprinted with additions in Fritz Machlup, *International Payments, Debts and Gold: Collected Essays*. New York: Charles Scribner's Sons, 1964, Part 4.

Machlup, Fritz, and Burton G. Malkiel, eds. *International Monetary Arrangements: The Problem of Choice*. Princeton, N.J.: Princeton University Press, 1964.

Meier, Gerald M. *Problems of a World Monetary Order*, 2nd ed. New York: Oxford University Press, 1974.

Mundell, Robert A., and Alexander K. Swoboda, eds. *Monetary Problems of the International Economy*. Chicago: University of Chicago Press, 1969.

Officer, L.H., and T.D. Willet (eds.). *The International Monetary System: Problems and Proposals*. Englewood Cliffs, N.J.: Prentice-Hall, 1969.

Posner, Michael (ed.). *Problems of International Money, 1972–85*. Washington, D.C.: IMF, 1986.

Tavalas, George, S. "The International Use of Currencies: The Dollar and the Euro." *Finance and Development* (September 1998), pp. 46–9.

Tew, Brian. *The Evolution of the International Monetary System, 1945–77*. New York: Wiley, 1977.

———. *The Evolution of the International Monetary System, 1945–81*. London: Hutchinson, 1982.

Triffin, Robert. *Europe and the Money Muddle*. New Haven, Conn.: Yale University Press, 1957.

———. *Gold and the Dollar Crisis*, rev. ed. New Haven, Conn.: Yale University Press, 1964.

———. *Our International Monetary System: Yesterday, Today and Tomorrow*. New York: Random House, 1968.

————. *The World Monetary Maze*. New Haven, Conn.: Yale University Press, 1966.

Tsoukalis, Loukas, ed. *The Political Economy of International Money*. London: Royal Institute of International Affairs, Sage, 1985.

Ungerer, Horst, et al. *The European Monetary System: Recent Developments*. Occasional Paper No. 48. Washington, D.C.: IMF, 1986.

von Furstenberg, George M., ed. *International Money and Credit: The Policy Roles*. Washington, D.C.: IMF, 1983.

Wrase, Jeffrey, M. "The Euro and the European Central Bank." *Business Review, Federal Reserve Bank of Philadelphia,* December 1999, pp. 3-13.

CHAPTER TWENTY-FIVE

MONETARY POLICY IN CANADA: A REVIEW

After reading this chapter you should be able to
1. Describe Canadian monetary policy during the Second World War
2. Argue that monetary policy eased after the Second World War
3. Relate how Canadian monetary policy changed in the 1950s and 1960s
4. Explain the role of exchange rates in the history of Canadian monetary policy
5. Provide a rationale for Canadian monetary policy in the 1970s and 1980s
6. Discuss the quest for price stability
7. Argue the pros and cons of using a monetary conditions index to guide monetary policy

The Early Preference for Cheap Money

The Bank of Canada was established in the midst of the economic depression of the 1930s. Demands for a coordinated easy money policy had been made for a long time in western Canada and were carried to the House of Commons in Ottawa by J.S. Woodsworth, the leader of the new political party, the Cooperative Commonwealth Federation. The government, cognizant of the chartered banks' opposition to a central bank, and itself not convinced of the necessity or possible role of such a bank, appointed the Royal Commission on Banking and Currency (the Macmillan Commission) to provide the answers. The Commission recommended the establishment of a central bank, but cautioned that it "could not cure all the economic ills of Canada" and that it "would not be a source of unlimited credit for all borrowers on all occasions."

The establishment of a central bank did not satisfy the demands of another new political group in Western Canada, the Social Credit Party, which swept into power in Alberta in 1935. Social Creditors, following the dogma of Major C.H. Douglas, saw economic stagnation as a way of life as long as orthodox institutions were allowed to maintain the chronic shortage of purchasing power. The Social Credit government of Alberta issued its own money, "stamp script." It was intended to increase the money supply in two ways. First, it was an addition to the existing stock and, second, the stamps that had to be attached to it to make it current increased the velocity of circulating money. This experiment with easy money ended in 1937 when the federal government (later confirmed by the Supreme Court of Canada) disallowed provincial legislation on matters that came under federal jurisdiction.

In the few years between its establishment and the Second World War, the Bank of Canada followed a policy of monetary expansion. Its open market operations were relatively small since it was able to provide the banking system with necessary reserves through its purchases of gold and foreign exchange. Moreover, it received substantial assistance in expanding the reserves of the chartered banks from the government's policy of building up its deposits with the chartered banks.

www.

The Wartime Monetary Policy

During the first few years of the war, monetary expansion was accelerated in a deliberate attempt to induce the economy to move as quickly as possible toward full-capacity output. The government increased the money supply by borrowing directly from the banking system. By mid-1941 the economy had reached potential output, and the government turned from the banking system to the general public as its chief supplier of funds. It tapped the general public through the sale of securities, by introducing new taxes, and increasing existing taxes. To further control inflationary tendencies, **price ceilings** were imposed, as were controls and rationing of supplies. Worker controls were also implemented and directives issued.

price ceilings
legal limits on how high price can go in a market

The prime role of the Bank of Canada throughout the war was to facilitate the sale of government securities. This required it to expand the reserves of the banks to allow them to make the necessary loans to the government and to the public. The public depended on temporary accommodation from the banks for its bond purchases. To ensure that the public would always remain receptive to the sale of government securities, the Bank also assumed the responsibility for maintaining orderly conditions in the securities market. This implied maintaining bond prices at an average level that would instil public confidence and at the same time allow the government to borrow at attractive rates. That the Bank was successful in its task is reflected in the amount of government securities taken up by the general public. Of all new funds required by the government during the war, the nonbank public supplied approximately 85 percent and the banking system supplied the remainder.

During the early part of the war the Bank provided the government with funds through the direct purchase of government securities. Throughout the war, however, it relied on its open market operations to provide the banks with reserves to allow them to purchase government securities and to make loans to the government and the public. Government loans from the banks took the form of nonmarketable deposit certificates that the government sold to them in an attempt to control their liquidity position. The Bank also provided temporary financing to the government from time to time by accumulating foreign exchange. In most cases, however, the potential effects of the Bank's foreign exchange purchases on the reserves of the chartered banks were offset by the switching of government deposits from the chartered banks to the Bank of Canada and by the Bank's open market operations.

The Postwar Easy Money Policy

Early in 1944, the Bank of Canada announced its intention to continue an easy money policy after the war. At the same time it reduced the Bank Rate and supplied the banks with more reserves than they had ever had before. The Bank's policy was part of overall government policy presented in the White Paper on Employment and Income in April 1945. In the White Paper the government committed itself to "the maintenance of a high and stable level of employment and income." Following the new Keynesian dogma, fiscal policy was to be the main technique for its accomplishment. To assure that there would be enough purchasing power available to maintain full employment, a comprehensive social welfare program was initiated, which included family allowances, liberal veterans' benefits, and housing legislation.

The expansionary programs introduced by the government, even before the end of the war, were based on two historical memories—the Great Depression, and the reconversion depression following the First World War. That depression did not follow as anticipated was in large part the result of government policies. The transition from a wartime to a peacetime economy took place much more quickly and smoothly than expected. A significant proportion of the demand for war materials was replaced by the demand for goods and services required for European aid and reconstruction. Purchasing power was provided to the European nations by the liberal credits and aid supplied by the Canadian and U.S. governments.

Domestic demand for goods and services also increased. An unprecedented proportion of the war had been financed through the sale of government securities. After the war the government viewed maintaining the price of bonds as a moral obligation so that their holders could sell them without loss. To keep faith with millions of investors, government accounts and the Bank of Canada were active purchasers of bonds in the market. Having deprived itself of many goods and services during the war, the public used its increased liquidity to satisfy its demands. With domestic demand added to foreign demand for Canadian production, prices moved up. Most of the government's policies to resist inflationary tendencies were accidental rather than planned. The only exception was the revaluation of the Canadian dollar in 1946 to insulate the Canadian economy from the increase in prices in the United States following the early abandonment of price controls there. However, any anti-inflationary effects the government's unplanned budgetary surpluses may have had were more than offset by its debt management program. Employing budgetary surpluses to redeem government debt not only returned cash to the public, but also maintained its liquidity by supporting bond prices.

Somewhat belatedly, the Bank of Canada attempted to control chartered bank expansion with moral suasion. In 1947 it suggested to the banks that they closely scrutinize the inventories and receivables of their customers before granting loans. Early in the following year it told the banks that financing capital development with bank credit was undesirable.

Beginning in 1948, yields on Canadian bonds were allowed to rise sharply. This resulted from the government's inability to support bond prices at their existing levels, rather than from any intention to allow higher interest rates to dampen inflationary tendencies. During the latter part of 1947, after the large drawing down of foreign loans and the sharp decline in foreign exchange reserves, the government introduced temporary direct import controls, special taxes, and exchange restrictions on foreign travel expenditure. The sale of foreign exchange had provided the government with additional funds to support the bond market. Now that it was faced with the task of building back these reserves and the possibility of smaller budgetary surpluses, the government's ability to support bond prices at higher levels appeared doubtful. The Bank of Canada's ability to provide further support was also restricted by a statutory provision prohibiting it from holding in excess of 50 percent of its note and deposit liability in securities of more than two years to maturity. By the end of 1947 this limit had been reached. In early 1948 the Bank and the government were obliged to abandon their policies of rigidly pegging bond prices. The resulting higher interest rates, however, were no longer required to dampen inflationary tendencies, which exhausted themselves by late 1948. From this time until late 1949, Canada experienced its first pause in the postwar upward spiral of prices.

The Return to Monetary Orthodoxy

After a brief pause, at the outbreak of the Korean War, inflationary tendencies returned to plague the Canadian authorities. Canadians, remembering previous wartime shortages, hurried to fill their larders. Added to this demand for goods and services was that by the government for defence. However, any attempts to deal with these demand pressures and the consequent upward movement in prices had to be deferred until a foreign exchange crisis was settled.

In 1949, following the realignment and devaluation of sterling and most European currencies, the Canadian dollar was devalued in terms of the United States dollar by about 9.1 percent. At the time, the Minister of Finance said that he was not at all sure that the new rate was the proper one for the Canadian dollar and that a subsequent change might have to be made. Because of an investment boom in Canada and rumours of possible revaluation of the Canadian dollar, speculators bought Canadian dollars in flood proportions during 1950. The consequent large increase in foreign exchange was purchased by the Bank of Canada and by the government's foreign exchange fund account with cash available from the federal Treasury and from the special sale of deposit certificates to the chartered banks. Because the Bank offset only part of its foreign exchange purchases by open market operations, the cash reserves of the banks were allowed to expand. Finally, to prevent any further inflationary consequences from its attempts to hold the external value of the dollar, the government freed the Canadian dollar to seek its own level.

With the exchange rate problem settled, the authorities set out to make a deliberate attempt to control inflation. In October, under the Consumer Credit Act, the government issued an order-in-council restricting consumer credit purchases. The Bank of Canada announced a policy of restriction with an increase in the Bank Rate from 1.5 percent to 2 percent. This was supported by a reduction in the net cash reserves provided to the chartered banks. Thus, by late 1950 the Bank of Canada had followed the lead of Western Europe and the United States and returned to monetary orthodoxy, controlling inflation with monetary measures along a broad front.

In 1951 the Bank of Canada supplemented its quantitative controls, which had reduced the cash reserves of the banks, with qualitative controls that restricted their lending. In February the banks agreed to a "credit ceiling" by refraining from buying corporate securities of more than one year to maturity and from extending term loans. In addition the banks agreed to impose margin requirements of at least 50 percent on loans on corporation stock, to increase margin requirements on instalment finance paper, and to tighten lending practices on commercial and personal loans. The life insurance companies also announced an anti-inflationary investment policy that may have been prompted by central bank moral suasion.[1] In both 1950 and 1951, monetary policy was assisted in fighting inflation by the government's fiscal policy, which included an increase in taxes and deferred depreciation allowances.

The return to monetary orthodoxy after 1950 proved fairly successful. Until almost the end of 1953, the economy operated at full employment with relatively little inflation.

Economic Contraction

By late 1953, the Korean War boom ended, and from then to mid-1954 Canada suffered its first real postwar recession. Reduced defence expenditures were accompanied by a series of setbacks, including a slackening demand for consumer durables; decreased expenditures on business inventories, machinery, and equipment; increased competition in export markets; and lower farm income resulting from poor crops and marketing and delivery difficulties. The Bank of Canada was slow to recognize the change in economic conditions, and when it finally initiated monetary expansion after 1954, recovery was already well under way. The same was true of the government's fiscal policy; in both its 1952 and 1953 fiscal years it had a budgetary surplus, while in the following two years, with economic recovery well under way, it had budget deficits.

1. The Bank of Canada also requested that the stock exchange impose more severe margin requirements.

Economic Recovery and Expansion

Economic recovery began in late 1954 with increased expenditures on residential construction encouraged by lower interest rates and the availability of mortgage money. The 1954 revisions to the Bank Act allowed the banks to make National Housing Act mortgage loans, and after only a brief period of reluctance the banks became major suppliers of mortgage funds. The revisions to the Bank Act also changed the statutory calculation of the banks' required reserves, which were increased from 5 percent to 8 percent. Paradoxically, however, this did not lead to contraction by the banks. Although the banks had been legally required to maintain cash reserves equal to 5 percent of their deposits, they actually held 10 percent. Now with the increase in the legal ratio they decided to work toward the new 8 percent ratio. This was prompted by the development of the money market initiated by the Bank of Canada and by the revisions to the Bank Act that allowed the banks to calculate their minimum required cash reserves on an average monthly basis rather than on an average daily basis.

During 1955 the economy was rapidly approaching full employment and the dangers of inflation were again present. Although the Bank of Canada contracted the reserve base of the banks through its open market operations, the banks were able to expand their loans by running down their treasury bills and day-to-day loans. Moreover, for the first time both the chartered banks and the approved money market dealers took substantial advances from the Bank of Canada. The Bank responded by increasing the Bank Rate in August and again in October and November. Late in the year it also used moral suasion on the banks to prevent them from making further commitments for "term" lending. The banks responded to moral suasion by agreeing to maintain a minimum liquid asset ratio of 15 percent by the end of May 1956. The intent of this new ratio was to prevent them from further switching from money market assets to loans and to render them more sensitive to official measures of monetary restraint.

During 1956 the Bank continued its restrictive monetary policy. The Bank Rate was again raised on three separate occasions. It now appeared that the Bank Rate was becoming a cost factor, not merely a psychological factor, in the market, as the banks adjusted their own rates in line with it after making public reference to the changes made by the Bank of Canada. Since the Bank Rate became an important factor in influencing market rates, it is difficult to explain why the Bank abandoned the fixed Bank Rate for a floating rate in November 1956. One explanation is that it wished to avoid being blamed by the public for rising interest rates. Moral suasion was again used in 1956, this time on nonbank institutions as well as on the banks. However, only the banks responded to the Bank of Canada's request for voluntary credit restraint by agreeing to restrict credit provided to instalment finance companies.

During 1955 and 1956 monetary policy proved generally successful. Interest rates were allowed to increase, and the money supply was held relatively stable. On the other hand, both wholesale and consumer prices showed remarkably small increases. During 1956 monetary policy was assisted by a large government budget surplus.

The Money Muddle

During 1957 the Canadian economy was showing signs of weakness as its export markets softened. Early the following year, although the rate of unemployment was very high, there were indications that recovery was in sight. However, any recovery that there might have been proved abortive, and the economy settled into a general state of stagnation. Throughout 1957 the Bank continued its policy of restraint, and only after a loud public outcry did it begin to expand chartered bank cash reserves in the following year; the Bank's timing was probably off by as much as six months. When the Bank finally leaned toward expansion, government debt management probably dictated its policy more than its acceptance that easier monetary conditions were appropriate.

In the first part of 1958, considerable uncertainty had developed in the securities market. Adding to this uncertainty was the large requirement for government financing and the large amount of Victory Bonds that were approaching maturity. To allay the uncertainties in the securities market, and partly as an anti-inflationary measure, the government embarked on a program to convert its maturing debt into long-term issues. With the conversion program between July and September, the average maturity of the public's holdings of government debt increased from eight years to almost fifteen years. In order to facilitate such a large conversion, the Bank of Canada embarked on a temporary expansionary policy. Soon thereafter, however, it withdrew support and interest rates rose to higher levels. Higher interest rates in Canada drove corporations, provinces, and municipalities to the U.S. capital markets, and the consequent inflow of foreign capital moved the external value of the Canadian dollar higher. This only added to the difficulties Canadian exporters already faced with weakening international markets.

During 1959 and through the first half of the following year, the Bank of Canada continued to restrict the money supply. The money market now came to play an important role in mobilizing the remaining available cash. For example, the developing commercial paper market temporarily made available excess corporate funds to firms requiring short-term credit. The increase in the velocity of circulation of money that resulted, as well as the sale of securities by the banks, made further monetary expansion possible.

The annual average unemployment rate exceeded 7 percent in 1958, and it did not fall below 6 percent until after 1962. Under these circumstances the Bank's reversion to monetary restraint after mid-1958 came under severe attack. It was seen to be inappropriate during a period of high unemployment and to be contributing to the capital inflow, an overvalued dollar, and the difficulties experienced by Canadian exporters. In August 1959 the minister of finance showed his concern over rising interest rates when he intervened in the Treasury bill auction by refusing bids "involving too high interest rates." However, James Coyne, then governor of the Bank of Canada, vigorously defended the Bank's policy of restraint with an unprecedented number of public speeches. Toward the end of 1959 the Prime Minister and the minister of finance attempted to answer the Bank's critics in turn by criticizing the chartered banks for not allocating credit equitably, and particularly for not looking after the needs of the small borrower—a criticism that was completely unjustified.

By 1960 it became apparent that the Bank's concern with inflation rather than with unemployment and slow economic growth was in conflict with the government's policy. Throughout 1960 and early 1961 the economy was again in a cyclical downturn. The Bank responded with only a mildly expansionary policy. Late in December the government, again somewhat belatedly, introduced a special budget that focused on the structural characteristics of the unemployment problem, on foreign ownership, and on foreign control of Canadian industry. The conflict between the governor of the Bank and the government should have been resolved by the governor's resignation, a move Coyne resisted even after it was requested by the government in May 1961. The government now took a definite stand: It announced an expansionary fiscal policy and presented a bill to the House of Commons declaring vacant the position of governor of the Bank of Canada. Although the Commons passed the bill, it was defeated in the Senate. Coyne, feeling vindicated, then resigned. The Senate had defeated the bill not because of the monetary policy of the Bank, but because the government had sought Coyne's resignation over a disagreement with a decision of the Bank's board of directors to raise his pension on retirement.

On July 24, 1961, the board of directors of the Bank of Canada announced the appointment of Louis Rasminsky as governor. On the same day both he and the minister of finance issued statements setting forth the future relationship between the Bank and the government. The basic principle of this relationship is that the government has the ultimate responsibility for monetary policy, and the governor of the Bank must either agree or resign.

The Exchange Rate and Monetary Policy

In July 1946, the Canadian dollar had been revalued and restored to parity with the U.S. dollar in a move to insulate the Canadian economy from postwar foreign inflationary spillovers, especially from the United States where wartime price controls had already been removed. Soon thereafter, a severe drain on Canada's foreign exchange reserves developed and a number of defensive measures, including import controls, were undertaken. In 1949, in response to realignments of foreign currency rates in Europe and in the sterling area, Canada depreciated its currency by 9 percent in terms of the U.S. dollar. At the time, the minister of finance noted that the "right rate" for the Canadian dollar at one time was unlikely to be the "right rate" at another, and that he might soon have to alter the official rate again, a premonition that soon proved to be correct.

With speculators expecting a near-term revaluation in response to a growing U.S. demand for Canadian raw materials, in the summer of 1950 an inflow of foreign capital increased Canada's foreign exchange reserves by over 50 percent. Reluctant to introduce severe monetary restraint to sterilize the impact of these capital inflows on the Canadian money supply, the government decided to allow the dollar to appreciate. However, rather than pegging it at a new value, which might shortly turn out to be inappropriate, it decided in

October to allow the dollar to float and to let market forces determine its proper value. Although the dollar's float was to be only a temporary expedient to determine its appropriate value, Canada did not return to the Bretton Woods pegged currency regime until June 1962.

For almost a decade after the Canadian dollar was allowed to float in October 1950, it displayed a remarkable degree of stability, fluctuating within a relatively narrow range. This was the result of stabilizing short-term international capital movements and the coincidental cyclical swings in Canada and the United States.

In 1959 and 1960, despite low growth and relatively high unemployment, the Bank of Canada conducted a restrictive monetary policy. The governor of the Bank defended this policy on the grounds that it was necessary because of inflationary threats to the economy and because of the unsatisfactory state of Canada's balance of payments. He characterized the latter as Canadians living beyond their means, with huge deficits in the country's current account balance, a growing volume of foreign debt, and an undesirable foreign predominance in Canadian business. By holding Canadian interest rates high, the governor hoped to encourage domestic saving and reduce aggregate demand and imports. However, rather than slowing capital inflows, high interest rates attracted them. This resulted in an appreciating Canadian dollar, which further exacerbated continuing high rates of unemployment. In June 1961, following the "Coyne Affair" and the departure of Governor James Coyne, the minister of finance announced that the resources of the exchange fund would be used to move the Canadian dollar to an unspecified "but significant" discount in relation to the U.S. dollar. This announcement immediately put downward speculative pressure on the Canadian dollar. To end the uncertainties created, on May 2, 1962, the government returned to a fixed exchange rate regime and fixed the value of the dollar at U.S.$0.925.

To convince currency speculators of its ability to defend the dollar's new par value, the government bolstered its foreign exchange reserves with foreign loans and standby agreements. In addition, the Bank of Canada lent its support with higher interest rates. As it turned out, once the speculators were driven off, the Canadian dollar at U.S.$0.925 was substantially undervalued; in every year between 1962 and 1970, with the exception of 1966, Canada's official foreign exchange reserves increased. Until 1964, the inflow of short-term capital allowed the Bank of Canada to frame monetary policy toward domestic objectives without serious exchange constraints.

In 1963 and again in 1968, the United States introduced remedial measures to deal with its growing balance of payments deficits by restricting capital exports. Canada sought and obtained exemption from the U.S. restrictions on capital exports. However, exemption was conditional on Canada's not allowing its foreign exchange reserves to increase beyond designated ceiling targets. As it turned out, ceilings on the amount of Canada's foreign exchange reserves resulted in a monetary policy dilemma.

Toward mid-decade, demand pressures in the United States because of the Vietnam War spilled over into Canada via growing merchandise surpluses. To hold the value of the dollar down to its fixed value and at the same time keep its foreign exchange reserves at their agreed ceiling level, the Bank of Canada had to allow monetary expansion and easier monetary conditions so as to discourage short-term capital inflows. Given domestic inflationary conditions, however, a restrictive monetary policy would have been a more appropriate policy.

In 1968 Canada was freed of its foreign exchange ceiling obligations. The Bank of Canada immediately introduced a restrictive monetary policy. Higher interest rates encouraged further short-term capital inflows. The Bank of Canada resisted upward pressure on the value of the dollar by intervening directly in the foreign exchange market. To sterilize the expansionary monetary effect of this intervention, it forced the chartered banks to buy a special issue of Treasury bills. By May 31, 1970, unable to resist upward pressures on the exchange rate without allowing an undesirable expansion of the money supply, the Canadian dollar was once again set free to float.

After the Canadian dollar was set free to find its own level at the end of May 1970, it immediately rose from its previous pegged level of U.S.$0.925, set in 1962, to parity with the U.S. dollar, and until 1976 it stayed a couple of cents above or below U.S.$1.00. The strength of the Canadian dollar was the result of large capital inflows from long-term external borrowing and an inflation rate below that of the United States. In 1970 and 1971, the Bank of Canada resisted the pace of appreciation of the Canadian dollar in relation to its U.S. counterpart with direct intervention in the foreign exchange market and a reduction in the Bank Rate. The Minister of Finance and the Bank also urged Canadian borrowers to consider the domestic capital market carefully before entering foreign markets. The Bank's intervention to moderate the upward pressure on the value of the Canadian dollar from 1970 to 1975 resulted in an excessive expansion of the money supply. In hindsight, this turned out to be a policy error, because it pushed the economy to double-digit inflation in 1974 and 1975.

Canada's inflation performance was better than that in the United States during the late 1960s and early 1970s, but generally worse thereafter. The higher inflation rates in Canada, together with a deteriorating current account in the balance of payments, resulted in a depreciation of the Canadian dollar against its U.S. counterpart. Between 1976 and 1986, the Canadian dollar depreciated by some 30 percent against the U.S. dollar. Sharp downward movements from its trend resulting from U.S. monetary shocks, changes in exchange rate expectations, and the conduct of Canadian monetary policy periodically punctuated the downward drift in the value of the Canadian dollar.

In 1977, interest rates in the United States started to move up sharply in response to a restrictive monetary policy introduced to control rising inflation and to defend the U.S. dollar against appreciating European currencies. Although the Bank of Canada also started to introduce a more restrictive monetary policy in 1978, following the failure of its policy of money growth targeting to cope with inflation, the Canadian dollar turned down sharply. To moderate the decline, the Bank intervened directly in the foreign exchange market with foreign assets borrowed by the federal government in external money and capital markets.

In 1982, another sharp run up of U.S. interest rates, which was not followed immediately in Canada, together with a loss of confidence in Canada's commitment to control inflation, resulted in speculative pressure against the

Canadian dollar. The consequent exchange crisis was resolved only after the Bank of Canada intervened directly and heavily in the foreign exchange market and pushed Canadian interest rates up to produce a wide interest rate differential in favour of Canada. In June and July of 1984, when the favourable interest rate differential narrowed, causing downward pressure on the Canadian dollar, monetary policy was again called upon to move Canadian interest rates up in order to allay exchange market uncertainty.

Another serious bout of downward pressure on the Canadian dollar occurred in February 1986. During the latter part of 1985, confidence in the Canadian dollar began to deteriorate as Canada's economic and financial prospects were perceived to be less promising. This view was based on a weakening in its current account balance due to a decline in international commodity prices, the failure of two chartered banks, and concern over the federal government's resolve to reduce its large fiscal deficits. Despite the relatively high short-term interest differential in Canada's favour, speculative pressure on the Canadian dollar forced its value to plunge to U.S.$0.69 on February 4, 1986. The minister of finance blamed the massive selling of Canadian dollars on a handful of traders on the Chicago Mercantile Exchange. The Canadian authorities put a sudden halt to the speculation against the Canadian dollar by unprecedented intervention in the foreign exchange market with funds borrowed from the commercial banks in the Eurocurrency market. In addition, the Bank of Canada sold Treasury bills, which rapidly increased the short-term interest rate differential vis-à-vis U.S. rates. The concerted actions immediately brought the exchange crisis to a halt.

Because of the close integration of Canadian and U.S. financial markets, changes in the U.S. dollar price of the Canadian dollar are extremely sensitive to changes in the differential between Canadian and U.S. short-term interest rates. When U.S. monetary policy changes, causing this differential to widen or narrow, Canada can respond by moving its interest rates to follow U.S. rates, by allowing the exchange rate to change, or by a combination of the two.

Between 1976 and 1986 the Bank of Canada managed domestic interest rates, and thereby the short-term interest rate differential between Canada and the United States, in order to prevent a sharp and persistent depreciation of the Canadian dollar that would exacerbate an already undesirable high domestic inflation rate. A depreciation of the Canadian dollar is directly transmitted to the domestic economy through higher Canadian dollar prices for imports, and indirectly through higher Canadian prices for import-competing and exportable goods in Canada. The possibility of these price changes increasing inflationary expectations, and hence creating a higher inflation rate, was a major concern for the governor between 1976 and 1986 and explains why the Bank attempted to resist any sharp and persistent depreciation of the Canadian dollar during this period.

Two major issues have confronted policymakers in the management of the exchange rate. The first relates to the tradeoff between charting an independent course for short-term interest rates and allowing greater exchange rate volatility. As we have seen, for the small, open Canadian economy in which financial markets are closely integrated with those of the much larger U.S. neighbour, U.S. monetary shocks must be absorbed either in the form of domestic interest rate changes, or foreign exchange rate changes, or a combination of the two. The Bank of Canada's choice has generally been the latter. However, as is indicated by the interest rate parity condition, the degree to which the Bank can follow a policy of "Made in Canada" interest rates depends on whether it can also manage changes in the expected rate of depreciation of the Canadian dollar.

The second policy issue that concerned the Bank during the period when the value of the Canadian dollar continuously depreciated against the U.S. dollar was the tradeoff between a persistent depreciation and the control of inflation. A depreciation of the Canadian dollar is directly transmitted to the domestic economy through higher Canadian prices for import-competing and exportable goods made in Canada. Empirical evidence indicates that import prices rise almost the full extent of depreciation within six months. Furthermore, because imports comprise some 25 percent of the value of domestic expenditures and about 20 percent of personal consumption expenditures, Canadian production costs and the Consumer Price Index are also immediately affected. In the longer run, the consequent change in inflationary expectations and attempts by labour to protect its real wage result in further cost and price increases. It was in this sense that the Bank of Canada saw persistent currency depreciation as having a high inflationary risk. However, these risks depended on the Bank accommodating a higher Canadian cost structure with monetary growth. In the absence of such accommodation, it is not at all clear that persistent depreciation of the Canadian dollar could have seriously exacerbated an already high rate of domestic inflation.

After 1986, both domestic interest rates and the value of the Canadian dollar, in terms of its U.S. counterpart, climbed upward. The Bank saw these increases as being necessary to control the inflation rate; others viewed these increases as seriously damaging Canada's international competitiveness and resulting in high rates of unemployment. It was also argued that with both high rates of interest and inflation, Canada could lose long-run competitive benefits from the implementation of the Canada–U.S. Free Trade Agreement. Some economists suggested that by again pegging the exchange rate on the U.S. dollar, Canada would have a better chance of preserving and enhancing its economic well-being in the competitive global economy.

Controlling Inflation

Although controlling inflation was a major concern of James Coyne during his tenure in the 1960s as governor of the Bank of Canada, with inflation running at less than 5 percent and unemployment rising, his concern did not receive much attention and at best was considered misplaced. It was not until the 1970s, when double-digit inflation arrived, that both the public and the Bank really started to take inflation seriously.

The acceleration in the rate of inflation in the 1970s was largely the result of higher rates in the United States. Higher inflation rates there can be traced to the second half of the 1960s, when excess demand was fuelled by a sharp increase in expenditures related to the Vietnam War and an accommodating monetary stance on the part of the Federal Reserve System. After Canada returned to a flexible exchange rate, an appreciation of the exchange rate could have provided insulation from the higher inflation rates in the United States. As already noted, the Bank's policy to resist the pace of appreciation of the Canadian dollar turned out to be a policy error. By allowing the M1 monetary aggregate to grow at rates of 12.7 percent, 14.2 percent, and 14.6 percent in 1971, 1972, and 1973, respectively, double-digit inflation was inevitable. Sharp increases in OPEC oil prices and world commodity prices in 1973 and 1974 further contributed to the inflationary pressures. With inflation running at close to 11 percent a year in both 1974 and 1975, the Bank made a dramatic change in policy. It adopted targets for the growth rate of the money supply.

monetary gradualism a policy of gradually reducing the rate of growth of the money supply to control inflation

In 1975, the Bank of Canada introduced its policy of **monetary gradualism**. At the same time, the federal government established the Anti-Inflation Board, which introduced wage and price controls.[2] The Bank policy of monetary gradualism may be summarized as follows:[3]

- The average rate of growth of the money supply as defined by M1 was to be gradually reduced until it was no higher than the long-term average growth rate of real output.
- Declining target ranges were pre-announced for the growth of M1.
- Short-term interest rates were controlled in order to make the demand for money consistent with the money-growth targets.

By gradually reducing the money supply, the Bank hoped to avoid the undesirable short-run consequences: the higher unemployment rates associated with rapid deceleration of money growth. The same purpose was to be served by pre-announcing growth targets to bring about a reduction in the public's inflationary expectations.

The Bank was initially successful in keeping M1 growth within its successive lower target ranges. In 1975 and again in 1978, it allowed M1 growth to exceed the upper limits of its targets to offset the effects of postal strikes on the demand for money. On the other hand, in 1978 short-term variability in M1 growth increased as the Bank began to give more weight to its conduct of monetary policy than to cushioning the depreciation of the Canadian dollar.

In the first three years of the Bank's program of monetary gradualism, the rate of inflation slowed. During these years monetary growth was checked, food costs were held down by special supply conditions, the increase in money wages

---

2. Empirical studies suggest that wage and price controls made a modest contribution to holding down wage and price inflation. See J.M. Cousineau and R. Lacroix, "L'impact de la politique de contrôle des prix et des revenus sur les ententes salariales," Economic Council of Canada Discussion paper 95, Ottawa 1977; D. Auld, L. Christofides, R. Swidinsky, and D. Wilson, "The Impact of the Anti-Inflation Board on Negotiated Wage Settlements," *Canadian Journal of Economics*, May 1979, pp. 195–227; Frank Reid, "Unemployment and Inflation: An Assessment of Canadian Microeconomic Policy," *Canadian Public Policy*, Spring 1980, pp. 283–99; and J. McCallum, "Two Cheers for the Anti-Inflation Board," *Canadian Public Policy*, March 1986, pp. 133–47.

3. See *Proceedings and Evidence of the Standing Committee on Finance, Trade and Economic Affairs*, No. 66, Ottawa, November 6, 1975; "Remarks by Gerald K. Bouey, Governor of the Bank of Canada," *Bank of Canada Review*, October 1975, pp. 23–30; "Remarks by R.W. Lawson, Senior Deputy Governor of the Bank of Canada, *Bank of Canada Review*, April 1976, pp. 17–26; and *Bank of Canada Annual Report of the Governor to the Minister of Finance and Statements of Accounts for the Year*, 1975 and 1976.

was slowed by the Anti-Inflation Board's constraints, the Canadian dollar grew stronger on foreign exchange markets, and fiscal expansion was contained. Toward the end of 1978, however, the downward trend in the underlying rate of inflation reversed, and by 1979 prices again started to advance at a double-digit pace.

With the return to a more rapid rate of inflation accompanied by high market rates of interest and no appreciable decline in the rate of unemployment, some observers concluded that the Bank's policy of restraining the rate of growth of M1 was misguided. Protagonists argued that the major effect of the Bank's policy was slower growth in the economy and an increase in the unemployment rate, with little effect on the rate of inflation.[4]

By 1980 the Bank of Canada realized that its implementation of monetary gradualism was too gradual for coping with inflation. For example, in a statement before the House of Commons Standing Committee on Finance, Trade and Economic Affairs in 1980, the governor of the Bank said:

> *The experience of the past few years appears to have led some observers to conclude that the Bank's approach to reducing inflation has failed. If they mean that progress in reducing inflation is less than the Bank hoped, I agree with them. But if they mean, as I think some of them do, that the Bank's approach was misconceived, then they have misread the history of the period. What they should conclude is that given the economic and financial developments over that period, many of which were unpredictable, it would have been better if the slowing of monetary growth had been less gradual so that it would have had more impact on inflation. That is the moral that should be drawn. In this connection I would point out that the rate of monetary expansion today is very much lower than it was five years ago and although we had arrived at this position through a very gradual process, the impact on total spending can be expected to be much firmer from now on than it was when we started on this path.[5]*

The Bank's approach of monetary deceleration was too gradual because much of the decline in M1 was offset by increases in its velocity of circulation due to financial innovations induced by higher levels of interest rates. For example, the demand for M1 shifted considerably with the introduction of daily-interest savings and chequing accounts and the development of cash management techniques for corporate accounts. Because of these financial innovations, M1 ceased to be a reliable guide to monetary policy.[6] Some economists argued that the Bank should have used a broader monetary aggregate as its target and that it should have implemented its policy by changes in the monetary base rather than by managing short-term interest rates.[7]

---

4. The vanguard of the attack was led by the Canadian Institute for Economic Policy. See, for example, the following two studies sponsored by the Institute: A.W. Donner and D.D. Peters, *The Monetarist Counter-Revolution: A Critique of Canadian Monetary Policy 1975–1979*; and C.L. Barber and J.C.P. McCallum, *Unemployment and Inflation: The Canadian Experience.*

5. Reprinted in *Bank of Canada Review,* November 1980, p. 17.

6. See Charles Freedman, "Financial Innovation in Canada: Courses and Consequences," *American Economic Review 73* (May 1983), pp. 101–06.

7. See Thomas J. Courchene, *Money, Inflation, and the Bank of Canada, Volume II: An Analysis of Monetary Gradualism, 1975–80* (Montreal: C.D. Howe Institute, 1981).

In November 1982 the Bank of Canada announced that it was abandoning the practice of establishing M1 targets. This came as no surprise, since in the previous two years it had already reduced the growth rate of M1 and at times allowed it to remain well below its target levels. Even before its November announcement, the Bank had already shifted from stabilizing monetary growth rates to stabilizing the exchange rates of the Canadian dollar, particularly in relation to its U.S. counterpart. Some economists argued that ever since 1978 the Bank had given more priority to the exchange rate than was consistent with monetary targeting.

Over the period 1981 to 1984, the Bank followed a very restrictive monetary policy with high interest rates. Starting in mid-1981 and continuing through the end of 1982, Canada, along with most other countries, experienced the most severe recession since the Great Depression of the 1930s. Inflation did not start to decline noticeably, however, before 1983. The federal government helped in the battle against inflation with its "6 and 5" program, introduced in 1982. It restricted wage increases in the federal public service and in Crown corporations to 6 percent in the first year and 5 percent in the second year. The private sector was asked to follow these guidelines but was not forced to do so.

Despite lower rates of inflation and relatively high rates of unemployment after 1982, the Bank of Canada did not significantly reverse its policy of monetary deceleration until 1985. Many economists believe that the Bank resisted lower interest rates because it feared that the consequent depreciation of the Canadian dollar against its U.S. counterpart would reignite inflation.[8] It was only after the Bank weakened its resistance against currency depreciation that it reversed its restrictive monetary policy. While it can be argued that the Bank's initial policy to control inflation was too slow and too weak, it can also be argued that its reluctance to allow the exchange rate to depreciate after the fight with inflation had been won unduly delayed recovery in the Canadian economy from the severe recession of 1981–82.

The Quest for Price Stability

In January 1988, the newly appointed Bank of Canada governor, John Crow, in his Hanson Memorial Lecture at the University of Alberta, explicitly announced that price stability was the Bank's long-term goal of monetary policy. According to the governor:

> *Monetary policy should be conducted so as to achieve a pace of monetary expansion that promotes stability in the value of money. This means pursuing a policy aimed at achieving and maintaining stable prices.*[9]

---

8. See Peter Howitt, *Monetary Policy in Transition: A Study of Bank of Canada Policy, 1982–85* (Montreal: C.D. Howe Institute, 1986).

9. John Crow, "The Work of Monetary Policy," *Bank of Canada Review,* February 1988, p. 4.

Over the next few years, in frequent speeches and appearances the governor underlined his quest for price stability, which became widely interpreted to imply a goal of zero inflation. The merits of achieving such a goal became a subject for debate by economists. Central to the debate was the question of whether the long-term benefits to society from zero inflation would outweigh the short-run costs associated with reducing monetary growth so as to achieve the long-run inflation target. The benefits enjoyed from a zero inflation rate are the avoidance of the costs associated with high and variable rates of inflation. These costs relate to the capricious redistribution of income and wealth, resource misallocation, and inefficiencies in the payments system. On the other hand, the short-run costs of reducing monetary growth to achieve zero inflation take the form of lost output and higher unemployment over the transitional period.

Starting in 1987, excess demand pressures again pushed the rate of inflation up, especially in Quebec and Ontario. The Bank of Canada responded with a much more restrictive monetary policy, which resulted in higher short-term interest rates and appreciation of the Canadian dollar. Beginning in 1990, the economy showed signs of slowing down and by the end of the year it was pronounced to be in recession.

On February 26, 1991, the governor of the Bank of Canada, in a joint announcement with the minister of finance, set out targets for reducing the rate of inflation to achieve price stability. The targets were specified in terms of the year-over-year increases in the consumer price index:

- 3 percent by the end of the year 1992
- 2.5 percent by the middle of 1994
- 2 percent by the end of 1995

Thereafter, further reductions in inflation were to be made until price stability was secured. From the Bank of Canada's point of view, price stability implied increases in the inflation rate of less than 2 percent per year.

The announcement of inflation targets for the framing of monetary policy over the intermediate run did not signal a change in the Bank's policy. The Bank had already been following a tight money policy since the late 1980s. The verbalization of the set inflation targets was aimed at providing the public with an anchor on which to base its inflationary expectations. In addition, it was intended to show that the adjustment to lower inflation and to price stability would be sustained.

Already after the first year, there were indications that the Bank's inflation targets were working and gaining credibility. Inflationary expectations were reduced dramatically and were reflected by labour's more modest demands for wage increases. Since interest rates fell, the Bank allowed the money supply to grow faster than was consistent with its intermediate-term inflation targets. This, however, is what one would have expected to accommodate the increase in the demand for money resulting from lower interest rates. The one disquieting note was the increase in the unemployment rate, which suggested that the short-run transitional costs in the quest for price stability could indeed be quite high.

In December 1993 the Bank and the federal government announced the objective of maintaining annual increases in the Consumer Price Index between 1 and 3 percent. This statement was meant to further bolster the credibility of the Bank's price stability objective. Indeed, the public statement that announced the commitment to price stability began with the premise that monetary policy should be concerned only with price stability:

> *High levels of economic growth and employment on a sustained basis are the primary objectives of monetary and fiscal policies. The best contribution that monetary policy can make to these objectives is to preserve confidence in the value of money by achieving price stability.*[10]

Critics of Bank of Canada policy argued that the pursuit of price stability caused the first "made in Canada" recession, in the early 1990s.[11] The unemployment rate rose on a national basis to above 10 percent, where it remained well into the mid-1990s. Some economists attributed the increase in unemployment to the Bank's high interest rate policy and a relatively noncompetitive banking system. When several chartered banks reported annual profits in excess of $1 billion, public criticism of the price stability objective came once again to the forefront of debate over monetary policy in Canada.

Figure 25–1 plots the actual change in the Consumer Price Index as well as its target band under the price stability objective. In the early 1990s the rate of increase in consumer prices fell well below the target band. Many economists believed the Bank of Canada induced a recession via the implementation of contractionary monetary policies (the price stability objective), and in 1994 Governor Crow was not reappointed when his term expired. At that point, Deputy Governor Gordon Thiessen took over the reigns. His term as governor of the Bank of Canada expires early in 2001.

core rate of inflation *the rate of inflation, net of changes in the prices of food, indirect taxes, and regulated prices*

Research at the Bank of Canada and elsewhere suggested that the inflation targets should be set in terms of the **core rate of inflation**: the underlying rate of inflation, net of changes in the prices of food (which can fluctuate with random changes in weather), indirect taxes, and regulated prices (such as energy prices and the price of communications services like telephones or cable).[12] Figure 25–1 demonstrates that the inflation rate calculated on the basis of the CPI less food, energy, and indirect taxes is much different from that based on the entire CPI. This was particularly true for 1994, when in an attempt to reduce smuggling, the federal government lowered taxes on tobacco products (thereby leading to a reduction in the rate of inflation—based on the entire CPI—to negative values in 1994).

---

10. *Bank of Canada Review*, Winter 1993–94.

11. For more on the critics and the Bank of Canada's response, see Pierre Fortin, "The Great Canadian Slump," *Canadian Journal of Economics* 29, 1996, pp. 761–89, Charles Freedman and Tiff Macklem, "A Comment on 'The Great Canadian Slump,'" *Canadian Journal of Economics* 31, 1998, pp. 646–65; and Pierre Fortin, "The Great Canadian Slump: A Rejoinder to Freedman and Macklem," *Canadian Journal of Economics* 32, 1999, pp. 1082–92.

12. See A. Dexter, et al., "Freely Determined versus Regulated Prices: Implications for the Measured Link Between Money and Inflation," *Journal of Money, Credit and Banking* 25 (May 1993), pp. 222–30, for some empirical work in this area.

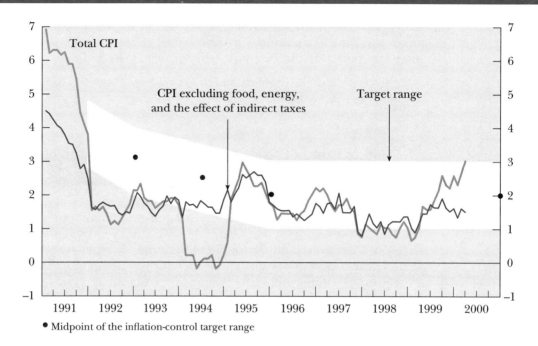

FIGURE 25–1   **CONSUMER PRICE INDEX**

* Midpoint of the inflation-control target range

As you can see, the Bank of Canada has maintained its target rate of inflation since late 1993.

SOURCE: Bank of Canada, *Monetary Policy Report*, May 2000, page 6.

As you can see from Figure 25–1, the Bank of Canada has had success in maintaining "price stability" in terms of its desire to see the inflation rate fall within a range of 1 to 3 percent. The price stability objective is the subject of considerable research at the Bank of Canada today, since the government and the Bank are committed to re-evaluating the target, and its range, by 2002. For example, empirical work at the Bank of Canada suggests that the CPI contains an inflationary bias of somewhat less than 1 percent—so it may not be the "best" indicator of inflation to use in setting policy.[13] Critics of the Bank's policies point to the potential for measurement errors in their attack on the price stability objective. Nevertheless, the Bank believes inflation control is the key to sustaining positive economic growth:

> *Canada has made significant progress in restoring the credibility of its macro-economic policies and making the adjustments necessary to lay the foundation for a more efficient, prosperous economy in the future.... The best contribution the Bank of Canada can make to sustaining these positive trends is to foster a monetary environment of confidence and stability. And that is what we intend to deliver with our commitment to targets for inflation control.[14]*

13. See Alan Crawford, *Measurement Biases in the Canadian CPI.* Technical Report 64 (Ottawa: Bank of Canada).

14. Bank of Canada, *Monetary Policy Report,* May 1997 (Ottawa: Bank of Canada), p. 2

BOX 25–1 CANADIAN INFLATION-CONTROL STRATEGY

Inflation Control and the Economy

- Inflation control is not an end in itself; it is the means whereby monetary policy contributes to solid economic performance.
- Low inflation allows the economy to function more effectively and thereby contributes to better growth over time.
- Inflation-control targets ensure that monetary policy works to moderate cyclical fluctuations in income and employment. These targets help the Bank to make more accurate judgments about the growth potential of the economy.

The Monetary Policy Instrument

- The Bank of Canada uses its influence on short-term interest rates to achieve a rate of monetary expansion consistent with the inflation-control target range. The transmission mechanism is complex and involves long and variable lags—the impact on inflation from changes in monetary conditions is usually spread over six to eight quarters.

The Targets

- In February 1991, the federal government and the Bank of Canada jointly announced a series of targets for reducing inflation to the midpoint of a range of 1 to 3 per cent by the end of 1995. In December 1993, this target range was extended to the end of 1998. In February 1998, it was extended again to the end of 2001.
- By the end of 2001, the government and the Bank of Canada plan to determine the long-run target for monetary policy consistent with price stability.

Monitoring Inflation

- In the short run, there is a good deal of movement in the CPI caused by transitory fluctuations in the prices of food and energy, as well as by changes in indirect taxes. For this reason, the Bank focuses on the CPI excluding food, energy, and the effect of indirect taxes. This measure is referred to as the *core CPI*.
- Over longer periods, the measures of inflation based on the total CPI and the core CPI tend to follow similar paths. In the event of persistent differences between the trends of the two measures, the Bank would adjust its desired path for core CPI inflation so that total CPI inflation would come within the target range.

SOURCE: Bank of Canada, *Monetary Policy Report*, May 2000, p. 6.

Operational Targets

monetary conditions index (MCI)
a blend of interest rates and exchange rates, meant to convey the stance of monetary conditions

THE MONETARY CONDITIONS INDEX   For several years the Bank used a **monetary conditions index** (**MCI**) to gauge the operational aspects of its price stability objective. The MCI plotted in Figure 25–2 is a combination of the exchange rate (the C-6 index) and short-term interest rates, and is meant to be an operational target.

The reasoning goes something like the following. If the economy were to experience an exogenous increase in aggregate demand, the inflation rate might rise—and exceed the upper target band. This would call for contractionary monetary policies, which would raise interest rates and the value of the

FIGURE 25–2 **MONETARY CONDITIONS INDEX**

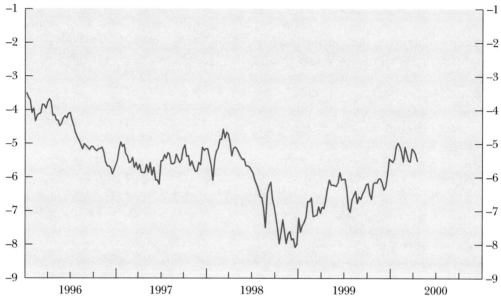

Wednesdays, January 1987 = 0

The Monetary Conditions Index provides information on the state of monetary conditions, as measured by the C-6 exchange rate and short-term interest rates.

Source: Bank of Canada, *Monetary Policy Report,* May 2000.

dollar. How far should this contractionary monetary policy go? How intense should it be? Just enough to bring monetary conditions back into line with the inflation objectives. But how does one measure monetary conditions? Sector-specific shocks to aggregate demand will have differential effects on interest rates and the exchange rate (say, for example, that the initial shock was that international investor confidence in the dollar fell and the dollar lost value). And trying to gauge monetary conditions based on just interest rates or just the exchange rate won't tell the whole story (of how the shock affects financial markets and the economy). So the use of a monetary conditions index, which blends changes in interest rates with changes in exchange rates (from some base period), will capture the salient features of these disturbances that may take the system away from price stability—requiring a monetary response. The Bank of Canada has used the MCI as a gauge and an operational target for monetary policies.

Now the Bank of Canada is the first to admit that monetary policy cannot be set purely based in some mechanistic fashion using the MCI.[15] And the Bank of Canada is not the only central bank to adopt an MCI for use in policy. (Central banks in Sweden and Norway use their own MCIs). However, critics

15. See Charles Freedman, *The Use of Indicators and of the Monetary Conditions Index in Canada, The Transmission of Monetary Policy in Canada* (Ottawa: Bank of Canada, 1996), pp. 67–80.

argue that MCIs are of dubious merit. For example, Eika, Ericsson, and Nymoen argue that the statistical models on which MCIs are constructed change as the structure of the economy changes; hence, MCIs based on historical relationships become unreliable over time. They argue that it is possible to use more sophisticated methods to construct a gauge by which economic policy—monetary policy in particular—could be set, but that central banks need to specify their objectives carefully during the process of constructing and evaluating their objective targets.

OVERNIGHT FINANCING RATE   How does the Bank actually implement policy on a day-to-day basis? Through its setting of the overnight financing rate, its primary instrument of monetary policy. As we learned previously, since February 1996, the Bank has established a target range in which it wants the overnight financing rate to lie, with the operational target the midpoint of the band. By intervening in the settlements process, the Bank of Canada directly affects the liquidity of the financial system, thereby achieving its target for the overnight interest rate. If there appears to be pressure for the overnight financing rate to rise above its targeted level, the Bank engages in a Special PRA to raise liquidity, which tends to bring the overnight rate back to its target. When the overnight financing rate falls below its target, the Bank of Canada undertakes a Special SRA to reduce liquidity and restore the overnight rate to its desired level.

The Bank also changes the target band to affect the level of aggregate demand in the economy. Figure 25–3 plots the overnight financing rate along with the operating band. Early in 2000, the Bank raised the operating band by 25 basis points, matching similar changes in U.S. interest rates, and in May

FIGURE 25–3 THE OVERNIGHT FINANCING RATE AND ITS TARGET RANGE

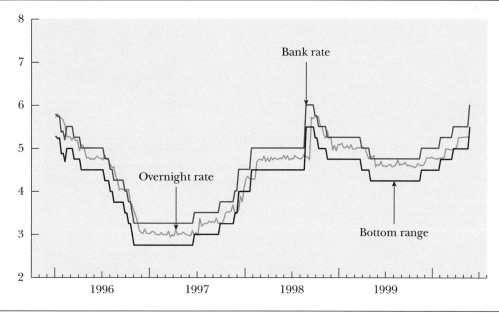

SOURCE: Statistics Canada, CANSIM DATABASE, Series B114038, B113862, May 2000.

2000, the Bank of Canada raised the band by a further 50 basis points the day after the Federal Reserve raised its interest rate target by 50 basis points. All of these increases are aimed at dampening increases in aggregate demand and thereby inflationary pressures, which both central banks thought were building throughout the North American economy.

Many economists were critical of the Bank of Canada's matching the hike in U.S. interest rates in May 2000. They believed that the Canadian economy was not experiencing significant inflationary pressures, as was the United States, and argued that Canadian monetary policy was overly concerned with how a widening interest rate differential would affect the value of the Canadian dollar. What they perhaps failed to consider was that central banks know that monetary policy operates with long and variable lags. Changes in interest rates have an impact on inflation and output some six to eight quarters into the future. While those shifts in interest rates may not appear to be consistent with current economic conditions, the central bank needs to consider where the economy will be in two years, and act accordingly, today. As Governor Thiessen indicated in a speech in New York early in 2000,

> *Up to now, our inflation performance has been somewhat better than we had expected.... This good inflation performance bodes well for the continued expansion of the Canadian economy. But what remains to be seen is whether this expansion will bring with it strong productivity gains for Canada similar to those witnessed in the United States. One thing is clear. The job of the Bank of Canada must be to keep inflation in Canada low and stable. Without that, we will be risking both the economic expansion and the potential productivity gains.[16]*

Finally, Michael Parkin provided an interesting essay on how monetary policy should be used to influence unemployment and inflation.[17] He concluded that "[t]he monetary authority should set a short-term interest rate according to a contingency rule to target zero inflation and, to the extent possible, smooth out fluctuations in unemployment." As we have seen, this is easier said than done.

The Lessons To Be Learned

Our review of monetary policy shows that in retrospect one can always discover policy errors. In a world of incomplete information, the conduct of monetary policy is at best one of successive approximation, with the hope that on balance the preponderance of policy initiatives turns out to be right. To expect more is to expect too much.

---

16. See Gordon Thiessen, "The Conduct of Monetary Policy When You Live Next Door to a Large Neighbour," Remarks to the Canadian Society of New York, March 2000.

17. Michael Parkin, "Unemployment, Inflation, and Monetary Policy," *Canadian Journal of Economics* 31, 1998, pp. 1003–32.

BOX 25–2   BACK TO THE FUTURE?

In its *Monetary Policy Report* of May 2000, the Bank of Canada noted that higher energy prices could raise inflation. Here's what the Bank said:

Rising Oil Prices: Implications for Inflation

The large swings in crude oil prices over the past two years and their effect on the total CPI underscore the importance of focusing monetary policy on a measure of core inflation that looks through such volatile factors. With major production cutbacks and stronger world demand, crude oil prices rose, on balance, by about 80 percent from just over U.S.$14 per barrel in October 1998 to about U.S.$25 per barrel in early April 2000. This largely explains the substantial jump in both gasoline and fuel oil prices at the consumer level and, in turn, most of the recent rise in the rate of increase in the total CPI—from less than 1 percent at the beginning of 1999 to 3 percent currently.

Prices for gasoline and fuel oil are highly sensitive to fluctuations in the international supply of and demand for crude oil. Changes in these prices are the most important first-round effect on the CPI from variations in crude oil prices. Swings in crude oil prices can also have first-round effects on the core CPI because energy costs represent an important share of the total costs of activities such as air and truck transportation and the manufacture of plastic products. Along with such cost-based effects on the core CPI, there could be second-round influences on wages and other prices if these first-round effects feed into expectations of higher ongoing inflation.

To date, the first-round effects on the core of CPI of the increase in crude oil prices appear to have been small. As of March, the estimated impact on the core CPI is less than 0.1 percent (mainly air fares), because of such factors as long-term contracts, the continued intense degree of competition in the retail sector, and the difficulty of passing on higher costs in the form of price increases. This contrasts with the estimated long-run effect on the level of the core CPI of a permanent 80 percent increase in oil prices (if there is full pass-through into consumer prices and no further major change in oil prices) of 0.5 to 0.7 percent. This longer-term effect would likely be spread over a period of more than one year. Moreover, in the current competitive environment, this long-run estimate should be considered an upper limit, since firms would be expected to achieve some cost savings through substitution towards cheaper sources of energy and by economizing on energy use.

By excluding energy prices from the core CPI, monetary authorities can better assess the underlying trend of inflation and, therefore, of future movements in inflation.* By focusing on a core inflation measure, the Bank has made it clear that it is prepared to accommodate the first-round effects of short-term movements in crude oil prices on the total CPI. Second-round effects, however, will not be accommodated. In the current circumstances, the impact of the sharp increase in crude oil prices on the total CPI appears to have been restricted to first-round effects. However, the Bank will be watching closely for significant evidence of broader second-round effects. If crude oil prices remain near U.S.$25, or fall further, the Bank expects that the total CPI will start to move down toward the core rate during the second quarter of this year.

In the 1970s, higher energy prices were presumed to have "caused" higher inflation. The Bank doesn't appear to believe the total CPI will move permanently away from the core CPI. Were they right? Explain.

---

* A similar principle of exclusion, or reduced weighting, of the more volatile CPI components is used to construct alternative statistical measures of trend inflation, such as CPIX and CPIW. Indeed, gasoline, fuel oil, and natural gas are three of the eight most volatile CPI components excluded from the CPIX measure. Also excluded from CPIX (but not from core CPI) is intercity public transportation (mainly air fares), which is very sensitive to oil prices.

KEY TERMS

core rate of inflation
monetary conditions index (MCI)

monetary gradualism
price ceilings

REVIEW QUESTIONS

1. What role did monetary policy play during the Second World War and in the period immediately after the war?
2. Why has the period between 1957 and 1960 been characterized as "the money muddle"?
3. How have the different exchange rate regimes affected the Bank of Canada's domestic policy objectives?
4. Describe how the Bank of Canada attempted to deal with inflation during the 1970s and early 1980s. Was it successful?
5. Outline the arguments in favour of price stability as the objective of monetary policy. Now argue against price stability. What is the current approach to monetary policy in Canada? Explain.

6. The Bank of Canada believes that higher energy prices will not necessarily raise the core inflation rate in Canada. Explain their reasoning and whether their predictions were realized in 2000.
7. Some economists believe the Bank of Canada caused the first made-in-Canada recession. Provide four reasons that support this view.
8. The Bank of Canada does not believe its critics when they say that the central bank created the recession of the early 1990s. Explain the reasons put forward by Bank economists in their defence of the Bank, and provide four criticisms of their analysis.
9. Is inflation too low? Would a higher rate of inflation make society better off? Explain.

SELECTED READINGS

Bank of Canada. *Annual Report of the Governor to the Minister of Finance.* Ottawa: Various Issues.

Binhammer, H.H. "Canada's Foreign Exchange Problems: A Review." *Kyklos* 17 (Nov. 4, 1964). Reprinted in John J. Deutsch et al., eds. *The Canadian Economy: Selected Readings*, rev. ed. Toronto: Macmillan, 1965.

Binhammer, Helmut, and L.C. McDonough. "The Canadian–U.S. Dollar Exchange Rate: History and Policy Issues," in W. Milberg and P. Bartholomew. *Research in International Business and Finance.* Greenwich, CT: JAI Press Inc., 1990, pp. 51–68.

Bouey, Gerald K. "Monetary Policy—Finding a Place to Stand." The 1982 Per Jacobssen Lecture, Toronto, September 5, 1982. Reprinted in Bank of Canada Review, September 1982.

Cairns, James P., H.H. Binhammer, and Robin Boadway. *Canadian Banking and Monetary Policy.* Toronto: McGraw-Hill Ryerson, 1972.

Canada. Government of Canada. *Policies for Price Stability.* Ottawa: Queen's Printer, 1968.

———. Senate. *Report of the Special Committee of the Senate on Manpower and Employment.* Ottawa: Queen's Printer, 1961.

———. *Report of the Standing Committee on National Finance, Growth, Employment and Price Stability.* Ottawa: Information Canada, 1971.

Courchene, Thomas J. *Monetarism and Controls: The Inflation Fighters.* Montreal: C.D. Howe Institute, 1976.

———. *Money, Inflation and the Bank of Canada: An Analysis of Canadian Monetary Policy from 1970 to Early 1975.* Montreal: C.D. Howe Institute, 1976.

———. *The Strategy of Gradualism: An Analysis of Bank of Canada Policy from Mid-1975 to Mid-1977.* Montreal: C.D. Howe Institute, 1977.

Courchene, Thomas J., Pierre Fortin, Gordon R. Sparks, and William R. White. "Monetary Policy in Canada: A Symposium." *Canadian Journal of Economics*, November 1979, pp. 590–646.

Crawford, Alan. *Measurement Biases in the Canadian CPI.* Technical Report No. 64. Ottawa: Bank of Canada, 1993.

Dexter, A., D. Levi, and B. Nault. "Freely Determined versus Regulated Prices: Implications for the Measured Link Between Money and Inflation." Journal of Money, Credit and Banking 25 (May 1993), pp. 222–30.

Dufour, Jean-Marie, and Daniel Racette. "Monetary Control in Canada," in *Fiscal and Monetary Policy*, research coordinator John Sargent. Collected Research Studies of the Royal Commission on the Economic Union and Development Prospects for Canada, No. 21. Toronto: University of Toronto Press, 1986.

Eika, Kari, Neil Ericsson, and Raynar Nymoen. *Hazards in Implementing a Monetary Conditions Index.* International Finance Discussion Paper 568. New York: Board of Governors of the Federal Reserve System, October 1996.

Fortin, Pierre. "The Great Canadian Slump." *Canadian Journal of Economics* 29, 1996, pp. 761–89.

———. "The Great Canadian Slump: A Rejoinder to Freedman and Macklem." *Canadian Journal of Economics* 32, 1999, pp. 1082–92.

Freedman, Charles. *The Use of Indicators and of the Monetary Conditions Index in Canada: The Transmission of Monetary Policy in Canada.* Ottawa: Bank of Canada, 1996, pp. 67–80.

Freedman, Charles and Tiff Macklem, "A Comment on 'The Great Canadian Slump.'" *Canadian Journal of Economics* 31, 1998, pp. 646–65.

Howitt, Peter. *Monetary Policy in Transition: A Study of Bank of Canada Policy, 1982–85.* Montreal: C.D. Howe Institute, 1986.

Lipsey, Richard, ed. *Zero Inflation: The Goal of Price Stability.* Toronto: C.D. Howe Institute, 1990.

Parkin, Michael. "Unemployment, Inflation, and Monetary Policy." *Canadian Journal of Economics* 31, 1998, pp. 1003–32.

Selody, Jack. *The Goal of Price Stability: A Review of the Issues.* Technical Report No. 54. Ottawa: Bank of Canada, 1990.

Sparks, Gordon R. "The Theory and Practice of Monetary Policy in Canada: 1945–83," in *Fiscal and Monetary Policy*, research coordinator John Sargent. Collected Research Studies of the Royal Commission on the Economic Union and Development Prospects for Canada, No. 21. Toronto: University of Toronto Press, 1986.

Thiessen, Gordon. "The Canadian Experience with Monetary Targeting," in *Central Bank Views on Monetary Targeting*. New York: Federal Reserve Bank of New York, 1982.

———. "The Conduct of Monetary Policy When You Live Next Door to a Large Neighbour." Remarks to the Canadian Society of New York, March 2000.

York, Robert C., ed. *Taking Aim: The Debate on Zero Inflation.* Toronto: C.D. Howe Institute, 1990.

GLOSSARY

absolute PPP   The exchange rate should be the ratio of the domestic price of a commodity relative to its foreign price.

absolute price   The price of one good in terms of the price of money.

Act Granting Additional Facilities in Commercial Transactions   A distinctive feature of Canadian banking that allowed banks early on to make loans secured by warehouse receipts.

adaptive expectations   Expectations formed by looking backwards; an average of past changes.

adverse selection   Tendency of worse risks to buy insurance, and of better risks not to buy it.

aggregate demand management policies   Economic policies aimed at manipulating the level of aggregate demand in the economy.

amero   The name suggested for the currency in a North American Currency Union.

amortized   When the principal amount borrowed is gradually repaid, along with interest during the life of the financial claim.

annuities   Bonds that promise to make equal annual payments until maturity.

annuity contract   A contract that provides income payments for a specified period.

annuity factor   Used to calculate the value of an annuity.

arbitrage   The simultaneous purchase (sale) in one market and sale (purchase) in another to profit from price differences across markets.

Arbitrage Pricing Theory (APT)   An alternative to the CAPM that assumes multiple sources (factors).

asked   The price at which someone is willing to sell.

asset transformation   Transformitory claims on borrowers into claims on intermediaries.

asymmetric information   Refers to imperfect distribution of information, allowing one party to a transaction to take unfair advantage of the other.

auction market   A market in which trades result from an organized bidding process.

availability doctrine   The idea that monetary policy works through restricting the availability of credit, and its effects on lenders.

balance of payments   A summary of all economic transactions between a country's residents and nonresidents during a given period.

bancor   The name for an international reserve asset proposed by John Maynard Keynes.

***Bank Act* of 1871**   The first permanent legislation governing Canadian commercial banks.

Bank of Canada   Canada's central bank.

Bank Rate   The rate of interest at which members of the Canadian Payments Association may borrow from the Bank of Canada.

bankers' acceptance   A time draft drawn on a bank by a borrower ordering the bank to pay a certain amount on a specified future date.

banking school   A view that bank deposits and circulating bills of exchange should be included in the definition of the money supply.

barter economy   An economy without money—all trade is based on exchange of goods and services.

base money   The monetary base comprising Bank of Canada notes and settlement balances held by the direct clearers with the Bank.

Basel Accord   An agreement among the Group of Ten countries covering regulatory risk-weighted capital requirements for internationally active banks.

Basel Concordant   An agreement among the Group of Ten countries establishing the principle that the home country is responsible for supervising the global operations of international banks in its jurisdiction.

basis   The cash price, or spot price, less the futures prices.

basis risk   Risk due to the fact that changes in the prices of futures contracts do not perfectly offset changes in the prices of assets being hedged.

beta   A measure of the systematic risk of an asset.

bid   The price at which someone is willing to buy.

bid–asked spread   The difference between the price at which someone is willing to buy and the price at which someone is willing to sell.

bilateral arbitrage   Arbitrage between two markets.

bilateral netting systems   A netting arrangement that periodically aggregates payments between counter-parties and calculates one payment per currency for each pair of counter-parties.

bimetallic standard   A metallic coin standard based on two metals.

BIS Capital Accord   International agreement for minimum capital requirements for banks.

black (parallel) markets   Illegal markets in controlled currencies.

bond   A promise by its issuer to pay a principal amount of money at a specified maturity date and, usually, to make regular interest payments in the interim.

book-based transactions   Transactions made by electronic book entry.

bought deal   The purchase by securities dealers of the entire issue of new securities for distribution.

brady bonds   Bonds issued under the Brady Plan for debt reduction and rescheduling.

branch banking   Where banks serve the public in different locations through branches.

brassage   A fee charged to cover the costs of coinage.

Bretton Woods System   The international monetary systems in existence from 1947 to August 1971, based on the concept of the adjustable peg for exchange rates.

brokerage fees   Charges made by intermediaries for cash withdrawal, transportation costs to and from the intermediary, and the subjective cost of having to make regular trips to get cash.

brokered deposits   Deposits placed by money brokers.

brokers   Parties acting as agents who bring buyers and sellers together.

Business Development Bank of Canada (BDC)   A federal government institution that provides specialized financing and business counselling to create and develop small and medium-sized businesses.

C-6 index   The value of the Canadian dollar relative to the currencies of the G-10 nations as well as those in the European Monetary Union.

call loans   Loans to securities brokers and dealers to finance their inventories of securities.

call option   An option giving its holder the right to buy financial assets.

Canada Deposit Insurance Corporation (CDIC)   The body that provides deposit insurance in all provinces except Quebec.

Canada Investment and Saving   The federal government agency responsible for all of the government's retail debt operations.

Canada Mortgage and Housing Corporation (CMHC)   A federal government institution that provides residential mortgage loan insurance and administers the government's financial assistance for housing.

Canadian Investor Protection Fund   A fund that protects the interests of investors.

Canadian Payments Association (CPA)   An association charged with clearing cheques for all financial institutions in Canada.

capital account   Net flows, both private and official (government), as a result of changes in Canadian claims on nonresidents and of changes in Canadian liabilities to nonresidents.

Capital Asset Pricing Model (CAPM)   A model that shows how the rate of return (or, alternatively, the price of an asset) is determined in an efficient market.

capital inflows   An increase in Canadian liabilities to nonresidents, or a decrease in Canadian claims on nonresidents.

capital market line (CML)   The efficient frontier of combined portfolios given the four underlying assumptions of the CAPM.

capital markets   Where assets with terms to maturity more than three years are traded.

capital outflows   A decrease in Canadian liabilities held by nonresidents, or an increase in Canadian claims on nonresidents.

capital-value intermediation   When the market value of the liabilities an intermediary issues against itself fluctuates less than the market value of the public's liabilities held by the institutions in their portfolios.

cash back   When debit cards are used to withdraw cash.

cash reserves   Cash held by financial institutions to meet the demand for cash.

cash setting   The Bank of Canada's use of drawdowns and redeposits to adjust the settlement of balances of the direct clearers following daily clearings.

cash surrender value   Accumulated savings in a policy paid at its termination.

cash-balance approach   A theory of the demand for money based on the transactions demand for money.

cash-balance equation   A relationship between the demand for money and nominal income.

Cedel   Depository for the settlement and clearing of foreign stock issues.

charters   Statutory authority to operate a bank requires a charter obtained by a special act of Parliament.

clean float policy   A policy of infrequent intervention in exchange markets.

clearing drain   The loss of cash reserves by one bank to another.

clearinghouse   An arrangement among depository institutions for settling balances that result from accepting one another's cheques and payments orders issued by their respective depositors.

clearing system   The system for collecting and processing cheques and other payment items.

closed mortgages   Mortgages that do not allow unscheduled payments.

closed-end investment companies   Investment companies that issue a fixed number of shares to invest in a portfolio of assets.

collar agreements   Agreements that combine buying a cap and writing a floor in which the cap rate differs from the floor rate.

commercial loan theory   Banks should make short-term self-liquidating loans.

commercial paper   Notes issued by nonfinancial corporations to borrow funds for short periods.

Committee of European Economic Cooperation (CEEC)   Committee formed in Europe to deal with post–Second World War recovery and aid programs.

commodity reserve dollar   Proposed by Benjamin Graham whereby the value of the dollar would be defined in terms of a specified bundle of commodities.

commodity reserve standard   When the monetary unit of account is defined in terms of a fixed combination of storable commodities other than metals.

commodity standard   A monetary system in which the value of the monetary unit is kept equal to the value of a specific quantity of a particular commodity or commodities.

common stock   A class of shares that represents ownership or equity in a business.

compounding   When an asset earns interest that is reinvested, generating additional income on both the principal and interest earned.

conditionality   A term employed by the IMF that refers to restrictions it imposes on borrowing countries.

conflict of interest   Where a financial institution must choose between its own interests and those of a client on whose behalf it is acting or whom it is advising.

contagion   The failure of one bank that sets off runs on other banks.

conventional mortgages   Mortgages not insured to the CMHC but that may be insured by a private investor.

convertible bonds   These bonds allow their holders to exchange them for another financial instrument, generally common stock.

core rate of inflation   The rate of inflation, net of changes in the prices of food, indirect taxes, and regulated prices.

corporate governance   Refers to rules, procedures, and standards of behaviour.

correlation coefficient   A measure of linear association; positive values suggest a direct relationship between two or more series, while negative values indicate that when one series rises, the other falls.

cost of carry   The cost of holding an asset until its delivery.

coupon rate   The yearly interest payment on a debt instrument divided by its face amount.

covariance   A measure of the degree to which two or more data series are linearly related.

covered (hedged) return   The return from an investment strategy in which futures or forward contracts have been employed to manage risk.

covered interest arbitrage   Arbitrage positions in which futures or forward markets have been used to set a price for delivery of an asset in the future.

covered interest rate parity   A relationship linking interest rates, exchange rates, and futures or forward exchange rates across nations.

Coyne Affair   The controversy between the government and the governor of the Bank of Canada that ended with the resignation of James Coyne, the governor.

crawling peg   The exchange rate is held fixed in the short run but is adjusted at regular intervals to reflect supply and demand conditions.

credibility   The extent to which the market believes what policy-makers have to say.

credit   Savings available to be lent to deficit economic units.

credit enhancement   Used to improve the marketability of the securities created through loan securitization.

credit transactions   Receiving payments from nonresidents.

cumulative computed settlement balance   The cumulative weighted sum of the daily settlement balances.

currency drain   The withdrawal of currency from the banking system into public circulation.

currency in public circulation   Currency outside banks and other financial institutions.

currency school   A view that only bank notes and coin supply made up the money supply.

currency swap   The exchange of debt or assets denominated in one currency for debt or assets denominated in another currency.

current account   The values of the flow of goods and services and other current receipts and payments between residents of Canada and residents of the rest of the world.

current accounts   Chequable bank accounts used by businesses for transactions purposes.

current yield   The annual interest payment divided by the price paid.

dealers   Parties acting as principals who underwrite and hold inventories of securities for resale.

debentures   Bonds secured by a claim on the general creditworthiness of the issuer.

debit cards   Cards that can be used to withdraw cash.

debit transactions   Making payments to nonresidents.

debt   A legal obligation to pay a specified amount at a specified time.

debt management   The management of the federal debt and its composition.

debt monetization   The transformation of financial assets into money.

debt rescheduling   A postponement of principal repayments but not interest payments.

debt securities   Securities such as bonds that represent a legally enforceable promise by the borrower to pay, in some future period, a stated amount of interest and the principal amount lent.

default (credit) risk   The probability that the borrower will be unable or unwilling to make agreed-on payments on time.

default-risk intermediation   The reduction in default risk resulting from holding indirect securities rather than primary securities.

deferred annuity   An annuity providing for income payments to begin at some future date.

deficit sector   Sector whose current income falls short of its current consumption expenditures plus investment expenditures.

defined benefit pension plan   A plan where benefits are predetermined by a formula and employer contributions depend on the cost of the benefit less the employee's contribution, if any.

defined contributing pension plan   A plan where contributions by employees and the employer are fixed and the benefits depend on the contributions and their earnings.

demand liabilities   Deposits that must be paid or transferred on demand.

demutualization The conversion of a mutual company to a company owned by shareholders.

denomination intermediation The transformation of financial assets into media of exchange of relatively small denomination.

deposit certificates Fixed-term deposit liabilities, usually in large denominations.

deposit insurance Insurance that provides guarantees for specified amounts of individual deposits.

derivative Financial instruments whose existence and values are derived from some other underlying financial asset.

derivative (secondary) deposits Newly created deposits that do not increase the reserves of a bank.

desired cash reserve ratio The ratio of total deposits that financial institutions desire to hold as cash to meet the demand for cash.

devaluation When a central bank reduces the value at which it will support its currency under fixed exchange rates.

direct clearers Members of the CPA who participate directly in the clearings and maintain settlement balances with the Bank of Canada.

direct securities Newly issued financial assets.

dirty float policy A policy of regular intervention in exchange markets.

discount When the market price of a bond is below its face value.

discount brokers Brokers offering low-cost execution of orders without investment advice.

discount rate The term used in the United States that is equivalent to the Bank Rate in Canada.

discount window Refers to borrowing from the U.S. Federal Reserve Bank.

discount yield The return for holding an instrument that is always sold at a discount.

disintermediation Loss of deposits by financial intermediaries because of higher returns in alternative capital market instruments.

diversification An investment strategy designed to avoid widespread portfolio losses by holding a variety of assets whose prices are not tied to one another and can be expected as a matter of random chance to have some offsetting movements.

dollarization Refers to the growing use of the dollar around the world.

Dominion Notes Act of 1870 The act that gave the federal government a monopoly on the issue of $1 and $2 notes for circulation.

double coincidence of wants A situation in which two or more individuals have what others want, and trade accordingly.

double liability Denotes that in case of bank failure, shareholders pay an additional amount equal to par value of shares.

drawdown The transfer of Government of Canada deposits with the direct clearers to the governments' deposit account with the Bank of Canada.

duration gap   The difference between the durations of an institution's assets and its liabilities, weighted by their total dollar amounts.

duration gap management   The management of risks due to the amount and timing of cash flows.

Economic Cooperative Administration (ECA)   Organization set up in the United States to administer Marshall aid funds for European recovery.

economies of scale   When output increases proportionately more than inputs increase; e.g., if inputs double and output more than doubles.

effective exchange rate   A weighted-average exchange rate based on merchandise trade.

effective interest rate   The rate of return on an asset after capital gains and losses are considered.

efficient   Markets are efficient when financial asset prices continually reflect all available information that bears on their evaluation.

efficient market hypothesis   The idea that no one can profit from forecasting security prices, since these prices are formed using all available information.

efficient portfolio   Portfolios that offer the highest expected return, given a constant level of risk.

electronic banking   Banking done by telephone, direct deposit, debit cards, payment cards, ABM, or personal computer.

electronic data interchange (EDI)   A system that companies use to exchange business information electronically.

electronic order books   A computerized facility that encourages trading.

EMR II   An exchange rate mechanism that links all EU members outside the Euro area to the Euro.

equation of exchange   An identity that relates the value of nominal transactions or income to the nominal money supply and the velocity of circulation.

equity funds   Mutual funds whose assets are invested primarily in equities or real estate.

equity securities   Securities such as stock that represent shares in the ownership of an enterprise and entitle owners to a pro rata share of any distributed profits of the enterprise.

EURIBOR (Euro Interbank Offered Rate)   A Euro-denominated benchmark interest rate.

EURO LIBOR   A Euro-denominated benchmark interest rate.

Euro   The name chosen for the new common currency by countries of the European Monetary System.

Eurobank   A bank that regularly accepts deposits denominated in foreign currency and makes foreign currency loans.

Eurobonds   Bonds that are denominated in a currency other than that of the country in which they are issued.

Euroclear   Depository for the settlement and clearing of foreign stock issues.

Eurocurrency A bank deposit held in one country that is denominated in another country's currency.

Eurodollar A U.S.-dollar-denominated deposit held with banks or bank branches outside the United States.

European Currency Unit (ECU) The currency unit used in the European Monetary System.

European Economic Community (EEC) An organization dedicated to the economic integration of Europe.

European Monetary System (EMS) An exchange rate system formed on March 13, 1979, that fixes the exchange rates of participating countries within a defined band.

European Payments Union (EPU) A clearing arrangement from 1951 to 1958 for the major European currencies.

exchange control regime Regulations used to control all of a country's economic transactions with the rest of the world.

Exchange Fund Account The fund managed by the Bank of Canada, on behalf of the government of Canada, that holds the country's official foreign exchange assets.

exchange rate The domestic currency price of foreign exchange.

Exchange Rate Mechanism (ERM) An exchange rate mechanism that provides for fixed but adjustable exchange rates for participating countries of the EMS.

exchange rate overshooting The tendency of exchange rates to overreact in the short run because of rigidities of one kind or another.

expectations theory A theory of the term structure of interest rates based on expectations of future interest rate movements.

expected rate of return The weighted average of all possible rates of return, where the weights are the probability of each rate of return occurring.

Export Development Corporation (EDC) A federal government institution that provides export credit insurance and export financing.

face value (par value) The principal amount promised at maturity.

factoring The purchase of receivables at a discount and the lending against receivables with an understanding to collect them.

factors The underlying determinants of the expected return, or price of an asset; examples include the inflation rate, the term structure of interest rates, and industrial production.

Farm Credit Corporation (FCC) A federal government institution that lends to farmers and farm-related enterprises.

fiat money Money that has no value in nonmoney use; it usually derives value from government decree of legal tender.

***Finance Act* of 1914** The act that allowed the federal Department of Finance to function as a pseudo-central bank.

finance paper Promissory notes issued by sales finance companies.

financial account Net flows, both private and official (government), resulting from changes in Canadian claims on nonresidents and of changes in Canadian liabilities to nonresidents.

Financial Flow Accounts Estimates of total gross saving and gross capital formation reported by Statistics Canada.

financial holding company A company that is the sole or major shareholder of a variety of different types of financial institutions.

financial option A right, but not an obligation, to buy or sell a financial asset at a specified price.

Fisher equation An equation linking the nominal interest rate to the real interest rate and the expected rate of inflation.

fixed Bank Rate regime Where the central bank uses its discretion to change its Bank Rate.

fixed exchange rate regime The central bank sets the exchange rate and intervenes to ensure the rate does not deviate substantially from its fixed level.

fixed income funds Mutual funds whose assets are invested primarily in longer-term fixed-income obligations such as bonds.

flexible exchange regime Nominal exchange rates are determined in competitive markets, without government intervention.

float The term used to refer to the value of funds in the process of being transferred from one deposit account to another.

floating Bank Rate regime Where the Bank Rate is tied to and varies with a specified market rate.

flow concept A variable that does have an associated time dimension.

foreign bonds Bonds issued by nonresidents in a country's domestic capital market.

forward contract In the foreign exchange market, a contract to convert a foreign currency investment back into Canadian dollars at maturity, at a set rate of exchange.

forward discount When a currency's forward value is less than its spot value.

forward premium When a currency's forward value is greater than its spot value.

four-pillar concept Separate legislation applying to four types of institutions: chartered banks, insurance companies, trust companies, and security dealers.

fractional reserve banking Where banks hold cash reserves equal to only a fraction of their deposits and formerly their note liabilities.

free banking Allowing banks to be formed without separate legislation in each case.

full-service brokers Brokers offering a full range of brokerage services.

funding risk Denotes when a depository institution does not retain sufficient primary deposits to fund its assets.

futures contract A transferable written agreement to buy or sell a specified amount of a financial asset at a stated price for delivery at a given future date.

futures markets Markets in which financial assets are bought and sold for future delivery.

General Arrangements to Borrow (GAB) Lines of credit from 11 industrial countries that are available for use by the IMF under specified circumstances.

geometric average A means of calculating an average when compounding is involved; values are multiplied, and the appropriate root is taken to determine an average.

Gibson Paradox A positive correlation between the price level and the interest rate.

global bonds Bonds issued simultaneously in more than one country.

gold arbitrage The process of simultaneous buying and selling of gold and currencies under the gold standard.

gold (mint) par of exchange The rate at which a country defines its monetary unit in terms of gold.

gold pool An arrangement between 1961 and 1968 to stabilize the price of gold.

gold standard When each country defines the value of its monetary unit in terms of a given amount of gold.

goldsmiths The activities of the London goldsmiths.

government regulations Rules and regulations governing behaviour of institutions as set out in laws, regulations, and guidelines.

government securities distributors Entities eligible to participate directly in the tender process for government securities; once called primary distributors.

Gresham's Law Bad money drives out good money.

Guaranteed Income Supplement (GIS) The OAS is supplemented by an income-tested Guaranteed Income Supplement.

guaranteed trust and investment certificates (GICs) Term deposits offering a guaranteed rate of return.

guarantees and letters of credit Assurances given by a bank that it will make payments on behalf of customers to third parties in the event that the customers default.

hedge Where a trader takes a position in one asset to offset the risk of a position in another asset.

hedging The act of matching one risk with a counterbalancing risk so as to reduce the overall risk of loss.

Herstatt risk The risk that after one counter-party delivers on one side of a foreign exchange transaction, the other counter-party will fail to deliver on the other side.

HIPC Initiative Joint World Bank–IMF initiative to provide debt relief to heavily indebted poor countries.

holding company   A firm that does not produce any output but owns other firms that do produce goods and services.

homogeneous expectations   When all market participants hold identical expectations.

identity   A relationship that always holds by definition, independent of any theory.

immediate annuity   An annuity providing for income payments to begin immediately after the contract is purchased.

impaired   Denotes when there is no reasonable assurance of repayment.

income effect   Captures the change in consumption that results from a change in the interest rate due solely to the ability to move to a different indifference curve.

income risk   The risk of loss in net interest income when the rates paid on deposits are not synchronized with rates earned on assets.

income–velocity equation of exchange   A relationship between money and prices based in part on nominal income.

indicators   Variables that provide the central bank with information for its conduct of monetary policy.

indifference curve   A curve relating the willingness of an individual to trade one commodity for another.

indirect clearers   Members of the CPA who do not maintain settlement balances with the Bank of Canada and who are represented by direct clearers in clearing and settlement processes.

indirect securities   Financial assets that trade after their original issue.

initial public offering (IPO)   An initial public offering of securities.

inside lag   The time between an economic disturbance and the policy response to correct it.

instalment debt contracts   Promissory notes signed by purchasers of durable consumer, commercial, and industrial goods.

Interac Association   A group of financial institutions that created an electronic switching network to connect ABMs.

interbank deposits   Loans from one chartered bank to another.

interest arbitrage   Arbitrage based on deviations between international interest rate differentials and expected changes in spot exchange rates.

interest equalization tax   A tax imposed in 1963 on foreign bonds issued in the United States and extended in 1964 to foreign loans by U.S. financial institutions. It was repeated in 1974.

interest rate   The stated rate of return on an asset.

interest rate cap   The ceiling or "cap" rate specified in an agreement.

interest rate intermediation   When financial intermediaries provide fixed interest rates to lenders but not to borrowers, or vice versa.

interest rate risk   Risk due to volatility in interest rates.

interest rate swap   Two borrowers exchange interest rate payments for a specified time.

intermediary   An institution bringing surplus and deficit economic units together.

intermediate target   A variable that can be directly influenced by central bank policy instruments.

intermediation   The process of bringing surplus and deficit economic units together.

International Bank for Reconstruction and Development   Known as the World Bank; makes long term loans to developing countries.

International Development Association (IDA)   An affiliate of the World Bank that offers concessional loans to the poorest developing countries.

International Finance Corporation (IFC)   An affiliate of the World Bank that provides loans and equity financing for private sector projects in developing countries.

International Monetary Fund (IMF)   An international body created after the Second World War to assist nations experiencing balance-of-payments difficulties.

intertemporal consumption decision   The decision to smooth consumption over time.

in-the-money   Denotes when an option has intrinsic value and, hence, can be exercised profitably.

inventory–theoretic approach   The idea that the demand for money is based on individuals desiring to hold an inventory of money for transactions purposes.

investment income   Interest, dividends, and miscellaneous investment income.

investment risk   The risk of loss in net worth due to unexpected changes in interest rates.

J-curve   The relationship between the exchange rate and the trade balance; a depreciation may temporarily reduce the trade balance, but eventually it should rise.

junk bonds   High-yield bonds usually rated as very risky.

Large Value Transfer System (LVTS)   An electronic funds transfer system that provides final settlement on a same-day basis.

legal tender   Financial assets that by law must be accepted for all payments.

lender of last resort   The central bank as the ultimate supplier of cash can come to the assistance of financial institutions in times of financial crisis.

lifecycle model of consumption   A theory attempting to describe consumption behaviour over an individual's lifetime.

line of credit   Commitment by a financial intermediary to stand ready to lend up to a specified amount to a customer.

liquid   An asset is liquid when it can be converted into money quickly, with little cost.

liquidity   The nearness to money or ease with which an asset can be sold or converted into money on short notice at a predictable price with little cost.

liquidity preference function   The relationship between changes in the quantity of money and interest rates.

liquidity preference theory   A theory that suggests the equilibrium interest rate is determined by the stock of money in the economy, in the short run.

liquidity premium   A premium paid to compensate lenders for capital risks.

liquidity risk   The risk of not having sufficient cash on hand to meet cash drain and clearing drain.

liquidity trap   A situation in which interest rates (bond prices) get so low (high) that everyone expects them to rise (fall); hence, no one will want to hold bonds (due to capital losses) and the speculative demand for money will become infinitely sensitive.

liquidity-risk intermediation   Involves financial institutions in transforming the public's illiquid claims into liquid claims on the institutions themselves.

loan loss provision   The provision reducing the outstanding value of a loan in the books of a bank to its estimated realizable value.

loan securitization   Involves the transformation of bank loans into marketable securities.

loanable funds theory   A theory that suggests the short-run equilibrium interest rate is determined by the supply of and demand for loanable funds.

London Interbank Offered Rate (LIBOR)   The interest rate at which banks in London, England, will lend Eurocurrencies in the interbank market.

long call   When one buys a call option.

long position   Buying the asset.

long put   When one buys a put option.

Louvre Accord   An international agreement (1987) aimed at reducing exchange rate volatility and coordinating monetary policies across countries.

Maastricht Treaty   The treaty sets out the framework for achieving monetary union in the European Economic Community.

margin requirements   The proportion of the price of a security that must be paid at time of purchase.

marginal productivity of capital   The additional output that results from using one more unit of physical capital.

market conduct regulation   Regulations designed to protect consumers.

market dollarization   The informal use of the American dollar alongside the local currency.

market makers   Those who hold inventories of securities and stand ready to buy and sell at quoted prices.

market portfolio   The optimum portfolio of risky assets.

market rate   When the yield on a debt instrument is equal to the contractual rate of interest.

market risk   The probability that the market price of an asset may decline for reasons other than default by the borrower.

market segmentation theory   A theory of the term structure that assumes that rates of return across different terms to maturity are unrelated.

market squeeze   Where market participants gain control of a particular securities issue and withhold its supply to manipulate its price.

marketability   An asset is said to possess marketability if there are readily available markets for its sale.

marketing-to-market risk   Refers to undesirable cash flows resulting from futures positions.

Marshall plan   Program of massive financial assistance proposed by American Secretary of State George Marshall for the postwar recovery of Europe.

Marshall–Lerner Condition   A condition required for a domestic deprecation to raise the trade balance.

master netting agreements   Agreement to sum all positive and negative values together to arrive at a net amount legally owed to or by a counter-party.

maturity gap (GAP)   The difference between the volume of an intermediary's interest-rate-sensitive assets and its interest-rate-sensitive liabilities.

maturity gap management   The management of risks due to differences in maturities of the assets.

maturity-risk intermediation   The holding of portfolios of assets with long-term maturities, and financing these portfolios with the issue and creation of short-term liabilities.

menu costs   The costs of frequent price changes.

merchandise trade   The value of all physical goods sold to nonresidents (exports) or purchased from them (imports).

metallic coin standard   A monetary system in which the value of the monetary unit is kept equal to the value of a specific metal.

metallic exchange standard   A form of metallic coin standard.

misalignment   When changes in the exchange rate are not related to changes in the fundamentals that determine it.

monetarism   A school of thought in which changes in the money supply are the primary cause of economic fluctuations, implying that a stable money supply would lead to a stable economy.

monetarist approach   The view that the quantity theory can be used to model the economy.

monetary aggregates   Money stock or money supply measures the sum of the values of financial assets in a specific definition of money, such as M1 and M2.

monetary base   The total amount of currency (Bank of Canada notes and coin) plus direct clearer's settlement balances at the Bank of Canada.

monetary conditions   An operational target that focuses on the movements of both short-term interest and exchange rates.

monetary conditions index (MCI)   A blend of interest rates and exchange rates, meant to convey the stance of monetary conditions.

monetary gradualism   A policy of gradually reducing the rate of growth of the money supply to control inflation.

monetary theory of the exchange rate   The theory that only a country's quantity of money determines its exchange rate.

money   Anything that provides monetary functions.

money growth targeting   The idea that monetary policy should be based on setting growth objectives for monetary aggregates.

money illusion   When individuals mistakenly care about nominal variables rather than real variables.

money laundering   The conversion or disposal of funds derived from illegal activity to conceal their illicit origin.

money market funds   A mutual fund that invests in money market securities.

money markets   Where assets with terms to maturity of fewer than three years are traded.

monometallic bullion standard   A form of metallic coin standard.

moral hazard   The tendency of insured parties to take more risk because they are insured.

moral suasion   Used by the central bank when persuading financial institutions to voluntarily pursue some objective of financial policy.

mortgage   A debt contract in which real property, usually land and buildings, serves as security for the contract.

mortgage-tilt problem   Rising interest rates that capture higher rates of inflation cause borrowers to make higher real payments in the early life of a mortgage loan rather than making constant real payment over time.

multilateral netting   Where each clearer's net credit or debit position vis-à-vis all other clearers is calculated for settlement.

multilateral netting systems   A netting system that nets the amounts among a group of counter-parties through a clearinghouse arrangement, resulting in one payment each day in a given currency to or from the clearinghouse by each counter-party.

multiple exchange rate system   A system of multiple exchange rates based on sources and uses of funds.

"National Dividend"   C.H. Douglas proposed that the central bank be mandated to increase the money supply, which would be distributed as a national dividend.

National Income and Expenditure Accounts   The accounts that show Gross Domestic Product (GDP) and record the saving and investment of each of four main sectors in the economy.

natural rate of unemployment   The rate of unemployment that results when expectations of inflation equal the actual inflation rate (implying all unemployment is structural and frictional); also referred to as NAIRU (nonaccelerating inflation rate of unemployment).

near-banks   Depository institutions other than the banks.

negatively correlated   Two series are negatively correlated when as one falls, the other rises.

neutral   When only nominal variables change (as opposed to real variables).

New Arrangements to Borrow (NAB)   Additional lines of credit from other financially strong countries that can be activated by the IMF in the event of systemic financial crisis.

New Classical   A school of thought emphasizing rationality, wage and price flexibility, and efficient information processing.

New Keynesian   A school of thought that blends traditional Keynesian models with market imperfections.

new money policy   A policy in which the premiums are revised periodically to reflect current and expected interest rates.

NHA mortgages   Mortgages insured under the *National Housing Act* by the CMHC.

nominal balances   The nominal amount of money held by individuals.

nominal exchange rate   The value of one currency in terms of another.

nominal rate of interest   The interest rate we see in the market.

nonmerchandise trade   The value of all services, investment income, and transfers sold to nonresidents less those purchased from nonresidents.

Old Age Security (OAS)   A universal benefit that provides a flat-rate government pension to all Canadians aged 65 or over (though it is taxed back for high-income earners).

"100-percent money"   A system of banking proposed by Irving Fisher in which a bank's deposit liabilities would be matched by an equal amount of cash reserves.

open mortgages   Mortgages that allow unscheduled principal payments.

open outcry   An auction whereby traders confront one another directly to bargain over price.

open-end investment companies (mutual funds)   Investment companies that issue new shares and redeem old ones according to demand.

operating band for overnight rates   Where the Bank of Canada monetary policy action keeps overnight interest rates within a band of 50 basis points.

operational target   A variable that the central bank can influence fairly directly by changing the setting of its policy instruments.

opportunity cost   The revenue or benefit forgone by using a resource one way rather than its best alternative use.

option premium   The price of an option.

Organization for European Economic Cooperation (OEEC)   An organization set up for promoting postwar recovery of Europe with American aid.

output gap   The difference between the current value of real output and its long-run value.

outside lag   The time between a policy response and its influence on the economy.

overconsuming   When consumption exceeds income.

overdraft loans   Overnight loans to direct clearers experiencing temporary shortfalls in balances as a result of daily clearings.

overnight financing rate   The rate of interest on overnight (one-day) securities.

over-the-counter (OTC) market   A market in which brokers and dealers directly trade.

paper standards   Paper money whose value is derived by government fiat.

par value   The value at which a monetary authority fixes its exchange rate.

Paris Club   An arrangement whereby the government of France hosts and chairs rescheduling negotiations between creditor and debtor countries.

Payment Clearing and Settlement Act   The Act gives the Bank of Canada explicit responsibility for regulatory oversight of Canada's major payments and settlement systems.

payments intermediation   The transformation of financial assets into media of exchange.

permanent real income   The average level of income expected to prevail over a long period.

perpetual bonds   Called perpetuities or consols, bonds that have no maturity date.

personal loan plan   An arrangement under which a bank provides loans to individuals.

Phillips curves   The inverse relationship between inflation and unemployment in the short run; the lack of a link between inflation and unemployment in the long run.

Plaza Accord   An agreement reached in 1985 by the G-5 nations to coordinate their efforts to lower the exchange value of the U.S. dollar.

pledge provisions   Historically a section in the *Bank Act* specifying assets the bank can accept to secure certain loans.

policy dollarization   The official adoption by a country of the American dollar as its legal currency.

policy ineffectiveness proposition   The idea that systematic monetary policy is known to all agents; hence, it will have no effect on the real side of the economy because it will have been planned for.

policy instruments   The techniques that allow the central bank to control base money.

portfolio balance approach   A theory attempting to determine the demand for money within a general portfolio approach to the selection of assets.

portfolio balance theory of the exchange rate   All financial assets denominated in a country's currency help determine its exchange rate.

Poverty Reduction and Growth Facility The principal means by which the IMF provides concessional support to low income countries.

precautionary balances Money held to meet unpredictable increases in expenditures and unpredictable delays in receipts.

preferred habitat theory A theory of the term structure based on expectations of future interest rates and a risk premium that rises as investors move away from their preferred term to maturity.

preferred stock A class of shares having privileges attached to it, usually a claim on dividends before common stock.

premium When the market price of a bond exceeds face value.

price ceilings Legal limits on how high price can go in a market.

price inflation A sustained rising trend in the general price level.

price stability A policy aimed at maintaining a low and stable rate of inflation.

price–specie flow mechanism If a country experienced balance of payments surplus, it gained gold (specie), this added to is money supply, its prices rose, and its balance of payments was restored to equilibrium.

primary dealers The federal government distributes its securities through a syndicate of investment dealers and banks. Members of the syndicate are called primary distributors.

primary deposit A deposit that may result not only from the deposit of currency (cash), but also from the deposit of cheques drawn on other banks.

primary market Where new issues of securities are bought and sold.

primary reserves Currency held by financial institutions and deposits at the central bank; held to meet the desired ratio of reserves to deposits.

prime rate The interest rate the banks traditionally charged their most creditworthy borrowers.

principal–agent relationship Where a principal delegates an agent to take some action on his or her behalf.

private placements Securities sold (placed) directly with buyers.

promissory notes Promises to repay a loan with principal and interest.

prudent portfolio approach Portfolio investment standards followed by a prudent person who holds a well-diversified portfolio.

prudential regulation Regulations designed to maintain a stable financial system and sound financial institutions.

P-Star Model An indicator model of inflation using the quantity theory.

Purchase and Resale Agreements (PRAs) Dealers can arrange to sell securities to the Bank of Canada with an agreement (a PRA) to repurchase them at an agreed-on price and future date.

purchasing power parity (PPP) Under ideal conditions, the exchange rate should reflect relative prices across countries.

put option An option giving its holder the right to sell financial assets.

quantity theory of money   The theory that the quantity of money or its growth is an important determinant of money income in the short run and of the price level in the long run.

Quebec Deposit Insurance Board   The body that provides deposit insurance in Quebec.

rational expectations   Expectations formed by looking forward and using all available information.

real balances   The purchasing power of money balances; nominal balances divided by the price level.

real bills doctrine (commercial loans theory)   If loans made by banks were based on "real bills" (promises backed by goods in the process of production or marketing), an optimum quantity of money would always be supplied.

real exchange rate   The relative price of the goods and services of two countries.

real rate of interest   The nominal interest rate, less an adjustment for what people believe inflation will be during the period.

real return bonds   Bonds whose principal amount is increased at maturity, or when sold, by the full increase in the Consumer Price Index.

reciprocal currency arrangement   Temporary currency swaps between central banks.

redeposit   The transfer of Government of Canada deposits from the Bank of Canada to the direct clearers.

registered pension plans   Pension plans registered and supervised under government pension legislation.

Registered Retirement Savings Plans (RRSPs)   Tax-sheltered arrangements for investing savings for retirement.

regulated markets   Markets in which securities trading is restricted to investment dealers and brokers who are registered to conduct business by a regulatory agency.

reinsurer   An insurance company that insures risks assumed by other insurance companies.

relative PPP   Exchange rates should change over time according to the relative changes in domestic and foreign prices.

relative price   The price of one item relative to that of another.

repurchase agreements (repos)   The immediate sale of securities and the simultaneous agreement to repurchase these securities at a pre-specified future price and date.

reserve asset   An asset held to allow a bank to convert the public's deposits into cash on demand or short notice.

revaluation   When a central bank increases the value at which it will support its currency under fixed exchange rates.

reverse mortgages   Mortgages designed to allow homeowners to borrow against the equity in their homes.

reverse repo   The immediate purchase of securities and a simultaneous agreement to resell the securities at a later date.

revolving credit   A contractual line of credit for a longer period than under a regular line of credit.

revolving underwriting facilities or note-issuance facilities   Undertakings from a bank where a customer issues short-term notes and, if unable to sell the notes at a prescribed price, the bank buys them at that price.

risk   A measure of the degree of certainty with which one can predict that actual rates of return will be close to the expected rate of return.

risk averse   When investors will only accept a greater amount of risk if it comes with a larger expected return.

risk of insolvency   The risk of not being able to make payments to creditors and depositors.

risk pooling   Writing insurance policies with a probability that risks are independent of each other.

risk premium   The difference between the expected rate of return on an asset and the risk-free rate of interest.

risk premium theory   A theory of the term structure based on expectations of future interest rates and a risk premium that rises with the term to maturity.

risk sharing   Where a very large insurance risk is shared by many insurers.

Royal Commission on Banking and Currency   In 1934 the commission proposed the formation of a central bank.

rules of the game   Refer to the practices governments of gold standard countries were supposed to follow to facilitate the operations of the gold standard adjustment mechanism.

Sale and Repurchase Agreements (SRAs)   The central bank sells securities to a chartered bank and agrees to repurchase them at a later date at its own initiative.

script money   The issue of paper money, which remained legal tender as long as a required monthly stamp was affixed to it.

secondary markets   Where previously issued securities are bought and sold.

secondary reserves   Very liquid assets held by financial institutions to ensure they meet their desired ratio of reserves and deposits.

security market line (SML)   The relationship between an asset's expected rate of return and the systematic risk of the asset, the risk-free rate of interest, and the market price of risk.

segregated funds   Life insurance assets dedicated to specific liabilities.

seigniorage   Profits from the issuing of money; the difference between the face value of money and its cost to produce.

self-dealing   Engaging in a nonarm's length transaction that benefits those undertaking it.

self-regulation   Enforcement of standards and rules by industry associations.

semi-strong efficiency   Economywide information is of no use in forecasting stock prices.

services   Travel, freight, shipping, and a broad range of professional and managerial services.

settlement system   The process whereby cash payment is made for net claims following clearing.

shiftability doctrine of liquidity   The idea that banks could protect themselves against large deposit withdrawals by holding government securities.

short call   When one sells a call option.

short position   Selling the asset.

short put   When one sells a put option.

short sale   Selling an asset that you don't currently own in anticipation of a decline in its price.

small-cap stocks   Shares of companies with low capitalization.

smart cards   Cards that have computer chips capable of storing and transferring money used for transaction purposes.

Smithsonian Agreement   An agreement between G-10 governments in December 1971 that provided for realignment of participating countries' exchange rules and the maintenance of their currencies within 2.25 percent on either side of their official par values.

snake in the tunnel   An arrangement among European governments dating from early 1972 to keep the market value of their currencies within 2.25 percent of each other.

Special Drawing Right (SDR)   Bookkeeping account created by IMF to serve as an international reserve asset.

Special PRAs (SPRAs)   Used when the central bank wants to increase liquidity in the financial system and put an upper "bound" on the overnight financial rate.

Special SRAs   Used when the central bank wants to reduce liquidity in the financial system and put a lower "bound" on the overnight financing rate.

specie   Gold and silver coin bullion.

speculative balances   Money held to finance a speculative opportunity in securities markets.

spot markets   Markets in which financial assets are bought and sold for immediate delivery.

standard deviation   A measure of dispersion about the mean used to measure risk; is the square root of the variance.

standby arrangements   An arrangement in which the IMF provides a line of credit to a borrowing country specifying the amount that can be borrowed during a specified period, provided IMF conditionality, if any, is satisfied.

statistical discrepancy   A data adjustment required to set the balance of payments equal to zero.

sterilization   Exchange market intervention that leaves the monetary base unchanged.

sterilized intervention   Exchange market intervention that does not lead to a change in a country's money supply.

stock concept   A variable that doesn't have an associated time dimension.

stock indexes   Weighted averages of the prices of shares trading on stock exchanges.

stock split   The division of a share into two or more shares.

straddle   A put and a call on the same currency, with identical strike prices and maturity dates.

strike price   The price at which an option may be exercised.

stripped zero-coupon bonds   Created when an investment dealer separates a conventional bond into its two constituent parts.

strong-form efficiency   Neither public nor private information can be used to forecast stock prices.

substitution effect   Captures the change in consumption that results from a change in the interest rate, when we restrict movement along the original indifference curve.

surplus sector   Sector whose current income exceeds its current consumption expenditures plus investment expenditures.

swap rate   The difference between the sale price of a currency and its repurchase price.

swapped deposits   Canadian dollar term deposits that a bank converts into foreign currency, for investment in foreign money markets.

swaps   Transactions in which two parties agree to exchange streams of payments over time.

symmetallism   When the monetary unit of account is defined as a combination of two metals in some specific proportion to each other.

synthetic loans   When the nature of a loan is changed by combining it with a futures contract.

systematic risk   That part in the variability of an asset's return that is attributable to economywide trends and events.

TARGET   An EU-wide system for euro payments.

target zone   Specifies a zone within which a currency is managed to fluctuate.

term insurance   Pure life insurance that pays a contractual amount in the event of a death.

term notes   A fixed-term deposit liability issued by a financial intermediary.

term structure of interest rates   The relationship between yields on securities of similar characteristics across different terms.

tied selling   When one purchase is conditional on another purchase.

time value of money   The increase in the value of an investment over time.

Tobin tax   Proposal for a universal tax on all spot conversions of one currency into another.

tranches Specifies the amount of other countries' currency that a member may draw (borrow) from IMF's ordinary resources.

transactions balances Money held for transactions purposes.

transactions demand The demand for money for transactions purposes.

transactions–velocity approach A relationship between money and prices based in part on the number of transactions that occur in the economy in a year.

transfers Inheritances and migrants' funds, personal and institutional remittances, official contributions, and withholding taxes.

Treasury bills Short-term, negotiable promissory notes issued by the federal government.

triangular arbitrage Arbitrage between three markets for three assets.

uncovered interest arbitrage Arbitrage positions in which futures or forward markets have not been used to set a price for delivery of an asset in the future.

uncovered interest parity A relationship linking interest rates, exchange rates, and expected changes in exchange rates across nations.

underconsuming When consumption falls short of income.

unit bank A bank limited to a single office.

universal life policy A policy under which the holder can vary the amount and timing of premium payments and change the amount of the insurance.

unsterilized intervention Exchange market intervention that leads to a change in a country's money supply.

unsystematic risk The variability in the return on an asset that is specific to that asset.

value-at-risk (VAR or VaR) An estimate of the largest loss that a portfolio is likely to suffer during all but truly exceptional periods.

variable life policy A policy under which benefits are not fixed, but vary with the market value of the assets in which the premiums have been invested.

variance A measure of dispersion about the mean; used to measure risk.

velocity of circulation The number of times money is turned over for transactions purposes in any given time period.

velocity of money The average number of times per year each dollar is spent, either on final goods and services (income velocity) or on everything (transactions velocity).

venture capital company A company that provides long-term capital and management assistance to new and expanding companies.

virtual banking Where all banking services are delivered electronically.

warrants Attached to bonds, they can be used to purchase the issuer's common stock at stated prices.

weak-form efficiency Security prices should not be "predictable" using past price data.

when-issued Treasury bill   A Treasury bill that is to be auctioned at the next weekly tender.

whole-life insurance   A policy with level premiums that combines saving with term insurance.

yield   The total rate of return on an asset.

yield curve   A graph describing yields across different terms to maturity.

yield to maturity   The interest rate that equates the present value of all expected future cash receipts from a debt instrument with its present value.

zero-coupon bonds   Bonds that promise to pay the principal amount at a specified maturity date.

Index

To the owner of this book

We hope that you have enjoyed *Money, Banking, and the Canadian Financial System*, Eighth Edition, (ISBN 0-17-616856-7), by H.H. Binhammer and Peter S. Sephton, and we would like to know as much about your experiences with this text as you would care to offer. Only through your comments and those of others can we learn how to make this a better text for future readers.

School _____   Your instructor's name _____

Course _____   Was the text required? _____   Recommended? _____

1. What did you like the most about *Money, Banking, and the Canadian Financial System*?

   _____

   _____

   _____

2. How useful was this text for your course?

   _____

   _____

   _____

3. Do you have any recommendations for ways to improve the next edition of this text?

   _____

   _____

   _____

4. In the space below or in a separate letter, please write any other comments you have about the book. (For example, please feel free to comment on reading level, writing style, terminology, design features, and learning aids.)

   _____

   _____

   _____

   _____

Optional

Your name _____   Date _____

May Nelson Thomson Learning quote you, either in promotion for *Money, Banking, and the Canadian Financial System*, or in future publishing ventures?

Yes _____   No _____

Thanks!

You can also send your comments to us via e-mail at
college@nelson.com

PLEASE TAPE SHUT. DO NOT STAPLE.

TAPE SHUT

TAPE SHUT

- - - FOLD HERE - - -

NELSON
THOMSON LEARNING ™

MAIL ✈ POSTE
Canada Post Corporation
Société canadienne des postes
Postage paid   Port payé
if mailed in Canada   si posté au Canada
Business Reply   **Réponse d'affaires**
0066102399   **01**

0066102399-M1K5G4-BR01

NELSON THOMSON LEARNING
HIGHER EDUCATION
PO BOX 60225 STN BRM B
TORONTO ON M7Y 2H1

TAPE SHUT

TAPE SHUT